# Abortion in Latin America and the Caribbean

## RECENT TITLES FROM THE HELEN KELLOGG INSTITUTE SERIES ON DEMOCRACY AND DEVELOPMENT

Paolo G. Carozza and Aníbal Pérez-Liñan, *series editors*

*The University of Notre Dame Press gratefully thanks the Helen Kellogg Institute for International Studies for its support in the publication of titles in this series.*

Ignacio Walker
*Democracy in Latin America: Between Hope and Despair* (2013)

Laura Gómez-Mera
*Power and Regionalism in Latin America: The Politics of MERCOSUR* (2013)

Rosario Queirolo
*The Success of the Left in Latin America: Untainted Parties, Market Reforms, and Voting Behavior* (2013)

Erik Ching
*Authoritarian El Salvador: Politics and the Origins of the Military Regimes, 1880–1940* (2013)

Brian Wampler
*Activating Democracy in Brazil: Popular Participation, Social Justice, and Interlocking Institutions* (2015)

J. Ricardo Tranjan
*Participatory Democracy in Brazil: Socioeconomic and Political Origins* (2016)

Tracy Beck Fenwick
*Avoiding Governors: Federalism, Democracy, and Poverty Alleviation in Brazil and Argentina* (2016)

Alexander Wilde
*Religious Responses to Violence: Human Rights in Latin America Past and Present* (2016)

Pedro Meira Monteiro
*The Other Roots: Wandering Origins in* Roots of Brazil *and the Impasses of Modernity in Ibero-America* (2017)

John Aerni-Flessner
*Dreams for Lesotho: Independence, Foreign Assistance, and Development* (2018)

Roxana Barbulescu
*Migrant Integration in a Changing Europe: Migrants, European Citizens, and Co-ethnics in Italy and Spain* (2019)

Matthew C. Ingram and Diana Kapiszewski
*Beyond High Courts: The Justice Complex in Latin America* (2019)

Kenneth P. Serbin
*From Revolution to Power in Brazil: How Radical Leftists Embraced Capitalism and Struggled with Leadership* (2019)

Manuel Balán and Françoise Montambeault
*Legacies of the Left Turn in Latin America: The Promise of Inclusive Citizenship* (2020)

For a complete list of titles from the Helen Kellogg Institute for International Studies, see http://www.undpress.nd.edu.

# Abortion in Latin America and the Caribbean

## The Legal Impact of the American Convention on Human Rights

**Ligia De Jesús Castaldi**

University of Notre Dame Press
Notre Dame, Indiana

University of Notre Dame Press
Notre Dame, Indiana 46556
undpress.nd.edu



Published in the United States of America

Library of Congress Control Number: 2020937032

ISBN: 978-0-268-10765-9 (Hardback)
ISBN: 978-0-268-10768-0 (WebPDF)
ISBN: 978-0-268-10767-3 (Epub)

*To Richard Stith,*
*Emeritus Professor of Law*

CONTENTS

# ACKNOWLEDGMENTS

The author wishes to thank former commissioners and judges who provided invaluable commentary on this research. She also wishes to thank Marel, Antonello, and Tommaso for their support. Opinions expressed in this work are exclusively the author's.

Unofficial translations are the author's, unless otherwise indicated.

The author intervened in *Artavia Murillo v. Costa Rica* as amicus curiae along with former Inter-American Court Judge Rafael Nieto Navia and law professors Jane Adolphe and Richard Stith.

# ABBREVIATIONS

| | |
|---|---|
| CEDAW | Convention on the Elimination of All Forms of Discrimination against Women |
| CRC | Convention on the Rights of the Child |
| ECJ | European Court of Justice |
| IACHR | Inter-American Commission on Human Rights |
| ICCPR | International Covenant on Civil and Political Rights |
| ICPD | International Conference on Population and Development |
| IVF | in vitro fertilization |
| OAS | Organization of American States |
| UDHR | Universal Declaration of Human Rights |
| UN | United Nations |
| VCLT | Vienna Convention on the Law of Treaties |

# Introduction

By ratifying the American Convention on Human Rights, most Latin American and Caribbean nations have undertaken an international obligation to legally protect every person's right to life from the moment of conception.[1] Article 4(1) of the convention has been identified by international human rights experts as the most emphatic recognition of the prenatal right to life to date in international human rights law:[2] "Every person has the right to have his life respected. This right shall be protected by law and, in general, from the moment of conception. No one shall be arbitrarily deprived of his life."

The recognition of a right to life from conception in the American Convention seems to have been distinctly inspired by a Catholic moral tradition of respect for prenatal life and a Latin American Catholic understanding of human rights law in general.[3] Direct and indirect references to the Catholic faith were made during the convention's drafting stages. The San José Conference, where the convention's text was adopted, began with opening speeches by the Costa Rican president and the first chief justice of the Inter-American Court of Human Rights, both of which invoked the Christian, particularly Catholic, inspiration of the human rights movement in Latin America.[4] Prior to the San José Conference, the Inter-American Commission on Human Rights (IACHR) had acknowledged the moral significance of the prenatal rights provision for states parties and cited "reasons of principle" to swiftly reject a proposal to remove the provision from the treaty text.[5]

Since the adoption of the treaty text including a prenatal right to life from conception in 1969, twenty-three countries have ratified the American Convention, namely Argentina, Barbados, Bolivia, Brazil, Chile, Colombia, Costa Rica, Dominica, Dominican Republic, Ecuador, El Salvador, Grenada, Guatemala, Haiti, Honduras, Jamaica, Mexico, Nicaragua, Panama, Paraguay, Peru, Suriname, and Uruguay.[6] The United States is a signatory but not a party: it signed the convention in 1977 but has never ratified it.[7] On the other hand, it has not as of 2019 withdrawn or expressed an intent to withdraw its signature.

In the last few decades, however, international human rights bodies have repeatedly urged Latin American and Caribbean nations to decriminalize and provide access to abortion, notwithstanding the American Convention's recognition of a general state duty to legally protect prenatal life. United Nations treaty bodies have repeatedly told Latin American and Caribbean states that international human rights treaties require the creation of abortion rights, as explained in chapter 6, and that legally authorizing abortion would reduce maternal mortality rates in the region.[8] The argument has been refuted in recent years by a number of medical studies that have found that legalization or availability of abortion is not one of the most relevant factors in maternal mortality reduction and that there is no correlation between restricted access to abortion and high maternal mortality rates.[9] For instance, Chile, a country that fully banned abortion for over a hundred years consistently had until 2017 the lowest maternal mortality rate in Latin America and the Caribbean. The United States, on the other hand, has the highest maternal mortality rate in the developed world, even though ample legal access to abortion—and even public subsidies—have been provided nationwide since 1973.[10]

Proposals to abolish prenatal life protections and to create a legal entitlement to abortion have also been advanced at the national level, and regionally through the Inter-American human rights system. Starting with the Inter-American Commission on Human Rights' *Baby Boy* report in 1981, a series of abortion-related hearings and petitions have provoked reports promoting decriminalization of abortion in several Latin American and Caribbean countries, as described in chapter 1. The Inter-American

Court then suggested in 2012 that decriminalization of abortion, especially at an early gestational age, may be legally compatible with the convention, in the *Artavia v. Costa Rica* judgment *dicta*, as discussed in chapter 2. The judgment, which cited *Roe v. Wade* along with German and Spanish high court judgments on abortion, suggested a desire to identify with Western European and North American feminist visions of human rights to the detriment of the prenatal right to life as recognized by states parties to the American Convention.[11]

As of 2019, no state party to the American Convention has fully decriminalized abortion despite a significant prevalence of advocacy for the creation of abortion rights in international human rights politics. Such advocacy has nevertheless deeply divided nations and individuals within the Inter-American human rights system, forcing them to take a position on a single issue that, since the 1970s, seems to have taken precedence over all other feminist causes. It has pitted believers against nonbelievers, liberals against conservatives, nationalists against globalists both in states parties to the American Convention and within the Inter-American system of human rights itself. It has raised larger jurisprudential questions regarding interpretation of international human rights treaties, how new rights are created, and who has the authority to do so—questions explored in this book. At the national level, advocacy for abortion rights has led to separation of powers issues and has brought constitutional procedures and federalism principles into question, as illustrated here.

The IACHR and the Inter-American Court are now at what may be a turning point in history, one where they may move forward with creating abortion rights or reverse course. Scholars have noted the state of uncertainty as to the scope of the rights of the unborn child in the Inter-American human rights system and as to the compatibility of decriminalization of elective abortion with the American Convention.[12] The Inter-American Court has never directly ruled on the issue, but the commission will probably deal with those questions as it continues to hear petitions challenging abortion bans in states parties to the American Convention, such as those described in chapter 1.[13] The Inter-American Court may thus be required—sooner rather than later—to address claims demanding the creation of abortion rights in one or more states parties to the American Convention.

This book proposes a nonrestrictive, good-faith interpretation of the convention that would comply with international treaty interpretation rules applied by the Inter-American Court of Human Rights, namely ordinary/textual interpretation; evolutive, systemic, and historic interpretation; and the *pro homine* rule, established by the Vienna Convention on the Law of Treaties (VCLT) and article 29 of the American Convention on Human Rights.[14] It also carries out a comparative analysis of interpretation of article 4(1) of the American Convention by Inter-American human rights bodies, on one hand, and by states parties to the convention, on the other. The book argues that only a nonrestrictive interpretation could be compatible with the object and purpose of the treaty, which, as evidence collected in this book demonstrates, is that of granting the unborn child broad and general, not exceptional, legal protection from elective abortion.

ONE

# The Inter-American Commission on Human Rights' Inconsistent Treatment of the Prenatal Right to Life

The American Convention on Human Rights in article 4(1) establishes an international duty to legally protect a prenatal right to life from the moment of conception: "Every person has the right to have his life respected. This right shall be protected by law and, in general, from the moment of conception. No one shall be arbitrarily deprived of his life."[1] Twenty-three nations—that is, the majority of Latin American and Caribbean members of the Organization of American States (OAS)—are legally bound by this provision and have made no reservations to it: Argentina, Barbados, Bolivia, Brazil, Chile, Colombia, Costa Rica, Dominica, Dominican Republic, Ecuador, El Salvador, Grenada, Guatemala, Haiti, Honduras, Jamaica, Mexico, Nicaragua, Panama, Paraguay, Peru, Suriname, and Uruguay.[2]

This chapter examines the inconsistent treatment of prenatal rights and abortion by the Inter-American Commission on Human Rights (IACHR), one of two human rights bodies created by states parties to oversee implementation of the American Convention on Human Rights. The chapter looks at the IACHR's human rights promotion activities as well as its individual complaints mechanism. Starting with *Baby Boy v.*

*United States*, the most influential IACHR report, the chapter surveys all Inter-American Commission on Human Rights reports on individual complaints that directly or indirectly relate to abortion and prenatal rights, including but not limited to *Paulina Ramírez v. Mexico*, and petitions filed by "Amelia," Mainumby, and "Manuela." Each report's merits, legal weight, and legal effects are also considered.

## Inter-American Human Rights Bodies

States parties created two human rights bodies to monitor the American Convention: the Inter-American Commission on Human Rights (IACHR) and the Inter-American Court of Human Rights.[3] The commission and the court have similar names but very different powers, mandates, and resources. The court is a regional international human rights tribunal created by the OAS to adjudicate individual complaints against states parties to the American Convention. It also issues advisory opinions and exercises oversight functions over the commission's practices.[4] The court's treatment of abortion and prenatal rights is described in chapter 2.

The United States is seat to the OAS and the commission in Washington, DC, and also has, at different times, been the commission's main donor. Its contribution of about $3 million to the IACHR in 2016, for instance, covered over half of the commission's budget.[5] The commission operates on a larger budget than the court (e.g., an estimated $5.3 million v. $2.7 million annually in 2016),[6] in part due to its significantly larger case load. In addition, both the Inter-American Court and Inter-American Commission have received considerable funding from nonmember states to the OAS, primarily European Union countries.[7] Funding by observer states has raised questions about the impact that foreign interests or visions of human rights may have on the Inter-American system.[8]

Both bodies are seeking to more than double their budgets and secure greater funding on the part of OAS member states.[9] In 2016, both Inter-American human rights bodies drew up a proposal which, if implemented, would make OAS member states primary contributors to the court and the commission's proposed annual budgets of 7 and 11 million US dollars, respectively.[10] The president of the court and the president of the commission both indicated that the proposal would give Inter-American human rights bodies "greater autonomy and independence."[11]

Other Inter-American advisory bodies on human rights issues include the Inter-American Human Rights Institute (IIDH), a specialized academic organization charged with promoting human rights education in the Americas; the Inter-American Commission of Women (CIM), a "principal forum for debating and formulating policy on women's rights and gender equality in the Americas"; and the MESECVI, "a systematic and permanent multilateral evaluation methodology" between the states parties to the Belém do Pará Convention and a committee of experts.[12] Reports and documents by these bodies will not be analyzed in any depth here, given their advisory, nonlegal nature, as opposed to the court and the commission's judicial and quasi-judicial authority.

Political trust in the Inter-American human rights system on the part of member states has varied within the last few decades, which may have affected the states' financial support thereof.[13] Criticism of the commission has come from both governments on the left and on the right. In 2019, for instance, Argentina, Brazil, Chile, Colombia, and Paraguay filed a joint declaration with IACHR executive secretary Paulo Abrão, in which they reaffirmed their commitment to the Inter-American human rights system but also expressed their concern for an apparent lack of compliance with some basic principles established by the convention.[14] Among other things, states called the Inter-American Commission and the court to respect national constitutional law and apply the principle of subsidiarity of Inter-American bodies and proportionality of reparations.

In the past, several states, like Colombia, Brazil, and Venezuela, questioned the powers and procedures of the IACHR.[15] In Brazil's case, the move purportedly came as a reaction to the commission's precautionary measures in the *Belo Monte Hydroelectric Plant* matter, an environmental controversy that seemed to affect the nation's economic interests.[16] In addition, Trinidad and Tobago denounced the American Convention in 1998, arguing that the commission's procedural delays in hearing petitions on capital cases interfered with the nation's application of the death penalty in its jurisdiction.[17]

Peru briefly denounced the convention in 1999, during the Fujimori administration. It withdrew its recognition of the contentious jurisdiction of the Inter-American Court in reaction to the *Castillo Petruzzi* judgment, which attempted to invalidate the conviction of four members of a guerrilla/group for terrorism and treason in military jurisdiction.[18] However, the next administration rescinded that withdrawal in 2001, stating that the denunciation should be deemed as never having occurred.[19]

Venezuela denounced the American Convention on Human Rights and withdrew from the Inter-American Court's jurisdiction in 2012, alleging politically motivated bias against Venezuela's *chavista* government on the part of Inter-American human rights bodies.[20] Among other things, Venezuela argued that the court and the commission demonstrated political bias by hearing petitions and cases against Venezuela where no domestic remedies had been exhausted (such as *Díaz Peña v. Venezuela* before the court) and by giving fast-track consideration to petitions against the *chavista* government (e.g., cases brought by journalists Ríos, Perozo, and others).[21] Venezuela also condemned the commission's position during the 2002 attempted coup d'état, where IACHR executive secretary Santiago Cantón allegedly recognized de facto authorities and the IACHR rejected requests for precautionary measures in favor of President Hugo Chávez, who had been kidnapped and remained incommunicado.[22]

An important factor in withdrawal from the Inter-American human rights system seems to have been the Inter-American Court's judgment in favor of Raúl Díaz Peña,[23] a "convicted terrorist," the state indicated, who had carried out bombings on Venezuelan diplomatic missions in Colombia and Spain and for whom the court requested an improvement of detention conditions even though he was a fugitive at the time.[24] The communication denouncing the convention, signed by then minister Nicolás Maduro, characterized the court and the commission's interventions as politically motivated and as a systematic transgression and manipulation of the convention's norms and spirit and made a point of explicitly withdrawing its acceptance of the Inter-American Court's contentious jurisdiction.[25]

## The Commission: A Sui Generis, Quasi-Judicial Regional Human Rights Body

The Inter-American Commission on Human Rights is a sui generis, quasi-judicial regional human rights body, not a court, with multiple functions established by the American Convention, the IACHR Statute, and its rules of procedure, including human rights advocacy and promotion in the region as well as reception of individual petitions against states parties to the American Convention.[26] Modeled on the now defunct European Commission of Human Rights, the IACHR is headquartered in Washington, DC, and is composed of seven part-time members serving in their individual capacity, not as representatives of their national state.[27]

In the context of its petition system, the Inter-American Commission has the power to issue nonbinding reports and recommendations for states parties on alleged individual human rights violations and has exclusive standing to take individual cases before the Inter-American Court.[28] The commission may also issue precautionary measures and request provisional measures before the court. It may mediate friendly settlements between states and alleged victims of human rights violations.

Given the two-tiered individual complaint system, which requires petitions to go to the commission before they can be heard by the Inter-American Court, the commission's practical role can be that of a filter to the Inter-American Court, often providing an opportunity for alternative dispute resolution between petitioners and their state before the complaint reaches the court. Friendly settlement agreements have been said to have a higher compliance rate than any other reports or resolutions issued by the commission.[29] The implementation of other reports, however, remains generally weak until cases reach the Inter-American Court for a binding decision.[30]

When a friendly settlement fails, the IACHR may submit a contentious case to the court; the court will then issue a legally binding judgment against the state party to the dispute.[31] The commission may also request an advisory opinion from the court on the interpretation of the American Convention, which the court may hear under its advisory powers.[32] Effects and authority of the Inter-American Court's judgments and advisory opinions are discussed in chapter 2.

The commission's authority is political rather than legal in nature. As a result, it may simultaneously play the role of victim's advocate, factual investigator, mediator, prosecutor, and adjudicator, which has led many to question the IACHR's credibility and impartiality in certain cases.[33] Aside from states parties, only the commission may bring lawsuits before the court; individuals having no standing.[34] The Inter-American Commission itself, however, does not have adjudication faculties, and its reports are not controlling on decisions of the court; in some instances, the Inter-American Court has in fact rejected the commission's claims, reasoning, or recommendations.[35]

Unlike Inter-American Court judgments, the commission's admissibility and merits reports and their corresponding recommendations in relation to individual petitions are not binding on states parties, as indicated by the Inter-American Court in *Caballero Delgado and Santana v. Colombia* and others: "[A] recommendation does not have the character of an obligatory judicial decision for which the failure to comply would generate State responsibility."[36] The court has, however, indicated that a state party to the American Convention "in accordance with the principle of good faith . . . has the obligation to make every effort to comply with the recommendations of a protection organ such as the Inter-American Commission."[37]

### The Commission's Abortion-Related Advocacy

The commission originally defended the American Convention's prenatal-right-to-life provision in article 4(1) during the convention's preparatory work (*travaux préparatoires*). During the treaty's drafting stages Brazilian commissioner Carlos Dunshee de Abranches proposed deleting the entire phrase recognizing a right to life from conception from the draft convention, but the commission refused to do so "for reasons of principle."[38] Some commission reports have subsequently interpreted article 1 of the American Declaration of the Rights and Duties of Man (American Declaration) and article 4(1) of the American Convention as incompatible with at least some elective abortions, particularly where the mother's motivation to abort was merely economic, that is, for poverty.[39] Such abortions, the commission has said, constitute a "patent and grave violation of human rights."

In recent years, however, the commission has urged countries to legalize abortion at least on the so-called *tres causales* (three grounds), namely the abortion of those conceived in rape, abortion of those with genetic disabilities (eugenic abortion), and abortion in cases where the pregnancy poses a risk to the life or health of the mother.[40] Advocates for abortion rights before the IACHR have identified decriminalization of abortion on three grounds as a gradual or incremental step toward full decriminalization of abortion and the creation of abortion rights.[41] The said rights would go beyond decriminalization on three grounds to *unrestricted* abortion, abortion subsidies, suppression of conscience rights of medical providers, and deregulation of abortion practices, among others.

Individual members of the IACHR and thematic reports have echoed this idea and have boldly promoted abortion legalization as a matter of "women's human rights to integrity and privacy," while making no mention to their potential incompatibility with article 4(1).[42] Through its periodic hearings system, a relatively informal procedure by which human rights organizations report to the IACHR on specific human rights issues in the region, the commission has also applied significant political pressure on individual states parties, such as Chile, to legalize abortion (as described in chapter 5). Little to nothing has been said, however, to encourage states to promote social services or financial assistance policies for women or families facing unexpected pregnancies.

Abortion providers and abortion rights advocates have shown remarkable influence over the IACHR in recent decades. Organizations that provide abortions, abortion equipment, and training, such as Planned Parenthood and Ipas, have had consistent presence at IACHR hearings on abortion in recent years, with the commission's approval despite their obvious conflict of interest.[43] Ipas, an organization that sells a handheld abortifacient device called a manual vacuum aspirator, its "signature product," has repeatedly appeared in public hearings before the IACHR, perhaps more than any other abortion rights organization, to demand legalization of abortion in countries where it is illegal.[44] It has also intervened as a petitioner, along with the Center for Justice and International Law (CEJIL), in at least one case, the *Beatriz* complaint against El Salvador, discussed in the next chapter.[45]

Organizations that advocate for the creation of abortion rights, such as the Center for Reproductive Rights, Women's Link Worldwide, CLADEM, and the International Planned Parenthood Federation (Western Hemisphere Region), routinely appear before the commission at its public hearings to argue that protection of the right to life from conception and abortion bans in states parties violate the American Convention.[46] Pro-life organizations, on the other hand, have been repeatedly denied participation in the commission's hearings.[47]

In 1981, the commission argued in *Baby Boy v. United States* that the American Convention does not protect the unborn child from at least some instances of elective abortion, and this idea set the foundation for the court's restrictive interpretation of the prenatal right to life in *Artavia v. Costa Rica*. Since then, the commission has supported abortion decriminalization in the context of individual petitions challenging abortion prohibitions in El Salvador, Mexico, Nicaragua, and Paraguay, as described below. The commission, however, has never explicitly recommended that a state party to the American Convention create a right to abort or legalize all abortions without restrictions.

### *Baby Boy v. United States*: A Restrictive Approach to the Right to Life from Conception

Not many are aware that *Roe v. Wade* and its companion case were challenged before the IACHR during President Jimmy Carter's administration, with a resolution being published shortly after Ronald Reagan took office in 1981.[48] The petition was brought by Catholics for Christian Political Action, an American pro-life organization, in 1977. The petitioners argued that the judicial legalization of abortion in *Roe v. Wade* by the US Supreme Court in 1973 resulted in the violation of the right to life of Baby Boy, an illegally aborted male fetus whose abortionist was acquitted by the Massachusetts Supreme Court.[49] They stated that the United States had incurred an international responsibility for a violation of the American Declaration of the Rights and Duties of Man, to which it is considered to be a signatory.[50]

In the *Baby Boy v. United States* report, the Inter-American Commission concluded that the abortion of Baby Boy was permissible under the American Declaration.[51] The American Declaration[52] is a regional human rights instrument adopted before the American Convention, in 1948. In it, all member states of the Organization of American States (OAS), including the United States, recognized a universal right to life of human beings: "*[E]very human being* has the right to life."[53]

The report's finding and resolutory section was based only on the American Declaration and not the American Convention, which the commission had no jurisdiction to apply because the United States is not a party to it. The complaint was filed in 1977, the year that the United States signed the Convention without ratifying it. In addition, the American Convention had not yet entered into force at the time of the complaint (it entered into force in July of 1978). Based on these two grounds, the IACHR lacked jurisdiction to apply the convention, as it admitted.[54]

The report nevertheless formulated the first restrictive interpretation of the convention's right to prenatal life. The commission's *Baby Boy* report stated, among other things, that the American convention's terms "in general, from the moment of conception" did not grant the prenatal right to life "absolute" protection.[55] This idea was later adopted by the Inter-American Court, almost thirty years later, in *Artavia v. Costa Rica*, where it held, among other things, that the American Convention did not grant prenatal life absolute protection and therefore did not protect the human embryo from artificial reproductive technologies.[56] *Baby Boy*'s interpretation, however, has been challenged from its inception. Commissioners Monroy Cabra and Tinoco asserted that such an interpretation was legally inappropriate and refused to endorse the majority opinion's understanding of the convention.[57] Commissioner Andres Aguilar, in his concurring opinion, suggested disagreement with this choice and pointed out that the convention did not apply to the petition at hand.[58]

## Who Was Baby Boy?

Baby Boy was a healthy male fetus of twenty-four to twenty-six weeks (approximately six months) gestational age (therefore potentially viable) who was intentionally aborted by hysterotomy,[59] a surgical procedure that resembles a caesarean section. Baby Boy's mother was a seventeen-year-old girl who, along with her mother, requested and consented to the procedure. Due to the unborn child's potential viability, the doctor who performed the abortion was convicted for manslaughter against Baby Boy and given a relatively light penalty of one year's probation but was subsequently acquitted by the Supreme Judicial Court of Massachusetts in *Commonwealth of Massachusetts v. Kenneth Edelin.*[60]

Given that *Roe v. Wade* tied state regulation of abortion to the state's legitimate interest in protecting prenatal life starting at viability, Baby Boy's ability to survive outside the womb became essential to determining whether his death by abortion had been legal or illegal. According to the reasoning in *Roe*, during the first trimester of gestation, a fetus may be aborted at any time for any reason.[61] After the first trimester, if a fetus is viable, a state, in promoting its interest in the potentiality of human life, may regulate, and even proscribe, abortion except where necessary for the "preservation of the life or health of the mother."[62]

Baby Boy's viability was undisputed at trial. He was found to have a regular heartbeat at the time of the abortion.[63] The autopsy demonstrated that he was "a normal child" with a body weight which was certainly small (600 grams, equivalent to approximately 1.54 pounds)[64] but with which other newborn children have survived.[65] There was evidence of respiratory activity and of a fetal age that would indicate viability. There was evidence that, given medical support, the baby would have probably survived and that his gestational age of up to twenty-six weeks placed him in the age bracket appropriate for legal viability, as indicated by Justice Reardon.[66]

Even though evidence indicated that Baby Boy could have survived the abortion had he been provided subsequent neonatal care, Dr. Kenneth Edelin caused his death in utero by deliberately delaying his live birth immediately following the detachment of the placenta, cutting his oxygen supply inside, rather than outside, of the uterus, in order to avoid legal restrictions surrounding viability.[67] Initially, Edelin attempted the abortion through the method of amniocentesis with saline infusion, an abortion that causes fetal death by draining off the amniotic fluid from the amniotic sac containing the fetus to replace it with a salt solution, causing contractions that would expel his body from the uterus.[68] Dr. Edelin inserted a long needle through the teenage mother's abdominal skin, hoping to reach into the amniotic sac.[69] The sac, however, failed to rupture; so, the next day, he proceeded to perform the abortion by hysterotomy, making an incision in the uterus to reach and extract the fetus.[70]

After Edelin detached the placenta from the fetus, a physician who witnessed the abortion testified that he saw Edelin remain motionless for at least three minutes with his hand in the uterus, his eyes fixed on a clock on the wall,[71] waiting for Baby Boy to die from oxygen deprivation. After a few minutes had elapsed, he delivered the child, placed him on a stainless steel basin, and put his hand on his chest wall for a few seconds, finding no heartbeat or sign of life.[72] Chief Justice Hennessey pointed out that there was evidence that "such a procedure is nowhere sanctioned as accepted medical practice. This was compared by one medical witness, Dr. Mecklenburg, to 'cutting the air hose on a salvage diver.' "[73]

The technique used by Edelin in the abortion of Baby Boy was found by the trial jury and later by the dissenting justices of the Massachusetts Supreme Court to be unethical and to constitute reckless homicidal conduct, "chosen without regard to the possibility of a live birth."[74] In addition, two doctors, Dr. Denis Cavanagh, a diplomat in the Royal College of Obstetricians and Gynecologists of England, and Dr. Norman L. Virnig, director of the Newborn Service at the St. Paul Ramsey Hospital, testified that the child would have survived the abortion had he been removed in a timely manner and given proper neonatal medical care.[75]

Given the fact that the child was, at the very least, potentially viable and that the abortion obtained by the teenager was not deemed to be "medically necessary," the prosecution could have pursued a claim of illegal abortion. However, due to the fact that the abortion took place between January 1973 and August 1974, the interregnum between *Roe v. Wade* and the approval of new state legislation, the prosecution brought manslaughter charges under Massachusetts' old abortion statute.[76]

Technically, manslaughter can only be committed on a live child, completely outside of the woman's body and homicidally destroyed.[77] Because the charge required a test of whether a live birth had occurred, the trial court examined a substantial amount of evidence in order to determine whether Baby Boy had taken a breath outside the uterus. Microscopic examination of lung tissue later fixed on slides showed partial expansion of some of the alveoli, which suggested respiratory activity outside the uterus. "Dr. John F. Ward, a pathologist, testified on the basis of his microscopic examination of lung tissue that the fetus 'did breathe outside the uterus.' "[78] Therefore, the jury found Dr. Edelin guilty of manslaughter, and the judge sentenced him to a relatively light penalty of one year's probation.

On appeal, the Massachusetts Supreme Court reversed the jury conviction for procedural reasons, concluding, among other things, that the case should not have been submitted to a jury trial at all.[79] The court found that there had been insufficient evidence of viability to proceed to a jury trial and that there was "prejudicial divergence" between the accusations against the defendant and instructions given to the jury.[80] For instance, the court found that showing Baby Boy's preserved body to the jury, placed in a 10 percent solution of formaldehyde by the resident pathologist, may have caused "unacceptable prejudice" among jurors.[81]

In addition, the court found the evidence that the fetus had taken a breath outside the uterus to be inconclusive.[82] The majority opinion stated that even if the fetus had swallowed amniotic fluid (as he might have done when distressed), there had been no evidence that he had taken a proper breath of oxygen in room air, either through the uterine incision or after delivery clear of the uterus, and the majority concluded that, therefore, his delivery did not technically qualify as a live birth. The court found that the three-to-five-minute wait by Dr. Edelin after detachment of the placenta did not constitute recklessness either, because he believed the fetus to be nonviable.[83]

Edelin was thus acquitted, and the abortion of Baby Boy, which could have been illegal even under *Roe v. Wade*'s standards, remained in impunity. Since then, Dr. Edelin has testified before Congress on numerous occasions promoting further deregulation of abortion in the United States, particularly for late-term abortions, as well as the reduction of state oversight on physicians who perform them.[84] He became a professor of obstetrics and gynecology at Boston University School of Medicine and was a member of the Committee on Ethics and Discipline of the Massachusetts Medical Society.[85] In addition, he was the chairman of the board of Planned Parenthood Federation of America from 1989 to 1992.

### The Petition Reaches the IACHR

In 1977, Christian B. White and Gary K. Potter, representing Catholics for Christian Political Action, filed a petition against the United States before the IACHR on behalf of Baby Boy.[86] They argued that the US Supreme Court decisions in *Roe v. Wade* and *Doe v. Bolton* had ended legal protection of unborn children in the United States and set the stage for the violation of Baby Boy's right to life in Massachusetts. Probably expecting a pro-life decision, they requested that the commission apply the American Declaration as interpreted by the American Convention, which explicitly protects the right to life from the moment of conception, and that it find the United States in violation of the right to life granted by article 1 ("Every human being has the right to life, liberty and the security of his person") and article 2 ("All persons are equal before the law . . . without distinction as to race, sex, language, creed or any other factor"—"age" being the key word here) of the American Declaration.[87]

Given the particular nature of individual petitions against countries such as the United States, which is a member of the Organization of American States but not a party to the American Convention, the IACHR has only limited jurisdiction over complaints against it.[88] Specifically, the commission may only accept complaints under the American Declaration, not the American Convention, according to the procedure established in the 1960 IACHR rules of procedure and the commission's statute.[89] The commission considers the United States to be automatically bound by the American Declaration since it became a member of the OAS in 1951 when in 1968 it ratified the OAS charter, which the Inter-American Court has deemed to interpret the American Declaration.[90] In terms of jurisdiction, the commission has deemed that both the American Declaration of the Rights and Duties of Man and the statute and rules of procedure of the IACHR have acquired "binding force" on the United States, according to the OAS charter, an assertion that the United States has repeatedly contested.[91]

Notwithstanding its objections, the US government has often responded to and defended itself against claims of human rights violations before the commission, inevitably submitting itself to the individual petitions system.[92] *Baby Boy* was one such instance. The procedure before the commission essentially involved an exchange of communications between the US government and the petitioners, culminating in a report, called IACHR Resolution 23/81, in which the commission assessed the United States' compliance with the American Declaration. Among other things, the petitioners stated that the US Supreme Court had sanctioned the arbitrary killing of human fetuses during the first six months of development by stating that the woman's right to abortion is absolute and that she is entitled to terminate her pregnancy at whatever time, in whatever way, and for whatever reason she alone chooses.[93] The State Department countered that in *Roe v. Wade* and *Doe v. Bolton*, the Supreme Court had protected the woman's right to privacy, deemed a fundamental right in the United States, implicitly enshrined in the Fourteenth Amendment of the US Constitution. The State Department affirmed that the court found that abortion prohibitions limited the exercise of the fundamental right to privacy in a manner inconsistent with "compelling state interests" that could justify the regulation of that right.

On July 27, 1979, Thomas Y. Yank, Henry Y. Hyde, Charles F. Dougherty, and Daniel E. Lungren, members of the US House of Representatives, requested that the commission inform them about related consequences of an eventual adverse decision of the commission against the United States.[94] Perhaps naively overestimating the political power of the IACHR, the congressmen posed the question of whether the United States could be subject to trade and diplomatic sanctions similar to those imposed upon Cuba by the OAS following the human rights violations of the Castro regime, should the commission find a violation of the declaration. In virtue of article 18 of the IACHR's statute, the commission declined to answer this consultation, invoking a procedural requirement that consultations be presented through the state party's delegation before the OAS in order for them to be considered.[95]

### A Partial Rapporteur

In its fiftieth session period (September–October 1980), the commission appointed pro-choice commissioner Carlos A. Dunshee de Abranches as rapporteur tasked with writing the *Baby Boy* report. This was highly irregular treatment for petitions in general, and no justification was given as to why the commissioners found it necessary or convenient to appoint a rapporteur to draft the report, contrary to usual practice of having the executive secretariat draft it.[96] Furthermore, Dunshee had unsuccessfully proposed to eliminate the prenatal right to life from conception from the draft convention on two occasions.[97] No explanation was provided as to why Carlos Dunshee, in particular, was chosen to write a report on a subject in which he had clear prejudice.

As a commissioner, Dunshee first proposed to eliminate the protection of the prenatal right to life from conception from the American Convention in 1969, during its preparatory work. A member of the IACHR at the time, Dunshee took part in an evaluation of the Inter-American Council of Jurists' draft for the American Convention.[98] On the occasion of the debate within the IACHR in 1968, then-Commissioner Dunshee unsuccessfully attempted to eliminate *all* protection from the time of conception by suggesting the deletion of the phrase "from the moment of conception."[99] The commission, however, rejected his proposal, stating that "for reasons of principle, it was fundamental to state the provision on the protection of the right to life in the form recommended to the Council of the OAS in its opinion [*sic*]."[100] It was thus decided to leave the right-to-life protections "from the moment of conception," as indicated by the Inter-American Council of Jurists.[101]

Later, in the following year, acting not as a commissioner but as a representative for the government of Brazil at the San José Conference, which approved the final text of the American Convention, Dunshee reiterated his formal proposal that states parties eliminate the prenatal right to life by deleting the expression "in general, from the moment of conception" from the text, in order to allow for individual states to legalize abortion in "a great variety of cases."[102] His proposal was also rejected at that stage. His subsequent appointment as rapporteur for the *Baby Boy* report thus raises legitimate questions about his impartiality and prejudice in light of his previous unsuccessful proposals to deprive the unborn child of human rights protection under the American Convention.[103]

## A Predictable Result

The report's conclusion was entirely unprecedented in the Inter-American human rights system but hardly surprising given the appointment of a pro-choice rapporteur and the petition's historical context. The *Baby Boy* report was issued in 1981, at a time when abortion advocacy was beginning to gain support in the Americas. It was also a time of enormous US political influence in Latin America. In *Baby Boy*, the commission seemed to rely entirely on the US government's interpretation of the declaration's preparatory work.[104] The commission also concluded that all other violations alleged by the petitioners—that is, violations of articles 2 (right to equality before law), 7 (right to special protection for mothers and children), and 11 (right to the preservation of health and to well-being) of the American Declaration—had "no direct relation to the facts set forth in the petition," and the commission dismissed them without any substantive examination.[105]

The *Baby Boy* report delved into an indirect interpretation of the American Convention, even though it acknowledged the convention's inapplicability to the United States and refused to read the American Declaration in light of the convention for the purposes of the prenatal right to life, as requested by the petitioners.[106] The commission did, however, read both instruments together to say that the *convention* did not grant an "absolute" right to life in light of the *declaration*'s preparatory work. The *Baby Boy* report held that the commission introduced the phrase "in general" during the convention's drafting to honor some political "compromise" that would have been reached during the Bogotá Conference—that is, the declaration's preparatory work, by which some states parties would have objected to a prenatal right to life in order to allow "life of the mother" or rape requirements for abortion in their jurisdictions.[107]

These conclusions, however, were not unanimously shared: four commissioners signed on to the report, and two dissented. Three separate opinions by Commissioners Andres Aguilar M., Marco Gerardo Monroy Cabra, and Luis Demetrio Tinoco Castro followed, evincing the lack of consensus among the commissioners. The concurring opinion by Commissioner Andres Aguilar hinted at having reservations about Carlos Dunshee's interpretation of the American Convention[108] but defended the report by stating that article 1 of the American Declaration only protects life from the moment of birth.[109] Commissioner Aguilar, however, concluded by stating that he shared the dissenting judges' view "based [on] the opinions of well-known men of science, that human life begins at the very moment of conception and ought to warrant complete protection from that moment, both in domestic law as well as international law."[110] Luis Demetrio Tinoco Castro (who had previously founded the first university in Costa Rica) and Marco Gerardo Monroy Cabra, who later went on to become a supreme court judge in his native Colombia, dissented on the report's substantive findings.

Both dissents by Commissioners Luis Demetrio Tinoco Castro and Marco Gerardo Monroy held that article 1 of the American Declaration, which protects the right to life of "every human being," also protects human life from the moment of conception and that abortion, particularly the one committed on Baby Boy, effectively violated the American Declaration.[111] Commissioner Tinoco found it self-evident that the declaration also protected life from conception—"life does not begin at birth—the final phase of the process of gestation—but at the moment of conception, which is the moment at which a new human being, distinct from the father and from the mother, is formed"—and that "in recognizing the right of the unborn to life, the Declaration rejects the legitimacy of any act that authorizes or considers acceptable acts or practices that will lead to its death."[112]

Commissioner Marco Gerardo Monroy Cabra pointed out that abortion is impermissible under the American Declaration: "[I]f conception produces a human life, and this right is the primary and fundamental one, abortion is an attack on the right to life and, therefore, runs counter to [a]rticle 1 of the American Declaration of the Rights and Duties of Man."[113] He referred to scientific evidence, such as the studies by geneticist Jerome Lejeune, demonstrating that the fetus is a human being and is genetically complete.[114] He also referred to Roman law precedents granting unborn children inheritance rights[115] and concluded that the voluntary interruption of pregnancy resulting in the destruction of the embryo or death of the fetus, like the one that ended the life of Baby Boy, "is unquestionably an offense against life and, consequently, a violation of [a]rticle 1 of the American Declaration of the Rights and Duties of Man."[116] He stated that "[i]n terminating legal protection of unborn children, the judicial decision of the [United States] constitutes a violation of Article 1 of the American Declaration of the Rights and Duties of Man."[117]

### Aftermath

Despite the Inter-American Court's reliance on its rationale in 2012, the *Baby Boy* report has been discredited by many commentators, including former Inter-American Court judges and IACHR commissioners.[118] Inter-American Court Judge Julio Barberis, for instance, was critical of the report and pointed out the inappropriateness of the IACHR's interpretation of the convention.[119] The existence of laws allowing abortion in some Latin American countries does not lead to the derogation of the right to life from conception in the American Convention, he said, but instead entails international responsibility.[120] Mexican Supreme Court Judge Sergio Salvador Aguirre Anguiano pointed out that the report interpreted the declaration and not the convention, since the commission had no power to interpret the convention in that case, and that the report was nonbinding on Mexico.[121]

American commissioner Dinah Shelton later wrote that the commission's conclusions in *Baby Boy* had been reached through "questionable reasoning, faulty analysis and little or no attention paid to the usual canons of construction of international documents."[122] She pointed out that the opinion of the commission did not, at any point, examine the meaning of the text of article 1 in the context of the declaration "as a whole" and that "this reliance on legislative history allows the majority to interpret the Convention to conform to its understanding of the Declaration in spite of obvious differences in language and purpose."[123] She also suggested that the commission in *Baby Boy* tacitly accepted *ratione personae* jurisdiction over the alleged victim, Baby Boy, by admitting the petition, therefore considering him a person with protectable rights in the Inter-American system. The assumption that a "person" had been subject to an alleged violation, she indicated, left open the possibility that other cases of fetal injury or death may be brought based on this report.[124]

### *Paulina Ramírez v. Mexico* (2007): A Wrongful Lifestyle Settlement

*Paulina* involved a friendly settlement procedure where the commission supported abortion rights advocates' demands for wrongful-birth-like reparations to Paulina, a rape victim whose mother had requested an abortion but later withdrew consent after receiving pro-life counseling.[125] The friendly settlement did not formally address the merits of the claim or interpret the convention in any way. For some time, it was politically influential in favor of abortion rights advocacy, but the state later adopted a constitutional amendment recognizing human life from the moment of conception that reversed the legislation prompted by the case in that state.

In 2002, an individual petition was brought before the IACHR by several organizations that advocate for abortion rights—the US-based Center for Reproductive Rights (CRR), some of its local affiliates, Alaide Foppa A.C., and the Grupo de Información en Reproducción Elegida (Reproductive Choice Information Group [GIRE])—representing Paulina del Carmen Ramírez Jacinto, a minor who had been impregnated at age fourteen.[126] Paulina was sexually assaulted by an adult man, who was later convicted and sentenced to sixteen years imprisonment; the rape resulted in pregnancy.[127] The child and her mother reported the assault and obtained legal authorization for the abortion at the public Prosecutor's Office, since the Baja California Criminal Code established a rape exception to criminal abortion.[128]

During their stay at the public hospital where the abortion was to be performed, Paulina and her mother were counseled by medical staff, pro-life individuals, and a Catholic priest, after which Paulina's mother withdrew her consent to the abortion.[129] They were exposed to pro-life materials and were told of the abortion's health risks by the hospital director.[130] Subsequently, Paulina's mother changed her mind about the abortion and asked hospital staff to refrain from carrying out the surgery. Paulina also refused the abortion, and in April 2000 she gave birth to a boy, whom she named Isaac de Jesús Ramírez Jacinto, effectively raising him at least until the time the petition was filed.[131]

The petition alleged human rights violations against a fourteen-year-old Paulina and her mother, arguing that the abortion had been intentionally delayed and that the counseling they had received constituted an "undue interference" with the pregnant child's purported right to an abortion.[132] They also claimed that the prosecution's failure to inform Paulina on the availability of abortifacients constituted a violation of her rights.[133] Even though Paulina and her mother voluntarily declined the abortion, the petitioners alleged that her case was "indicative of those of a countless number of girls and women *forced* into motherhood after being raped."[134] They demanded that the state adopt regulations forcing physicians to perform abortions and restricting rape victims' access to pro-life materials or health-related information on abortion risks that might lead them to change their minds on their decision to abort.[135]

Even though the commission never actually examined the petition's admissibility or merits, it endorsed all of the petitioners' demands and cooperated in their practical enforcement from the outset.[136] From 2002 to 2007, the IACHR facilitated at least four meetings between government representatives of the Mexican state of Baja California and the abortion rights advocates that filed the petition.[137] In them, it cooperated with the petitioners in getting the government to accept responsibility for the alleged violations and reaching a friendly settlement, the written agreement of which was signed on March 8, 2006.[138] The commission then held a follow-up meeting in October of the same year to verify state compliance with the commitments assumed vis-à-vis the petitioning abortion rights advocates.[139]

Had an admissibility analysis been carried out, the petition could have probably been defeated due to the petitioners' failure to exhaust any and all domestic remedies. No domestic *amparo* (constitutional application for appeal) or judicial remedy of any sort, other than the complaint before the local Prosecutor's Office, was filed at the local level.[140] Instead, the claim was directly submitted before the IACHR, in contravention of general principles of international law recognized by the American Convention, which provides that remedies under domestic law must have been pursued and exhausted before a party resorts to international human rights bodies.[141] The commission never addressed whether the petitioners were effectively denied a right to access domestic remedies or whether they simply chose not to.

Similarly, potential conflict with the unborn child's right to life from conception, children's rights, freedom of expression for pro-life individuals, and conscience rights for physicians arising from the petition were never examined by the commission. The question of whether children, or adults for that matter, had a protected right to abortion under the American Convention was not addressed. The fact that Paulina, like the victim's mother in *Baby Boy*, was a minor child was ignored. Eventually, without any substantial analysis or interpretation, the commission simply stated that the settlement was "compatible with the object and purpose of the American Convention" and approved the friendly settlement signed by the parties in March 2006.[142] The state of Baja California made no challenges to the petition's admissibility or merits and accepted full responsibility for all of the petitioners' allegations, pledging to comply with all of their demands.[143]

The friendly settlement agreement strikingly resembled a tort settlement in an American "wrongful birth" action (except for the fact that this case involved an entirely healthy child). In it, the state agreed to give generous reparations in cash, around 700,000 pesos—the equivalent of approximately US$66,000 in March 2006—to Paulina and her son, Isaac de Jesús, whose unwanted birth had allegedly resulted in "consequential damages" and "moral damages" to his mother.[144] The amount included, aside from said damages, assistance for housing and maintenance expenses, school enrollment fees, school supplies, and transportation.[145] The state thus assumed full financial "liability" for all expenses relating to Isaac's maintenance and education. In addition, it committed itself to granting Paulina and Isaac generous social assistance (the kind that perhaps should be made available to all low-income single mothers) such as school vouchers, free health care until Isaac's age of majority, free counseling, financial and technical assistance in setting up a grocery store, and permanent education assistance for Isaac.[146]

Reparations were also to be paid to abortion rights advocacy organizations, such as a computer and a printer that were handed out to them "as a one-off presentation,"[147] although it was unclear what human rights violations *they* had suffered. In addition, the government of Baja California took extraordinary commitments vis-à-vis the Center for Reproductive Rights, including to consult with it before the approval of the preliminary draft of an amendment to the government protocol (official standard) for treatment of victims of sexual violence and to carry out comprehensive research on abortion in Mexico for this organization.[148]

At the time of the IACHR's report, March 2007, the commission found that state had actually complied with most of the agreed-upon reparations.[149] Baja California Sur eventually reformed its criminal code to create an additional "health of the mother" requirement to the criminalization of abortion and to establish lower penalties for illegal abortion.[150] The state also reformed its criminal procedure code to facilitate access to abortions following rape. These reforms entered into force in September 2005. The state of Baja California also issued a "public acknowledgment of responsibility," published in the local newspapers *La Voz de la Frontera* and *La Crónica* on December 30, 2005, as well as in the official gazette of the state of Baja California on February 10, 2006.[151]

The commission celebrated the agreement while vaguely alluding to the Convention of Belém do Pará, women's rights, health care services, right to equality, nondiscrimination, and gender-based violence.[152] It welcomed the state's good faith "in complying with its treaty obligations"[153] and exhorted other states' parties to adopt criminal, civil, or administrative measures in order to ensure that "incidents," such as counseling of a pregnant teen to carry her pregnancy to term or delaying a minor's abortion, "are duly sanctioned and do not enjoy impunity."[154] The report did not, however, identify an actual legal basis for these conclusions in the American Convention.

The friendly settlement only produced temporary effects in Baja California. After *Paulina*, in October 2008, the state legislature approved a constitutional amendment protecting the right to life from conception, stating: "[F]rom the moment in which an individual is conceived, he enters under the protection of the law, and is treated as a born person for all corresponding legal effects, until his natural or non-induced death."[155] The constitution prevails over states in Mexican states, so the amendment voided incompatible provisions in the criminal code and similar laws adopted as a result of *Paulina.*

### *James Demers v. Canada*: Partial Acceptance of a Pro-life Claim

*James Demers v. Canada*,[156] an admissibility report involving a pro-life activist's freedom of speech and a claim for violation of unborn children's right to life, did not interpret the American Convention either but implicitly recognized that unborn children can be victims under the American Convention if certain conditions are met. The petitioner, James Demers, a resident of British Columbia, Canada, was arrested pursuant to the Canadian Abortion Services Act in December 1996 for peacefully protesting outside a Vancouver abortion clinic.[157] He was found to be in violation of the Abortion Services Access Zone Regulation, a zoning regulation that made it illegal to disseminate pro-life materials and information within thirty meters of an abortion clinic.[158]

Remarkably, the day Demers was arrested he was standing quietly with a sign bearing a citation of article 4(1) of the American Convention.[159] In 1997, Demers was convicted in the Provincial Court of British Columbia at Vancouver.[160] His appeals to the Supreme Court of Columbia in 1999 and the Court of Appeals for British Columbia in 2003 were subsequently dismissed, thus exhausting all domestic remedies. In 2005, Demers submitted the petition against Canada before the IACHR, alleging human rights violations against himself as well as hundreds of thousands of unborn children and their mothers.[161]

Like the United States, Canada never signed or ratified the American Convention on Human Rights, nor did it accept the convention's additional protocols or the jurisdiction of the Inter-American Court.[162] Therefore, the commission, consistent with its practice for petitions against Canada and the United States, applied the American Declaration only, in virtue of article 23 of its rules of procedure and deriving its jurisdiction from the OAS Charter.[163] The report thus examined whether James Demers's petition was admissible for violations of the American Declaration only.

The commission found that the facts pertaining to alleged violations of article 4 of the American Declaration (right to freedom of expression), as stated in the petition, constituted prima facie violations of the American Declaration, and the petition was declared admissible in that regard.[164] The petition was, however, declared inadmissible regarding claims of violations against aborted children and their mothers under articles 1, 7, 13, 17, and 29 of the American Declaration, due to the stated vagueness of the petitioner's claim, which derived from a lack of jurisdiction *ratione personae*.[165] The petitioner made a general claim for right-to-life violations "against hundreds of thousands of unborn children and their mothers."[166] The unnamed and indeterminate number of victims was found by the commission to be insufficient to satisfy the requirements of article 23 of the commission's rules of procedure, which requires petitioners to point out individual victims of human rights violations.[167]

On one hand, the commission correctly stated that while a petitioner has liberal standing before it—meaning he can bring a claim on behalf of others—he or she must indicate a specific victim whose rights under the convention have been specifically violated.[168] The *Baby Boy* petition can be distinguished here by the fact that the victim, Baby Boy, was a distinct individual: the aborted viable male child of a pregnant teenager. The commission recalled that it previously disallowed petitioners to represent an "indeterminate group of persons,"[169] and it applied the same reasoning in *Demers*, where it deemed that the petitioner's mere reference to "unborn children and their mothers" was insufficient and that victims should be "sufficiently specific, defined and identifiable" in the petition.[170] On the other hand, it seems unusual for the commission to partially reject a petition on a procedural objection without allowing the petitioner to amend his complaint, despite the fact that Mr. Demers attempted to do so.[171]

The commission has allowed petitioners to amend similar anonymous and generic complaints in other cases, such as Petition 12.361 against Costa Rica, which later became the *Artavia* case (discussed in chapter 4).[172] In that case, the IACHR not only allowed petitioners to amend their complaint by identifying alleged victims of reproductive rights' violations almost two years after the petition had been submitted, but it also allowed them to expand on the substantive allegations against the state.[173] Given that abortion enjoys legal protection in Canada, the petitioner faced exceptional difficulties in accurately identifying specific, defined victims (i.e., unborn children or their mothers), since identifying information about women who had abortions is protected by privacy laws and not available to the public. The petitioner thus experienced genuine obstacles in overcoming the commission's active legitimation standard, which required Demers to prove that he was a representative of the said abortion victims in order to justify his liberal standing before the commission.[174]

In Petition 12.361, the commission applied a greater degree of flexibility toward petitioners at the admissibility stage: "To accept the argument of the state that the complaint should be inadmissible because the individual victims were not identified in the initial petition, although they were subsequently identified, would imply a formalistic decision inconsistent with protecting the human rights enshrined in the Convention, and would place the presumed victims in a position of defenselessness."[175] In addition, "[t]he Inter-American Court of Human Rights has declared that it is a commonly accepted principle that the procedural system is a means for seeing that justice is done, and that it is not sacrificed for the sake of mere formalities."[176] A similar degree of flexibility could have been applied in *Demers*.

In any case, the IACHR accepted that unborn children could be victims in the Inter-American system as long as they were individual cases and not complaints *in abstracto* or *actio popularis*.[177] As of 2019, there is no public record that the case has been archived or resolved through the friendly settlement process in any of the IACHR annual reports, which contain information on the status of individual petitions.[178] It is unlikely that the petition is still open for resolution by the commission due to the over-ten-year hiatus since the admissibility report, but no public record of the case's archive can be found in the IACHR annual reports either.

## The Case of "Amelia": A Challenge to Nicaragua's Full Abortion Ban

Advocates for the creation of abortion rights have challenged the validity of the full abortion bans in Nicaragua and El Salvador mostly by seeking the recognition of a right to "therapeutic abortion," as in the matter of *Beatriz*, brought before the Inter-American Court (described in chapter 2).[179] The term has been interpreted both narrowly and broadly by abortion rights advocates to include many forms of abortion decriminalization, from life and health exceptions to rape and eugenic exceptions to abortions on female prisoners to abortions on pregnant children on account of age alone.[180] The *Amelia* petition was introduced at a time when Nicaragua, in particular, was being subjected to significant international pressure, including withdrawal of foreign aid on the part of some European countries, to reinstate its decriminalization of so-called therapeutic abortion.[181]

In *PM 43-10 "Amelia," Nicaragua*,[182] the commission heard a request for precautionary measures, filed by several abortion rights advocates, including US-based Catholics for Choice, that indirectly challenged Nicaragua's abortion ban. There was no interpretation of the prenatal right to life from conception in *PM 43-10 "Amelia," Nicaragua*; but the commission failed to order an abortion among its precautionary measures or to urge Nicaragua to change its abortion law, despite being urged to do so.

The complaint involved Amelia (pseudonym), a pregnant twenty-six-year-old woman suffering from an unspecified form of metastatic cancer, whose doctors allegedly refused to treat her with chemotherapy or radiotherapy due to her pregnancy and the high risk that treatment could cause a miscarriage. Petitioners argued that Amelia was in need of an immediate abortion and requested the IACHR to order one through precautionary measures, which are applicable "in serious and urgent situations," "to prevent irreparable harm to persons," according to its rules of procedure.[183]

The precautionary measures issued by the commission were confined to recommending measures to preserve a cancer patient's right to medical treatment but did not order an immediate abortion as the petitioning organizations requested. The IACHR asked the state of Nicaragua "to adopt the measures necessary to ensure that the beneficiary has access to the medical treatment she needs to treat her metastatic cancer; to adopt the measures in agreement with the beneficiary and her representatives; and to keep her identity and that of her family under seal," but it did not recommend the requested abortion.[184]

The state of Nicaragua complied with the precautionary measures, and "Amelia" received chemotherapy, which eventually led to a stillbirth.[185] Organizations involved in the petition—the Strategic Group for the Decriminalization of Therapeutic Abortion, Catholics for Choice, Feminists of León, Nicaraguan Center for Human Rights, and the Latin American and Caribbean Women's Health Network—later deplored the fact that Amelia had carried the pregnancy to term as "inhuman," arguing that the allegedly unviable child took away her energy to fight the illness. They insisted that she should have been given an abortion.[186]

### The Case of "Mainumby": A Challenge to Paraguay's Full Abortion Ban

In 2015, the IACHR was asked to issue precautionary measures against Paraguay recommending that an immediate abortion of a female fetus be performed on a pregnant indigenous child.[187] The commission recommended that medical treatment and "all available options" be presented to the child, without specifically alluding to abortion but coming close to doing so.[188] Commissioner Paulo Vannuchi later stated that, in granting the precautionary measures, the commission "did not include one of the requests, *that there be a clear defense of a right to abortion*," because they understood "that the issue of abortion involves such delicate questions, religious convictions [*sic*]."[189]

The state of Paraguay openly resisted the claim that the American Convention required it to order an abortion on a minor, and the country categorically affirmed that its international human rights obligations under the American Convention involved a duty to protect both the health of mother and that of her unborn child. Particularly, the state defended its constitutional protection of a prenatal right to life as consistent with the American Convention: "The state had complied with the norms established in Article 4 of the National Constitution of the Paraguay Republic, consistent with Article 4 of the Pact of San Jose [American Convention]."[190]

Mainumby (pseudonym) was an indigenous ten-year-old child who was raped and impregnated by her stepfather. The perpetrator was captured and jailed.[191] He was tried together with Mainumby's mother, whom authorities prosecuted for complicity due to her failure to protect her child from sexual abuse.[192] The complaint before the IACHR, however, did not request that the perpetrator and his accomplice be brought to justice. Instead, it requested that the child be given access to abortion and that the mother be granted greater access to the child and restored custody of her.[193]

The request for precautionary measures was filed on behalf of Mainumby and her mother by two abortion rights advocacy organizations: CLADEM, a Peru-based organization, and Equality Now, a US-based organization.[194] The petitioners requested that the Paraguayan state immediately provide Mainumby with information about access to abortion in order to "protect her right to life, health, physical and mental integrity, both on the short and long term," as well as information on the health risks involved with carrying the pregnancy to term.[195] The request seemed to be based on the assumption that the child would have chosen abortion had she been informed about the option to abort.

The demand seemed somewhat disingenuous given that (a) abortion was not, in fact, legally available for Mainumby under Paraguayan law, and (b) the assumption that Mainumby would have wished to abort contradicted her express desire to give birth and raise her daughter, as reflected in the record.[196] There are no criminal exemptions for rape or minority alone under Paraguayan law; abortion is legally permitted only when the mother's life is endangered by the pregnancy, and in that case, abortion is understood as a medical procedure that may indirectly cause fetal death, not one intended to destroy the unborn child.[197]

The petition's purpose thus seems to have been to make abortion available to the child and to indirectly challenge Paraguay's full abortion ban by getting the commission to order the creation of a criminal exemption for abortion following rape, and on account of minority alone, as Commissioner Vannuchi later suggested.[198] The commission, however, stopped short of doing so although it vaguely alluded to the idea.

### Mainumby's Stated Wishes and Mainumby's Mother as Alleged Victim

Even though the petition was nominally filed on behalf of the child, it appears that the petitioning organizations did not represent the child's views before the commission, since it later transpired that Mainumby herself did not actually want or request an abortion.[199] Despite the commission's emphasis on a child's right to participate in health care decision-making, neither the IACHR, CLADEM, nor Equality Now reported any contact with Mainumby or any inquiry into Mainumby's wishes about getting an abortion. Their only statement in that regard was that the girl had not objected to her mother's petition for abortion, that "there was no manifestation of disagreement between the mother and the child" at the time her mother petitioned for an abortion.[200]

The record, in fact, specifically indicated that Mainumby expressed a wish to have the baby, even though she was apparently being "pressured" to ask for an abortion, according to witness testimony.[201] Petitioners themselves reported that, with time, after therapy and institutional placement, the child "was enthusiastic about her pregnancy" and that she "had a good bond with the pregnancy."[202] She also told her fellow institutionalized girl friends that "she always wanted a girl" and that she wanted to work on embroideries for the baby.

The petitioners chose to file for precautionary measures on behalf of both the child and the mother even though the mother had been convicted for failure to protect her child from sexual abuse.[203] The petition itself indicated that the mother knew of the abuse for at least two years: she denounced her partner's rape of the child when she was eight years old, apparently to no avail, yet she continued to cohabit with the rapist, and the abuse continued until the child became pregnant at the age of ten.[204] The mother then petitioned for an abortion on her minor daughter, first before a hospital, then before a juvenile court.[205]

The Paraguayan Prosecutor's Office indicated that the woman had been placed in temporary imprisonment in order to prevent undue influence on Mainumby, suspecting that the child's contact with her mother "could affect potential elements of proof" and interfere with the sexual assault investigation.[206] Furthermore, the child was appointed independent counsel through the child protective services office.[207] The petitioners were aware of all of these facts but nevertheless petitioned for the mother's access and custody of Mainumby, the improvement of the mother's incarceration conditions, and her eventual acquittal of all charges.[208] Perhaps these facts motivated the commission to eventually refuse precautionary measures for the mother and grant them only for Mainumby.[209]

### UN Group of Human Rights Experts Demands an Abortion for Mainumby

A month before the precautionary measures were issued, a United Nations (UN) working group of four human rights experts, which included former commissioner Juan Méndez,[210] issued a statement saying that "the Government of Paraguay has failed in its responsibility to act with due diligence" in the case of Mainumby for refusing "access to treatments to save her life and preserve her health, including safe and therapeutic abortion in a timely manner."[211] Unlike CLADEM and Equality Now, the UN expert group statement did mention that "[i]t is crucial that the alleged rapist, who has just been arrested, be duly prosecuted," but the statement said nothing about the mother and focused on the supposed need for an immediate abortion on Mainumby.[212]

The group explicitly advanced the idea of abortion as a life-saving health treatment, and as the only alternative to serve the pregnant child's best interests: "[D]espite requests made by the girl's mother and medical experts to terminate this pregnancy which puts the girl's life at risk, the [s]tate failed to take measures to protect the health as well as the physical and mental integrity and even the life of the 10-year-old girl."[213] It also demanded the creation of a governmental body that would authorize the abortion to be performed on the child: "No proper interdisciplinary and independent expert assessment with the aim to insure the girl's best interests was done before overturning [*sic*] life-saving treatments, including abortion."[214]

Paraguay's Ministry of Foreign Relations issued a press release protesting UN experts' issuance of the statement without even requesting any information from the Paraguayan government.[215] The ministry emphasized its commitment to protecting the rights of the child and cited article 4 of its constitution, which protects the right to life from the moment of conception. It reported that Mainumby was receiving medical and psychological treatment, that she had been placed under permanent medical supervision, and that an interdisciplinary board had been created to evaluate her state of health. The ministry reported that the perpetrator had been arrested and imprisoned and was awaiting trial. It invited the independent group of experts to visit Paraguay in order to see the measures implemented to care for Mainumby.

Shortly after the UN expert statement was issued, the interdisciplinary panel issued a report that did not make the expected recommendation—namely, an immediate abortion. The panel recommended that the child's pregnancy be "interrupted" upon "the materialization of any risk."[216] It also recommended that contact with her mother and her family be reestablished as requested by petitioners. A few days later, a congressional committee for the "study of the criminal code reform" hosted a hearing on the potential reform of abortion prohibitions contained in article 109 of Paraguay's criminal code.[217] The hearing, however, did not lead to the creation of any criminal exemptions for abortion.

Given that the hospital's medical board and Mainumby's attending physician reported no complications, an immediate abortion or a termination of pregnancy was never ordered. The petitioners filed for precautionary measures before the IACHR nine days after the interdisciplinary panel report.[218] The day after, the Ministry of Foreign Relations issued another press release directed to the IACHR and the abortion rights advocacy organizations involved, describing the measures it had taken to protect the child's mental and physical health, her contact with extended family members and her mother, and the legal and psychological assistance provided to the mother, who was imprisoned due to her failure to protect the child and her complicity with the sexual abuse.[219] The press release indicated that the health minister had discussed Mainumby' s situation with the Office of the UN High Commissioner for Human Rights, and had called international human rights experts and organizations to "stick to [international] norms of cooperation, coexistence and respect."[220]

### Paraguay's Response to the IACHR Complaint

The Paraguayan government authorities understood their international human rights obligations as involving a duty to protect both the health of mother and that of the unborn child and rejected the suggestion that Mainumby should automatically be given an abortion. The state reported to the commission that it had created a medical team in order to "evaluate and monitor the health of the pregnant child and the developing fetus" in order to fulfill "the state's obligation, through its public health system, to safeguard the life and health of persons."[221]

The Paraguayan government authorities reported to the IACHR that Mainumby, who was also found to have signs of malnourishment, had been placed under permanent medical observation in a public hospital and then transferred to a home for pregnant teenagers, with weekly hospital visits and daily monitoring.[222] The Health Ministry created a medical team and implemented a work plan to provide comprehensive nutritional, dental, obstetric, and mental health assistance to Mainumby.[223] Child protection authorities provided Mainumby with assistance from a social worker and continued psychological therapy for her and one of her siblings; they facilitated contact between the child and her extended family and made plans for family reunification.[224] The child also received elementary school instruction and child care preparation from two professionals assigned by the ministry of education at the institution where she resided.[225] Visitation with Mainumby's mother was also allowed.[226]

Mainumby's pregnancy evolved favorably: her attending obstetrician reported that she was suffering no complications and was gaining appropriate weight and that the fetus was also developing normally.[227] The medical team assisting her reported that the child was in stable condition and that she responded well to medication in one episode of some discomfort and irritability.[228] The hospital where Mainumby was receiving health care later issued a report stating that the attending physician advised against an interruption of pregnancy and that a late-term abortion could have been psychologically harmful to the child.[229] CLADEM and Equality Now were dissatisfied with these medical treatment choices and insisted that the child be evaluated by a different medical board that would recommend an abortion, even though the child was at the beginning of her third trimester (twenty-sixth week) of pregnancy at the time of the complaint before the IACHR.[230]

The commission's resolution favorably noted the comprehensive measures implemented by Paraguay to protect the child's rights and health, as well as the visitation granted to the mother and other family members.[231] However, it noted the absence of a specific plan in case of an emergency, which, according to the commission, should include "all available options, in light of WHO guidelines . . . on sexual and reproductive health of children and adolescents" and of the "highest applicable international standards."[232] It vaguely noted a lack of information on the decision-making process regarding the child's health care and on the application of the best-interests-of-the-child principle, but did not specifically refer to abortion.[233]

### IACHR Conclusions

The IACHR finally issued precautionary measures against the state of Paraguay in June 2015, in Resolution 178/15, which did not actually recommend any specific measures that the state was not already taking, but generally asked Paraguay to protect Mainumby's "life and personal integrity" and "to ensure the child's right to be informed and to participate in decisions affecting her health in accordance with her age and maturity."[234] While the commission indirectly alluded to abortion by recommending that Paraguay ensure adequate medical treatment for Mainumby "in light of the technical guidelines of the World Health Organization and other similar sources," "in which all the options available are assured," it did not specifically refer to abortion.[235]

The resolution stated that Mainumby's pregnancy, her age, the sexual violence she endured, and the alleged lack of contact with family members, among other factors, placed her at grave, urgent risk of irreparable harm, therefore satisfying the standard for precautionary measures.[236] The commission also stated that the Paraguayan state had failed to give proper legal representation to the child, even though the Paraguayan child defender's office had legally represented Mainumby.[237] The IACHR did not explain why it considered that representation improper.

The resolution condemned the lack of information to Mainumby and her family on the supposed availability of abortion and suggested that carrying the pregnancy to term may have caused the child "unnecessary physical and mental suffering."[238] Throughout, however, it avoided the use of the term *abortion* by deferring to the UN Expert Group Statement (which did explicitly allude to it) and indicating that the child should have been given information on "possible risks" of carrying the pregnancy to term and on "all necessary alternatives" from an "integral perspective."[239]

Regarding Mainumby's mother, the commission entirely ignored the mother's potential complicity in the child's sexual abuse. It did not reach any specific findings and indicated that it would need further information from both parties to do so.[240] Eventually, however, only Mainumby was named as beneficiary of the commission's precautionary measures and not her mother.[241]

### Aftermath and Compliance with Precautionary Measures

Paraguay rejected the IACHR's precautionary measures, characterizing them as untimely (*extemporáneas*), indicating that it had already taken all measures to prevent the impunity of the child's sexual assault and to "ensure the life and integrity of the pregnant child as well as prenatal" life.[242] Its Ministry of Foreign Relations understood its actions as consistent with the American Convention: "The state complied with the norms established in article 4 of the National Constitution of the Paraguay Republic, consistent with article 4 of the Pact of San José [American Convention]."[243] The ministry noted the case's large media exposure and reminded the media and public opinion of the need to safeguard the child's identity in order "to respect her right to privacy and nonexposure, both of the child and of her baby in gestation," in accordance with Paraguayan child protection statutes.[244]

In the meantime, Mainumby delivered a healthy baby girl via C-section in August 2015.[245] Her mother served two months' imprisonment and was then granted supervised visitation with Mainumby. She was reunited with her daughter as of October 2015 and received cash benefits as well as welfare assistance from the Paraguayan government.[246] Petitioners, however, continued to protest that Mainumby had been subjected to "forced pregnancy" and "forced motherhood," while advocating for decriminalization of abortion for minors and rape victims in Paraguayan jurisdiction, as well as the creation of broadly defined exceptions for the life and health of the mother.

Almost one year after the precautionary measures had been issued, in April 2016, four commissioners revisited the case and confronted Paraguayan state officials during a public hearing in Washington, DC, reprimanding the state of Paraguay for its failure to give Mainumby access to an abortion.[247] The hearing itself was conducted in a highly irregular manner. A working meeting on the *Mainumby* request for precautionary measures had originally been scheduled between the petitioners (Equality Now and CLADEM) and state representatives, but Paraguay declined to attend, given the IACHR's denial of its request for confidentiality.[248] It is unclear why Paraguay requested confidentiality, but commissioners ultimately forced a public hearing on the *Mainumby* matter anyway by using a hearing originally designated to deal with the general situation of victims of sexual violence in Paraguay to discuss the *Mainumby* request for precautionary measures, despite Paraguay's protests.[249]

Rather than following up on the precautionary measures as a whole, the commissioners focused on the petitioners' request for an abortion alone and Paraguay's failure to provide it. No questions were asked about Mainumby's health or that of her newborn child. Commissioner Esmeralda Arosemena de Troitiño questioned Paraguayan officials on why Mainumby's pregnancy had not been interrupted.[250] Commissioner Paulo Vannuchi complained about "fundamentalist, pro-life organizations" in Paraguay, which he said led to Amnesty International calling *Mainumby* a high-profile case at the global level.[251] Commissioner Enrique Gil Botero suggested that children had a right to informed consent in abortion situations as they do in gender reassignment surgeries.[252] Commissioner Margarette May Macaulay said that for "a child who is forced to have a child, [their] childhood is completely arrested, they can no longer enjoy the rest of their childhood," and indicated that the child's opinions must be taken into account under the Convention on the Rights of the Child.[253]

The state officials representing Paraguay reiterated the state's rejection of the commission's measures as untimely (*extemporáneas*) given that, at the time, Paraguay had already complied with its obligation to protect both mother and child.[254] Throughout, state delegates seemed confused about the commission's focus on abortion, whereas the state had applied all sorts of protective measures given to child rape victims and had made sure that Mainumby had a safe delivery, which she did. One of the state's representatives expressed some frustration, indicating that the commission's measures had "not contributed to dialogue with civil society" at the national level.

Ricardo Gonzales Borgue, from the Secretariat for Childhood and Adolescence, indicated that Paraguay had seriously undertaken its commitment to protect Mainumby's rights but that the Paraguayan Constitution protects life from the moment of conception and that its interpretation made it impossible to comply with the commission's recommendation that she be given an automatic abortion. He indicated that the actions of the secretariat had saved two lives, that of the mother and the child, and that Mainumby's attending medical professionals had evaluated the child's pregnancy and "did not, at any moment, recommend that she be given an abortion according to current law in Paraguay." He explained that Paraguayan law prohibits abortion and only grants a punishment exemption for indirect abortion in situations where the mother's life or health is at serious risk, which was not the case with the minor.

### *Manuela* Petition against El Salvador

The *Manuela* petition was filed in the context of repeated demands on the part of advocates and Commissioner Margarette May Macaulay that El Salvador stop enforcing its full abortion ban immediately and then take steps to overturn it.[255] Advocates for abortion rights had previously made several appearances at the commission's public hearings attacking the abortion ban by arguing that overzealous prosecution on the part of state officials had resulted in many women being imprisoned for involuntary miscarriage or obstetric emergencies in El Salvador.[256] Those allegations, however, have been categorically rejected by Salvadorian authorities, who have repeatedly held that the said cases involved infanticide, not involuntary miscarriages.[257] The *Manuela* individual petition, involving a woman who allegedly had a spontaneous abortion and would have been wrongfully convicted, was declared admissible by the IACHR in 2017.[258]

The petition's facts are quite grotesque: Manuela (pseudonym) was convicted by a Salvadorian court for the aggravated murder of her newborn baby (El Salvador's statutory equivalent of infanticide) by violently ripping the umbilical cord off his body and throwing him into a latrine, where the baby drowned in excrement.[259] Her family apparently provided crucial evidence regarding the circumstances of the child's death.[260] The petitioners—namely the CRR, the Citizens Group for the Decriminalization of Therapeutic, Ethical and Eugenic Abortion, and another local organization—dispute the judicial fact-finding itself: they allege that Manuela did not know that she was pregnant, had an unexpected delivery in the latrine, lost consciousness, was not responsible for her baby's death, and was therefore wrongfully convicted.[261]

The case's connection to abortion seems relatively tenuous: petitioners do not say that Manuela wanted an abortion, requested one, or tried to have one, and she was not convicted for abortion but instead for aggravated murder, but the admissibility report somehow blames it all on El Salvador's abortion ban,[262] without identifying a clear connection. Other facts involving Manuela's cancer diagnosis, her lack of medical care, and her subsequent death in custody seem more persuasive in terms of characterizing potential human rights violations,[263] but those had nothing to do with her conviction or with the country's abortion ban. The state does not seem willing to readily accept the allegations, but the petition was declared admissible by the commission.[264] Therefore, whether the case results in either a friendly settlement, a merits report, or even a lawsuit before the Inter-American Court may depend on how much resistance the state will offer to the commission's recommendations.

In any case, it is hard to see how the commission could reach a merits decision without violating its "fourth instance" doctrine, according to which Inter-American human rights bodies should not hear requests to retry matters of fact or domestic law. The Inter-American Court has repeatedly defined this doctrine as meaning that the court "cannot serve as an appellate court to examine alleged *errors of internal law or fact* that may have been committed by the domestic courts acting within their jurisdiction."[265] Such examination would be appropriate only insofar as "the mistakes entailed a possible violation of any of the rights set forth in the Convention," and it is unclear how the alleged errors could lead the commission to conclude that El Salvador violated the convention here.[266]

To conclude that El Salvador has violated the convention would essentially require a fact-based review of the national trial court's decision by the commission; it would require the commission to act exactly as a national court of appeals. To reach the conclusion that Manuela was wrongfully convicted, the commission would inevitably have to reweigh the evidence and reassess the credibility of witnesses to potentially reach new factual conclusions and substitute its judgment for the national trial court's.

Taking such a step could be a reckless move, not only because the commission has no capacity, in terms of resources, to reassess forensic and other criminal evidence presented at trial but also because it would be missing its main witness, Manuela, who passed away in 2010, two years before the petition was filed.[267]

## Future of IACHR's Enforcement of the Prenatal Right-to-Life Provision

During the drafting or preparatory work (*travaux préparatoires*) that led to the American Convention on Human Rights, the commission refused to reverse the convention's recognition of a right to life from conception "for reasons of principle," when it was so suggested by Commissioner Carlos Dunshee de Abranches, who later authored the *Baby Boy* report. Since then, however, the commission has been relatively inconsistent in asserting the incompatibility of article 4(1) with elective abortion. In *Baby Boy v. U.S.*, the IACHR interpreted article 4(1) of the American Convention on the prenatal right to life and article 1 of the American Declaration on a universal right to life in a restrictive manner, as being compatible with the creation of a constitutional right to abortion in the United States. That interpretation was later used by the Inter-American Court in the *Artavia Murillo* case, discussed in chapter 2.

Since *Baby Boy v. United States*, the Inter-American Commission on Human Rights has been mostly unwilling to promote enforcement of article 4(1)'s protection of prenatal life in the context of abortion. In fact, it has sometimes actively promoted decriminalization of abortion and creation of abortion rights in states parties to the American Convention, as in the *Paulina* settlement, in the *Mainumby* hearing, and in many of the commission's promotional activities. Petitions by pro-life advocates, such as those in *Baby Boy* and *James Demers*, have generally not been well received by the commission, which has often sided with pro-choice petitioners such as in *Paulina*, *Amelia*, *Mainumby*, and *Manuela*.

No case or petition before the IACHR has so far actually involved a woman who was prosecuted or sanctioned for abortion, not even the *Manuela* petition, pending at the commission as of 2019, which involves a conviction for infanticide, not induced abortion. Instead, petitions have involved authorization for abortions on pregnant minors on account of their age alone, as in *Paulina* and *Mainumby*, and for immediate abortions on impoverished women suffering from serious health conditions, as in *Amelia* and *Beatriz* (addressed in the next chapter). The commission has demanded little accountability from petitioners on abortion-related matters; it has permitted abortion rights advocates to get away with deception, for instance, in claiming to speak for Mainumby before the commission or in presenting her mother as a victim.

The IACHR has stopped short of formally requiring states to provide or facilitate an immediate abortion through individual petitions or precautionary measures procedures. It has failed to directly recommend decriminalization of abortion when hearing challenges against full abortion bans such as those of Nicaragua and Paraguay, although it came close to doing so in *Mainumby*. The commission has, on the other hand, sometimes used its political rather than legal powers to pressure individual states to decriminalize abortion and to ignore their prenatal-right-to-life protections, as in the *Paulina* settlement.

The commission's abortion-related advocacy has, in addition, led to political repercussions that may partially affect its own proper functioning. In 2013, US senators Marco Rubio and Mike Lee sent a letter to then US secretary of state John Kerry expressing concern about the promotion of an ideological agenda by the OAS with financial support from the United States. Citing complaints from Central and South American officials that their national sovereignty is being threatened by "cultural imperialism imposed by an organization that is seemingly more concerned with pushing an ideological agenda than respecting the local rule of law," the letter described the Inter-American Court of Human Rights as "often subverting laws on matters pertaining to issues like abortion and marriage."[268]

Starting in 2017, over six hundred legislators from at least eighteen countries in Latin America and the Caribbean signed a declaration denouncing Inter-American bodies' promotion of abortion legalization as contrary to the letter and spirit of the American Convention.[269] The American Declaration Regarding the Independence and Self-Determination of Peoples on Matters Relating to Life, Family and Religious Freedom denounced "aggressive and continued efforts by the OAS, the Inter-American Commission on Human Rights and the Inter-American Court of Human

Rights to advance and impose on [m]ember [s]tates certain ideological policies and perspectives that threaten the right to life."[270] It also rejected any interpretation of the American Convention that "seeks to limit or exclude the right to life[;] . . . that promotes the creation of an alleged international obligation to authorize or subsidize voluntary abortion or expand scenarios where abortion is not punishable; or that limits the right of conscience of those that for serious reasons refuse to cooperate with voluntary abortions."

The most serious blow to the commission's abortion-related activities came in 2019, during President Donald Trump's administration, when the US government withdrew funds from the Inter-American Commission due to its promotion of abortion legalization in states parties to the American Convention.[271] The withdrawal was requested by nine US senators who, in a public letter to Secretary of State Mike Pompeo, denounced both the commission and the Inter-American Commission on Women (CIM) for "aggressively lobby[ing] pro-life sovereign nations to legalize abortion," in violation of the Siljander Amendment, which prohibits US federal funds from being used to "lobby for or against abortion."[272]

In particular, the senators denounced public statements by which the commission urged Argentina, Chile, and El Salvador to change their abortion laws, pointing out that "these ideologically-motivated actions are especially egregious when one considers the American Convention on Human Rights[, which] recognizes that 'every person has the right to have his life respected . . . from the moment of conception.'"[273] They lamented that both the commission and CIM "have completely ignored the OAS mandate to protect the right to life in favor of an ideological commitment to abortion."[274] Four former American commissioners and one nominee unsuccessfully pleaded for a rejection of the request, arguing that the commission's activities could not be categorized as lobbying given its intergovernmental nature and public advocacy activities.[275]

Ultimately, a reported US$210,000 was cut from the US contribution to the commission in March 2019, in the context of an expanded Mexico City policy that withholds federal funds from organizations that advocate for or provide abortions abroad.[276] Secretary Pompeo indicated that funding to the OAS was reduced by the "estimated U.S. share of possible O.A.S. expenditures on these abortion-related activities" and stated that the OAS should focus on "addressing crises in Cuba, Nicaragua and Venezuela and not on advancing the pro-abortion cause."[277] The relatively low amount of US$210,000, equivalent to less than half of the US contribution to the commission's regular budget, suggests that the State Department may have intended to send a clear antiabortion message rather than substantially affect the IACHR's budget. Many Latin American pro-life legislators expressed their support for the US government's decision and echoed its request for the commission not to promote abortion using states parties' funding.[278]

Advocacy for the creation of abortion rights could, at least temporarily, become attenuated in light of the 2019 partial funding sanctions applied by the United States against the commission for its abortion-related advocacy. If such advocacy were to resume, however, states parties should keep in mind that the commission is a quasi-judicial, nonjudicial body and that although its reports may have relative political weight, they are essentially nonbinding soft law, as recognized by many a high court judge.[279] States parties have no legal duty to accept an IACHR interpretation of the American Convention, particularly where that interpretation would be based on a restrictive reading of the convention's prenatal right to life as requiring either the creation of abortion rights or the decriminalization of abortion in domestic jurisdictions.

TWO

# The Inter-American Court of Human Rights' Restrictive Approach to the Prenatal Right to Life

The Inter-American Court of Human Rights is a permanent international human rights tribunal with jurisdiction over states parties to the American Convention. It is a relatively small court composed of only seven part-time judges who integrate a single chamber.[1] These judges serve in their individual capacity, not as representatives of their national states.[2] The court was created by the OAS (Organization of American States) to adjudicate individual complaints against states parties to the American Convention and to exercise oversight functions over the commission's practices.[3] Only states parties and the commission may bring lawsuits before the court; individuals have no standing.[4] Out of twenty-three states parties to the American Convention, all but three nations—Dominica, Grenada, and Jamaica—have recognized the Inter-American Court's jurisdiction to hear individual complaints against them.[5]

Before 2012, the Inter-American Court of Human Rights historically recognized the American Convention's protection of a prenatal right to life of unborn children without much controversy. It had acknowledged the unborn child's humanity and had granted reparations for the death of unborn children and for violations of prenatal rights against them and their mothers, as explained below. However, in 2012, in *Artavia Murillo et al. v. Costa Rica*, the court favored a restrictive interpretation of the prenatal child's right to life in the context of artificial reproduction.

The Inter-American Court's interpretation forced the state of Costa Rica, which recognizes the unborn as a person entitled to a right to life, to diminish its level of constitutional protection for the human embryo in favor of artificial reproduction practices.[6] Although international rules of treaty interpretation were invoked, their application was superficial, one sided, and incomplete, as shown by the analysis below. The judgment's use of questionable evidence, selective exclusion of unfavorable evidence, and inaccurate reporting have attracted criticism throughout Latin America.[7]

The decision, however, stopped short of creating a right to artificial reproductive technologies. Even though it ordered subsidy of in vitro fertilization (IVF), it did so only as a form of reparation in this particular case and did not declare that a right to personal decisions on IVF always involved a positive state duty to subsidize or provide them. Likewise, the judgment failed to articulate a right to abortion or related state duties, although some of its language favored a gradual protection of the unborn child.

Six months after *Artavia*, the court was prompted by the IACHR to carry out an indirect interpretation of article 4(1) as containing a state duty to decriminalize so-called therapeutic abortion in *In Matter of B. regarding El Salvador*, discussed in this chapter. The court, however, stopped short of doing so and instead deferred to medical criteria and ordered that the state ensure that the alleged victim's medical team take all medical measures they considered opportune to protect her right to life, health, and personal integrity. This chapter reveals that a medical need for abortion has never been proven before the IACHR, only the need for what some statutes call an indirect abortion, akin to a premature delivery, where medical procedures are required to attempt to preserve both the life of mother and that of the child. It illustrates how medical opinion prevailed in *Beatriz*, as it did in *Amelia* and *Mainumby*, discussed in the previous chapter. In all three cases, Inter-American bodies ultimately ordered medical treatment, rather than abortions, for the pregnant children and women involved.

## The Inter-American Court of Human Rights' Interpretation Authority and Relevant Rules

The court has been given the authority to issue legally binding interpretations of the American Convention in its judgments against states parties to a dispute.[8] The Inter-American Court has reiterated its authority to interpret the convention, emphasizing that "this Court is the ultimate interpreter of the Convention," which is true in the sense that its judgments are final and "not subject to appeal."[9] The court, however, has no power to amend the treaty, as indicated by the court's vice-president, Judge Eduardo Vio Grossi, who has stressed the court's interpretive rather than legislative function in his dissenting opinions, stating that only states parties have normative powers through their treaty-making and amendment authority and that the court should be careful not to tread on them.[10]

The court has also been given jurisdiction to issue nonbinding advisory opinions upon request from member states or the commission, regarding the interpretation of the convention and the compatibility of domestic laws with the same.[11] The court has historically recognized the nonbinding nature of its advisory opinions: "[T]he advisory opinions of the Court, . . . because of their advisory character, lack the same binding force that attaches to decisions in contentious cases." But its 2017 advisory opinion on same-sex unions and gender identity suggested that advisory opinions may be binding through an application of the *control de convencionalidad* doctrine, explained below.[12]

The Inter-American Court has made important contributions to international human rights law, such as its judgments on recognition of *habeas corpus* as a nonderogable right and on forced disappearances, among other matters; it has not, however, been free of moral controversy.[13] One of its most controversial moves in recent years has perhaps been to interpret the convention as containing a right to same-sex marriage in a 2017 advisory opinion, despite the convention's definition of marriage as a "right of men and women," rather than an individual right like all other rights in the convention.[14] The opinion also declared the existence of a right to administrative procedures for birth certificate modification for persons who identify as transgender.[15] The opinion was requested by outgoing Costa Rican president Luis Guillermo Solís Rivera, whose proposals to legally recognize same-sex unions and a right to change birth certificate sex designations were rejected by national legislators.[16]

The court's advisory opinion validated his proposed legislation and also held that approval of the legislature is unnecessary for the creation of transgender birth certification alteration or legal recognition of same-sex unions.[17] The holding that Costa Rica must recognize same-sex unions and same-sex marriage, in particular, generated significant resistance from the local population, to the point where it nearly swayed the country's presidential election in favor of an evangelical Christian candidate who opposed the court's opinion.[18] The opinion also drew criticism from national civil society organizations in other countries in the region, which denounced the court's "judicial activism."[19]

### *Control de Convencionalidad* Doctrine: Self-Execution and *Erga Omnes* Effects of Inter-American Court Judgments

The court has also created controversy in regard to its *control de convencionalidad* doctrine, a court-created principle that attempts to expand the authority of the court's judgments beyond the parameters established in the American Convention, which only allows for limited binding effects and self-execution of the court's decisions.[20] Created by Judge Sergio García Ramírez in 2006 in *Almonacid Arellano v. Chile* and reiterated in at least twenty-nine subsequent court decisions, the doctrine essentially promotes the idea that Inter-American Court judgments are self-executing in national jurisdictions and may prevail over a state party's domestic, even constitutional, laws.[21] It also submits that Inter-American Court decisions are binding on all states parties to the American Convention, regardless of whether they were a party to the dispute or not.[22]

The theory appears to have drawn inspiration from the European Court of Justice (ECJ), which has long insisted that its interpretations of European law are superior to national laws (including national constitutions) as well as directly effective in conferring individual rights and duties (a doctrine originally limited to constitutional courts).[23] Acceptance of the ECJ's claims to supremacy of its treaty interpretations over the courts and nations of Europe, however, has been neither complete nor unanimous. For instance, the German Constitutional Court, in a decision known as *Solange I*, determined[24] that the fundamental individual rights found in the German constitution take precedence over any conflicting doctrines developed by the ECJ.

Under the American Convention article 68(2), self-execution of the court's judgments is limited to any given judgment's reparations ordering compensation for victims of human rights violations: "That part of a judgment that stipulates compensatory damages may be executed in the country concerned in accordance with domestic procedure governing the execution of judgments against the state."[25] The specific reference to a particular section of the judgment clearly indicates that states did not intend for *all* of the judgment to be self-executing in domestic courts or to prevail over domestic law, and certainly not automatically. The mention of "compensatory damages" also indicates that, notwithstanding the court's ability to order other forms of reparation (such as restitution, bringing individual perpetrators to justice, public apologies, or training of law enforcement authorities),[26] only reparations ordering financial compensation for material or moral damages are self-executing in domestic courts.

The *control de convencionalidad* doctrine, however, claims that Inter-American Court judgments, including their "interpretation" of the convention, have an immediate, direct effect in national jurisdictions and are automatically enforceable in domestic courts, requiring no action by the legislature, such as an implementing statute, or by the judiciary, such as a criminal trial.[27] An application of this doctrine can be found, for instance, in the implementation phase of the *Artavia* judgment described below, where the court declared that its order to modify domestic law to allow reproductive technologies was directly enforceable in Costa Rican jurisdiction.[28] In that case, the court itself adopted enforcement powers and reversed a national Supreme Court decision by declaring the validity of a presidential order.[29]

The American Convention, like other Romano-Germanic treaties, also provides in article 68(1) that Inter-American Court judgments are binding only on states parties to a case, without any *stare decisis* binding force over future cases: "The States Parties to the Convention undertake to comply with the judgment of the court *in any case to which they are parties.*"[30] The doctrine of *control de convencionalidad*, however, asserts that Inter-American Court judgments have prospective *erga omnes* effects on all states parties to the convention—as held in the case of *Gelman v.*

*Uruguay*[31]—a proposition that may be in direct contradiction with the treaty text itself.

A strict application of *control de convencionalidad* would effectively create a system of binding international precedents—that is, case law or jurisprudence—as well as a duty to follow *stare decisis*, even though the states parties to the convention appear to have intended the exact opposite, according to the language in article 68. Such an interpretation would create centralized judicial supremacy and make the Inter-American Court's pronouncements almost as binding as those of the US Supreme Court under the Anglo-Saxon doctrine of *stare decisis*, a practice that is almost entirely unfounded within the jurisprudence of the Americas, even in federal states like Mexico and Argentina. It would also enable any national public officials to exercise their own *control de convencionalidad*; according to the court: "[T]he organs of any of the branches whose authorities perform judicial duties exercise . . . a control of 'conventionality' *ex officio* between the domestic norms and the American Convention."[32]

Judges who sympathize with the doctrine seem to view the Inter-American Court of Human Rights as "[a]n agency for generating renewed Inter-American human rights law," as expressed by Judge Sergio García Ramírez, who referred to the court as "an organ that emits general—but mandatory—guidelines for the formation of an *American ius commune* in its subject matter."[33] Former judge García Sayán has similarly stated that the application of this doctrine would enable the court's jurisprudence to be "multiplied in hundreds or perhaps thousands of domestic courts in cases that it would never have been able to hear directly"[34] and to become a source of doctrinary and jurisprudential inspiration for national courts.[35]

Not all judges have agreed with the *control de convencionalidad* doctrine, however. Founding judge Rafael Nieto Navia has indicated that Inter-American Court judgments in contentious cases are only binding on states parties to a dispute and do not have general, *erga omnes* effects under the convention.[36] Current judge and vice-president Eduardo Vio Grossi would probably support a more moderate version of the doctrine: he sees value in the guidance that Inter-American Court judgments may provide to prevent human rights violations of the American Convention.[37] He believes, however, that some of the doctrine's tenets would give the court a supranational character that would erode the Inter-American human rights system's subsidiarity and complementarity and that such a reading of the convention would violate the norm mandating that its interpretation be carried out in "good faith."

Even though no state has questioned the binding nature of Inter-American Court judgments in which they are parties, five states parties to the American Convention have signed a declaration rejecting any *erga omnes* effects of Inter-American Court judgments. In 2019, Argentina, Brazil, Chile, Colombia, and Paraguay signed a declaration reminding the commission and the court that "the resolutions and judgments of Inter-American bodies are only effective against parties to the litigation."[38]

The highest courts of Argentina, Mexico, and Uruguay have rejected at least some elements of the *control de convencionalidad* doctrine. In 2017, the Argentinian Supreme Court refused to overturn a civil appeals court decision despite the Inter-American Court's order to do so in *Fontevecchia and D'Amico v. Argentina*, rejecting the alleged self-executing character of Inter-American Court orders on noncompensatory reparations.[39] In *Fontevecchia*, the Inter-American Court condemned Argentina for restricting two journalists' freedom of expression by imposing a fine for their publication of a tabloid story on then-president Menem's presumed illegitimate child.[40]

Among the reparations granted to the victims, the Inter-American Court had ordered that "the State must revoke the [civil court of appeals] decision in its entirety" and stated that "[i]n order to comply with this reparation, the State must adopt all judicial, administrative, or other measures as may be necessary, and has a period of one year as of legal notice of this Judgment to do so."[41] The Argentinian Supreme Court en banc accepted the Inter-American Court decision's binding nature, but it found that the court's order to overturn a domestic court judgment was beyond the attributions granted by the American Convention article 63(1) on reparations, which do not include the power to overturn national court judgments.[42] The Supreme Court held that such an order violated the Inter-American Court's subsidiarity principle and its fourth instance doctrine.[43]

The idea that Inter-American Court judgments have *erga omnes* effects on all states parties to the convention has also encountered resistance from the Uruguayan Supreme Court. In the *Two Coronels* case, the court held that the American Convention contains no duty to abide by Inter-American Court jurisprudence, either in judgments against other states parties or in consultative opinions, and that Inter-American Court decisions in which Uruguay is a party are only binding on domestic courts in their dispositive section—that is, the section of the judgment containing the court's resolution.[44] It also held that that no duty to abide by the *control de convencionalidad* doctrine can be found in the American Convention and that the ultimate interpreter of the Uruguayan constitution is the Uruguayan Supreme Court.[45]

Some high courts of Latin America have invoked Inter-American Court judgments in their own decisions, but have only attributed to them nonbinding authority.[46] The Argentinian Supreme Court, for instance, has stated at least once that Inter-American Court decisions have no binding authority over domestic courts but only "moral significance."[47] The Mexican Supreme Court has interpreted its 2011 constitutional amendment on international human rights treaties to mean that Inter-American Court judgments to which Mexico was not a party may be binding on national courts but only *as long as the legal issue decided in a judgment is identical to the legal question before the court*, and *only where the judgment favors the human person* and the protection of his or her rights.[48] Inter-American Court judgments where Mexico was not a party would therefore not be binding where their interpretation is more restrictive than the Mexican constitution or where domestic law grants greater protection than the American Convention according to the court's interpretation.

Peru's highest court, on the other hand, seems to have adopted the *control de convencionalidad* doctrine almost entirely. The Constitutional Court of Peru has held that the judgments of the Inter-American Court of Human Rights, including their *ratio decidendi*, are "binding for all public authorities," "even in those cases in which the Peruvian State has not been a party to the proceeding."[49] But even in that case, the Constitutional Court of Peru specifically limited the judgments' authority to the *ratio decidendi* and not the *dicta*, or the decision as a whole.

## Recognition of Prenatal Rights by the Inter-American Court of Human Rights

The Inter-American Court has granted reparations for the death of unborn children. In the 2004 *Gómez-Paquiyauri Brothers v. Peru* judgment, the court granted reparations to a pregnant mother for the miscarriage of her unborn child following the murder of her family members. The Court specifically referred to Jorge Javier, the deceased fetus, as a "baby" and a "child."[50] Jorge Javier's mother was Marcelina Haydée Gómez Paquiyauri, who was nine months pregnant at the time of her siblings' murders.[51] Marcelina suffered a nervous ailment that eventually resulted in the child's death before birth. The court ordered reparations for the loss of her child, referring to the miscarriage as one of the "devastating consequences of the facts of the instant case on the [victims'] family as a whole, and individually on each of its members."[52] Later, in 2009, the court called forced abortion a "barbaric act" in the case of *Las Dos Erres v. Guatemala.*[53]

The court has acknowledged the unborn's humanity by repeatedly referring to unborn children as "children," "minors," and "babies" in at least three cases: *Gómez-Paquiyauri Brothers v. Peru*, *Miguel Castro-Castro Prison v. Peru*, and *Goiburú et al. v. Paraguay.*[54] Likewise, in *Artavia v. Costa Rica*, the court referred at least a dozen times to the human fetus as an "unborn child," despite its conclusion that human embryos created in vitro are not "persons" under the convention.[55] In *Goiburú et al. v. Paraguay*, the court found that the state of Paraguay violated article 5(1) of the convention to the detriment of a pregnant woman and her then-unborn child, Carlos Marcelo Mancuello Ríos.[56] The mother, Gladis Esther Ríos de Mancuello, was the wife of Carlos Jose Mancuello, a victim of torture and forced disappearance. The judgment indicated that she was unlawfully imprisoned after her husband's arrest and spent most of her pregnancy in prison. Her child, Carlos Marcelo, who was in utero at the time of his father's forced disappearance and was born in prison, where he remained with his mother until they were both released almost three years later.[57] The court granted Carlos Marcelo thirty-three thousand US dollars in compensation, indicating he was a "minor" at the time of his father's forced disappearance, that is, before birth.[58]

In the 2006 ruling of *Miguel Castro-Castro Prison v. Peru*, dealing with a military bombing of the Miguel Castro-Castro Prison in Peru, three pregnant inmates were among the victims of the attack.[59] Eva Sofía Challco, Sabina Quispe Rojas, and Vicenta Genua López, who were, respectively, seven, eight, and five months pregnant at the time of the events, were forced to lie on their stomach and suffer other threats to their bodily integrity.[60] Ms. Sofía Challco was gassed, exposed to submachine gun fire, kicked, and locked in a cell with no bathroom, and had rats thrown at her by her captors.[61]

The women gave birth in prison and did not receive opportune prenatal medical care. Ms. Quispe did not receive any medical care at all either before or after her child's birth.[62] The court granted them compensation for their nonpecuniary damages, such as "feelings of anguish, despair, and fear for the lives of their children."[63] Judge Sergio García Ramírez, in his concurring opinion, lamented "the extreme pre-natal violence, put in evidence in the brutalities to which pregnant women were submitted in the Castro-Castro prison," as he wondered about "the consequences of this situation of extreme violence in the mind—or the subconscious—of the children born from the mother's womb so disrespected and violated, even before their birth."[64]

In 2006, in *Sawhoyamaxa Indigenous Community v. Paraguay*,[65] the court recognized an entitlement of unborn children to children's rights, particularly the right to prenatal health. The court interpreted the convention's article 19 on the rights of children to mean that measures of protection owed to children "shall also be granted to pregnant women."[66] It indicated that, especially during pregnancy, delivery, and breastfeeding, the state must guarantee vulnerable indigenous women access to health services, while adopting special measures based on the best interests of the child, according to children's rights enunciated in article 19 of the American Convention.

### The IVF Cases against Costa Rica: A Restrictive Interpretation of the Human Embryo's Right to Life

In *Artavia Murillo et al. v. Costa Rica*, decided in 2012, the Inter-American Court of Human Rights found that Costa Rica's ban on IVF violated the American Convention. The judgment held that (a) "personal decisions" to produce biological children by IVF are protected under the American Convention on Human Rights and (b) before implantation, the human embryo is not a person entitled to a right to life.[67] The court defined the term "conception" in article 4(1) to mean "implantation" of the human embryo in the maternal womb.[68] It read article 4(1)'s phrase "in general, from the moment of conception" to mean that only gradual or incremental protection should be given to prenatal life, depending on the unborn child's physical stage of development.[69] In addition, the court ordered Costa Rica to authorize, regulate, and subsidize IVF services through its social security system.[70] Finally, the court reiterated some of these findings and ordered similar reparations in *Gómez Murillo v. Costa Rica*, an identical case decided in 2016.[71]

The cases are significant not only because *Artavia* was the Inter-American Court's first interpretation of article 4(1) on the prenatal right to life from conception but because they may come up in future abortion litigation, since, like abortion, artificial reproduction inevitably involves the destruction of prenatal life, as recognized in the *Artavia* judgment: "[T]o date, there is no option for practicing IVF without some possibility of embryonic loss."[72] The question addressed by the court in *Artavia* was not whether embryos died during IVF procedures or how many died but whether human embryos had a right to life at all,[73] a discussion that an abortion claim would similarly provoke.

### Background: Costa Rica's Ban on In Vitro Fertilization

A strong supporter of the Inter-American system on human rights, Costa Rica hosted the adoption of the American Convention in 1969; hence the convention's designation as *Pact of San José*, in honor of Costa Rica's capital city. Costa Rica has also been seat to the Inter-American Court headquarters since 1979.[74] In addition, Costa Rica fully ratified the American Convention without reservations and recognized the commission and the court's jurisdiction.[75]

Costa Rica's unique ban of IVF[76] was motivated by moral concern over the loss and destruction of human embryos during IVF procedures, the mortality rate of which was estimated at 90 percent by expert witness testimony in the *Artavia* trial.[77] In addition to embryonic death, IVF involves ethical dilemmas regarding selective abortions—euphemistically called "fetal reductions"—in instances of multiple pregnancy, where some fetuses are selectively aborted in order to maximize other fetuses' chances of survival and to minimize health risks to the mother.[78]

Costa Rica, a Catholic country, has a religious tradition of respect for the prenatal right to life and recognizes the unborn as a human person in its domestic laws.[79] Its children's code, for instance, recognizes the human embryo as a person who is entitled to the right to life from conception onward.[80] The so-called ban on IVF, however, did not entirely mirror Catholic teaching, which opposes all IVF both due, on one hand, to embryonic death involved in IVF procedures and, on the other, because of the sexless production of children, which undermines the unitive purpose of marriage.[81] The ban contemplated an exception: IVF would be constitutionally permissible as long as intentional embryonic death was not involved in the procedure.[82] The ban was thus limited to protecting the human embryo's right to life from intentional death, but did not apply Catholic teaching on a child's moral right to be conceived as the result of a conjugal act.

The ban originated in 2000, when the constitutional chamber of the Costa Rican Supreme Court struck down Executive Decree N. 24029-S, which authorized and regulated artificial reproductive technologies in Costa Rica.[83] Chief Justice Rodolfo Piza Escalante, who had previously been a founding Inter-American Court judge and the court's first president, wrote the opinion for the majority, finding that IVF violated the human embryo's right to life and human dignity under the Costa Rican constitution and the American Convention article 4(1), among other arguments.[84] Shortly thereafter, in 2003, the judgment was praised by Roberto Cuéllar, executive director of the Inter-American Institute of Human Rights, an institution created by the Inter-American Court and the government of Costa Rica.[85] Cuéllar characterized the judgment as, among other things, an important contribution to a "wealth of jurisprudence in defense of human rights."[86]

The Supreme Court judgment did not criminalize IVF clinics or their users; it did not declare a criminal prohibition on all in vitro fertilization or order the legislature to establish criminal penalties for users or providers. Rather, by striking down the executive decree that regulated IVF, it made most IVF procedures unconstitutional and therefore illegal on Costa Rican soil, an action that the Inter-American Court of Human Rights later found to have a "prohibitive effect."[87] The executive decree allowed up to six human embryos to be inoculated for implantation in the womb and prohibited embryo destruction, disposal, and preservation.[88] The decree allowed heterologous IVF—that is, artificial reproduction involving gamete donors; it protected donor anonymity and exemption from paternity or maternity suits.

The constitutional chamber expressed concern over intentional embryonic death in IVF procedures and about constitutional issues relating to gamete donation, namely surrogacy contracts, preadoption contracts, and a donor-conceived child's right to know the identity of his or her biological parents. The court found that the executive decree violated the principle of *reserva de ley* (translated by the Inter-American court as "legal reserve"), according to which all limitations to constitutional rights ought to be established through the legislature and not the executive.[89] The chamber's judgment held that according to Costa Rican law and international human rights instruments, particularly the American Convention article 4(1), the human embryo is fully recognized as a human person from the moment of fertilization and is entitled to the right to life and to human dignity.[90] The judgment found that IVF procedures, as practiced in 2000, involved a deliberate manipulation of embryonic life, which presented a "disproportionate risk of death" for the great majority of human embryos produced by IVF.[91]

The ban was qualified in the sense that it contained a limited exception under which IVF could be constitutionally acceptable: the Supreme Court stated that the procedure may eventually meet constitutional scrutiny if it evolves into techniques that would not entail deliberate or predictable embryonic death.[92] In 2008, Ileana Henchoz and Karen Espinoza, who later became petitioners in *Artavia*, tested this exception by obtaining administrative court approval of IVF procedures involving single-embryo transfer.[93] But the resolution was struck down by the Supreme Court, given that single-embryo transfer would be preceded by embryo selection and disposal before inoculation in the womb, which also involved intentional embryonic death.[94] It thus seems that only a procedure involving successive attempts at single-embryo production and single-embryo transfer would have met the Supreme Court's requirements for a legitimate exception to the human embryo's right to life.

Complaints challenging the Costa Rican ban's legality under the American Convention were filed by fifteen couples in two petitions before the Inter-American Commission on Human Rights from 2001 to 2010: *Ana Victoria Sanchez Villalobos v. Costa Rica*[95] and *Daniel Gerardo Gómez, Aída Marcela Garita et al. v. Costa Rica.*[96] Both petitions were declared admissible by the IACHR and subsequently sent to the Inter-American Court for review.[97]

Most plaintiffs did not fit Judge García Sayán's description of the group most affected by the IVF ban, namely childless, infertile couples whose only option to become biological parents was to use IVF and who could not afford to travel abroad for treatment.[98] In fact, most of the alleged victims in the lawsuit had either biological or adopted children of their own: some had biological children from a previous marriage and desired children with a new partner, others had adopted children, and others had actually conceived biological children naturally, in time.[99]

Only one out of fifteen couples argued that IVF was their only reproductive option, while most petitioners indicated IVF had been recommended to them by physicians as "one option" to conceive a biological child and did not show any evidence of having pursued any fertility treatments at all prior to IVF.[100] Most couples eventually did use IVF outside of Costa Rican jurisdiction, often without success.

The plaintiffs' essential complaint was not that the IVF ban deprived them of a "presumed right to have children," since there is no guarantee that the procedure can, in fact, produce children in every instance, as the court correctly observed; the plaintiffs' complaint was that they had been unable to get IVF in Costa Rica at the time that they had decided to do so.[101] The court thus identified their complaint as one relating to autonomy rather than one based on the right to found a family. The petitioners' representatives at the court initially requested reparations of around twenty million euros and later lowered the requested amount to 2.3 million US dollars in compensation for the alleged victims.[102] Those who had gone through IVF procedures abroad also sought compensation for costs of traveling abroad for IVF and paying for the procedure in a different country.[103]

*Withdrawal of Ana Victoria Sanchez Villalobos from the Complaint.* It is worth noting that two of the main petitioners, Ms. Sanchez Villalobos and her husband, the poster couple after whom the petition had been initially named, formally withdrew from the petition in 2008, expressing moral concerns over embryonic deaths during IVF procedures. Ms. Sanchez Villalobos and her husband wrote a letter to then IACHR executive secretary Santiago Cantón,[104] indicating that they had a change of heart and they now realized that IVF violates a human person's right to life and poses health risks to both the mother and the unborn child.[105] After adopting two children, the couple thought of parenting as a privilege, not a right, and spoke of IVF as objectifying to children.

Both the commission and the court failed to acknowledge the Villaloboses' withdrawal and their letter to Cantón in any of their reports, judgments, or resolutions. The omission seems anomalous given that at least one procedural issue arose due to the withdrawal: the petition was twice renamed, as *Petition 12.361* and later as *Gretel Artavia Murillo v. Costa Rica.*[106] In addition, IACHR merits reports and Inter-American Court judgments usually give a recitation of the proceedings before the commission, but in this case this important issue—the withdrawal of two petitioners—was omitted.[107]

It is unclear why both the commission and the court chose to omit this detail. One could argue that perhaps the withdrawal of the poster couple was perceived as weakening the petitioners' case, and since both bodies supported their cause, the omission could have been intentional. Alternatively, one could argue that the omission was a mere oversight, since the withdrawal of two petitioners did not invalidate the complaint. However, the fact that the petition was initially named after one of the petitioners who later withdrew and that they made a formal withdrawal stating moral and legal arguments makes the insignificance argument harder to believe. Likewise, the fact that the Villaloboses' reasons for withdrawal supported the state of Costa Rica's defense should have given their withdrawal at least some significance in regard to the lawsuit's merits.

*Involvement of IVF Clinics in IACHR and Court Proceedings.* Another important fact omitted from the *Artavia* and *Gómez* judgments is that the petition was originally brought by private IVF clinics that, along with infertile couples, were seeking financial compensation for the prohibitive effect that the constitutional chamber judgment had in Costa Rica. Initially, the complaint in *Ana Victoria Sanchez Villalobos v. Costa Rica* included two private IVF clinics: Costa Rica Ultrasonografia S.A. and Instituto Costarricense de Fertilidad.[108] The petitioners' legal representative, local attorney Gerardo Trejos, asked that the status of "victim" be accorded to the companies that acquired medical equipment to practice IVF in Costa Rica. The reasoning was that, since the companies were unable to make use of the equipment they had purchased due to the IVF ban, they ought to be granted fair compensation.[109]

Given the private IVF clinics' lack of standing, the IACHR appropriately found that part of Trejos's petition was inadmissible.[110] The IACHR's decision was consistent with previous decisions in which the commission declined jurisdiction *ratione personae* over legal persons and private entities for certain claims, on the grounds that article 1(2) of the convention limits the scope of some of its protections to natural human beings.[111]

IVF clinics, however, continued to be involved in the international litigation all the way to the Inter-American Court proceedings. The Inter-American Court allowed expert witness testimony "for informational purposes" from IVF clinic employees Gerardo Escalante Lopez and Delia Ribas Valdés, overruling objections from the state regarding an evident economic conflict of interest.[112] Unsurprisingly, the testimony of these witnesses favored the legalization of IVF in Costa Rica, arguing for the consideration of sterility as a public health issue and praising the procedure's supposed high rate of success around the world.[113] Later on, the petitioners requested, during the judgment's implementation phase, that the court grant provisional measures "to permit that specific clinics offer, under supervision, IVF services."[114]

A year and a half after the *Artavia* judgment, the plaintiffs in the case requested, among other provisional measures to the Inter-American Court of Human Rights, authorization for IVF clinics to operate in the country as well as an order from the court that "the [Costa Rican Social Security Institute] . . . be ordered to provide this service within no more than six months."[115] Lawsuits to the same effect were filed in Costa Rican tribunals, demanding immediate authorization and subsidy of IVF in Costa Rica.[116] The Inter-American Court denied the provisional measures request because it sought "to benefit an undetermined number of persons that are not victims in this case."[117]

*IACHR Advocacy for IVF and Domestic Legislative Proposals.* Throughout the friendly settlement process, the IACHR urged Costa Rica to authorize and subsidize IVF as soon as possible. The commission suggested that legislators could appropriately pass "a regulation that reduced the number of eggs fertilized," as long as it would otherwise allow IVF.[118] According to Costa Rican press, the commission established three different deadlines for the Costa Rican Congress to pass a legislative bill authorizing IVF and other artificial reproductive technologies and to provide public funds for the same.[119]

Costa Rican legislators did not comply with the commission's recommendation to authorize IVF via statute. It must be said, however, that in 2011, when the merits report became public and *Artavia Murillo v. Costa Rica* was filed before the court, at least one IVF bill was still pending approval in the Costa Rican Congress.[120] In addition, one bill was introduced in an attempt to legalize the procedure in a manner that would aim at reducing embryo mortality.[121] The bill aimed to accomplish this by requiring inoculation of all embryos created during each IVF cycle. The bill also prohibited selective abortions of surplus fetuses after implantation.

The Pan-American Health Organization (PAHO) was critical of the bill given that transferring all embryos in the same cycle would increase the risk of multiple pregnancy and, in turn, the risk of fetal reduction. The IACHR, on the other hand, expressed its support for a bill that would revert to the standards established by the 1995 executive decree regulating IVF.[122] In 2010, however, legislators rejected the bill.[123] Meanwhile, the Costa Rican executive branch banned an ad campaign launched by Radio Fides, a Catholic radio station, which sought to raise awareness about the harms of IVF and the embryonic lives lost as a result of the procedure.[124] In 2012, the Costa Rican Supreme Court declared that the ban violated freedom of expression and allowed the campaign to resume.[125]

### The Creation of International Human Rights Obligations to Facilitate IVF via Treaty Interpretation in *Artavia v. Costa Rica*

In November 2012, the Inter-American Court issued its judgment *Artavia Murillo et al. v. Costa Rica*, holding that "personal decisions" to produce biological children by in vitro fertilization are protected under the American Convention, in spite of the absence of any provision addressing reproductive rights or artificial reproduction in the American Convention.[126] The court ordered Costa Rica to legally authorize IVF and create a regulatory framework for it, as well as to subsidize it through its social security system, as a form of reparation.[127]

The judgment found, via treaty interpretation, an existing international obligation to authorize artificial reproduction.[128] According to the

*Artavia* judgment, a right to make "personal decisions" to produce biological children through IVF and a corresponding state duty to authorize it would implicitly arise from existing rights, namely the right to privacy (article 11), the rights of the family (article 17), the right to personal liberty (article 7), the right to personal integrity (article 5), and the right to health (Protocol of San Salvador).[129] They would also arise from previously unrecognized principles of "reproductive autonomy" and "reproductive freedom."[130]

Still, in the judgment, the Inter-American Court refused to address the question of whether "a presumed right to have children or a right to have access to IVF" exists,[131] which restricts the scope of the holding. Such a right could imply a *positive* state duty to provide IVF, but the court articulated only a *negative* state duty not to interfere with the right to "personal decisions" to use IVF to conceive biological children. Although it ordered Costa Rica to subsidize IVF as a form of reparation, it did not state that it had a general positive obligation to do so arising from the American Convention.

Since the court's reasoning began with the premise that "personal decisions" to produce biological children by IVF were protected under other rights in the American Convention and that the human embryo's life was not, the latter had no possibility of withstanding the court's proportionality calculus.[132] The logical conclusion could therefore not have been any other than one finding that "personal decisions" to produce biological children by IVF must prevail over any considerations regarding the human embryo's right to life, which the court found to be nonexistent before implantation.[133]

The argument that the IVF ban interfered with "personal decisions" may not have been entirely accurate in the sense that Costa Rica did not prohibit couples from reproducing via IVF and did not impose any kind of sanctions on couples who decided to get IVF or who underwent IVF procedures abroad; it only prohibited IVF from being performed in Costa Rican jurisdiction. Many petitioners did travel abroad for IVF and reported no legal repercussions whatsoever. Perhaps it would have been more accurate to state that the Costa Rican ban interfered with personal decisions to obtain IVF *in Costa Rica.*

The proportionality test probably emulated the European Court of Human Rights' identical abortion standard, which has required states that allow abortion to use a balancing test that weighs the "state interests in protection of the unborn" against the "conflicting rights of the mother" for abortion cases.[134] This test applies in the European system because no specific definition of the unborn as a person exists in the European Convention, as opposed to the American Convention article 4(1), which recognizes the unborn as a person who is entitled to the right to life from the moment of conception.

The IACHR initially proposed the application of the arbitrariness test, which required the following criteria: (1) legality, (2) legitimate aim, (3) suitability, (4) necessity, and (5) proportionality.[135] The commission accepted that the IVF ban met the first two requirements but found that the ban did not meet the requirements for suitability, necessity, and proportionality.[136] The commission also conceded that the prohibition had been legally issued and that protecting embryonic life constituted a legitimate purpose.[137] However, in regard to the necessity requirement, the commission argued that Costa Rica could have used less restrictive measures in regulating IVF.[138] Ultimately, however, the court entirely avoided the application of the commission's proposed arbitrariness test or even a balancing test between competing rights by finding that the human embryo was not a person.[139]

A balancing test would have required weighing the human embryo's right to life against a parent's privacy and autonomy. Such an analysis could have probably led to the conclusion that the right to individual privacy, the right to nondiscrimination, the right to personal integrity, or the right to have a family cannot prevail over the right to life, given the latter's fundamental and nonderogable nature, as suggested by Judge Vio Grossi.[140] Instead, the court upheld a right to make personal decisions on artificial reproduction in an isolated manner, disregarding the state's interest in protecting embryonic life and limiting its analysis to the severity of the ban's restrictions on the petitioners' rights.[141] The state invoked principles of indivisibility and interdependence of human rights, according to which upholding a right at the expense of another's right to life would be an illegitimate application of the convention, but the argument was ignored.[142]

The judgment's proportionality calculus represented Costa Rica as wielding "absolute," unreasonable protection of the unborn over adults' decisions, without exception, but that representation was inaccurate.[143]

The Costa Rican Supreme Court did not grant the human embryo's right to life "absolute" protection, as the court characterized it, but only protection from IVF; Costa Rica permits, for instance, a "life of the mother" exception to criminal abortion.[144] It does not protect the human embryo in any and all contexts, but only in the context of this particular reproductive technology: Costa Rica allows for artificial insemination, among other methods.[145] Even protection from IVF was not absolute, given that the Costa Rican Supreme Court interpreted the American Convention to only prohibit those procedures that would entail embryonic death and specifically stated that it would allow the procedure in the absence thereof.[146] Nevertheless, the Inter-American Court found that the ban was, "in practice," an "absolute" ban, given that the Costa Rican Supreme Court requirement of no deliberate or predictable embryonic death would be "impossible" to fulfill because "to date, there is no option for practicing IVF without some possibility of embryonic loss."[147]

*Costa Rica's Violations of the American Convention.* The *Artavia* judgment was not about "facilitating, in the broadest possible terms, the development and strength of the family unit," and not even about the right to have children, as stated by the court itself.[148] Even if petitioners had been able to access IVF, the court noted, it would be impossible to determine whether the procedure would have been successful in producing genetically related children in any instance.[149] That was the case for several petitioners who were unable to conceive notwithstanding several IVF attempts at pregnancy in foreign countries.[150]

The holding, instead, seemed to focus on the autonomy of couples that wished to use artificial reproductive technologies and were not legally allowed to do so in Costa Rican jurisdiction.[151] Compensation for moral damages was awarded in regard to the right to privacy: "[T]he Court recalls that the damage does not depend on whether or not the couples were able to have children . . . , but corresponds to the disproportionate impact on their lives of the inability to exercise their rights autonomously."[152] The court found Costa Rica to be in violation of both the right to privacy and the right to raise a family, although it did not award compensation for moral damages based on the latter.[153]

The judgment gave great weight to the feelings of infertile individuals seeking legal IVF in Costa Rica, "the feelings of anguish, anxiety, uncertainty and frustration, and the effects on the possibility of deciding their own, autonomous and independent life project," while expressing no sensitivity for embryonic death, fetal reductions, and potential harmful effects of IVF on women and children.[154] Petitioners expressed mental anguish and depression and reported marital problems or dissolution over their childlessness or the lack of genetic children as well as over failed IVF attempts.[155] Some petitioners who already had children of their own expressed their desires and frustration at not having a genetically related child with a new spouse.[156] Despite testimony of depression and other psychological issues, none of the petitioners actually completed psychological treatment later offered by the state free of charge: some of them did not even start it, and at least two of them, including Ms. Artavia Murillo, declined to continue treatment.[157]

In addition, expert witness testimony presented by Costa Rica indicated that health risks associated with IVF for women include ovarian hyperstimulation syndrome and multiple pregnancy.[158] One petitioner, Andrea Bianchi, spoke about the mental suffering caused by the IVF procedure itself: she spoke of the invasive nature of IVF "treatment" and of the stress caused by the ethical dilemmas surrounding her treatment, which made her constantly question herself on the consequences of her choice to undergo IVF, but these statements were omitted from the judgment.[159] Additional evidence was presented that IVF poses health risks to children conceived via IVF, including increased risk of rare genetic disorders and premature birth.[160] The merits of this evidence relative to the right to health presented by the state went unexamined on the basis of a formalistic excuse, namely, that the Costa Rican constitutional chamber's decision did not address the argument.[161]

The argument seems weak, since the Inter-American Court is not a fourth instance whose role would be limited to reviewing elements of the lower court's decision, and therefore the court was not procedurally precluded from examining the right-to-health arguments.[162] In *Artavia*, the court certainly examined other substantive issues that the Costa Rican Supreme Court had not addressed, such as the definition of conception as implantation and the compatibility of legal abortion with the American Convention. Therefore, nothing seems to have truly precluded the court from analyzing the substantive claims on the right to health, which directly related to the merits of the lawsuit.

An inappropriate analogy between IVF and natural conception was used by the commission and the court to conclude that the ban was ineffective in achieving its purpose of protecting embryonic life.[163] The analogy, proposed by expert witness Fernando Zegers-Hochschild, trivialized embryonic death in IVF by arguing that embryonic loss during IVF was no different from embryonic loss in natural pregnancy.[164] Judge Margarette Macaulay reiterated this idea at the public hearings by making the bizarre suggestion that if Costa Rica wanted to protect embryos from death through IVF, it should also ban sex or natural conception to protect embryos from natural death.[165] The analogy seems highly questionable for obvious reasons: if the standard were to tolerate violations of the right to life simply because natural death is inevitable, or because death exists in nature, then almost any other violation of the right to life would have to be permitted.[166]

Obvious differences exist between embryonic death in IVF and in the process of natural conception, primarily the element of intent or foresight, as discussed by the Costa Rican Supreme Court, which stressed, in regard to artificial reproduction, that the problem was "not limited to the number of human lives lost, but has to do primarily with the predictability of those deaths."[167] First, the Costa Rican Supreme Court found that embryonic death in IVF is not only highly foreseeable but may even be intentional (in instances of selective abortions and disposal of frozen embryos), as opposed to early miscarriages in natural procreation, which are neither intentional nor foreseeable.[168] Second, witness testimony indicated that the rate of embryonic death in IVF procedures (90–92 percent) is much higher than that in natural pregnancy,[169] even though large numbers of embryos die at all stages of the reproductive process, both in vitro and in vivo. The Inter-American Court, however, discredited this evidence as inconclusive and entirely ignored the element of foresight or intent.

Since the court spoke of a violation of the right to health, it could have recommended state funding for a comprehensive program of fertility treatments along with IVF, but it did not.[170] It merely ordered the state to "include the availability of IVF within the infertility treatments and programs offered by its health care services, in keeping with the obligation of guarantee in relation to the principle of non-discrimination."[171]

Three members of the commission had previously rejected the argument that banning IVF constituted discrimination against women, the disabled, or the poor. Dinah Shelton, Felipe Gonzalez, and Rodrigo Escobar Gil wrote a dissent to the IACHR merits report where they stated that the IVF ban was not discriminatory given its applicability to all individuals and couples in the country.[172] They found that the State's *legitimate* objective was to protect human embryos, not to regulate who is entitled to reproduce.[173] The Inter-American Court nevertheless found that the IVF ban constituted discrimination based on gender, disability, and economic status, heeding the commission's request that the court take this opportunity to "build up its case law on the subject of equality and non-discrimination."[174] As a result, Costa Rica was ordered to promote trainings on reproductive rights and nondiscrimination for all employees of the judiciary.[175]

The majority's discussion of discrimination in the IVF ban as discrimination against women was partially based on the idea that the principle of equality and nondiscrimination requires that precedence be given to the rights of women over those of the unborn child, citing committee reports from the CEDAW (Convention on the Elimination of All Forms of Discrimination Against Women).[176] An obvious refutation of this premise is that the principles of equality and nondiscrimination require giving *equal* weight to the rights of women and those of unborn children, especially since both groups can be considered vulnerable and disadvantaged for different reasons.

The idea that an IVF ban constitutes discrimination against women can be similarly challenged by pointing out that the ban would affect any infertile individual, whether male or female, who seeks to produce a genetic child, but that point was not addressed in any depth.[177] The court's statement that "women may resort to IVF without the need for a partner" seems incomplete, since men can resort to IVF without the need for a partner also, if using a surrogate mother or gestational carrier.[178] In addition, the court explained that the ban had a discriminatory impact on women because Latin American sexist gender stereotypes promoted a cultural expectation for women to bear children.[179] In another statement, it declared that "motherhood is an essential part of the free development of a woman's personality," without making any similar statements about fatherhood, which seemed to reinforce the very stereotypes that the court purported to reject.[180]

The court's argument that the ban had a disproportionate effect on women who had interrupted IVF procedures when the Supreme Court handed down its judgment could have been more persuasive if it had been supported by some kind of evidence.[181] However, the judgment cites no evidence showing that any of the alleged female victims were undergoing ovarian hyperstimulation or any similar procedures at the time of the constitutional chamber judgment or that any had suffered negative health-related consequences attributable to the interruption of treatment.

In regard to infertility as a form of disability, amici curiae pointed out that IVF can be used to alter or change the social condition of childlessness by artificially producing a child but that IVF is not directed toward restoring or preserving an individual's fertility and reproductive health.[182] The court admitted that expert witness testimony demonstrated that there is no scientific consensus that infertility can be categorized as a disability, but nevertheless concluded that it was, citing an unidentified WHO definition.[183]

The finding led the court to hold that infertile individuals enjoy the same protections granted to disabled persons under international law and that IVF is a health service to which they are entitled.[184] The court adopted a broad, vague definition of disability based on a "social model" under which disability would not be limited to the presence of a physical, mental, intellectual, or sensorial impairment, but also related to "limits or barriers that are commonly encountered in society by individuals with functional diversity includ[ing] those that are attitudinal or socio-economic."[185]

The finding that the ban discriminated against infertile couples who could not afford IVF procedures abroad likewise enabled the court to order that IVF services be provided by the state.[186] The convention prohibits discrimination on the basis of "economic status," but an individual's inability to afford IVF procedures outside of Costa Rica does not seem to be an economic status per se.[187] Given the high cost of IVF for the average citizen in any developing country (estimated by petitioners to be of around fifteen thousand US dollars per trial),[188] the category of persons who cannot afford IVF procedures outside of Costa Rica could probably include most persons in the country, whether poor or middle class.[189]

The judgment cites no record of the petitioners' actual income and no evidence that they were, in fact, a part of the class of "poorer households," as indicated by Judge Diego García Sayán;[190] in fact, many petitioners could and actually did pay for IVF abroad. This fact could have made the discrimination finding moot in regard to those alleged victims, as the court itself seemed to admit.[191] Instead, the state was eventually ordered to pay up to twenty-five thousand US dollars in material and immaterial damages to each person who had to travel abroad for IVF treatment, regardless of their income level or financial need.[192]

*State Funding of IVF as a Form of Reparation.* The most extravagant reparation ordered by the *Artavia* court was perhaps the mandate that the state of Costa Rica subsidize IVF by providing it through its social security health system, a measure that neither the petitioners nor the commission had requested.[193] Judge García Sayán's separate opinion tried to minimize the irrationality of this reparation by dwelling on the duty to provide "gradual" and "progressive" availability only.[194] Nevertheless, this one-of-a-kind reparation may seem excessive because Costa Rica is a developing country with limited resources and more important health concerns, as Judge García Sayán acknowledged. The reparation also seems disproportionate to the supposed violations committed by the state against fifteen couples. Even in cases involving collective rights, such as those of indigenous peoples, where proven claims for compensation were involved, the court has been generally conservative in awarding collective and individual economic reparations.[195]

The mandate to subsidize IVF was given without any meaningful consideration of the financial resources available to Costa Rica, even though Judge García Sayán pointed out that a country's level of economic development was an important factor.[196] The judgment merely stated that Costa Rica never demonstrated the nonexistence, unavailability, or insufficiency of economic and budgetary resources to subsidize artificial reproduction. Because Costa Rica already subsidizes some fertility treatments, Judge García Sayán voiced suspicion that there might be enough financial resources to subsidize IVF, which the state must be deliberately withholding.

The reparation, coupled with the court's construction of the Protocol of San Salvador[197] and references to potential IVF subsidies in Latin American countries, suggests an incipient attempt to convert a negative state obligation to *allow* IVF into a positive state obligation to *fund* it or *subsidize* it.[198] The view that IVF should be a state-funded practice was supported by petitioners and Judge García Sayán throughout the proceedings.[199]

The court seemed to sympathize with the idea when holding that the right to privacy in the American Convention and the right to enjoy the benefits of scientific and technological progress in the Protocol of San Salvador would create state obligations vis-à-vis reproductive technologies, even though no evidence of state intent to that effect was provided.[200]

Other courts have already realized that creating a right to state-funded IVF would be hardly justiciable, not to mention impractical. The European Court, for instance, has never held that states parties to the European Convention on Human Rights have a duty to sponsor IVF, even though most of them have significantly greater resources than Costa Rica. The European Court has, in fact, stated that the European Convention does not guarantee the right to a specific level of health care in any area.[201] A right to state-funded IVF may not even have significant support among pro-choice scholars, some of whom have admitted that there is no state duty to subsidize IVF, which, like cosmetic surgery, "fall[s] into the category of 'luxury medicine.' "[202] They have also said that "no state funding supports natural conception . . . and states may accordingly decline funding of [artificial reproduction]."[203] Just as it analogized natural conception to IVF in some scenarios, the court could have similarly applied that analogy in relation to government funding.

*Restrictive Interpretation of the Right to Life from Conception in* Artavia. The *Artavia* judgment stated that "there is no one agreed definition of the beginning of life," but it nevertheless chose a preferred definition, one that defined the term "conception" as equivalent to "implantation" in the maternal womb, rather than "fertilization," the most common meaning attributed to the term in medical science.[204] Thus, it rejected a prenatal right to life of human embryos created through IVF in Costa Rican jurisdiction. The court also read article 4(1)'s phrase "in general, from the moment of conception" to mean that there is no absolute protection for the prenatal right to life, only "gradual or incremental" protection depending on the unborn child's physical stage of development.[205]

The judgment did not deny that life begins at conception, a fact that even the petitioners admitted, but redefined the term "conception" in the most restrictive possible manner, as meaning pregnancy or implantation of the human embryo in the maternal womb rather than fertilization.[206] In other words, as pointed out by Judge Vio Grossi, the court ignored the ordinary, most commonly understood meaning of conception as fertilization in order to give the term a special meaning.[207] Yet it gave no proof that the parties so intended, as required by the Vienna Convention article 31(4).

In fact, no national statute of any state party to the American Convention defined conception as implantation when *Artavia* was decided, but many defined it as fertilization.[208] Ecuador's juvenile code, for instance, establishes a right to life from conception and, in the same provision, prohibits genetic research or manipulation from fertilization until birth.[209] Five Latin American supreme and constitutional courts (those of Argentina, Chile, Ecuador, Honduras, and Peru) defined conception as fertilization when banning abortifacient drugs, invoking the American Convention.[210] An amicus brief submitted in support of Costa Rica by founding Inter-American Court judge Rafael Nieto Navia and this author emphasized those precedents.[211] The decision, however, did not acknowledge their existence. The judgment also misrepresented Judge Nieto Navia's former membership as a founding judge of the Inter-American Court of Human Rights and merely identified him as a "professor" when listing amicus briefs for Costa Rica, even though he did not identify himself as anything other than a former Inter-American Court judge in the brief.[212] Such a deliberate alteration of a former judge's title on the part of the court's secretariat and its acceptance on the part of judges seem to show a lack of good faith and may indicate that the secretariat sought to minimize the appearance of support for the prenatal right to life from conception in the *Artavia* case.

It must be said, in any case, that the court's interpretation of article 4(1) was not a part of the judgment's resolutory dispositions, as pointed out by Judge Vio Grossi, which means that the court's construction of the right to life from conception was not legally binding on Costa Rica nor created an authoritative interpretation, making the scope of the *Artavia* holding relatively limited.[213] In fact, a different composition of the court in 2016 in *Gómez v. Costa Rica* and in *Matter of B.* failed to even mention the *Artavia* interpretation of article 4(1) on the prenatal right to life, even though both cases dealt with the prenatal right to life.

Both before and after the adoption of the American Convention, the ordinary meaning of the term "conception" has been understood to be that of fertilization of the ovum by the sperm, as pointed out by Justice Vio

Grossi: "[A]n important part of medical science—if not the majority—shares this understanding," he indicated.[214] The court, however, relied on the minority view presented by Dr. Fernando Zegers-Hochschild, the Commission's expert witness, a Chilean expert on artificial reproduction and the founder and former director of the Unit of Reproductive Medicine at a private IVF clinic, in which he continued to work as senior staff at the time of the *Artavia* trial.[215]

Prior to the *Artavia* decision, Zegers-Hochschild had written, "We are convinced that a new life begins at *fertilization*," but in *Artavia*, Zegers-Hochschild argued that "the starting point for the development of the embryo, and subsequently of its human life, is its *implantation* in the uterus."[216] These contradictory statements could have raised questions about Zegers-Hochschild's credibility as a witness. In addition, the fact that Zegers-Hochschild was an IVF practitioner who was directly involved in the artificial reproduction industry, and therefore had a direct economic interest in the decision's outcome, raised conflict-of-interest issues that could have disqualified him as a witness, but they did not.[217]

Expert witness testimony of former IACHR commissioner Marco Gerardo Monroy Cabra and medical school professor Maureen L. Condic, on the other hand, was given little credibility by the *Artavia* court.[218] The court rejected their definition of conception as fertilization, arguing that that definition was "associated with concepts that confer certain metaphysical attributes on embryos" and with "beliefs" that should not be imposed "on others who do not share them," even though none of the witnesses' testimony or scientific literature submitted to the court referred to the metaphysical attributes of embryos.[219] Judge Eduardo Vio Grossi later criticized these conclusions in his *Gómez* dissent, indicating that they had been reached "on the basis of some medical positions on the matter," while the court had discarded other positions "without any justification."[220]

Zegers-Hochschild stated that "conception or gestation is a phenomenon of the woman, not the embryo," a view that led the court to conclude that the American Convention protected unborn human life only through the woman, and not as independent life itself.[221] Vio Grossi's dissent pointed out that such an interpretation disentitled the human embryo from human rights protection and contradicted the spirit of the American Convention, which specifically sought to protect the human embryo independently of the mother, as illustrated in article 4(5) of the convention, which prohibits the application of the death penalty to pregnant women, thus protecting the unborn child, and only him, from execution.[222]

The court's choice to use the 1946 edition of the Dictionary of the Royal Spanish Academy, which defined conception as pregnancy, seems to have been inappropriate for at least three reasons. First, no reference was made to reliable Portuguese, English, or French dictionaries, some of which did define conception as fertilization, even though the Inter-American system reunites Spanish- and non-Spanish-speaking countries.[223] Second, the 1946 edition preceded the convention's adoption in 1969 and its entry into force in 1978; the 1970 edition of the dictionary was closer in time to 1969 and should have been taken into account when reporting on common usage in 1969.[224] In fact, the 1970 edition defined conception and fertilization as synonymous, as pointed out by Judge Vio Grossi.[225] These synonymous definitions remain until the present day, reflecting the ordinary understanding that the terms "fertilization" and "to make a woman conceive" are synonyms, he indicated.[226]

Third, human fertilization and implantation had not been scientifically distinguished in 1946, as acknowledged by the court.[227] The use of "conceive" to mean "receive " or "take in and hold" is ancient, perhaps even approaching archaic.[228] Prior to the discovery of the ovum in the 1830s, it had long been common to imagine that a "fertile" woman simply "conceived," that is, took in and held the male seed and gave it a place to grow.[229] Since the Spanish Royal Academy long understood itself to be a guardian of tradition in language, it is not surprising that its 1946 edition contained this early meaning in defining the word "conceive." But that very old meaning was not the ordinary way that the word "conception" was used in educated discussion of human gestation during the time relevant for the interpretation of article 4(1), that is, in 1969 and onward. In light of modern genetic knowledge about the human embryo, it certainly was not the ordinary way in which it was understood in 2012, at the time of *Artavia.*

At the time of the convention's adoption, states parties could not have been thinking of in vitro fertilization, given that in vitro fertilization was practiced for the first time only in 1978, as acknowledged by the court, and "prior to IVF, science had not considered the possibility of carrying out fertilization outside a woman's body."[230] The inexistence of IVF at the time of the drafting of the convention may explain why there was no debate at all during the *travaux préparatoires* about affirming a right to life from "fertilization" versus waiting until "implantation" before affirming that right.[231] Given the presence of a concern to protect all human life among by the drafters, as demonstrated by the American Declaration's universal right-to-life provision, it seems unlikely that, had such distinction been known, states would have, without any discussion at all, intentionally left new life wholly unprotected in the period between fertilization and implantation.[232] Therefore, the "fertilization" meaning of "conception" must never have been in doubt among the drafters, as indicated by Judge Vio Grossi.[233]

### Partial Compliance with Inter-American Court Judgment

Immediately after the judgment was issued, Costa Rica swiftly complied with most of the judgment's reparations, as acknowledged by the Inter-American Court in the implementation phase.[234] Costa Rica paid the plaintiffs financial compensation for material and immaterial damages and attorneys' fees; it published the court's judgment in several venues, including the Supreme Court's website; and it organized reproductive rights trainings on artificial reproduction and the *Artavia* judgment for members and employees of the judiciary.[235] It did not immediately comply with the portion of the judgment ordering a change in domestic constitutional law to authorize, regulate, and subsidize IVF, and in this noncompliance it seemed to indicate a fundamental moral disagreement with the *Artavia* judgment rather than the state's apathy about complying with international judgments.

The Inter-American Court judgment in *Artavia* did not put an end to the ethical controversy over IVF at the national level. Costa Rica's government branches were strongly divided over the subject of artificial reproduction: President Luis Guillermo Solís Rivera favored the authorization and liberalization of IVF, while the constitutional chamber of the Supreme Court and the Attorney General's Office rejected it. The legislative branch was undecided on the issue. Until September 2015, however, there was a clear agreement between all state powers that the legislature would be the entity to approve and regulate IVF.[236] For three years after the judgment, various bills were introduced in the Costa Rican Congress, none of which obtained enough political consensus to pass, due to the ethical concerns that persisted among the legislators over the death and destruction of human embryos in IVF procedures.[237]

President Solís Rivera, with the Inter-American Court's support, sought to authorize and liberally regulate IVF in Costa Rica, but a group of legislators and the constitutional chamber of the Supreme Court got in the way of his efforts. In September 2015, the Inter-American Court held a public hearing where it urged Costa Rica to immediately proceed to legally authorize IVF.[238] A few days later, the president published Executive Decree 39210 authorizing and regulating IVF, against which a group of four congresspersons, supported by the Attorney General's Office, requested a writ of *amparo*, which later turned into a constitutional action.[239] On February 3, 2016, the constitutional chamber of the Costa Rican Supreme Court declared the presidential decree to be unconstitutional and invalid, invoking the principle of *reserva de ley* recognized in article 2 of the American Convention, which provides that any changes to states parties' national legal systems should take place through legislative measures and in observance of their constitutional processes.[240]

The essential holding of the constitutional chamber of the Costa Rican Supreme Court was that Inter-American Court judgments are not self-executing in their entirety in national courts and that some reparations require legislative action. The chamber struck down the presidential decree, citing Supreme Court precedent holding that all restrictions to fundamental rights and liberties ought to be established through a formal lawmaking process by the legislature.[241] The executive did not, according to the constitutional chamber, have the constitutional prerogative to limit fundamental rights or liberties—in the instant case, a woman's right to health and the implanted embryo's right to life and human dignity. Furthermore, the chamber found that the decree violated the principle of separation of powers, which, according to its jurisprudence, demanded democratic legitimacy of limitations to human rights, which only the legislature could approve.[242]

The constitutional chamber did not reject Costa Rica's obligation to authorize and regulate IVF as per *Artavia*. On the contrary, it recognized its "unavoidable duty to comply with the court's judgment."[243] It did not favor all unconstitutionality arguments advanced by the plaintiffs either, most of which challenged the decree's authorization of heterologous IVF procedures (i.e., those involving gamete donors) and its designation of the human embryo as "fertilized egg." The constitutional chamber rejected the argument that the decree impinged on a child's constitutional right to know the identity of his or her parents because it allowed gamete donation and preempted paternity suits against donors; the court held such provisions do not preempt a child's right to know the identity of his or her biological parent, that is, the gamete donor.[244] In addition, it did not find that the decree objectified the human embryo or that it was inconsistent with international human rights law as interpreted by the Inter-American Court in *Artavia*, as it placed some limitations on embryo preservation and destruction.

The constitutional chamber acknowledged the self-executing character given to Inter-American Court judgments in general by Costa Rican law but found that that character did not apply to the judgment's provisions ordering a modification of the national legal system where constitutional rights were involved.[245] Costa Rican Act N. 6889, the Agreement for the Seat of the Inter-American Court of Human Rights, establishes that all Inter-American Court of Human Rights judgments and resolutions, including resolutions by the court's chief justice, are as binding on Costa Rican state authorities as judgments issued by Costa Rican courts, thus regarding them as self-executing.[246] The constitutional chamber held, nevertheless, that the American Convention article 2 specifically defers to state sovereignty when modifications of domestic law provisions are involved and mandates that national constitutional processes be followed, such as the Costa Rican rule that only the legislature may enact limitations to fundamental rights.[247]

In the meantime, while the constitutionality action was pending a resolution by the Costa Rican Supreme Court, the commission issued precautionary measures and filed a second lawsuit before the Inter-American Court against Costa Rica.[248] The commission justified its premature filing by arguing the "need to obtain justice for the victims in the case" given that the state had failed to immediately comply with its prior recommendations to restore the executive decree's legal validity.[249] The day after the constitutional chamber's decision, upon the executive's request to intervene, the Inter-American Court gave the government of Costa Rica a seven-day deadline to declare the chamber's decision invalid and to validate the presidential decree that had attempted to authorize IVF.[250]

The Costa Rican Supreme Court did not overturn its decision as ordered, so, in a shocking move, the Inter-American Court intervened to directly authorize IVF and impose the president's regulation, against the chamber's decision, in national jurisdiction. On February 26, 2016, the Inter-American Court issued a resolution that declared, despite the national Supreme Court's decision, that "it is understood that IVF is now authorized in Costa Rica" and that access to IVF must be permitted "immediately."[251] The court also ordered that the executive decree "be maintained as valid" and that any subsequent regulation that the legislature may adopt should follow the *Artavia* judgment's standards.[252]

*The Court's Supraconstitutional Claims.* This extraordinary intervention on the part of the Inter-American Court in a state party's constitutional legal process to legally authorize IVF raises jurisprudential questions about the court's implementation authority and about the self-execution of its judgments. The court's blunt move to enforce this sort of supraconstitutional authority over the Costa Rican Supreme Court and the legislature was criticized by many Latin American academics and by Judge Vio Grossi himself.[253] Vio Grossi pointed out that the court should not create supranational powers for itself and should not dictate which government body ought to comply with the court judgment, nor add new obligations that had not been previously established.[254] He indicated that a judgment's implementation process should not turn into a new trial and that the court's resolutions on compliance should not constitute a new judgment, given their lesser weight under the American Convention and the court's statute.[255]

The court's reaction may have been motivated at least in part by a desire to impose its own vision of human rights on a traditional, religious society that hesitated to embrace it.[256] The judges openly expressed their frustration with the country's moral qualms about reproductive technologies and their irritation with "arguments that *insist* on the protection of human embryos' right to life, contrary to the reasoning of this court."[257] The court reprimanded the constitutional chamber for failing to ensure that the judgment by the former prevailed over moral arguments against reproductive technologies, and the court went as far as saying that the constitutional chamber should have contributed to "*putting an end* to the discussion on the prohibition of the in vitro fertilization technique."[258] Eventually, in *Gómez Murillo v. Costa Rica*, decided in November 2016, the court expressed satisfaction over having unilaterally settled the debate, with the assumption that "the controversy over arguments relating to the rights established by article 4(1)(right to life) . . . has ceased."[259]

In addition, the court may have wished to assert its relatively weak authority, given that a staggering 77 percent of all Inter-American Court judgments have not been fully complied with.[260] Setting an example with Costa Rica, a small Central American nation that also happens to be the seat of the Inter-American Court, could logically minimize any possibilities of resistance. Furthermore, the Costa Rican president's invitation to intervene in defense of his decree probably contributed to the court acting as a fourth instance or supranational tribunal.[261] After all, it was the executive together with the *Artavia* plaintiffs that requested the Inter-American Court to nullify the constitutional chamber's decision because, they argued, it contradicted the judgment, and that is exactly what the Inter-American Court did in its implementation resolution of February 2016.[262]

The court's direct enforcement of a supraconstitutional authority in the implementation of *Artavia* may also be a product of Costa Rica's unique situation as headquarters to the court itself, which may give the court a greater degree of influence in national politics and public opinion. Costa Rica's agreement with the Inter-American Court to make that court's judgments and resolutions self-executing is exceptional in the region, as indicated by Santiago Cantón, former IACHR executive secretary: "[S]tates should pass internal legislation to ensure compliance with the decisions of the Commission and Court. In the region, only three countries have such legislation (Peru, Costa Rica, and Colombia)."[263] Other states, like Argentina, have rejected claims of supraconstitutional authority on the part of the Inter-American Court.[264]

Costa Rican law is unique in that it grants a great deal of deference to the Inter-American Court's authority by making that court's judgments and resolutions against Costa Rica, including those issued by the court president alone, self-executing in national jurisdiction under Act 6889 of

1983.[265] This status has not been free of criticism: Rodolfo Piza Escalante, founding Inter-American Court judge, expressed some discomfort with the fact that Costa Rican law grants such authority to Inter-American Court decisions and resolutions "without qualification, not even a condition of reciprocity."[266] Act 6889's language, however, only says that Inter-American Court judgments and resolutions "will have the same executive and executory weight as those dictated by Costa Rican tribunals"; it does not say which Costa Rican tribunals.[267] Costa Rica had modified its domestic laws to comply with Inter-American advisory opinions before *Artavia*, but never in contradiction with a constitutional chamber judgment.[268]

Thus, it is unclear whether Inter-American Court resolutions and judgments always prevail over Costa Rican Supreme Court judgments, as they did over the constitutional chamber's in this case. The Costa Rican legislature has not made distinctions between higher courts and lower courts, but it may wish to do so in the future. In any case, members of the Costa Rican constitutional chamber have now accepted the Inter-American Court's resolution reversing their decision as authoritative, and no formal resistance has been offered to the resolution.[269] Therefore, it does not seem that Costa Rican courts will be limiting the authority of the Inter-American Court's judgments any time soon.

*Friendly Settlement of* Gómez Murillo v. Costa Rica. A second judgment against Costa Rica was issued in November 2016, *Gómez Murillo v. Costa Rica*, in which the court expanded *Artavia*'s reparations, with full cooperation of the government of Costa Rica.[270] New reparations consisted in creating training programs for all government employees (not just those of the judiciary, as previously established) and strengthening public school education on "human rights, non-discrimination and respect for individual autonomy," as well as "starting an ample and participatory discussion on surrogate motherhood."[271] In addition, the Costa Rican government pledged to pay petitioners an amount of twenty-five thousand US dollars each in reparation for human rights violations committed against them and to pay attorney's fees to the petitioners' lawyer, Huberth May Cantillano.[272] The court added that these reparations ought to be tax free and that the state should pay interest on arrears if payment was delayed.[273] The judgment also reiterated the Inter-American Court's decision that

Presidential Decree 39210-MP-S was now valid and IVF was now authorized in Costa Rica.[274]

The lawsuit, filed by five additional infertile couples in January 2016, presented virtually the same allegations as the *Artavia* complaint, but the political context was now very different. The new government of Costa Rica, represented by the Presidency and the Foreign Affairs Ministry, was now fully compliant with the court's orders and accepted full international responsibility for human rights violations against the petitioners.[275] In addition, the state entirely abandoned its defense of a state interest in protecting embryonic life, which left the issue uncontroverted, as noted by the court.[276] Soon after the court issued its resolution nullifying the constitutional chamber's decision, the government of Costa Rica and the petitioners reached a friendly settlement favoring the petitioners' requests.

The Inter-American Court's composition had changed almost entirely too, with the exception of Judge Vio Grossi, who dissented in *Artavia*.[277] The new members of the court reaffirmed most of the *Artavia* judgment's findings and resolutory dispositions, albeit not all of its reasoning. In a very unusual move, the court issued a judgment that approved the friendly settlement and reiterated *Artavia*'s interpretation of the American Convention as it pertains to the existence of an international obligation to authorize IVF.[278] The judgment could have simply ruled on the friendly settlement's terms and admissibility, as established by article 63 of the court's rules of procedure, which provide that, in the event of a friendly settlement, the court shall "rule upon its admissibility and juridical effects."[279] Instead, the judgment validated the *Artavia* judgment's *ratio decidendi* in regard to a state obligation to authorize reproductive technologies, as pointed out by Judge Vio Grossi, who also dissented in the *Gómez* judgment.[280]

The *Gómez Murillo v. Costa Rica* judgment, however, failed to uphold the prior court's restrictive interpretation of article 4(1) even though it fully supported that court's creation of international obligations to authorize IVF. While the *Gómez* judgment concurred with the *Artavia* judgment's *ratio* on an international obligation to authorize and facilitate artificial reproductive technologies arising from several articles in the convention, it was silent on *Artavia*'s interpretation of article 4(1) on the prenatal right to life.[281] The judgment noted that the controversy over arguments regarding a violation of article 4(1) "has ceased," but it did not make any reference whatsoever to *Artavia*'s reasoning or findings on the definition of the term "conception," the human embryo's personhood, and her supposed gradual and incremental protection, even though it could have.[282] The fact that in *Gómez* the court did not validate the earlier court's interpretation of article 4(1) on the prenatal right to life suggests that that earlier interpretation may constitute part of the decision's *dicta* rather than *ratio*. *Gómez*'s silence about the prenatal right to life, even though the court frequently cites its own *dicta*, could also indicate that the new judges found the *Artavia* judgment's interpretation of the right to life from conception less persuasive than that same court's opinion on artificial reproductive technologies, even though it may agree with the earlier judgment's conclusions.

In both *Artavia* and *Gómez*, the commission appropriately held, among other things, that the petitioner provided no basis in fact or law that would indicate how the rights of the named adult victims were affected by the state under article 4 (right to life) of the American Convention.[283] The IACHR therefore found both petitions inadmissible as they related to articles 4 (right to life), 5 (right to humane treatment), 8 (right to a fair trial), 25 (right to judicial protection), 26 (progressive development), and 32 (relationship between duties and rights) of the American Convention, mostly because the petitioners failed to characterize any specific violations of these rights.[284]

Closure on the case remains pending given the Inter-American Court's express commitment to supervise enforcement of the settlement agreement as part of the procedure for supervision of compliance, which the dissent believed to be inappropriate.[285] In any case, the *Artavia* and *Gómez* judgments should not prevent Costa Rican legislators from adopting relatively restrictive legislation on IVF, as suggested by the commission itself that "regulation that diminishes the number of fertilized ovules" would be acceptable.[286] Commissioners Dinah Shelton, Felipe González Morales, and Rodrigo Escobar Gil indicated "nothing in the decision suggests that the State is precluded from also regulating to protect maternal health and life. . . . The risks of pregnancy increase with age and the State may very well set an upper age limit (as well as a lower one to protect girls from abuse)."[287] Other "less restrictive" regulations suggested by the commission as a whole include limiting IVF access to married couples or cohabiting couples who had no impediments to legally marry and prohibiting embryo freezing, embryo destruction, and embryonic research, as was done in other Latin American countries like Chile and Panama.[288]

## *Control de convencionalidad* and Potential Effects of the IVF Judgments

The *Artavia* judgment cannot be properly said to be a "Latin American Roe v. Wade," given its narrow effects, in the sense that the judgment does not legally apply to any state party other than Costa Rica, as pointed out by the judgment itself and all separate opinions. The judgment's interpretation of the prenatal right to life was titled "Interpretation of Article 4(1) of the Convention *as relevant in this case*," which clearly indicates that the interpretation would be relevant to that case only.[289] Judge García Sayán, who wrote the majority opinion, confirmed this understanding by indicating, in his concurring opinion in *Artavia*, that "the Court has proceeded to interpret this article *for the effects of this case*."[290] Judge Vio Grossi, in his *Gómez* dissent, also pointed out that "the judgment issued by the court is binding *only* to the state party to the dispute *and in regards to that state only*," citing article 68(1) of the American Convention.[291]

Since the Inter-American Court is not bound by *stare decisis*, Judge Vio Grossi correctly pointed out that "another judgment may reach a different pronouncement."[292] The holding is unlikely to be factually or legally relevant to any other state party to the American Convention for two reasons. First, that no other country has an explicit comprehensive ban on IVF, and such a situation is now unlikely to repeat itself.[293] Second, the judgment's definition of "person" and "conception" should not affect most abortion bans in the region given that they usually apply *after*, not *prior* to the human embryo's implantation in the womb. Alejandro Pérez Hualde, a former judge on the supreme court of the Argentinian province of Mendoza, pointed this out and added that the *Artavia* judgment dealt with the beginning of human life, not with putting an end to human life.[294]

The Brazilian attorney general (*Advogado-Geral da República*), Grace Mendonça, also indicated that the *Artavia* judgment was inapplicable to abortion debates in 2018, during the hearings before the Federal Supreme Court concerning first-trimester abortion (discussed in chapter 5).[295] Specifically, *Artavia* was cited as supporting the argument that the American Convention does not grant absolute protection to the unborn child, which would allow for legalization of first-trimester abortions in Brazil.[296] In response, Mendonça pointed out that "although the IACHR stated that it is not possible to confer the status of a person to the embryo, it has not at any time rejected the need to protect the fetus after fertilization. In fact, the argument developed in this case *Artavia v. Costa Rica* refers *essentially to the embryo produced through in vitro fertilization and not yet implanted, and not to the intrauterine embryo*."[297] She stated that the allegation that the Inter-American Court of Human Rights would have reduced the degree of protection of the right to life of the unborn was unfounded since the *Artavia* decision applies only to exceptional situations of the not-yet-implanted human embryos created in vitro.

Even assuming that the *control de convencionalidad* doctrine was widely accepted, which it is not, a single judgment with explicitly limited effects would not create the kind of uniformity needed to generate what the court wants to characterize as jurisprudence, especially in light of *Artavia*'s restrictive interpretation and its lack of reiteration in subsequent cases, including one on the same facts and against the same state. In addition, uniform international court decisions may create customary international law if unobjected to, but an individual decision deviating from custom would have no such power.

The effect of the in vitro judgments may be broad only in the sense that their language can be and has been used to support political efforts for the creation of abortion rights in general and reproductive technologies in particular. The decision's broad language on privacy as an absolute right that prevails over the embryo's right to life and the decision's reiterated claim that the right to life can be subject to multiple limitations easily lend themselves to interchangeable use as arguments for the creation of abortion rights.[298] In a way, *Artavia*'s legal-realist reasoning went beyond Justice Blackmun's *Roe v. Wade*, for *Artavia* not only extended a privacy doctrine to include a right to destroy human embryos without any textual basis, as *Roe* did, but it did so while interpreting a treaty that explicitly recognizes a right to life from conception.

As of 2018, *Artavia* has been mostly invoked at the national level in litigation dealing with artificial reproductive technologies, often without success. For instance, in 2016, the Argentinian federal Supreme Court, in the *L.E.H.* case, rejected a constitutional claim where plaintiffs invoked the *Artavia* judgment. The lawsuit sought public funding of unlimited IVF attempts at pregnancy through a particular IVF technique, intracytoplasmic sperm injection (ICSI), as well as funding of preimplantation genetic diagnosis (PGD).[299] The federal Supreme Court upheld a ruling by the supreme court of the Argentinian province of Mendoza that, among other things, declined to give the *Artavia* judgment any weight in its jurisdiction, given the existence of specialized national laws prohibiting certain practices, such as genetic modification and disposal of human embryos.[300]

One of the Mendoza Supreme Court judges specifically addressed the applicability of the *Artavia* holding according to *control de convencionalidad*. Judge Alejandro Pérez Hualde, in a concurring vote, agreed that Inter-American Court decisions provided "guidance" about the interpretation of the American Convention but held that the *Artavia* judgment had been wrongfully decided, in contradiction with the Inter-American Court's prior judgments on the right to life and with the convention itself.[301] He indicated that nothing in Argentinian law gave Inter-American Court judgments power to supersede Argentina's own law, particularly because the *Artavia* judgment was issued against another nation, nonunanimously, and the judgment itself along with two separate opinions had indicated that its effects were limited to that case. Judge Pérez Hualde pointed out that the court's "opinions" on the definition of the term "person" were only *dicta*—that is, not part of the decision's *ratio*—and the court's related holding would be incompatible with Argentinian law, particularly its civil code and its declaration in favor of a prenatal right to life upon ratification of the Convention on the Rights of the Child.

The Argentinian Federal Court of Salta, in the *L.O.A.* case, similarly held that the *Artavia* decision was not binding on the state of Argentina, given that Argentina was not a party to the dispute and that Inter-American Court judgments have no *erga omnes* effects.[302] In that case, plaintiffs also sought public funding of unlimited attempts at pregnancy through the ICSI technique. Their request was partially granted, but domestic legal prohibitions of embryo freezing, selection, disposal, reduction, or destruction, as well as other restrictions, were upheld. Among other things, the court held that *Artavia*'s rejection of the human embryo's personhood conflicted with Argentina's own laws and with precedent such as the *R.N.F.* decision, which had recognized the embryo as a human person starting at fertilization. The ruling was confirmed in subsequent judgments, such as the *C.D.M.* case, where the court allowed public funding of IVF procedures but prohibited embryo freezing.[303]

The constitutional chamber of the Paraguayan Supreme Court in A.I. No. 4/2019 denied review of a juvenile court of appeals judgment that authorized implantation of human embryos postdivorce and disregarded the *Artavia* judgment.[304] The chamber's *in limine* dismissal upheld an appeal that granted the ex-wife's petition to carry out PGD tests and implant selected human embryos created with her ex-husband, against his objections. The husband had unsuccessfully invoked the *Artavia* decision to argue that the human embryo is not a person and therefore has no right to life. Court of Appeals judge Clara Estigarribia Mallada suggested that the *Artavia* decision's reading of the convention was incompatible with Paraguayan law and was therefore inapplicable.[305]

As of 2018, the *Artavia* judgment has been invoked only once by a high court in a state party in support of abortion decriminalization, but not as a binding source of interpretation. In 2017, the Constitutional Court of Chile cited the *Artavia* judgment in support of its argument for nonabsolute protection of the unborn, but also held that the decisions of the Inter-American Court of Human Rights in disputes to which Chile was not a party are not binding on the court, particularly where there is "a lack of complete uniformity in its decisions."[306] The court did acknowledge that even if nonbinding, its judgments are important tools for interpretation.

*Effects on Ratification of American Convention and Acceptance of Court's Jurisdiction.* The universal ratification of the American Convention by the OAS members has been a long-standing priority for Inter-American human rights bodies, but the *Artavia* judgment may do little to contribute to greater ratification.[307] While some nonparties to the convention may agree with *Artavia*'s tenets, the Inter-American Court's lack of flexibility in refusing to grant state deference in controversial matters of moral relevance may do little to reinforce its authority in the long term. Restricting national judges' ability to interpret national constitutions and imposing interpretive uniformity according to the personal opinions of judges of the Inter-American Court may dissuade some states parties from submitting to its jurisdiction.[308] Furthermore, the requirement that Costa Rican judges and their staff be retrained in proper judging on matters of abortion and reproductive technologies[309] could strike some national judges as arrogant and paternalistic, while others may view such trainings as a tool of ideological imposition of pro-choice views on the judiciary.

*Artavia*'s disregard for national sovereignty may also dissuade nonparties, like the United States, Belize, and other English-speaking nations, from ratifying the American Convention.[310] Even though state representatives may agree with some parts of the holding and *dicta*, the court's overruling of a supreme court decision and its imposition of a duty to provide IVF through government agencies and subsidize it may prove unacceptable for traditional US constitutional standards.[311] For similar reasons, nonparties to the Inter-American Court's statute (Dominica, Grenada, and Jamaica) may be dissuaded from recognizing the court's jurisdiction.[312]

Former commissioner Paolo Carozza has pointed out that an aggressively monist and hierarchical application of the *control de convencionalidad* doctrine, in particular, may reinforce what he calls the "Anglo-Latin divide" of human rights in the Americas—that is, the predominance of the Latin American legal and political traditions coupled with a general disengagement from the Inter-American human rights system on the part of English-speaking states parties.[313] Commissioner Carozza has also pointed out that the court's restrictive interpretation of the American Convention in *Artavia* itself would probably inhibit ratification of the convention by the United States, given that "for some time, the clear trend in both popular opinion and in law has been to back away from the earlier and more extreme versions of the constitutional right to an abortion."[314]

### Provisional Measures in *Matter of B. regarding El Salvador*: An Unsuccessful Challenge to a State's Full Abortion Ban

The court and the commission have both dealt with the issue of abortion when the pregnancy causes a risk to the mother's life, a question that, in theory, could lead to the lawful authorization of an abortion even under the least restrictive interpretation of a prenatal right to life, as suggested by Judge Vio Grossi.[315] In reality, however, such situations are more complex than they appear, and both human rights bodies have declined to order or recommend an abortion on the sole basis that a woman suffers from a serious medical condition, even though they were prompted to do so. Both the court, in *Matter of B.*, and the commission in *Amelia (Nicaragua)* (discussed in chapter 1) have instead ordered or recommended medical treatment for the pregnant woman involved.

*Matter of B. regarding El Salvador* was decided only six months after *Artavia*, in May 2013; nevertheless, it made no reference to the court's interpretation of article 4(1) of the convention therein, even though it could have, since the provisional measures involved an abortion request. In the complaint, the IACHR requested the court to authorize an abortion and to prevent El Salvador from enforcing its abortion ban through the provisional measures procedure; the court, however, failed to do so. The request for an immediate termination of pregnancy was filed before the Inter-American Court on behalf of Beatriz, a twenty-two-year-old lupus patient who was carrying an anencephalic female child.[316]

The complaint requested authorization for the abortion of Beatriz's anencephalic fetus as a provisional measure, while indirectly challenging El Salvador's ban on all abortions by asking the court "[to] establish in its order that immediate and effective compliance with the provisional measures that it orders cannot, in any way, result in the exercise of the State's punitive powers."[317] The court, however, deferred to Beatriz's attending physicians and only ordered that the state ensure that her medical team could take, without any interference, all medical measures they considered opportune and desirable to protect Beatriz's right to life, health, and personal integrity.[318] Beatriz's pregnancy was eventually interrupted, but the child received neonatal care upon birth, succumbing to her condition five hours after birth.

Throughout, the El Salvador Supreme Court's detailed analysis, thorough fact finding, and nuanced reasoning demonstrated the irrationality of a supposed right to abortion arising out of "risk to the life of the mother" scenarios, where the *direct killing* of a fetus has never proven to be medically necessary, as illustrated below.[319] Furthermore, the constitutional chamber of the Salvadorian Supreme Court reiterated that life-saving medical procedures that do not entail the intentional destruction of a human fetus are not prohibited under its criminal abortion ban.[320]

### The Complaint's Threefold Purpose

At the national level, the complaint's purpose was initially unclear. Supreme Court judge Florentín Meléndez, a former member of the IACHR, pointed out that the initial purpose of the *amparo* petition was unclear, since it seemed to be only about the protection of Beatriz's life and health, but as the process unfolded, it became clear that the plaintiffs were requesting that she be given an abortion and that therefore "the fundamental rights of the child" were also involved.[321] Judge Sydney Blanco later indicated his suspicions that the court system may have been manipulated by the fraudulent use of Beatriz's case to promote the legalization of abortion in El Salvador.[322]

Even though the *amparo* petition generally requested the protection of Beatriz's right to life and health, it presented the immediate termination of her pregnancy as the only way to preserve them; there was no request for any medical treatment of her condition (lupus).[323] No efforts to preserve the life of her child were requested either, as observed by Judge Meléndez.[324] On the contrary, because the child's anencephaly was deemed "incompatible with extra-uterine life," Beatriz's representatives requested that Beatriz be given an immediate termination at "an early stage" in order to prevent the pregnancy from progressing.[325] Former commissioner Florentín Meléndez indicated that the plaintiffs' lack of concern for the protection of the rights of the unborn child did not inhibit the constitutional chamber from making a pronouncement in her favor.[326] He affirmed that under El Salvador's constitution, the unborn child is recognized as a person and entitled to life from conception and that, therefore, both the mother and the *nasciturus* are subjects of constitutional protection.

The *amparo* also requested an immediate interruption of pregnancy without any authorization by public authorities, even though one of the plaintiffs themselves had actually submitted one such authorization request.[327] The defendants—namely the hospital director, its legal representative, and the chief perinatology physician—had formally requested a legal opinion on the abortion from the Human Rights Department of the Attorney General's Office (*Procuraduría General de la República*).[328] Beatriz's attorneys deemed the request for authorization to be "unnecessary and irrelevant," but one of them, Denys Muñoz Rosa, participated in a similar request for a technical opinion from the Prosecutor's Office (*Ministerio Público*), which seems strange and raises professional ethics questions.[329]

The IACHR recommendations to El Salvador were similarly vague in appearance: the commission requested that the state adopt "necessary measures to protect the life, personal integrity, and health of B" but did not, in fact, request any specific measures other than the termination of her pregnancy.[330] According to the commission, the "urgent and imminent risk of irreparable damage" to Beatriz's life and health had been caused by "the failure to implement the treatment indicated by the Medical Committee of the . . . National Maternity Hospital," and that committee had recommended only one thing: the termination of Beatriz's pregnancy.[331]

Once the complaint reached the Inter-American Court, however, the commission's purpose was much more straightforward: (a) to have the court order an immediate abortion for Beatriz without medical or judicial authorization and (b) to have the court declare that the state of El Salvador could not enforce its abortion ban against anyone involved in the said abortion.[332] The commission also condemned El Salvador's ban on all abortions, which it identified as constituting the "key obstacle" to the protection of Beatriz's right to life and health, denouncing El Salvador's law for seeking "to protect the life of the fetus, even in exceptional circumstances such as those of this case," namely, an anencephalic fetus's disability and her low probability of survival after birth.[333]

No evidence, however, was provided that El Salvador's ban on abortion was standing between Beatriz and her right to health: no cases were documented of women or physicians in analogous situations being prosecuted or imprisoned in El Salvador. No indication was given that any health care practitioners involved in Beatriz's care were under any threat of prosecution. The sole evidence presented in this regard was the statement that the Medical Committee that recommended termination of Beatriz's pregnancy refused to perform the procedure because they had a subjective belief that they might be subject to criminal sanctions under El Salvador's criminal code.[334]

At the evidentiary hearing before the national constitutional chamber, however, the physicians themselves admitted their knowledge that other interruptions of pregnancies had been performed in the same hospital to protect a mother's health "without a need for legal authorization and with no criminal or any other kind of consequences whatsoever."[335] For that reason, Judge Florentín Meléndez suggested that the hospital's medical authorities' alleged fear of prosecution was not only unfounded but fabricated.

### The Complaint's Anonymity and Beatriz's Consent

The petition before the IACHR was filed by attorneys affiliated with national and international organizations that provide abortions or promote the creation of abortion rights in Latin America and the Caribbean: Ipas Central America, Center for Justice and International Law (CEJIL, *Centro por la Justicia y el Derecho Internacional*), the national Citizens' Group for the Decriminalization of Therapeutic, Ethical and Eugenic Abortion (*Agrupación Ciudadana por la Despenalización del Aborto Terapéutico, Ético y Eugenésico*), and the local Feminist Coalition for Local Development (*Colectivo Feminista para el Desarrollo Local de El Salvador*).[336] These petitioning organizations, however, went entirely unnamed in the Inter-American Court provisional measures resolution and in the commission's precautionary measures without any stated reason.

It is unclear why the commission and the court chose to conceal the identity of organizations representing Beatriz at the Inter-American level, even though the petition itself only requested anonymity for Beatriz.[337] No indication of any real or potential risks for the groups in question were given to justify their anonymity, and no pseudonym was assigned, as was done for Beatriz. In any case, the petitioning organizations publicly identified themselves as Beatriz's representatives immediately after the provisional measures were issued, which seems to suggest the existence of some strategy for temporary anonymity only, rather than safety concerns.[338] The organizations' public stance for abortion rights could have given away the ulterior motive of legalization of abortion in El Salvador, which the petitioners were initially hesitant to assert, as noted by Supreme Court judges.

It was also unclear to the judges at the domestic level that Beatriz, a poor and uneducated woman, was freely making decisions about her abortion request. Psychiatric evaluation reports indicated that Beatriz was being pressured to abort: "[W]ith regard to the emotional state of the individual examined, as she herself has said, she is under pressure, because she has been told that she is in danger of dying if they do not decide 'to remove the child.'"[339] Beatriz also believed that she would die if she didn't get an abortion: "I want to live . . . yes, I want to live for my other child. I think that as this child is unfortunately ailing, and is going to die, then they should remove it . . . because my life is in danger."[340] She was also under the impression that she would go to jail if the pregnancy was terminated: "[Beatriz]'s emotional state is also affected by the belief that a possibility exists that she will be given a prison penalty."[341]

In addition, the director of the Institute of Forensic Medicine, José Miguel Fortín, reported that false information led Beatriz to believe that she would die if she did not make up her mind about getting rid of her child and that she was not informed of alternatives to terminating the pregnancy.[342] Fortín lamented the fact that Beatriz had been given false information: "What she's been told is untrue . . . the end does not justify the means. It is not okay to say something false to persuade someone," he said, suggesting that Beatriz had been misled in an unacceptable way so that those misleading her could get political support for the abortion rights position.[343] The president of feminist organization CEMUJER, speaking for the organizations involved in the petition, did not deny these allegations when asked about them.[344]

National judges were skeptical about Beatriz's informed consent. Judge Florentín Meléndez indicated that, during the evidentiary hearing, Beatriz had expressed a decision to get an interruption of pregnancy because the child had little chance of survival, but that she did not necessarily understand this procedure as involving fetal destruction.[345] Justice Sydney Blanco made similar observations.[346] No evidence whatsoever was presented that Beatriz herself believed that El Salvador's abortion ban should be abolished, only that "[t]he emotional situation of the individual examined is also affected by her belief that she could be faced with a prison sentence."[347]

### Fast-Track Procedure and Nonexhaustion of Domestic Remedies

While *Matter of B.* was going through the Inter-American Court, Amnesty International simultaneously requested and obtained a joint statement by a group of four United Nations experts who urged El Salvador to provide Beatriz with an abortion. The UN experts group included the UN special rapporteur on torture, Juan Méndez, a former IACHR commissioner, who had also taken part in another UN expert statement, urging that an abortion be performed on "Mainumby," whose case was brought before the IACHR.[348]

The statement urged El Salvador "to provide life-saving treatment" for Beatriz, while arguing that carrying the pregnancy to term would constitute "a cruel, inhumane and degrading situation" for her.[349] Like the commission's complaint before the court, the joint statement called for an overturn of El Salvador's abortion ban but perhaps with greater specificity: "This case exemplifies the urgent need to launch a national dialogue on abortion legislation, in order to consider the introduction of exceptions to its general prohibition, especially in cases of *therapeutic abortion and pregnancy resulting from rape or incest.*" [350]

Neither the constitutional chamber nor the Inter-American Court seems to have given the joint statement any weight, since they did not even mention it when both of their resolutions subsequently came out. The statement probably did, however, contribute to the international pressure and media attention generated by the case, which caused the complaint to move with significant speed through the national and international court systems.[351] Judge Rodolfo González Bonilla indicated that no other *amparo* case had ever been decided so quickly by the constitutional chamber, that is, in forty-eight days from the time it was filed, the shortest time between a filing and a resolution having been two months in the past.[352] He also indicated this *amparo* was given priority over others that were pending.[353]

The commission and court likewise admitted and issued resolutions on the petition even though constitutional remedies were being simultaneously pursued at the national level, which seems to violate article 46 of the convention, requiring exhaustion of domestic remedies, especially since no evidence was presented that those remedies would be ineffective. The IACHR took the complaint up to the Inter-American Court while El Salvador's constitutional chamber was still hearing the *amparo* and had not yet issued a resolution on it.[354] The commission granted precautionary measures twelve days after the constitutional chamber's own granting of precautionary measures, perhaps in an attempt to pressure the chamber to favorably resolve the petitioners' requests on the merits.[355] Interestingly enough, the Inter-American Court ruled on the provisional measures request the day after the constitutional chamber issued its judgment, which may raise serious questions about the commission and the court's observance of the convention's subsidiarity principle in abortion-related cases.[356]

### Nuanced Findings at the National and Inter-American Levels

The Constitutional Chamber distinguished a lawful termination of pregnancy from abortion in that the latter seeks not only to terminate the pregnancy but to terminate the child's life, which is prohibited by El Salvador's Constitution, whereas the former does not. A lawful termination of pregnancy "would not entail, much less seek, the destruction of the fetus, and [the infant] would be tended to with all measures necessary to ensure, as far as possible, her life outside the womb."[357] The distinction is quite important for legal purposes because a lawful termination of pregnancy is not criminally prohibited under Salvadorian law. It is also important in medical terms, given that a lawful termination of pregnancy and an abortion are two entirely different procedures: the first would consist in premature birth through either induced labor or a caesarean section, such as the one eventually performed on Beatriz, whereas the second would involve the deliberate destruction of the human fetus.

The distinction was also recognized by the Attorney General's Office, which opined that there should be no legal impediment to the interruption of Beatriz's pregnancy and that both the mother's and child's rights could be protected by inducing or accelerating delivery, a process during which the infant may die of natural causes, "not due to human action seeking to provoke her death *in utero*."[358] Likewise, the representative of the national Medical Union stated that, under the college's Ethics and Deontology Code, which is binding for all licensed medical professionals in El Salvador, "there is no situation in current medical practice that justifies the deliberate termination of fetal life for the purpose of saving the mother's life."[359] He also stated that a doctor should always strive to do everything in his or her power to save the life of both patients.

There was unanimous agreement at the constitutional chamber that a termination of pregnancy during which physicians strove to save both the life of the mother and that of the child would not be subject to criminal sanctions under El Salvador's criminal law.[360] Judge González Bonilla specifically indicated that such a termination of pregnancy would not constitute a crime—or, in any case, would fit under the criminal code exceptions of article 27 on intent.[361] The language used by the constitutional chamber, only a part of which was quoted by the Inter-American Court, read: "While we respect these requirements, the circumstances that authorize the medical intervention and the appropriate moment for this are *decisions that correspond strictly to the medical professionals* who must assume the risks involved in the exercise of their profession and decide, according to up-to-date scientific knowledge and an analysis of medical records, exams and the patient's physical health, whatever is clinically suitable to ensure *the life of both the mother and the nasciturus*."[362]

Similarly, Judge Meléndez indicated that, whereas an interruption of pregnancy is needed under circumstances such as those of Beatriz's case, it should be up to medical specialists, not the constitutional chamber, to determine the procedure to be performed and the timing, while minimizing risks to the life of the mother and providing adequate medical care for the infant, protecting both the mother's right to life and health and the *nasciturus*'s right to be born with dignity and to receive medical care.[363] In such instances, medical personnel, he stressed, have a duty to preserve the life of both human beings, providing adequate and timely medical care.[364] The constitutional chamber thus ruled against the *amparo* seeking an abortion but warned that the hospital authorities were still obligated to continue monitoring Beatriz's state of health, to "provide her the treatment that at every moment [was] suitable for her medical condition," and to take whatever measures they found necessary to deal with future complications that might arise.[365]

Judge Meléndez's dissenting vote indicated that both the mother and the hospital's physicians requested the constitutional chamber to authorize a lawful medical procedure at the evidentiary hearing, not an unlawful abortion.[366] In his dissent, he asserted that the majority opinion should have stressed the fact that such a procedure would be followed by medical care for the unborn child; thus the procedure was substantially different from an abortion and therefore licit, requiring no authorization whatsoever. He found it procedurally contradictory to deny the *amparo* petition and yet order medical authorities to continue monitoring Beatriz's health and provide her with medical treatment, but clarified that his dissenting vote should not be interpreted as an approval of abortion procedures but as an endorsement of the "defense of the life of both [mother and child] in accordance with the Constitution and with international law."

Judge Florentín Meléndez dissented from the majority's finding that the hospital's medical authorities had not violated Beatriz's rights by failing to terminate Beatriz's pregnancy. The evidence proved, he stated, that physicians were aware that the procedure they would perform to terminate Beatriz's pregnancy would be licit and quite different from an abortion: it would consist in a small C-section to be performed on the patient while she was stable, not in critical condition. The doctors indicated that the infant would receive medical care and assistance until her death, which according to medical prognosis was inevitable.

Judge Meléndez concluded that the attending physicians knew what to do, knew that the procedure was licit, knew of potential health risks for Beatriz, and yet failed to perform it based on the argument that they had no legal authorization to do so. Therefore, Judge Meléndez believed the doctors in question had engaged in unlawful conduct by "omitting to act" in providing Beatriz with an interruption of pregnancy and that the majority opinion had erred in failing to clarify that an eventual termination of pregnancy to be carried out on Beatriz, if necessary to preserve her life, would be a lawful act, not prohibited nor penalized by the law.[367] The head of the Prosecutor's Office made a similar suggestion when he stated that the doctors could be subject to criminal sanctions for the lack of due diligence in omitting medical assistance under pretext of requiring prior authorization.[368]

The lack of regulation for termination of pregnancy when a pregnancy causes risk to a mother's life was identified by the constitutional chamber as a contributing factor in the confusion over the distinction between illegal abortion and a lawful termination of pregnancy when the mother's life is endangered.[369] There seemed to be some uncertainty among at least some authorities. The Ministry of Health, for instance, seemed to associate the lawful termination of pregnancy with abortion and indicated there were no applicable medical protocols or guidelines for complicated pregnancies such as the petitioner's.[370] The fact that the criminal code does not include a definition of abortion may have also contributed to confusion over the term's definition.[371]

The constitutional chamber called the state to issue public health guidelines for health care personnel that would indicate how to proceed in cases where specialists have identified the "existence of a real and imminent danger to the life of the pregnant mother and, naturally, for that of the *nasciturus*" posed by carrying a pregnancy to term.[372] Specifically, it referred to the issuance of such guidelines as a duty that lay on public health authorities but also, the court said, on medical authorities, who could adopt whatever guidelines or protocols they found suitable, in the absence of government guidelines.

Even though the country's legal and medical authorities had explained that a termination of Beatriz's pregnancy would not violate Salvadorian laws, the IACHR singled out El Salvador's full ban on direct abortion as the "main obstacle," the "key obstacle," to the lawful termination of Beatriz's pregnancy.[373] In spite of the distinction being recognized by several entities even before the commission heard the petition, the IACHR complaint before the court made no distinction between abortion and a lawful termination of pregnancy under Salvadorian legal standards. The terms "abortion," "termination," "ending," and "interruption of pregnancy" were used interchangeably, which, as one American commentator pointed out, could have been a calculated effort to obscure the above distinctions in order to claim broader decriminalization of abortion.[374]

*Division at the National Level concerning the Need for Immediate Termination of Pregnancy.* Medical opinion at the national level seemed to be divided over Beatriz's need for an immediate interruption of pregnancy or an eventual one, contingent on her suffering serious complications. An early termination of pregnancy had been recommended by a medical committee and by a clinic funded by the Pan American Health Organization (PAHO), on the basis that pregnancy alone could aggravate Beatriz's lupus and that the child's anencephaly implied an added risk of intravascular disseminated coagulation.[375] Health Minister María Isabel Rodríguez favored this opinion.[376] The hospital director and the chief of the perinatology unit, on the other hand, did not find that anencephaly posed the said risk, but only a risk of polyhydramnios, that is, an excess of amniotic fluid in the amniotic sac which could occur after the twenty-sixth week of pregnancy.[377] Other government institutions, such as the Children and Adolescents' Protection Board (*Junta de la Protección de la Niñez y de la Adolescencia*) and the LEPINA (Child Protection Act) Juvenile Court declined jurisdiction to issue an opinion on the matter or to authorize the procedure.[378]

The hospital director and the Institute of Forensic Medicine shared the medical opinion that the need for interruption of the patient's pregnancy was contingent on her clinical evolution.[379] The institute's director,

José Miguel Fortín, explained the forensic report's conclusion that there was no imminent risk because Beatriz's lupus and hypertension were, at the time, in remission, that there were no medical reasons, at the time, for interrupting the pregnancy, and that "to do so [to interrupt the pregnancy] [would] not revert the chronic pathologies that she [suffered] from, nor prevent the complications that [might] derive therefrom."[380] He explained that lupus is a serious illness that would not disappear regardless of whether Beatriz's pregnancy was interrupted or not, especially given her prior deterioration due to lack of proper care. Dr. Fortín cited international research studies indicating that the mortality due to lupus-related complications in pregnant patients was about 1 percent and that in forty years there were only seventeen cases of documented maternal deaths in such cases.[381] He indicated the risk would be higher if her lupus was reactivated and that in that case termination of pregnancy might be required, but that was not the case with Beatriz at the time.

Fortín denounced misrepresentations that were addressed to his office and the public in an effort to promote the cause of abortion rights. He indicated that the Health Ministry had given his institution false information: its report indicated that Beatriz was suffering from kidney failure and was at "imminent risk of death," which forensic medicine found to be incorrect.[382] He also indicated that the population had been "sold" an untrue story regarding the case's facts: "It is not true that she is imminent risk, it is not true that she will get better by taking the child out of her womb."[383] Regarding the child's anencephaly, Dr. Fortín said it was unclear how severe the anencephaly itself was, but in any case, he pointed out that it would be a eugenic abortion, not one based on risk to the mother's life.[384]

The constitutional chamber came to the same conclusion after examining all evidence submitted by the parties. Initially, the chamber granted precautionary measures ordering medical treatment for Beatriz while the *amparo* was being processed but did not order an immediate termination of pregnancy, given that the court believed the attending physicians should make such a decision.[385] For the first time since 1984, the constitutional chamber held an evidentiary hearing where final arguments were also presented.[386] Judge González Bonilla indicated that this hearing gave the chamber the most important elements for the court to issue its decision on the merits of the *amparo* claim: "We thought it indispensable to do two things: to hear Beatriz herself and the various specialists who could evaluate her physical and mental health. . . . In this case, it was the evidence provided by medical specialists that determined the judgment's outcome."[387] The constitutional chamber also opened a 24/7 communication mechanism with the hospital so that the former could be notified of any developments in Beatriz's state of health during the *amparo* process.[388]

Most of the medical evidence presented at the hearing—such as the risk of polyhydramnios starting at twenty-six weeks' gestation or the risk of developing preeclampsia, as she did in her first pregnancy—was characterized by physicians as an "eventual and future risk," not as a "current and imminent" risk to Beatriz's life or health, as reported by Judge González Bonilla.[389] Still, the court was aware that her status at the time was "not necessarily a permanent situation that [would] not vary over the course of time and, for this reason, the defendant health authorities [were] obliged to continue monitoring the petitioner's health and to provide her with the treatment that, at all times, [was] appropriate for her medical condition."[390]

The constitutional chamber therefore declined to order an immediate interruption of pregnancy based on expert witness testimony indicating that Beatriz's condition was stable, that it had significantly improved with medical treatment, and that, despite the risks inherent to her condition, she did not, at that moment, need a termination of pregnancy.[391] The chamber found no violation of the patient's right to life or health, particularly since she had received medical treatment in a timely fashion since the moment when she first sought medical assistance, whereas medical personnel had striven to preserve both her health and that of her unborn child.[392]

After the constitutional chamber judgment was issued, the organizations representing Beatriz reiterated before the IACHR their request for an immediate interruption of pregnancy, even though they acknowledged that Beatriz's health was "clinically stable" and that there was "no imminent risk of death."[393] The commission granted precautionary measures, asking El Salvador to protect Beatriz's right to life, health, and personal integrity by interrupting her pregnancy, as recommended by a medical committee of the hospital she was evaluated in.[394] Since Beatriz was not given an abortion, the commission then took the complaint up to the

Inter-American Court, arguing the existence of a situation of "extreme gravity, urgency and the irreparable nature of the damage" posed by the ongoing pregnancy.[395]

The Inter-American Court found that all requirements for provisional measures had been met, noting the medical recommendations for Beatriz's treatment, including but not limited to the interruption of pregnancy.[396] It did not, however, order an immediate termination of pregnancy but only that the state "adopt and guarantee, urgently, all the necessary and effective measures so that the medical team who [were] treating B. [could] take, without any interference, the medical measures they consider[ed] opportune and desirable" to protect Beatriz's right to life, health, and personal integrity.[397]

*El Salvador's Abortion Ban Immaterial to the Complaint.* The commission's request that the court denounce El Salvador's full abortion ban and declare that the abortion of Beatriz's child could "not, in any way, result in the exercise of the State's punitive powers" would have required the Inter-American Court to interpret article 4(1) and to declare its incompatibility with full abortion bans, even though the IACHR denied this. Such a declaration would have most likely exceeded the scope of provisional measures.[398] The court, however, seems to have declined to go that far.

The Inter-American Court did not find that an abortion involving fetal destruction was, at the time, material to the complaint, citing the Salvadorian Supreme Court holding that "after the twentieth week, an eventual interruption of the pregnancy would not lead to or, in particular, have the purpose of the destruction of the fetus and, also, that the latter would be provided with the necessary measures to ensure, insofar as possible, its life outside the uterus."[399] It also cited testimony by the Institute of Forensic Medicine certifying that "from an obstetric perspective, [Beatriz] is in the second trimester of her second pregnancy, so that, from a medical standpoint, one can no longer speak of abortion."[400] The court therefore did not order that El Salvador refrain from enforcing its abortion ban, as requested, but only that the state adopt all necessary measures to ensure that the medical team treating Beatriz could take whatever medical measures they found suitable to protect her life and health, which, by their own words, did not include the abortion of her anencephalic female child.[401]

## Aftermath

A few days after the provisional measures were granted, on June 3, 2013, Beatriz's pregnancy was terminated via caesarean section.[402] Her anencephalic female infant was born alive and cared for by a neonatology team; the infant died that same day of natural causes associated with her anencephalic condition.[403] Following the C-section, Beatriz's health condition was monitored and found stable and normal. She was released from the hospital a week later, and a follow-up visit was scheduled.[404]

It should be noted that although the state did attempt to preserve the unborn child's life, it did not try to preserve it at all costs.[405] At twenty-six weeks' gestation, the risk for infant mortality was certainly greater than later in the pregnancy, but the hospital's team did not follow the standard protocol for preterm labor, which would have been to administer drugs to delay labor in order to maximize the chances of infant survival.[406] The reason given for the lack of attempts to ensure fetal viability was the child's disability: "The requirements for detaining the uterine activity with medication were not met because this was contraindicated in the case of fetuses with fetal abnormalities incompatible with life."[407]

The Inter-American Court followed up with the provisional measures three months later, in August 2016, when the petitioning organizations challenged the state of El Salvador to prove a negative: that irreparable harm had not been caused to Beatriz's health, personal integrity, and quality of life by her carrying the fetus for twenty-six weeks.[408] The stated concern was Beatriz's continued medical treatment after her child's birth, but the organizations complained, among other things, that they had covered the cost of her transportation for each medical appointment and requested government reimbursement for it.[409] The bottom-line request, however, was that the state document "the impact of the late-stage interruption of her pregnancy" and the "negative consequences that may have been caused by the delayed response by the authorities."[410] The commission echoed this request.[411]

In the absence of any actual evidence that Beatriz's life or health had been compromised solely by the progression of the pregnancy, the court found that these expectations on the part of the commission and petitioners were unsubstantiated, particularly since evidence was presented that her condition was actually stable.[412] Finding that the situation which motivated the provisional measures no longer existed, and commending the state of El Salvador's positive efforts to comply with the same, the court lifted the provisional measures and closed the matter on August 19, 2013.[413]

Although it is hard to see any remaining substantive claims based on the August 2013 follow-up court hearings, the IACHR resuscitated the petition by issuing an admissibility report in September 2017.[414] This is technically permissible given that provisional measures do not preempt the outcome of an eventual decision on the merits of the claim, nor do they "prejudge the State's responsibility for the facts denounced," according to the court.[415] In theory, nothing prevents the report from being followed by a merits report at a later date and potentially a new complaint before the Inter-American Court on the merits.

The commission's admissibility report claims that El Salvador's criminal law on abortion is "ambiguous, incomplete," because it applies subsequent, and not prior, to an abortion and allegedly "impose[s] gender stereotypes and roles that materialize as a form of discrimination against girls and women."[416] The commission supports the petitioners' demand for "therapeutic, ethical and eugenic abortion," a designation used by some abortion rights advocates to refer to the life/health of the mother, rape, and eugenic grounds for abortion.[417] The commission again admits all claims on the merits on the part of abortion rights advocates, including the argument that Beatriz's own right to life was affected by her inability to obtain the abortion of her anencephalic child—an odd claim, since Beatriz did not lose her life, or even come close to losing it, by giving birth.[418] The report characterizes the government's failure to provide Beatriz with an abortion as a violation of the American Convention on Human Rights, the Convention to Prevent and Punish Torture, and the Convention of Belém do Pará.[419]

Given the court's 2013 finding that the complaint did not involve an abortion, properly speaking, the *Beatriz* case seems to have exhausted its potential as the test case for abortion rights advocacy in the region. In addition, other arguments regarding the inexistence of effective domestic remedies seem unpersuasive, given the national Supreme Court's expedited review of the complaint and the petitioners' lack of a direct challenge to the country's abortion ban in national courts. The requirement of non-duplicity of international proceedings does not seem to be met, given that, as the petitioners pointed out, "four special United Nations mechanisms had asked the State for information regarding the case in question," although those, they argued, did not qualify as "international governmental organizations."[420] On the other hand, the case may have contributed to the education of doctors, judges, and the general public at the national and Inter-American levels on the difference between abortion procedures that deliberately seek to end prenatal life and termination of pregnancy where efforts are made to save both the life of the mother and that of the child.

### Future of Article 4(1)'s Interpretation and Jurisprudential Issues

Both the *Gómez* and *Beatriz* decisions suggest weaker support for the creation of a right to abortion by the Inter-American Court in the aftermath of the IVF cases against Costa Rica. The outcome of future abortion litigation before the Inter-American Court may therefore not be as predictable as *Artavia* may suggest. The judgments have, however, raised larger jurisprudential issues regarding the court's authority and the principle of subsidiarity or "complementarity," established in the American Convention's preamble and in articles 46(1) and 61(2), under which the Inter-American human rights system only applies once domestic jurisdiction remedies have been exhausted, thus "reinforcing or complementing the protection provided by the domestic law of the American states."[421] Judge Manuel Ventura Robles explained that under this principle, "Inter-American jurisdiction for the protection of human rights has limits that states parties to the American Convention on Human Rights established. First, its complementarity. That is, its jurisdiction was not established so that all cases would be submitted to it."[422] Both Inter-American human rights bodies have reiterated that they are not to be used as a "fourth instance," that is, as an appeals or cassation court to examine supposed errors of fact or law allegedly committed by national courts.[423]

The Inter-American Court's battle with the Costa Rican constitutional chamber in the implementation phase of *Artavia* brought up serious questions about the proper role of the court in enforcing its own judgments, not to mention issues of subsidiarity and the propriety of adding new obligations after a judgment has been issued, as pointed out by Judge Vio Grossi. Furthermore, the fact that the *Beatriz* complaint was handled in parallel processes at the national Supreme Court, a UN expert group, and the Inter-American Court of Human Rights also raises questions about nonduplicity of international proceedings and subsidiarity of the Inter-American system.

*Artavia* and *Beatriz* involved challenges to pro-life national Supreme Court decisions handed down by constitutional chambers, both of which had, interestingly, been decided by former members of the court and the commission (founding judge Rodolfo Piza Escalante and former commissioner Florentín Meléndez, among others). But the Inter-American Court seemed much more deferential to the Salvadorian constitutional chamber than it was to its Costa Rican counterpart in *Artavia*, perhaps in part due to the former's detailed analysis, thorough fact-finding, and nuanced reasoning.

Whether or not future abortion litigation before the Inter-American Court results in a restrictive interpretation of the prenatal right to life is to be determined by the future composition of the court and the assent that states parties give to Inter-American Court judgments. An eventual restrictive interpretation may legally bind an individual Latin American or Caribbean state to liberalize its abortion laws and may also have the broader effect of altering the current understanding of the American Convention's protection of the prenatal right to life among states parties to the treaty. It is unclear whether a weakening of the right-to-life provision could be limited to the prenatal right to life only. It is not unimaginable that it may affect the right to life of other vulnerable persons such as the elderly, terminal patients, and severely disabled persons, for whom a "right to die" is currently being promoted in national and international human rights politics.

Restrictive interpretations of the right to life from conception could also create political strife and resistance to the court's authority on the part of some states parties, and even provoke counterlegislation. The *Artavia* judgment, for instance, was met with significant resistance by Costa Rican legislators, the constitutional chamber, and the attorney general, in spite of the country's general deference to the Inter-American Court's authority. Depending on the reparations ordered and the means of enforcing its judgments, any future supraconstitutional claims on the part of the Inter-American Court could probably deter nations, such as the United States, that traditionally believe in the subsidiarity of international tribunals, from ratifying the convention. Perhaps for that reason the court has used judicial restraint in *In the matter of B.*, refraining from addressing the overall legality of abortion in El Salvador and deciding only on the issue that was necessary for resolution of the case.

THREE

# Toward a Nonrestrictive Interpretation of the American Convention's Prenatal Right to Life from Conception

A nonrestrictive interpretation of the American Convention's prenatal right to life, recognized in article 4(1), should look at the convention's own rules of interpretation and other international norms and principles of human rights treaty interpretation, namely (a) the *pro homine* principle, (b) the ordinary meaning rule, (c) "evolutive" interpretation, (d) "systemic" interpretation, and (e) "historic" interpretation, analyzed from this chapter onward. These interpretation methods are essentially those established in the Vienna Convention on the Law of Treaties, which the court has recognized as an authoritative statement of international norms of treaty interpretation, and in article 29 of the American Convention on rules of interpretation, which the court is charged to abide by.[1]

This chapter does not question the use of these methods. Instead, it proposes a good-faith, nonrestrictive application thereof, one that would be more consistent with the treaty text; its context, object, and purpose; the convention's golden *pro homine* standard; and the Inter-American Court's own jurisprudence. The chapter focuses on the *pro homine* principle and the ordinary meaning rule. Chapters 4 and 5 deal with evolutive interpretation, and chapter 6 looks at systemic and historic interpretation.

## The Convention's *Pro Homine* Rule

The American Convention's only rule on treaty interpretation can be found in article 29, which prohibits restrictive interpretations of human rights recognized in the American Convention.[2] The provision proscribes any interpretation that would *restrict* human rights to a greater extent than that provided in the convention or in the laws of a state party, one that would *preclude* rights that are inherent in the human personality or are given recognition in another treaty, or one that would *limit* the protection granted by the American Declaration of the Rights and Duties of Man and other international human rights instruments.[3]

Article 29 codifies the *pro homine* principle, also called the *pro personae* principle, which, as indicated by former judge Sergio García Ramírez, is designed to "[resolve], in terms favorable to the human being, the tension between the internal and international legal orders," especially since it allows domestic law to prevail over restrictive interpretations of the convention.[4] Judge Julio Barberis described the rule as one that gives the human person "greater and better protection."[5]

Founding judge Rodolfo Piza Escalante described this principle as establishing that human rights norms should be interpreted "extensively in everything that favors the human being and the full enjoyment of human rights, and restrictively in anything that excludes, restricts and conditions or qualifies them. Conflicts of norms should always be resolved in the most favorable way to the human being."[6] Judge Vio Grossi has described the rule as mandating "the most extensive possible interpretation," "under which the human rights norms must be interpreted in the terms most favorable to the holders of the rights," particularly when applied to the right to life.[7]

The *pro homine* rule has been repeatedly applied by the Inter-American Court to children and migrants, and by Latin American high courts to the human embryo and the human fetus.[8] When applied to the unborn child, the principle is usually articulated as a presumption of entitlement in virtue of which, when in doubt, a statute should be given the most favorable interpretation for the unborn, as described in chapter 4.[9] The constitution of Peru, article 2(1), for instance, establishes that every person has a right to life, identity, mental and physical integrity, unrestricted development, and well-being and that, from conception, the unborn shall be a subject of rights in everything that favors him or her.[10] The Honduran constitution contains a similar principle in article 67, which provides that the unborn shall be considered as born for all rights accorded within the limits established by law.[11] Mexico's constitution, in its transitory provision, holds that laws adopted before the reform's entry into force shall be effective only as long as they favor or benefit the unborn.[12]

Several Latin American high courts have applied the *pro homine* principle to the human embryo's right to life when interpreting the convention's article 4(1). For instance, the Constitutional Court of Peru noted the divide over the definition of "conception" among scientists and jurists and applied the *pro homine* principle, concluding that when in doubt, the court should err on the side of preserving fundamental rights.[13] Likewise, the Argentinian, Peruvian, and Honduran highest courts have applied the *pro homine* principle when protecting human life from the time of fertilization onward.[14] The Chilean Constitutional Court held in 2008, as the Argentinian Supreme Court had held in 2002, that judicial reasoning should defer to the interpretation that would favor a person's right to life vis-à-vis any other construction that would presuppose denying that right.[15] The Mexican Supreme Court has found that Inter-American Court judgments to which Mexico was not a party are only binding on Mexican judges as long as they favor the human person and the protection of his rights, not where their interpretation is more restrictive or where domestic law grants greater protection.[16]

### Restrictive Interpretation of the Right to Life

The Inter-American Court has consistently noted that the right to life has been too often narrowly interpreted, and the court has indicated that the inherent right to life cannot be properly understood in a restrictive manner: "[T]he right to life is a fundamental human right, and the exercise of this right is essential for the exercise of all other human rights. If it is not respected, all rights lack meaning. Owing to the fundamental nature of the right to life, *restrictive approaches to it are inadmissible*."[17] Prior to *Artavia*, the court consistently favored nonrestrictive approaches to the recognition of the right to life, particularly that of children. In *Servellón García*, the court stated that children have special rights derived from their condition and that these are accompanied by specific duties of the family, society, and the state; violations against their right to life are especially gross, the court indicated.[18] Indifference or disdain for the life of unborn children should then have equally grave connotations.

In the *Artavia* judgment, the Inter-American Court carried out exactly the type of restrictive interpretation prohibited by the *pro homine* rule in article 29: it read article 4(1) of the American Convention as providing only limited and gradual protection to the unborn child's right to life, therefore restricting human rights to a greater extent than that provided in the convention. It suppressed and restricted the prenatal right to life to a greater extent than that provided under Costa Rican constitutional law, which the Inter-American Court overturned and replaced with its preferred and more restrictive law through direct intervention in domestic jurisdiction.[19]

The *Artavia* judgment precluded rights that are inherent in the human personality by rejecting the human embryo's personhood before implantation and recognizing a right to life only gradually after that.[20] The restrictive interpretation of article 4(1) in *Baby Boy* and *Artavia* limited human rights protection granted by the American Declaration of the Rights and Duties of Man and other international treaties to which Costa Rica was a party, including the Universal Declaration on Human Rights, the International Covenant on Civil and Political Rights (ICCPR) and the Convention on the Rights of the Child (CRC), as explained in chapter 6.

The court's restrictive interpretation has attracted reactions and criticism from civil society, judges, former members of Inter-American bodies, and academics throughout Latin America, with reason.[21] Former IACHR president Paolo Carozza pointed out: "With its recent decision in *Artavia Murillo v. Costa Rica* . . . the Inter-American Court has given a strikingly narrow reading of the relevant language of article 4 of the Convention—a reading not only quite *contrary to the treaty's intent and its manifest recognition* of the right to life from conception, but also one which in fact *impedes states* from according legal protection to human embryos, and which signals that the legal protection of unborn human life in later stages will also have to give way always to the protection of other interests."[22]

Several Latin American courts have criticized *Artavia*'s interpretation of article 4(1) as an overly restrictive interpretation. For instance, a federal court of appeals in Argentina indicated that the *Artavia* judgment had noted different perspectives on the definition of conception and human personhood and had chosen the most restrictive interpretation of the prenatal right to life, in contradiction with the *pro homine* principle in the convention, noting that it represented an involution (*retroceso*) rather than an evolution for the protection of the prenatal right to life.[23] The supreme court of the Mendoza Province in Argentina declined applying the *Artavia* judgment in its jurisdiction, pointing out that incorporating its tenets would replace the national constitution with the Inter-American Court's "opinions," which improperly rejected preventive protection of human life, running counter to the American Convention itself.[24]

### Legislative Prerogative/Recognition

Article 29(c) provides that "[n]o provision of this Convention shall be interpreted as . . . precluding other rights or guarantees that are inherent in the human personality or *derived from representative democracy as a form of government*."[25] This language may suggest that an Inter-American decision that attempted to overturn democratically enacted legal protections for the unborn child would violate the convention's rules of interpretation and be therefore invalid. The American Convention also establishes that restrictions to human rights recognized in the convention may only be lawfully enacted by legislative authority: "The restrictions that, pursuant to this Convention, may be placed on the enjoyment or exercise of the rights or freedoms recognized herein may not be applied except in accordance with *laws enacted* for reasons of general interest and in accordance with the purpose for which such restrictions have been established."[26] The Inter-American Court has historically interpreted the term "laws" to mean legislative action by "democratically elected legislative bodies established by the Constitution."[27]

Judge Humberto Sierra Porto has argued that euthanasia and abortion on three grounds could be lawfully authorized by a state party's executive or judiciary branches, requiring no legislative enactment.[28] No need for legislation exists, he contended, where a right is clearly established in the convention; "the 'requirement of law' cannot be used as a mechanism to obstruct real compliance with the fundamental rights or to suspend the full force of human rights."[29] His arguments can be challenged on multiple fronts, starting with the fact that the convention contains no "clearly described" right to euthanasia or abortion on three grounds, in contrast with a clearly recognized right to life, as Sierra Porto himself has admitted.[30]

Creating legal grounds for abortion would restrict the right to legal protection of prenatal life from conception recognized in article 4(1); therefore the convention would require legislative action at the national level for the creation of such grounds. The language of article 30 explicitly rules out enactment of human rights limitations by executive regulations or court decisions, perhaps because of the relatively ample discretion that presidents and judges enjoy when making unilateral decisions, which may lend itself to arbitrariness when improperly used.

The Inter-American Court should therefore not promote or legitimize the creation of abortion grounds via executive regulations or court decisions, regardless of their level of authority within their government corresponding branches. Founding judge Rafael Nieto Navia has also suggested that the commission should only recommend that states adopt progressive measures in favor of human rights recognized in the convention, not against them, and that Inter-American bodies may not lawfully recommend the legalization of abortion and abolition of its right-to-life protections for the unborn.[31]

## Ordinary Meaning of Article 4(1)

The American Convention establishes an international duty to legally protect a prenatal right to life from the moment of conception and does not contain a provision on reproductive rights or abortion. According to international rules of treaty interpretation, as codified in the Vienna Convention on the Law of Treaties (VCLT) article 31(1), the text of the American Convention should be used as a primary source of interpretation, using the ordinary meaning rule: "[A] treaty shall be interpreted in *good faith* in accordance with the *ordinary meaning* to be given to the terms of the treaty in their *context* and in the light of its *object and purpose*."[32] This section analyzes the ordinary meaning of the terms of article 4(1), that is, the article's recognition of the unborn child's personhood, the right to life from conception, potential exceptions to the said right, and the arbitrariness test, all in good faith, as follows.

### Good Faith and Prejudice

The Vienna Convention requires that treaties be interpreted in "good faith" as a starting point for a proper reading of any treaty.[33] A judge who openly disagrees with the American Convention's protection of the prenatal right to life from the moment of conception in article 4(1) or has advocated against it would then have to be disqualified from hearing any related cases on the ground of prejudice; otherwise, treaty interpretation is unlikely to be carried out in good faith. The principle of good faith can also be defined as "assuming that what was agreed was for its effective implementation," as indicated by Judge Vio Grossi.[34] In that vein, a judge who argued that prenatal-life protections in the convention are only aspirational or one who advocated to make those protections unenforceable in practice would also have to be recused for prejudice. Such cases are relatively common in the commission, where some members such as Margarette Macaulay, a former Inter-American Court judge, have routinely recommended that states lift their legal bans on abortion or stop enforcing them and that they decriminalize elective abortion on multiple grounds.[35]

Some Inter-American Court judges have openly expressed opinions against any legal protection of the prenatal right to life from elective abortion. Judge Elizabeth Odio, for instance, has advocated for a removal of all legal barriers to abortion practices.[36] Judge Humberto Sierra Porto, as a member of the Colombian Constitutional Court, authored the 2006 judgment C-355, which created four grounds for decriminalized abortion, as described in chapter 5.[37] The judgment also gave an even more restrictive interpretation of the American Convention than the *Artavia* decision, arguing that the human fetus, or *nasciturus*, is not recognized as a human person entitled to the right to life therein and that any eventual rights would have to be outweighed by female autonomy and dignity.[38] As a constitutional court judge, Sierra Porto minimized the prenatal constitutional right to life and promoted the recognition of elective abortion as a "fundamental right."[39] He actively restricted conscience rights of physicians and health care institutions, particularly those of religious institutions that morally object to performing abortions.[40]

The *Baby Boy* report illustrates exactly how the lack of good faith can distort a proper interpretation of the American Convention by a human rights body charged with its application.[41] The report was written by Carlos Dunshee, a commissioner who had actively opposed the inclusion of the right to life from conception in the convention's text during its drafting stages, both as a delegate of his native Brazil and as a commissioner.[42] As a result, the *Baby Boy* report gave a partial account of the provision's preparatory work, presenting Dunshee's rejected proposals as authoritative and giving the American Declaration the most restrictive interpretation possible, while minimizing the American Convention's prohibition of elective abortion, as explained in chapter 1.

The majority in the *Artavia* case also consisted of judges who had previously expressed opposition to legal protection of the unborn child from abortion in states parties, such as Judge Diego García Sayán and Judge Alberto Pérez Pérez.[43] During the public hearing at the Inter-American Court, Judge Pérez Pérez mocked Costa Rica's argument that conception happens at fertilization by referring to it as a "magical moment" of sorts.[44] Judge Leonardo Franco expressed concern over Costa Rica's stunted development in terms of "progressive" human rights causes.[45] In addition, Judge Macaulay angrily asked if the state of Costa Rica intended to "ban sex," arguing that nature is as inefficient in protecting embryos as IVF, while García Sayán congratulated IVF practitioner Zegers-Hochschild on his presentation and praised the birth of babies conceived by IVF in Chile.[46] Pro-life organizations that were present at the public hearing reported that the judges' contempt for state arguments regarding the human embryo's right to life was so blatant that the judges "constantly gesticulated" and visibly showed their disapproval of the state's arguments during the hearing.[47]

In theory, judges should be able to transcend personal values or beliefs and apply the American Convention nonrestrictively, but in practice, the *Artavia* decision's language and reasoning revealed significant dissent from the convention's recognition of a prenatal right to life from conception and its recognition of the human embryo's personhood, which the judgment attempted to reduce to its minimal expression, and to some extent amend.[48] Some may argue that a pro-life judge—if the contemporary world of international human rights ever came to tolerate one—might not have negative prejudice against the convention's implementation because the American Convention protects the life of the unborn child. Nevertheless, nonrestrictive interpretations of article 4(1) in the commission and the court have not necessarily been written by individuals who identified as "pro-life," but by independent judges who simply had no prejudice against the convention's recognition of a right to life from conception and had no personal opposition to states parties' respect for prenatal life.

### Ordinary Meaning of the Unborn as a "Human Being" and a "Person"

The prenatal child's nature as a person and a human being is plainly and unambiguously stated in the text of articles 1(2) and 4(1) of the American Convention. Article 1(2) of the American Convention establishes a definition of the term "person" as synonymous with "human being."[49] The court has repeatedly held that this provision must be read in relation to article 4(1).[50] In addition, article 3 says, "Every *person* has the right to recognition as a person before the law." The treaty then goes on to state that "this" right (the right to life of every human being/person) shall enjoy general legal protection from the time of conception, thus reemphasizing that personhood begins at conception too: "*Every person* has the right to have *his life* respected. This right shall be protected by law and, in general, *from the moment of conception.*"

Putting these clauses together, with attention to their grammatical structure, we may conclude first and above all that *the convention grants legal personhood and a right to life inclusively to "every" human being.* Inter-American Court judges like Julio Barberis have recognized that the ordinary meaning of this provision is that personhood begins before birth, at conception: "[T]he Convention leaves no room for doubt that a 'person' is every human being from the moment of conception," which is simply "accepting in the law what is real in nature," he said.[51] Judge Rafael Nieto Navia has also indicated that a good-faith interpretation according to the ordinary meaning of the terms would lead to the self-evident conclusion that, in article 4(1), states parties recognized the unborn as persons from the moment of conception.[52] Inter-American founding judge

Rodolfo Piza Escalante, in the decision later challenged in *Artavia*, indicated that, by recognizing that every person is a human being and that every person has a right to recognition as such before the law, the convention clearly recognized "real and legal personhood of the unborn and his rights."[53]

Commissioner Marco Gerardo Monroy Cabra has also shared this understanding and indicated that the ordinary meaning of the terms "human being" and "person" included the human embryo starting at fertilization of the ovum by the sperm: "Most scientists agree that the fetus is a human being and is genetically complete . . . [at] fertilization in the true sense of the word."[54] In 2010, Judge Ricardo Lewandowski of the Brazilian Supreme Court read article 4(1) of the convention in a similar way, pointing out that "[e]ven when the expression 'in general' is relativized, that phrase does not affect the idea, for legal purposes, that life begins at conception, beginning either *in utero* or in vitro," he stated.[55]

Inter-American Court judgments have recognized the unborn not only as a person but as a "child," by referring to unborn children as "children," "minors," and "babies," as in *Gómez-Paquiyauri Brothers v. Peru*, *Miguel Castro-Castro Prison v. Peru*, and *Goiburú et al. v. Paraguay*.[56] Even the *Artavia* judgment referred at least a dozen times to the human fetus as an "unborn child."[57] When looking at the convention's *travaux préparatoires*, the judgment pointed out that "during the preparatory work the words 'person' and 'human being' were used without the intention of making a distinction between the two terms. Article 1(2) of the Convention specifies that the two terms must be understood as synonyms."[58] Even though the *Artavia* court did not find that the human embryo was a human person before implantation, it did not deny that the human embryo is a person after implantation, or a human being, for that matter.[59]

A few years after *Artavia*, in 2016, the court issued Advisory Opinion OC-22/16, where it established, among things, that the ordinary meaning of the terms "human being" and "person" was that of "a member of the human species."[60] This ordinary meaning, according to the court, was reflected in the Royal Spanish Academy Dictionary and non-Spanish versions of the American Convention and was consistent with the convention's use of the terms "person" and "human being" as synonymous.[61] It would thus be difficult for the court to argue, at present, that the human embryo or human fetus is not a member of the human species, either before or after implantation.[62]

### Ordinary Meaning of "From the Moment of Conception" as Fertilization, Incompatibility with Gradualism

For states parties to the American Convention, the text of article 4(1) settles the debate over the moment when human life begins and when a human person begins to have a right to life, as pointed out by Judge Alvaro Tafur Galvis of the Colombian Constitutional Court.[63] Inter-American founding judge Piza Escalante also indicated that the convention took a "decisive step" by protecting the right to life starting at conception.[64] Likewise, Commissioner Monroy Cabra has indicated that "[i]f international agreements are to be faithfully and literally interpreted, in keeping with the meaning that should be attributed to the terms of a treaty and read in-context, taking into account the objective and purpose of that treaty, there is no doubt that the protection of the right to life should begin at the moment of conception."[65]

The *Artavia* judgment's restrictive reading of the term "in general" to mean that under the American Convention "the protection of the right to life under this provision is not absolute, but rather gradual and incremental according to its development" directly contradicts the text of article 4(1), which provides that the prenatal right to life shall be protected "in general, from the moment of conception," not gradually or incrementally.[66] Judge Vio Grossi said that the interpretation suggested support for the idea that the convention would allow abortion as long as it was early in the pregnancy.[67] Former court of appeals judge and distinguished Argentinian academic Nestor Pedro Sagüés called it a "fabrication" (*invención*).[68]

The phrase "from the moment of conception" plainly excludes graduality or incrementalist models (*modelos de plazos*), which would fully decriminalize abortions during the *first trimester* or *before viability*, since the convention's language grants general, ample protection to prenatal life "from the moment of conception." Alejandro Pérez Hualde, Argentinian former state supreme court judge, incisively pointed out that full decriminalization of first-trimester abortions waives all legal protection of the human fetus before the first trimester, leaving him or her in a state of "absolute vulnerability" (*desprotección absoluta*), graduality beginning only at day one of the second trimester, which would certainly *not* constitute a gradual or incremental model of legal protection from the time of conception.[69]

By establishing an international obligation to legally and generally protect human life from the moment of conception onward, states have waived their discretion to legally protect prenatal life starting later in pregnancy, or gradually depending on the fetal stage of development; they have undertaken a legal obligation to generally protect life *beginning at conception.* As of 2019, no state party has made a reservation on this point.

Prior to *Artavia*, the highest courts of five Latin American countries (Argentina, Chile, Ecuador, Honduras, and Peru) interpreted "conception" to mean "fertilization" and invoked the American Convention when doing so.[70] For instance, Ecuador's Constitutional Court and Peru's Constitutional Court banned emergency contraception due to its abortifacient effects in 2005 and 2009, respectively.[71] Both states invoked their national constitutions and the American Convention when recognizing the human embryo's entitlement to the right to life before implantation.[72] In 2001, the Argentinian Supreme Court banned an abortifacient drug, affirming that Argentina is under an international obligation, in virtue of its ratification of international treaties, to protect human life from the moment of conception.[73]

*Artavia*'s redefinition of the term "conception" as implantation does not seem to have had much resonance with the highest courts of states parties to the American Convention, none of which have echoed the judgment in that regard. After *Artavia* was decided, in 2014, the Bolivian Constitutional Court emphasized that, under its constitution, "life and everything that may potentially generate it, is protected" from the moment of fertilization of the ovum by the sperm and that "the fetus is entitled to the protections stemming from the Constitution of the State and the laws."[74]

### "In General," Even If Not Absolute

There have been two main interpretations of this term over time within the Inter-American human rights system: the first, reading "in general" as allowing exceptions to the unborn child's right to life, the second, understanding these terms as merely recognizing a general right to life of unborn children rather than exceptions. On one hand, Inter-American bodies have interpreted the terms rather restrictively in *Baby Boy* and then *Artavia*, as indicating that "the protection of the right to life under this provision is *not an absolute* and unconditional obligation, but entails understanding that *exceptions* to the general rule are admissible."[75] That interpretation is mostly based on a supposed compromise during the convention's preparatory work between states that legally authorized abortion and others that did not.[76] No evidence of the said compromise was ever provided, as shown in chapter 6. However, the court has stated that the ordinary meaning of the term "in general" could also support that understanding.[77] This section focuses on the ordinary meaning.

On the other hand, some Inter-American Court judges have interpreted the term "in general" in a minimally restrictive manner as designed to extend right-to-life protections to the unborn child and not as creating exceptions to the unborn child's right to life in particular. In his *Artavia* dissent, Judge Eduardo Vio Grossi observed that states parties did not give the terms a special meaning and that therefore the ordinary meaning rule should apply.[78] He read the term as a synonymous with "common," "universal," or "usually," "mainly," "concerning all or most people," as opposed to "extraordinary" or "infrequent."[79] The terms, he indicated, allude not to exceptions but to inclusivity of the unborn child under the American Convention since article 4(1) protects the right to life of "every person": the expression "and, in general" was added "to permit the protection," which by law must be given to the right of "[e]very person . . . to have his life respected . . . to be accorded also to the unborn child."[80]

In his view, the term was simply meant to extend right-to-life protection to the unborn, to include rather than exclude the unborn: "[T]he expression 'and, in general' makes no reference to an exception, to an exclusion. Quite the opposite, this expression is inclusive. It makes applicable the obligation, to protect the right to life of every person by law, from the moment of conception," he said.[81] He found that the clause provides that legal protection of the right to life from conception "will be granted always and in every case or circumstance—although perhaps in a somewhat different fashion—from the moment of conception."[82]

Founding judge Rafael Nieto Navia has also read the expression "in general" this way. He has indicated that its ordinary meaning is that of "commonly" or "generally," which does not support the idea that the American Convention allows taking the unborn child's life through abortion under any circumstances.[83] He suggested that capital punishment rather than abortion may have been the exception that state parties had in mind when adopting the text of article 4(1) and including the phrase "in general." Judge Julio Barberis likewise understood "in general" as a nonlegal term that could apply starting at conception but not necessarily ending at birth, suggesting that it could have been designed to apply in the context of the death penalty.[84]

Three reasons seem to support Judge Barberis's understanding. First, the fact that the paragraphs immediately following article 4(1) deal with the death penalty. Second, three states (Barbados, Guatemala, Trinidad and Tobago) made reservations on article 4, indicating an understanding that, according to the convention, the death penalty could be considered a legitimate exception to the right to life in limited circumstances.[85] Third, legislative history shows that states parties discussed the death penalty, and not abortion, during the Declaration's *travaux préparatoires* at the Bogotá Conference.[86] The American Convention's final text restricted application of the death penalty in articles 4(2) and (3), and states parties eventually abolished it in 1991 through the Protocol to the American Convention on Human Rights to Abolish the Death Penalty.[87]

*A Nonrestrictive Spin on a Restrictive Interpretation.* Even if "in general" was restrictively interpreted, as Inter-American bodies would currently have it, the existence of exceptions would not negate the general rule, that is, the international legal obligation to protect the unborn child's ever-present and personal right to life. The terms of article 4(1) itself, "This right shall be protected by law and, *in general*, from the moment of conception," distinctly acknowledge the existence of an international obligation to enact general, not exceptional, legal protection for the unborn child's life. This understanding remains undisputed by the Inter-American Commission and Court, which, even in their restrictive interpretations of these terms, have never questioned the existence of a general international duty to protect prenatal life from the time of conception.

Inter-American Court judges have understood the expression to mean that states parties ought to protect the right to life from conception in most cases, even where they make exceptions for few and exceptional cases in which protection may be waived. In 2010, Judge Augusto Cançado Trindade read the expression as equivalent to "in principle" and suggested that article 4(1) would allow only very limited exceptions to the right to life, which would probably exclude broad legalization of abortion such as Canada's.[88] Judge Julio Barberis read the ordinary meaning of the expression to mean "generally," "commonly," "in most instances," or "in most cases," as opposed to "exceptionally," "occasionally," "singularly," "unusually, or "infrequently."[89] Even where exceptions may be admissible, he said, they should only occur "in a few instances or exceptionally," and they should never be arbitrary, as required by the same provision in the convention itself.

Even pro-choice decisions have recognized the existence of a general state duty to protect prenatal life. For example, judgment C-355 of the Constitutional Court of Colombia accepted a general duty of legal protection when it read the expression "in general" to "allow *exceptions* to the protection of the product of conception," "notwithstanding the fact that the protection granted [from conception] applies *in general*."[90] Colombian Constitutional Court judge Tafur Galvis likewise conceded that the convention did not mandate absolute protection of the right to life, but held that the term "in general" means that legal protection ought to be given "always," referring to "the majority of things"; therefore criminal exceptions could apply for abortion only under "exceptional" circumstances, in a "strictly regulated" manner that would leave little room for judicial discretion that could lead to arbitrariness.[91]

High courts and supreme court judges of some states parties—namely Bolivia, Chile, Colombia, El Salvador, Mexico, and to some extent Brazil—have given a nonrestrictive spin to the commission and the court's restrictive interpretation of the prenatal right to life. The said courts and judges have found their nations' relatively strict abortion bans to be compatible with a "nonabsolute" protection to the unborn child's right to life. In 2014, for instance, the Constitutional Court of Bolivia sympathized with the idea of gradual and incremental legal protection for the human fetus, although it did not at any point cite the *Artavia* decision.[92]

Differing from the judgment's reasoning, however, the Bolivian Constitutional Court held that even though legal protection of the human embryo and fetus increases with fetal development, in an incremental manner, it never disappears. The court found that its domestic laws did not grant "absolute protection" to the unborn child, citing *Baby Boy v. United States*, where the commission indicated that the American declaration and convention did not grant an "absolute" right to life from the moment of conception. It did not find that its criminal law granted the said "absolute protection" because (a) the unborn are not treated as citizens under Bolivian law; (b) criminal law establishes lower criminal penalties for abortion than for homicide; (c) criminal law allows nonpunishment for abortions of those conceived in rape; and (d) where conflict between the life of the mother and the life of the unborn child exists, the law gives preference to the mother's life over the life of the unborn.

The Bolivian Constitutional Court found its restrictions on abortion therefore compatible with the American Convention and upheld its ban on most elective abortions and its criminal penalties for abortion practitioners as constitutional.[93] It held that a human "embryo may not be considered to be property of the woman" and rejected the idea that pregnancy alone implies a threat to the mother's right to health, that it can be legitimately compared to an illness or a threat to a woman's personal integrity, or that it can be labeled as "cruel, inhuman or degrading treatment."[94]

El Salvador's constitutional chamber of the Supreme Court seems to have understood a nonabsolute protection of the unborn child in the same way as the Bolivian Constitutional Court. In its *amparo* judgment 310-2013, denying an automatic abortion on a lupus patient carrying an anencephalic child, the Salvadorian court did not specifically cite the *Artavia* case, but it agreed with the understanding that the convention does not require absolute protection of unborn life.[95] The constitutional chamber pointed out that the American Convention and the CRC, which protect the *nasciturus*'s right to life, "do not demand that the State guarantee an absolute and unconditional protection of incipient life; to the contrary, their systematic interpretation reveals the need, in specific cases, to weigh the right to life of each element of the mother-child duo."[96] Still, it found that the country's full abortion ban, which allows termination of pregnancy only upon risk to the mother's life, followed by neonatal care for the child, allowed a balance of rights between the right to *life* of the mother and that of the child and was therefore compatible with the state's obligations under international human rights law.[97]

The constitutional chamber held that the unborn child's right to life "is not absolute and unlimited" in such a way that the *nasciturus*'s rights would be given a greater, superior status over the mother's, but held that its national criminal law did not treat it that way because it allowed exceptions to abortion for the same mitigating or exonerating factors that apply to other crimes, such as lack of intent, lack of consent, mental incapacity, and so on.[98] In addition, the judgment interpreted article 27 of the national criminal code, prohibiting abortion, as allowing for a balance of rights between the unborn child's right to life and the mother's, where conflict may arise.[99] The court therefore found that the country's full abortion ban, allowing termination of pregnancy only upon risk to the mother's health, followed by neonatal care for the child, was entirely compatible with the state's obligations under international human rights law.[100]

Unlike the *Artavia* court, which applied a proportionality test, the Salvadorian court used the method of *ponderación*—that is, balancing of rights, which applies when two legal rights or interests of the same status are involved. The *amparo* judgment held that when two fundamental rights are in conflict, such as in situations where the pregnancy poses real, imminent risk to the mother's life, the method of *ponderación* applies, and only if no equilibrium can be found may one right take precedence over another.[101] Precedence, however, cannot be given to a right over another *in abstracto*—that is, as a general rule, but only on a case-by-case basis, through judicial application of the constitution.[102]

Chilean judges likewise found that Chile's long-standing full abortion ban had never been an "absolute" ban on abortion in Chile, given that indirect abortion where the mother's life was at risk was never included in the criminal abortion prohibitions.[103] The Chilean Constitutional Court upheld three grounds for abortion in 2017, citing, among other evidence, the *Artavia* judgment's *dictum* on the "nonabsolute" character of the unborn child's right to life, as described in chapter 5.[104] Concurring judge Domingo Hernandez, however, pointed out that, regardless of the ruling, human life continued to be an "absolute" value and explained that the law created requirements for nonpunishment of abortion as a mere absolutory excuse (*excusa legal absolutoria*) to an otherwise unlawful act.[105] He indicated that abortion lacked the ethical and social value that was normally recognized for other health treatments and that the act itself continued to be considered a crime in Chile and legally "unjust."[106]

Colombian Constitutional Court judges Marco Gerardo Monroy Cabra and Rodrigo Escobar Gil, who went on to become IACHR commissioners, have similarly found that the direct abortion of a child where the pregnancy presents some risk to the mother's health does not pass the proportionality test given its lack of strict proportionality between the full sacrifice of the fetus's rights—*certain* death—and the benefit to the mother of avoiding *potential* death.[107] They found that indirect abortion, where the end is not to destroy the fetus but to preserve the mother's health and life from serious risk of death, was the only legally acceptable alternative from a proportionality perspective and that this practice was never penalized in Colombia nor included among criminal penalties for voluntary abortion.

Judge Ricardo Lewandowski of the Brazilian Supreme Court has also read the clause "in general" as allowing only narrow exceptions to legal protection of the unborn child's life: "Even when the expression 'in general' is relativized, . . . the signatory state may eventually waive its protection under exceptional circumstances, when other rights are at stake. A typical example would constitute the lifting of legal sanctions for so-called 'necessary abortion,' established in art. 128, paragraph I, of the Brazilian Criminal Code, which refers to that practiced by a medical doctor when there is 'no other means to save the life of the pregnant woman.' "[108] He later added: "[I]t is possible to make exceptions to that absolute right when other rights are at stake; in which case it would require a balancing of rights [*ponderação de valores*]." And "the expression 'in general' allows exceptions to the protection owed, in principle, in an absolute manner to life from the moment of conception. For that reason, I held that the Brazilian Criminal Code in article 128, paragraph I allows necessary abortion, taking away its illegality."[109]

Mexican Supreme Court judges have interpreted "in general" this way, having indicated that the words "in general" mean that prenatal life protection will be waived "only by exception" under the circumstances established by national legislation, not broadly for first trimester abortions.[110]

The president of the national human rights commission similarly stated that the expression "in general" may allow for criminal liability to be waived under exceptional circumstances where national legislators thought a justification existed, but *not on the grounds of gestational period*, such as in Mexico City's first-trimester abortions (discussed in chapter 5), which left prenatal life wholly unprotected during the beginning of pregnancy.[111]

The interpretation of the American Convention given by constitutional courts and supreme court judges demonstrates that national courts may not be as willing to restrictively interpret the prenatal right to life in the American Convention as the Inter-American Court, even where the prenatal right to life was found to allow exceptions. They also show that domestic abortion bans may be defended even under a restrictive interpretation of article 4(1), which no state party is legally required to adopt.

In any event, even if exceptions to the enforcement of the prenatal right to life were permissible in the court's understanding of the words "in general," they would not be lawfully *required*; there would be no state *duty* to reduce legal protection for prenatal life, as pointed out by Judge Sergio García Ramírez.[112] The words "in general" are preceded by "This right shall be *protected by law*," which suggests that exceptions to the legal protection or *enforcement* of the right to life from conception may be permissible, but the prenatal right to life itself must be recognized "in general." Therefore, the convention may permit, but does not require, that domestic legal *protection* of this treaty-based right, not the treaty-based right itself, be abated in minor ways, but not "in general," after the moment of conception. The right to life remains even if, by law, its protection is not enforced.

*Proposals for a "Margin of Appreciation" Doctrine.* The application of the margin of appreciation doctrine to the issue of abortion in the Inter-American system has been proposed as a solution that may, at least temporarily, relieve tensions that may arise between Inter-American human rights bodies and states parties to the American Convention over this very polarizing moral issue in international human rights law. The idea is not unthinkable since both the *Baby Boy* and the *Artavia* judgments suggested that the convention's term "in general" was intended to leave the issue of abortion as a matter of state sovereignty during the treaty's preparatory work.[113] Brazilian Supreme Court justice Carlos Britto has similarly suggested that the convention's term "in general" should be read that way: "Brazil also opposed, in that conference, the original text so that it would include—as it eventually did—the caveat of 'in general.' That is, as a rule, to submit that matter *to the legislation of every sovereign state.*"[114]

In 1981, Mexico made an interpretive declaration at the time of its ratification of the convention indicating its understanding that the term "in general" created some margin of appreciation in regard to the international obligation to legally protect prenatal life: "With respect to article 4, paragraph 1, the government of Mexico considers that the expression 'in general' does not constitute an obligation to adopt, or keep in force, legislation to protect life 'from the moment of conception,' *since this matter falls within the domain reserved to the States.*"[115] The Mexican Supreme Court has confirmed its understanding, as stated in its reservation, that the convention's words "in general" "grant states a *margin*" to regulate abortion.[116]

Five states parties to the convention—namely Argentina, Brazil, Chile, Colombia, and Paraguay—signed a declaration recognizing, among other things, a "margin of appreciation of states in complying with the obligations established by the convention."[117] Judge Vio Grossi, in the *Artavia* judgment and subsequent opinions he has written since, has supported the idea of applying the margin of appreciation doctrine in the Inter-American human rights system for controversial moral matters that are not "expressly and specifically regulated" by international human rights law, such as reproductive technologies, abortion, or same-sex marriage.[118] His *Gomez* dissent indicated that "[f]or now, given that *in vitro* fertilization has not been regulated under international human rights law, it is therefore understood as a matter of domestic, internal jurisdiction, of exclusive concern to the state and expressly within its margin of appreciation."[119] He later pointed out, in 2017, that "not everything is regulated by international law" and that the domain of exclusive national jurisdiction of states parties still exists under international treaties.[120]

Former commissioner Paolo Carozza has also supported the application of a functional equivalent of the European Court's margin of appreciation doctrine, pointing out that the absence of constitutional-pluralism doctrines may have been reasonably justified in the past due to the weakness of democratic institutions and the rule of law and the gross human rights violations endemic to the region.[121] He finds it highly doubtful, however, that the same kind of rigidity and uniformity is justified at present, when the human rights violations that states engage in have become more sophisticated. In addition, "[i]f the Anglophone world is to be taken more seriously in the Inter-American system, a greater tolerance of constitutional pluralism akin to the European model needs to be cultivated in this hemisphere as well. This means, concretely, not only a much more robust use of comparative law in general, but the development of some formal doctrines of pluralism that are analogous to the margin of appreciation."[122]

The Inter-American Court and the Inter-American Commission often seek to emulate the European Court of Human Rights, and for some, there is no reason why it should not emulate it on the margin of appreciation doctrine, particularly when it comes to morally controversial, politically polarizing issues such as abortion. In particular, the European Court of Human Rights has given states a "wide margin of appreciation," that is, "considerable room to maneuver" in "sensitive" areas over which the European Convention has no express provisions, such as in the context of abortion and artificial reproductive technologies, as well as other issues like same-sex marriage and assisted suicide.[123] Requirements for the application of a wide margin of appreciation usually include a lack of European consensus on the subject and a lack of clarity in the text of international human rights instruments on the subject.[124]

Such requirements may or may not be met in the Inter-American system, depending on the issue at hand. The text of the American Convention certainly leaves no doubt that domestic authorities have a duty to enact and enforce laws that protect prenatal life from any acts that deliberately seek to take it. Likewise, one could argue that some areas, such as the recognition of the unborn child as a person entitled to the right to life and the view of elective abortion as a violation of that right, enjoy broad consensus among states parties, as described in chapter 5. Less consensus can be found, however, in other areas such as statutory provisions for nonpunishment of abortions where, aside from the life-of-the-mother requirement, there is no majority state practice favoring a particular provision, as explained in chapter 5.

Key differences exist between the two systems' legal protection of prenatal life. In *Vo v. France*, the European Court recognized that the American Convention's protection of the unborn child's life beginning at conception may be incompatible with legal abortion, as opposed to the European Convention on Human Rights, which is silent on the subject.[125] Unlike the American Convention, the text of the European Convention contains no explicit protection of prenatal life; therefore the European Court of Human Rights allows states, within their margin of appreciation, to determine in their internal order "when the right to life begins."[126]

In light of the European Convention text's silence on prenatal life, the European Court has so far refused to address whether the unborn is a "person" within the meaning of article 2 of the convention and has deferred to state jurisdiction on this matter, while stating that such margin of appreciation is not unlimited and may entail an obligation to protect the unborn.[127] It has also stated that where there is no consensus among states parties over legal protection of public policy interests, "particularly where the case raises sensitive moral or ethical issues, the margin will be wider."[128] In that vein, the European Parliament has also recognized that, "considering the ethical, social and cultural dimension of abortions, it is for Member States to develop and implement their policies and legal frameworks. The Commission does not have the intention to complement national health policies in this respect."[129]

Unlike the European Court, the Inter-American Court has not fully developed doctrines that defer some matters to national sovereignty or promote plurality of interpretation.[130] In *Artavia*, the court specifically refused to borrow from the European Court's doctrine of the margin of appreciation even though the state of Costa Rica specifically asked it to do so.[131] Although the *Artavia* court relied heavily on European Court jurisprudence, it refused to apply the same safeguards that the European system provides against judicial arbitrariness. Such doctrines, however, seem desirable given the region's cultural, political, and social diversity and would allow for a response to criticism on the "democratic deficit" of international courts.[132]

Judge Diego García Sayán has identified at least one set of circumstances where local specification of human rights can be considered acceptable by the court, regardless of such specification's results. In the context of nondiscrimination and the rights of indigenous peoples, García Sayán has promoted such juridical pluralism: "[I]ndividual rights are exercised in communities and they must be interpreted precisely in each specific context," and "juridical pluralism is a concept with increasing acceptance and legitimacy that the Inter-American Court applies when developing its jurisprudence in cases of this type."[133] That rationale could also apply to juridical pluralism in allowing states parties to interpret prenatal rights in their own specific context, especially given that legalization of abortion involves local values, moral perspectives that may vary according to local religious and cultural norms.

For as long as the Inter-American Court and Inter-American Commission continue to be unwilling to enforce protection of the prenatal right to life, a holding that abortion is a matter within states' margin of appreciation may be the only nonrestrictive alternative to a restrictive reading of the convention or the creation of a new right to abortion. On the other hand, such a doctrine may in the long term render article 4(1)'s protection of prenatal life relatively ineffective, *if defined broadly*. If the margin of appreciation were to be broadly understood simply as "leaving the issue of induced abortion for states to decide" as in the European human rights system, it might in the long term render article 4(1)'s protection of prenatal life virtually ineffective. Such a definition of the doctrine could be inconsistent with what treaty itself stipulates, that is, a clear legal duty to generally protect prenatal life from the moment of conception and limit practices that undermine an unborn child's right to life, including elective abortion. A *broad* margin of appreciation on abortion could theoretically gut the prenatal-right-to-life provision of any enforcement potential, if Inter-American human rights bodies were willing to hold states accountable for violations of the prenatal rights provision, which, as of 2018, they are not.

A broad margin of appreciation on voluntary abortion, additionally, does not seem to be consistent with states parties' legislative intent when they drafted the convention. During the convention's preparatory work, Brazil proposed an amendment to the American Convention article 4(1) to delete "in general, from the moment of conception" to essentially make abortion a state issue for legislatures in particular to decide, as expressed by Carlos Dunshee, the Brazilian delegate.[134] But this proposal was rejected by states parties, which suggests that they did not want to leave the issue of abortion up to state discretion or to leave legal protection of prenatal life as an optional clause. The amendment's rejection indicates that states had the explicit intent to recognize a state duty for all parties to the American Convention to legally protect prenatal life, as the final text indicates. Only one nation, Mexico, made a reservation to this provision.

If the prenatal right to life is to be interpreted nonrestrictively, a consistent margin of appreciation could only be defined *narrowly* to generally protect the prenatal right to life from abortion while allowing states parties some flexibility in preserving statutory requirements for nonpunishment of abortion. A margin of appreciation would have to be limited by the convention itself if it were to respect the convention's *pro homine* rule and promote an effective implementation of the convention in states parties. Arbitrariness limitations would still be legally required under article 4(1), and decriminalization of elective abortion for arbitrary reasons should still constitute a check on states parties' international obligation to protect a person's right to life from the time of conception generally, rather than exceptionally, as explained below.

### Arbitrariness Test Applied to Elective Abortion

The article 4(1) text on the prenatal right to life from conception is immediately followed by the prohibition of arbitrary exceptions to the right to life: "*No one* shall be *arbitrarily* deprived of his life."[135] Judge Julio Barberis has indicated that the first words in the clause, "no one," suggest the inadmissibility of *any* exceptions to the arbitrariness requirements, even where exceptions to the right to life were admissible.[136] The Inter-American Court has consistently stressed a negative state duty to refrain from depriving anyone of their right to life in an arbitrary manner, and that duty clearly extends to any deprivations of the prenatal right to life, given the article's text.[137] If the general obligation to protect prenatal life allows for exceptions, then those exceptions should meet the arbitrariness test.

Arbitrariness standards should apply even in the case of nonpunishment of abortions in domestic jurisdiction. Judge Ferrer Mac-Gregor has indicated, in the context of the death penalty, that article 4(1)'s prohibition of arbitrariness applies in the context of any legal and non-legal deprivations of the right to life: "The mandate applies not only as a prohibition of those executions that have been committed outside the law . . . , but also to those that occur even when the state acts within the limits of the law."[138] Therefore the mere legality or nonpunishability of some abortions (see chapter 5) would not exclude them from the requirement that such deprivations of the right to life not be arbitrary.

Article 30 of the American Convention, which requires that human rights restrictions be enacted *by law* for a *legitimate purpose* and for "reasons of general interest," may also require that grounds for abortion in states parties be enacted by the legislature, not the judiciary, for a legitimate purpose and for reasons of general, rather than private, interest.[139] The Inter-American Court has interpreted article 30 as requiring that restrictions are not "abusive or arbitrary," that they be "*substantively and formally established by law*, pursue a *legitimate* aim, and comply with the requirements of *suitability, necessity and proportionality*" as well as "*humanity*."[140] It has also indicated that arbitrary deprivations of the right to life are those that, "for example, [involve] the *use of force* in an *illegitimate, excessive or disproportionate* manner."[141]

Some elements of this test have been clearly defined by the court. For instance, in the context of legitimate use of lethal force, the Inter-American Court has defined the "absolute necessity" test, stating that "[lethal force] must be forbidden as a general rule" and only employed in "extraordinary" cases "as a measure of last resort."[142] In the context of abortion, it seems that the only case where a termination of pregnancy may objectively constitute an absolute necessity would be the "life of the mother" (or a narrow health) provision. Proportionality, in the context of right-to-life violations, has been determined to imply that the level of lethal force should not be greater than the level of resistance offered.[143] Since the unborn child is obviously unable to raise any resistance at all, this test would also justify the termination of pregnancy only when the mother's life is endangered by the continuation of the pregnancy.

Some judges have found that any direct abortion would fail to pass all elements of the arbitrariness test under the American Convention. Judge Julio Barberis, for instance, has indicated that according to Inter-American Court decisions, it would be arbitrary to deprive any human being of the right to life for reasons to which he is entirely foreign and in relation to which he has no responsibility whatsoever, as occurs in a direct abortion.[144] Any abortion performed by public or private actors where the intent is to end the unborn person's life is an arbitrary act, he said, as would be a court judgment ordering the abortion of an unborn person or the killing of a disabled minor due to his disability.

Some judges have found that laws that allow first-trimester abortions, thus granting impunity for all abortions regardless of reason before a certain gestational age, are arbitrary. One Mexican Supreme Court judgment held in 2008 that legalization of first-trimester abortion was compatible with the American Convention because the latter did not include an "absolute right to life" of the *nasciturus*.[145] That judgment, written by Judge José Ramón Cossío Díaz, did not create binding precedent (*jurisprudencia*) on that court due to absence of a majority opinion and the narrow margin in favorable votes, but it did uphold Mexico City's legalization of first-trimester abortion. Three judges—Genaro David Góngora Pimentel, Sergio A. Valls, and José de Jesús Gudiño Pelayo—concurred with Cossío Díaz on that point.[146] The opinions opposed the finding by the Mexican president of the National Human Rights Commission that the first-trimester abortion statute violated the American Convention's right to life from conception given that, by criminally punishing only those abortions that occurred after twelve weeks' gestation, the district left unborn life disproportionately unprotected.[147]

Three dissenting judges, however, found that first-trimester abortions were not permissible under the American Convention, even if the right to life was given a nonabsolute character. Judge Sergio Salvador Aguirre Anguiano held that first-trimester abortions do not meet the reasonableness and proportionality requirements given that they "nullify in an absolute manner the *nasciturus*' right to life during a certain stage of pregnancy."[148] He found that a woman's rights are not permanently affected by pregnancy and that her life and health are placed at greater risk by abortion than by pregnancy, whereas the unborn child's life will be permanently affected by abortion.[149] He indicated that first-trimester abortions did not satisfy the "necessity" test either, given that alternatives to abortion are available that do not require the obliteration of one right in favor of another and allow for a balance of rights (*ponderación*).

It is clear, in any case, that decriminalization or legalization of abortion on the sole basis of convenience, personal autonomy, privacy, or individual choice would be arbitrary and violate the American Convention, as the United States admitted in the *Baby Boy* case, indicating that "[a]n abortion which was performed without substantial cause based upon the law could be inconsistent with article 4."[150] The ordinary meaning of "arbitrariness," as articulated by Judge Vio Grossi, is "what is understood by it today . . . an 'act or procedure contrary to justice, reason or the law, issued only by personal choice or random whim.'"[151] In a similar sense, Colombian Constitutional Court judge Tafur Galvis indicated that even if protection of unborn life may not be absolute under the American Convention, a woman's decision to terminate a pregnancy that she does not desire is not absolute either, and that abortion may be legally permissible only under "exceptional" and "strictly regulated" circumstances in the Inter-American human rights system, not for *arbitrary* or *capricious* decisions on the part of the mother or other persons.[152]

### Treaty Context of Prenatal Right to Life from Conception

According to article 31(2) of the Vienna Convention on the Law of Treaties, the context of the American Convention comprises the treaty's entire text, including its preamble and annexes, any reservations, and the American Declaration of the Rights and Duties of Man, given the convention's nature as a related agreement.[153] In particular, this section also analyzes Inter-American Court interpretation of article 4 on the right to life in other contexts, such as the death penalty; the court's application of article 3 on the right to identity; and its application of article 19 on the rights of the child and the need for consistency with its interpretation of article 4(1) on the right to life from conception. This section also looks at the American Declaration in detail, the interpretation of which is inextricably linked to the understanding of the American Convention.

The court has consistently held that the fundamental right to life is a prerequisite for the enjoyment of other rights: "[T]he right to life is a fundamental human right, the full enjoyment of which is a *precondition* for the enjoyment of all the other human rights."[154] The court has also recognized a "*supreme entitlement* that every human rights treaty and declaration recognizes and protects . . . : human life."[155] The IACHR has similarly said that "the right to life is widely recognized as the *supreme right* of the human being, and the *conditio sine qua non* to the enjoyment of all other rights."[156] Furthermore, the court has recognized the right to life as an international norm of *jus cogens.*[157]

In a sense, the American Convention does establish an "absolute" right to life because article 27(2) prohibits its derogation or suspension, even in time of war or public danger or state of emergency. Inter-American

Court judgments have characterized the right to life as a "nonderogable" right, as part of a "nonderogable nucleus" of fundamental rights that cannot be repealed.[158] The preamble of the Protocol to the American Convention on Human Rights to Abolish the Death Penalty likewise states that the inalienable right to life cannot be suspended for any reason, not even in times of war, public danger, emergency, or constitutional suspension of guarantees, thus preempting utilitarian calculations weighing the person's rights versus public interests, however important.[159] This supreme, nonderogable, fundamental right to life also belongs to unborn children from the moment of conception, according to article 4(1) of the convention.

The court has articulated a state duty to prevent violations of the right to life stemming from article 1(1) on the state "obligation to respect rights": "The obligation to guarantee the rights to life and personal integrity presuppose the duty of States to prevent the violation of those rights."[160] It has held that article 4(1) requires not only legislative action but also public health measures, investigation of deaths, identification of perpetrators, punishment of offenders, victim compensation, and the prevention of certain forms of violence and life-threatening situations.[161] It has found that the duty to respect the right to life obligates states and all of their agencies to refrain from directly engaging in killing and to refrain from engaging in collaboration to kill, acquiescence of killing, or tolerance thereof.[162] The court has also found state responsibility where private parties carried out right-to-life violations, for a state's failure to comply with its duty to protect and respect the right to life and prevent the infringement of that right.[163]

Under these criteria, criminal abortion bans and their enforcement are directly related to the treaty's duty to legally protect the unborn, to investigate possible violations, to punish offenders, and to prevent future violations, as indicated by Colombian Constitutional Court judge Tafur Galvis.[164] On the other hand, creating a legal duty of public health facilities or even private health care facilities to provide abortions would violate the said duty to prevent and protect. In the case of *Gonzales Lluy v. Ecuador*, the court held that the state has an "obligation to monitor and supervise the provision of health care services . . . and [an] *obligation not to endanger life*, which violates Articl[e] 4."[165] Forcing health care providers to perform abortions would certainly run counter to that interpretation.

Article 4(3) of the convention mandates that "the death penalty shall not be reestablished in states that have abolished it." It would then be inconsistent for the court to order a state to overturn their constitutional or criminal law protections of the right to life from conception, to preclude a state from enforcing its elective abortion ban, or to order a state to reestablish legal authorization of abortion where it has been abolished.

Article 2 of the convention, on domestic legal effects, has been repeatedly interpreted as establishing a general obligation of states parties to adopt domestic laws that will render compliance with the convention's human rights norms effective and to put those laws into actual practice at the national level (principle of *effet utile*).[166] The court should then consistently require states to do the same to protect the prenatal right to life both in the context of abortion and in other scenarios where the unborn child's life is intentionally taken, such as those described in chapter 5.

The Inter-American Court has interpreted article 4(1) to contain both a negative state duty to ensure that no one is arbitrarily deprived of their right to life and a positive state obligation to "adopt all the appropriate measures to protect and preserve the right to life," to "adopt a normative framework that dissuades any threat to life," and to "establish an effective legal system to investigate, punish, and redress deprivation of life by State officials or private individuals."[167] Abortion bans make investigation and prosecution of induced abortion possible; legalization would make it *impossible.*

The sole fact that criminal abortion bans cannot stop any and all abortions and that abortions continue to happen does not justify legalization of abortion according to previous jurisprudence, given that the state duty to prevent violations of the right to life is "an obligation of means, rather than of results," and that the state's violation of this duty cannot be shown "by the mere fact that a right has been violated."[168] The court can only make that determination on a case-by-case basis, previous decisions have stated.[169]

According to the Inter-American Court, legislation that precludes criminal prosecution of serious human rights violations, such as amnesty laws, violates, among others, article 2 of the convention. Broad legalization of all first-trimester abortions or of all previability abortions essentially precludes criminal prosecution of anyone involved in the killing of an unborn child in the first trimester or before viability and may therefore violate article 2 of the convention as well. The court has held that states have a duty to "to establish an effective system of administration of justice able to *investigate, punish and repair* any deprivation of lives."[170] To decriminalize abortion would *preclude* investigation of, prosecution of, or sanctions against abortion providers, who, in practice, are mostly prosecuted under abortion bans, rather than mothers (see chapter 5).

These holdings have not been isolated findings in relation to some violations of the right to life and not to others. Judge Vio Grossi noted that "this has been the Court's constant and consistent case law. . . . It has been stated in more than 12 cases and has even been reiterated on two occasions [in 2012]," the year *Artavia* was decided.[171] In 2008, the court recommended "the elimination of any norms and practices that in any way violate the guarantees provided under the Convention or disregard the rights therein enshrined or obstruct its exercise" and recommended "the promulgation of norms and the development of practices conducive to the effective observance of those guarantees."[172]

States parties should therefore be legally permitted, if not required, to ban most practices that intentionally cause the death of an unborn child, such as elective abortion. They should also be legally able to discourage those practices and to encourage nonviolent alternatives for girls, women, and parents facing an unplanned pregnancy, such as financial assistance, psychological support, and adoption placement services.

The prenatal right to life and any exceptions thereto should be read within the treaty's context, including the nondiscrimination clause in article 1(1), which provides that states ought to "ensure to all persons subject to their jurisdiction the free and full exercise of those rights and freedoms, without any discrimination for reasons of race, color . . . *birth*, or *any other social condition*." A domestic law that would grant impunity for abortion for any reason whatsoever before birth, or when the child is below some particular gestational age, such as first-trimester abortions in Mexico City and Uruguay, may constitute discrimination on the basis of age, in violation of article 1 and article 24 of the convention, the latter of which provides for the right to equal protection. In that regard, Judge Guillermo I. Ortiz Mayagoitia of the Mexican Supreme Court stated that "the interruption of pregnancy during the first 12 weeks of gestation constitutes *discrimination* towards the embryo during that period and suppresses his fundamental rights," given that the human embryo is thus "targeted only *because of his stage of development* and not his nature."[173]

Eugenic abortion may similarly constitute arbitrary discrimination under the right to equality, which the Inter-American Court has found to be a norm of *jus cogens*.[174] The eugenic abortion of children whose mothers were affected with the Zika virus, for instance, which OAS secretary general Luis Almagro advocated for, may be contrary to the court's prior holdings that "any exclusion, restriction or privilege that is not *objective* and *reasonable*, and which adversely affects human rights," is forbidden and that states may only grant *distinct treatment* when this "is reasonable, proportionate and objective."[175] It may also violate the Convention on the Rights of Persons with Disabilities, to which many Latin American and Caribbean states are parties.[176]

Former IACHR commissioners Marco Gerardo Monroy Cabra and Rodrigo Escobar Gil have suggested that eugenic abortion violates human dignity. They have pointed out that the presence of fetal malformations or disabilities cannot be lawfully considered to take away the person's human dignity, neither does the child's disability or malformation take away the mother's human dignity.[177] In addition, Judge Cristina Pardo Schlesinger of the Colombian Constitutional Court found that an authorization of eugenic abortion on the basis of a child's cerebral malformation undermined the rights of persons with disabilities, which are incompatible with eugenic abortion.[178] Disability-based abortion, she held, reinforces social discrimination against disabled persons and signifies a step backward in the protection of the rights of persons with disabilities.[179]

The abortion of unborn children affected by conditions diagnosed as "incompatible with life"—that is, of unborn children given a life-limiting diagnosis, indicating that their condition is expected to result in death shortly after birth—has been designated by some as "euthanasic abortion," in order to void it of eugenic motivations.[180] Former commissioners Monroy Cabra and Escobar Gil granted some analogy to the practice to euthanasia, or mercy killing, in the sense that the stated justification is to spare the fetus and the mother future sufferings in light of malformations that may make the child unviable.[181] Euthanasia, they indicated, involves the patient's request or consent, whereas the abortion of an unviable child cannot possibly involve the child's consent and therefore is no different from eugenic abortion, where "the life of a defenseless human being is disposed of in impunity."[182]

Abortion rights advocates sometimes argue that abortion bans are discrimination against women because only women can become pregnant.[183] That argument, however, can be rebutted by the fact that many—if not half—of all aborted fetuses are female. In some cultures, the abortion of female fetuses has been called gendercide and has been denounced by the International Beijing Conference on Women as a human rights violation.[184]

*Judicial Guarantees, the Death Penalty, and Elective Abortion.* Judicial guarantees have been recognized for those sentenced to death in states parties to the convention; unborn children should be entitled to—at the very least—equal protection. For instance, the Inter-American Court has established that intentional deprivations of life such as the death penalty may *only* be imposed for the most serious crimes "and pursuant to a final *judgment* rendered by a competent court and *in accordance with a law* establishing such punishment."[185] A death "sentence must be *individualized* in conformity with the characteristics of the crime"; mandatory death sentences are impermissible.[186]

A nonrestrictive interpretation of the prenatal right to life from conception would have to, at the very least, extend that reasoning to intentional deprivation of human life by abortion and require that any exceptions to the general duty to protect the prenatal right to life in states parties to the convention be enacted by law, that abortion authorizations be made on an individualized, case-by-case basis, and that they be subject to judicial review. Abortion decriminalization would be especially arbitrary if it allowed little room for individualized consideration, especially where no judicial or medical authorization or no police report was required, as advocates for abortion rights usually propose.

Statutory provisions for nonpunishment of abortions in cases of serious risk to the life or health of the mother are usually subject to this type of individualized consideration, as explained in chapter 5. A blanket authorization for the abortion of a category of unborn children, however, such as those suffering from a certain type of severe disability or those conceived in rape, is more likely to be arbitrary given that it would treat human beings in that category "not as uniquely individual human beings, but as members of a faceless, undifferentiated mass to be subjected to the blind infliction of the death penalty."[187] A law that authorized abortions on the basis of parental poverty or similar social grounds may also preclude the possibility of individualized consideration and contradict Inter-American Court decisions holding that "children cannot be discriminated against based on the conditions of their parents."[188]

When speaking about the death penalty, which, under the American Convention, is a permissible but discouraged exception to the right to life, the Inter-American Court has held that "[b]ecause execution of the death penalty is *irreversible*, the strictest and most rigorous enforcement of judicial guarantees is required of the State so that those guarantees are not violated and a human life not arbitrarily taken as a result."[189] The Inter-American Commission has similarly stated "that the right to life holds a special primacy, and any deprivation of that right must be subject to the *highest possible level of scrutiny*," thus proposing that a "strict scrutiny" standard akin to the US Supreme Court's standard for review involving fundamental rights be applied to domestic death penalty laws.[190]

It would therefore be inconsistent for the court and the commission to refer to a "supreme right to life" of death row inmates but no "absolute" right to life of unborn children, especially given that the consequences of both abortion and the death penalty are equally irreversible. It would be equally incoherent for the court to apply the highest level of scrutiny to death penalty convicts and apply a lesser standard for children facing abortion, in particular since the latter are in a position of greater disadvantage because they do not enjoy any due process rights and cannot possibly assert a right to judicial remedies in cases of legal abortion.

The death penalty and abortion are similar in that they both involve an intentional deprivation of the right to life. They are different, however, in the sense that "the death penalty is accepted as a legal exception to the protection of the right to life" under the American Convention and "is not illegal *per se* in the Inter-American system," as Judge Eduardo Ferrer Mac-Gregor Poisot has recognized.[191] The convention, on the other hand, prohibits most acts that deliberately deprive the unborn child from her right to life with very limited exceptions. Judge Rafael Nieto Navia would entirely reject the analogy between the death penalty and abortion for this reason.[192]

Abortion and the death penalty are also different in the sense that abortion affects an entirely innocent life, as opposed to the death penalty, which affects the lives of individuals who have been tried and convicted "for the most serious crimes."[193] For that reason, article 4(5) of the American Convention specifically prohibits the imposition of the death penalty on pregnant women, a norm designed to protect the unborn child, and only him, from execution, as pointed out by Judge Nieto Navia.[194] The fact that prenatal children are entirely innocent (even when conceived in rape, an unborn child is not himself guilty of the sexual crime) and that committing any legal offense is entirely *impossible* for them, together with their specific general protection under the American Convention as children, should certainly grant them under the convention a level of protection superior to that granted for persons sentenced to death, according to founding judge Nieto Navia.[195]

If a country's domestic laws do not allow the death penalty to be applied to a perpetrator of rape, no matter how grave or violent the circumstances of the assault, it certainly should not legally allow the abortion of a child conceived in rape, who could not possibly have any responsibility for the crime. Such a double standard would be arbitrary and therefore legally intolerable under the convention. If a state party went even further by allowing the abortion of children conceived in rape with no individualized consideration and with no criminal complaint, investigation, or even a police report, thereby protecting potential perpetrators of such abortions from prosecution, the argument of arbitrariness and lack of judicial guarantees would seem equally persuasive.

*The Right to Recognition as a Person.* The Convention's preamble recognizes that "the essential rights of man are not derived from one's being a national of a certain state, but are based upon *attributes of the human personality*."[196] Article 1(2) and article 3 of the American Convention affirm the right of every human being to recognition as a person before the law.[197] The Inter-American Court itself has stated that the breach of such recognition implies the absolute denial of the possibility of being a holder of any rights and of assuming any obligations and renders individual human beings vulnerable to human rights violations by the state or private parties.[198]

Judges and former IACHR commissioners Monroy Cabra and Escobar Gil of the Colombian Constitutional Court read the preamble together with article 1(2) on the definition of "person" as "human being" to indicate that the American Convention clearly establishes that every human being is entitled to human rights.[199] "[T]here is no doubt that the unborn human being has a right to be recognized as a person, in virtue of which he is entitled to the right to life," the justices pointed out.[200] Article 1(2), they said, leaves states no margin to interpret the international norm in any other way than according to its literal terms, that is, as asserting that the unborn child is a human being and is therefore entitled to the convention's protection.

A nonrestrictive interpretation of the convention would therefore find that denying the unborn child's humanity and personhood violates the right to recognition as a person before the law, as it has in past cases of forced disappearance. In such instances, the court has said that denying a person legal recognition as a person is "one of the most serious forms of placing the person outside the protection of the law, [but] it also entails to deny that person's existence and to place him or her in a kind of limbo or uncertain legal situation before the society, the State and even the international community."[201]

Judge Manuel Ventura, in a case involving children's rights, held that "personal identity starts *from the moment of conception* and its construction continues throughout the life of the individual" and that the "elements and attributes, which comprise personal identity, include such varied aspects as a person's origin or 'biological reality.' "[202] Since the unborn child's biological existence is undeniable even under a restrictive interpretation of the convention, denying his or her legal personhood may, therefore, be a serious violation of article 3 of the American Convention.

The court has held that the right to legal recognition as a person "implies the capacity to be the holder of rights (capacity of exercise) and obligations," but in the context of children, it has held that *capacity to exercise rights* is irrelevant.[203] In Advisory Opinion OC-17/02 the court held that "pursuant to contemporary provisions set forth in international human rights law, including article 19 of the American Convention on Human Rights, children are subjects entitled to rights, not only objects of protection."[204] It recognized that "[a]dulthood brings with it the possibility of fully exercising rights, also known as the capacity to act. . . . Children do not have this capacity, or lack this capacity to a large extent. . . . But they are all *subjects of rights*, entitled to inalienable and inherent rights of the human person."

Judge Cançado Trindade, in his concurring opinion, added that "[t]he limitations of legal capacity nothing subtract [*sic*] from legal personality. The *titulaire* of rights is the human being, of flesh and bone and soul, and not the existential condition in which he finds himself temporarily."[205] Later, he described the court's advisory opinion as holding that "the Law accords juridical personality to every human being (child and adolescent included), irrespective of his existential condition or of his juridical capacity to exercise his rights for himself (capacity of exercise)."[206]

Since the unborn child has been referred to as a child by the court, including in the *Artavia* decision, the argument that the unborn child is not a person because he or she cannot possibly be entitled to all rights attributed to persons in the American Convention fails in light of previous court decisions.[207] In addition, states parties have never understood the unborn's right to life and his or her right to be recognized as a person to be contingent on the ability to exercise all other civil and political rights, as explained in chapter 4. In fact, most Latin American and Caribbean civil codes largely recognize unborn children to be generally entitled to the right to life before birth, even where he or she lacks legal capacity for civil transactions.

*Article 19 and the Convention on the Rights of the Child.* Children are human rights subjects, not state interests or social values, according to Inter-American Court decisions. In its Advisory Opinion OC-17/2002 the court held that "pursuant to contemporary provisions set forth in International Human Rights Law, including article 19 of the American Convention on Human Rights, children are *subjects* entitled to rights, not only *objects* of protection."[208] Judge Cançado Trindade, in his concurring opinion, added that "[i]n fact, the subjects of law are the *children*, and not *infancy or childhood*."[209] Therefore the subject of law should be the unborn child and not prenatal life in general, or a state interest therein.

The Inter-American Court has given the Convention on the Rights of the Child a preferential status as a primary source of interpretation of the

American Convention's article 19 on the rights of the child, holding that the CRC "comprise[s] the *corpus juris* of the rights of the child," "which should be used as a source of law by the Court to establish 'the content and scope' of the obligations undertaken by the State through article 19 of the American Convention."[210] The Inter-American Court has adopted the CRC definition of the term "child" as "every human being below the age of eighteen years," and in *Sawhoyamaxa Indigenous Community v. Paraguay*, the court included unborn children in this definition by recognizing an entitlement of unborn children and pregnant mothers to the right to prenatal health.[211]

The text of the CRC explicitly protects the unborn child's rights by recognizing, in its preamble, that "*the child*, by reason of his physical and mental immaturity, *needs* special safeguards and care, including appropriate *legal protection, before as well as after birth*," a recognition that was previously affirmed in the 1959 Declaration on the Rights of the Child.[212] The preambular paragraph's relationship to the provision on the child's "inherent" right to life and a duty of states to take measures to ensure the survival and development of the child in article 6, in particular, was highlighted during the convention's *travaux préparatoires*.[213]

The CRC preamble, in particular, explains the treaty's object and purpose, which would never be in contradiction with a lawful interpretation of the treaty, according to the VCLT. According to the Vienna Convention, a treaty's provisions should be interpreted in context with the preamble and not in isolation.[214] The *Artavia* judgment attempted to diminish the preamble's interpretive value by relying on its *travaux préparatoires*, as discussed in chapter 6 on historic interpretation.[215] Any claims that the preamble has no interpretive value, however, have been preempted by the VCLT, which establishes that a treaty's preamble *is an essential part of the treaty text itself* for the purposes of interpretation.[216]

High courts of states parties to the convention have consistently read the CRC text in conjunction with its preamble, literally, as applying to unborn children. The CRC also recognizes the child's unqualified right to life, health, and development, including a right to "adequate pre-natal . . . care" of the child and the mother.[217] The Mexican Supreme Court, in 2002, read the CRC as establishing that the child's right to life is protected before as well as after birth.[218] The Argentinian Supreme Court, in *Portal de*

*Belén*, read the CRC preamble in conjunction with its articles as recognizing a right to life of unborn children.[219] Argentinian federal courts have recognized the CRC's applicability to the human embryo and fetus.[220] El Salvador's Supreme Court has also understood the Convention on the Rights of the Child and its corresponding declaration as protecting the *nasciturus*'s right to life.[221] The Chilean Constitutional Court has made similar references to the CRC as prohibiting direct abortion.[222]

Florentín Meléndez, a former member of the IACHR and supreme court judge in El Salvador's constitutional chamber, held in 2013 that under international human rights law—particularly the American Convention, the International Covenant on Civil and Political Rights (ICCPR), and the CRC—the unborn child's right to life from the moment of conception is recognized as a nonderogable, fundamental right.[223] According to Judge Meléndez, the CRC applies to the unborn child; he referred to "the rights of children, the protection of which according to . . . international human rights law begins from the moment of conception."[224] Specifically, he interpreted article 6 on the right to life and article 24 in light of the preamble, emphasizing a state duty to provide prenatal and postnatal health care to the child and the mother. Mexican Supreme Court judges Aguirre Anguiano and Pardo Rebolledo reached a similar conclusion based on the CRC preamble.[225]

Founding judge Rafael Nieto Navia has also read article 6 of the CRC, recognizing "that every child has the *inherent* right to life," as having the ordinary meaning that the right to life may not be alienated from any children, that the state must protect their survival, and that no right to abortion may be lawfully inferred from the convention, under any circumstance.[226] Commissioner Luis Demetrio Tinoco Castro, in 1981, pointed out that the CRC preamble's expression "*before as well as after birth*" "recognized that the human being exists, has rights, and needs protection, including legal protection, in the period preceding his birth," and inspired the Juridical Committee, which drafted the American Declaration of the Rights and Duties of Man, which gave the unborn child similar protection.[227] Most Latin American states parties to the American Convention participated in the CRC's preparatory work meetings, including Argentina, Brazil, Colombia, Honduras, Mexico, Nicaragua, Panama, Peru, and Venezuela, so that assertion may very well be accurate.[228]

The court has emphasized the "particular gravity" of violations of the right to life against children.[229] When it comes to the right to life of children, states parties to the American Convention have twofold obligations under article 4 and article 19 of the American Convention. The state obligation to respect the right to life of every person under its jurisdiction takes on special dimensions in the case of children, and it becomes an obligation to "prevent situations that might lead, by action or omission, to breach it," compounded by the added obligation established in article 19 of the American Convention to promote the rights of the child.[230]

The court has also indicated that article 19 of the convention must be understood as complementary to article 4, requiring special measures of protection for children, due to their physical and emotional development.[231] In Advisory Opinion on the Juridical Status and Human Rights of the Child, the Inter-American Court indicated that the child's right to life enshrined in article 4 included a state obligation "to provide the measures required for life to develop under decent conditions."[232] A nonrestrictive interpretation of the convention would therefore find that legalization of elective abortion constitutes not only a violation of article 4(1) but also a violation of article 19 for failure to prevent the violation of the rights of the child and to ensure special measures to protect her life and development.

The Inter-American Commission has recognized that the right to life, especially that of children, is a norm of *jus cogens*, that is, a norm that cannot be validly derogated, whether by treaty or by the unilateral objection of a state, but only by the formation of a subsequent customary rule to the contrary.[233] In 2002, in *Michael Domingues v. United States*, the Commission held that the prohibition of imposing the death penalty on children was an international *jus cogens* norm.[234] It explained that norms of *jus cogens* derive their status from fundamental values held by the international community, that is, peremptory norms, the violations of which are considered to shock the conscience of humankind and therefore bind the international community as a whole, such as the prohibition of genocide, slavery, forced disappearance, and torture.[235]

Likewise, in *Villagrán Morales*, the commission, in its final arguments before the court, underscored the *jus cogens* nature of the right to life referring to children, in particular, and the fact that it is the essential basis for the exercise of the other rights. It emphasized that "[t]he right to life cannot be annulled" and that "[t]he violation of that norm . . . has not been the object of any corrective."[236] Inter-American Court judges Cançado Trindade and Alirio Abreu-Burelli agreed with the commission and stated, in their concurring opinion, that "there can no longer be any doubt that the fundamental right to life belongs to the domain of *jus cogens*."[237] Since the unborn child has been recognized as a child that enjoys right-to-life protection from the moment of conception, the same standard should apply to violations of his or her right to life, under the convention.[238]

*Mexico's Interpretive Declaration.* Treaty reservations or declarations are also a part of the treaty context as long as they are accepted by other states parties; no reservations on article 4(1) were filed to create abortion rights in any jurisdiction, but one was filed to leave protection of prenatal life as a matter of state sovereignty.[239] Mexico is the only state that has filed an interpretive declaration to article 4(1) of the American Convention; no state party has—at least formally—objected to it. The declaration asserts that the federal Mexican government does not consider itself obligated to pass legislation to protect the right to life from the time of conception because the issue is a matter of state jurisdiction: "Interpretative declaration. With respect to article 4, paragraph 1, the Government of Mexico considers that the expression 'in general' [used in that paragraph] does not constitute an obligation to adopt, or keep in force, legislation to protect life 'from the moment of conception,' *since this matter falls within the domain reserved to the States*."[240]

The declaration seems to be more about national sovereignty than about the prenatal right to life, although it certainly concerns both. At first glance, it may seem that the declaration may allude to federalism principles, given Mexico's regime on abortion, which leaves the issue of abortion up to the state rather than federal government to decide. That may explain why other states parties (including federal states like Brazil and Argentina) that support prenatal rights have not objected to it. Most Mexican Supreme Court judges, however, seem to have discarded this interpretation and have found that the term "states" referred to other nations and that the declaration was meant to leave abortion as a matter of domestic policy.[241]

Mexican Supreme Court judges have been split on whether or not Mexico meant to make a virtual reservation on the prenatal right to life to the treaty on the prenatal-right-to-life provision. In 2007, a majority of the Mexican Supreme Court agreed with the opinion that invoked the reservation to reject a challenge to the legalization of first-trimester abortion in Mexico City, stating, among things, that "Mexico is not bound to protect life from the moment of conception or any other specific moment [in virtue of the scope of] its interpretative declaration."[242] Three judges dissented and held that the interpretive declaration was not meant to be a rejection of the convention's legal obligation to protect life from the time of conception but was simply intended to mean that that obligation may not conflict with Mexico's national constitution unless constitutional reform procedures are followed.[243] A reservation that would have been intended to exclude an obligation to protect the right to life from the moment of conception, they said, would have violated article 29 of the convention, which prohibits limitations of rights recognized in the convention or that are inherent in the human personality.[244]

While the declaration's language itself indicates that Mexico did not intend to comply with the convention's mandate to enact laws protecting life from the time of conception, it does not create abortion rights for Mexico either, nor does it prevent Mexican states from protecting the prenatal right to life, as they have in fact done (see chapter 5). It simply categorizes the duty to legally protect prenatal life as a matter of domestic law, which suggests support for a margin of appreciation on legal protection of prenatal life, particularly on the issue of elective abortion.

*The American Declaration and Its Universal Protection of the Right to Life.* The American Declaration of the Rights and Duties of Man (American Declaration) is a nonbinding agreement adopted by states parties to the American Convention in direct connection with the treaty and can therefore be considered a part of the treaty context, according to article 31(2)(a) of the Vienna Convention on the Law of Treaties. The American Declaration's close relation to the American Convention is explicitly indicated in article 29 of the convention and in its preamble.

The American Declaration of the Rights and Duties of Man plainly establishes a universal right to life of each human being: "*Every* human being has the right to life."[245] Given that the American Convention defines the term "human being" as "person" and recognizes a right to life from conception of all persons, many could logically conclude that the two instruments, read together, recognize a universal right to life of all persons, including unborn children. Judge Piza Escalante read the declaration this way, as well as some members of the commission.[246] In addition, article 7 of the American Declaration closely ties the right to protection for pregnant mothers to children's rights: "All women, *during pregnancy* and the nursing period, and all *children* have the right to special protection, care and aid."[247]

Commissioner Luis Demetrio Tinoco has read the term "human being" as including the unborn child from the moment of conception: "[T]he American Declaration of the Rights and Duties of Man refers to the complete period of human life—from conception to death—when it states that 'every human being has the right to life.' "[248] Both Commissioners Monroy Cabra and Tinoco interpreted the declaration text as prohibiting abortion. Commissioner Tinoco indicated: "[I]n recognizing the right of the unborn to life, the Declaration rejects the legitimacy of any act that authorizes or considers acceptable acts or practices that will lead to its death."[249] Likewise, Commissioner Monroy Cabra declared that "if conception produces a human life, and this right is the primary and fundamental one, abortion is an attack on the right to life and, therefore, runs counter to article 1 of the American Declaration of the Rights and Duties of Man."[250]

Draft article I of the American Declaration submitted by the Juridical Committee in 1947 initially contained a right to life of "[e]very person . . . including those who are not yet born[,] as well as the incurable, the insane, and the mentally retarded."[251] Commissioner Tinoco explained that this was an express recognition that "the human being exists, has rights, and needs protection, including legal protection, in the period preceding his birth."[252] At the Bogotá Conference, a working group amended the committee's draft article 1 so that it read, "Every human being has the right to life, liberty, security and integrity of this person," thus removing the section that stated that "[t]his right extends to the right to life from the moment of conception; to the right to life of incurables, imbeciles and the insane. Capital punishment may only be applied in cases in which it has been prescribed by pre-existing law for crimes of exceptional gravity."[253]

On April 30, 1948, the seventh plenary session of the conference approved the final text of article 1, establishing a universal right to life, liberty, and personal security.[254] The final act was signed on May 2, 1948.[255] In *Baby Boy*, the commission suggested that the legislative intent in excluding "those who are not yet born" and a right to life "from conception" from the declaration's final text was to deny a prenatal right to life and thus allow states parties to legally permit some abortions.[256] The nonbinding report proposed the unsubstantiated theory that the elimination of the term "unborn" and the existence of laws authorizing abortion under some circumstances in Latin American countries in 1947, at the time of the declaration's adoption, meant that the states parties intended the American Declaration to make right-to-life exceptions for elective abortion at the domestic level.[257]

The dissents by commissioners Monroy Cabra and Tinoco Castro challenged the majority opinion by pointing out that no evidence of a compromise on abortion existed in the declaration's *travaux préparatoires*: there was no actual discussion on abortion at all, no delegations raised objections or amendment proposals for article 1 on account of abortion, and no other legislative history exists that would warrant a conclusion that states meant to disentitle unborn children from the right to life for elective abortion.[258] Commissioner Tinoco specifically indicated that he found "no mention whatever" of the said political compromise, problems, or objections in the minutes of the working group or of the sixth committee or of the plenary session of the conference that met in Bogotá.[259]

No motion or written draft by any delegation explicitly requesting the elimination of that phrase from the juridical council's draft can be found, either. No record of the declaration's *travaux préparatoires* provided "any specific explanation of the reasons that motivated the elimination of the supplementary phrase" contained in the Draft Declaration of the International Rights and Duties of Man presented by the Inter-American juridical committee, which recognized "the right to life for all persons, including (a) the unborn, as well as (b) 'incurables, imbeciles, and the insane.'"[260]

Commissioner Monroy Cabra pointed out that the conference records are silent on the reason for removing the said phrases.[261] His examination of the *travaux préparatoires* yielded no evidence whatsoever that the removal of that phrase was motivated by an intent to protect life only from the moment of *birth* onward, "much less to allow abortion."[262] He also mentioned that the topic of abortion was not addressed at all during the Bogotá Conference, given that, at the time, the biological, scientific fact that life begins at conception was not a matter of controversy among Latin American states. Commissioner Tinoco further explained that the agreement on the unborn child's entitlement to the right to life at the time of the declaration's drafting was so complete that it "was not discussed or put in doubt by anyone."[263]

Both Commissioner Monroy Cabra and Commissioner Tinoco pointed out that just as the deletion of the phrase "this right extends . . . to the right to life of incurables, imbeciles, and the insane" cannot reasonably lead to a conclusion that states did not intend to protect the life of the disabled, neither can the mere deletion of the sentence warrant a presumption that states parties rejected the Inter-American proposal to protect unborn children.[264] Commissioner Monroy Cabra articulated that, according to the declaration, "the life of the unborn child, the infant, the young, the old, the mentally ill, the handicapped, and that of all human beings in general, must be recognized."[265]

The only reason given for the elimination of the unborn (as well as the "imbeciles and mentally weak") from the final draft was to refrain from giving exhaustive lists of protected categories under article 1, as expressed by the sixth committee rapporteur, Mr. Lopez de Mesa, in these terms: "[L]ikewise, it was decided to draft them (the rights and duties) in their mere essence, *without exemplary or restrictive listings*, which carry with them the risk of useless diffusion and of the dangerous confusion of their limits."[266] Commissioner Tinoco also wrote: "Now: if the elimination of the phrase that concerns those persons has no other moral, logical, and legal justification than the purpose of the Sixth Committee—and later of the plenary session of the Conference—to avoid 'exemplary or restrictive listings,' for the same reason it is necessary to admit that it was the purpose of avoiding its 'listing'—and no other—that led the Committee and the Conference also to eliminate the unnecessarily explanatory expression 'the right to life from the moment of conception.' "[267] Thus, he explained, it was the need for conciseness and inclusiveness, rather than exclusivity, that accounted for dropping the specific inclusion of unborn children and the mentally disabled from article 1 of the American Declaration.

## Object and Purpose

The object and purpose of the treaty is a primary source of interpretation along with the treaty text and context, according to the Vienna Convention.[268] The object and purpose of the American Convention, as stated in its preamble, is to complement, not diminish, human rights protection in domestic jurisdiction:[269] "[T]he essential rights of man are not derived from one's being a national of a certain state, but are based upon attributes of the human personality, and . . . they therefore justify international protection in the form of a convention *reinforcing* or *complementing* the protection provided by the domestic law of the American states."[270] The court should not, therefore, carry out an interpretation that would derogate or reverse prenatal-right-to-life protections provided by national laws of states parties. The object and purpose of article 4(1), according to its plain language, is to recognize the unborn child as a human person from the moment of conception and to establish a state duty to recognize her inalienable human right to life, one that should be generally and broadly protected.

The object and purpose of the American Convention's provision on the right to life from conception could also be relevant in the event of a new complaint against the United States' abortion laws, since it is the only country that has signed but not ratified the American Convention. The United States is not a party because it has not ratified the American Convention, but it is a signatory, given that it signed the convention in 1977. Therefore, it is not legally bound by the convention but may have a minimal legal duty to "refrain from acts that would defeat the object and purpose" of the convention, according to article 18 of the VCLT, which some scholars believe to bind the United States as customary international law.[271]

The relevant question for the commission would not be whether the convention applies to the United States, because it does not, and the United States is not legally bound by it. It would be whether the United States has complied with its minimal legal duty to "refrain from acts that would defeat the object and purpose" of the convention, unless it can prove that it has "made its intention clear not to become a party to the treaty."[272] Whether the United States has expressed this intention is unclear, but it has not withdrawn its signature, and no official statements seem to have been made against becoming a party to the American Convention.

If a future composition of Inter-American bodies did address the issue, however, it would mean that they may look, among others, at whether the United States engaged in any acts that would "substantially reduc[e] either its ability to comply with its treaty obligations after ratification or the ability of the other parties to obtain the benefits of the treaty."[273] A wide breadth of state actions would have to be analyzed in order to reach a determination on whether the United States has either breached or observed the object and purpose of the treaty. In any case, the Inter-American Court would have no authority to hear any petitions against the United States under the American Convention unless the United States ratified the treaty.

Effet Utile. The Inter-American Court of Human Rights has repeatedly held that "[t]he object and purpose of the Convention, as an instrument for the protection of the human being, requires that the right to life be interpreted and enforced so that its guarantees are truly practical and effective (*effet utile*)."[274] The majority opinion in *Artavia* also looked at the object and purpose of article 4(1), in particular, and read the term "in general" as intended "to permit, should a conflict between rights arise, the possibility of invoking exceptions to the protection of the right to life from the moment of conception. In other words, the *object and purpose* of article 4(1) of the Convention is that the right to life should *not* be understood as an absolute right, the alleged protection of which can justify the total negation of other rights."[275]

To conclude that the *object and purpose of the treaty* was *to permit exceptions to the right to life from conception*, rather than protect it, is no doubt a restrictive interpretation of the provision's language. In his *Gómez* dissent, Judge Vio Grossi pointed out that such an interpretation "could be eventually used to attempt to justify that the Convention permits abortion, which would be incompatible with its letter and spirit."[276] Such an interpretation would deprive the American Convention's express provision protecting the unborn of its *effet utile*, which was to give ample, not exceptional, protection to the unborn child, as pointed out by Judge Vio Grossi:[277] "I could not disagree more with this assessment, because the object and purpose of article 4(1), considered from the perspective of the principle of good faith, the terms of the treaty and their context, can only be that the . . . the right of every person is truly protected, including, therefore, that of the conceived or unborn child."[278]

Judge Vio Grossi rejected this restrictive reading of the convention's object and purpose and indicated: "The 'object and purpose' of the said provision [. . . ] was established so that it would *really* achieve what it was designed for and not for it to be *emptied of content*."[279] The object and purpose of the treaty should also be kept in mind when one is interpreting the terms "in general" in article 4(1), according to Judge Vio Grossi: "[T]he said words 'and, in general' should be understood . . . so that they effectively *contribute to the general object and purpose* sought and not that they constitute an exception to it, and even less, particularly, a *denial* of the right to life."[280]

### Creation of Abortion Rights and International Obligations to Legally Authorize Abortion under the American Convention

The plain language of article 4(1) establishes a general obligation to legally protect the unborn child from acts that deliberately seek to take his or her life, such as elective abortion. Since as early as 1972 until present day, Inter-American Court judges and states parties have understood the terms of article 4(1) as generally prohibiting abortion and allowing criminal abortion bans. For instance, Judge Eduardo Vio Grossi, in his 2016 *Gómez* dissent, plainly indicated that the convention's text does not permit abortion and that such an interpretation would be "*contrary to its letter and spirit*."[281] Former Inter-American Court judge Thomas Buergenthal, an American national, pointed out in 1972 that article 4(1) "introduce[s] some highly controversial issues relating to . . . abortion."[282] No Inter-American human rights decision has ever suggested that states parties to the convention may not ban elective abortion or that they are legally prohibited from enforcing abortion bans or that abortion providers should operate with impunity, without threat of criminal prosecution. Likewise, no state party has ever interpreted the American Convention as prohibiting abortion bans.

States parties have traditionally understood article 4(1) as generally prohibiting abortion. El Salvador's Supreme Court has repeatedly interpreted its full ban on abortion as consistent with the American Convention, most recently in 2013, in the judgment regarding B., described in chapter 2.[283] In 2017, the Guatemalan Supreme Court interpreted the American Convention as recognizing prenatal personhood and a right to life and found that abortion rights advocacy by the country's attorney general was unconstitutional and a violation of international treaties ratified by Guatemala, including the American Convention.[284] As explained in chapter 6, states parties like Argentina, Chile, Dominican Republic, El Salvador, Guatemala, Honduras, and Nicaragua have invoked the American Convention when formally objecting to the inclusion of abortion rights language in international conference outcome documents, such as those of the Beijing Conference on Women and the Cairo Conference on Population and Development, among others.

The American Convention contains no reference to abortion; it contains no provision on sexual and reproductive rights that could be reasonably interpreted to contain abortion rights either. The Inter-American Court has so far never interpreted the convention to contain a human right to abortion or a state duty to legalize abortion deriving thereof. While the American Convention allows for "progressive development" of human rights, it only refers to "rights implicit in [the] economic, social, and cultural" category of rights and rights that are "recognized by virtue of the laws of any State Party or by virtue of another convention to which one of the said states is a party" as well as "rights or guarantees that are inherent in the human personality."[285] None of these can be interpreted to include abortion because abortion is not an economic, social, or cultural right; it is not recognized as a right by virtue of the laws of any state party or any international treaty to which parties to the convention are parties, as explained in chapter 5; and it is not inherent to human personality.

Other rights not recognized in the American Convention may be included within its scope of human rights protection only via the amendment process or subsequent treaties called protocols, according to article 31 of the convention: "Other rights and freedoms recognized in accordance with the procedures established in articles 76 and 77 [on amendments and protocols to the Convention] may be included in the system of protection of this Convention."[286] No amendments or protocols on abortion have been approved as of 2019.

If abortion is indeed a human right, abortion rights advocates should not have insurmountable difficulty in persuading states to recognize it as such by either amending the American Convention, adopting a protocol, or adopting a new treaty on reproductive rights. Several new protocols and treaties recognizing implicit rights that are not explicit in the convention have been successfully promoted and adopted by states parties, even though they may raise controversial issues, such as the Protocol of San Salvador, on social, cultural, and economic rights, and the Convention of Belém do Pará, on violence against women.[287]

An Inter-American convention on sexual and reproductive rights has never materialized even though a campaign for one has been promoted since 2008, at one point with the OAS secretary general José Miguel Insulza's support.[288] The campaign's draft text includes a right to "safe and voluntary maternity" and an unlimited right to abortion, specifically, a right to access abortion services as part of a right to reproductive health.[289] It would create a state duty to provide free, quality abortion services and to "eliminate legislation that interferes with the exercise of this right," among others.[290]

The campaign's draft convention text has never gathered enough support from states parties for its introduction before the OAS General Assembly, unlike other human rights treaties that have been introduced, debated, adopted, and ratified after passage of the American Convention. Controversy over recognition of international human rights obligations has not precluded the adoption and entry into force of treaties like the Inter-American Convention on the Elimination of All Forms of Discrimination Against Persons with Disabilities and the Inter-American Convention Against Racism, Racial Discrimination and Related Forms of Intolerance, in 2013 and 2017, respectively.[291] The fact that states parties have not supported the introduction of a reproductive rights treaty seems to indicate their lack of support for abortion rights.

One could argue that the new meaning given to the word "conception" as implantation and the new meaning given to "in general" as "gradually and incrementally" in the *Artavia* judgment are so distant from the ordinary meanings of those terms that their adoption would, if accepted, constitute a treaty amendment, which the Inter-American Court has no unilateral legal power to do, as indicated by Judge Vio Grossi in his *Gómez* dissent. In that judgment, he reminded the rest of the court that "the court's job is to interpret and apply the Convention, that is, to say what the Law says and not what it wishes; it should not assume, therefore, the normative function expressly assigned [by the Convention and international law] to states parties."[292]

The Inter-American Court and the Inter-American Commission have been previously accused of having "distanced themselves from the sacred principles they are called upon to protect . . . and even overlooking the very content and provisions of the [convention]."[293] Bypassing the amendment and treaty process by distorting the American Convention's prenatal-life protection with its relatively easy proabortion rights majority and unilateral interpretation power only reinforces this criticism. The only legitimacy that the politically expedient tactic of judicial treaty amendment by stealth could enjoy would be in virtue of its substantive content, that is, its recognition as a noble enterprise, but not many states parties are currently decided about the morality and altruism of abortion rights advocacy.

Reading an international obligation to legally authorize abortion under the American Convention or devising a human right to abort would require an even greater stretch of interpretation than that of the *Artavia* judgment. It would necessarily reduce the scope of the prenatal right to life to its minimal expression and would reverse human rights protections originally established for unborn children in the American Convention. It would require a departure from the convention's usual canons of human rights treaty interpretation: the ordinary meaning of the convention's text, the object and purpose of the treaty, the American Declaration, the *travaux préparatoires*, state practice, the *pro homine* principle, and international law favoring the unborn child would all have to be deliberately ignored, distorted, and obscured in order to create abortion rights or related obligations.

Imaginary rights conflicts are often presented to justify the creation of abortion rights through stealth amendments. The rights of the unborn children and their mothers are artificially pitted against each other to justify the judicial creation of abortion rights, but the conflict is only apparent, even in situations where the mother's right to life is endangered by the pregnancy, as explained by different courts cited in previous chapters. In fact, the convention and other international human rights treaties invariably protect the right of pregnant women and their children jointly in the context of maternity, pregnancy, prenatal health, and childbirth. Abortion rights claims before Inter-American human rights bodies present no real conflict between two rights in the convention, because abortion and the prenatal right to life are not equally recognized as human rights under the convention or in any other international norm binding on states parties, as explained in chapters 5 and 6.[294]

## The State Duty to Generally Protect the Unborn Child's Right to Life by Law

The American Convention, as expressed by former commissioner Paolo Carozza, "is, *on its face*, the international human rights treaty that is most clearly protective of the right to life of the unborn."[295] A nonrestrictive interpretation of the American Convention, carried out in good faith, would honor the plain language and ordinary meaning of the treaty text, which clearly recognizes the unborn child's right to life and a related state duty to legally and effectively protect it in general, not exceptionally.

The treaty terms, read in their context, support the understanding that the unborn child is a human being entitled to broad and general human rights protection from elective abortion. The Inter-American Court's interpretation of the prenatal right to life in *Artavia* characterized almost exactly the kind of restrictive interpretation prohibited by article 29 of the convention. However, future compositions of the Inter-American Court of Human Rights are not bound to follow that interpretation. A future composition of the court could also disregard *Baby Boy*'s restrictive and incorrect interpretation of the American Declaration of the Rights and Duties of Man, which recognizes a universal right to life without any exclusions for the prenatal child or any other human being.

Even a restrictive interpretation that would read the term "in general" to legally allow or tolerate some abortions would, in any case, be lawfully required to adhere to the arbitrariness test required by article 4(1) for any intentional deprivations of the right to life. Such an interpretation should apply at least the same standards used for the death penalty, namely strict scrutiny, judicial guarantees, and the right to individualized consideration.

The legal authorization of abortion on the sole basis of individual choice, autonomy, or privacy would certainly be arbitrary under both a restrictive and a nonrestrictive interpretation of the convention. In addition, the treaty's duty to generally protect the prenatal right to life applies "from the moment of conception," not from a later point in pregnancy, such as twelve weeks or viability; it is also incompatible with gradualist or incrementalist models. Therefore, legalization of first-trimester abortions also constitutes a clear violation of the American Convention.

Even under a restrictive interpretation of the term "in general," some statutory provisions for nonpunishment of abortions may be *permissible* under a state's margin of appreciation, but nothing in the convention suggests that decriminalization of direct, voluntary abortion may be legally *required.* No lawful exception to the unborn child's right to life could defeat the object and purpose of the treaty, which is to reinforce rather than overturn human rights protections in domestic law. No good faith interpretation of article 4(1) could grant exceptional, rather than general, protection to the unborn child's right to life, in violation of the *pro homine* rule. If Inter-American human rights bodies are unwilling to enforce article 4(1) in regard to its general protection of the unborn child's right to life, a middle-ground approach could be to give states parties a *narrow margin of appreciation* in legislating on grounds for nonpunishment of abortion. A margin of appreciation doctrine seems much needed to restore the Inter-American system's subsidiarity and would probably be well received by states in general, regardless of their attitude toward abortion.

FOUR

# Evolutive Interpretation

## *State Practice on Prenatal Personhood and Human Rights Entitlement*

States parties to the American Convention on Human Rights have adopted domestic laws to protect the prenatal right to life and recognize the unborn child's entitlement to human rights, as mandated by article 2 of the American Convention: "[T]he States Parties undertake to adopt, in accordance with their constitutional processes and the provisions of this Convention, such legislative or other measures as may be necessary to give effect to those rights or freedoms."

This chapter analyzes state practice subsequent to ratification of the American Convention, which, according to the Vienna Convention, constitutes a primary source of treaty interpretation.[1] The Inter-American Court of Human Rights has acknowledged and applied this rule, designating it as "evolutive interpretation" and indicating that comparative law analysis of domestic norms and domestic case law are essential in identifying the same.[2]

### Constitutional Recognition of a Prenatal Right to Life and Prenatal Personhood

Before the adoption of the American Convention on Human Rights only two current states parties to the American Convention, Ecuador and

Paraguay, recognized a right to life from conception.[3] After signature or ratification of the convention, eight Latin American and Caribbean states parties have explicitly protected the right to life from the time of conception in their national constitutions and recognized prenatal personhood from conception in their national constitutions: Chile, Ecuador, El Salvador, Guatemala, Honduras, Paraguay, and Peru.[4] It must be said, however, that other states implicitly recognize prenatal rights, such as the Argentine Constitution article 75(23), which provides that Congress shall have the power to enact a special and integral social security system that protects *needy children, from gestation* through the end of elementary schooling, and that protects the mother during pregnancy and nursing.[5]

### Incorporation of Prenatal Right to Life in National Constitutions

States have mirrored the American Convention's language in articulating a "right to life from conception" belonging to every "person" or "human being."[6] The Constitution of El Salvador, article 1, recognizes every *human being* as a *person* from the moment of conception, using the two terms interchangeably and stating that El Salvador recognizes the human person as the origin and the end of the activity of the state.[7] The Constitution of Paraguay, article 4, amendment in 1992, to use wording similar to the convention's, provides that the right to life from conception is inherent to the *human person.*[8] The Constitution of Peru likewise establishes that every "person" has a right to life and that, from conception, the unborn shall be a *subject of rights* in everything that favors him or her.[9] The Guatemalan Constitution declares, in article 3, that the state guarantees and protects *human life* from the time of conception, as well as the integrity and security of the *person.*[10] The Guatemalan Supreme Court has recognized this article as consistent with the American Convention.[11] The Honduran Constitution includes the "unborn" ("*al que está por nacer,*" one about to be born) in the section dealing with "individual rights" of persons in the constitution.[12] The Dominican Constitution also includes the right to life from conception under its section on fundamental rights, that is, civil and political rights of *persons.*[13]

Some constitutions refer to *prenatal rights* as *children's rights.* For instance, the Ecuadorian Constitution article 45 provides that (1) *children and adolescents* shall enjoy the rights common to all human beings, in addition to those specific to their age; (2) the state shall recognize and ensure their right to life, care, and protection *from the moment of conception*; and (3) their other rights shall be protected—including their right to a family, to full health and nutrition, to social security, and to respect for their dignity.[14] This provision expands the state's duty of protection toward the child from conception recognized in Ecuador's prior constitution of 1967, before the American Convention was adopted.[15] The Chilean Constitutional Court has found an implicit constitutional right to life of the unborn in article 19(1) of the Constitution of Chile, which declares that the constitution guarantees to all persons the right to life and to physical and psychological integrity of the person.[16] The Chilean Constitutional Court held that legislators had left a record of their interpretation of this article, which stated that the *nasciturus*, from conception, is a *person* in the constitutional sense and, therefore, entitled to the right to life.[17] It also held that the rights of gestating mothers and those of unborn children deserved *equal protection* under the Chilean Constitution.[18]

The Constitutional Court seems to have taken a step back, however, in 2017, albeit in a 6 to 4 decision, which may not create the required majority for authoritative precedent, according to Chilean law professors Hernán Corral and José Manuel Díaz de Valdés.[19] In 2017, the Constitutional Court declared that the *nasciturus* was not, after all, a person under the constitution until birth, but it recognized that prenatal life is "a juridical interest of the utmost importance," that "the unborn is a legal good of the utmost importance for the Constitution," and that the *status of person need not be recognized* for prenatal life to be protected.[20]

### Incorporation of Prenatal Right to Life in Federal States Parties

In 2002, the Mexican Supreme Court recognized that prenatal life is protected under the Mexican Constitution, federal law, and *international law* and that the unborn is also entitled to the right to life, without which no other rights may come into existence.[21] Although the federal constitution of Mexico does not contain specific provisions on the right to life beginning at conception, its article 123 establishes that an employer shall be required to ensure the greatest possible guarantees for the health and life of their workers *and of the product of conception* when pregnant women are involved.[22] The Mexican Supreme Court read this provision in conjunction with article 4 of the constitution (on equality before the law) and held that it protects the right to life from the moment of conception regardless of the unborn's stage of development.[23] This jurisprudence remains effective today, as indicated by several supreme court judges.[24] In 2008, the Supreme Court composition that upheld Mexico City's first-trimester abortion legalization failed to recognize the existence of abortion rights when prompted to do so.[25]

In 2008, Mexican Supreme Court judges Sergio Salvador Aguirre Anguiano, Mariano Azuela Güitrón, and Guillermo I. Ortiz Mayagoitia interpreted the American Convention as treating the *nasciturus*—that is, the unborn child—as a *human person* entitled to the right to life.[26] Judge Aguirre Anguiano stated that it is *self-evident* that the American Convention protects the unborn child.[27] He interpreted the convention's terms "person" and "no one" in article 4(1) and article 2 to include the unborn child and to therefore entitle her to a right to life as well as a right to not be deprived of her life arbitrarily and to have her life legally protected.[28] He indicated that to deny the unborn child recognition as a human being is to "repeat the historical error of objectifying certain human beings for reasons of political and ideological convenience."[29] He also suggested that doing so contradicted the principle of *progressive development* of human rights as well as national Mexican law, which recognized the *humanity* of the product of conception. In 2011, the Supreme Court upheld two state constitutional amendments on human life beginning at conception, finding that they were consistent with *international obligations* contracted by Mexico and therefore valid.[30]

Most Mexican state constitutions also recognize the unborn child's right to life from conception. Between the years of 1989 and 2019, twenty-one out of thirty-one Mexican states amended their state constitutions to protect the right to life from the time of conception.[31] The amendments remain in force in twenty-one of these: Baja California, Chiapas, Chihuahua, Coahuila, Colima, Durango, Guanajuato, Jalisco, Morelos, Nayarit, Nuevo León, Oaxaca, Puebla, Querétaro, Quintana Roo, San Luis Potosí, Sinaloa, Sonora, Tamaulipas, Veracruz, and Yucatán.[32] The state of Campeche had passed a constitutional amendment recognizing the right to life from conception but repealed it in 2010.[33] The state of Sinaloa was one of the last states, as of the beginning of 2019, to amend its state constitution to protect the right to life from the time of conception.[34] The state of Nuevo León considered passing such an amendment since 2016 but delayed its passing until 2019 due to political pressure from several international organizations that opposed the amendment, including the UN High Commissioner for Human Rights, the United Nations Population Fund (UNFPA), and UN Women.[35]

The amendments have survived constitutional scrutiny despite repeated instances of constitutional challenge, where the Mexican Supreme Court has relied on principles of federalism and legislative deference.[36] The Federal Mexican Supreme Court upheld the amendments in San Luis Potosí and Baja California in 2011, refusing to hear the unconstitutionality claim; it upheld the amendments in Oaxaca and Guanajuato in 2013, rejecting the proposition that right-to-life amendments violated reproductive rights or separation of church and state.[37] The court partially struck down the Querétaro amendment on narrow, procedural grounds (statute of limitations) and only in regard to the Arroyo Seco municipality.[38] However, "[s]everal justices commented that the State was free to revisit the issue and follow the proper procedure in passing the amendment."[39]

The constitutions of Chiapas, Chihuahua, Colima, Durango, Guanajuato, Jalisco, Morelos, Nayarit, Oaxaca, Querétaro, San Luis Potosí, Tamaulipas, and Yucatán designate the unborn as a "human being" who is entitled to human rights—in particular, the right to life from conception.[40] The Constitution of Campeche designates the unborn as a "person."[41] The Constitution of Guanajuato, like the American Convention article 1, expressly rejects any distinction between the terms "person" and "human being," as in the American Convention, by affirming that "a person is any human being from conception until natural death."[42] Furthermore, the state of Coahuila refers to the unborn as "children" and provides that they should be protected by law from the time of conception.[43] The Constitution of Baja California recognizes the unborn's right to life from conception until "natural or non-induced death."[44]

Some Mexican state constitutions (Campeche, Chiapas, Puebla, Querétaro, Quintana Roo, Sonora, San Luis Potosí, Tamaulipas, Veracruz, and Yucatán[45]) allow exceptions to the right to life from conception, but only under very limited circumstances and not necessarily for abortion. The language in the constitutions of Campeche, Chiapas, Puebla, Quintana Roo, Tamaulipas, Veracruz, and Yucatán generally refers to exceptions established by criminal law, without specifying whether those would include elective abortion, fetal homicide, or involuntary miscarriage (see definitions in chapter 5). The Querétaro Constitution indicates that the provision for a right to life from conception does not derogate "absolutory excuses" established by criminal law.[46] San Luis Potosí and Sonora specifically include "life of the mother" exceptions and an exception for the abortion of children conceived in rape.[47]

Several Mexican states have specifically defined conception as *fertilization* in their constitutions. In 2010, for instance, the Nayarit Constitution was amended to specifically recognize and protect the right to life from fertilization, *whether natural or artificial.*[48] The constitutions of Campeche, Durango, Jalisco, Nayarit, Oaxaca, Sonora, Querétaro, Tamaulipas, and Yucatán expressly recognize conception as the moment of *fertilization.*[49] This definition may prevent potential claims that human embryos are not entitled to constitutional rights before implantation—that is, when artificially conceived in vitro or when unable to implant in the uterus lining due to abortifacient drugs.

Similarly, after Argentina's adoption or ratification of the American Convention,[50] over half of all Argentinian provinces—namely Buenos Aires, Catamarca, Córdoba, Chaco, Chubut, Entre Ríos, Formosa, Salta, San Luis, Santiago del Estero, Tierra del Fuego, Antártida and Islas del Atlántico Sur, and Tucumán—adopted constitutional provisions explicitly recognizing a *right to life from the moment of conception.* The constitutions of Salta, Chubut, Catamarca, San Luis, Tucumán, and Córdoba, for instance, state that life is protected from the time of *conception* and that everyone, particularly public authorities, has a *duty to respect and protect it.*[51] The Constitution of Entre Ríos adds the *arbitrary deprivation* of life from conception as a constitutional violation.[52] In addition, the constitutions of Entre Ríos and Buenos Aires specifically protect life *from the moment of conception until natural death.*[53]

The constitutions of Entre Ríos, Tucumán, Chaco, San Luis, Córdoba, Tierra del Fuego, Antártida, and Islas del Atlántico Sur recognize that "every person" in the province is entitled to a right to life from conception.[54] The Formosa Constitution establishes that "every human being" shall have a right to life from conception as well as a right to personal integrity.[55] The Constitution of Santiago del Estero uses language similar to that of the American Convention by stating that "every person" shall be entitled to the right to life, in general, from the moment of conception.[56]

Some provincial constitutions, such as the constitutions of Chubut, Chaco, San Luis, and Córdoba, recognize both the unborn child's *right to life* and to *personal integrity*—defined as physical and moral integrity—from conception.[57] In addition, the constitutions of Tucumán, Chaco, San Luis, and Córdoba recognize the unborn's right to a "dignified existence" from conception.[58] Moreover, the Formosa Constitution establishes the provincial government's obligation to raise awareness on the responsibilities of procreation, and the Catamarca Constitution suggests the unborn child is also entitled to *social rights.*[59]

## The Unborn Child's Personhood and Right to Life in Primary Laws

### Personhood Recognition

Most primary laws of states parties to the American Convention—that is, laws of higher hierarchy such as codes or legislative acts, which prevail over secondary regulations and executive orders—refer to the unborn as a "person," a "human being," or a "child." For instance, the newer Argentinian Civil Code, which became effective in 2015, uses the term "unborn person" throughout to designate the human fetus and the human embryo.[60] The civil code recognizes human life and personhood beginning at conception in article 19: "[T]he existence of the human person begins at conception."[61] The previous civil code also recognized the beginning of human life at conception, in articles 63 and 70: "Unborn persons are those not yet born but conceived in the maternal womb," and "the existence of persons begins at conception in the maternal womb."[62]

Interestingly enough, the expression "in the maternal womb" was removed in the 2015 code, a deletion that could support a definition of conception as *fertilization* rather than implantation according to law professor Nicolás Lafferriere.[63] Prior Argentinian Supreme Court decisions in

*T.S. v. Buenos Aires*, recognizing an anencephalic fetus as a human person, and *Portal de Belén*, defining conception as fertilization, would also seem to support that interpretation. In addition, the executive branch of Argentina's federal government proposed to define the beginning of human life as implantation for the purposes of in vitro fertilization in the new code, but this proposal was rejected, which suggests that legislators did not agree with this understanding of the term.[64]

Children's codes of Costa Rica, El Salvador, Honduras, Ecuador, Guatemala, Nicaragua, and Panama refer to the unborn child as a person or a human being who is entitled to legal rights, including the right to life.[65] The Children and Adolescents Code of Nicaragua refers to the unborn as *children* and as *human persons* with special characteristics, in the process of development, and establishes that they are entitled to constitutional rights and human dignity.[66] The Nicaraguan Civil Code designates *unborn persons* as having a "natural existence" that should be protected, even if they do not yet possess all legal rights.[67] Paraguay's current Code of Childhood and Adolescence, article 9, mandates that "unborn persons" shall be protected from the time of conception.[68] On the other hand, Honduras's Children's Code establishes that, for the code's purposes, childhood begins upon birth, but refers to the unborn as a human being and a person and recognizes his or her right to life from conception as well as a right to be born in conditions compatible with human dignity.[69] Peru's Act on National Population Policy establishes that every human person is entitled to the right to life from conception.[70]

Many Latin American and Caribbean children's codes and other primary laws explicitly include unborn children in their definition of children. For instance, the Argentinian Act on Rights of Parents and Children during Childbirth speaks of the unborn as a "person to be born" (*persona por nacer*), as a "child," and as a "boy or girl."[71] El Salvador's Act on Comprehensive Protection of Children and Adolescents repeatedly uses the terms "person" and "child" interchangeably when referring to the unborn and specifically defines the term "child" as referring to any person from the moment of *conception until eighteen years of age*.[72] The act declares *all* children, including unborn children, to be human rights subjects from the moment of *conception* and to be entitled, in particular, to the right to life and the right to be born in conditions compatible with *human dignity*.[73] El Salvador's Family Code also refers to the unborn as a minor and provides he is entitled to rights from the moment of *conception.*[74] Its health code also refers to the unborn child as a *child*, existing as such from conception onward.[75]

Likewise, the Bolivian Code of Children and Adolescents defines *children* as all human beings *from conception* up to the age of eighteen.[76] Children's codes of Costa Rica[77] and Guatemala[78] define a *child* as any person *from conception* to the age of twelve and an adolescent to be any person between twelve and eighteen years of age. Panama's Act 14, which created the National Ministry for Children, Adolescents, and the Family, defines children as "every person from conception up to the age of 14," and adolescents as those between fourteen and eighteen years of age.[79] Panama's Family Code defines "minor" as any human being from conception until the age of eighteen.[80] The Paraguayan Act 2169 Establishing the Age of Majority and the Paraguayan Health Code define "child" as any human person from *conception* until eighteen years of age.[81] Paraguay's former Juvenile Code defined the term "child" in a similar manner but did not explicitly refer to the unborn as a *person*; the amended code includes this recognition.[82]

Peru's Code of Children and Adolescents defines "child" as "every human being from the moment of conception up to 12 years of age" and adolescents as those aged twelve to eighteen.[83] The children and adolescents codes of Paraguay and Ecuador designate the miscarried fetus as a "child," and Ecuador's code also uses the word "boy" or "girl" when referring to the child in utero.[84] Nicaragua's Family Law Code, adopted in 2014, also recognizes "conceived and unborn" children as *persons* and *children*, mandating that the Ministry of Children and Adolescents be automatically involved in any claim affecting their rights.[85]

March 25 has been declared by legislative or executive decree as the Unborn Child Day in Argentina, Bolivia, Chile, Costa Rica, Dominican Republic, Guatemala, Honduras, Nicaragua, and Peru, and some of these decrees have invoked the American Convention.[86] For instance, the Guatemalan National Congress decree of 1999 declaring March 25 as the day of the unborn child held that "the state guarantees human life from its conception *in accordance with the American Convention on Human Rights* [Article 4(1)] of which Guatemala is a signatory."[87] The Peruvian congressional decree issued in 2001 invoked articles 1(2) and 4(1) of the American Convention when indicating that "these international instruments reinforce the purpose of this legislative proposal, which is to sensitize persons about the child's right to life, in order to find ways to fight the causes that lead to abortion (poverty, fear, prejudice, sexual and reproductive education, etc) [*sic*]."[88]

### The Right to Life from Conception in Primary Laws

After ratification of the American Convention, the children's codes and other primary laws of most states parties have mirrored the American Convention's prenatal right-to-life provision by explicitly recognizing the unborn's *right to life from conception.*[89] The children's codes of Bolivia, Colombia, Costa Rica, Ecuador, El Salvador, Guatemala, Honduras, Nicaragua, Paraguay, and Peru explicitly contain, like the American Convention, a right to life of children from the moment of conception.[90]

Many national civil codes not only recognize the unborn's entitlement to life but also *enable the judiciary* to protect it via civil, in addition to criminal, jurisdiction. The Chilean, Colombian, Honduran, Nicaraguan, Peruvian, and Salvadorian civil codes, using virtually identical language, allow *judges* to take any measure they find suitable when they believe that the life of the unborn may be at risk, as long as those measures do not endanger the child's life or health.[91] The Colombian Civil Code provision was upheld by the Constitutional Court in Judgment C-591 of 1995.[92]

The Brazilian Civil Code stipulates that civil capacity begins at the moment of birth, but "the law protects, from the moment of conception, the *unborn child's rights*"—a provision that was interpreted by Federal Supreme Court Justice Lewandowski as protecting the right to life from conception.[93] Likewise, Brazil's Act on Children and Adolescents provides that children have a right to life that should be protected through the implementation of *social policies that promote births.*[94]

National family codes and other primary laws also protect unborn life beginning at conception. For instance, Panama's Family Code establishes that every *minor* shall have a right to protection of his or her *prenatal* life.[95] El Salvador's Family Code states that the life and health of the *child* shall be protected by a range of legal, social, and support measures from *conception* until majority.[96] In addition, Paraguay's Health Code, Title I, relating to the health of persons, provides that *unborn persons'* lives and health shall be protected "from their conception."[97] Likewise, Peru's Act on National Population Policy establishes that every human person is entitled to the right to life from conception.[98]

## The Right of Unborn Children to Health, Social Protection, and Equal Protection before Birth

After signature or ratification of the American Convention, most states parties to the American Convention have recognized and protected the unborn child's right to health, survival, and development through children's codes, family codes, health codes, and national constitutions. The unborn child's right to health, survival, and development is usually framed in these laws as a social and economic right that entails a positive state duty to provide, subsidize, and ensure access to prenatal health services as well as to enact and implement related social policy. In addition, prenatal health is not merely perceived as a right belonging to mothers, but as a right of unborn children, entitling both to equal protection.

National constitutions that recognize the unborn child's right to health, social protection, and equal protection include the Argentinian Constitution, which mandates a social security system that grants special and comprehensive protection to both children and their mothers throughout pregnancy.[99] The Brazilian Constitution provides for the protection of maternity and childhood, granting special social rights to pregnant women.[100] Likewise, the Honduran Constitution establishes a child's right to prenatal health and development—the fulfillment of which is found in the state's assurance of access to prenatal health for both the child and his or her mother.[101]

Primary laws of the majority of states parties to the American Convention recognize a right of unborn children to health, survival, and development. For instance, El Salvador's Act on Comprehensive Protection of Children and Adolescents specifically recognizes the unborn child's right to life, prenatal health, survival, growth, and birth in circumstances that promote his or her biological, psychological, and social development.[102] Similarly, El Salvador's Family Code expressly recognizes the child's fundamental right to life, health, and development from conception until the age of majority, which shall be safeguarded by means of a wide range of legal protections and social policies including prenatal health services.[103]

Honduras's Code of Children and Adolescents establishes that every human being has a right to development before birth and that the state shall adopt all measures necessary to ensure that gestation, birth, and development take place in conditions compatible with human dignity.[104]

The Guatemalan Act on Comprehensive Protection of Children and Adolescents recognizes a right to care, protection, and development (including physical, mental, and social development) from conception.[105] Likewise, Ecuador's Code of Childhood and Adolescence also establishes a state duty to ensure children's survival and development from conception through gestation.[106] The Nicaraguan Children and Adolescents Code provides that the state shall promote public policies that ensure prenatal care, safe births, survival, and comprehensive development from gestation onward.[107] Peru's Code of Children and Adolescents establishes a state duty to provide access to prenatal health care throughout pregnancy for teenage mothers.[108]

El Salvador's Act on Comprehensive Protection of Children and Adolescents contains perhaps the most progressive language in terms of recognition of a prenatal right to health as a social and economic right. The act establishes a state duty to protect the unborn child's life by ensuring prenatal health care and psychological assistance for mothers from conception to birth.[109] It also recognizes a state duty to provide free, government-funded health services, treatment, medication, food, and nutritional counseling for pregnant women and girls facing disability or poverty.[110] Remarkably, the act establishes a legal duty of both public and private health care institutions to provide emergency obstetric care for pregnant women or teenagers. The act also prohibits the government from using scarcity of resources as a defense for refusing to provide care.[111] The act specifies that the prenatal right to development includes appropriate nutrition, secure and hygienic housing, drinking water, sewage, and electricity, among other things. It also affirms that the state shall have a subsidiary responsibility to ensure that parents and the family can provide for these needs in accordance with their financial means and resources.[112]

Similarly, the Panama Family Code recognizes a child's right to health and survival before birth and mandates state subsidy of medical and health services to poor pregnant mothers as well as food subsidies for unemployed mothers.[113] The Paraguay Children and Adolescents Code contains similar provisions and establishes that such assistance shall be provided even if the child dies before birth.[114] The Costa Rica Children's Code affirms a prenatal right to life and development as well as a right to economic and social protection by mandating that the state ensure and protect that right through economic and social policies that promote dignified conditions for gestation, birth, and overall development.[115] For this purpose, the Costa Rican Code of Children and Adolescents establishes a public health subsidy for poor pregnant women consisting in cash assistance, equivalent to minimum wage, to be paid by the Social Assistance Bureau during gestation and lactation.[116]

Similar language recognizing a child's right to prenatal health care can be found in the Brazilian Children's Act, which mandates that these health services should be rendered through public policies that enable healthy births and development.[117] It provides for a state duty to ensure prenatal care and food assistance for pregnant women in need.[118] Likewise, the Bolivian Children's Code provides that the state should ensure and protect the unborn child's right to life by implementing social policies that ensure dignified conditions for his or her birth and that provide for comprehensive development.[119] It also mandates that the state offer free health services and food assistance to pregnant mothers, particularly teenage mothers and pregnant inmates.[120] Colombia's Code on Children and Adolescents also mandates the development of public policies that ensure the right to life, care, and protection, as well as the right to survival, health, and development from conception.[121]

The Mexican Federal Act for the Protection of Children and Adolescents also recognizes a right to health of unborn children by establishing that federal, state, and local authorities shall offer access to prenatal care.[122] In addition, the Mexican Federal Constitution provides that employers shall ensure that working conditions do not harm the health or life of pregnant women and their unborn children.[123] The Peruvian Public Health Act declares an inherent right to health from conception and creates a duty of individuals and society at large to protect it.[124] Paraguay's current Code of Childhood and Adolescence stipulates that unborn persons shall be protected through the provision of health care for pregnant women, from conception until forty-five days after delivery and that the state has only subsidiary, not primary, responsibility to provide it.[125] The Dominican Republic Children's Code provides for a state duty to ensure prenatal health, including free health services.[126]

In addition, the laws of many states parties to the American Convention recognize equal protection of mothers and their unborn children. For instance, the Paraguayan Health Code establishes that the unborn child enjoys a right to have their life and health protected from conception and that, during pregnancy, the mother and unborn child shall be protected as a biological unit.[127] El Salvador's Health Code mandates preventive and therapeutic health services for the pregnant woman and the child, from conception onward.[128] The Panama Family Code establishes preferential treatment for pregnant women in public health and social services and in alimony actions.[129] Barbados grants pregnant women preferential status in nutrition programs.[130] The Costa Rica Children's Code establishes that pregnant children and teenagers shall be given free prenatal health services for both themselves and their unborn children; it also establishes that they shall be given preferential treatment in public health facilities, particularly in situations of risk to their own health and the health of their unborn children.[131] The code also establishes a state duty to provide medical treatment to pregnant mothers infected with HIV or AIDS directed to avoiding transmission to the *nasciturus* child.[132]

Similarly, the Chilean Health Code provides for equal protection of mother and child during pregnancy by establishing a state duty to protect the child and to ensure that the mother has access to prenatal health care; this health care should be provided free of charge for indigent women and children.[133] Ecuador's Code of Childhood and Adolescence establishes a state duty to ensure access to prenatal health care for both the mother and unborn child, particularly for pregnant teenagers.[134] Specifically, the code provides that a child's right to health includes maternal health and prenatal care.[135] The Honduran Code of Children and Adolescents establishes a state duty to provide both the mother and the child with prenatal health care, through public health agencies, as well as food assistance when necessary.[136]

## Parental Rights and Duties toward the Unborn

Many civil laws of states parties to the American Convention recognize parental authority over unborn children and parental duties toward them, treating the unborn as born for legal purposes. Chile's Civil Code recognizes biological parental authority over their children's property, including future property or assets of unborn children.[137] Brazil's Civil Procedure Code recognizes only a biological mother's parental authority over her unborn child.[138] Paraguay's Health Code establishes parents' obligation and right to care for their children's health from gestation onward.[139] El Salvador's Family Code emphasizes a parental duty of care toward children from their conception onward.[140]

Most states parties legally authorize voluntary or involuntary establishment of paternity before birth. Domestic laws of Bolivia,[141] Brazil,[142] Costa Rica,[143] El Salvador,[144] and Panama[145] allow for voluntary or involuntary paternity recognition by fathers and the filing of paternity actions by mothers against fathers before a child's birth. Costa Rica's Family Code also provides that paternity recognition of children born within marriage—that is, legitimation—shall apply retroactively to the time of the child's conception.[146] Argentina, Colombia, Dominican Republic, Honduras, Mexico, Nicaragua, Paraguay, and Peru allow for voluntary paternity recognition before birth or allow a father to contest paternity claims before the child's birth.[147] The Honduran Family Code requires notarization and registration of voluntary paternity recognition and provides that paternity will become effective upon the child's birth.[148] Paraguay and Peru preempt fathers from disputing paternity before the child's birth.[149]

### Prenatal Alimony

Over half of all civil codes, family codes, and children's codes of states parties to the American Convention recognize prenatal alimony rights to which both the unborn child and the mother are entitled. For instance, Brazil's 2008 Statute N. 11.804 allows a pregnant woman to collect prenatal alimony (*alimentos gravíticos*) from the potential father of her unborn child throughout pregnancy, from the child's conception to his or her birth.[150] This "supplementary financial aid throughout pregnancy" would account for half of a pregnant woman's expenses for food or health care costs.[151] Upon the child's birth, the financial aid turns into child support unless paternity is successfully contested.[152] Likewise, Nicaragua's Family Code, adopted in 2014, allows a pregnant mother to collect *prenatal alimony* from an estranged husband or partner before the child's birth.[153] In

Paraguay, juvenile courts—rather than family courts—hold jurisdiction to hear prenatal alimony complaints, demonstrating a view of prenatal alimony primarily as a right of children.[154]

Prenatal alimony normally covers the mother's health care expenses during gestation delivery and after birth, under the codes of Colombia, Costa Rica, Chile, Dominican Republic, Ecuador, El Salvador, Honduras, Panama, Paraguay, Peru, and Uruguay.[155] According to Ecuador's Code of Childhood and Adolescence, in addition to maternity and prenatal health care expenses, prenatal alimony may cover the pregnant mother's food, clothing, and shelter expenses and may apply even in the event of miscarriage or unintended fetal death.[156] The Civil Code of Peru also mandates coverage of food expenses—limiting them to sixty days before and after delivery—as well as shelter, clothing, and even education or employment training costs.[157]

Generally, alimony is not gender-neutral in Latin America, and prenatal alimony obligations, in particular, belong to fathers. Bolivia's Family Code provides that alimony, including prenatal alimony, shall be paid to pregnant women and children.[158] Costa Rican courts may order a father to reimburse the mother of his child for pregnancy and prenatal care expenses as long as his paternity is established within twelve months of the child's birth.[159] Panama's Family Code provides that fathers shall be subject to prenatal alimony obligations to be paid to the child's mother during pregnancy and lactation.[160] This obligation can be binding on the father's estate in countries like Peru and Panama, where, if the child should die before birth, the mother would have no obligation to reimburse any payment made to her under this obligation.[161] In addition, the Honduran Family Code provides that perpetrators of sexual assault may be ordered to pay prenatal and postnatal alimony for any children conceived in rape.[162]

### Balance of Parental Rights v. Prenatal Rights

Some Latin America and Caribbean Codes protect the unborn child's best interests over parental rights or wishes under certain circumstances. For instance, Ecuador's Children's Code, which defines "child" as any human being from conception to the age of eighteen, stipulates that the principle of the best interests of the child applies to unborn children and that, when in conflict with other rights, children's rights shall have absolute priority.[163] Panama's Family Code mandates state action, for the sake of the unborn children, to combat improper use of drugs, alcohol, or medication by pregnant women.[164] In the realm of family planning, Paraguay's Health Code stipulates that reproductive health services shall be supervised by health authorities that shall oversee respect for the fundamental rights of human beings and the dignity of the family.[165] The Bolivian Children's Code prohibits adoption of children before birth and invalidates parental consent given to that effect.[166] The Mexican Health Act prohibits organ or tissue donation by pregnant women that implies "risk to the health of the woman or that of the product of conception."[167]

In the context of reproductive technologies, Peru's Health Act prohibits in vitro fertilization for nonreproductive purposes as well as for human cloning.[168] Furthermore, Colombia,[169] Honduras,[170] and Ecuador[171] categorically prohibit prenatal adoptions, perhaps to prevent surrogacy arrangements or baby trafficking. The Honduran Children's Code categorically prohibits artificial procreation involving the use of sperm donation, probably to prevent a child from having more than two (biological and legal) parents.[172] El Salvador's Act on Comprehensive Protection of Children and Adolescents prohibits genetic or medical research that may place the human embryo's life, physical integrity, or dignity at risk.[173] Its criminal code establishes jail penalties and professional sanctions for human genetic modification for nontherapeutic purposes; it bans reproductive cloning and the use of prenatal technologies for sex selection purposes.[174] Fines may also apply for fetal injury resulting from genetic modification.[175]

Similarly, Peru's Code of Children and Adolescents protects the unborn child's life from embryonic research or genetic modification which may be contrary to personal integrity and development.[176] The Colombian Criminal Code prohibits genetic modification of embryos for reproductive purposes, as well as human cloning and trafficking of human embryos, and establishes jail penalties for violators.[177] Nicaragua also bans nontherapeutic genetic modification, race selection of human embryos, and all human cloning, imposing imprisonment penalties and professional sanctions on perpetrators.[178] Likewise, embryonic research would be included in its prohibition to create human embryos for nonreproductive purposes. Criminal codes of Panama and Guatemala contain similar provisions.[179]

## Civil Inabilities, Legal Protection, Succession, and Property Rights of Unborn Children

Most civil codes in states parties to the American Convention establish that the prenatal right to life is protected by law even where the unborn child may not enjoy legal capacity or legal personhood for civil law purposes.[180] The civil codes of Bolivia, Brazil, Chile, Colombia, Ecuador, El Salvador, Honduras, Mexico, Nicaragua, Panama, Paraguay, and Peru specifically recognize that the law protects the life of the unborn despite his or her lack of legal personhood or civil capacity, which begins at birth.[181] The language in these codes varies: the Mexican Federal Civil Code establishes that "physical persons" only acquire legal capacity at birth, but "from the moment an individual is conceived" he is protected by law.[182] The Peruvian Civil Code proclaims that human life begins at conception, the unborn are subject to all rights that may benefit them, and only property rights can be made contingent on birth.[183]

According to civil codes of Chile, Colombia, Ecuador, El Salvador, Honduras, Nicaragua, and Panama, judges are authorized to order, either at their own initiative or upon a third party's request, any measures they may deem convenient "to protect the unborn's life " whenever they believe that prenatal life may be endangered.[184] The Chilean Supreme Court, for instance, invoked this provision when banning emergency contraception in 2001 and 2008.[185] Judicial measures may include legal sanctions on the mother who seeks to end her child's life, but punishments that may endanger prenatal life or health can be deferred until after birth.[186]

The Argentinian Supreme Court has affirmed a textual interpretation of a provision in the former civil code (which can also be found in the newer one) establishing that even though the unborn are civilly incapacitated, human existence begins at conception in the maternal womb, and persons may acquire some rights before they are born.[187] In *Sánchez, Elvira Berta v. the National Ministry of Justice and Human Rights*, a grandmother sought victim compensation for the forced disappearance of her daughter, nine months pregnant at the time of her execution, and compensation for the loss of the daughter's unborn grandchild.[188] The grandmother's claim had been rejected in lower courts based on the argument that, according to the Argentinian Civil Code, the unborn child did not acquire rights that could be transferred to his heirs. The Supreme Court, however, rejected that reasoning on the basis that the grandmother's claim was not for a hereditary right that depended on the child's live birth but one depending on his or her existence. The court thus acknowledged the existence of the unborn child as a human person and allowed compensation for his grandmother.

Some civil codes of states parties to the Convention identify the unborn as "natural persons"—recognizing their natural existence and entitlement to life, health, and personal integrity—distinct from the designation of "legal persons," which is often characterized as legal capacity to enter contracts or to be the subject of property and succession rights. For instance, virtually all Mexican states and Mexico City distinguish between legal and physical persons, finding that the unborn fit into the latter category.[189] For instance, the states of Aguascalientes, Baja California, Baja California Sur, Campeche, Chiapas, Chihuahua, Coahuila, Colima, Durango, Guanajuato, Guerrero, Hidalgo, Jalisco, Michoacán, Morelos, Nayarit, Nuevo León, Oaxaca, Puebla, Querétaro, Quintana Roo, San Luis Potosí, Sinaloa, Tabasco, Tamaulipas, Tlaxcala, Veracruz, and Yucatán use nearly identical language when essentially stating that a natural person's "legal capacity is acquired at birth," but that "from the moment an individual is conceived, he is entitled to legal protection."[190]

National laws of most states parties to the American Convention allow unborn children to be entitled to property and succession rights as well as other benefits before birth. For instance, Suriname's civil law generally affords unborn children the legal capacity to inherit, to receive gifts, and to be granted some property rights.[191] Chilean tax law allows for the creation of trusts in the name of unborn children.[192] Paraguay's Civil Code stipulates that, for the purposes of life insurance, the term "child" shall include unborn children as beneficiaries and enables individuals to recover tort remedies for prenatal injuries.[193]

Entitlement of an unborn child to property and succession rights is usually conditioned on her live birth, in which case the corresponding legal effects become retroactive to the time of the gift, bequest, or death of the testator—for example, in Brazil, Ecuador, El Salvador, Mexico, and Honduras.[194] In Argentina and Paraguay, those rights become irrevocable upon the child's live birth, no matter how brief his or her survival.[195]

Many national civil codes refer to the unborn child's rights as deferred or suspended until live birth, such as the civil codes of Bolivia, Colombia, Costa Rica, Ecuador, El Salvador, Honduras, Panama, and Peru.[196] Other codes, like the Nicaraguan Civil Code, refer to the unborn child's "eventual" property rights that become effective upon the child's live birth.[197] Civil codes of Argentina, Bolivia, Costa Rica, Chile, the Dominican Republic, Mexico, Nicaragua, Paraguay, and Peru, among others, establish, in similar terms, that the unborn may be entitled to inheritance and gifts only if they are born alive and that children who die before birth will be reputed as having never existed for succession purposes—that is, their parent(s) may not claim successorship.[198]

Criteria for what constitutes live birth have been codified in lesser or greater detail in different states parties to the convention. Most countries, such as Colombia, Ecuador, El Salvador, and Nicaragua, require that the child survive after complete separation from the mother.[199] In Mexico, either complete separation from the mother and survival for a minimum of twenty-four hours or presentation of the live child before the civil registrar's office is required.[200] In Paraguay, breathing or crying attested to by witnesses, no matter how brief, can constitute evidence of a live birth.[201]

Most states parties to the convention authorize the appointment of a legal representative or guardian ad litem for an unborn child in administrative or judicial proceedings involving property or inheritance rights. For instance, the civil codes of Argentina, Brazil, Costa Rica, Ecuador, El Salvador, Honduras, Nicaragua, Panama, Paraguay, and Peru allow unborn children to be legally represented by either their parents or third parties.[202] In addition, Chile, Colombia, Ecuador, El Salvador, Honduras, Nicaragua, and Peru allow for the judicial appointment of a guardian.[203] A parental preference applies in Brazil, Bolivia, El Salvador, and Paraguay; a paternal preference applies in Peru.[204] Interestingly, Peru specifically prohibits anyone convicted for abortion to serve as a guardian ad litem for an unborn child.[205]

A posthumous child—that is, the child born after his or her biological father's death but conceived during his lifetime—is entitled to succession rights upon live birth, at which point their rights become retroactive to the time of conception. For instance, when an unborn child's father dies before his or her birth, Brazil, Panama, Honduras, and Suriname allow a pregnant woman to claim intestate succession on behalf of her unborn child.[206] The laws of Colombia, Chile, Ecuador, Honduras, Nicaragua, and Peru allow a dying parent—usually the father—to appoint, through his will, a guardian ad litem to defend the unborn child's eventual property rights.[207] The laws of some Mexican states, such as the State of Mexico and Querétaro, contain similar provisions.[208]

A few civil codes restrict the powers of the unborn child's representative or guardian to exclusively administrative functions. The civil codes of Chile, Colombia, Ecuador, Nicaragua, and El Salvador provide for the appointment of a guardian of the property for unborn children (*curatela*, distinct from *tutela*, which usually implies a guardianship of both the property and the person), whose sole powers shall be to represent the child in property or inheritance proceedings.[209]

## Application of *Pro Homine* Principle to Unborn Children

Several constitutions and primary laws of states parties to the American Convention codify the *pro homine* principle in favor of the unborn child, according to which a law should be given an interpretation that ensures—to the maximum extent—the unborn child's right to life and development. The principle, when applied to the unborn child, is usually articulated as a *presumption of entitlement* in virtue of which, when doubt exists, a statute should be given the most favorable interpretation for the unborn (*in dubio pro nasciturus*).[210] The national constitutions of Peru, Honduras, Chile, and Mexico have codified or expressly applied the *pro homine* or *pro personae* principle in favor of the unborn child, beginning at conception (*in dubio pro nasciturus*).[211]

The Constitution of Peru, article 2(1), for instance, establishes that every person has a right to life and unrestricted development and that, from conception, the unborn shall be a subject of rights in everything that favors him or her.[212] The Honduran Constitution contains a similar principle in article 67, which provides that the unborn shall be considered as born for all rights accorded within the limits established by law.[213] Mexico's Constitution, in its transitory provision, holds that laws adopted before the reform's entry into force shall be effective only as long as they favor or benefit the unborn.[214] The Constitutional Court of Chile found that, when doubt exists, the *pro homine* principle should apply to the *nasciturus* or unborn child, given that the Chilean constitution's purpose was to serve the human person.[215] The Guatemalan Supreme Court interpreted the *pro homine* principle in the Constitution of Guatemala as protecting all citizens equally but granting preference to the weakest.[216]

Primary laws of several states parties to the convention, like the civil codes of Bolivia and Peru, establish that "the unborn is considered to be born whenever it is in his or her interest" in virtually identical terms.[217] Peru's Criminal Code indicates that abortion prohibitions protect the unborn child's right to life, which is constitutionally recognized, and that the unborn is deemed to have been born whenever his or her best interests are concerned.[218] Peru's Code of Children and Adolescents contains a similar provision and mandates a presumption of minority when doubt exists regarding a child's minority.[219] Mexican federal civil law also recognizes the *in dubio pro nasciturus* principle by establishing that "from the moment an individual is conceived" he is protected by law and "held out as born for all purposes indicated in this Code."[220] The Costa Rican Civil Code provides that the "physical person" is deemed born for legal purposes, in anything that favors him, starting three hundred days before his or her birth.[221] The civil codes of Guatemala and Panama limit the application of this principle to viable unborn children.[222] Suriname's civil law establishes that "the child of which [*sic*] a woman is pregnant must be considered already born as often as (his) self-interest requires this."[223]

## States Parties' Understanding of Prenatal Rights

States parties to the American Convention have a long-held juridical tradition of recognizing and protecting the unborn child's right to life from conception, one that is very much alive. After ratification of the American Convention, states parties to the American Convention have enacted laws providing comprehensive recognition and protection of prenatal rights. Such laws include constitutional and legal recognition of the unborn as a person entitled to a right to life and health, parental duties toward unborn children, conditional entitlement to property and succession rights, and even a right to social and economic protection from the state.

Most states parties to the American Convention have incorporated into their domestic laws the treaty's acknowledgment of the humanity and personhood of the unborn child as well as the treaty's recognition of a right to life of every person from the moment of conception. States parties to the convention have been pioneers of explicit recognition of prenatal personhood in their national constitutions, which often have used terms identical to those of article 4(1) in the convention. At least eight states parties to the American Convention have adopted explicit constitutional provisions recognizing and protecting a right to life from conception in their constitutions, mirroring the American Convention's language in attributing humanity and personhood to the unborn child.

Most primary laws of states parties to the convention likewise recognize a right to life from conception and include unborn children in their definition of "children." Several domestic laws codify the *pro homine* principle in favor of the unborn child (*pro nasciturus* principle). Most civil codes of states parties to the convention establish that the unborn is entitled to legal protection even though he or she may not enjoy legal capacity or legal personhood for the purposes of civil transactions. A general presumption for unborn children's entitlement to property and succession rights is recognized in national civil codes. Entitlement of unborn children to property and succession rights, however, is usually contingent upon a child's live birth, in which case it applies retroactively. Civil statutes of states parties to the convention also recognize a right to life before birth, and some jurisdictions enable civil judges to order any measures a judge may deem convenient "to protect the unborn's life" when he or she believes it may be endangered.

Some Latin American and Caribbean states parties to the American Convention have gone beyond mere recognition of humanity and a right to life in their children's codes, family codes, health codes, and national constitutions by recognizing economic and social rights belonging to unborn child, such as the right to health, survival, and development. Prenatal health is perceived as not merely a right belonging to mothers but also as a right of unborn children, and equal protection is granted to both. In addition, most states parties have recognized a legal parent-child relationship between biological parents and their unborn children, involving parental rights and duties, such as the right of fathers to establish paternity over unborn children and the duty of fathers to pay prenatal child support.

Furthermore, most states authorize the appointment of a legal representative or guardian for an unborn child in administrative or judicial proceedings involving property or inheritance rights.

The consistent recognition of prenatal rights, particularly the right to life from conception, in states parties after ratification of the American Convention on Human Rights indicates that these states have interpreted the American Convention's protection of the right to life from conception in a nonrestrictive manner. Such a recognition usually includes positive state obligations to secure prenatal rights to life, health, and development for all unborn children through law and public policy.

FIVE

# Evolutive Interpretation

## *State Practice on the Treaty Obligation to Legally Protect Prenatal Life from Abortion*

States parties to the American Convention undertook a legal duty to enact and enforce laws to protect the prenatal right to life by ratifying the American Convention, which mandates that "[the right to life] *shall be protected by law* and, in general, from the moment of conception."[1] Article 2 of the American Convention stipulates that states give domestic legal effects to the rights recognized in the treaty through constitutional and legislative provisions.[2] By prohibiting voluntary, elective abortion and legally combating abortion practices, states parties have taken steps to comply with their obligation to "take affirmative action, avoid taking measures that restrict or infringe a fundamental right, and eliminate measures and practices that restrict or violate a fundamental right."[3] Criminal bans on induced abortion are designed to contribute to the deterrence and "elimination of any norms and practices that in any way violate the guarantees provided under the Convention or disregard the rights therein enshrined or obstruct its exercise."[4]

This chapter analyzes state practice on abortion following ratification of the American Convention; it carries out a comparative law analysis of domestic norms and of national court decisions, which, according to the Inter-American Court, is essential in determining the "evolutive interpretation" of the convention's prenatal right to life.[5] The chapter examines the question of whether states parties have established criminal penalties for any acts that deliberately take the life of an unborn child in compliance with the convention's requirement that states "adopt all the appropriate measures to protect and preserve the right to life" and to "adopt a normative framework that dissuades any threat to life."[6] Evolutive state practice after adoption of the American Convention on Human Rights demonstrates that states have banned abortion out of a sense that they are legally compelled to do so under the American Convention. Legislatures and high courts, such as those in Bolivia, Chile, El Salvador, Mexico, and others, have cited the American Convention when upholding abortion bans. On the other hand, no court or legislature has alluded to a supposed international obligation to legally authorize abortion deriving from the American Convention.

## General Duty to Legally Protect the Prenatal Right to Life from Abortion

### Abortion Defined

Since the ratification of the American Convention, all states parties have adopted criminal statutes that include abortion as a criminal offense and categorize it as a "crime against persons," a "crime against human life," or a "crime against personal integrity," alluding to the personhood of the unborn human being.[7] For instance, in Argentina and Brazil, abortion is included among "crimes against persons."[8] In Brazil, Costa Rica, and Ecuador abortion is listed under "crimes against life."[9] El Salvador's legislators titled the criminal code chapter on abortion as "Crimes against the Life of the Developing Human Being."[10] Common law Caribbean countries like Dominica generally prohibit abortion in their national "offenses against the person" acts.[11]

Criminal laws of most countries, such as those of Guatemala, Mexico, and Panama, list abortion under crimes against life (or human life) and crimes against personal integrity.[12] The Nicaraguan Criminal Code adds "personal security" and devotes an entire chapter to "abortion, genetic modification and injuries to the unborn."[13] Peru classifies abortion under "crimes against life, the body and health."[14] The Uruguayan code characterizes abortion as a crime "against the physical and moral personhood of man."[15] Bolivia adds the designation of a crime "against the dignity of the human being."[16] Chile classifies abortion under crimes "against the safety of families, public morality and sexual integrity."[17] Abortion is generally listed under the same category as homicide, manslaughter, and murder, but penalties are almost always lighter.

When defined, the term "abortion" is usually described as the intentional or deliberate destruction of an unborn child. For instance, Grenada's criminal code defines "abortion" as follows: "The offence of causing abortion can be committed by causing a woman to be prematurely delivered of a child, with intent unlawfully to *cause or hasten the death of the child*."[18] The Bolivian Criminal Code defines "abortion" as any act causing the death of a human fetus or causing her premature birth and subsequent death.[19] Costa Rica's criminal code defines it in similar terms.[20] Suriname's penal code defines it as the willful interruption of a pregnancy or causing the expulsion or death of a fetus.[21]

The term "abortion" may apply to induced fetal death at any point of gestation. The Honduran criminal law, for instance, defines "abortion" as an act that intentionally causes the "death of a human being at any time during pregnancy or labor."[22] Guatemala and Mexico also apply the definition throughout gestation.[23] The Paraguayan criminal code defines abortion as "killing a fetus," and "fetus" is defined as the human embryo from the moment of conception up to labor.[24] Other terms akin to "infanticide" may be used for late-term abortions: Dominica's "Offenses against Persons Act," for instance, designates abortions under twenty-eight weeks of gestation (called the point of viability) as an "unlawful miscarriage" and designates abortions beyond the twenty-eight weeks as "child destruction."[25]

*Miscarriage Distinguished.* Spontaneous abortion is clearly distinguished from induced abortion in criminal codes of states parties to the convention. The legal meaning of the term "abortion" has not always coincided with the common understanding or even the medical definition of the term. According to the Royal Spanish Academy Dictionary, which the Inter-American Court has used to determine the ordinary meaning of other terms in article 4(1), the term *aborto* (abortion) alone implies the natural or induced death of the fetus, not necessarily the crime of induced abortion, forced abortion, or fetal homicide.[26]

Spontaneous abortion or involuntary miscarriage—that is, the involuntary death of an unborn child—is not punishable by law under *any* criminal statute. Statutory language often distinguishes *aborto involuntario, aborto culposo,* and *aborto espontáneo* (Spanish terms for involuntary, negligent, or spontaneous abortion), which does not constitute a criminal offense, from *aborto inducido* and *aborto provocado* (induced, procured, or elective abortion), which does.

No criminal statute of any state party to the American Convention penalizes a woman for the miscarriage of her unborn child. El Salvador has been repeatedly accused by abortion rights advocates of doing so, and a petition to that effect has been filed before the IACHR (see chapter 1, "*Manuela* Petition against El Salvador"). The state, however, has consistently denied those allegations, which as of 2018 remain unproven.

Even where the mother's conduct may have unintentionally contributed to an abortion (Nicaraguan law designates this conduct as *aborto imprudente* [imprudent/negligent abortion]), the criminal statutes of El Salvador, Guatemala, and Nicaragua specifically provide that no penalty shall apply for such cases.[27] Mexico's Federal Criminal Code also provides that a miscarriage resulting from a woman's imprudence is not subject to criminal punishment.[28] Similarly, nearly all criminal laws in Mexican state laws provide no criminal punishment for involuntary miscarriages, even if caused by negligence or imprudence.[29]

Some statutes mandate humane disposition of miscarried fetuses and authorize the issuance of fetal death certificates. For instance, Chile's Decreto 216/03 orders surrender of fetal remains for burial upon parental request, as well as the issuance of a death certificate or a "fetal death and fetal mortality statistic" certificate, depending on whether the child was born alive.[30] In 2017, Paraguay also passed a law allowing fetal death certificates for children who die in spontaneous abortions.[31]

*Indirect Abortion Distinguished.* No statute in a state party to the American Convention penalizes a woman where fetal death occurs as the unintended result of life-saving medical treatment or procedure.[32] Indirect abortion resulting from medical treatment on a pregnant woman, where the physician's intent is to treat her condition, not to end the life of her unborn child, is not subject to criminal punishment by law under any of the region's criminal statutes. Such situations, which tend to be very rare in practice, could include treatment of ectopic pregnancy, uterine cancer during the first trimester of pregnancy, preeclampsia and other maternal conditions such as hypertension, and so on.[33]

Some states parties have recognized an important distinction between direct and indirect abortion. Indirect abortion is understood as a life-saving medical intervention that indirectly provokes a miscarriage, where the purpose of terminating the pregnancy is to treat the pregnant woman, not to destroy the unborn child (principle of double effect), as recognized by high courts of El Salvador, Chile, and Guatemala.[34]

Certain criminal codes explicitly provide criminal liability waivers for abortions where medical doctors perform life-saving or therapeutic medical treatment on pregnant women: for example, Guatemalan law shields physicians from criminal liability for abortion when they perform a life-saving medical procedure on the mother without the intent to "directly provoke" fetal death.[35] The Guatemalan Supreme Court, invoking the bioethical principle of double effect, held that a life-saving medical procedure that unintentionally causes fetal death—that is, indirect abortion—is not prohibited under the national criminal statute.[36] A direct abortion—that is, any act or procedure intended to destroy the human fetus—on the other hand, is subject to criminal penalties.

The laws of Paraguay and Dominica have similar provisions.[37] Paraguay explicitly exempts physicians and mothers from criminal punishment in situations involving a life-threatening condition of the mother where a medical procedure indirectly causes fetal death but is not intended to destroy the unborn child.[38] Likewise, Dominica allows this exception when the act that caused the death of the child can be proven to be "in good faith for the purpose only of preserving the life of the mother."[39]

*Forced Abortion.* The majority of criminal statutes of states parties to the American Convention penalize forced abortion (*aborto sin consentimiento de la mujer*), meaning an abortion caused without the mother's consent, and establish severe penalties for it—for instance, in Ecuador, Peru, and Uruguay.[40] In some countries like Brazil, Ecuador, El Salvador, and

Paraguay, a forced abortion is described as one where the mother's consent is absent and where fraud, duress (grave threats), or coercion (violence) has been used against her.[41] Chile categorizes forced abortion as a "crime against humanity" and imposes severe penalties, comparable to those for genocide or war crimes.[42]

In addition to standard criminal penalties for abortion, aggravated penalties apply to persons who provoke or participate in a forced abortion in Argentina, Bolivia, Brazil, Colombia, Costa Rica, Guatemala, Mexico, Nicaragua, and Suriname.[43] Some criminal codes, such as the Guatemalan, Nicaraguan, and Mexican codes, mandate aggravated penalties where a forced abortion involved fraud, threats, or violence to the mother.[44] Nicaraguan law establishes aggravated professional sanctions for physicians who engage in forced abortions, such as suspension of professional authorization to practice medicine or to provide any health care services for up to ten years.[45]

Criminal laws of Panama also provide for aggravated penalties for husbands or unmarried partners who force a woman to abort.[46] Ecuador, Panama, Paraguay, Peru, and Suriname have additional punishments when a forced abortion results in the mother's death.[47] In addition, Ecuador's criminal code provides for aggravated penalties for perpetrators of sexual assault or human trafficking who force their victims to abort.[48]

*Fetal Homicide.* Fetal homicide, *aborto preterintencional* or *aborto culposo* in Spanish, is regarded as a crime in the majority of states parties to the American Convention; it is usually defined as a fetal death resulting from acts of violence against a pregnant woman.[49] Imprisonment penalties usually apply only where the perpetrator is aware of the woman's pregnancy or her state was noticeable at the time the crime was committed—for instance, in Argentina, Bolivia, Chile, Guatemala, Honduras, and Peru.[50] Other countries, however, punish fetal homicide even in cases where a woman's state of pregnancy was unknown to the perpetrator, but only if culpability, negligence, or imprudence existed on his part—for example, in Bolivia, Colombia, Ecuador, El Salvador, and Nicaragua.[51]

In addition to imprisonment sanctions, some countries, like Bolivia, establish community service penalties.[52] Others, like Costa Rica and Peru, explicitly mandate fines or civil sanctions for fetal homicide.[53] Some criminal codes, such as Nicaragua's, apply professional sanctions for medical malpractice cases resulting in fetal death, which is treated as fetal homicide for statutory purposes.[54] The criminal codes of some nations also include aggravated penalties for a husband or unmarried partner who causes a miscarriage through acts of violence against a pregnant woman—for instance, in Panama, Paraguay, and Uruguay.[55] Moreover, an act of violence against a pregnant woman that ultimately results in fetal death can receive an aggravated penalty in domestic violence trials in Bolivia and Costa Rica.[56]

Like the American Convention's article 4(5), Dominica's Offences against the Person Act prohibits the execution of pregnant women: "[W]here a woman convicted of an offence punishable with death is found, in accordance with the provisions of the Act, to be pregnant, the sentence to be passed on her shall be a sentence of imprisonment for life instead of sentence of death."[57] A state report to the Convention on the Rights of the Child (CRC) Committee affirmed that the legislators' intention here was to preserve the life of the unborn child.[58] Jamaica's Offences against the Person Act contains a similar provision.[59]

*Fetal Injury.* The crime of fetal injury is usually defined as nonlethal injuries perpetrated on a human fetus and resulting in harmful consequences to his or her health or development, either as a result of violent acts against a pregnant woman or medical malpractice—for example, in Colombia's criminal statutory definition.[60] Nicaragua and El Salvador define "fetal injury" more narrowly as any act causing bodily harm that gravely affects fetal development or provokes serious or permanent physical or mental injury in an unborn child.[61]

Provisions on fetal injury are usually found in newer criminal statutes, adopted subsequent to the ratification of the American Convention: the Peruvian Criminal Code, for instance, was amended in 2002 to include fetal injury, among things.[62] Penalties consist in imprisonment and professional sanctions for physicians or health professionals—for instance, in Colombia and Nicaragua.[63] El Salvador also punishes fetal injury with civil fines.[64]

Several states parties to the convention further protect the unborn's health and personal integrity by prohibiting prenatal paternity testing, embryonic research, and cloning or genetic modification. For instance, Ecuador's Code of Childhood and Adolescence orders that no paternity deoxyribonucleic acid (DNA) tests be performed on an unborn child.[65] Peru's Code of Children and Adolescents protects the unborn child's life from embryonic research or genetic modification that may be contrary to his or her integrity and development.[66] Ecuador's Constitution and the criminal codes of Panama and Guatemala contain similar provisions.[67]

Chile's Human Genome Act also protects the human embryo by prohibiting human cloning, whether reproductive or therapeutic; embryonic stem cell research; and any research that involves the "destruction, death, [or] severe or permanent injury in a human being."[68] Argentina's new civil code prohibits any practice directed to genetically modify a human embryo, affecting his or her offspring.[69] The code recognizes the need to protect human embryos before implantation and establishes that further legislation shall be adopted for that purpose.[70] El Salvador's Act on Comprehensive Protection of Children and Adolescents prohibits genetic or medical research that may place the human embryo's "life, physical integrity or dignity" at risk, as well as ethnic, cultural, or social practices that may have a similar effect, and includes a mandatory reporting requirement.[71]

### Elective Abortion

Elective abortion—that is, the induced or procured abortion of a human embryo or fetus upon the mother's request or otherwise involving her consent—is called *aborto inducido* (induced abortion), *aborto consentido* (consensual abortion), or *aborto con consentimiento de la mujer* (abortion with a woman's consent) in states parties' criminal statutes. Elective induced abortion is consistently punished by criminal law in states parties to the American Convention. Mitigated penalties can legally apply to mothers under domestic criminal laws—for example, when the woman has acted under duress or been subject to fraud. Criminal sanctions for mothers may be waived where "the consequences of the infraction affect the perpetrator in such a serious way, that criminal punishment becomes unnecessary," such as in some elective abortions, or under *estado de necesidad* (state of necessity—e.g., risk to the mother's life).

In practice, the primary effect of abortion prohibitions in protecting prenatal life appears to be deterrence, since mothers are very rarely prosecuted, whereas abortion providers may face serious criminal, civil, and professional penalties for performing abortions and even more serious sanctions where women are injured in the process.[72] Enforcement of abortion prohibitions on women or convictions of pregnant women who abort are uncommon; enforcement on abortion providers, however, is more frequent. For instance, the Chilean Constitutional Court found that only 378 women had been prosecuted for abortion between 2005 and 2016, a span of eleven years, and only 148 of them had been convicted (an average of about 13 per year).[73] Abortion rights advocacy organizations presenting at IACHR hearings have also indicated that criminal penalties for abortion are very rarely applied and have "almost exclusively a symbolic value."[74]

Common enforcement of abortion bans in the region tends to consist in arrests of abortion clinic owners and providers and detention and conviction of individuals who sell or distribute abortifacient drugs to pregnant women seeking to abort.[75] One reason for this practice may be that selective prosecutions are often allowed by statute; for instance, the Honduran Criminal Procedure Code grants the prosecutor's office prosecutorial discretion against crimes that have a maximum penalty of five years' imprisonment (elective abortion is one of them) where the accused is not dangerous and the public interest is not greatly affected.[76]

*Criminal Sanctions for Mothers and Abortion Providers.* Criminal statutes of states parties to the American Convention establish criminal liability of mothers who intentionally abort their own children, regardless of whether they induced their own abortion or had the abortion performed by a third party.[77] Criminal penalties generally consist of imprisonment and are relatively light, often subject to commutation: criminal statutes of most states parties to the American Convention impose six months to three years imprisonment for mothers who abort—for instance, in Bolivia, Brazil, Colombia, Costa Rica, Ecuador, Panama, and Suriname.[78] Criminal codes of Argentina and Chile establish similar imprisonment penalties of up to four years.[79]

Chile reconsidered these penalties during the criminal code reform in 2017, and legislators chose to maintain them even though they created three statutory provisions for nonpunishment of abortion.[80] Penalties range from a maximum of five to nine years in the Dominican Republic, El Salvador, Haiti, and Honduras to a maximum of ten years in Grenada.[81] On the other hand, some states establish significantly lighter sentences, such as up to two years in Nicaragua, Paraguay, and Peru, where community service is also applicable, and up to nine months' imprisonment in Uruguay, the only national jurisdiction to allow first-trimester abortions in the region, where the criminal code applies only beyond the first trimester.[82]

The most severe penalties in the region are theoretically established by the Jamaican Offences against the Person Act of 1864, which establishes a penalty of life imprisonment and hard labor for mothers who abort their children.[83] Likewise, Dominica establishes a life imprisonment penalty—equivalent to infanticide or homicide in terms of punishment—for the crime of "child destruction," that is, late-term abortions starting at twenty-eight weeks gestation, which the Offenses against the Person Act identifies as the point of viability.[84] There is no publicly available evidence, however, that these provisions have ever been enforced.

Imprisonment punishments are ordinarily equal for the mother who aborted her child and the individual who performed the abortion in Argentina, Bolivia, Colombia, Grenada, Dominican Republic, El Salvador, Guatemala, and Haiti.[85] Sanctions are more severe for abortion practitioners in Ecuador, Nicaragua, Panama, Paraguay, Peru, and Uruguay, but they are more severe for mothers in the criminal statutes of Chile and Jamaica.[86]

Individuals who perform elective abortions, regardless of their methods, may generally be punished with imprisonment sanctions in states parties. Sentences range from a maximum of two to twelve years in different countries. For example, sentences are up to two years in Dominica and Uruguay; up to three years in Bolivia, Costa Rica, Ecuador, Jamaica, and Nicaragua; up to four years in Argentina, Peru, and Suriname; up to five years in Dominican Republic and Paraguay; up to six years in Panama; up to eight years in Guatemala and Chile; and up to twelve years in El Salvador.[87] Parole requirements and civil fines may also apply in the Dominican Republic.[88]

Health care professionals who perform abortions may be subject to aggravated jail penalties in most states parties. Aggravated prison sentences for performing or facilitating abortions may apply to any person who practices the healing arts, including, in most countries, physicians, surgeons, midwives, nurses, pharmacists, other health care personnel, medical students, residents or interns, assistants to a health professional, and even abortifacient drug manufacturers or salespersons.[89] Individuals who routinely perform abortions may receive additional jail sentences in Bolivia and Suriname.[90] The criminal laws of Jamaica and Haiti also provide for hard labor sanctions.[91]

In many states parties to the American Convention, courts may also apply civil fines and professional sanctions to individuals who perform elective abortions. For instance, in Honduras, civil fines may apply for physicians, medical students, paramedics, nurses, or midwives who participate in induced abortions.[92] Costa Rica and Suriname also impose civil fines on those who perform abortions and those who advertise or sell abortifacient drugs, substances, instruments, or procedures.[93] Professional sanctions, including temporary suspension from professional practice, may apply to health care professionals, nonprofessional midwives, or pharmacists who "abuse their science or knowledge" by performing or assisting in abortions in Argentina, Brazil, El Salvador, Guatemala, Mexico, Nicaragua, Peru, and Suriname.[94]

Some jurisdictions also establish criminal penalties for anyone who directly or indirectly aids and abets an elective abortion, such as by counseling a woman to get an abortion, assisting her in obtaining an abortion, or paying for one. For instance, the Dominican Republic's criminal code provides for six months' to two years' imprisonment for any person who facilitates communication between an abortionist and a pregnant woman if the abortion actually takes place.[95] El Salvador similarly prohibits advising a pregnant woman to get an abortion, paying for a woman's abortion, or otherwise assisting her in getting the abortion—all of which can lead to relatively light jail sanctions.[96] Uruguay's criminal code also establishes jail penalties for those who participate directly or indirectly in an illegal induced abortion, that is, one that does not fit into the criminal punishment exemptions provided by law.[97]

Attempted abortion is an absolutory excuse in most states parties to the American Convention, with a few exceptions. In Argentina, Bolivia, Guatemala, and Haiti, for example, criminal codes specifically stipulate that no penalty shall be imposed for attempted abortion.[98] On the other hand, Jamaica's criminal statute imposes criminal penalties for attempted abortion.[99] Paraguay punishes only the abortionist for attempted abortion, not the woman who seeks it.[100] Grenada punishes attempted forced abortion and attempted fetal homicide but does not punish attempted elective abortion.[101]

While mothers who intentionally abort their children may be subject to imprisonment, most jurisdictions establish mitigating factors that may reduce or waive criminal penalties. The most common mitigating factor in the criminal laws of several states parties is *honoris causa* motivation, that is, when a woman aborted or was assisted in aborting for the purpose of hiding her dishonor. This antiquated mitigating factor may be based on the recognition of social stigma attached to unwed pregnancy in traditional societies and still warrants a reduced sentence for mothers and abortionists in Uruguay, Bolivia, Chile, and Costa Rica.[102] Judges are given discretion to waive all criminal responsibility for *honoris causa* motivation on a case-by-case basis in Guatemala and in Uruguay, where the criminal code applies to cases beyond the first trimester.[103] A perpetrator of incest, however, may not invoke the *honoris causa* mitigating factor when he coerced his victim to abort in Uruguay.

The Mexican Federal Criminal Code allows for a similar mitigating factor, namely, a reduced sentence if the woman who aborted had a "good reputation," if her pregnancy was the product of an "illegitimate" relationship, and if her state of pregnancy was unknown to others.[104] In contrast, the Honduran Criminal Code eliminated this factor during the 1996 reform.[105] It was also eliminated as a mitigating factor in Nicaragua and Ecuador.[106]

A few states parties to the convention also establish other circumstances, such as rape, physical or mental health condition of the mother, the unborn child's disability, and parental poverty as mitigating—not exculpatory—factors. For example, rape or error in artificial insemination can be a mitigating factor in Peru, but a criminal police investigation is legally required in both instances.[107] A mother's grave or serious health condition can be a mitigating factor in Uruguay after the first trimester.[108] In Guatemala, a mother's pregnancy-related psychological disorder may decrease her sentence for induced abortion.[109] In Costa Rica, an abortion under six months' gestation may result in mitigated penalties.[110] The Peruvian criminal code establishes mitigated penalties for an abortion where a child can be proven to potentially suffer serious physical or mental disabilities, but a medical diagnosis is required.[111] Economic distress, or *angustia económica*, is a mitigating factor in Paraguay and after the first trimester in Uruguay.[112]

Virtually all states parties to the American Convention mandate aggravated penalties for abortion providers where an induced abortion procedure results in a woman's death or severe injury. According to Brazilian law, sentences are increased by one-third if the mother is severely injured and are duplicated if she dies as a result of the abortion.[113] Argentina, Bolivia, Costa Rica, Ecuador, Guatemala, Paraguay, Peru, and Uruguay contemplate similar criminal sanctions.[114]

*Abortifacient Drugs.* Generally, criminal codes of states parties to the convention prohibit abortions performed "by any method."[115] Many, however, specifically penalize the advertisement and distribution of abortifacient drugs or substances (called medication abortion in the United States).[116] For instance, Brazilian criminal law punishes the advertisement of "methods, substances or objects designed to provoke abortion."[117] Dominica's Offenses against the Person Act, like those of other Caribbean nations, prohibits giving a pregnant woman "any poison or other noxious thing" that would cause an abortion, and it establishes a penalty of two years' imprisonment for individuals who violate that norm.[118] Likewise, the Dominican Republic prohibits the sale or use of any abortifacient substances.[119]

The highest courts of five Latin American states parties—Argentina, Chile, Ecuador, Honduras, and Peru—have upheld bans on so-called emergency contraception due to its abortifacient effects. In *Portal de Belén—Asociación Civil sin Fines de Lucro v. Ministerio de Salud y Acción Social de la Nación*, the Argentinian Supreme Court revoked the ministry of health's authorization to produce, distribute, or sell an emergency contraception drug called Imediat due to its abortifacient effects and on the grounds that it violated the human embryo's right to life.[120] The court declared that Argentina is under an international obligation, in virtue of its ratification of international treaties to protect human life from the moment of conception, holding that any method that prevents implantation of the embryo is considered to be abortifacient.[121]

Both Chile's Supreme Court and its Constitutional Court rejected emergency contraception drugs as unconstitutional on two occasions.[122] First, in 2001, the Supreme Court reversed sanitary registration for Postinal, a drug that was determined to be an abortifacient and potentially in violation of the unborn human being's right to life.[123] In 2008, the Constitutional Court banned the sale and distribution of the said "emergency contraception" in the country's public health facilities due to the drug's abortifacient effects by declaring the executive regulation unconstitutional, namely the "Normas Nacionales sobre Regulación de Fertilidad" (National Norms on Fertility Regulation) on hormonal emergency contraception.[124]

The Constitutional Court also held that persons under Chilean jurisdiction were entitled to life from conception, understood as fertilization, and that when doubt exists, judicial interpretation that favors the unborn's right to life shall prevail over arguments that seek to obliterate that right. The court held that the verdict had *erga omnes* effects; in other words, it was applicable to both individuals and governmental agencies. In 2010, Chilean legislators passed a statute regulating state subsidy of family planning methods that specifically excluded from the category of approved contraceptives drugs or methods designed to "directly provoke an abortion."[125]

Ecuador's Constitutional Court also held that an emergency contraception drug was unconstitutional by reversing sanitary registration and authorization for distribution of Postinor, given that its main component, levonorgestrel, prevented implantation of the human embryo in the uterus. The court found that this violated the right to life from conception, which is protected under article 49 of the Ecuadorian Constitution.[126] It also ordered a revision of similar drugs that had been previously registered by an agency of the ministry of health.

In 2009, Peru's Constitutional Court banned the free distribution of the morning-after pill as a national health policy in virtue of its national constitution and the American Convention on human rights.[127] It also ordered that laboratories that produced, sold, or distributed the drugs include a warning on their labels that the product could inhibit the implantation of the embryo.

In 2011, the Constitutional Chamber of the Honduran Supreme Court gave a favorable consultative opinion on a bill prohibiting the use, distribution, and commercialization of emergency contraception due to its abortifacient effects on the human embryo.[128] The court ruled that the drug's potential to prevent implantation of the human embryo in the uterine lining would have an abortifacient effect, which would be incompatible with public policy granted in favor of the human embryo or zygote. In 2009, the ministry of health had issued Executive Decree 2744, prohibiting emergency contraception along the same terms, but emergency contraception later became de facto available in the country.[129]

The Guatemalan Supreme Court has also held that contraceptive methods that do not prevent conception, but only implantation of the human embryo in the uterus, can be categorized as abortifacient.[130] In addition, the Inter-American Commission on Human Rights has reported that emergency contraception is de facto unavailable in other countries like Costa Rica and Nicaragua, given a general understanding that the drug is illegal due to its abortifacient effects.[131] It is also de facto illegal in El Salvador, where the Children's Code indicates that sexual and reproductive health services shall ensure and promote respect for human life from conception.[132]

## Statutory Provisions for Nonpunishment of Abortion

A slight majority of states parties to the American Convention (fourteen out of twenty-three) establish one or more types of exemptions from criminal punishment for abortions that nevertheless remain illegal. States parties usually designate these punishment exemptions as *supuestos de aborto no punible* (requirements or prerequisites for the nonpunishment of abortion), *excusas absolutarias* (absolutory excuses), or *supuestos de inexigibilidad* (requirements for nonenforcement, nonexactability or nondemandability). The Chilean abortion statute and the Colombian Constitutional Court use the word *causales*, which can be translated as "grounds" for nonpunishment of abortion.

As the terms themselves indicate, requirements for nonenforcement of abortion bans are situations where legislators recognize the existence of a crime but decide to waive criminal punishment in certain situations defined by statute. Such requirements are characteristic of Romano-Germanic criminal law in general, and thus of most European and Latin American legal systems, but have little or no equivalent in Anglo-American law, as noted by comparative law scholars.[133] Such nonpunishment must be understood to depenalize (not decriminalize) abortion in the narrow linguistic sense, in that it removes criminal penalties for abortion under certain circumstances.[134] It is unlike decriminalization, in the broad sense, in that even in these select circumstances abortion remains criminal, despite its lack of any legal penalty.

The Supreme Courts of Mexico, Bolivia, and El Salvador have explained the nature of these provisions for nonpunishment of abortion. The Bolivian Constitutional Court explained that where statutory requirements are met, the nonenforcement of abortion bans is a waiver of criminal penalty that does not imply a legal entitlement to abort under some set of circumstances, nor a duty of the state to provide legal protection for abortion in those situations.[135] Chilean Constitutional Court judges explained that a mere penalty waiver does not constitute a "justification" for abortion, nor does it turn abortion into "licit conduct"; instead, abortion continues to be a crime but is unenforceable (*inexigible*) by means of penalty.[136]

The Mexican Supreme Court distinguished "absolutory excuses" for abortion from *eximentes de responsabilidad* ("exculpatory defenses," where the word "excuse" is commonly used in Anglo-American law, such as for insanity or mistake of fact). The court indicated that absolutory excuses involve situations where someone has actually committed a crime under the law but where a statutory punishment exemption nevertheless prevents the application of the corresponding penalty.[137] Such exemptions are not, as in lawful killings, *ex ante* permissions, but rather *ex post* excuses, where conduct is criminal but not subject to criminal punishment, the court explained. They do not relieve the subject of personal criminal culpability; they merely relieve him or her of the sanction or punishment.[138]

The Argentinian statement at the Beijing World Conference on Women illustrates a similar understanding: "[T]he Argentine delegation participated in the consensus on [the section recommending] that Governments should consider reviewing laws containing punitive measures against women who have undergone abortions. This position was taken in view of the legal tradition of Argentina, the practice of our courts and the attenuating circumstances that have generally been considered; this does *not* constitute, however, a proposal to decriminalize abortion or exempt from criminal responsibility those who may be accomplices or participants in this offence."[139]

Analogous exemptions from punishment for other crimes can be found in criminal laws of some states parties. For instance, scholars have compared absolutory excuses for abortion to criminal waivers for the crime of theft or fraud between close relatives, where some legislatures have waived criminal penalties for the sake of preserving family unity, the idea being that criminal sanctions would do more harm than good to the family relationship.[140] Some jurisdictions also waive punishment in cases of involuntary manslaughter "where the consequences of the infraction affect the perpetrator in such a serious way, that criminal punishment becomes unnecessary," such as in the accidental death of a child at the hands of his or her parent.[141] Punishment exemptions under these circumstances, however, do not turn theft, fraud, or manslaughter into a legally permissible act, much less into one that is justified or that constitutes a legal entitlement.

### A Comparative Look at States Parties' Provisions for Nonpunishment of Abortion and Constitutional Reasoning

*"Life of the Mother" Requirement.* A majority of states parties to the American Convention (fourteen out of twenty-three) explicitly waive punishment for abortion where the mother is affected with a life-threatening condition.[142] State parties' statutory definitions of a "life of the mother" requirement may vary and do not necessarily include intentional, voluntary abortion. Chile's life of the mother provision, for instance, was interpreted by Constitutional Court justice Domingo Hernández Emparanza as allowing only indirect, not direct, abortion.[143] Dominica, Guatemala, and Paraguay have statutory provisions to that effect.

Criminal statutes typically require that abortion under these circumstances be used only as a measure of last resort, and many require proof that there are no other means to save the mother's life. For instance, Brazil's criminal code calls this ground for nonpunishment of abortion *aborto necessário* (necessary abortion), allowing it only "if there is no other way to save the pregnant woman's life" and if the abortion is performed by a physician.[144] Peru designates the criminal punishment exemption as *aborto terapéutico* (therapeutic abortion) and requires that the abortion be the "only means" to save a pregnant woman's life.[145]

The criminal codes of Argentina, Bolivia, Costa Rica, and Ecuador contain broader language exempting abortion from criminal punishment if carried out to avoid "endangerment" to the life of the mother, rather than imminent death, but they add that the abortion shall be allowed only if the risk "cannot be avoided through any other means."[146] Likewise, Uruguay's criminal law requires "grave" risk to the woman's life beyond the first trimester and requires that attempts be made to preserve the fetus's life.[147] Jamaica has no legislative provision allowing these abortions, but it has reported that a life-of-the-mother requirement is legally allowed on the basis of common law.[148]

Generally, medical authorization or a formal recommendation by an ethics committee is required and, only rarely, judicial authorization. The Mexican Federal Criminal Code, which applies in federal jurisdiction only—for example, in maritime or federal territory such as Mexican embassies or consulates—requires the favorable opinion of two medical doctors "where possible" and if the delay would not pose a risk to the mother's life.[149] Colombian law requires a determination that carrying a pregnancy to term "represents a risk" to the life of the mother, as certified by one physician.[150]

The Barbados Medical Termination of Pregnancy Act similarly requires the opinion of two physicians, acting in "good faith, that the continuance of the pregnancy would involve risk to the life of the pregnant woman."[151] Further, abortions after twenty weeks gestation may require the recommendation of three physicians and the determination that the abortion is "immediately necessary to save the life of the pregnant woman."[152] Panama requires "grave" or serious medical circumstances that endanger the mother's life, to be determined by a multidisciplinary commission, appointed by the minister of health, and allows physicians who conscientiously object to abortion to refuse to perform the procedure.[153] The Bolivian Criminal Code requires judicial authorization.[154]

*"Health of the Mother" Requirement.* Fewer than half of all jurisdictions in the region (nine out of twenty-three) waive penalties for abortion in situations where pregnancy poses nonlethal health risks to the mother.

In contrast with nonparties to the convention like the United States, where the health exception is broadly construed, the health ground has been narrowly defined in states parties to the American Convention.[155] In these jurisdictions, the health ground for nonpunishment of abortion applies only to instances of "grave" or "serious" risk to the mother's physical, not mental health (with the exception of Colombia), and where that risk cannot be avoided through any other means than the interruption of pregnancy.

For instance, Peru, which designates this ground for nonpunishment of abortion as *aborto terapéutico*, requires that abortion be the "only way" to avoid "grave and permanent injury" to the mother's physical health.[156] The criminal codes of Argentina, Bolivia, Costa Rica, and Ecuador require proof that the risk to the mother's health cannot be avoided using any means other than abortion.[157] Fewer than half of all the Mexican states allow for this criminal punishment exemption, and those that do only allow it upon a serious or grave health condition.[158] The Barbados Medical Termination of Pregnancy Act requires a determination that the mother may suffer "grave permanent injury" to her physical or mental health for an abortion beyond twenty weeks' gestation.[159] Grenada's health ground for nonpunishment of abortion includes a good faith requirement, allowing procedures carried out "in good faith and without negligence for the purpose of medical or surgical treatment of a pregnant woman," even if a procedure "causes or is intended to cause" a miscarriage, premature delivery, or the child's death.[160] Uruguay's criminal code requires the existence of "grave" health-related reasons beyond the first trimester and mandates that attempts be made to preserve the fetus's life, if possible, without causing harm to the mother's health.[161]

Generally, a formal medical recommendation is required, and under limited circumstances, judicial authorization. For example, the Barbados Medical Termination of Pregnancy Act requires a good faith opinion of one physician that the continuance of the pregnancy would involve risk to the health of the mother.[162] Moreover, the act instructs that the physician carrying out the risk assessment "must take into account the pregnant woman's social and economic environment, whether actual or foreseeable," meaning that additional factors such as poverty may indirectly lift punishment for abortion under this provision.[163]

In Bolivia, abortions after the twenty-week gestation period under the health provision may require the recommendation of three physicians who certify that the abortion is "immediately necessary . . . to prevent grave permanent injury to the physical and mental health of the woman."[164] Judicial authorization is required before such abortions are performed.[165] Colombia is probably the most liberal jurisdiction in regard to this requirement. Colombia's Constitutional Court created a criminal punishment exemption for the physical or mental health of the mother and included a requirement of certification by one physician for this ground, which it later waived in individual cases as discussed below.[166]

*Rape/Incest Requirement.* Around half of all states parties to the American Convention (twelve out of twenty-three) make criminal punishment exemptions for the abortion of unborn children conceived in sexual crimes, typically rape and incest.[167] The criminal codes of Barbados and Bolivia exempt mothers and any party involved in the abortion of a child conceived in the commission of any sexual crime.[168] The codes of Brazil, Panama, and Uruguay specifically refer to "rape" only, not incest.[169] In addition, the Brazilian criminal code waives culpability for this factor as long as a physician performed the abortion.[170] Brazilian Act 12845 of 2013 mandates that rape victims be given "pregnancy prophylactic" treatment, which probably alludes to emergency contraception rather than abortifacient drugs.[171]

Judges in Costa Rica are given discretion to waive all criminal responsibility for this factor on a case-by-case basis.[172] Jamaica has no legislative provision allowing abortion of those conceived in rape, but has reported allowing it on the basis of common law.[173] The Federal Criminal Code of Mexico and the codes of several Mexican states include rape as a requirement for nonpunishment of abortion.[174] Likewise, the federal Victim's General Law (Ley General de Víctimas) was amended in 2013 to authorize "access to services of emergency contraception and elective interruption of pregnancy" in cases of rape.[175] The statute applies to federal, state, and municipal public hospitals.[176]

In addition, the highest courts of Argentina and Colombia created a new statutory provision for nonpunishment of abortion in cases of rape in their jurisdictions. The criminal code of Argentina formerly allowed abortions of those conceived in rape only where the mother could be categorized as mentally disabled or insane.[177] This rather eugenic requirement was essentially designed to prevent the birth of mentally disabled children.[178] Ecuador has a similar stipulation at present.[179]

In 2012 in its *F.A.L.* decision, the Argentinian Supreme Court interpreted the criminal code to allow the abortion of children conceived in rape for any pregnant woman or child, regardless of her mental health.[180] It also held that judicial authorization should not be required; only a sworn affidavit by the woman stating that she was a victim of sexual assault would be necessary, a controversial holding that would allow sexual aggressors to escape prosecution.[181] The court recognized an individual right of conscientious objection to abortions but suggested that institutions may not have a right to object to performing abortions.[182]

The *F.A.L.* decision was not, however, readily accepted in all Argentinian provinces. Even though the Argentinian Supreme Court has federal jurisdiction, its decisions do not generally have *erga omnes* effects; that is, they bind only the parties to a particular dispute.[183] In this case, however, where the issue involved the Province of Chubut, the court ordered that all Argentinian provinces issue their own protocols or regulations allowing for the abortion of children conceived in rape and that both provincial and federal courts abstain from denying access to the said abortions—a mandate that seemed to exceed the court's authority, according to some Argentinian state officials, jurists, and scholars.[184]

As of 2019, around half of all provinces (thirteen out of twenty-five) have passed regulations for abortions of children conceived in rape, and some lower courts have refused to comply with the Supreme Court decision.[185] In June 2015, the Argentinian Federal Health Ministry issued an executive regulation, the Protocol for Comprehensive Care of Persons with a Right to Interruption of Pregnancy (Protocolo para la atención integral de las personas con derecho a la interrupción del embarazo), which sought to enforce the *F.A.L.* decision's expansion of the rape ground for nonpunishment of abortion in provincial jurisdiction.[186] Its implementation, however, remains weak, given that some provinces, including Buenos Aires, Córdoba, Mendoza, and Tucumán, have rejected its adoption.[187]

Similarly, rape used to be only a mitigating factor for abortion in Colombia but became a criminal punishment exemption via Constitutional

Court Judgment C-355.[188] Prior to the ruling, when rape was a mitigating factor, penalties for aborting a child conceived in rape could be lessened up to three-quarters of the full prison term, and judges had discretion to waive penalties entirely under "extraordinary circumstances."[189] The judgment converted mitigation for rape into a provision for nonpunishment of abortion, stating that abortion would not constitute a crime when pregnancy resulted from sexual assault, rape, or any nonconsensual sexual act, but only if the act was properly denounced before authorities.[190] One of the court's chambers subsequently rejected the requirement for a police report in an individual implementation ruling (*sentencia de tutela*).[191]

Most countries that allow absolutory excuses for the abortion of a child conceived in rape require that the abortion be performed within a certain period, as well as requiring a criminal complaint and sometimes judicial authorization. These requirements may significantly limit the practice, since this particular ground for abortion has greater potential for manipulation where no criminal report or investigation is required. For instance, Panama requires a criminal complaint, corroborated in summary instruction with judicial authorization, and prohibits abortions under the rape requirement after the first two months of pregnancy.[192] Uruguay's abortion law requires a criminal complaint and allows the abortion only within the first fourteen weeks of pregnancy.[193]

Chile's law places a similar gestational limit of twelve weeks' gestation for adult women and fourteen weeks' gestation for pregnant minors but does not require a criminal complaint, even though health personnel are subject to mandatory reporting duties.[194] Judge Hernández Emparanza's concurring opinion in the judgment that upheld the statute suggested that any regulations of the act should ensure that the mother's motivations are based on the actual existence of a sexual crime rather than a procedural subterfuge to obtain an otherwise unlawful abortion.[195] A loose application of this criminal punishment exemption, he emphasized, would be unconstitutional, he said.

The Argentinian *F.A.L.* decision, on the other hand, required only a sworn affidavit by the alleged victim.[196] Barbados law likewise requires only a "written statement of a pregnant woman stating that she reasonably believes that her pregnancy was caused by an act of rape or incest."[197] In addition, the Panamanian criminal code also specifically recognizes the right of physicians or other health care personnel to refuse to perform these abortions for reasons of conscience, whether religious or not.

Bolivia's criminal code used to require that the victim press criminal charges and that the abortion be judicially authorized, but Bolivia's Constitutional Court struck this requirement down in 2014 as unconstitutional.[198] It held that a woman's report to public authorities at a health facility should suffice to authorize the practitioner to perform the abortion.[199] The Constitutional Court nevertheless cited its prior decisions reiterating the holding that the state could, through its legislature, constitutionally choose to punish most abortions through criminal law, and it explicitly rejected the existence of a right to abortion: "[O]ur Political Constitution does not contain a supposed right to abortion nor can [abortion] be recognized as a reproductive health method."[200]

*Inviability/Eugenic Requirement.* Only about one-third (eight out of twenty-three) of states parties to the American Convention waive criminal punishment for eugenic abortion, typically the abortion of unborn children that have been medically diagnosed as nonviable, that is, suffering from a condition designated as "incompatible with life"; only three states allow it for other serious disabilities.[201] "Incompatible with life" conditions are those where the children are said to have very small chances of survival, like anencephaly or trisomy 18. Other disabilities, like a child's Down syndrome or trisomy 21 would not meet the requirement. Uruguay's abortion law, for instance, includes a limited eugenic abortion provision for nonpunishment of abortion of children who suffer from malformations that are "incompatible with extra-uterine life."[202] The law requires the favorable opinion of two physicians if the delay would not pose a health risk to the mother. In addition, the constitutional courts of Colombia and Brazil have created a eugenic ground specifically designated to authorize the abortion of anencephalic children and others whose condition is deemed to be incompatible with extrauterine life.

The Chilean criminal punishment exemption for eugenic abortion likewise applies only to unborn children suffering from a "lethal" condition that would be "incompatible with extra-uterine independent life" as determined by two separate and concurring diagnosis by "two specialist medical doctors."[203] Constitutional Court justice Hernández Emparanza suggested that a *pro homine* interpretation would require that inviability be rigorously verified by diagnosis of two subspecialists in maternal-fetal medicine rather than two obstetrician specialists who would lack the necessary expertise to properly diagnose lethal conditions in unborn children.[204] He found that the risk of an erroneous diagnosis was too great to be constitutionally tolerable when issued by a nonspecialized physician.[205]

Colombia's Constitutional Court, in Judgment C-355, also created a criminal punishment exemption for situations where the unborn child suffers from a serious condition that is diagnosed as incompatible with viability, as certified by a physician.[206] In a subsequent judgment, however, Judgment SU-096, the court applied this exception to a viable fetus that suffered from undiagnosed, nonfatal brain malformations and validated an authorization for his late-term abortion at twenty-four weeks' gestation.[207] Two vigorous dissents by Judge Cristina Pardo Schlesinger and Judge Bernal Pulido followed.

Judges Pardo and Pulido interpreted the nature and limits of the eugenic ground for abortion created in Judgment C-355. Judge Pardo indicated that the court should have strictly applied the eugenic abortion ground as established in Judgment C-355, which required fetal inviability, that is, more than mere fetal malformation or disability.[208] She found that the court's application of the eugenic ground in SU-096 was inappropriate because any abortion based on disability discrimination is unconstitutional in Colombia. She held that the purpose of the eugenic ground "is not to end the life of the unborn, but to protect the rights of the pregnant woman, and only in that way the measure becomes ethically acceptable and legally admissible."[209] Judge Bernal Pulido also pointed out that when a disability cannot be accurately diagnosed prenatally and is not categorized as "incompatible with life," it does not fall within Colombia's eugenic ground abortion, which permits only the abortion of those diagnosed as suffering from "incompatible with life" conditions.[210]

Brazil's Federal Supreme Tribunal likewise created an absolutory excuse for the abortion of anencephalic children in decision ADPF 54 in 2012.[211] The tribunal based its decision on the premise that the interruption of pregnancy due to anencephaly is not to be considered an abortion since anencephalic fetuses do not have "the ability or natural capacity to be a person" and therefore cannot be victims of the crime of abortion.[212]

The decision created jurisprudence and was therefore binding on all Brazilian states.[213]

Dissenting opinions criticized the majority's reasoning. Chief Justice Cezar Peluso wrote a dissenting opinion in which he manifested his complete disagreement with the verdict and affirmed that the anencephalic fetus is a bearer of life and that aborting him is therefore prohibited conduct.[214] He characterized appeals to personal autonomy and individual freedom as "void" and discriminatory against anencephalic fetuses and emphasized that the tribunal did not have the legitimate authority to create new legal measures.

Judge Ricardo Lewandowski dissented based on balance-of-powers arguments, indicating that the issue should have been decided by parliament, which had previously rejected legislative bills on anencephaly and abortion, and that the court exceeded its jurisdiction by legislating this instance of nonpunishment of abortion.[215] He also disagreed with the majority opinion's substantive arguments, indicating that the decision may entail future disentitlement of the right to life for other unborn children suffering from serious congenital malformations and chromosomal abnormalities.[216] Concurring Judge Gilmar Mendes agreed with the majority but conceded that the termination of pregnancy involving an anencephalic fetus was, indeed, an abortion.[217]

The Mexican Federal Criminal Code and Panama's criminal statute contain a similar criminal punishment exemption that, ironically, applies "when the unborn child's life is endangered."[218] Facially, the provision seems incoherent since an abortion would end the endangered life of the child anyway, a result that the code seeks to avoid. In Panama's criminal statute, the article's context deals with health-related issues, so the provision could be referring to either induced labor for the sake of the child's health or to children affected with conditions designated as "incompatible with life," although the latter seems more likely.[219] In any case, the code requires authorization by a multidisciplinary commission, appointed by the health minister, that would determine whether or not the child's condition is serious enough. The code also allows physicians who conscientiously object to abortion to refuse to perform the procedure.

The Barbados Medical Termination of Pregnancy Act, probably the most liberal statute in terms of the eugenic abortion provision, authorizes first-trimester abortions of children who may "suffer such physical or mental abnormalities as to be seriously handicapped."[220] Certainty of the said disability is not required, but only that a medical practitioner, in good faith, finds a "substantial risk" thereof.[221] This ground for nonpunishment of abortion in Barbados, however, only allows for abortion of fetuses of up to twelve weeks' gestational age; the statute also provides that any person may object to participating in an abortion to which he or she has a conscientious objection.[222] Although Jamaica has no legislative provision allowing eugenic abortion, it has reported allowing it on the basis of common law, but only for the most serious disabilities.[223]

*Multiple Provisions for Nonpunishment of Abortion in States Parties to the American Convention.* About one-third of all states parties to the American Convention (eight out of twenty-three) have established statutory provisions for nonpunishment of abortion under all, or almost all, of the circumstances indicated above, namely life/health, an inviability/eugenic provision, and rape. Those states are Barbados, Bolivia, Brazil, Chile, Colombia, Jamaica, Panama, and Uruguay. Abortion rights advocates have identified these as three grounds rather than four,[224] counting the life and health exemptions as one provision, perhaps because the health and life grounds can be similarly defined. Depending on the health definition, however, the life and health provisions can be two very different grounds, particularly where health is broadly defined to include mental health. In addition, rape and incest can be two different grounds where involving adults, since adult incest can involve consent.

Two countries stand out among all states parties to the convention as the most liberal jurisdictions in terms of abortion decriminalization, namely Colombia and Uruguay. Colombia has, through constitutional interpretation, broadly constructed criminal punishment exemptions to abortion. Uruguay has passed legislation allowing first-trimester abortions, which, to date, probably makes it the most liberal jurisdiction on abortion legalization among states parties to the American Convention.

Bolivia could have become one of these most liberal jurisdictions on abortion in 2017 with the criminal code reform that created eight different grounds for abortion; the code, however, was abolished by the legislature less than two months later in January 2018, at President Evo Morales's initiative.[225] The amended code's abortion provision, which was apparently drafted by a coalition of abortion rights advocacy organizations and providers including Ipas, generally maintained penalties for induced abortion, but added new grounds for abortion.[226] The latter included previously unheard-of social grounds based on a pregnant woman's or teen's social condition, namely having existing caregiving duties to an elder or child or being a student.[227] Age alone—that is, being a minor—was also an exculpatory ground for abortion with no similar precedent in the region. Press reports indicate that poverty was discussed and then ruled out as a potential ground for nonpunishment of abortion.[228]

The legislation certainly had the potential to decriminalize many abortions in practice, due to its vague language and broad social grounds. After all, caregiving duties, having other children, and being enrolled in a study program are probably ordinary situations for most Latin American girls and women. In addition, the code's loose verification requirements preempted state oversight: no medical or police reports or technical or judicial certification or authorization would have been required from a pregnant woman who requested an abortion, only a hospital form, which would have made enforcement virtually impossible.[229]

In spite of the government's reassurances that abortion had not been decriminalized in the country, the code generated a great deal of backlash from civil society, particularly from pro-life and religious organizations that expressed concern with abortion and religious freedom provisions in the new code.[230] President Morales acknowledged that "different civil society groups expressed their rejection of the law, arguing different reasons but in agreement that the new criminal code violated, rather than protected, their fundamental rights and human dignity."[231] He called legislators to pass a new criminal code that would "promote social justice and peace."[232] As of 2018, Bolivia seems to have returned to a relatively conservative abortion regime allowing criminal punishment exemptions only where the mother's life or health is endangered and following rape or incest.[233]

Ecuador likewise refused to expand legalization of abortion on multiple grounds in 2019. A legislative bill sought to legalize abortion on four grounds, namely rape, fetal malformation, and "nonconsensual insemination" (*inseminación no consentida*), a term that may or may not have alluded to error in artificial insemination procedures. The proposal fell five votes short of the seventy votes required for the National Congress to amend the criminal code.[234] Ecuador maintains existing statutory provisions on nonpunishment of abortion where the mother's life or health is endangered and in cases of rape of a mentally disabled woman.

*Nonpunishment of Abortion on Three Grounds* (Tres Causales). In 2017, the Chilean Constitutional Court upheld the constitutionality of three grounds (*tres causales*) for abortion—namely life, health of the mother, and rape—established by Act N. 21.030, which was introduced by President Michelle Bachelet and narrowly approved by congress.[235] Prior to 2017, Chile had a full abortion ban for over 140 years since 1875, as well as the lowest maternal mortality rate in Latin America.[236] The full abortion ban allowed only a narrow "therapeutic purpose exception" in the national Health Code from 1931 to 1989, which permitted only indirect abortion in situations of risk to the mother's life or health and required certification by two to three physicians.[237] The "therapeutic purpose exception" was derogated in 1989 and replaced with a similar provision, article 119 of the Health Code, which provided that no action or medical interventions may legally seek to cause a direct abortion, thus allowing only life-saving medical interventions that treat the mother's condition, not those that are intended to end the fetus's life.[238]

Several initiatives to amend the code to create additional absolutory excuses for abortion were rejected until 2017, when President Bachelet, also a previous executive director of UN Women, introduced the legislation and obtained congressional approval by a slim margin.[239] The legislative decree amended Chile's Criminal Code and Health Code to create criminal punishment exemptions to criminal abortion bans allowing both direct and indirect abortion, as indicated by the dissents, under three relatively narrow grounds: (a) risk to the mother's life, (b) fetal pathology that is "incompatible with extrauterine life, in any case, of a lethal nature," and (c) abortion of those conceived in rape up to twelve or fourteen weeks' gestation. The Constitutional Court upheld most of the bill, with the exception of conscientious objection restrictions, by a six-to-four majority.[240]

Prior to passage of the bill, the IACHR had urged Chile to abolish its full abortion ban. While the Constitutional Court was hearing the challenge against the bill, the commission held hearings in Argentina, where celebrity abortion rights advocate Isabel Allende, along with US-based Center for Reproductive Rights and others, requested the commission to contact the Chilean congress in support of the legislation.[241] The commission followed suit and urged Chilean legislators not to delay in passing President Bachelet's proposed legislation given that her term was about to expire, as it did six months later in December of 2017 when conservative president Sebastián Piñera was elected.[242]

Upon the passage of the bill, a group of congresspersons and senators that made up about one-quarter of each chamber unsuccessfully challenged the legislation as unconstitutional, invoking Chile's constitutional article 19, which mandates legal protection of prenatal life: "... the right to life and to physical and psychological integrity of the person. *The law shall protect the life of the unborn.*"[243] The Constitutional Court, however, interpreted the provision to mean that "the Constitution mandates protecting the life of the unborn [but] does not speak of protecting a right to life."[244] The court found that lawmakers had discretion in regard to protecting prenatal life and were therefore constitutionally allowed to place limitations on such protection, since the right to life is "not absolute," citing the *Artavia* judgment.[245] The court then applied a proportionality test between women's rights and a legally protected "interest" in prenatal life to conclude that women's rights must, under the three circumstances above, take precedence.[246]

Even though the judgment announced it would not deal with the ontological status of the unborn, it went on to declare that the human embryo or fetus is *not* a person under the constitution, albeit with only five out of ten judges agreeing on the issue, which may not be enough to create authoritative precedent, according to Chilean legal scholar Hernán Corral.[247] The reasoning was mostly based on a part of the constitution's legislative history, on a "dynamic" rather than originalist constitutional interpretation, on the idea that the *nasciturus* cannot benefit from the legal status of personhood until birth, and on her unique dependency on the mother for survival.[248] Despite previous constitutional precedent finding that human life begins at conception and that the unborn is a human person under the constitution, the Constitutional Court chose to rely on an alternative decision that authorized organ donation from patients diagnosed with brain death, holding that defining death was a matter for legislators to decide, among other things.[249] The Constitutional Court interpreted that decision as meaning that legislators also had historical discretion in defining the beginning of human life and that creating grounds for nonpunishment of abortion was included within those constitutional powers.[250]

Four dissenting judges found that the majority had carried out an irrational interpretation of the constitutional text and disagreed with its conclusions, indicating that the national constitution (and the civil code) contained a duty for legislators to protect the prenatal right to life from direct abortion and that reversing constitutional rights is not within the legislature's power.[251] Their dissent stated that the majority had "forced" an inappropriate reading of the terms "person" and "conception," in contradiction with legislative history, constitutional precedents, Chilean codes protecting prenatal life, the Medical Association Ethics Code (which prohibits direct abortion under all circumstances), and scholarly doctrine.[252] They also affirmed that no constitutionality test could lead to the nullification of one person's right to life over another's, citing the German Constitutional Court's recognition that "the interruption of pregnancy always constitutes the destruction of the unborn's life."[253] Dissenting judge Juan José Romero Guzmán characterized the majority's interpretation of article 19 as "argumentative gymnastics" in his dissent and pointed out that the court did only a partial reading of the relevant constitutional provision recognizing a right to life of the unborn.[254]

The decision was, in any event, relatively narrow: despite some broad statements on individual autonomy and women's rights, the Constitutional Court clarified that abortion continued to be a crime in Chile.[255] One of the judges in the majority, Hernández Emparanza, categorically rejected the idea that the law could be interpreted as creating abortion rights, which at least six other judges agreed with.[256]

In addition, the judgment struck down the legislation's prohibition of conscientious objection by institutions and by nonprofessional individual personnel in health care facilities.[257] The bill attempted to force medical doctors to perform abortions where a pregnancy resulting from rape was approaching the twelfth or fourteenth week limit for abortion, but the Constitutional Court found that provision to be unconstitutional.[258]

Despite its reference to the *Artavia* judgment, the judgment held that Inter-American Court decisions are not binding on the Chilean Constitutional Court, particularly in areas where they lack uniformity, such as conscience rights.[259] It is also worth mentioning that the act contains a couple of provisions that went unchallenged and were therefore upheld, such as that prohibiting the donation or sale of human tissue, fluid, or organs for profit or for any purpose that did not relate to the termination of pregnancy, which could have been inspired by the organ trafficking scandal surrounding Planned Parenthood in the United States.[260] The act also prohibits the advertisement of abortion clinics, abortion procedures, and abortion services for terminations that do not fit within provisions for nonpunishment of abortion.[261]

Notwithstanding the decision's limits and its rejection of a strict application of the *control de convencionalidad* doctrine, the Inter-American Commission celebrated the Constitutional Court's decision as a fundamental step in favor of women's and girls' rights.[262] The commission urged the Chilean government to ensure immediate promulgation of the bill (signing into law and publication) and encouraged other states in the region to follow in Chile's footsteps, "cognizant that the denial of the right to voluntarily interrupt a pregnancy in certain circumstances can constitute a violation of the fundamental rights of women, girls, and adolescents."[263] In addition, the CEDAW Committee called on Chile to "[e]xtend the scope of Law No. 21.030 in order to decriminalize abortion *in all cases*."[264]

In December 2018, a new executive regulation that limited individual and institutional conscience rights was struck down by the Constitutional Court.[265] The regulation would have forced health care personnel and health care institutions to perform abortions where a woman required an "immediate and urgent" (*inmediata e impostergable*) abortion.[266] It would have applied institutional conscientious objection to private hospitals only, not to public institutions or private institutions that had entered any service agreements or contracts with the public health system.[267] The regulation would have also created a duty of objecting institutions to transfer pregnant women seeking abortions to other facilities that would provide them.[268]

*Regulation of Provisions for Nonpunishment of Abortion: Clinic Regulations, Counseling Requirements, Abortions on Minors and Disabled Women.* Where statutory provisions for nonpunishment of abortion are established, states parties generally regulate abortion practices and require informed consent and counseling of pregnant women seeking abortions. The Barbados

Medical Termination of Pregnancy Act, for instance, authorizes unannounced inspection of abortion clinics and facilities: "[T]he Chief Medical Officer or other person authorized by him in writing, may at all reasonable times enter any premises for the purpose of ascertaining whether there has been any contravention of this Act or the regulations."[269] The Barbados Medical Termination of Pregnancy Regulations of 1983 mandates that any medical practitioner who carries out abortions must "be familiar with counseling functions with particular reference to family life education and child-birth."[270] Specifically, a physician who performs abortions must counsel the woman requesting the abortion, or at least ensure that a person authorized by the minister has counseled her prior to performing any abortion.[271] The act allows the minister to place residential requirements on women seeking abortions,[272] probably in order to avoid abortion tourism or evasion of foreign abortion laws. Abortion providers who violate informed consent or parental consent regulations, or perform second-trimester or late-term abortions outside of hospitals, may be subject to imprisonment and fines.[273]

In Chile, informed consent must include oral and written information on alternatives to abortion, such as social services, welfare assistance, and adoption services.[274] The national abortion statute also states that health care workers must ensure that the pregnant woman or child is not making a decision based on coercion.[275] A counselor must also advise the woman on the possible immediate and long-term effects of abortion, on methods of contraception, and on the availability of family planning services.[276] The statute refers to a pregnant woman's "right to a support program" that would include shelter, nondissuasive counseling, and prenatal health care.[277] Conscientious objection by individuals and institutions is explicitly allowed and constitutionally protected in Chile. The act's original criminal punishment exemptions for nonmedical personnel and for objections close to the end of the first trimester of pregnancy were struck down by the Constitutional Court.[278]

Similarly, the Colombian General Attorney's Office (Procuraduría) issued strict guidelines for implementation of the Constitutional Court Judgment C-355 regarding informed consent.[279] According to the guidelines, a woman requesting an abortion should be given information regarding the risks of abortion as opposed to childbirth; she should be given counseling encouraging her to carry her pregnancy to term and information on alternatives to abortion, such as medical treatment or adoption; she should also be offered ultrasound images of her unborn child.[280]

Uruguay's abortion law, which authorizes first-trimester abortions, mandates counseling of every single woman or adolescent considering abortion.[281] The Voluntary Interruption of Pregnancy Act requires physicians to refer women to a three-member committee, integrated by a gynecologist, a social worker, and a mental health professional. The committee is required by law to inform the woman about potential risks of the abortion procedure and alternatives to abortion, including adoption or social welfare government programs that may help alleviate the mother's poverty. The committee is also required to ensure that the woman considering abortion is not being coerced or pressured by third parties, to provide her with information on family planning methods, and even to interview the unborn child's father, with her consent. According to the act, counseling must aim to help the woman overcome the situation that led her to choose abortion, and it must ensure that she is making an informed decision.[282] A five-day waiting period must elapse before a woman considering abortion can sign informed consent documents and have the abortion.[283]

Where statutes allow nonpunishment of abortions on pregnant children or mentally disabled women—for example, for rape—such statutes generally require parental consent or the consent of a legal guardian.[284] Uruguay's abortion law, for instance, requires a guardian's consent *and* judicial authorization for abortions on mentally disabled women.[285] Some jurisdictions like Chile and Colombia, however, are comparably liberal in allowing abortions on minors with little to no parental consent requirements, particularly where the alleged absolutory excuse is sexual assault. In Colombia, for instance, minors over the age of fourteen are presumed to be able to give informed consent and to not require parental consent, according to the Constitutional Court's decision in C-355.[286]

Chile's abortion statute is also relatively weak in regard to parental consent and notification requirements. It requires either one-parent consent, one-parent notification, one "responsible adult" notification, or a judicial bypass, depending on whether a girl is under or above the age of fourteen years and on whether she is at risk of violence, abandonment, coercion, homelessness, or any acts that violate her integrity, as determined by a medical team.[287] Only judicial resolutions denying an abortion, not those granting it, can be subject to appeal.[288] Similar requirements apply for abortions on mentally incapacitated or intellectually disabled women.[289]

Some states parties to the American Convention, on the other hand, have legally prohibited all elective abortions on pregnant minors and disabled women subsequent to their ratification of the American Convention. For instance, criminal statutes of Bolivia and Brazil categorize abortions on pregnant children under sixteen and fourteen years of age, respectively, as forced abortions.[290] Cases of abortion on minors may be prosecuted as child abuse, as reported in Jamaica.[291] Parents who facilitate their child's induced abortion may get aggravated penalties in El Salvador, even if the child is not a minor.[292] These provisions may also apply to abortions on mentally disabled women.[293]

### First-Trimester Abortions in States Parties to the American Convention

Colombia and Uruguay stand out as the most liberal jurisdictions on abortion compared to other states parties to the American Convention. The first, because of its Constitutional Court's advocacy for a constitutional right to abortion on three grounds, the second, because of its decriminalization of first-trimester abortions. In addition, Brazil's Supreme Court has considered legally authorizing first-trimester abortions but has failed to do so as of 2018. While the Colombian Constitutional Court has advocated for the creation of a right to abortion on three grounds, Uruguay has not categorized its decriminalization of first-trimester abortions as a constitutional right per se, therefore permitting substantive regulation thereof, such as legal requirements for the procedure, in the absence of which an abortion would be illegal.

*First-Trimester Abortions in Uruguay.* Uruguay is the only national jurisdiction among states parties to the American Convention to have legally authorized first-trimester abortions; outside the first trimester, however, induced abortion continues to be a crime. In October 2012, the Uruguayan General Assembly (Asamblea General) adopted, by a narrow vote, the Voluntary Interruption of Pregnancy Act, legalizing elective abortions during the first trimester of pregnancy.[294] More liberal legislative bills were rejected in years prior, notably in 2008, when President Tabaré Vázquez, a socialist and former obstetrician, vetoed the legislation invoking article 4(1) of the American Convention.[295]

The Voluntary Interruption of Pregnancy Act (Ley de Interrupción Voluntaria del Embarazo) waives criminal penalties for all abortions performed during the first twelve weeks of pregnancy but establishes several mandatory requirements for legal abortions, in the absence of which the procedure is illegal.[296] Requirements include (a) a medical consultation or evaluation in a public hospital or a government affiliated institution; (b) that the woman inform the physician of the reasons why she wishes to terminate the pregnancy, whatever their nature (for statistics collection purposes); (c) that a three-member interdisciplinary committee counsel the woman considering abortion; and (d) that a five-day waiting period be exhausted, after which ratification of the decision to abort would be attested by signing informed consent documents.[297] According to the act, abortions beyond twelve weeks of pregnancy may only be performed under circumstances of grave risk to the mother's health or life, the child's inviability, or rape (up to fourteen weeks only, for the latter).[298]

The Uruguayan legislature included several restrictions on first-trimester abortions in the act, such as citizenship and residence requirements for women requesting abortions, perhaps in order to prevent "abortion tourism," as well as a prohibition of economic profit from abortions in the public health system or affiliated hospitals.[299] In addition, the act establishes that first-trimester abortions shall not be used as a method of birth control.[300] The act also allows for conscientious objection of physicians or health care personnel, which requires minimal formalities and is characterized as "portable" (applicable in every health institution where the objector is employed); exceptions are made only for circumstances of grave risk to the mother's life or health.[301] This right was subsequently challenged and upheld and recognized by a high administrative court (Tribunal de lo Contencioso Administrativo de Montevideo).[302]

Since 2013, the Uruguayan Health Ministry has reported an average number of about 8,923 abortions per year, with abortions increasing roughly 10 percent every year.[303] Reported reasons for abortion in 2017 were as follows: the mother's choice (99.84 percent), rape (0.01 percent), risk to the mother's health (0.06 percent), and fetal inviability (conditions incompatible with life) (0.09 percent).[304] Previous years indicated similar statistics. These numbers indicate that the overwhelming majority of elective abortions in the country were legally authorized and performed based on the child's gestational age and the mother's individual choice and that they probably would not have been legally performed under previous stipulations for nonpunishment of abortion. They also suggest that life/health, rape, and inviability situations are relatively rare in practice.

Neither the statute nor Uruguay's highest courts have created a constitutional right to abort during the first trimester, however. In addition, the issue of father's rights has been raised, and no constitutional entitlement of a pregnant woman to abort has, as of 2018, been articulated. A denial to an abortion request was reported, interestingly enough, where the unborn child's father objected to the abortion on the grounds that he was willing to raise and care for the child immediately after the birth.[305] The family court in question denied the abortion request on that basis, but the issue later became moot because the woman said that she had a miscarriage.

*First-Trimester Abortion Proposals in Brazil and Mexico.* Since 2016, members of the Brazilian Federal Supreme Court have expressed sympathy with proposals to legally authorize first-trimester abortions in Brazil, but the court itself has not ruled on the matter. In 2016, a chamber of the Brazilian Federal Supreme Court declared that temporary incarceration of abortion providers violated the right to habeas corpus; the majority opinion, written by Ministro Luis Alberto Barroso, also advocated, *in dicta*, for the decriminalization of all abortions during the first trimester of pregnancy.[306] Judges Edson Fachin and Rosa Weber sided with Barroso; two judges, Luis Fux and Marco Aurélio, dissented and would have based their decision on exclusively criminal procedure grounds.[307]

Barroso argued that the criminal code provisions banning most abortions should be interpreted to apply only beyond the first trimester and argued that the nation's Federal Constitution contained a right to women's autonomy and to physical and psychological integrity that translated into a right to abortion.[308] His basis for that conclusion was that abortion bans in the first trimester violated principles of gender equality and discriminated against poor women; he cited no legal authority.[309] Citing abortion statistics by the Guttmacher Institute and the World Health Organization

(WHO) as well as foreign decisions that have no legal effect in Brazil, such as *Roe v. Wade* and *R. v. Morgentaler*, a Canadian Supreme Court decision, he found abortion bans to be inadequate, unnecessary, and disproportionate in promoting a state interest in protecting fetal life.[310] He noted that many "democratic and developed" nations in the world allowed abortion in the first trimester.[311] He also argued that first-trimester abortion bans violated women's sexual and reproductive rights, citing soft law instruments like the Cairo and Beijing conferences, but making no reference whatsoever to the American Convention.[312]

The decision did not have *erga omnes* effects—that is, was not legally binding for anyone outside the parties to the dispute—but could create jurisprudence (*sumula vinculante*) if followed by a series of similar decisions or a decision by the Supreme Court en banc (including all of its eleven judges).[313] Notwithstanding its limited value as binding precedent and poor legal reasoning, the judgment may have had the political effect of creating momentum for those who advocate for first-trimester abortion legalization through the judiciary. In March 2018 the *Partido Socialismo e Liberdade* (PSOL, Socialism and Freedom Party) directly challenged the criminal code provisions as unconstitutional and sought the legal authorization of first-trimester abortions by the Federal Supreme Court, in Argumentation of Noncompliance of Fundamental Precept (ADPF) No. 442.[314]

As of 2019, the Federal Supreme Court has not reached a verdict on PSOL's claims, and it is uncertain that it will do so anytime soon, given the lack of a voting deadline in standard ADPF procedures such as this. Justice Rosa Weber did, however, admit the claim and conduct public hearings in August 2018 to debate legalization of first-trimester abortion, where medical doctors, public health professionals, psychologists, bioethicists, scientists, legal scholars, and religious groups presented views in favor of and against legalization of first-trimester abortions.[315]

Brazil's attorney general (Advogado-Geral da República), Grace Mendonça, questioned the court's jurisdiction to hear the claim based on balance-of-powers principles. She criticized the court's conducting of public hearings as improperly taking over the legislative role and not allowing the kind of broad debate that would take place within the National Congress, where proposals to decriminalize first-trimester abortions were already pending before the Chamber of Deputies.[316] She argued that the Supreme Court should conduct an abstract review of constitutionality and not act as a legislator in order "to create an exclusionary criminal criterion of a formal nature," that is, to decriminalize abortion in the first trimester of pregnancy.[317] Mendonça also noted that under constitutional principles the court may not act as a positive legislator, and that for the court to expand the list of grounds for nonpunishment of abortion would constitute extrapolation of political power, as the court's function is to interpret laws, not create them.

Elective abortion during the first trimester of pregnancy has also been decriminalized in Mexico's Federal District—that is, Mexico City. In 2007, the city's legislative assembly amended the district's criminal code and health act, redefining abortion as the interruption of pregnancy after the twelfth week of gestation, in contrast with virtually all Mexican states, which define abortion as the death of an unborn child from conception throughout pregnancy, even before implantation in the maternal womb.[318] The amendment legally authorized abortion on demand during the first trimester, but the city's law continues to penalize second- and third-trimester abortions that do not involve health risks, rape, or disability of the unborn child.[319]

The president of the National Human Rights Commission and the attorney general (Procurador General de la República) denounced legalization of first-trimester abortions as incompatible with Mexico's human rights obligations under the American Convention and challenged the law in May 2007 before the Federal Supreme Court.[320] In 2009, the court upheld the legislative reform in a split decision with no majority opinion.[321] There were as many dissenting opinions as judges, which showed strong discomfort with even the narrow reasoning in upholding the law. The minority opinion dissented on the basis of existing constitutional protection of the unborn child.[322]

Nonetheless, there was significant consensus on the idea that abortion decriminalization and legalization remains a matter of state sovereignty in Mexico, according to Mexico's interpretive declaration to the American Convention.[323] Following the verdict, twenty-one out of thirty-one Mexican states adopted amendments to their constitutions recognizing the unborn child's right to life from conception, some of which specifically expressed their rejection of the Federal Supreme Court decision in their legislative records.[324] In the meantime, reported abortions in Mexico City have increased from 4,799 to 18,104 per year from 2007 to 2017.[325]

### Advocacy for the Creation of Abortion Rights before High Tribunals in States Parties: A Comparative Look at Six Constitutional Decisions

No state party to the American Convention has allowed unrestricted abortion or categorized abortion as a constitutional right or a human right under the American Convention, but, instead, states parties have continued to generally prohibit elective abortion, thus creating a large body of counterpractice vis-à-vis claims arguing the existence of abortion rights. States parties' national criminal statutes continue to generally prohibit abortion, even where criminal punishment exemptions are permissible on certain grounds.

No Latin American or Caribbean national constitution contains or has explicitly been interpreted to contain "a human 'right' of women to exterminate their unborn children," as Inter-American Court judge Julio Barberis characterized abortion rights claims.[326] Colombia is alone in having granted some constitutional protection for abortions, although only in nonauthoritative judgments and only insofar as criminal punishment exemptions apply for life, health, rape, or fetal disability, not for a broad right to abort. No state party currently mandates government funding of abortions or constitutionally protects abortion providers or designates abortion rights advocates as human rights defenders.

As of 2019, no constitutional or supreme court of any state party to the American Convention has found a human right to unrestricted abortion (*aborto libre*) as deriving from that treaty, even though high courts in at least six states parties have been compelled to do so. Four national supreme courts and constitutional courts—those of Bolivia, Chile, El Salvador, and Guatemala—have found that no national or international right to abortion derives from their constitutions or international treaties ratified by them, including the convention. Supreme courts of two states parties, Mexico and Colombia, have found limited abortion rights deriving from their national constitution and primary legislation, but not from the American Convention. Chambers of the Mexican and Colombian supreme courts have referred to abortion as a constitutional and fundamental right, albeit only on limited grounds, and in semiauthoritative decisions.

Neither chamber found an unlimited right to abort outside of those grounds, based solely on the mother's choice, autonomy, or privacy.

*Colombian Constitutional Court's Right to Abortion on Three Grounds.* The Colombian Constitutional Court is alone among states parties to the American Convention in treating abortion as a constitutional right, albeit only on three grounds (life/health, rape, and eugenic abortion) which would entail an entitlement to abort at any point in pregnancy. Abortions where those grounds are absent, however, have not been decriminalized and remain technically illegal. The court, however, has never invoked the American Convention as containing or requiring the creation of a right to abortion but instead has relied on other international treaties such as the Convention on the Elimination of All Forms of Discrimination against Women (CEDAW).[327]

In 2006, the Colombian Constitutional Court amended the Criminal Code article 122 prohibition of abortion by creating what it counted as three absolutory excuses for abortion (life and health of the mother, inviability, rape or incest, the last including IVF error, which the court called "forced insemination"). In decision C-355, Colombia's Constitutional Court, headed by Judge Humberto Sierra Porto, who later went on to become a member of the Inter-American Court, derogated the criminal code provision on mitigating factors for abortion and converted it to a stipulation on grounds for nonpunishment of abortion, adding an absolutory excuse for the abortion of human fetuses conceived by error in IVF procedures and another for the abortion of inviable fetuses.[328]

Before the C-355 judgment of 2006, the Colombian Constitutional Court had upheld abortion bans in at least three previous decisions starting in 1994.[329] It had also recognized the unborn child's personhood, her entitlement to constitutional rights from the moment of conception, and her entitlement to constitutional protection under *amparo* (a constitutional writ) in at least eight previous decisions.[330] With a new composition in 2006, the court departed from its previous jurisprudence. Dissenting judges Rodrigo Escobar Gil, who later became a member of the IACHR, and Marco Gerardo Monroy Cabra, who had been a commissioner in years prior, as well as many other commentators have harshly criticized the court's judicial activism in the decision.[331]

The C-355 Constitutional Court originally rejected the existence of a right to abort arising from either its constitution or international treaties: "[N]o duty to decriminalize abortion can be inferred from constitutional and international norms, nor a prohibition for national legislators to adopt criminal laws in that area. Therefore, Congress has ample margin to configure public policy in regards to abortion."[332] The judgment also affirmed that the state had a duty to protect prenatal life since the *nasciturus*'s life is a constitutionally protected "good" (*bien de relevancia constitucional*) and that the state is not required, but may opt to protect such life through criminal law.[333] Judges Monroy Cabra and Escobar Gil maintained that the unborn child holds a fundamental right to life, not an abstract constitutionally protected interest, and in making these assertions the judges invoked the American Convention's recognition of the unborn child as a person in the preamble, article 1(2) and 4(1).[334]

Since then, however, provisions for nonpunishment of abortion evolved into a constitutional right to abortion on three grounds. Constitutional Court chambers, integrated by three-judge panels, promoted the creation of a constitutional right to abortion through a series of judgments on individual implementation called *sentencias de tutela* and *sentencias de revisión*, which according to national constitutional statutes are technically meant to affect only individual plaintiffs and not to create constitutional jurisprudence.[335] Starting in 2006, the Constitutional Court began to hear all kinds of abortion requests, thus effectively becoming an abortion authorization tribunal, something that other courts, such as El Salvador's supreme court, have actively sought to avoid.[336] Whether hearing abortion authorization requests was a proper judicial or constitutional role was not examined in much depth by the court, however.

The chambers sometimes went beyond the rules established in Judgment C-355. For instance, the Eighth Chamber ordered health care centers that had denied abortion requests to pay compensation for their failure to provide abortions, and, in one case where a child had been born, for altering the mother's "life plan" (*proyecto de vida*), a finding akin to a wrongful birth tort in US jurisdiction.[337] The court also upheld authorization for late-term abortions at twenty-four and twenty-seven weeks gestation where a medical certificate indicated fetal disability or a risk to the woman's life or health.[338]

Judges Pardo and Pulido vigorously dissented on the 2018 judgment that validated a late-term abortion for inviability, indicating, among other things, that the eugenic ground for abortion does not apply after viability. Judge Pardo dissented, explaining that having no term limits for abortions on three grounds was inconsistent with national and international norms on abortion and with the court's own principle of "gradualism," which grants greater legal protection for viable fetuses.[339] On this point, she cited the *Artavia* decision as favoring the protection of viable fetuses and requiring that their rights be proportionally balanced against the mother's.[340] She held that Judgment C-355 should not be interpreted to allow abortions after viability, a point at which medical procedures for safe abortion require fetal homicide prior to fetal extraction, given that the child may otherwise be born alive and provoking her death after birth would constitute homicide.[341] "In that sense," she said, "the decriminalized grounds established by Judgment C-355 must ensure protection to the life of the unborn, which increases with the course of several weeks of gestation, particularly at 24 weeks where the fetus reaches independent viability."[342] Judge Bernal Pulido also suggested that a viable fetus that may survive outside of the mother's womb may not constitutionally have his life ended via judicial order based on the mere "possibility that he may have a disability" after birth.[343]

Through implementation judgments in individual cases, the Eight Chamber restricted conscience rights by creating new requirements for the admissibility of conscientious objection to abortion.[344] The chamber prohibited judges from conscientiously objecting to hearing abortion petitions and ordered professional investigations to be opened against them. It also ordered that a professional investigation be opened against a physician who had previously registered as a conscientious objector to abortion.[345] Finally, just as it amended the criminal code in Judgment C-355, the constitutional court subsequently amended Act 1719 of 2014 to create a legal obligation for health care providers to apply a certain protocol on sexual violence issued by the health ministry that would restrict conscientious objection of health care personnel that refused to perform abortions.[346]

The judgments met with strong resistance from the Attorney General's Office (Procuraduría General de la República), headed by Alejandro Ordóñez Maldonado, a pro-life Catholic who attempted to counteract the court's expansion of abortion rights beyond Judgment C-355. For instance, the attorney general issued administrative guidelines on conscience rights, misoprostol, and emergency contraception, which were not covered by Judgment C-355. The guidelines prompted a lawsuit by Women's Link Worldwide, an abortion rights advocacy organization, against the attorney general and two of his assistant attorneys on the grounds that the guidelines interfered with access to abortion.[347] The Eighth Chamber ruling sided with abortion rights advocates and ordered the attorney general to refrain from treating conscientious objection as a human or constitutional right, to refrain from referring to emergency contraception as an abortifacient, and to stop interfering with the approval of abortion-inducing drug misoprostol by the health ministry.

In 2010, in implementation judgment (*sentencia de tutela*) T-585, a three-judge panel of the Eighth Chamber interpreted Judgment C-355 as creating a right to abort in instances of absolutory excuses for abortion: "[It is] undeniable that out of Judgment C-355 a *true right* to voluntary interruption of pregnancy for women arises who are included in the *three decriminalized grounds*."[348] The chamber concluded that because abortion is a constitutional entitlement under those circumstances, both the government and health care providers have a duty to protect and enforce it; thus the chamber turned a negative obligation to abstain from prosecution into a positive obligation to protect and ensure access to abortion.[349]

In 2014, the Third Chamber used the original expression "decriminalization" of abortion from Judgment C-355, but in 2016 the same chamber specifically referred to a "fundamental right" to abort as included in a right to reproductive autonomy.[350] In 2018, the *full* Constitutional Court validated a "right of women to autonomously decide to [get] a voluntary interruption of pregnancy *under the permissible grounds*."[351] The court nevertheless limited itself to reiterating the grounds established in Judgment C-355 "without going further than the grounds established in that decision," while, at the same time, "urging Congress" to regulate the practice.[352]

Colombia's legislature has, since 2006, when Judgment C-355 was issued, been silent on the criminal code reform and creation of a right to abortion on three grounds carried out by the Constitutional Court, probably because of conflicting messages from the court itself. The court originally acknowledged the legislators' ability to regulate abortion and at times even urged legislators to assert their legislative authority to do so.[353] In other instances, however, it has seemed to preempt counterlegislation on abortion by stating that there is "no need for legislative or regulatory development whatsoever," except where such development is in accordance with the legislature's judgment or in order to expand the grounds for non-punishment of abortion created therein.[354] Such legislative void may reflect either legislative uncertainty or approval of the Constitutional Court's decisions, or a lack of political consensus on abortion regulation among Colombian voters.

*Mexican Supreme Court's* Amparo *on Right to Abortion of those Conceived in Rape.* In a 2018 *revisión de amparo* judgment, the Second Chamber of the Mexican Supreme Court found that denying an abortion to a sexual assault victim violated its Federal Constitution and federal law.[355] The plaintiffs—the minor and her parents—argued, among other things, that a right to abortion derived from the American Convention article 5 on the right to personal integrity as well as the Convention on Torture.[356] The judgment made no finding regarding such claims, but it did find that denial of abortion to a rape victim violated its Constitution's article 1, on the state's duty to protect human rights, and a federal statute, the Victim's General Law (Ley General de Víctimas), which mandates access to abortion for rape victims.[357]

The facts, as indicated in the judgment, involve a request for eugenic abortion and abortion following rape. In November 2015, a minor pregnant girl and her mother reported the child's sexual assault to law enforcement authorities in the state of Morelos.[358] In January 2016, the unborn child was diagnosed with an unidentified genetic disability, the designation of which was redacted from the judgment.[359] The minor and both of her parents then requested an abortion at the Cuernavaca General Hospital, a public state hospital. The hospital denied the abortion request due to the "lack of a medical justification," adding that the mother was not suffering any medical pathologies and that the fetal condition did not "pose any risk to the life of the mother."[360] A lower court ordered that the minor be given medical treatment but failed to order the abortion; therefore, the plaintiffs filed an action called *revisión en amparo* before a chamber of the Mexican Supreme Court. No petition was made regarding prosecution or conviction of the perpetrator, and the judgment didn't include any specific information on the perpetrator's identity or prosecution either.[361]

The Second Chamber found that both eugenic abortion and abortion of those conceived in rape were not subject to criminal punishment under the Morelos Criminal Code, that the federal Victim's General Law authorized abortion following rape, and that therefore public hospital authorities could not lawfully deny an abortion request by the minor.[362] The chamber did not find a right to abortion of those conceived in rape to be explicitly contained in the national Constitution, but repeatedly referred to human rights violations against the pregnant minor, stemming from a violation of the Constitution's provision on the government's duty to safeguard human rights.[363] In a five-to-one vote, the chamber ordered that the lower court order reparations, compensation, satisfaction, and nonrepetition to the minor and her parents.[364] Although not legally binding on all Mexican states, the decision suggests support for the creation of a right to abortion of those conceived in rape and sets an interpretive precedent for the rest of the federal circuit. The judgment did not, however, find a right to abortion following rape in the American Convention.

*Rejection of a Right to Abortion by High Courts of Bolivia, Chile, El Salvador, and Guatemala.* In 2014, the Constitutional Court of Bolivia explicitly rejected the existence of a right to abortion in any international treaties ratified by that state, including the American Convention.[365] The mixed decision struck down, on one hand, the requirement for judicial authorization for abortions of those conceived in rape but, on the other, categorically rejected the existence of a right to abortion: "[O]ur Political Constitution does not contain a supposed right to abortion nor can [abortion] be recognized as a reproductive health method."[366] "Unconditional abortion and in all stages of embryo development is not constitutionally admissible," it held. It did not find a right to abortion in any international treaties ratified by Bolivia either, including the American Convention.[367]

The Constitutional Court found its restrictions on abortion to be compatible with the American Convention, and it upheld its ban on most elective abortions and its criminal penalties for abortion practitioners as constitutional.[368] It held that a human "embryo may not be considered to be property of the woman" and rejected the idea that pregnancy alone implies a threat to the mother's right to health or that it can be legitimately compared to an illness or a threat to a woman's personal integrity or labeled as "cruel, inhuman or degrading treatment."[369]

It reasoned that existing constitutional protection of the unborn child's right to life was "sufficient reason" for the legislature to enact "public policies needed for his protection, which necessarily includes criminal law."[370] Criminal law was not found, however, to be the only way to address abortion, as pointed out by dissenting judge Andrade Martínez: "[I]f a state prohibits abortion, in virtue of the principle of solidarity, it must assume the responsibility of caring for the newborn child without arguing pretext of structural deficiencies or economic scarcity."[371] Interestingly, the Constitutional Court of Bolivia identified the practice of induced abortion as incompatible with indigenous culture and indigenous spiritual values and cosmological vision. It indicated that some indigenous women had resorted to induced abortions after being raped by white Europeans, which constituted a "break" or "conflict" with ancestral principles and values of indigenous communities.

The Chilean Constitutional Court that upheld three grounds for non-punishment of abortion also made a point of clarifying that abortion continued to be a crime; despite the number of separate opinions, a majority of seven to three judges explicitly rejected a right to unrestricted abortion.[372] Judge Hernández Emparanza, who voted with the majority and wrote a concurring opinion, specifically rejected the creation of a right to abortion on the sole basis of a pregnant woman's will to abort or on the basis that she is a woman.[373]

El Salvador's Supreme Court has repeatedly held that the *nasciturus* has a right to life from conception under the nation's constitution and that a woman cannot constitutionally demand a "right to one's own body or one's own womb" or a "right to the interruption of pregnancy" that would "nullify" the *nasciturus*'s right to life.[374] Since 2007, the Supreme Court has held that, while the right to life of the unborn child may be balanced against other rights, the constitution's legislative intent behind providing for that right was to preempt constitutional claims to a right to abortion that would place disproportionate limitations on the prenatal right to life.[375] Full decriminalization of elective abortion, according to the Supreme Court, would be such an instance.[376]

Judge González Bonilla explained that, by reforming article 1 of the Constitution to recognize the unborn child as a human person, the legislature recognized prenatal life as deserving constitutional protection and placed the unborn child in an equal constitutional position and status before the law, so that her rights could be weighed in cases of conflict with other rights.[377] Her status, he said, places her on the same level as the mother by recognizing an entitlement to life from conception; article 1 rejects criteria that would condition her rights on viability (as in the case of anencephalic children, he pointed out) or gestational age.

The judges agreed that any changes to current abortion law in El Salvador should come from the legislature and not the courts. Supreme Court judge Florentín Meléndez, who was a member of the IACHR in years prior, pointed out that under current law the Constitutional Chamber of the Supreme Court could never authorize abortion in any of its forms or circumstances. He indicated that such a decision could only come from the Legislative Assembly, through the approval of a law, as previously stated by the Constitutional Chamber itself.

The Guatemalan Supreme Court similarly rejected the existence of a right to abortion, that is, the right to choose to end a human life in a direct and intentional manner and a right to safe abortion, pointing out that abortion is never safe for the unborn, whose death is sought.[378] It also rejected the notion of abortion as included within a woman's right to life, given that it would certainly affect the life of aborted female fetuses.[379] In regard to abortion being included within a right to personal liberty or privacy, the court noted that abortions freed only males from the responsibilities of fatherhood and, in cases of sexual violence, offered perpetrators a false remedy for their actions.[380]

The legalization and normalization of abortion, the court indicated, will not address any of the difficulties associated with pregnancy; a truly holistic and comprehensive public policy must be adopted, one that strengthens the family unit through social and economic benefits—that encourages adoption, among other things.[381] The judgment also listed abortion's negative physical and psychological effects on women and noted that the state had a duty to protect women from the physical and psychological violence of abortion.[382]

*Argentina's Legislative Rejection of Abortion Rights.* Argentina, one of South America's most socially liberal countries—the first in the region to legalize same-sex marriage—shocked the rest of the Western world in 2018 by rejecting the creation of abortion rights in its national jurisdiction. The decision by Argentinian senators to reject a bill that would have created abortion rights at the national level reflected a strong sense of respect for the unborn child's right to life, not only on the part of legislators but of Argentinian society as a whole, which massively mobilized like never before in favor of "saving both lives" ("salvemos las dos vidas"), a pro-life campaign to promote alternatives to abortion.[383] The bill's contents are worthy of a closer look in order to understand the law that Argentinian legislators considered and ultimately rejected.

The legislative bill, drafted by the Campaña Nacional por el Derecho al Aborto Legal Seguro y Gratuito (National Campaign for the Right to Safe, Legal, and Free Abortion) and introduced into the lower chamber by Congresswoman Victoria Donda Pérez, contained most elements that abortion rights advocates would probably identify as essential to the creation of abortion rights in domestic jurisdictions. First, the bill categorized abortion as a legal right of the mother.[384]

Second, it legally authorized abortion for any reason from conception until the end of the first trimester and gave the unborn child only gradual protection starting at fourteen weeks' gestation in the second trimester of pregnancy.[385] The bill also decriminalized abortion beyond the fourteenth-gestational-week limit on four grounds: life, broadly defined mental or physical health, rape, and "incompatible with life" fetal conditions.[386]

Third, the bill explicitly authorized all abortion methods recommended by the World Health Organization.[387] According to official WHO publications, those methods include pharmacological abortion through the use of misoprostol and mifepristone; surgical methods including vacuum aspiration, dilation, and evacuation; and dilation and curettage.[388] The WHO also recommends preprocedure methods to produce "fetal demise" for abortions beyond twenty weeks gestation, such as injection of potassium chloride into the fetus's heart and intraamniotic or intrafetal injection of digoxin, the latter of which "requires time for fetal absorption" leading to death.[389]

In terms of its effects on medical and health care providers, the law would have, on one hand, exempted those who perform abortions from previously applicable criminal and civil penalties and would have reduced penalties where an abortion resulted in the pregnant woman's death.[390]

On the other hand, the bill would have imposed a duty on health care personnel to provide abortions within a five-day period, regardless of any medical considerations.[391] It would have imposed criminal, civil, and professional penalties on health care professionals and institutions that refused to perform abortions or delayed them, greatly restricting their conscience rights.[392]

The radical abortion rights bill also mandated public funding of abortion, mandatory training on abortion for all health care personnel in the country, and mandatory comprehensive sexual education, which was also categorized as a right, in all education institutions in the country, whether public or private.[393] The law would have allowed abortions on minors aged sixteen to eighteen years of age without parental consent and would have allowed substitution of parental consent with that of any adult friend ("referente afectivo") for younger children, as Argentinian legal experts pointed out.[394]

The bill did not require a criminal investigation for child rape where a minor would be seeking an abortion. In addition, the law would have prohibited dissuasive counseling, particularly counseling that involved moral considerations.[395] Finally, it would have undermined Argentina's federal system by regulating abortion at the national level and taking away the provinces' autonomy to legislate on abortion-related matters.[396]

Significant international pressure was applied on Argentinian legislators to adopt the proposed bill on the part of the IACHR and other international human rights bodies including the UN Committee on the Rights of the Child and the UN Working Group on Discrimination against Women.[397] In the course of a public hearing requested by abortion rights advocates including Amnesty International, Catholics for Choice, and the Center for Legal and Social Studies (CELS), the IACHR demanded that Argentinian legislators "carry out a detailed review of any normative framework that may have discriminatory effects on women's exercise of their sexual and reproductive rights," reminding them of supposed "international standards on this issue, in order to inform the ongoing debate in Congress."[398] In addition, Luz Patricia Mejía, former IACHR member, rapporteur on women's rights, and, at the time, technical secretary of the MESECVI (Follow-up Mechanism to the Belém do Pará Convention), spoke to Argentinian lawmakers in favor of the abortion rights bill.[399]

The American Convention's right-to-life provision, however, was repeatedly cited by legislators, academics, and medical associations in congressional hearings as incompatible with the abortion rights bill. Members of the Chamber of Deputies invoked the American Convention as prohibiting legalization of abortion during the chamber debates.[400] During public hearings before the Senate, high-profile academics, including Nestor Pedro Sagüés, also a former court of appeals judge, invoked the American Convention's obligation to protect prenatal life from conception and to reject the creation of abortion rights.[401] Furthermore, the Argentinian medical community publicly expressed its opposition to the abortion bill and expressed its understanding that it was contrary to international law. The National Academy of Medicine (Academia Nacional de Medicina), for instance, issued a public statement declaring their recognition of the unborn child as a human being and as a subject of human rights under "international treaties."[402]

The Argentinian Chamber of Deputies initially approved the bill by a narrow margin (129–125, with 1 abstention), but the Senate ultimately rejected it with a relatively narrow margin too (38–31, with 2 abstentions).[403] These results seem to suggest that a more moderate bill, one that did not create abortion rights, could have been passed by the Senate at the time. The fact that the Chamber of Deputies had previously rejected more radical bills, including one that would have created a right to unrestricted abortion throughout pregnancy ("aborto libre") is also indicative that abortion rights are mostly disfavored by the Argentinian legislature.[404]

## Full Bans on Induced Abortion in States Parties to the American Convention

Since their signature and ratification of the American Convention, more than one-third of states parties to the American Convention (nine out of twenty-three) have adopted full abortion bans through their legislatures, that is, criminal norms that prohibit direct voluntary abortion under any and all circumstances. It must be said, however, that no state party seems to have a full legal ban on all procedures directed to the interruption of pregnancy. No state party, for instance, stipulates criminal penalties for indirect abortion where the mother's life is at grave risk. No jurisdiction among states parties to the American Convention has a judicial interpretation to that effect either, as explained above. To do so, as noted by the Constitutional Chamber of El Salvador's Supreme Court, would be to "legally demand heroic behavior" from the pregnant mother, meaning the sacrifice of her own life, something that the law cannot do, even in states with full abortion bans.[405]

Advocates for the creation of abortion rights have characterized full abortion bans as those that have no provision on nonpunishment of abortion or that have a single "life of the mother" requirement.[406] One of the reasons for including jurisdictions with a single absolutory excuse may be that the situation of a risk to a mother's life tends to be very rare and would therefore only allow a minimal number of abortions in practice.[407] This classification goes a step further by referring to countries that allow indirect abortion only as having full abortion bans, given that the said procedures are not considered to be elective abortion at all in most states parties to the convention (see section on indirect abortion above).

The countries listed here are therefore states parties to the convention where either no explicit criminal statutory provisions for nonpunishment of abortion exist or where the sole explicit punishment exemption applies where the mother's life is at serious risk, and that rule is narrowly defined to allow only indirect but not direct abortion. Both instances amount to a full ban on abortion because no provision for nonpunishment of direct abortion exists under either modality, and therefore a full legal prohibition of induced abortion can be properly said to exist under both sets of jurisdictions.[408]

Six states parties to the American Convention prohibit all abortions with no explicit life-of-the-mother provision for nonpunishment of abortion in their criminal statutes: Dominican Republic, El Salvador, Haiti, Honduras, Nicaragua, and Suriname.[409] Chile used to be in this category until it decriminalized abortion on three grounds in 2017. The Supreme Court of El Salvador, in 2007, recognized an implicit life-of-the-mother criminal punishment exemption in its criminal code in cases of necessity, that is, where the mother's life is endangered by carrying the pregnancy to term (*estado de necesidad*) and where mental incapacity is involved.[410] A commission of the Honduran Congress also interpreted its criminal code as containing an implicit life-of-the-mother provision under the "necessity" defense (*estado de necesidad*) applicable to any crime under the criminal code.[411] In addition, some jurisdictions, like Suriname, define "abortion" only as direct abortion. That definition may explain the absence of an explicit life-of-the-mother ground for nonpunishment of abortion allowing indirect abortion, which is probably not legally regarded as abortion at all and may therefore be permitted under current criminal statutes.

Three other countries—namely Dominica, Guatemala, and Paraguay—similarly outlaw all abortions but explicitly establish a single absolutory excuse only for indirect abortion in situations of serious risk to the life of the mother.[412] Their criminal statutes have the same legal effect as a full ban on direct abortion with no explicit life-of-the-mother criminal punishment exemption since all direct or induced abortions are equally prohibited by law. Paraguay, for instance, defines its criminal punishment exemptions in this context as situations involving a serious health risk to the mother where a medical procedure "involving acts associated with labor" indirectly causes fetal death but is not intended to destroy the unborn child.[413]

Other jurisdictions may also understand the "life of the mother" provision as implicitly authorizing indirect abortion only, but have no explicit statutory language or high court interpretation to that effect as of 2018, and have therefore not been included in this category. Should a state party interpret its life-of-the-mother provision to allow indirect abortion only, that jurisdiction would best be classified as having a full abortion ban, for the reasons indicated above.

Legislatures in Dominican Republic, El Salvador, and Nicaragua eliminated all criminal punishment exemptions to abortion prohibitions between 1997 and 2006. El Salvador's 1973 criminal code used to contain life-of-the-mother, rape, and eugenic provisions for nonpunishment of abortion, which were derogated upon the code's reform in 1997.[414] In Nicaragua, article 165 of the criminal code, a provision dating from 1893 that permitted "therapeutic abortion" (characterized as abortion upon a mother's life-threatening health condition, to be decided by three physicians and the woman's husband or closest relative), was abolished by the National Congress in October 2006.[415]

In 1985, the Honduran legislature also rejected previously approved stipulations for nonpunishment of abortion in the criminal code, thus effectively eliminating all cases of legal abortion. Derogated provisions in the 1983 criminal code, articles 130 and 131, allowed for abortion in cases of rape, where the mother was mentally disabled, or where she was a minor under fifteen years of age.[416] It also allowed for "therapeutic" abortion and for eugenic abortion in very broad terms in order to "prevent the birth of a potentially defective being."[417] However, these articles were derogated by the National Congress before they became effective in 1985, during a period of *vacatio legis*, through a legislative decree that found them unconstitutional (violating the Constitution's right-to-life provisions).[418] In addition, Honduras's social security regulations have prohibited classification of induced abortion as an illness for subsidy purposes since 1971.[419]

Haiti's criminal code has prohibited abortion under all circumstances since the nineteenth century and still prohibits it today, without exceptions.[420] Likewise, criminal codes of the Dominican Republic and Suriname make no criminal punishment exemptions for abortions, thereby prohibiting abortion under all circumstances.[421]

### Attempts to Decriminalize Some Abortions in the Dominican Republic and Honduras

In 2014, Dominican Republic president Danilo Medina, with the support of the House of Representatives, attempted to modify the country's criminal code by including a provision that would have decriminalized abortion on three grounds (life/health, rape, and eugenic abortion). Two grounds were eliminated after the House vote, leaving only a life-of-the-mother ground for nonpunishment of abortion. Immediately after the vote, a United Nations Expert Group urged the Dominican Republic to create abortion grounds in cases of "risk to the health, including mental health, of the woman or girl, of rape and incest and of fatal impairment of the foetus," which the president partially acceded to.[422]

The national Constitutional Court, however, declared the new criminal code to be unconstitutional due to constitutional procedural violations, namely that the criminal code reform required approval by both chambers of Congress.[423] The president had only obtained approval from the House of Representatives and proceeded to sign the bill into the law, which the court found to constitute a violation of constitutional dispositions on the lawmaking process.[424] The entire code was challenged and declared unconstitutional during the *vacatio legis* period; therefore, it never became binding. The reformed provision was submitted for Senate approval and rejected by nineteen out of twenty senators in 2016.[425] It was then reintroduced in the House of Representatives and rejected in 2017.[426]

Honduran legislators also reconsidered and rejected proposals to decriminalize abortion on three grounds in 2017. Feminist organizations and minority political parties advocated for criminal law reform that would have decriminalized abortion on the grounds of life or health of the mother, rape, and eugenic purposes.[427] A United Nations Expert Group urged Honduran legislators to adopt these grounds for legal abortion and to make emergency contraception available in the country.[428] The Honduran president, Juan Orlando Hernández, on the other hand, urged legislators not to pass the proposed decriminalization of abortion and suggested he would veto any legislation to that effect.[429]

The proposed amendment was first rejected by a multipartisan congressional commission charged with evaluating the proposal, then by Congress as a whole. The congressional commission concluded, among other things, that a "life of the mother" criminal punishment exemption was unnecessary because terminating a pregnancy under true medical emergency situations is already permitted under the "necessity" defense (*estado de necesidad*) that applies to all crimes in the criminal code.[430] A large majority of the National Congress then ratified the committee's report in plenary session, rejecting the proposed decriminalization of abortion.[431] The Honduran Medical College then issued its position statement—which, they clarified, was based on lay, nonreligious considerations—against any decriminalization of intentional abortion and other acts against human life, which the college found contrary to professional ethics and to the country's laws.[432]

In April 2018, El Salvador's national legislative assembly rejected two proposals seeking to overturn the country's full abortion ban by declining to vote on them.[433] Together, the proposals created four grounds for abortion, namely life and health of the mother, age (minority), rape of a minor, and a eugenic purpose. International human rights bodies like the IACHR and the UN high commissioner for human rights, Zeid Ra'ad al-Hussein, urged Salvadorian lawmakers to overturn their full abortion ban and decriminalize abortion on at least these grounds.[434] Nevertheless, strong opposition from civil society, pro-life organizations, and the Catholic and evangelical churches reduced the amount of political support for decriminalization, ultimately leading to the rejection of the proposed legislative bills.

### Constitutional Challenges to El Salvador's Abortion Ban

El Salvador's Supreme Court has thrice upheld its full ban on abortion, finding it consistent with the American Convention on Human Rights and the Convention on the Rights of the Child, most recently in 2013 in the judgment regarding *Matter of B.* described in chapter 2.[435] Prior to the challenge brought by Beatriz's representatives, in 2013, the Supreme Court had interpreted the national Constitution—which defines the term "person" as "every human being from the moment of conception" and establishes that "every person has a right to life"—as recognizing an inherent right to life of every person starting at conception.[436] In 2007, the Constitutional Chamber of the Supreme Court upheld its abortion ban against a challenge by two individuals who argued that the criminal code was unconstitutional because it lacked criminal punishment exemptions for the life and health of the mother, for the abortion of those conceived in rape, and for eugenic purposes.[437]

After hearing opinions from the Legislative Assembly, the president, vice-president, and the attorney general (Fiscal General de la República), the Constitutional Chamber found no violation of the national constitution given that the criminal code contained a provision on exculpatory factors (article 27) that includes necessity ("estado de necesidad") and mental incapacity.[438] The court found that, under this provision, judges could decide, on a case-by-case basis, to waive punishment for abortions performed in cases of risk to the mother's life, where the risk is actual and imminent and where abortion is the only alternative to protect a superior juridical interest or right.

The basis for the court's findings was the constitution's text, which treats "prenatal life" as essentially "human life" from conception until death.[439] The court found that provisions for nonpunishment of abortion could be constitutionally acceptable if passing a test of "ponderación" that would involve the balancing of constitutional rights of the mother and those of the unborn child, as rights holders of equal status.[440] Just as the unborn's right to life is not absolute, the court indicated, a woman cannot constitutionally assert an absolute liberty or "right to her own body" or a "right to the interruption of pregnancy" that would nullify or obliterate the *nasciturus*'s right to life.[441] The effects of constitutional rights limitations should be proportionate to the rights protected, the court indicated, such as in the case of risk to the mother's life, which is equal in value to the child's.[442] It also held that legislators have a duty to criminalize abortion where it disproportionately affects the unborn's life but must regulate situations where conflict arises between the right to life of the mother and that of the child.[443]

The decision was upheld in 2011 when a similar challenge was filed by different plaintiffs.[444] The court rejected the claim, invoking its 2007 decision, which had settled the question regarding a criminal punishment exemption for abortion where the pregnancy poses a risk to the life of the pregnant woman, noting that the mere fact that the abortion regulation did not satisfy every person's vision of how abortion should be regulated was insufficient for a constitutional claim.[445] In regard to other criminal punishment exemptions, the court indicated that the legislature was within its discretion to decide to waive or not to waive punishment according to societal standards and criminal policy considerations and that nothing in the Constitution compelled the Constitutional Chamber to substitute its judgment for theirs.[446]

In 2013, the Constitutional Chamber of the Supreme Court rejected the existence of a right to abortion and reaffirmed the constitutionality of its full ban on abortion, while indicating that the criminal code allows for termination of pregnancy in cases of risk to the mother's life, as long as fetal death is not deliberately caused. While the court held that the unborn child's right to life is fully protected under the constitutions and international treaties ratified by El Salvador, it held that this right "is not absolute and unlimited" in a way that would give the *nasciturus*'s rights a greater, superior status over the mother's.[447] Exemptions from criminal punishment may apply for the same mitigating or exonerating factors that apply to other crimes, such as *estado de necesidad* (grave, imminent risk to the mother's life), lack of intent, lack of consent, mental incapacity, and so on, it indicated.[448] The chamber also expressed a preference for specificity in criminal statutes and called legislators to issue legal norms to govern situations of conflict between the mother's life and the life of the unborn child "prior to, and not as a result of a criminal court process," warning that "this Chamber cannot become 'a court for authorization of pregnancy interruptions.' "[449]

### Unconstitutionality of Advocacy for the Creation of Abortion Rights in Guatemala

In 2017, the full Guatemalan Supreme Court (en banc) unanimously found that advocacy for the creation of abortion rights violated Guatemala's constitutional protection of human life from conception and its criminal statutes prohibiting abortion, invoking the American Convention, albeit in a decision that did not, at that point, create binding precedent.[450] The judgment ordered the national ombudsman (Procurador de los Derechos Humanos), Jorge Eduardo De León Duque, to stop his advocacy for the creation of abortion rights, which consisted in the promotion of a reproductive rights handbook intended for mandatory use in public schools and health care government agencies.[451]

The handbook, titled *Human Rights, Sexual and Reproductive Rights and Pregnancy Care in Children and Adolescents* (*Manual de derechos humanos, derechos sexuales y reproductivos y atención de embarazos en niñas y adolescentes*), promoted abortion legalization and referred to abortion as a right, among other assertions.[452] Its language, according to the court, promoted the transgression of the right to life and the commission of a crime, that is, the intentional destruction of innocent human life under the guise of a right that could be demanded from the state.[453] The judgment also pointed out that the handbook used euphemisms and misleading language that deliberately concealed or trivialized the gravity and violence of abortion, which entails the destruction of a human being.[454]

The Supreme Court strongly rejected abortion rights advocacy language: it rejected the existence of a right to choose to end another's life, the idea that legal abortion meant safe abortion, and the claim that abortion was necessary to protect a woman's life, liberty, privacy, or health.[455] The court found that the state of Guatemala had a duty to protect the right to life from conception and prevent violations thereof, affirming that innocent human life is protected under the national Constitution and under the American Convention on Human Rights, which recognizes prenatal personhood.[456] It also noted that the state had a duty to protect women from the physical and psychological violence of abortion.[457]

The court emphasized that public officials such as the ombudsman, who freely accept public office, have a serious and solemn obligation to protect the national Constitution and enforce national criminal statutes, and therefore have a duty to defend prenatal life from the moment of conception rather than promote its destruction.[458] Rather than promoting legalization of abortion, the court indicated, the ombudsman should promote a truly holistic and comprehensive public policy that protects both maternity and prenatal life—such as strategies that strengthen the family unit through social and economic benefits—and should encourage adoption.[459]

The court rejected the ombudsman's argument that abortion rights advocacy was consistent with the "progressive development" of human rights and his appeal to a "global movement" that advocated for abortion legalization; the court found that legally authorizing abortion would constitute a reversal of rights previously recognized.[460] Rather than progress, legalization of abortion would cause a regression by authorizing a barbaric practice that would give a parent a right over the life of her child and would deny the child's legal personhood, as occurred at certain points in ancient history.[461] A truly progressive interpretation, the judgment stated, would protect incipient, innocent, weak, and defenseless life and ethically reduce maternal and child mortality.[462]

Guatemalan constitutional law, however, requires three consistent findings by the same court in order for precedent to become binding—that is, to constitute jurisprudence.[463] The Supreme Court decision was appealed to the Constitutionality Court, which may uphold or overturn the decision; therefore, the judgment alone does not create binding precedent for future similar cases.

## Other Relevant Aspects of State Practice for Interpretive Purposes

### Evolution in State Practice since Adoption of the American Convention

For the purposes of treaty interpretation, it is subsequent and not previous state practice that matters; but practice prior to the adoption of the American Convention may be relevant in demonstrating the evolution of state practice since the adoption of the treaty.[464] In 1981, the Inter-American Commission gave an overview of prior state practice in the *Baby Boy v. United States* report, where it looked at 1946–48 abortion prohibitions in the region and found that states were relatively permissive of abortion.[465] Assuming those findings are correct, which is admittedly debatable, they would demonstrate that the general consensus on abortion prohibitions has not evolved toward liberalization since 1946, a year that preceded both the adoption of the American Declaration of the Rights and Duties of Man in 1948 and the adoption of the American Convention in 1969. To a significant extent, restrictions on abortion in states parties to the American Convention have increased since 1946, with the exception of Colombia and Uruguay.

In *Baby Boy*, the commission's analysis of state practice in 1946 concluded that abortions were legally permissible "*in the majority* of the American States."[466] The *Baby Boy* report listed multiple grounds for abortion in twelve countries that "excluded the penal sanction for the crime of abortion if performed in one or more of the following cases: A - when necessary to save the life of the mother; B - to interrupt the pregnancy of the victim of a rape; C - to protect the honor of an honest woman; D - to prevent the transmission to the fetus of a hereditary or contagious disease; E - for economic reasons (*angustia económica*)."[467]

If the commission's analysis was accurate, a comparison of subsequent practice after ratification of the convention and present-day abortion laws would reveal a much higher awareness of the incompatibility of direct elective abortion with the American Convention. As of 2019, nine countries (most of which were original drafters of the American Convention) have full bans on induced abortion, while no full abortion bans existed in 1948, according to the commission. Today, only about one-third of all states parties have created multiple absolutory excuses for abortion, but those cannot be properly said to have decriminalized abortion, with the exception of Colombia and Uruguay, because abortion continues to be a crime; only the punishment is waived. Furthermore, no state party to the convention recognizes a constitutional right to abortion or a right to abortion deriving from any international treaty.

Requirements for nonenforcement of abortion bans usually necessitate proof, for example, that there are no other means to avoid harm to the mother's life or health, that abortion is a measure of last resort, or that sexual assault has been reported to law enforcement. Judicial authorization, medical opinion, or ethics committee opinions recommending an abortion may be required. In the great majority of countries, absolutory excuses do not require participation of public hospitals or state funding, but those few countries that do require some form of state cooperation allow conscientious objection of health care personnel.

In addition, two of the five criminal grounds for nonpunishment of abortions listed in *Baby Boy* have been virtually abolished in states parties to the American Convention: categories C and E, nonpunishment of abortion for *honoris causa* or economic reasons, were the broadest grounds in the *Baby Boy* report's list and would have probably allowed "the most diverse cases of abortion."[468] While the former only exists as a criminal punishment exemption in two states parties, where judges may apply it on a case-by-case basis, the latter has been universally abolished: poverty does not constitute a ground for abortion in any state party to the American Convention.

Since the American Convention's adoption, respect for prenatal life and legal protection of the unborn child's right to life in states parties to the American Convention has transcended governments and partisan politics. Traditional allies of abortion rights advocates in other regions of the world have actively resisted decriminalization of abortion in Latin America. For instance, socialist presidents Tabaré Vázquez from Uruguay and Rafael Correa from Ecuador have opposed decriminalization of abortion; the leftist *Sandinista* government of Nicaragua has fiercely defended its full abortion ban against international objections.[469] Medical organizations and professional colleges, as well as top academics, have spoken against abortion in Argentina, Honduras, and other countries, in contrast with North American and Western European professional organizations and academics, who generally sympathize with abortion rights.

### Abortion Regulation in Nonparties to the Convention

Nations that are not parties to the American Convention but are members of the OAS, such as the United States, Canada, Cuba, and Guyana, have significantly more liberal laws on abortion than states parties to the treaty. Some of these nonparties have expressed an understanding that the convention bans at least some forms of abortion and includes a legal obligation to protect prenatal life, and this perception, among other factors, has dissuaded them from ratification. For instance, in 2010, Inter-American Court judge Augusto Cançado Trindade stated that delegates of the United States and Canada before the OAS had told him that the convention's legal obligation to protect a prenatal right to life was one of the reasons they had not ratified the convention, given their countries' broad legalization of abortion.[470]

Virtually all nonparties to the American Convention that are also members of the Organization of American States (OAS) have more liberal laws on abortion than states that have ratified the treaty. Cuba, notably, allows abortion on demand and has one of the highest abortion rates in the world.[471] Guyana also allows abortion on demand, according to the Guttmacher Institute.[472] Abortion rights advocates report that St. Kitts and Nevis allows a broad mental health ground for abortion, aside from life-and-physical-health grounds.[473] Trinidad and Tobago allows common law grounds for eugenic abortion (of those suffering from most serious disabilities), aside from life-of-the-mother, physical-health, and rape grounds. St. Lucia allows life, physical-and-mental-health, rape, and incest grounds. Belize allows life and physical-and-mental-health criminal punishment exemptions along with eugenic abortion and poverty grounds. St. Vincent and the Grenadines allows the same grounds as Belize, plus rape and incest criminal punishment exemptions.

Only two Caribbean states that are not parties to the American Convention, Antigua and Barbuda and Bahamas, place substantive restrictions on abortion by contemplating the life of the mother and the physical health of the mother as grounds for abortion only. Venezuela is the only nonparty having a full abortion ban, but the country was a party to the convention for thirty-five years until 2012, when it denounced the treaty as described in chapter 1.[474]

The United States government, which signed the American Convention but did not ratify it, has expressed an understanding that "an abortion which was performed without substantial cause based upon the law could be inconsistent with Article 4 [of the American Convention]."[475] Even though the United States currently allows abortion on demand, the

US Supreme Court has upheld a great deal of restrictions on abortion in recent decades, such as a federal partial-birth abortion ban prohibiting dilation and extraction, an inhumane abortion procedure that Justice Antonin Scalia characterized as bordering on infanticide.[476] The US Supreme Court has also found that states are not required to fund abortions or to allow the use of public facilities and employees for abortion, and it has repeatedly stated that states may use funds to encourage childbirth over abortion, among other things.[477]

Canada, which did not sign or ratify the convention but is a member of the OAS, has generally read the treaty to contain a legal obligation to legally protect prenatal life. Canadian debates on the ratification of American Convention illustrate the understanding that article 4(1) of the convention would conflict with Canadian law, where abortion is currently widely available, even in the absence of a constitutional right to abortion in that country.[478] In 2003, a parliamentary committee examined the possibility of Canadian ratification of the American Convention and identified the right to life from conception in article 4(1) as "the main source of concern" according to their expert witness testimony.[479] Noting the IACHR's interpretation of "in general" in *Baby Boy* as not imposing any specific obligation on states with respect to abortion, the committee reported that Canadian abortion rights advocates feared that article 4(1) "could be used to prohibit abortions in Canada, or even prevent access to some contraceptives such as the 'morning-after pill,' intra-uterine devices or RU-486, which act after conception."[480] Even after the *Artavia* decision's interpretation, members of the Canadian Congress may still have concerns over the understanding that "[e]ven though Article 4(1) does not impose an obligation to prohibit abortions, it may impose an obligation to regulate them."[481]

Nonparties that are not members of the OAS also have more liberal abortion laws even if they share the states parties' Catholic culture, such as Italy, Portugal, or Spain, which have very liberal abortion laws, restricting only late-term abortions and only under certain circumstances.[482] In addition, Ireland became the last Western European country to legalize abortion in 2018 by repealing its national constitutional provision recognizing the constitutional protection of the unborn child's life, while in the same year, Argentina rejected legalization of abortion through the legislature.

The two countries were similar in the sense that they are traditionally Catholic and relatively liberal on the moral issues (both countries have, for instance, recognized same-sex marriage). They were different, however, not only in that one is Latin American and the other European but in that Argentina recognizes an international obligation to legally protect the prenatal right to life, codified in the American Convention, whereas Ireland does not.

SIX

# Systemic and Historic Interpretation

## *Relevant Rules of International Law and the Convention's Preparatory Work*

All states parties to the American Convention have ratified the Convention on the Rights of the Child (CRC), which explicitly recognizes the prenatal right to life, and other international treaties that generally recognize a universal right to life without exceptions, such as the International Covenant on Civil and Political Rights (ICCPR). These treaties are relevant to the American Convention's systemic interpretation since, according to the Vienna Convention on the Law of Treaties, "There shall be taken into account, together with the context . . . any relevant rules of international law applicable in the relations between the parties."[1]

This chapter looks at relevant rules of international law pertaining to the prenatal right to life and applicable in the relations between the parties, such as article 6(4) of Additional Protocol II to the Geneva Conventions and the United Nations Declaration on Human Cloning.[2] It also examines Latin American and Caribbean states' interpretive declarations upon ratification of the CRC as well as over twenty years of periodic reports to the CRC Committee and their implications of those reports for interpretation of the American Convention.[3] It describes Latin American and Caribbean states parties' statements on abortion and prenatal rights in international fora, particularly those invoking article 4(1) of the American

Convention at the International Conference on Population and Development and the Fourth World Conference on Women in Beijing, among others.[4] The chapter's last two sections explore the historic interpretation of American Convention article 4(1), according to its *travaux préparatoires*, which, according to the VCLT article 32, are complementary means of interpretation.

Out of all interpretation rules distorted by the *Artavia* judgment, systemic interpretation was probably the one approached with the least precision and good faith; this chapter addresses its misrepresentations and completes the information provided therein. The judgment skipped the analysis of international treaty texts by carrying out a "joint" systematic and historical interpretation of some international human rights treaties. Proving that the Inter-American Court is poorly suited to *historically* interpret any treaties other than the American Convention, the judgment carried out a superficial and partial analysis of selected portions of the CRC and of the preparatory work of the Universal Declaration of Human Rights (UDHR) in order to prove that they supposedly disentitled the unborn child from a right to life, in direct contradiction with the *pro homine* interpretation rule in article 29.

## Systemic Interpretation Defined

The Vienna Convention's definition of what the Inter-American Court calls "systematic" interpretation is compatible with article 64 of the American Convention, which grants the court the authority to interpret the American Convention along with "other treaties concerning the protection of human rights *in the American states*."[5] The Inter-American Court has interpreted article 64 in Advisory Opinion OC-1/82 as meaning that the court has the power to interpret a treaty only as long as it is "directly related to the protection of human rights in a Member State of the Inter-American system"; that is, it has power to interpret only a "human rights treaty *to which [states] are parties*, but which has been adopted outside the framework of the Inter-American system."[6]

The Inter-American Court has sometimes recognized its lack of interpretive authority in regard to treaties to which no member state of the Inter-American system is a party: "[T]he Court can exercise neither its contentious nor advisory jurisdiction to establish the scope of international agreements, whatever be their character, concluded by non-Member States of the Inter-American system, or to interpret legal provisions governing the structure or operation of international organs or institutions not belonging to that system."[7] Accordingly, the court could properly rely on the Convention on the Rights of the Child or the International Covenant on Civil and Political Rights, which all states parties to the American Convention have ratified, but not on the European Convention on Human Rights or the Maputo Protocol, regional treaties to which no Latin American or Caribbean state can be a party.[8]

The court, however, has sometimes applied systemic interpretation incorrectly by relying on the entire *corpus juris* of international human rights law rather than on "rules of international law applicable in the relations *between the parties*," as established in the Vienna Convention.[9] In the *Artavia* judgment, for instance, the court relied on international treaties of regional human rights protections systems like the European and African systems, to which no state party to the American Convention can possibly be a party.[10]

The court's lack of rigor on systemic interpretation has been pointed out as one of its greatest weaknesses—for instance, when five states parties to the convention signed a declaration calling Inter-American bodies to "a strict application of the sources of international human rights law."[11] Former commissioner Paolo Carozza referred to the existence of a general "Inter-American liberality of the use of sources," which he has described as the institutions' appeal to a variety of nonconsensual sources of law coupled with relative disregard for orthodox practice in any legal tradition or jurisdiction in the region.[12] The practice is certainly not unanimously accepted within the court itself, since both Judge Alberto Pérez Pérez and Judge Eduardo Vio Grossi have criticized the court's reliance on other regional human rights systems, particularly on the European system.[13]

Assuming that judgments by the European Court of Human Rights were relevant to interpretation of the American Convention—which they are not—the *Artavia* judgment selectively invoked only those decisions that supposedly favored its interpretation of the human embryo's nonpersonhood, but omitted European instruments and decisions that contain explicit human rights protections for the human embryo. For instance, the European Court has found that the unborn may be included in the convention's scope of protection, even when the national legislation allows abortion.[14] The court has also stated that states may have a legitimate interest in limiting the number of abortions and in protecting morals.[15]

The European Court of Human Rights, in *A, B and C v. Ireland*, unambiguously stated that article 8 of the European Convention on the right to privacy "cannot . . . be interpreted as conferring a right to abortion."[16] Subsequent case law has reaffirmed the principle that there is no right to have an abortion or to perform it.[17] The European human rights bodies have held that the autonomy of the woman per se does not suffice to justify abortion under the European Convention.[18] In *A, B and C v. Ireland*, for instance, the European Court acknowledged that Ireland's nearly full abortion ban constituted a legitimate restriction to the right to respect for private life.[19] In *Brueggemann and Scheuten v. Germany*, the European Commission of Human Rights had similarly held that "pregnancy cannot be said to pertain uniquely to the sphere of private life. Whenever a woman is pregnant her private life becomes closely connected with the developing fetus."[20]

*Artavia*'s reliance on national judicial decisions on abortion in nonparties to the American Convention, such as the United States, Germany, and Spain, to decide a claim against Costa Rica was also entirely inappropriate. These judgments are irrelevant to the interpretation of the American Convention because they come from domestic, not international, courts, and they apply to states that are not parties to the American Convention. Even assuming that US or European domestic courts had any relevance as sources of interpretation of the American Convention, which they do not, the court did not cite abortion laws of Eastern European nations like Poland or Croatia or those of Western European nations like Ireland, which, at the time of the *Artavia* decision, recognized the unborn child's right to life in the Eighth Amendment to its Constitution Act.

Some decisions cited were, to boot, mischaracterized by the Inter-American Court, notably the 1975 German Constitutional Court that struck down West Germany's liberal abortion statute while holding that abortion decriminalization may be permissible under some circumstances. The judgment repeatedly affirmed the constitutional right to life of the unborn, even in the embryonic stage, and interpreted the term "everyone" in its Constitution (article 2(2) of the Grundgesetz: "everyone possesses the right to life") to include the unborn human being.[21] The decision spoke of the legal irrelevance of distinctions among the various stages of "self-developing life" ("sich entwickelnden Lebens").[22] It came to the conclusion that the legal order was always required to condemn abortion as wrong, even when it decided to tolerate it and exempt women from punishment. As a consequence, before having an abortion, women were expected to go through explicitly dissuasive counseling and to be reminded of their fundamental duty to respect the life of the unborn.[23]

In 1993, the German Constitutional Court reaffirmed most of that earlier judgment, holding that the constitution guarantees the "unborn" a right to life and that abortion is "an act that kills."[24] It established that the abortion concerns "an individual life, one that in the process of growing and unfolding itself does not develop into a human being but rather develops as a human being," with its "own" ("eigenen") constitutional right to life.[25] The German court added that the degree of legal protection owed to the fetus is independent of the stage of pregnancy.[26] It further pointed out that this protection was valid independent of any particular religious beliefs, over which the legal order of a religion-and-worldview-neutral state can make no judgments.[27]

### The CRC's Protection of Prenatal Rights and the American Convention's Interpretation

All states parties to the American Convention have, in contrast, ratified the Convention on the Rights of the Child (CRC).[28] The CRC entered into force in 1990, twelve years after the American Convention, and can therefore be considered a "subsequent agreement between the parties regarding the interpretation of the treaty or the application of its provisions" as well as a "relevant rule[s] of international law applicable in the relations between the parties."[29]

An international obligation to legally protect prenatal life can be clearly and explicitly found in the text of the CRC. The Convention preamble explicitly stipulates that "*the child*, by reason of his physical and mental immaturity, needs special safeguards and care, including appropriate *legal protection, before as well as after birth*."[30] Articles 6 and 24 recognize every child's unqualified right to life, health, and development, including the right to "adequate pre-natal . . . care," thus explicitly including the unborn child.[31] Article 41 of the CRC prohibits restrictive interpretations of the rights contained therein. The Human Rights Committee has indicated that the convention provides that when taking special measures of protection, "[s]tates parties should be guided by the *best interests of the child*, by the need to ensure the survival and development of *all* children and their well-being," in articles 3 and 6.[32]

Former IACHR commissioners Marco Gerardo Monroy Cabra and Rodrigo Escobar Gil, who were also Constitutional Court judges in Colombia, read the CRC preamble and CRC articles 1 and 6 (on the right to legal recognition as a person) together as "leading to the conclusion that the term 'child' includes unborn human beings, and therefore extends to them the special protection granted by the treaty, among them the right to life."[33] They thus rejected the idea that international human rights law is imprecise about the unborn human being's right to life, as often stated by those who advocate for the creation of abortion rights.

### Interpretation of Article 1—Definition of "Child"

The understanding that the CRC article 1 includes the unborn child in the definition of "child"[34] can be traced back to the *travaux préparatoires* of the 1959 Declaration on the Rights of the Child's, where several Latin American states affirmed their view that the child's right to life was protected from the moment of conception in a proposal to that effect, introduced by Argentina and supported by Bolivia, Colombia, Costa Rica, Ecuador, El Salvador, Guatemala, Haiti, Honduras, Paraguay, Peru, the Dominican Republic, Uruguay, and Venezuela, among others.[35]

Following their signature and ratification of the CRC, some Latin American states parties, such as Argentina, Ecuador and Guatemala, have laid down their interpretation of article 1 by filing interpretive declarations affirming that the term "child" refers to every person from the moment of conception.[36] Argentina's declaration upon ratification of the CRC specifically stated that "[c]oncerning article 1 of the Convention, the Argentine Republic declares that the article must be interpreted to the effect that a *child means every human being from the moment of conception* up to the age of 18."[37] This declaration has been interpreted by Argentinian courts as prohibiting the destruction of human embryos.[38] Similarly, Ecuador filed a declaration that stated that the CRC Preamble protected the unborn child, which "should be borne in mind in interpreting all the articles of the Convention."[39] Guatemala likewise filed an interpretive declaration indicating that it understood article 1's definition of the word "child" to be the same as in its national constitution—that is, it understood both as stipulating that a child's right to life starts "from the time of its conception."

In addition, state reports to the CRC monitoring body, which the Inter-American Court has regarded as evidence of subsequent state practice, have demonstrated states parties' understanding of article 1 as including unborn children.[40] For instance, Argentina's Act incorporating the CRC into domestic law held that "regarding article 1 of the Convention [on the Rights of the Child], the Republic of Argentina declares that it must be interpreted in the sense that it is understood that the child is every human being from his conception until the age of 18."[41] Before the CRC Committee, Argentina reported that "for the purposes of the Argentine legal system a child is 'any human being from conception up to the age of 18' . . . without deference to semantic designations for each phase of the child's life."[42]

Other states parties like Guatemala, El Salvador, Bolivia, Honduras, and Peru have explicitly affirmed in their reports to the CRC Committee their understanding that the CRC applies to the unborn child from the moment of conception. Guatemala reported that both its constitutional protection of the right to life from conception and the definition of "child" as a person from conception found in its Act on the Comprehensive Protection of Children and Adolescents, were "consistent with the definition in article 1 of the Convention."[43] El Salvador reported that an amendment to its constitution recognizing every human being as a person from the moment of conception "was adopted in response to the letter and spirit of the preamble to the Convention on the Rights of the Child."[44] Bolivia reported to the CRC Committee that its Code for Children and Adolescents was in agreement with the convention in its definition of "children" as all human beings from the moment of conception.[45] Honduras reported that its definition of "child" protected children in the same terms as the CRC and that those terms therefore included unborn children since the time of conception.[46] Similarly, Peru indicated that its Children's and Adolescents' Code, which protects life from the time of conception, "uses the same upper and lower age limits as the Convention on the Rights of the Child."[47]

Some states parties have incorporated the definition of "children" as starting at conception in their national constitutions and primary laws, particularly children's codes, under a sense of a legal obligation arising from article 1 of the CRC. For instance, Paraguay has reported on its compliance with the CRC by legislating into its Constitution and Children's Code a definition of "child" as any human being from conception onward.[48] Ecuador has reported on its general compliance with the CRC by providing protection for a child's right to life from conception in its constitution as well as its Children's Code's definition of minor as "any human being from the prenatal stage to the age of 18 years."[49] Honduras has also reported on its definition of "children" as starting from the moment of conception and continuing until the age of eighteen in its Children's Code as a measure of compliance with the CRC.[50] Colombia has indicated that article 17 of its Minors' Code, recognizing the child's existence from conception, had been modified to comply with its international obligations under CRC to reflect the child's right to life, health, and development from conception.[51] Furthermore, Uruguay reported on its Children's Code's comprehensive protection of children from conception to the age of majority as part of its implementation of article 3 of the CRC regarding protection of children.[52]

Bolivia, Costa Rica, Nicaragua, Panama, and Paraguay have specifically referred to the CRC's article 1 when reporting on their national statutory definitions of children as human beings from conception until eighteen years of age.[53] Panama, for instance, reported that its Family Code definition of "minor" as a human being from his or her conception up to eighteen years of age and its Family Code's provisions on child support, which apply from conception onward, are in compliance with the CRC.[54]

In 2008, Mexican Supreme Court judge Sergio Salvador Aguirre Anguiano acknowledged the preamble's significance when interpreting the CRC as a whole, according to the Vienna Convention article 31, and interpreted that treaty to define "child" as "any human being from the moment of conception until the age of 18" and to recognize an entitlement of the child to the right to life.[55] He indicated that, in light of the CRC preamble and articles 1 and 2 of the convention, the CRC is "designed to ensure the well-being of the product of conception" and that such product—the child—should not be discriminated against on the basis of birth.[56] His fellow Supreme Court judges Mariano Azuela Güitrón and Guillermo I. Ortiz Mayagoitia supported that interpretation.[57]

### Interpretation of Article 6—Prenatal Right to Life

States parties to the American Convention including Guatemala,[58] Nicaragua,[59] Paraguay,[60] and Venezuela[61] have reported to the CRC Committee on their constitutional and legal recognition of the right to life from conception in compliance with article 6 of the CRC, which recognizes a child's right to life, survival, and development.[62] Peru has reported on existing legal protections to the unborn child from the moment of conception and specifically stated in 2005 that "[h]uman life is the period of time lived by a person from conception in the womb until death and consists of the manifestation and activities of a human being. Once conceived, every child has the right to life; article 6 of the Convention therefore declares this right to be an inherent right."[63]

Notably, Latin American and Caribbean states parties have also reported to the CRC Committee on their domestic criminal prohibitions on abortion when describing their compliance with article 6 of the CRC on the right to life, health, and development.[64] Costa Rica has reported on its criminal prohibition of abortion as a measure designed to comply with article 6 of the CRC.[65] Likewise, Honduras has reported on its criminal code reforms expanding prohibitions on abortion and its legal protections for the unborn child.[66] Panama has reported on its fetal death statistics and on its criminal law regarding elective abortion as compliant with CRC.[67] Chile has reported that its constitution and its laws protect "the lives of persons yet to be born" and that its legal system "prohibits abortion."[68]

While reporting on its obligations under article 6, El Salvador reported that all types of conduct constituting abortion were punishable under criminal law "in order to protect life from conception."[69] Colombia affirmed that "practices involving abortion are never acceptable" and reported that Colombian legislation protects the right to life of both the mother and the unborn child.[70] Haiti also reported on its criminal penalties for voluntary abortion as consistent with article 6 of the convention.[71]

Most Caribbean countries, like Dominica,[72] Grenada,[73] Haiti,[74] and Suriname,[75] have also reported on their criminal penalties for induced abortion as consistent with article 6 of the convention. In addition, Haiti reported in 2002 that prison sentences of pregnant women "may be suspended in order to protect the unborn child."[76] Similarly, Dominica reported in 2003 on its prohibition against applying the death penalty to pregnant women, indicating that "the intention here no doubt is to preserve the life of the unborn."[77]

Latin American and Caribbean states have also reported to the CRC Committee on prenatal health in relation to their obligations under article 24 (right to health) of the CRC.[78] Brazil, for instance, recognized "the vulnerability of the human being from conception up to approximately 6 years of age."[79] Mexico stressed the need to protect prenatal survival, health, and development from the time of conception and during life in utero and reported on its policies to that effect under article 6 of the CRC.[80]

### The CRC *Travaux Préparatoires*

The preparatory work of the Convention on the Rights of the Child (CRC) confirms the ordinary meaning of the preamble text, which establishes a state duty to legally protect the unborn child "the child, by reason of his physical and mental immaturity, needs special safeguards and care, including appropriate *legal protection, before as well as after birth.*"[81] As illustrated below, the CRC preparatory work shows that the treaty was originally intended to apply to the unborn child and, at the very least, to allow states parties to legally prohibit any deliberate acts against her life, including elective abortion.

The CRC's protection of the unborn child was initially brought up during the *travaux préparatoires* discussions on the definition of "child" in article 1. The question of whether "child" should be defined therein as any human being starting at conception or birth was vehemently debated by states parties to the treaty. The wording was left broad, establishing a ceiling for the definition (eighteen years of age) but no floor. Finally, agreement was reached on inserting a sentence in the convention's preamble recognizing that the child needs "appropriate legal protection before as well as after birth," as had also been previously recognized in the Declaration on the Rights of the Child.[82]

The first draft of the convention, proposed by Poland, had established in article 1 (final article 2) the convention's protection of all children without discrimination.[83] Barbados, a state party to the American Convention on Human Rights, brought up the need for a definition of the term "child" and suggested that states address whether that definition should include the human fetus and thus imply a prohibition of abortion.[84] Portugal asserted that "the rights of the child prior to birth could be more clearly defined."[85]

The second draft of article 1 was created by a working group and subsequently rejected by states parties: "According to the present Convention a child is every human being *from the moment of his birth* to the age of 18 years unless, under the law of his State, he has attained his age of majority earlier."[86] Some countries supported this text, but many states opposed the definition of "childhood" as beginning at birth and "indicated that this is contrary to [their] legislation. They argued that the concept should be extended to include the entire period from the moment of conception."[87] Finally, "Morocco proposed that the words 'from the moment of his birth' should be deleted from the article in order to solve the difficulty," and that amendment was adopted.

The debate over the CRC's inclusion of the unborn child was settled with the adoption of the preamble text "before as well as after birth."[88] According to the representative of Poland, who was a member of the working group, the expression "before as well as after birth" struck "a delicate balance which the working group had reached in the course of continued discussions."[89] The said compromise, he said, was intended to allow states to legally protect the unborn child: "[It] did not exclude the protection of the child before birth, nor did it contradict a wider interpretation of the text or the application of other, more comprehensive provisions, as laid down in article 21 of the draft convention [dealing with the nonrestrictive interpretation of the Convention and mandating that precedence be given to national norms or other international norms 'that are more conducive to the realization of the rights of the child].' "[90]

According to the preparatory-work records, the language "before as well as after birth," literally quoting the Declaration on the Rights of the

Child, was first introduced in 1980 "by the Holy See, in accordance with other delegations," and then in 1989 by the Federal Republic of Germany, supported by the Holy See, Ireland, Malta, and the Philippines, which had introduced a parallel proposal.[91] These states, along with "a number of delegations," explained their intent that their national laws contained provisions "protecting the rights of the unborn child from the time of conception" and that "the future convention could not ignore an [*sic*] important issue of the rights of the unborn child."[92] The preambular paragraph containing those terms was so important to the Federal Republic of Germany that its delegation indicated that it "would formally request a vote in the Working Group if his proposal was not duly reflected in the text of preambular paragraph 6."[93]

The 1989 *travaux préparatoires* records also indicate that "a number of delegations," including but not limited to Italy, Senegal, Kuwait, Austria, Egypt, and three Latin American states (Argentina, Colombia, and Venezuela), vocally supported the inclusion of the term "before as well as after birth": "The importance of protection of the child even before it is born was repeatedly stressed in this connection. It was further stressed that in all national systems protection was provided to the unborn child and the draft convention should not ignore this fact."[94] Italy emphasized its interpretation that "no state was manifestly opposed to the principles contained in the Declaration of the Rights of the Child, and, therefore ... the protection of life before birth could be considered as 'jus cogens' since it formed part of the common conscience of members of the international community."[95]

It is worth noting that Latin American civil society groups also agreed at the time with the CRC's application of the phrase "from the moment of conception": during the convention's preparatory work, in 1988, a Latin American meeting of nongovernmental organizations (NGOs) proposed a draft text for article 35 which included the unborn child's protection from sale and organ trafficking, among things. The Latin American NGO meeting proposal, submitted by the government of Argentina by *note verbale*, stated: "The States parties to the present Convention shall enact laws to prevent the abduction, sale or traffic of children in any form *from the time of conception* up to the age of 18 and/or of human organs and shall take all appropriate national, bilateral and multilateral measures to avoid and penalize these actions."[96]

A handful of state representatives—namely, the United States, Norway, the Netherlands, India, China, the Soviet Union, Denmark, Australia, Sweden, the German Democratic Republic, and Canada—wanted to eliminate prenatal rights protections from the CRC and opposed the language applying the convention to the child "before birth," but the wording favored by the majority ultimately prevailed.[97] Some of these delegations expressed their belief that the unborn child is not a person and that the declaration was outdated.[98]

There seemed to be some concern among states with national laws that permitted some abortions, but supporters of the preamble' amendment responded to this concern by saying that the "purpose of the amendment was not to preclude the possibility of abortion [particularly in situations such as] threat to the health of the mother."[99] Nevertheless, some states still recognized that the preamble text was not neutral on abortion, and they requested that the "before as well as after birth" phrase be placed in square brackets under a new section entitled "proposals on which no consensus was reached"; that proposal was rejected too, as indicated in the preparatory work records.[100]

On two different occasions, states opposing language that recognized the child's need for legal protection "before as well as after birth" filed proposals to eliminate or qualify those terms, and both proposals were ultimately rejected. First, in 1980, the United States proposed a compromise text that would have eliminated the phrase "before as well as after birth."[101] The text stayed in the draft convention for a few years but was replaced by the Federal Republic of Germany's counterproposal reintroducing the terms in 1989.

Then, "an informal drafting group was set up to undertake [informal] consultations," and that group eventually approved the wording "before as well as after birth."[102] The informal drafting group was composed of countries from both sides of the abortion issue: on one hand, the Federal Republic of Germany, Ireland, Italy, and Poland, and on the other, the Netherlands, Sweden, and the United States. The chairman of the group submitted the agreed-upon draft text that included the said terms, but he added a statement requesting that the preparatory work record reflect that "[i]n adopting this preambular paragraph, the Working Group does not intend to prejudice the interpretation of article 1 or any other provision of the Convention by States Parties."[103] Ireland later protested the inclusion of that statement in the committee's report given its lack of discussion in committee.[104]

The *Artavia* judgment relied on that single statement to deny that the Declaration and Convention on the Rights of the Child protected a prenatal right to life or recognized the human embryo as a person, and the judgment omitted any reference to the existence of the UN Juridical Counsel's response indicating that the statement might be invalid and ineffective in interpreting the convention.[105] This deliberate omission on the part of the judgment seemed to show a lack good faith given that the legal counsel's report was also a part of the preparatory work records cited in the judgment.

The report by United Nations Juridical Counsel Carl August Fleschnauer evaluated the validity of the chairman's statement and concluded that it might be invalid and ineffective in interpreting the convention, pointing out that its obvious intent was to undermine the preamble's protection of the unborn child.[106] The report was issued upon the United Kingdom's request that the UN Legal Counsel clarify whether the UK could legally interpret the statement as applying to its interpretation of the child's-right-to-life provision.[107] The UN Juridical Counsel's report responded that although there is no prohibition against the inclusion of such statements in the preparatory work records, the value of the chairman's statement for interpretative purposes in regard to article 1 is uncertain, given that the statement sought to "deprive a preambular paragraph of its usual purpose," which is to be a part of the treaty context for the purposes of interpretation.[108]

The legal counsel also suggested that such a "strange" statement might have no effect on an eventual interpretation of the Convention on the Rights of the Child, given that article 32 of the Vienna Convention establishes the preparatory work of a treaty as a supplementary means of interpretation only, where the treaty terms are unclear. Furthermore, the VCLT expressly provides that "interpretative agreements" of this sort are only binding if they are agreed upon by all states parties to the treaty or accepted by them as an instrument related to the treaty, which was not the case with the chairman's statement.[109] The United Kingdom and Luxembourg seem to have taken the legal counsel's report seriously, as they both filed reservations on the right to life from conception, which would have been unnecessary if the informal drafting group's statement had been deemed to have any significant interpretive value.[110]

The statement's language, in any case, would only *allow* individual states to opt out of the preamble when defining the term "child," but it certainly would not *require* any states to do so. The statement did not allude to abortion either.[111] It did not imply, as the *Artavia* judgment incorrectly asserted, that the preparatory work "did not intend to extend to the unborn child the provisions of the Convention, *especially* the right to life."[112] Such a restrictive interpretation of the CRC is in open contradiction with article 29 of the American Convention, which forbids a restrictive interpretation of other international treaties to which states are parties.[113] It also violates the court's own holding that "the interpretation of other international instruments cannot be used to limit the enjoyment and exercise of a right; also, it must contribute to the most favorable application of the provision to be interpreted."[114]

## Other International Treaties

Latin American and Caribbean states parties have ratified other international human rights treaties, both global and regional, that establish positive state obligations to secure prenatal rights to life, health, personal integrity, and development of unborn children, both independently and through the mother. For instance, regional agreements contain provisions granting human rights protection for expectant mothers in close connection to children's rights. Among these is the Protocol of San Salvador, which connects unborn children's rights to the family setting, stipulating in article 15(3) that states shall "provide special care and assistance to mothers during a reasonable period before and after childbirth" as well as provide protection for children.[115] Article 2 of the Inter-American Convention on Support Obligations defines a child as any person below the age of eighteen, thereby establishing a ceiling, but no floor, to the definition.[116] When ratifying that treaty, Panama submitted a declaration stating: "A person who is not yet born (*nasciturus*) shall have the right to prenatal support."[117]

At the global level, article 14 of the Geneva Convention (IV) Relative to the Protection of Civilian Persons in Time of War provides for and mandates protection of expectant mothers from the effects of war.[118] Similarly, the majority of states parties to the American Convention, except for El Salvador, Haiti, Jamaica, and Nicaragua, have ratified the Rome Statute of the International Criminal Court, which includes in its definition of genocide in article 6(d) "measures intended to prevent births"—that is, abortions—with the intent to destroy a particular group.[119] At the regional level, the Inter-American Convention on the Prevention, Punishment and Eradication of Violence Against Women ("Convention of Belém do Pará"), ratified by all states parties to the American Convention, also mandates, in article 9, that special attention be given to violence against pregnant women.[120]

Furthermore, a right to prenatal health has been recognized in article 12(2)(a) of the International Covenant on Economic, Social and Cultural Rights (ICESCR), ratified by virtually all states parties to the American Convention.[121] A right of pregnant women to prenatal health is also recognized in article 12(2) of the Convention on the Elimination of All Forms of Discrimination Against Women (CEDAW), ratified by several countries in the region.[122] Mexican Supreme Court judge Sergio Salvador Aguirre Anguiano interpreted ICESCR articles 5, 10, and 12 as prohibiting treaty interpretation that would create a right to acts directed to the destruction of any rights recognized in the covenant, such as the right to prenatal life and health.[123] "If states have a duty to prevent child mortality under the Covenant, what greater violation of this obligation could there be than legalizing the interruption of pregnancy up to the 12th week?" he reasoned in regard to Mexico City's legalization of first-trimester abortion.[124]

In addition to major human rights treaties, Latin American and Caribbean states have consistently recognized the unborn child's right to life in international declarations in the United Nations context. For instance, Latin American and Caribbean states overwhelmingly voted in favor of the United Nations Declaration on Human Cloning. This declaration calls upon states to prohibit both therapeutic and reproductive human cloning and genetic engineering techniques on human embryos, which the declaration denounces as incompatible with human dignity and the protection of human life.[125]

During the declaration's approval, Mexico and Costa Rica voiced their intent to protect "human dignity" and "human life" through the adoption of the said declaration.[126] Costa Rica's statement was actually the precursor of the United Nations ban on all forms of human cloning, and Costa Rica was the first state to introduce a draft international convention for the prohibition of all forms of human cloning, which referred to the human embryo before implantation as a human being.[127]

Central American countries, in particular, have adopted a subregional declaration reiterating their commitment to protect the unborn child from abortion. The Declaration of the Central American Presidents and the Prime Minister of Belize on the International Conference on Population and Development to be Held in Cairo in September 1994, for instance, was adopted by the 15th Summit of Central American Presidents.[128] The declaration stated, among other things: "The family must be based on *respect for life as of its conception* and the union of man with a woman as it is established by our customs."[129]

### The Universal Declaration on Human Rights

All states parties to the American Convention have signed the Universal Declaration of Human Rights (UDHR), which establishes a universal, unrestricted right to life in article 3: "Everyone has the right to life, liberty and security of person."[130] Article 25(2) establishes that "[m]otherhood and childhood are entitled to special care and assistance."

The UDHR also implicitly protects the unborn child by establishing a right to health services and social security for everyone, including expectant mothers, in article 22 (right of social security) and article 25(1) (right to a standard of living adequate for health and well-being).[131] Former commissioners Monroy Cabra and Escobar Gil have read articles 3 and 6—establishing that "everyone" has a right to life and to recognition of their legal identity as those possessing such rights—as a "clear and precise mandate to recognize every human being's individual entitlement to rights, regardless of the state of development" in which they may find themselves.[132]

The *Artavia* judgment stated that the UDHR's term "human being" did not include the unborn child because, according to the preparatory work, the word "born" in article 1 ("All human beings are *born* free and equal in dignity and rights") "was used *precisely* to exclude the unborn child from the rights recognized in the Declaration."[133] However, no evidence was provided to support that assertion—no reference to any language actually stating an intent to exclude unborn children from human rights recognition in the declaration's preparatory work or to determine that human life begins at birth.[134]

A closer look at the cited *travaux préparatoires* records in fact shows that states understood a right to life from conception to be either implicit or contained in the general right to life; the Soviet Union, Lebanon, China, and the United Kingdom expressed concern over this point.[135] The document also shows that the reference to the unborn, as well as the reference to the disabled, was removed only "in the interests of brevity."[136] The declaration's *travaux préparatoires* indicate, however, in the words of Chilean representative Eduardo Cruz-Coke, that the "silence [of the declaration's text] on so grave a question as this showed great restraint," not an intent to exclude the unborn child from human rights protection.[137]

The Universal Declaration's *travaux préparatoires* contains evidence that signatory states actually rejected the second paragraph of the draft article of the declaration that recognized potential exceptions to the right to life for eugenic abortions and abortions of those conceived in rape.[138] Chile, Panama, and Uruguay, three Latin American states parties to the American Convention, in particular, opposed that article in the strongest terms, and the language on abortion was rejected by a majority of ten votes against three.[139]

### International Covenant on Civil and Political Rights

All states parties to the American Convention have ratified the ICCPR, which contains a universal right to life of every human being, using language similar to that of the American Convention: "Every human being has the inherent right to life. This right shall be protected by law. No one shall be arbitrarily deprived of his life."[140] Uruguay and Colombia, two states parties to the American Convention, originally proposed that language, with the intent that the article on the right to life "begin with an affirmation of the inherent right to life of everyone," a proposal that was overwhelmingly accepted by other states parties.[141]

During the ICCPR's *travaux préparatoires*, Latin American states proposed including language that would recognize a prenatal right to life from conception in the ICCPR's current article 6. In 1957, Brazil, El Salvador, and Mexico, along with Belgium and Morocco, proposed that article 6 begin with the following words: "The right to life is inherent in the human person. *From the moment of conception,* this right shall be protected by law."[142] Several proposals to include a recognition of a right to life from conception had previously been offered in 1947 and 1950 by Lebanon but had not been voted on by the states parties as a whole.[143]

The countries proposing the amendment held that life began at conception, that right-to-life protection should be extended "to all unborn children," and that "the legislation of many countries accorded protection to the unborn child."[144] The inclusion of the terms "from the moment of conception" was, however, rejected by thirty-one votes to twenty.[145] The *Artavia* judgment cited this vote as its basis to conclude that "the preparatory work for article 6(1) of the ICCPR reveals that the States did not seek to treat the unborn child as a person and grant it the same level of protection as those who are born."[146]

The ICCPR drafting (Third Committee) records indicate the reason for the rejection of the term "from conception": "[T]he amendment was opposed on the grounds that it was impossible for the State to determine the moment of conception and, therefore, to undertake to protect life from that moment. Moreover, the proposed clause would involve the question of the rights and duties of the medical profession. Legislation on the subject was based on different principles in different countries and it was, therefore, inappropriate to include such a provision in an international instrument."[147] The record does not allude to a general intent of states parties to deny the unborn child's personhood and ensuing human rights protection, as the *Artavia* judgment misrepresented.

The ICCPR also prohibits imposing the death penalty on pregnant women in article 6(5), the drafting of which was actually proposed by Guatemala, a state party to the American Convention.[148] The ICCPR's *travaux préparatoires,* namely the records of the Commission on Human Rights for 1952 and 1957, reveal that the legislative intent behind this provision was "to prevent the carrying out of the sentence of death *before the child was born.*"[149] The provision was "interpreted as applying solely to the period preceding childbirth."[150] The records further state that "the intention of paragraph 4 [5] was inspired by humanitarian considerations and *by consideration of the interests of the unborn child*, was that death sentence [*sic*], if it concerned a pregnant woman, should not be carried out at all."[151] Drafting states disagreed as to whether or not a pregnant woman given a death sentence should be executed at all after the child's birth given that "the normal development of the unborn child might be affected if the mother were to live in constant fear that, after the birth of her child, the death sentence would be carried out."[152]

The language in article 6 of the ICCPR probably inspired the subsequent recognition of a prenatal right to life from conception in the American Convention, given that the former preceded the latter and that similar terms on legal protection of the right to life can be found in article 4(1) of the American Convention, which added the explicit recognition of the right to life from conception. As pointed out by former IACHR member Dinah Shelton, "[B]oth regional and global human rights instruments contain provisions which seek to guarantee the basic needs of mother and fetus during maternity. There is, undoubtedly, general agreement that protection should be afforded to allow for healthy development of the fetus and the well-being of the mother."[153] A similar ban on imposing the death penalty on pregnant women can be found in the American Convention in article 4(5), as well as in other international humanitarian law instruments ratified by nearly all Latin American and Caribbean states, such as article 6(4) of Additional Protocol II to the Geneva Conventions.[154]

States parties to the American Convention have interpreted the ICCPR to protect the right to life of unborn children. For instance, the Supreme Court of El Salvador read the ICCPR as protecting the right to life from the time of conception, albeit in a way that allowed for exceptions where the mother's life is at risk.[155] Judge Florentín Meléndez, in particular, emphasized that under the ICCPR and the CRC, the unborn child's right to life from the moment of conception is recognized as a nonderogable, fundamental right.[156] Likewise, the Mexican Supreme Court has repeatedly read the Federal Constitution's protection of the right to life from the moment of conception as consistent with the CRC and the ICCPR's universal right to life and prohibition of execution of pregnant women.[157] In 2008, for instance, the court held that Mexico's Federal Constitution protects the right to life from the moment of conception regardless of the unborn's stage of development, in consistency with the CRC and the ICCPR.[158]

Members of treaty-monitoring bodies that promote abortion rights have often minimized the treaties' protection of unborn life in order to politically pressure countries into legally authorizing or liberalizing elective abortion.[159] Human Rights Committee recommendations, for instance, were cited in the *Artavia* judgment to support the holding that "an absolute protection of the prenatal life or the life of the embryo cannot be inferred from the ICCPR."[160] In 2018, the Human Rights Committee advocated for the creation of abortion rights, ironically in General Comment No. 36 on article 6 of the ICCPR on the right to life. The general comment entirely ignored the prenatal right to life and instead stated that "the right to life is not absolute" and called on states parties to legalize abortion, particularly in cases of risk to the life or health of the mother, rape, and where "the pregnancy" is "not viable."[161] The committee also urged states to decriminalize abortion providers and to restrict individual conscientious objection by medical providers, among others.[162]

Nonjudicial international human rights bodies, however, lack the power to issue legally binding (or persuasive) treaty interpretations, especially when those interpretations fail to follow rules of international treaty interpretation and mandate acts that contradict the object and purpose of a treaty, as indicated by international law experts.[163] Former IACHR commissioners Monroy Cabra and Escobar Gil have pointed out that treaty body recommendations do not create legally binding obligations for countries unless a country decides to incorporate such recommendations into its domestic law via constitutional court jurisprudence—that is, unless uniform jurisprudence exists making that treaty a part of its constitutional law (*bloque de constitucionalidad*).[164] Chilean Constitutional Court judges rejected the proposition that the commentaries, observations, and recommendations of international human rights bodies such as the Human Rights Committee, which advocated for abortion rights, had any binding force in the national legal system, and the judges reiterated that such statements only constitute international *soft law*, citing constitutional precedent to that effect.[165]

The IACHR has, in any event, rejected the idea that the ICCPR somehow allows abortion and could therefore be incompatible with the American Convention's prenatal right to life. During the American Convention's preparatory work, in 1968, the commission debated a proposal from

Commissioner Carlos Dunshee de Abranches. Dunshee proposed that the draft article on the right to life be amended to eliminate *all* protection of prenatal life from conception, arguing that the provision would have created conflict with article 6(1) of the ICCPR.[166] The commission, however, found no conflict with the covenant and rejected his proposal, leaving the right-to-life protection "from the moment of conception" as indicated by the Inter-American Council of Jurists.[167]

## Nonexistence of Abortion Rights in International Human Rights Law

No global or regional international treaty ratified by states parties to the American Convention contains a human right to take the life of an unborn child through elective abortion or mandates the legal authorization of such an act.[168] This fact has also been occasionally acknowledged by high UN officials like Anand Grover, UN Special Rapporteur for Health, who recognized in 2011, during his presentation of a report on the right to health to the United Nations General Assembly, that there is "no international law on the matter [of abortion]."[169]

Former commissioners Monroy Cabra and Escobar Gil recognized this fact when they wrote that "no international obligation to decriminalize abortion emanates from international law."[170] "Instead," they said, "international treaties . . . expressly recognize the right to life of all human beings from the moment of conception."[171] High court judges have also recognized this. Colombian Constitutional Court judge Alvaro Tafur Galvis, for instance, pointed out that "no international human rights instrument . . . clearly establishes a right to access abortion" or leads to the conclusion that regarding abortion as a crime is a human rights violation.[172]

Contrary to common misconceptions, CEDAW and other international nonbinding instruments, such as the Cairo and Beijing international conferences, do not create abortion rights. CEDAW does not even contain the term "abortion" or its equivalent, or "reproductive rights." In fact, CEDAW article 12(2) protects a mother's health in connection with pregnancy.[173] Likewise, the Rome Statute of the International Criminal Court has sometimes been cited as supporting a right to abortion, to which former commissioners Monroy Cabra and Escobar Gil have replied that the terms of the treaty itself evidently reject an international obligation to decriminalize abortion, whether broadly or specifically.[174] The statute states that "'[f]orced pregnancy' means the unlawful confinement of a woman forcibly made pregnant, with the intent of affecting the ethnic composition of any population or carrying out other grave violations of international law. *This definition shall not in any way be interpreted as affecting national laws relating to pregnancy.*"[175]

The outcome documents for the international conferences of Cairo and Beijing—that is, the ICPD Programme of Action adopted at the 1994 International Conference on Population and Development and the Beijing Declaration and Platform for Action adopted at the 1995 Fourth World Conference on Women (the nature of which is entirely nonbinding)—are often cited as authorities supporting the creation of international abortion rights, but neither document comes close to doing so.[176] The documents contain mixed language on abortion, some of which exhorts countries to "deal with the health impact of unsafe abortion as a major public health concern" and to ensure "safe" abortion "[i]n circumstances *where abortion is not against the law.*"[177] However, such language does not explicitly advocate for authorization of abortion where illegal, much less the creation of abortion rights. The Beijing Declaration only encouraged states to "consider reviewing laws containing punitive measures against women who have undergone illegal abortions"; it did not demand that states fully decriminalize or legally authorize elective abortion.[178]

Both the ICPD Programme of Action and the Beijing Declaration and Platform for Action explicitly indicated that abortion is a practice that must be combated, stating that "every attempt should be made to eliminate the need for abortion" and that "[g]overnments should take appropriate steps to help women *avoid abortion.*"[179] In addition, both the ICPD Programme of Action and the Beijing Declaration specifically affirmed that abortion may never be promoted as a method of family planning.[180] They also declared that the need exists to "reduce the recourse to abortion" through expansion of family planning services.[181] Countries in transition—for example, Eastern European countries—were urged in Cairo to "address their current reliance on abortion for fertility regulation" as an urgent matter.[182] All countries were exhorted to help women "avoid repeat abortions."[183]

The Cairo and Beijing outcome documents also asserted the right of individual nations to make decisions regarding abortion by providing that "[a]ny measures or changes related to abortion within the health system *can only be determined at the national or local level* according to the national *legislative* process."[184] In addition, the conferences condemned "prenatal sex selection" carried out through the abortion of female fetuses.[185] The UN Conference on Women held in Beijing condemned prenatal sex selection against female unborn children as a human rights violation, calling nations to "eliminate all forms of discrimination against the *girl child* which result in harmful and unethical practices such as *prenatal* sex selection."[186]

In addition, the United States, a signatory to the American Convention, introduced a reservation in the ICPD Programme of Action indicating that it did not support the creation of an international right to abortion. Represented by Al Gore, during President Bill Clinton's administration, the United States made the following statement:

> We believe that making available the highest quality family-planning and health-care services will simultaneously respect women's own desires to prevent unintended pregnancies, reduce population growth and the rate of abortion.
>
> The United States Constitution guarantees every woman within our borders a right to choose an abortion, subject to limited and specific exceptions. We are committed to that principle. But let us take a false issue off the table: *the United States does not seek to establish a new international right to abortion, and we do not believe that abortion should be encouraged as a method of family planning.*
>
> We also believe that policy-making in these matters should be *the province of each Government, within the context of its own laws and national circumstances,* and *consistent with previously agreed human rights standards.*
>
> In this context, we abhor and condemn coercion related to abortion or any other matters of reproduction.
>
> We believe that where abortion is permitted, it should be medically safe and that unsafe abortion is a matter of women's health that must be addressed.[187]

### Persistent Objection to the Creation of Abortion Rights by States Parties to the American Convention

States parties to the American Convention have expressly rejected treaty interpretations that would unilaterally create abortion rights or create human rights obligations to legally authorize elective abortion. For instance, at the Beijing conference, Argentina stated that no reference to sexual and reproductive health may be interpreted as including legal abortion.[188] Argentina declared that terms such as "reproductive health services" or "regulation of fertility" may not be interpreted "as restricting the right to life or abrogating the *condemnation of abortion* as a method of birth control or an instrument of population policy," while invoking article 75(23) of the Constitution of Argentina, article 16 of CEDAW, and paragraph 42 of the Vienna Programme of Action adopted by the World Conference on Human Rights.[189] In Beijing, Argentina also indicated that even though their delegation supported a Platform of Action recommendation that suggested reviewing laws criminalizing abortions, this participation "does not constitute, however, a proposal to *decriminalize abortion* or *exempt from criminal responsibility* those who may be accomplices or participants in this offence."[190]

States parties to the American Convention represented at Cairo and Beijing rejected the interpretation of terms like "reproductive health," "sexual health," "maternity without risk," "reproductive rights," "sexual rights," and "regulation of fertility" as including a duty to decriminalize elective abortion. For instance, the Dominican Republic at Cairo rejected the interpretation of these terms as including abortion or termination of pregnancy.[191] At the Beijing Conference on Women, the Dominican Republic objected to the interpretation of "reproductive rights" and related terms as including abortion or the interruption of pregnancy, stating that the "Dominican Republic, as a signatory to the American Convention on Human Rights, and in accordance with the Constitution and the laws of the Republic, confirms that every person has a right to life, and that life begins at the moment of conception."[192] Ecuador filed a similar written statement, making a reservation excluding abortion from legitimate interpretations of the phrase "reproductive rights" and related terms due to the principle of "the inviolability of life, the protection of children from the moment of conception," and "responsible paternity," a principle embodied in its constitution.[193]

Guatemala, appealing to the American Declaration of the Rights and Duties of Man and the American Convention on Human Rights, entered a reservation in chapters 2 and 7 of the ICPD Programme of Action regarding abortion as a reproductive or sexual right or as a reproductive health service, noting that "life exists from the moment of conception and that the right to life is the source of all other rights."[194] At Beijing, Guatemala reiterated this reservation and expressed its "unconditional respect for the right to life from the moment of conception."[195] El Salvador objected to the understanding of abortion as a reproductive right, a related reproductive health service, or a family planning service in the ICPD Programme of Action, stating: "We Latin American countries, *are signatories to the American Convention on Human Rights* (Pact of San José). Article 4 thereof states quite clearly that life must be protected from the moment of conception. . . . For this reason . . . we consider that life must be protected from the moment of conception."[196] In 2010, El Salvador withdrew its reservations to the terms "reproductive health" and "reproductive rights," on the understanding that "abortion shall not be promoted as a birth control method under any circumstances."[197]

When filing its declaration to the ICPD Programme of Action, Honduras referred to the American Convention on Human Rights and the Declaration of Guácimo, noting that the language of the Programme of Action should not be interpreted as overriding international obligations, stemming from the American Convention, to protect human life from the moment of conception.[198] At both Cairo and Beijing, Honduras specifically rejected the interpretation of terms relating to reproductive health, sexual health, and family planning as including abortion, in light of the American Convention on Human Rights, which "reaffirms that every individual has the right to life from the moment of conception, on the basis of the moral, ethical, religious and cultural principles that should govern human behaviour."[199]

In both the Cairo and Beijing conferences, Nicaragua filed a declaration stating that an implicit understanding that abortion could be included as a reproductive or sexual right was not acceptable on the basis that "*as a signatory of the American Convention*, [Nicaragua confirms] that every person has a right to life, this being a fundamental and inalienable right, and that this right begins from the very moment of conception."[200] Also at Beijing and Cairo, Paraguay rejected the interpretation of the regulation of fertility as including abortion, declaring that such interpretation was "totally unacceptable"; and at Cairo, Paraguay affirmed that "the right to life is the inherent right of every human being from conception to natural death," in accordance with article 4 of its constitution.[201]

During the adoption of both conference outcome documents, Peru rejected the interpretation of reproductive health–related terms as including abortion on the grounds that it is inconsistent with the right to life and indicated that "the right to life and the consideration of a person from the moment of conception as a subject of law in every respect are fundamental human rights."[202] In Cairo, Peru declared that "the right to life [exists] from the moment of conception; abortion is rightly classified as a crime in the Criminal Code of Peru, with the sole exception of therapeutic abortion"; it also cited the CRC when reiterating its objection to the international legalization of abortion and stated that "Peru regards abortion as a public health problem" and that family planning methods should not "place life at risk."[203]

States parties to the American Convention have also demonstrated opposition to the creation of abortion rights in other fora. For instance, Nicaragua, Chile, Honduras, the Dominican Republic, and Costa Rica rejected the introduction of the term "reproductive rights" as including legal abortion in the outcome document of the UN Conference on Sustainable Development.[204] Likewise, based on the universal character of the right to life, Argentina objected to abortion as included among reproductive rights and reproductive health services at the Sixth Session of the Regional Conference on the Integration of Women into the Economic and Social Development of Latin America and the Caribbean in 1994, at the said conference's twentieth board meeting in 1997, at the World Summit for Social Development in Copenhagen and Johannesburg in 1995, and at the Second United Nations Conference on Human Settlements (Habitat II) in Istanbul in 2002 ("Habitat II").[205] At the First Regional Conference on Population and Development, held by the Economic Commission for Latin America and the Caribbean (ECLAC) in

2013, Guatemala filed a reservation reiterating its unrestricted respect for human life from conception onward.[206]

At Habitat II, Ecuador, Guatemala, and Honduras rejected abortion "as a method of family planning, fertility regulation or birth control."[207] In addition, at the Tenth and Eleventh sessions of the Regional Conference on the Integration of Women into the Economic and Social Development of Latin America and the Caribbean, Nicaragua, Chile, Costa Rica, and El Salvador rejected abortion as a reproductive health service or right.[208] Chile declared in writing that "in accordance with the Political Constitution of the Republic of Chile, which protects life before birth, [Chile] subscribes to the Brasilia Consensus on the understanding that this does not imply an endorsement of abortion."[209] Costa Rica stated that "[t]he Constitutional Chamber of the Republic of Costa Rica has repeatedly affirmed that 'a person is a person from the moment of conception, and we are dealing with a living being, with the right to protection under the legal system,' in accordance with the juridical norms and Political Constitution in force in Costa Rica."[210] Nicaragua indicated that "[a]bortion or the interruption of pregnancy may not, under any circumstance, be considered a means of fertility regulation or of birth control; all internal legislation governing this matter falls under the sovereignty of the nation of Nicaragua."[211] El Salvador made a similar statement rejecting abortion as a legitimate reproductive health service or family planning method, adding that "article 1 of our Constitution, which relates to the human person, states that 'Every human being is recognized as a human person from the moment of conception.'"[212]

Some states parties to the American Convention have also opposed the creation of abortion rights before United Nations committees and officials when admonished for retaining their abortion prohibitions. In 2007, for instance, upon suggestions by CEDAW Committee experts Ms. Shin and Ms. Pimentel that Honduras legalize abortion, the Honduran delegates reminded the committee that under article 67 of the Constitution of Honduras, which focuses on individual rights, the fetus was considered a human being.[213] In 2011, upon the presentation of a report on the right to health by the UN Special Rapporteur on Health at the United Nations General Assembly, which urged states to legalize abortion as a human rights obligation, Latin American states, among other states, objected to the alleged existence of abortion rights.[214] Argentina stated that it did not endorse the report with regard to abortion, given that Argentina's legislation banned abortion and recognized a universal right to life for all. "Chile's delegate said the report did not give a balanced view, since it emphasized abortion as a health service."[215] Chile's delegate further stated that Chile "did not recognize a right to abortion" given that the nation essentially recognized the right to life of all human beings. The delegate from Honduras endorsed Chile's comments.

### Historic Interpretation of the Right to Life from Conception

The *travaux préparatoires* are supplementary methods of interpretation that, according to the Vienna Convention, may be used either to confirm the treaty's ordinary meaning or to clarify an ambiguity, not to reverse or obscure the treaty's explicit terms.[216] Article 32 of the VCLT, titled "supplementary means of interpretation," stipulates: "Recourse may be had to supplementary means of interpretation, including the preparatory work of the treaty and the circumstances of its conclusion, in order to *confirm* the meaning resulting from the application of article 31, or to *determine the meaning* when the interpretation according to article 31: (a) leaves the meaning ambiguous or obscure; or (b) leads to a result which is manifestly absurd or unreasonable."[217] When a textual analysis produces an interpretation that is unambiguous and reasonable, the legislative records can be used only to confirm that reading.

The text of the American Convention on Human Rights contains no ambiguity regarding the unborn child's personhood and right-to-life entitlement, wrote former judge Julio Barberis. The convention's historic interpretation should not be used to replace the convention's ordinary meaning with the judges' preferred interpretation, he said in reference to the *Baby Boy* report, although the same could be said of the *Artavia* judgment.[218] The reliance on complementary means of interpretation as primary means of interpretation is contrary to international norms of treaty interpretation, he pointed out.[219] The historic interpretation should therefore confirm, not distort, a good-faith, nonrestrictive interpretation of the prenatal right-to-life provision, even if judges can find other readings that they agree with or like better.

## The Convention's Preparatory Work

The prenatal right to life applying "from the moment of conception" was included by states parties since the American Convention's very first draft in 1959 until present day. The first draft American Convention was created by the Inter-American Council of Jurists in 1959.[220] In it, the right to life from the moment of conception was explicitly recognized, and it remained so until the adoption of the final text.[221] At the Second Inter-American Extraordinary Conference in Rio de Janeiro (held in 1965), the OAS General Assembly charged the OAS Permanent Council with completing a second draft American Convention that incorporated the first draft, two independent drafts presented by Chile and Uruguay, and IACHR recommendations which were issued as a two-part report in 1966 and 1967.[222] The council then asked OAS member states to present their observations on the question of whether the draft American Convention could conflict with UN international human rights treaties, to which states parties responded in the negative.

The Inter-American Commission on Human Rights created a second draft American Convention upon the council's request; this draft was approved in an extraordinary period of sessions; and the commission presented its final draft convention text to the council on July 18, 1968. As indicated in previous chapters, during the commission's debates, Commissioner Carlos Dunshee proposed a removal of the right to life from conception as a whole, allegedly due to incompatibility with the ICCPR, but the commission decided to keep this provision "for reasons of principle."[223] The commission's second draft convention was presented to OAS member state governments for their observations and commentary and discussed at the Inter-American Specialized Human Rights Conference, held November 7–22, 1969, in San José, Costa Rica, where the final convention text was adopted and opened for signature.[224] The convention entered into force on July 18, 1978, upon the eleventh ratification.

Several proposals were made regarding the expression "and, in general, from the moment of conception" at the San José Conference, most of which did not make it to a vote. Ecuador proposed the deletion of the term "in general."[225] Colombia proposed that the phrase "the right to life is inherent to the human person" be added to the article on the right to life.[226] El Salvador (and the United States) supported this proposal.[227] Uruguay and Panama found it to be unnecessary. The Dominican Republic proposed amending the right-to-life article to make it identical to the ICCPR's provision: "Regarding the right to life, we believe that universal concepts of human rights would be strengthened if the Inter-American was identical to that adopted by the United Nations in article 6(1) of the Covenant."[228] This proposal made no allusion to abortion and seemed to be clearly distinct from Brazil's, as noted by the *Artavia* court, which pointed out that Brazil and the Dominican Republic had introduced two "separate amendments."[229] In fact, Brazil itself objected to the Dominican Republic's proposal, on the basis that strict adherence to the covenant's text was unnecessary.[230]

*Brazil's Rejected Proposal at the San José Conference.* Brazil's delegate, Carlos Dunshee, suggested the deletion of "and, in general, from the moment of conception."[231] According to the *Baby Boy* report, which he authored, the proposal was based on concern over "the abortion laws in force *in the majority* of the American States."[232] However, the preparatory-work records indicate that no reference was made to such an issue during the discussion of the right to life from conception. Instead, the stated justification for the proposal was that the said language was "vague" and would not be effective in preventing states parties to the future convention from legally authorizing "the most diverse cases of abortion."[233] Brazil's observations to the draft indicated that "[t]he said clause may therefore raise questions that, if the current drafting remained, could render the article's acceptance and implementation more difficult."[234] Brazil also pointed out that its civil and criminal codes protected the right to life from conception and prohibited abortion at the time, except for rape and situations in which the mother's life was at risk.

The United States, which did not ultimately become a party to the convention, supported Brazil's proposal invoking only an intent to allow the application of the death penalty in its jurisdiction, but did not make any observations about abortion in regards to that proposal.[235] Chile rejected the Brazilian proposal.[236] Venezuela, a state that was party to the convention for over thirty-five years, spoke out against Brazil's proposal, indicating that "in the matter of civil and political rights, this is not up for state legislatures to decide on," referring to the right to life in particular.[237] Venezuela's delegation used some strong language in opposing the amendment by declaring that "regarding the right to life from conception of a human being there can be *no concessions*" and that a convention that would not recognize that principle would be "unacceptable."[238]

Ultimately, the Brazilian proposal in favor of allowing legal abortion in some jurisdictions was, unlike other proposals, explicitly voted on and rejected by states parties present at the conference, which demonstrates that states parties did not favor a reading of the convention that would have left the unborn child unprotected from elective abortion under domestic law.[239] Even if the proposal had passed, which it did not, the question of abortion would have simply been left open for states to decide, as Dunshee indicated: "[the right to life from conception] is a subject that should be left to each country's legislature," and so the proposal would not have created a right to abortion or a state duty to legally authorize it.[240]

*Adopted Text.* After rejection of the Brazilian proposal, the phrase "and, in general, from the moment of conception" made it to the final text. Upon approval of the final text, Brazil's delegate , Dunshee filed a statement reiterating his opposition to the adopted language.[241] Brazil and the United States also filed a joint statement regarding their own interpretation of article 4(1), without making any direct reference to abortion: "The United States and Brazil interpret the language of paragraph 1 of article 4 as preserving to State Parties discretion with respect to the content of legislation in the light of their own social development, experience and similar factors."[242]

Costa Rica seems to have rejected this statement by filing a counter-declaration. In it, it invoked its founding fathers, its humanitarian tradition, its opposition to the death penalty, and its cultural identity to reiterate its firm support of "the principle of inviolability of human life, recognized in article 21 of the Costa Rican Constitution," affirming "that it cannot accept . . . norms that do not aim at protecting, *in an absolute manner*, this sacred principle."[243] Ironically, Costa Rica's interpretation was not even mentioned in the court's historical interpretation of article 4(1) in the IVF cases against it, or even brought up in its *pro homine* analysis, even though such a statement should have been given interpretive weight, at least in regard to that particular state.

Although the expression "in general," added by the commission, was eventually adopted, no intent to qualify the prenatal right to life in favor of abortion or to create abortion rights can be found in the Inter-American Conference, not even on the part of Brazil, which actually expressed concern that a restrictive reading of the term might make the convention's prohibition of abortion ineffective.[244] As for the *Artavia* court's argument that states parties had intended to give the term "in general" in article 4(1) a special meaning—namely, that of excluding human embryos from the category of persons—the convention's *travaux préparatoires* show absolutely no evidence confirming that assumption, as pointed out by Judge Vio Grossi.[245]

In *Artavia*, the Mexican interpretive declaration to the American Convention was discussed within the historic interpretation of the American Convention, even though that declaration had nothing to do with the *travaux préparatoires* and was actually introduced twelve years after the Inter-American Conference and two years after the convention went into force.[246] In fact, the Mexican declaration has no bearing on the convention's historical interpretation. It does, however, have some interpretive value as part of the treaty context, and certainly has binding interpretive value for the application of the convention as it pertains to Mexico.

The American Convention's historic interpretation confirms that the convention was intended to mandate general legal protection for the right to life from conception from the very first draft of the American Convention all the way to the adopted text. The personhood of the unborn child was never challenged during the preparatory work. Two objections were filed against the prenatal right to life by one single individual, and both were rejected, first in the commission, then at the Inter-American Specialized Human Rights Conference in San José, Costa Rica.

The court's statement that "the preparatory work does not provide a clear answer to [the dispute over the prenatal right to life]" denies the demonstrable fact that the term "from the moment of conception" "received strong support from other representatives and remained unchanged," as human rights experts on both sides of the abortion issue have recognized.[247] The statement also obscures, rather than clarifies, the treaty's meaning. The *Artavia* judgment's historic interpretation of the convention's prenatal right-to-life provision is not only a restrictive interpretation that violates article 29 but also an unlawful supplementary interpretation of the convention under VCLT article 32 and therefore deserves little deference by the states parties and the court itself.

# Conclusion

Despite previous good-faith interpretations, Inter-American human rights bodies have, in recent decades, either refused to enforce the prenatal right-to-life provision or handed down a restrictive interpretation thereof, creating confusion among states parties as to the proper meaning of the right to life from conception in the American Convention. The IACHR and the Inter-American Court of Human Rights, the bodies theoretically charged with monitoring compliance with the American Convention's right to life from conception, have instead advocated for the creation of abortion rights in states parties to the treaty, which led to the commission's partial loss of US funding in 2019. Notably, the *Artavia* judgment issued by the Inter-American Court against Costa Rica has been the most restrictive interpretation of article 4(1) to date. That said, the decision was not binding on any other nation, its *ratio* was limited to in vitro fertilization and not abortion, and it does not seem to have had much resonance within the court itself or among states parties to the American Convention.

The great majority of states parties, on the other hand, have given article 4(1) a nonrestrictive interpretation and have adopted a variety of domestic laws protecting the unborn child from intentional death and destruction, including induced abortion bans. States parties have adopted criminal prohibitions on elective abortion pursuant to article 2 and article 4(1), and these prohibitions have established a general obligation of states parties to adopt domestic laws that will give the prenatal right to life from conception an *effet utile*.[1] States parties to the American Convention universally categorize elective abortion as a criminal practice and continue to generally regard it as a violation of the unborn child's right to life and personal integrity, even where statutory provisions for nonpunishment of abortion exist. Other practices that directly affect prenatal life, such as forced abortion, fetal homicide, and fetal injury, are also sanctioned with criminal and civil penalties in the great majority of countries in the region.

States parties generally establish narrow exceptions to the rules regarding abortion as a crime and waive criminal punishment for abortion under limited circumstances, mostly when the mother is suffering from a life-threatening health condition. Other criminal punishment exemptions vary, and their regulation is not homogenous in the region. Around half of all states parties have exempted abortions from criminal punishment where a pregnancy results from a sexual crime such as rape or incest, and only about one-third have passed exceptions for nonlethal health risks to the mother or for fetal inviability or disability. Only one-third of all jurisdictions currently allow multiple exceptions for nonpunishment of abortion (usually life/health, rape, and eugenic abortion).

Depenalization of abortion in the region has been irregular, partial, and often advanced by national judiciaries rather than the legislatures. Some states parties' courts, notably Colombia's Constitutional Court, have played a peculiar, quasi-legislative role in decriminalizing abortion and in eventually creating a constitutional right to abort on three grounds. High courts have been responsible for the creation of some absolutory excuses for abortion in states parties, such as for the abortion of anencephalic children in Brazil and of children conceived in rape in Argentina. It must be said that no decision authorizing the nonpunishment of abortion in domestic high courts in the region has been unanimous: one or more judges dissented in every instance, and courts have been deeply divided over the issue, as observed by the Chilean Constitutional Court in 2017.[2]

No state party to the American Convention has decriminalized any abortions through popular vote. As of 2018, Uruguay's legislature stands alone in choosing to substantially depenalize abortions via a legislature-adopted statute. More importantly, no court or legislature has depenalized or decriminalized abortion indicating that they were doing so out of a sense of legal obligation under the American Convention.

Even where statutory dispositions for nonpunishment of abortion have been adopted, abortion cannot be properly said to have been decriminalized in the region, with the exception of Uruguay and Colombia. Even where criminal penalties are unenforceable under criminal statutes, elective abortion continues to be legally regarded as a crime, one that may be legally tolerated, but not celebrated as a constitutional right. Other than in Colombia, elective abortion on three grounds is not understood as an entitlement of the pregnant woman or as a constitutional right in any state party to the convention.

Despite a restrictive interpretation of the prenatal right to life on the part of Inter-American human rights bodies, the American Convention continues to be cited as protecting the unborn child from elective abortion, as the 2018 Argentinian debates on abortion legalization demonstrate. States that grant higher levels of protection to prenatal rights have actively resisted abortion rights advocacy by Inter-American human rights bodies. Nicaragua, Paraguay, and El Salvador, for instance, have rejected the idea that the convention requires them to authorize direct, elective abortions in *Amelia*, *Mainumby*, and *Beatriz*. A fundamental disagreement on interpretation of the American Convention's prenatal right to life thus seems to have emerged between most states parties and Inter-American human rights bodies.

A good-faith, nonrestrictive interpretation of article 4(1) of the American Convention, according to its ordinary meaning, in light of its context and in accordance with the object and purpose of the treaty, would recognize that this provision unambiguously mandates that states parties give the unborn child general, ample legal protection from direct abortion. The language of article 4(1) of the convention not only allows but requires states parties to legally protect the unborn child from any practice that deliberately and arbitrarily violates her right to life from conception ("This right *shall* be protected by law and, in general, from the moment of conception. *No one shall be* arbitrarily deprived of his life." (emphasis added)), such as fetal homicide, forced abortion, and elective abortion. Evolutive, systemic, and historic interpretation confirm this understanding, which remains undisputed by Inter-American human rights bodies.

Under article 4(1) of the American Convention, states parties are under the obligation to protect the unborn child from abortion "in general," not exceptionally. Full abortion bans may thus be consistent with a *pro homine* interpretation of the American Convention as long as a statutory provision for nonpunishment of indirect abortion exists to protect the mother's equal right to life in situations where her life is endangered by carrying the pregnancy to term. That requirement has been codified in some states parties to the American Convention either as a necessity defense (*estado de necesidad*) or as a statutory "life of the mother" or "health of the mother" provision for nonpunishment of abortion that is usually defined as applying in cases of serious, imminent risks to the mother's physical health and survival. No duty to decriminalize the intentional destruction of the unborn child could be reasonably imposed under the convention in the "life of the mother" scenario, however, since fetal demise has never been proven to have any medical benefit for the mother's health or life, as demonstrated before the commission and the court in *Amelia*, *Mainumby*, and *Beatriz*.

Other grounds for nonpunishable abortion or absolutory excuses may fall under a margin of appreciation granted to states by the convention and would be permissible under the American Convention only as long as they are exceptional and not arbitrary, according to article 4(1), and as long as they are enacted by the legislature, as required by article 30. Serious objections based on arbitrariness could be raised, for instance, against the abortion of those conceived in sexual crimes or eugenic abortion, specially where those exceptions are broadly defined or procedural safeguards are lax. A nonrestrictive interpretation of the prenatal right-to-life rule could tolerate, but would not require, absolutory excuses for rape or fetal inviability only if these are not applied in an arbitrary manner. Narrowly defined statutory provisions that include significant procedural safeguards to protect both the life of the mother and the *nasciturus* to the greatest extent possible and that provide for meaningful enforcement, for instance, could demonstrate that a state is not authorizing deprivation of the prenatal right to life in an arbitrary manner.

Almost unanimously, states parties have expressed the understanding that legally authorizing abortion on the sole basis that a pregnant woman wants one, or the woman's choice, would constitute an arbitrary reason under article 4(1). Abortion on the sole basis of a pregnant teen's age or a woman's chronic health condition, in the absence of any serious, actual medical complications, as requested in *Beatriz*, *Mainumby*, and *Paulina*, has also failed the arbitrariness test in some states parties, such as El Salvador, Nicaragua, and Paraguay. A broad legal authorization of abortion on eight grounds, including social reasons and poverty, such as that of Bolivia's short-lived criminal code, would have been likely to fail the nonarbitrariness requirement under the convention as well.

Gradual or incremental protection of the unborn child starting at viability or at the beginning of the second trimester of pregnancy would directly contradict the convention's language, which requires general protection "from the moment of conception." No state party has understood first-trimester abortions to be compatible with the American Convention, not even Uruguay, which did not rely on the convention when it became the first and only state in the region to decriminalize first-trimester abortion. In fact, former Uruguayan president Tabaré Vázquez, when he vetoed legislation, warned the National Assembly that due to the American Convention's recognition of the unborn as a person entitled to a right to life from conception, Uruguay might have to withdraw ratification of the treaty.[3]

A nonrestrictive interpretation of the American Convention could never reasonably create a state obligation to fully decriminalize elective abortion or mandate states to legalize first-trimester or previability abortions, given the convention's explicit mandate to *generally* protect the unborn child's right to life *from conception*, as many states parties' high courts have noted. The American Convention does not contain a provision on reproductive rights or abortion, nor can such a provision be inferred from any other treaty ratified by states parties to the convention. Given article 4(1)'s context, Inter-American human rights bodies could not lawfully categorize induced abortion as a human right, even on three grounds, just as it has never categorized any direct intentional taking of human life, such as the death penalty, as a right either, even where such an act is legal.

Unless the American Convention was amended to include a right to abortion or a new treaty to that effect was adopted, such a distortion of the one global treaty that most explicitly recognizes a person's right to life from the moment of conception would violate every applicable international rule of treaty interpretation, especially the *pro homine* rule in the convention itself. It would effectively amend the convention by stealth. Creating an international duty to decriminalize abortion could have several consequences, the least of which would be to create a state duty to give abortion providers immunity from prosecution since, in practice, penalties are very rarely enforced against women. An international entitlement to elective abortion would expose states parties to international complaints where an elective abortion is denied or delayed in their jurisdiction. It could probably, depending on the interpretation given, create related duties (1) to force health care personnel to provide immediate abortions, thereby restricting their conscience rights, (2) to eliminate or weaken requirements for abortions on minors, or (3) to publicly fund elective abortions.

Nothing prevents, however, a future composition of Inter-American human rights bodies from enforcing article 4(1) on the prenatal right to life. As of 2019, there is no uniform jurisprudence on the unborn child's right to life in the Inter-American system, as pointed out by scholars.[4] *Artavia* may one day be denounced as a decision bringing shame on the court, the way that the *Dred Scott* and *Roe* decisions have been denounced in the United States. Only by interpreting and applying the right to life from conception in good faith, in a nonrestrictive manner, in accordance with the *pro homine* principle, will Inter-American human rights bodies be able to promote nonviolent and compassionate support for girls, women, children, men, and families facing unplanned pregnancies. A truly progressive interpretation of the American Convention may one day promote the "progressive and irreversible" abolition of elective abortion in an "incremental" manner in order to bring about abortion's "gradual disappearance" just as the court has said in regard to the death penalty.[5] Only then will the rest of the world recognize the American Convention's protection of the right to life of unborn children as one of the greatest contributions by Latin America and the Caribbean to international human rights law.

# NOTES

## Introduction

1. Organization of American States, American Convention on Human Rights art. 4(1).

2. *See, e.g.*, Shelton, "International Law on Protection of the Fetus." (Professor Shelton, who then went on to become a member of the Inter-American Commission on Human Rights, points out that the American Convention stands out among other international human rights instruments in its explicit establishment of a prenatal right to life.) *See also* Carozza, *Anglo-Latin Divide and the Future of the Inter-American System of Human Rights*, 164 (former president of the Inter-American Commission on Human Rights Paolo Carozza indicates that the American Convention "is, *on its face*, the international human rights treaty that is most clearly protective of the right to life of the unborn" [emphasis added]).

3. *See Abortion, in* Catechism of the Catholic Church § 2271 (indicating that the Catholic Church has affirmed the immorality of abortion since the first century). *See also* Carozza, *From Conquest to Constitutions*, 281 (tracing Latin American human rights tradition back to sixteenth-century Catholic thinker Bartolomé de Las Casas; commenting on the influence of Catholic social doctrine in Latin American understanding of French Declaration on the Rights of Man and its understanding of the citizen in Simón Bolívar's thought and the Mexican Constitution of 1917, among things).

4. *See* Inter-American Yearbook on Human Rights (1968), 97 (tracing human rights movement back to the colonization era when Catholic voices rose up in condemnation of slavery and racial segregation). *See also Palabras pronunciadas por el doctor Rodolfo Piza Escalante*, 22–23 (speech by first Inter-American Court chief justice Rodolfo Piza Escalante at the court's inauguration, where he describes the Christian origin of international human rights law, particularly the concept of human dignity, derived from divine revelation in the book of Genesis).

5. *See, e.g.*, Organization of American States, *Actas y Documentos of the Interamerican Specialized Conference on Human Rights*, 408–9.

6. *See* Signatories and Ratifications: American Convention on Human Rights.

7. For more information on US obligations under the American Convention, *see* discussion on the *Baby Boy* petition against the United States in chapter 1 and discussion on object and purpose of the treaty in chapter 3.

8. *See, e.g.*, Callamard, *Rep. on a Gender-Sensitive Approach to Arbitrary Killings* (indicating that "[t]reaty bodies and special procedures mandate holders have consistently condemned countries that criminalize and restrict access to abortion, making direct links between the criminalization of abortion, maternal mortality and the right to life. Noting that such laws violate the right to life of pregnant women and other rights, the Human Rights Committee and the Committee against Torture, for example, have expressed concerns about restrictive abortion laws, including absolute bans on abortion, as violating the right to life and prohibition of torture and other ill-treatment"). *See also Maternal Mortality in 2005* (World Health Organization (WHO) suggests that the realization of the fifth MDG goal to reduce maternal mortality will require, among other things, prevention of unsafe abortions by legalization of abortion).

9. *See* Loudon, *Death in Childbirth, 1800–1950*; Kassembaum et al., *Global, Regional, and National Levels and Causes of Maternal Mortality During 1990–2013*, 980–1004; *Trends in Maternal Mortality: 1990 to 2008* (WHO report); Koch et al., *Women's Education Level, Maternal Health Facilities, Abortion Legislation and Maternal Deaths* (all finding that access to maternal and obstetric health care, skilled birth attendants, women's education, and the overall level of health care in a given country or region, rather than abortion, are the most important factors in reducing maternal mortality rates).

10. *See* Koch, *Epidemiology of Abortion and Its Prevention in Chile*, 71 (demonstrating that after Chile's adoption of a full abortion ban in 1989, abortion-related maternal deaths decreased and became "an exceptionally rare phenomenon in epidemiological terms (a risk of about 1 in 4 million pregnant women of fertile age or 0.4 per 100,000 live births for abortion of any type, excluding ectopic pregnancy)"); Agrawal, *Maternal Mortality and Morbidity in the United States of America* (reporting that the United States has a higher maternal mortality rate than most high-income countries and the Islamic Republic of Iran, Libya, and Turkey). *See also* Martin, *U.S. Has the Worst Rate of Maternal Deaths in the Developed World* (citing studies comparing maternal mortality rates in developed countries).

11. *See* Artavia Murillo v. Costa Rica n.283. *Cf.* Stith, *The Fabrication of Human Rights as a World Religion*, 859–61 (noting that Latin Americans, as well as those from other traditional cultures, tend to be utterly deferential to international agents of human rights in a quasi-religious way).

12. *See* Antkowiak and Gonza, *The American Convention on Human Rights: Essential Rights*, 74–75 (noting that the Inter-American Court has, as of 2017, left "the rights of unborn children in a state of significant uncertainty").

13. *See, e.g.*, Murillo, *Costa Rica ofrece a CIDH posible arreglo en aborto terapéutico* (indicating the existence of a petition on behalf of two women, A.N. and

Aurora, against Costa Rica arguing a state duty to provide the abortions of their severely disabled fetuses). *See also El Salvador 2016 Human Rights Report*, 23 (report from US Department of State indicating that a petition had been submitted to the Inter-American Commission on Human Rights by nongovernmental organizations claiming a human rights violation against seventeen women who were allegedly convicted for abortion in El Salvador).

14. *See* Vienna Convention on the Law of Treaties arts. 31–32; Organization of American States, American Convention on Human Rights art. 29.

## ONE. The Inter-American Commission on Human Rights' Inconsistent Treatment of the Prenatal Right to Life

1. Organization of American States, American Convention on Human Rights art. 4(1).

2. *See* Signatories and Ratifications: American Convention on Human Rights. The Organization of American States (OAS), a regional international governmental organization composed of most of the nations of the Western Hemisphere, including the United States, Canada, and most Latin American and Caribbean states, was created by the Charter of the Organization of American States. *See* Charter of the Organization of American States art. 106. Out of thirty-five OAS member states, ten have never ratified the American Convention, notably the United States, Canada, Belize, Cuba (the last was only readmitted to the OAS in 2009 through resolution AG/RES. 2438 (XXXIX-O/09), and other Caribbean states: Antigua and Barbuda, The Bahamas (Commonwealth of), Guyana, Saint Lucia, Saint Kitts and Nevis, and Saint Vincent and the Grenadines. Trinidad and Tobago and Venezuela initially ratified but later withdrew from the treaty. Foreign territories in the Caribbean, such as Puerto Rico, Guadeloupe or French Guyana are not independent states and therefore cannot become members of the OAS.

3. *See* Organization of American States, American Convention on Human Rights art. 33.

4. *See id.* arts. 61–62, 64. *See also* Advisory Opinion OC-19/05, ¶ 13.

5. *See IACHR Thanks the United States for Additional Financial Contribution.*

6. *See Financial Resources.*

7. *See* Vio Grossi, *Reflexión sobre la justicia interamericana en DD.HH* (indicating that 50 percent of the Inter-American Court's funding is provided by European states, such as Spain, and Norway). *See also IACHR Thanks Donors*; *Recursos Financieros 2014* (indicating that, until 2014, European Union states contributed about 50 percent of the Commission's budget).

8. *See IACHR and Inter-American Court Present a Joint Proposal for the Financing of the Inter-American System of Human Rights* (Judge Roberto Caldas and IACHR president James Cavallaro indicate that Inter-American system bodies have too often depended on nonstates parties and non-OAS states).

9. *See* Letter from Roberto F. Caldas and James Cavallaro (proposing a total budget of around $18 million, 57 percent of which would be allocated for the IACHR and 43 percent for the Inter-American Court). *See also* Orozco, *La reforma de la Comisión Interamericana de Derechos Humanos*, 8 (where Commissioner Orozco calls for greater financial resources for Inter-American human rights bodies).

10. See IACHR, *IACHR Strengthened.* The court and commission experienced a growing financial crisis that seems to have peaked in 2016, but the commission seems to have been more effective in fundraising. The commission's president, James Cavallaro, indicated in October 2016 that many states parties had contributed to overcoming the financial crisis, namely Argentina, Chile, Panama, Colombia, Mexico, Peru, and Uruguay. Funding by nonstates parties, however, seems to have been significant. For instance, the European Commission, Denmark, Spain, Sweden, and Switzerland donated to the commission's 2016 crisis.

11. *See* Letter from Roberto F. Caldas and James Cavallaro.

12. *See About Us*, INTER-AMERICAN HUMAN RIGHTS INSTITUTE.

13. *See* Cassel, *Regional Human Rights Regime and State Pushback*, 1; Picq, *Is the Inter-American Commission of Human Rights Too Progressive?* (describing the commission's strained relationship with countries like Bolivia, Brazil, and Ecuador).

14. *See Chile, Argentina, Brasil, Colombia y Paraguay piden a la Corte de DD.HH. respetar "margenes de autonomía" de los estados.*

15. *See* Shelton, *Rules and the Reality of Petition Procedures in the Inter-American Human Rights System*, 3–5 (discussing underlying causes of a "crisis of commitment" on the part of states parties to the Inter-American system on human rights).

16. *See id.* at 5 (describing how the Belo Monte precautionary measures led to Brazil's campaign to reduce the commission's powers from 2011 to 2013).

17. *See* Signatories and Ratifications: American Convention on Human Rights.

18. *See* Márquez Luzardo, *La denuncia de la Convención Americana sobre Derechos Humanos y otros casos paradigmático*, 37–40.

19. *See* Signatories and Ratifications: American Convention on Human Rights (Peru's withdrawal of its denunciation considered the denunciation to be null and void: "[T]he declaration of recognition should be understood to have been in effect without interruption since its deposit with the General Secretariat of the Organization of American States (OAS) on January 21, 1981").

20. Letter from Minister of Popular Power for Foreign Affairs of the Bolivarian Republic of Venezuela to José Miguel Insulza, 5.

21. *Id.* at 3–7 (Annex).

22. *Id.* at 6–7 (Annex).

23. *See* Case of Díaz-Peña v. Venezuela.

24. Letter from Minister of Popular Power for Foreign Affairs of the Bolivarian Republic of Venezuela to José Miguel Insulza, 9–10 (Annex).

25. *Id.* at 3–4, 10–11.

26. *See* Organization of American States, American Convention on Human Rights arts. 41–51; Statute of the Inter-American Commission on Human Rights art. 18; Rules of Procedure of the Inter-American Commission on Human Rights art. 1 (2013); Charter of the Organization of American States art. 106.

27. *See* Organization of American States, American Convention on Human Rights arts. 34, 36. *See also What Is the IACHR?*

28. *See* Organization of American States, American Convention on Human Rights arts. 41–51, 61–65, 63(2); *see also* Statute of the Inter-American Commission on Human Rights art. 18; Rules of Procedure of the Inter-American Commission on Human Rights arts. 23, 25.

29. *See* Dulitzky, "50 años del sistema interamericano de derechos humanos," 496.

30. *See* Commissioner Felipe González, Address at the O.A.S. General Assembly.

31. *See* Organization of American States, American Convention on Human Rights arts. 61(1), 63(2), 64; *see also* Statute of the Inter-American Commission on Human Rights art. 19 (d).

32. *See* Organization of American States, American Convention on Human Rights art. 64; *see also* Annual Report of the Inter-American Commission on Human Rights (1980), 10.

33. *See* Shelton, *Rules and the Reality of Petition Procedures in the Inter-American Human Rights System*, 317; Carozza, *Anglo-Latin Divide and the Future of the Inter-American System of Human Rights*, 168.

34. *See* Organization of American States, American Convention on Human Rights art. 61.

35. The court has deviated from the commission's recommendations, either totally or partially, on several occasions. *See* the following cases heard before the Inter-American Court of Human Rights: Case of Palma Mendoza et al. v. Ecuador, Las Palmeras v. Colombia, Constitutional Court v. Peru, Nogueira de Carvalho et al. v. Brazil (total deviation from commission's recommendations on the merits), Cayara v. Peru (deviation from commission's procedural analysis).

36. *See* Case of Caballero Delgado and Santana v. Colombia, para. 67, where the Inter-American Court indicates that "the term 'recommendations' used by the American Convention should be interpreted to conform to its ordinary meaning, in accordance with Article 31(1) of the Vienna Convention on the Law of Treaties. For that reason, a recommendation does not have the character of an obligatory judicial decision for which the failure to comply would generate State responsibility. As there is no evidence in the present Convention that the parties intended to give it a special meaning, Article 31(4) of the Vienna Convention is not applicable.

Consequently, the State does not incur international responsibility by not complying with a recommendation which is not obligatory." *See also* Case of Genie Lacayo v. Nicaragua, paras. 93–94; Advisory Opinion OC-19/05, ¶ 13 (c) (under "Guarantees in the petition proceedings").

37. *See* Case of Loayza Tamayo v. Peru, paras. 79–82; Case of Baena Ricardo et al. v. Panama, paras. 191–92.

38. Inter-American Yearbook on Human Rights, 97 (1968).

39. Campos en los cuales han de tomarse medidas, parte II, p. 1 ("El uso del aborto para ayudar a resolver los problemas económicos y de subsistencia derivados de la explosión demográfica constituiría patente y grave violación de los derechos humanos" [The use of abortion to help solve economic problems of subsistence caused by demographic explosion would constitute a patent and grave human rights violation]).

40. *See IACHR Urges All States to Adopt Comprehensive, Immediate Measures to Respect and Protect Women's Sexual and Reproductive Rights*; *see also* Rep. on Public Hearings from the 162nd Session (noting, in regard to abortion bans in the region that "the laws in place are restrictive and hamper access to reproductive health services, which are essential so that women can make free and autonomous decisions about their reproductive and family life").

41. *See, e.g.*, *Thematic Hearing "Derechos sexuales y reproductivos de las mujeres en América del Sur."* The three grounds could be four in practice since life and health can be two distinct grounds, depending on how broadly or narrowly "health" is defined, as discussed in chapter 5.

42. *See, e.g.*, *Access to Maternal Health Services from a Human Rights Perspective*, 86, 99, 102. *See also* IACHR, *Third Report on the Human Rights Situation in Colombia*, chapter XII, ¶ 49.

43. *See, e.g.*, *Human Rights Situation of Pregnant Women in the Americas* (featuring Planned Parenthood Global—which describes itself as "the international arm of Planned Parenthood Federation of America," the latter being the United States' single largest abortion provider—appearing before the IACHR to promote legalization of elective abortion in Latin American and Caribbean countries that currently ban it). *See also About Planned Parenthood Global.*

44. *See Woman-Centered, Comprehensive Abortion Care Trainer's Manual, 2nd edition*; *Our Work*; *Steps for Performing Manual Vacuum Aspiration Using the Ipas MVA Plus and EasyGrip Cannulae. See also, e.g., Derechos Humanos y Criminalización del Aborto en Sudamérica.*

45. *See Nicaragua Before the Inter-American Commission for Violations of the Human Rights of Girls, Women, Indigenous Peoples and People of African Descent*; *CIDH le exige explicaciones a El Salvador por el caso de Beatriz.*

46. *See* participants list at *IACHR Hearings and Other Public Events, Sessions by Topic, Rights of Women. See also Thematic Hearing "Risks and Vulnerabilities Affecting Defenders of Women's Rights in the Americas"*; *Thematic Hearing "Human*

*Rights Situation of Women in Nicaragua.*" The acronym CLADEM stands for Comité de América Latina y El Caribe para la Defensa de los Derechos de la Mujer (Latin American and Caribbean Committee for the Defense of Women's Rights).

47. *See* Ramos, *CIDH favorece a ONGs pro aborto y discrimina a las que defienden la vida, denuncian.*

48. Roe v. Wade and Doe v. Bolton.

49. *See* Commonwealth of Mass. v. Kenneth Edelin.

50. Baby Boy v. United States, para. 18(e).

51. *See id.* para. 1 (under "Resolves").

52. *See* American Declaration of the Rights and Duties of Man.

53. *Id.* art. 1 (emphasis added).

54. *See* Baby Boy v. United States, paras. 1, 14, 20 (under "Whereas").

55. *Id.* paras. 30, 31 (under "Whereas").

56. *See* Artavia Murillo v. Costa Rica, ¶ 273.

57. *See* Baby Boy v. United States, para. 2. (Dr. Luis Demetrio Tinoco Castro, dissenting).

58. *Id.* paras. 2, 4 (Dr. Andrés Aguilar M., concurring).

59. The *Baby Boy* report mistakenly states that Edelin performed a hysterectomy (extraction of the uterus) on the pregnant teenager; *see* Baby Boy v. United States, para. 8. The actual term used in national court records indicates that it was actually a hysterotomy. See Commonwealth of Mass. v. Kenneth Edelin, 498.

60. *See* Commonwealth of Massachusetts v. Kenneth Edelin, 498–99.

61. *See* Roe v. Wade, 732.

62. Commonwealth of Massachusetts v. Kenneth Edelin, 528 (citing *Roe* at 501).

63. *See id.* at 505.

64. *Id.* at 504.

65. *Id.* at 529 (Reardon, J., dissenting).

66. *Id.* at 528–29.

67. *Id.* at 540–41 (Hennessey, C.J., dissenting in part).

68. *Id.* at 503 (majority opinion).

69. *Id.* at 502.

70. *Id.* at 503.

71. *Id.* at 541 (Hennessey, C.J., dissenting in part).

72. *Id.* at 504 (majority opinion).

73. *Id.* at 541 (Hennessey, C.J., dissenting in part).

74. *Id.* at 540.

75. *Id.* at 535–36.

76. *See* Baby Boy v. United States, paras. 1–2.

77. *See* Commonwealth of Massachusetts v. Kenneth Edelin, 508.

78. *Id.*

79. *Id.* at 524–25.

80. *Id.* at 497.

81. *Id.* at 504.

82. *Id.* at 505.

83. *Id.* at 543 (Hennessey, C.J., dissenting in part). (Chief Justice Hennessey dissented in part, indicating that "the defendant formed his judgment of non-viability either in bad faith, or unreasonably, based upon facts he knew or reasonably should have known.")

84. *See, e.g., Testimony of Dr. Ken Edelin.*

85. McFadden, *Kenneth C. Edelin, Doctor at Center of Landmark Abortion Case, Dies at 74* (on the life of Dr. Kenneth Edelin).

86. *See* Baby Boy v. United States, para. 3.

87. *Id.* at paras. 1–13.

88. *See* American Convention on Human Rights art. 20; *see also* Statute of the Inter-American Commission on Human Rights art. 18 (commission's functions with respect to state members of the Organization of American States and nonparties to the American Convention).

89. *See* Baby Boy v. United States, paras. 2–3 (under "Whereas") (citing articles 53–57 of the 1960 Rules of Procedure of the Inter-American Commission on Human Rights, article 35(1) of the 1980 Rules of Procedure). Articles 20 and 24 of the Statute of the Inter-American Commission on Human Rights also deal with states that are nonparties to the American Convention. For more on the application of the declaration to nonparties to the American Convention, *see* Case of Caballero Delgado and Santana v. Colombia.

90. Interpretation of the American Declaration of the Rights and Duties of Man Within the Framework of Article 64 of the American Convention on Human Rights, ¶ 17.

91. *See* Andrews v. United States, ¶¶ 59, 77 (citing articles 3(i), 16, 51(e), 112, and 150 of the OAS charter, ratified by the United States on April 23, 1968) (In Andrews v. United States, the US government cited *Baby Boy* when arguing that the commission had no authority to impose upon a state, by means of "interpretation," an international obligation based upon an international instrument that the state had not duly accepted or ratified, such as the declaration. Here, the State Department stated: "[T]he United States categorically rejects the petitioners' contention that the American Declaration and the Statute and Regulations of the Commission has acquired legally binding force for all OAS member countries. As the United States has previously noted, the Declaration is not a treaty and has not acquired binding legal force" (¶ 59). "In this respect, the Commission has no authority to rewrite the American Declaration, which is what the petition has invited it to do" (¶77)). *See also* Case No. 9647. *See also* Buergenthal, *Advisory Practice of the Inter-American Human Rights Court*, 7–8 (where a former Inter-American Court judge points out that, even though the declaration is clearly not a "treaty" within the meaning of article 64(1) of the American Con-

vention, "it is generally recognized, that the Protocol of Buenos Aires, which amended the OAS Charter, changed the legal status of the Declaration to an instrument that, at the very least, constitutes an authoritative interpretation and definition of the human rights obligations binding on OAS member states under the Charter of the Organization").

92. *See* Inadmissibility Report 12.379, para. 31.

93. *See* Baby Boy v. United States, para. 15.

94. *Id.* para. 19.

95. *Id.* paras. 12–14.

96. Shelton, *Rules and the Reality of Petition Procedures in the Inter-American Human Rights System*, 9 (former commissioner Dinah Shelton indicates that IACHR reports or resolutions are exclusively drafted by the IACHR executive secretariat). *See also* García Elorrio, "Protección de los niños no nacidos en el Sistema Jurídico Interamericano de Derechos Humanos: La integración normativa con el *jus cogens*," 130 (pointing out the subjectivity of Dunshee's perspective as a rapporteur in this petition).

97. *See* Baby Boy v. United States, para. 20.

98. Inter-American Yearbook on Human Rights, 97 (1968).

99. *See* Baby Boy v. United States, para. 26.

100. See Inter-American Yearbook on Human Rights, 97 (1968).

101. *See* Baby Boy v. United States, para. 27. *See* Inter-American Yearbook on Human Rights, 97 (1968).

102. *See* Organization of American States, *Actas y Documentos of the Inter-american Specialized Conference on Human Rights*, 408–9.

103. *See* García Elorrio, "Protección de los niños no nacidos en el Sistema Jurídico Interamericano de Derechos Humanos: La integración normativa con el *jus cogens*," 124.

104. *See* Baby Boy v. United States, para. 19(h).

105. *See id.* para. 33.

106. *Id.* para. 31.

107. *Id.* paras. 19(e), 25, 30.

108. *See id.* (concurring opinion of Dr. Andrés Aguilar M., paras. 1–4).

109. *Id.* paras. 5–7.

110. *Id.* para. 8.

111. *See* Baby Boy v. United States (Dr. Marco Gerardo Monroy Cabra, dissenting), para. 9; *see also id.* (Dr. Luis Demetrio Tinoco Castro, dissenting).

112. *See* Baby Boy v. United States (Dr. Luis Demetrio Tinoco Castro, dissenting).

113. *See* Baby Boy v. United States (Dr. Marco Gerardo Monroy Cabra, dissenting), para. 9.

114. *See id.* paras. 5, 8.

115. *Id.* para. 7.

116. *Id.* para. 8.

117. *Id.*

118. *See*, Barberis, *El derecho a la vida en el pacto de San José de Costa Rica*, 11–26 (critiquing the commission's interpretation of the American Declaration in Baby Boy v. United States).

119. *Id.* 13.

120. *Id.* at 17.

121. *See* Acción de inconstitucionalidad 146/2007 y su acumulada 147/2007, Suprema Corte de Justicia de la Nación [SCJN] [Supreme Court], *Intervención del Ministro Sergio Salvador Aguirre Anguiano en sesión extraordinaria celebrada el 25 de agosto de 2008*, 10.

122. *See* Shelton, *Abortion and Right to Life in the Inter-American System*, 312–14.

123. *Id.* 312–13.

124. *Id.* 312.

125. *See* Paulina del Carmen Ramírez Jacinto v. Mexico, 9.

126. *See Center's Cases* (the Center for Reproductive Rights has often used pregnant children in their abortion impact litigation citing L.C. v. Peru, before UN Committee on the Elimination of Discrimination against Women; KL v. Peru, before the United Nations Human Rights Committee; and Paulina del Carmen Ramírez Jacinto v. Mexico).

127. *See* Paulina del Carmen Ramírez Jacinto v. Mexico, 9.

128. *Id.* at 10, 11.

129. *Id.* at 11–12.

130. *Id.* at 13.

131. *See id.* at 15 (petitioners argued that Paulina had given her "forced" consent when declining the abortion). *See also id.* Annex.

132. *Id.* at 1, 10–12.

133. *Id.* at 9.

134. *Id.* at 14 (emphasis added).

135. *See* Paulina del Carmen Ramírez Jacinto v. Mexico, Annex.

136. *Id.* at 24.

137. *Id.* at 5–8.

138. *Id.* at 16.

139. *Id.* at 8.

140. *See* Center for Reproductive Rights, *Paulina: Five Years Later*, 72–73.

141. Organization of American States, American Convention on Human Rights art. 46(1)(a).

142. *See* Paulina del Carmen Ramírez Jacinto v. Mexico, 18, 24.

143. *Id.*

144. The Economist Currency Converter. *See* Paulina del Carmen Ramírez Jacinto v. Mexico, 16 (numbers 1, 9).

145. Paulina del Carmen Ramírez Jacinto v. Mexico, 16 (numbers 2–3, 6).
146. *Id.* at 16 (numbers 2–4, 6, 8).
147. *Id.* at 16 (number 7).
148. *Id.* at 16 (number 12).
149. *Id.* at 22.
150. *See* Código Penal para el Estado de Baja California, art. 252 (Mex.).
151. *See* Paulina del Carmen Ramírez Jacinto v. Mexico, Annex.
152. *Id.* at 18–19.
153. *Id.* at 17.
154. *Id.* at 26.
155. Constitución Política del Estado Libre y Soberano de Baja California, art. 7 (Mex.).
156. James Demers v. Canada, 3.
157. *Id.* 12–13.
158. *Id.* 13.
159. *Id.* 12.
160. *Id.* 16.
161. *Id.* 2.
162. *See* Signatories and Ratifications: American Convention on Human Rights.
163. James Demers v. Canada, 40.
164. *Id.* at 62.
165. *Id.* at 45.
166. *Id.* at 2.
167. *Id.* at 45.
168. *Id.* at 44.
169. *Id.* (citing inadmissibility of the petition in Felix Roman Esparragoza González et. al. v. Venezuela, Petition 12.210, Inter-Am. Comm'n H.R., Report No. 48/04, OEA/Ser.L/V/II.122, doc. 5 rev. 1 (2004)).
170. James Demers v. Canada, 45.
171. *Id.* at 3.
172. Ana Victoria Sánchez and Others v. Costa Rica, ¶ 69.
173. *Id.* at 4, 14, 41, 46, 47.
174. *Id.* at 41–42.
175. *Id.* at 46.
176. *Id.*
177. *Id.* at 4, 42, 44.
178. *See* IACHR Annual Reports.
179. *Cf.* Colectivo Feminista para el Desarrollo Local de El Salvador, Agrupación Ciudadana por la Despenalización del Aborto Terapéutico, Ético y Eugenésico de El Salvador, Ipas, CEJIL, *Petición Inicial "Beatriz vs. Estado de El Salvador,"* 5, 8.

180. *E.g.*, *Audiencia CIDH Nicaragua Derecho a la integridad personal de niñas y mujeres en Nicaragua*, at 12:04 (Ipas representative refers to the abortion of children conceived in rape as "therapeutic abortion"). *See id.* at 54:53 (Ipas representative refers to abortions on minors as "therapeutic abortion"). *See also* Annual Report of the Inter-American Commission on Human Rights 2002, para. 70 (reporting that "[w]hen a prisoner is pregnant after a conjugal visit or when she enters prison, the prison administration does everything possible to get the woman to have a *therapeutic abortion*" (emphasis added)).

181. *See* San José Articles, note to article 8 (describing political pressure to legalize abortion on the part of several United Nations agencies and Sweden's withdrawal of foreign aid to the country).

182. *See PM 43-10 "Amelia."*

183. *See* Rules of Procedure of the Inter-American Commission on Human Rights art. 25(1).

184. *See PM 43-10 "Amelia."*

185. *Id. See Aborto en Centroamérica.*

186. *See Aborto en Centroamérica.*

187. Asunto Niña Mainumby respecto de Paraguay, Medidas Cautelares No. 178/15.

188. *Id.* paras. 2, 23.

189. *See Paraguay: Violencia sexual*, at 48:42 (emphasis added).

190. *Comunicado de Prensa*, Ministerio de Relaciones Exteriores, República del Paraguay (June 11).

191. *See Paraguay: Violencia sexual*, starting at 1:00:47. *See also Comunicado de Prensa No. 2*, Ministerio de Relaciones Exteriores, República del Paraguay (May 21, 2015), para. 4.

192. *See* Asunto Niña Mainumby respecto de Paraguay, Medidas Cautelares No. 178/15, paras. 3(G), 6(B), (E).

193. *Id.* paras. 1, 2, 5(F).

194. Código Penal (Para.) art. 109 (4).

195. Asunto Niña Mainumby respecto de Paraguay, Medidas Cautelares No. 178/15, para. 1.

196. *Id.* para. 10(D).

197. Código Penal art. 109 (4) (Para.).

198. *See Paraguay: Violencia sexual*, at 51:20 (at a public hearing on the petition, Commissioner Vannuchi asks if Mainumby's case has provoked further dialogue in regard to legal reform on abortion in Paraguay, comparing it to lessons learned by Honduras from the murder of environmental activist Berta Caceres).

199. *See* Asunto Niña Mainumby respecto de Paraguay, Medidas Cautelares No. 178/15, para. 10(D).

200. *Id.* para. 3(E).

201. *Id.* para. 10(D).

202. *Id.*

203. *Id.* paras. 3(G), 5(D), 5(F), 10(B), (D).

204. *Id.* para. 3(A). *See Niña de 11 años dio a luz* [Eleven-year-old child gives birth].

205. *See* Asunto Niña Mainumby respecto de Paraguay, Medidas Cautelares No. 178/15, para. 3(E).

206. *Id.* para. 3(G).

207. *Id.* paras. 5(F), 6(D).

208. *Id.* paras. 10(B), (C), 21.

209. *Id.* paras. 21–22.

210. *See* UN News Centre, *Paraguay: UN Experts Deplore Government's Failure to Protect 10-Year-Old Rape Survivor* (the statement was signed by UN experts Ms. Emna Aouij, chair-rapporteur of the working group on the issue of discrimination against women in law and in practice; Ms. Rashida Manjoo, special rapporteur on violence against women, its causes and consequences; Mr. Dainius Púras, special rapporteur on the right of everyone to the enjoyment of the highest attainable standard of physical and mental health; and Mr. Juan E. Méndez, special rapporteur on torture and other cruel, inhuman, or degrading treatment or punishment). *See also Special Procedures of the Human Rights Council* (the United Nations human rights experts are part of what is known as the Special Procedures of the Human Rights Council, which designates independent fact-finding and monitoring mechanisms of the Human Rights Council that address either specific country situations or thematic issues in all parts of the world).

211. *Human Rights: Paraguay Has Failed to Protect a 10-Year Old* [*sic*] *Girl Child Who Became Pregnant after Being Raped, Say UN Experts.*

212. *Id.*

213. *Id.*

214. *Id.*

215. *Comunicado de Prensa,* Ministerio de Relaciones Exteriores, República del Paraguay (May 13, 2015).

216. *See* Asunto Niña Mainumby respecto de Paraguay, Medidas Cautelares No. 178/15, paras. 3(G), 14(i).

217. *See* Diputado [Congressman] Eber Ovelar, *Debatirán sobre el aborto en una audiencia pública.*

218. *See* Asunto Niña Mainumby respecto de Paraguay, Medidas Cautelares No. 178/15, paras. 1, 9(A).

219. *Comunicado de Prensa No. 2,* Ministerio de Relaciones Exteriores, República del Paraguay (May 21, 2015).

220. *Id.*

221. *See* Asunto Niña Mainumby respecto de Paraguay, Medidas Cautelares No. 178/15, paras. 6(A), 9(A), (B).

222. *Id.* paras. 6(A), (C), 9(A).

223. *Id.* paras. 6(A), (C), 18.

224. *Id.* para. 6(B).

225. *Id.* paras. 6(C), 9(B).

226. *Id.* paras. 6(C), 9(B), 18.

227. *Id.* para. 9(A).

228. *Id.* paras. 14(ii), 18.

229. *Id.* para. 10(A).

230. *Id.* para. 10(A)–(D). *Id.* para. 5(E).

231. *Id.* para. 18.

232. *Id.* para. 19.

233. *Id.* para. 19.

234. *Id.* paras. 2, 23.

235. *Id.* para. 2.

236. *Id.* paras. 14–19.

237. *Id.* paras. 5(F), 6(D).

238. *Id.* paras. 15–16.

239. *Id.*

240. *Id.* para. 21.

241. *Id.* para. 22.

242. *Comunicado de Prensa*, MINISTERIO DE RELACIONES EXTERIORES, REPÚBLICA DEL PARAGUAY (June 11, 2015).

243. *Id.*

244. *Id.*

245. *See Niña de 11 años dio a luz.*

246. *See* López Garelli, *Liberan a la madre de la niña paraguaya embarazada*; López Garelli, *Prueba de ADN confirma que padrastro embarazó a la niña paraguaya de 11 años. See also Abogada afirma que el Estado miente a la CIDH.*

247. *See* IACHR, *Paraguay: Violencia sexual*, at 1:00:47.

248. *Id.* at 1:02:15.

249. *See id.* at 1:00:47 (the hearing's original title was Sexual Violence and Human Rights of Girls and Adolescents in Paraguay. The state officials representing Paraguay protested that the hearing was used to discuss the *Mainumby* matter even though it was supposed to address more general matters and even though the Commission had denied their request for a confidential hearing on the case).

250. *See Paraguay: Violencia sexual*, at 38:40.

251. *See id.* at 49:00

252. *See id.* at 44:48.

253. *See id.* at 55:06

254. *See id.* at 55:06, 1:00:47.

255. *See IACHR Urges El Salvador to End the Total Criminalization of Abortion* (indicating that the IACHR calls on El Salvador to launch a moratorium on the enforcement of Criminal Code Article 133 and to review the convictions of twenty-seven women allegedly convicted for abortion, citing Commissioner Macaulay's statements to that effect).

256. *E.g., Thematic Hearing "Human Rights Situation of Women Deprived of Liberty due to Obstetric Emergencies During Pregnancy in El Salvador"* (where several NGOs, including Center for Reproductive Rights and Agrupación Ciudadana por la Despenalización del Aborto Terapéutico, Ético y Eugenésico de El Salvador [Citizens group for the decriminalization of therapeutic, ethical, and eugenic abortion] state that women have been imprisoned for obstetric emergencies in the country, while El Salvador state representatives categorically reject such allegations). *See also Thematic Hearing "Situación de derechos humanos de las mujeres y las niñas en El Salvador"* (where Commissioners Tracy Robinson, Rose Marie Antoine, and Rosa Maria Ortiz express their concern over El Salvador's full ban on abortion and alleged wrongful prosecution of women who miscarry, in agreement with Ipas, CEJIL, and other nongovernmental organizations).

257. *See El Salvador 2016 Human Rights Report*, 23 (describing complaint by human rights organizations that seventeen women had been convicted for abortion in El Salvador and indicating that the Legal Medicine Institute responded that the women had committed infanticide instead). *See also* Schumacher-Matos, *Abortion or Infanticide in El Salvador?* (pointing out inaccuracy in NPR reporting about El Salvador's prosecution of Cristina Quintanilla for abortion, whereas her case actually involved infanticide and mercy killing, not abortion). *See also* Baklinski, *NPR Says El Salvador Mom Was Charged for "Having an Abortion"—but Evidence Shows She Murdered Her Newborn* (indicating that abortion complaint against El Salvador actually involved infanticide, not abortion).

258. *See* Manuela and family v. El Salvador.

259. *Id.* at paras. 4, 5.

260. *Id.* at para. 5.

261. *Id.* at para. 2.

262. *Id.* at para. 1.

263. *Id.* at paras. 2, 6, 7.

264. *Id.* at paras. 10–11.

265. Case of Genie Lacayo v. Nicaragua, para. 94; Case of Perozo et al. V. Venezuela, para. 64 (emphasis added).

266. *Id. Cf.* Santiago Marzioni v. Argentina, ¶¶ 48–51 (under the "fourth instance formula," "if [a petition] contains nothing but the allegation that the decision was wrong or unjust in itself, the petition must be dismissed," since "the Commission cannot review the judgments issued by the domestic courts acting within their competence and with due judicial guarantees, unless it considers that a possible violation of the Convention is involved").

267. *See* Manuela and family v. El Salvador, 3.

268. Letter [from Sen. Mike Lee and Sen. Marco Rubio] to State Department to fully implement the Organization of American States (OAS) Revitalization and Reform Act of 2013.

269. *Mexico Declaration, American Declaration Regarding the Independence and Self-Determination of Peoples on Matters Relating to Life, Family and Religious Freedom.*

270. *Id.*

271. *See* Morello, *Pompeo Cuts OAS Funds over Advocacy of Legal Abortion.*

272. Letter from James Lankford, Thom Tillis, Michael B. Enzi, Michael S. Lee, James M. Inhofe, John Kennedy, Roy Blunt, Ted Cruz, and Joni K. Ernst, U.S. senators, to Mike Pompeo, sec'y of state.

273. *Id.*

274. *Id.*

275. Letter from Tom Farer, Robert Goldman, Dinah Shelton, James Cavallaro, presidents and members of the Comm'n, and Douglas Cassel, U.S. nominee to the Comm'n, to Mike Pompeo, sec'y of state.

276. *See* Morello, *Pompeo Cuts OAS Funds over Advocacy of Legal Abortion.*

277. *Pompeo Announces Expansion of Pro-life "Mexico City Policy,"* at 1:05.

278. *Legisladores de toda América piden a la OEA que no se promueva el aborto con dinero de sus países* [Legislators from all over America ask the OAS not to promote abortion with their money].

279. *See* Acción de inconstitucionalidad 146/2007 y su acumulada 147/2007, Suprema Corte de Justicia de la Nación, *Intervención del Ministro Sergio Salvador Aguirre Anguiano en sesión extraordinaria celebrada el 25 de agosto de 2008* (Mexican Supreme Court Judge Sergio Salvador Aguirre Anguiano points out that the *Baby Boy* report is not binding on Mexico given the nature of the commission's powers and its resolutions' limited authority).

## TWO. The Inter-American Court of Human Rights' Restrictive Approach to the Prenatal Right to Life

1. Compare, for instance, to European Court of Human Rights, which is composed of forty-seven full-time judges, four chambers, and a full bench. *See Composition of the Court.*

2. *See* Organization of American States, American Convention on Human Rights arts. 4(1), 52 (judges serve only part-time in the court and may simultaneously have full-time professional activities).

3. *Id.* arts. 41, 44–51; *see also* Control of Due Process in the Exercise of the Powers of the Inter-American Commission on Human Rights, para. 13.

4. *See* Organization of American States, American Convention on Human Rights art. 61.

5. *See* Signatories and Ratifications: American Convention on Human Rights.

6. *See* Corte Suprema de Justicia, Sala Constitucional, marzo 15, 2000, Expdte. 95-001734-0007-CO (Costa Rica), ¶ 5 (attorney general argues that the

court's decision in *Artavia* forced the state of Costa Rica to carry out a new *ponderación*, i.e., balancing test, that would diminish constitutional protection of the unborn).

7. *See, e.g.*, Rocha da Silva and Dantas Echeverria, *Tentativas de contenção do ativismo judicial da Corte Interamericana de Direitos Humanos*, 397–400 (characterizing the *Artavia* decision as an illustration of judicial activism); Silva Abbott, *Jurisdicción de Corte Interamericana* (law professor Max Silva Abbott critiques evolving interpretation by the Inter-American Court); *Nicaragua propone someter a reforma la Convención Americana sobre Derechos Humanos*; Andújar de Zamora, *Instrumentalización del embrión humano* (analyzing *Artavia*'s arguments on conception as implantation and the nonpersonhood of the human embryo from a bioethical perspective); *Gobiernos de América Latina.*

8. *See* Organization of American States, American Convention on Human Rights arts. 61, 62(3), and 64(1).

9. *See* Cabrera-García and Montiel-Flores v. Mexico, ¶ 225. *See also* Artavia Murillo v. Costa Rica, ¶ 171. *See* Organization of American States, American Convention on Human Rights arts. 62(3), 64(1), and 67.

10. Case of Lagos del Campo v. Peru, partially dissenting vote of Judge Eduardo Vio Grossi, 2–3 (where Judge Vio Grossi indicates that the court's jurisprudence should be understood as an auxiliary rather than as a primary source of international law or as a maker of international rights or obligations per se).

11. *See* Organization of American States, American Convention on Human Rights arts. 64(1) and (2).

12. *See* Inter-Am. Ct. H.R., Advisory Opinion OC-1/82, para. 28.

13. *See* Ferrer Mac-Gregor and González Domínguez, *Death Penalty, Amnesty Laws, and Forced Disappearances*, 105–11 (describing substantive contributions of the Inter-American Court to international human rights law in regard to forced disappearances); Castillo Córdova, *La Corte IDH, o El mito de la infalibilidad* (Peruvian law professor critiques the Inter-American Court's provisional measures following the Durant and Ugarte judgment against Peru—which ordered that four constitutional actions against Constitutional Court judges be archived—characterizing the measures as unlawful and *ultra vires*).

14. *See* Organization of American States, American Convention on Human Rights art. 17(2) ("The right of men and women of marriageable age to marry and to raise a family shall be recognized, if they meet the conditions required by domestic laws, insofar as such conditions do not affect the principle of nondiscrimination established in this Convention"). *See also* Gender Identity, and Equality and Non-discrimination with regard to Same-Sex Couples.

15. See Gender Identity, and Equality and Non-discrimination with regard to Same-Sex Couples, ¶¶ 161, 171.

16. *See* Madrigal, *Costa Rica consulta a Corte IDH si es necesaria legislación que regule uniones homosexuales. See also* Request for Advisory Opinion (requesting an advisory opinion on the existence of a requirement under the American

Convention to legally authorize name and gender change in official government identification documents and to grant patrimonial rights to individuals living in same-sex unions).

17. See Gender Identity, and Equality and Non-discrimination with regard to Same-Sex Couples, ¶¶ 161, 171, 228.

18. *See* Aréchaga, *Despotismo ilustrado de hoy* (describing the advisory opinion's effect in Costa Rican politics, indicating that evangelical candidate Fabricio Alvarado won the first electoral round mostly on the basis of his opposition to the court's advisory opinion and proposal to withdraw Costa Rica from the its jurisdiction, and indicating that thirteen presidential candidates opposed the opinion while only one of them supported it).

19. *See, e.g.*, Vásquez, *La Corte Interamericana se debilita* (Cato Institute commentator who supports same-sex marriage argues that the Inter-American Court's position on the advisory opinion diminishes its legitimacy as an institution and its ability to protect traditional human rights causes in the region).

20. *See* Panel I, Diálogo jurisprudencial y control de convencionalidad (for further discussion of the *control de convencionalidad* doctrine). *Compare to* Organization of American States, American Convention on Human Rights art. 68. *See also Opinión sobre las sentencias de la #CIDH–Parte 1–FEB 11–1/4 | Willax* (Francisco Tudela, former foreign relations minister of Peru, critiques the *control de convencionalidad* doctrine).

21. Almonacid Arellano v. Chile; Redilla Pacheco v. Mexico; Cabrera-García and Montiel-Flores v. Mexico, ¶¶ 7, 12, 21; Case of Loayza Tamayo v. Peru, ¶ 35 (reiterating the *control de convencionalidad* doctrine). *See also* Vio Grossi, *Jurisprudencia de la Corte Interamericana de Derechos Humanos*, 94 (mentioning twenty-nine decisions as of 2015). *See* Enforceability of the Right to Reply or Correction (arts. 14(1), 1(1), and 2 American Convention on Human Rights) (where the court holds that the right to reply is self-executing in states parties under the American Convention). *See also* Gender Identity, and Equality and Non-discrimination with regard to Same-Sex Couples, Concurring Vote of Judge Humberto Sierra Porto, ¶¶ 14, 18 (arguing that the American Convention is self-executing: "[T]he Convention—and the rights recognized therein—have direct legal effects, which supposes or signifies that all judicial agents have a direct application mandate and, in general, this does not require *interpositio legislatoris*, legislative interpretation"). *See also* Becerra Ramírez, "La jerarquía de los tratados en el orden jurídico interno," at 303; Ferrer Mac-Gregor, "Interpretación conforme y control difuso de convencionalidad, ¶¶ 386–87; Ferrer Mac-Gregor, *Eficacia de la sentencia interamericana y la cosa juzgada internacional*, ¶¶ 652–88.

22. *See* Case of Gelman v. Uruguay, ¶¶ 67–90.

23. *See* Weiler, *Transformation of Europe*; Stith and Weiler, *Can Treaty Law Be Supreme, Directly Effective and Autonomous—All at the Same Time?* (for an introduction to the constitutional tensions within the European Union).

24. *See* BVerfGE May 29, 1974 (Ger.), 37, 271; BVerfGE Oct. 22, 1974 (Ger.), 73, 339 (subsequent decision known as *Solange II* that drastically raised the burden of proof on opponents of the ECJ but nevertheless reaffirmed that treaty interpretations in conflict with fundamental German constitutional rights do not, in principle, have domestic validity).

25. Organization of American States, American Convention on Human Rights art. 68(2).

26. Organization of American States, American Convention on Human Rights art. 63(1).

27. *See* Cabrera-García and Montiel-Flores v. Mexico, ¶ 225 (asserting that national judges must "take into account not only the treaty, but also the corresponding interpretation made by the Inter-American Court, which is the ultimate interpreter of the American Convention"). *See* Control de Convencionalidad, Cuadernillo de Jurisprudencia de la Corte Interamericana de Derechos Humanos No. 7 (2015 publication by the Inter-American Court summarizing its own jurisprudence on the *conventionality control* doctrine).

28. *See* Silva Abbott, *El caso Artavia Murillo vs. Costa Rica* (for a discussion and critique of the *control de convencionalidad* doctrine and its application in *Artavia*).

29. *See* section III(E) *infra.*

30. Organization of American States, American Convention on Human Rights art. 68(2) (emphasis added).

31. *See* Case of Gelman v. Uruguay, ¶ 69 (where the court says that states parties to the convention should follow "precedent or jurisprudential guidelines of the Inter-American Court" even where they have not been parties to a dispute). *See also* García Ramírez, *El control judicial interno de convencionalidad*, 128–29; Hitters, *Un avance en el control de convencionalidad*, 695–710; Hitters, *El control de convencionalidad y el cumplimiento de las sentencias de la Corte Interamericana*, 543–44; Nogueira Alcalá, *Diálogo interjurisdiccional, control de convencionalidad y jurisprudencia del Tribunal Constitucional en el período 2006–2011*, 65, 83–84, 71–75, 82, 91, 94, 104–5, 126, 128; Meier García, *Nacionalismo Constitucional y Derecho Internacional de los Derechos Humanos*, 334, 371; Pereyra Zabala, *El control de convencionalidad en el sistema interamericano de derechos humanos*, 167, 173; Sagüés, *El "control de convencionalidad" como instrumento para la elaboración de un ius comune interamericano*, 462, 468, 458–60; Sagüés, *Obligaciones internacionales y control de convencionalidad*, 1330.

32. *Vélez-Loor v. Panama*, ¶ 287.

33. García Ramírez, *Relationship Between Inter-American Jurisdiction and States (National Systems)*, 124 (emphasis added).

34. García-Sayán, *Inter-American Court and Constitutionalism in Latin America*, 1836.

35. *See* García-Sayán, *Exámenes del horizonte*, 54.

36. *See* Nieto Navia, *Aspectos internacionales de la demanda contra la penalización del aborto*, 31, 35.

37. *See* Vio Grossi, *Jurisprudencia de la Corte Interamericana de Derechos Humanos*, 93–112 (2015).

38. *Declaración sobre el Sistema Interamericano de Derechos Humanos. See also Chile, Argentina, Brasil, Colombia y Paraguay piden a la Corte Interamericana de DD.HH. respetar "margenes de autonomía" de los estados.*

39. *See* Corte Suprema de Justicia de la Nación, 14/02/2017, 368/1998 (34-M)/CS1 Ministerio de Relaciones y Culto "s/informe sentencia dictada en el caso 'Fontevecchia y D'Amico vs. Argentina' por la Corte Interamericana de Derechos Humanos" [Fallos: 340:47] (Arg.). *See also La Corte sostuvo que la Corte Interamericana de Derechos Humanos no puede revocar sentencias del Máximo Tribunal argentino.*

40. *See* Corte Suprema de Justicia de la Nación, 14/02/2017, 368/1998 (34-M)/CS1 Ministerio de Relaciones y Culto "s/informe sentencia dictada en el caso 'Fontevecchia y D'Amico vs. Argentina' por la Corte Interamericana de Derechos Humanos" [Fallos: 340:47] (Arg.).

41. *Id.*

42. *See* the judgment in Corte Suprema de Justicia de la Nación, 14/02/2017, 368/1998 (34-M)/CS1 Ministerio de Relaciones y Culto "s/informe sentencia dictada en el caso 'Fontevecchia y D'Amico vs. Argentina' por la Corte Interamericana de Derechos Humanos" [Fallos: 340:47] (Arg.), 4, 7–8.

43. *See id.*, 4–6, 11–12.

44. *See* Suprema Corte de Justicia del Uruguay [S.C.J.] [Uruguay Supreme Court of Justice], 22/02/2013, M. L., J. F. F., O.—Denuncia—Excepción de inconstitucionalidad arts 1, 2 y 3 de la ley 18831, No. 20/2013 (Uru.) (see consideration points, ¶ III(a)).

45. *See id.*

46. *See* García-Sayán, *Inter-American Court and Constitutionalism in Latin America*, 1841 (according to former judge García-Sayán, Inter-American Court decisions have been mostly cited in domestic high court decisions involving four issues: amnesties, the obligation to investigate human rights violations, the right to an effective remedy, and nondiscrimination and the rights of indigenous peoples).

47. *See* Juzgado Federal de Salta No. 1, 8/7/2013, "Lodi Ortiz Andrea Melisa—Larran Cristian c/Swiss Medical s/amparo," Expdte. No. 61000007/13 (Arg.) (citing Fallos: 330:4040, 332:1488). *See also* Rabbi Baldi Cabanillas and Fléming Cánepa, *El caso "Artavia Murillo vs. Costa Rica" de la CIDH*, 551–95 (for an analysis of the Argentinian Supreme Court's treatment of *control de convencionalidad* starting with the *Ekmekdjián v. Sofovich* decision).

48. *See* Jurisprudencia emitida por la Corte Interamericana de Derechos Humanos, 204 (original Spanish text states: "siempre que sea más favorable a la persona," and "cuando el criterio se haya emitido en un caso en el que el Estado

Mexicano no haya sido parte, la aplicabilidad del precedente al caso específico debe determinarse con base en la verificación de la existencia *de las mismas razones que motivaron el pronunciamiento*" (emphasis added)).

49. *See* García-Sayán, *Inter-American Court and Constitutionalism in Latin America*, 1840 (citing TC, Pleno Jurisdiccional, June 19, 2007, Colegio de Abogados del Callao c. Congreso de la República, No. 00007-2007-PI/TC, ¶ 36).

50. Gómez-Paquiyauri brothers v. Peru, ¶¶ 67(x), 216.

51. See *id.* ¶ 67(x).

52. *Id.* ¶¶ 197, 216.

53. Las Dos Erres Massacre v. Guatemala, ¶ 139 (where the court stated that "pregnant women were subject to induced abortions and other barbaric acts").

54. Gómez-Paquiyauri brothers v. Peru, ¶ 71; Castro Prison v. Peru, ¶ 61; Goiburú et al. v. Paraguay.

55. *See* Artavia Murillo v. Costa Rica, ¶¶ 222, 224–26, 231, 236, 252, 261, 269.

56. Goiburú et al. v. Paraguay, ¶ 104.

57. *Id.* ¶ 56(d).

58. *Id.* ¶¶ 160(b)(iii), 161. *See* Provisional Measures Requested by the Inter-American Commission on Human Rights in the Matter of the Republic of Argentina, Reggiardo Tolosa Case.

59. Castro Prison v. Peru.

60. *Id.* ¶¶ 197(57), 290.

61. *Id.* ¶ 186(a)(6).

62. *Id.* ¶ 197(57).

63. *Id.* ¶ 292.

64. Castro Prison v. Peru, Merits, Concurring Opinion, ¶ 61. *Id.*

65. Sawhoyamaxa Indigenous Community v. Paraguay.

66. *Id.* ¶ 177.

67. *See* Artavia Murillo v. Costa Rica, ¶¶ 136–62, 223, 264.

68. *Id.* ¶ 189 et seq.

69. *Id.* ¶ 264.

70. *Id.* ¶ 338.

71. Case of Gómez Murillo et al. v. Costa Rica.

72. *See* Artavia Murillo v. Costa Rica, ¶ 159.

73. *Id.* ¶¶ 174–90.

74. *See I/A Court History*.

75. *See* Signatories and Ratifications: American Convention on Human Rights (Costa Rica ratification/accession: 03/02/70, recognition of the jurisdiction of the court and recognition of competence of the commission in February 1980).

76. *See* Artavia Murillo v. Costa Rica, ¶¶ 67, 255 (according to the Inter-American Court, in 2012 Costa Rica became the only country in the world to explicitly ban IVF, although a number of other countries, including Latin American nations, simply had no legal regulation of it and others were beginning to restrict

and limit the practice). *See, e.g.*, Evans v. United Kingdom, 382–83 ("Certain [European] States have enacted primary or secondary legislation to control the use of IVF treatment."); *see also* S.H. v. Austria, ¶ 34–40 (enumerating European IVF prohibitions on heterologous in vitro fertilization in Croatia, Germany, Italy, Lithuania, Norway, Turkey, and Switzerland).

77. *See* Public Hearings of the 133 Period of Sessions, Inter-Am. Comm'n Human Rights, *In Vitro Fertilization, Costa Rica*, at 33:17–33:20 and 1:25:20–1:26:27. *See also* Case of Gómez Murillo et al. v. Costa Rica, ¶ 24, indicating that fifteen children conceived by IVF were born between 1995 and 2000, which seems a relatively low birth rate considering that the procedure was practiced nationwide for a period of five years. Still, without accounting for the number of IVF attempts, successful pregnancies, or human embryos created through the procedure, the number does not give any meaningful indication of the procedure's success rate—i.e., live births versus embryonic death.

78. *See* Artavia Murillo v. Costa Rica, ¶ 213.

79. Roman Catholicism is Costa Rica's official religion, according to its national Constitution. *See* Constitución Política de Costa Rica, art. 75 (Costa Rica).

80. Código de la Niñez y la Adolescencia [Childhood and Adolescence Code] arts. 2, 12 (Costa Rica).

81. *See Gift of a Child.*

82. *See* Artavia Murillo v. Costa Rica, ¶ 156.

83. Corte Suprema de Justicia, Sala Constitucional, marzo 15, 2000, Expdte. 95-001734-0007-CO (Costa Rica), ¶ 1.

84. *See* Artavia Murillo v. Costa Rica, ¶¶ 73–76.

85. *See* Cuéllar M., Justicia, libertad y derechos humanos (*Prólogo* [Prologue]).

86. *See id.* at XII.

87. Case of Artavia Murillo et al. ("In vitro fertilization") v. Costa Rica, Monitoring Compliance with Judgments, Order of the Inter-American Court of Human Rights, ¶ 4 (Inter-Am. Ct. H.R., Feb. 26, 2016).

88. *See* Corte Suprema de Justicia, Sala Constitucional, marzo 15, 2000, Expdte. 95-001734-0007-CO (Costa Rica).

89. *See* Artavia Murillo v. Costa Rica, ¶ 273. Corte Suprema de Justicia, Sala Constitucional, marzo 15, 2000, Expdte. 95-001734-0007-CO (Costa Rica), ¶ III.

90. *Id.* at ¶¶ V–IX.

91. *Id.* at ¶ IX.

92. *See* Artavia Murillo v. Costa Rica, ¶¶ 76, 155–56.

93. *Id.* at ¶¶ 78–83.

94. *Id.* at ¶¶ 79–81.

95. Ana Victoria Sánchez Villalobos and Others v. Costa Rica, ¶ 1.

96. Gómez v. Costa Rica, Case 1368-04, Inter-Am. Comm'n H.R., Decision on Admissibility, 237.

97. *See* Artavia Murillo v. Costa Rica, ¶ 75. *See also* Gómez v. Costa Rica, Case 1368-04, Inter-Am. Comm'n H.R., Decision on Admissibility, ¶ 69.

98. *See* Artavia Murillo v. Costa Rica (García-Sayán, J., concurring) at 3.

99. *See* Artavia Murillo v. Costa Rica, ¶¶ 89, 101, 116 (mentioning couples that already had biological children and desired children with a new spouse). *See id.* ¶¶ 100, 105, 111 (mentioning couples that had adopted children). *See id.* ¶¶ 111, 115 (mentioning couples that had eventually conceived children naturally).

100. *See* Case of Artavia Murillo et al. ("In vitro fertilization") v. Costa Rica, Request for Provisional Measures, ¶ 3(A.1.1.) (petitioner Andrea Bianchi, for instance, indicated that she never sought treatment for endometriosis in Costa Rica).

101. Artavia Murillo v. Costa Rica, ¶ 326.

102. *See* Public Hearings of the 133 Period of Sessions, Inter-Am. Comm'n Human Rights, *In Vitro Fertilization, Costa Rica*, at 55:25–56:55 (The plaintiffs' legal representative, Gerardo Trejos, initially announced that the victims would request reparations of around 20 million euros for the creation of a publicly funded national IVF clinic). *See also* Artavia Murillo v. Costa Rica, ¶¶ 346–47, 358.

103. *See* Public Hearings of the 133 Period of Sessions, Inter-Am. Comm'n Human Rights, *In Vitro Fertilization, Costa Rica*, at 13:10–13:25, 34:27–34:57.

104. *See* Letter from Ana Victoria Sánchez Villalobos, Plaintiff, Inter-Am. Comm'n on Human Rights Case 12.361, to Santiago A. Cantón, Exec. Sec'y, Inter-Am. Comm'n on Human Rights. *See also Mujer comprende que vida comienza en concepción y retira demanda contra Costa Rica.*

105. Letter from Ana Victoria Sánchez Villalobos, Plaintiff, Inter-Am. Comm'n on Human Rights Case 12.361, to Santiago A. Cantón, Exec. Sec'y, Inter-Am. Comm'n on Human Rights.

106. *See* Gómez v. Costa Rica, Case 1368-04, Inter-Am. Comm'n H.R., Decision on Admissibility, ¶¶ 9, 13, 14, 17, 21, 24, 45, 56 (Ana Victoria Sánchez Villalobos v. Costa Rica was simply referred to as "Case 12.361," the name "Ana Victoria Sánchez Villalobos" being omitted from the admissibility report). *See also* Artavia Murillo v. Costa Rica, Case 12.361, Inter-Am. Comm'n H.R., Merits, Rep. No. 85/10 (2011) (commission's merits report submitting the case to the court's jurisdiction, including for the first time the petition's designation as Gretel Artavia Murillo vs. Costa Rica).

107. *See, e.g.*, Inter-Am. Comm'n H.R., Luis Godoy v. Argentina (IACHR report reciting commission proceedings).

108. *See* Ana Victoria Sánchez Villalobos and Others v. Costa Rica, ¶ 2.

109. *Id.* at ¶¶ 27–28.

110. *Id.* at ¶ 49.

111. *See* Banco de Lima v. Government of Peru (recognizing IACHR's jurisdiction to protect the rights of an individual whose property was expropriated, but not to protect "the rights of juridical beings" such as corporations or banking institutions); Tabacalera Boquerón v. Paraguay; Mevopal v. Argentina, ¶ 20;

Bendeck-Cohdinsa v. Honduras, ¶ 17 (cited in Inter-Am. Comm'n H.R., Ana Victoria Sánchez Villalobos and Others v. Costa Rica, ¶ 49).

112. Artavia Murillo v. Costa Rica, ¶¶ 19, 21, 23.

113. *See id.* at ¶¶ 9, 11.

114. *See* Case of Artavia Murillo et al. ("In vitro fertilization") v. Costa Rica, Request for Provisional Measures, ¶ 4.

115. *Id.*

116. *See* Jorge Oviedo, *Costa Rica después de la sentencia de la CIDH en Artavia Murillo* (state attorney Oviedo describes the status of lawsuits before Costa Rican courts seeking further damages and judicial authorization for private practitioners to carry out IVF procedures, as well as administrative action against the Costa Rican social security system for delaying implementation of IVF subsidies).

117. *See* Case of Artavia Murillo et al. ("In vitro fertilization") v. Costa Rica, Request for Provisional Measures, ¶¶ 5, 6.

118. *See* Artavia Murillo vs. Costa Rica, ¶ 265.

119. *See generally* Avendaño, *Fecundación in vitro: Trámite exprés*; *CIDH Extends Deadline for Approval of Law for In-Vitro Fertilization in Costa Rica.*

120. *See* Artavia Murillo v. Costa Rica, Case 12.361, Inter-Am. Comm'n H.R., Merits, Rep. No. 85/10 (2011), ¶¶ 89–90.

121. Artavia Murillo v. Costa Rica, ¶ 84 (citing bill on in vitro fertilization and embryo transfer, File 17,900, October 22, 2010).

122. *See* Exec. Order. No. 24029-S (Executive Decree 24029-S of 1995 allowed all artificial reproduction techniques including IVF but restricted the latter to homologous procedures between married couples). *See also* Ana Victoria Sánchez Villalobos and Others v. Costa Rica, ¶ 16 (fertilization of more than six ova was prohibited, and all embryos were to be transferred to the woman's uterus, thus preventing embryo cryopreservation, destruction, or disposal).

123. *See* Artavia Murillo v. Costa Rica, ¶ 84.

124. *See* Luis Díaz, *Radio Fides interpondrá recurso de amparo por censura a campaña contra FIV.*

125. *Levantan censura a anuncios católicos sobre fecundación in vitro en Costa Rica.*

126. *See* Artavia Murillo v. Costa Rica, ¶¶ 136–62.

127. *Id.* ¶ 338.

128. *Id.* ¶ 143.

129. *Id.* ¶ 143.

130. *Id.* ¶¶ 146, 150.

131. *Id.* ¶ 326.

132. *See id.* ¶ 314 (concluding that the IVF ban constituted "severe interference" with the right to make "personal decisions" to produce biological children by IVF).

133. *Id.* (Vio Grossi, J., dissenting) at 3–4 (criticizing the court's subordination of the right to life to reproductive rights); Artavia Murillo v. Costa Rica, ¶¶ 136–62, 264.

134. *See* A, B & C v. Ireland, 185, 261.

135. *See* Artavia Murillo v. Costa Rica, Case 12.361, Inter-Am. Comm'n H.R., Merits, Rep. No. 85/10 (2011), ¶¶ 89–90.

136. *See* Artavia Murillo v. Costa Rica, ¶ 265.

137. *Id.* ¶¶ 266–65.

138. *Id.* ¶ 265.

139. *Id.* ¶¶ 260, 273.

140. *See* Artavia Murillo v. Costa Rica (Vio Grossi, J., dissenting), 21. *See also* Case of Gómez Murillo et al. v. Costa Rica, Opinion: Judge Vio Grossi, 6. *Cf.* Villagrán-Morales v. Guatemala, ¶ 144; Xákmok Kásek Indigenous Cmty. v. Paraguay, ¶ 186.

141. *See* Artavia Murillo v. Costa Rica, ¶ 263 (judgment indicates that analysis of arbitrariness-test requirements is unnecessary, then elaborates on the excessive protection given to the embryo vis-à-vis the plaintiffs' rights). *See id.* ¶ 273; Artavia Murillo v. Costa Rica (Vio Grossi, J., dissenting), 19 (where Judge Vio Grossi points out the awkwardness of the conflict between the said rights and "a technique," rather than between those rights and other rights or state interests).

142. Artavia Murillo v. Costa Rica, ¶ 35. *See also* Gómez v. Costa Rica, Case 1368-04, Inter-Am. Comm'n H.R., Decision on Admissibility, ¶ 40.

143. *See* Artavia Murillo v. Costa Rica, ¶¶ 158–62.

144. *Id.* ¶¶ 171, 270.

145. *See id.* ¶ 312.

146. *See id.* ¶ 156.

147. *Id.* ¶ 159.

148. *See id.* ¶¶ 145, 161, 326, 350, 363 ("[T]his case is not related to a presumed right to have children or a right to have access to IVF. To the contrary, the case has focused on the impact of a disproportionate interference in decisions regarding private and family life, and the other rights involved").

149. *See id.* ¶ 161.

150. *See id.* ¶¶ 104, 114. *See also* Case of Gómez Murillo et al. v. Costa Rica, ¶¶ 41–42. *See also* Case of Artavia Murillo et al. ("In vitro fertilization") v. Costa Rica, Request for Provisional Measures, ¶¶ 3(A.1), 3(A.2).

151. *See* Artavia Murillo v. Costa Rica, ¶¶ 278–79, 326.

152. *Id.* ¶ 363.

153. *Id.* ¶¶ 317, 363.

154. *Id.* ¶ 363.

155. *Id.* ¶ 161. *See also* Case of Gómez Murillo et al. v. Costa Rica, ¶¶ 37–43.

156. *See* Artavia Murillo v. Costa Rica, Case 12.361, Inter-Am. Comm'n H.R., Merits, Rep. No. 85/10 (2011), ¶ 114. *See* Artavia Murillo v. Costa Rica, ¶ 283.

157. *See* Case of Artavia Murillo et al. ("In vitro fertilization") v. Costa Rica, Monitoring Compliance with Judgments, Order of the Inter-American Court of Human Rights, ¶¶ 51–53 (Inter-Am. Ct. H.R., Feb. 26, 2016). *See also* Caso Artavia Murillo y otros ("fecundación in vitro") vs. Costa Rica: Reparaciones declaradas cumplidas.

158. *See* Case of Artavia Murillo et al. ("In vitro fertilization") v. Costa Rica, Monitoring Compliance with Judgments, Order of the Inter-American Court of Human Rights, ¶ 128 (Inter-Am. Ct. H.R., Feb. 26, 2016).

159. *See* Public Hearings of the 133 Period of Sessions, Inter-Am. Comm'n Human Rights, *In Vitro Fertilization, Costa Rica*, at 10:13–12:34, 38:24–40:44.

160. *See* Artavia Murillo v. Costa Rica, ¶ 128.

161. *Id.* ¶¶ 134–35.

162. *See* Santiago Marzioni v. Argentina, ¶¶ 48–51 (on fourth-instance doctrine). *See also* Andrews v. United States, ¶ 170 (where IACHR affirms that the subsidiarity principle does not preclude the commission from considering a case where the petitioner's allegations entailed a possible violation of any of the rights set forth in the American Convention).

163. *See* Artavia Murillo v. Costa Rica, ¶¶ 274, 314–16.

164. *Id.* ¶¶ 265, 309.

165. *See* IACHR, Public Hearings of the 96 Regular Session from Aug. 27 to Sept. 7, 2012, at 2:38:00–2:50:21 (see part 4).

166. *See* Carranza Latrubesse, *Las perplejidades de los derechos humanos.*

167. *See* Ana Victoria Sánchez Villalobos and Others v. Costa Rica, ¶ 30.

168. *See* Artavia Murillo v. Costa Rica, ¶¶ 76, 305, 308 (citing the Costa Rican Supreme Court, which emphasized that IVF involves "conscious [and] voluntary manipulation" of human embryos).

169. *See id.* ¶ 308 (stating that expert witness Martha Garza estimated that "embryo mortality is around 30% in natural circumstances and, for IVF, it is calculated that embryonic loss is around 90%").

170. *See* Artavia Murillo v. Costa Rica, ¶¶ 146–50 (the judgment mentioned the right to health but did not adjudicate on its violation, perhaps because of its jurisdictional limitations over social and economic rights).

171. *Id.* ¶ 107 (see number 4).

172. *See* Artavia Murillo v. Costa Rica, Case 12.361, Inter-Am. Comm'n H.R., Merits, Rep. No. 85/10 (2011) (Explanation of Dissenting Opinion).

173. *See id.* at 30.

174. *See id.* at 4, 31.

175. *See* Artavia Murillo v. Costa Rica, ¶¶ 341, 345.

176. *See id.* at ¶ 227.

177. *See* Artavia Murillo v. Costa Rica, Case 12.361, Inter-Am. Comm'n H.R., Merits, Rep. No. 85/10 (2011) (Explanation of Dissenting Opinion).

178. Artavia Murillo v. Costa Rica, ¶ 300. *See also* Case of Gómez Murillo et al. v. Costa Rica, ¶ 24.

179. *See* Artavia Murillo v. Costa Rica, ¶¶ 294–96.

180. *Id.* at ¶ 143.

181. *Id.* ¶¶ 161, 300.

182. Brief for Asociación para la Defensa de la Vida, 6–7.

183. *See* Artavia Murillo v. Costa Rica, ¶¶ 62, 271, 288–91 (citing expert witness Fernando Zegers-Hochschild's testimony at the public hearing before the court).

184. *Id.* ¶¶ 288–93.

185. *Id.* ¶ 291.

186. *Id.* ¶¶ 303–4.

187. *See* Organization of American States, American Convention on Human Rights art. 1(1).

188. *See* Public Hearings of the 133 Period of Sessions, Inter-Am. Comm'n Human Rights, *In Vitro Fertilization, Costa Rica*, at 34:22–34:50, 37:02–37:39 (where petitioner Andrea Bianchi indicates that each attempt at pregnancy using IVF outside of Costa Rica had cost her around fifteen thousand US dollars).

189. *See Latin America & Caribbean (Developing Only)* (indicating that gross national income per capita was $8,981 per year in 2012, the year that *Artavia* was decided).

190. *See* Artavia Murillo v. Costa Rica (García-Sayán, J., concurring), ¶ 11(c).

191. *See* Artavia Murillo v. Costa Rica, ¶¶ 92, 95, 97, 104, 118, 125, 314, 351 (indicating that discrimination based on financial situation occurred against some petitioners, not all).

192. *See id.* ¶¶ 355, 363. *See* Public Hearings of the 133 Period of Sessions, Inter-Am. Comm'n Human Rights, *In Vitro Fertilization, Costa Rica*, at 13:10–13:25, 34:27–34:57 (petitioner Bianchi requesting compensation for her IVF treatments in Colombia).

193. *See* Artavia Murillo v. Costa Rica, ¶ 338.

194. *See id.* (García-Sayán, J., concurring), ¶¶ 10–11.

195. *Cf.* Antkowiak, *Dark Side of Virtue*, 1–80 (indicating that the Inter-American Court's collective and individual monetary reparations for indigenous peoples' ancestral property claims are overly restrictive and undermine collective rights).

196. *See* Artavia Murillo v. Costa Rica (García-Sayán, J., concurring), ¶ 11.

197. Additional Protocol to the American Convention on Human Rights in the Area of Economic, Social and Cultural Rights (Protocol of San Salvador) art. 15.

198. *See* Artavia Murillo v. Costa Rica, ¶ 255 (the judgment cited two then-bills in Argentina and Uruguay that would mandate some state funding of IVF, if approved, and referred to expert witness Zegers-Hochschild's statements affirming that the Chilean government had begun funding some IVF procedures. At the date of the judgment, however, not a single state party to the American Convention had mandated public funding of artificial reproduction in its domestic jurisdiction).

199. *See* Public Hearings of the 133 Period of Sessions, Inter-Am. Comm'n Human Rights, *In Vitro Fertilization, Costa Rica*, at 37:02–37:39, 55:25–56:55; *see also* Artavia Murillo v. Costa Rica (García-Sayán, J., concurring).

200. *See* Artavia Murillo v. Costa Rica, ¶ 150.

201. *See* Glass v. United Kingdom, 46–49; P. & S. v. Poland, ¶ 96.

202. *See* Cook, Dickens, and Fathalla, *Reproductive Health and Human Rights*, 312.

203. *Id.*

204. *See* Artavia Murillo v. Costa Rica, ¶¶ 185, 189 et seq.

205. *Id.* ¶ 264.

206. *See* Public Hearings of the 133 Period of Sessions, Inter-Am. Comm'n Human Rights, *In Vitro Fertilization, Costa Rica*, at 01:07:49–01:08:46.

207. Artavia Murillo v. Costa Rica (Vio Grossi, J., dissenting), 9.

208. *Id.* (indicating that most countries in the region treat conception and fertilization as synonymous).

209. Código De La Niñez Y Adolescencia, art. 20 (Ecuador).

210. *See* chapter 5.

211. *See* Artavia Murillo v. Costa Rica, ¶ 13.

212. *Id.* Brief by *Rafael Nieto Navia and Three Law Professors* as Amici Curiae Supporting Costa Rica, 12–13 (see cover page, where Judge Rafael Nieto Navia identified himself as founding Inter-American Court Judge and not as a professor).

213. *See* Artavia Murillo v. Costa Rica (Vio Grossi, J., dissenting) at 23.

214. *See Id.* at 9, 14 (citing majority opinion, ¶¶ 79, 266–84). See also Case of Gómez Murillo et al. v. Costa Rica, Opinion: Judge Vio Grossi, 6.

215. *See Fernando Zegers-Hochschild.*

216. Croxatto and Zegers-Hochschild, *Anticoncepción de emergencia, ciencia y moral*, 400–401 (arguing that levonorgestrel prevented fertilization, not implantation of the human embryo, stating: "Estamos convencidos de que una nueva vida comienza con la fecundación" [We are convinced that a new life begins with fertilization]). *See* Artavia Murillo v. Costa Rica, ¶ 183 (citing summary of expert opinion provided by Fernando Zegers-Hochschild at the public hearing before the court) (emphasis added).

217. *See* Lafferriere, *La Corte Interamericana de Derechos Humanos y un injusto fallo sobre el embrión humano ante las biotecnologías*, 179–97.

218. Artavia Murillo v. Costa Rica, ¶ 182.

219. *Id.* ¶ 185.

220. *See* Case of Gómez Murillo et al. v. Costa Rica, *Opinion: Judge Vio Grossi*, 5.

221. Artavia Murillo v. Costa Rica, ¶¶ 181, 187.

222. *See* Artavia Murillo v. Costa Rica (Vio Grossi, J., dissenting), 19. *Cf.* Henríquez Herrera, *Comentario al Fallo de la Corte*, 55, 61 (a Chilean scholar qualifies the court's conclusion as absurd and with no basis in the convention's text).

223. *See Conceive*, Oxford Dictionaries (the modern *Oxford English Dictionary* defines *conception* as both fertilization and impregnation, using the terms as synonymous).

224. See Signatories and Ratifications: American Convention on Human Rights.

225. *See* Artavia Murillo v. Costa Rica (Vio Grossi, J., dissenting) at 9, 16, 19.

226. *Id.* (Vio Grossi, J., dissenting) at 9. *See also Preñar*, in *Diccionario de la lengua española.*

227. *See* Artavia Murillo v. Costa Rica, ¶¶ 181, 187–89.

228. *See Conceive*, Oxford Dictionaries (from the late-thirteenth-century *conceiven*, "take (seed) into the womb, become pregnant," from stem of Old French *conceveir* (Modern French *concevoir*), from Latin *concipere* (past participle *conceptus*), "to take in and hold; become pregnant").

229. Baer, *Epistola de Ovo Mammalium et Hominis Genesi.*

230. Artavia Murillo v. Costa Rica, ¶ 179.

231. *See id.* ¶¶ 187, 194–221.

232. *See id.* ¶¶ 194–221.

233. *Id.* ¶ 179. *See also* Case of Artavia Murillo et al. v. Costa Rica, Preliminary Objections, Merits, Reparations, and Costs, Judgment (Vio Grossi, J., dissenting), 15 (indicating that the majority implicitly admitted that states parties did not originally understand *conception* to mean implantation: "[T]he definition of conception that the drafters of the American Convention had at the time *has changed*") (emphasis added).

234. *See* Case of Artavia Murillo et al. ("In vitro fertilization") v. Costa Rica, Monitoring Compliance with Judgments, Order of the Inter-American Court of Human Rights, ¶ 26 (Inter-Am. Ct. H.R., Feb. 26, 2016) (resolution items 1 and 2).

235. Artavia Murillo v. Costa Rica, ¶¶ 56, 65, 67–69.

236. *Id.* ¶ 10.

237. *See* May, *El Estado incumple la sentencia FIV.*

238. *See* Public Hearings of the 133 Period of Sessions, Inter-Am. Comm'n Human Rights, *In Vitro Fertilization, Costa Rica.*

239. *See CSJ, Costa Rica (2016)*, ¶ 5.

240. *Id.* ¶ III, V.

241. *Id.* ¶ III (citing the Constitutional Chamber's wealth of jurisprudence to this effect).

242. *Id.* ¶ IV.

243. *Id.* ¶ II, 6.

244. *Id.*

245. *Id.* ¶ IV.

246. Case of Artavia Murillo et al. ("In vitro fertilization") v. Costa Rica, Monitoring Compliance with Judgments, Order of the Inter-American Court of

Human Rights, ¶ 8 (Inter-Am. Ct. H.R., Feb. 26, 2016). *See also* Corte Suprema de Justicia, Sala Constitucional, Exp. 15-013929-0007-CO, Res. N. 2016001692, febrero 3, 2016, SISTEMA COSTARRICENSE DE INFORMACIÓN JURÍDICA, ¶ III (Costa Rica).

247. *See* Corte Suprema de Justicia, Sala Constitucional, Exp. 15-013929-0007-CO, Res. N. 2016001692, febrero 3, 2016, SISTEMA COSTARRICENSE DE INFORMACIÓN JURÍDICA, ¶ IV (Costa Rica).

248. *See CIDH presenta caso sobre Costa Rica a la Corte IDH. See also* Resolución de levantamiento de medidas cautelares (the IACHR did not lift precautionary measures until 2018, indicating that the couples in question had not provided any observations to the state's communications since the court's *Gómez Murillo* judgment was issued).

249. Case of Artavia Murillo et al. ("In vitro fertilization") v. Costa Rica, Monitoring Compliance with Judgments, Order of the Inter-American Court of Human Rights, ¶ 21 (Inter-Am. Ct. H.R., Feb. 26, 2016). *See also* Case of Gómez Murillo et al. v. Costa Rica, ¶ 3(f).

250. *See* Franck, *Costa Rica: Por segunda vez llevada a la Corte Interamericana con motivo de la FIV.*

251. Case of Artavia Murillo et al. ("In vitro fertilization") v. Costa Rica, Monitoring Compliance with Judgments, Order of the Inter-American Court of Human Rights, ¶ 13 (Inter-Am. Ct. H.R., Feb. 26, 2016).

252. *See id.* ¶¶ 26–27 (resolution items 3–5).

253. *Id.*, Dissenting Vote Judge Eduardo Vio Grossi (in Spanish only). *Cf.* Case of Duque v. Colombia, Opinion: Judge Ventura Robles, 1, 2; Case of Duque v. Colombia, Opinion: Judge Vio Grossi. (In Alberto Duque v. Colombia, a judgment that was published on the same day as the implementation resolution, the court was criticized for not adhering to the principle of subsidiarity, also by its own judges. In the judgment, which found a state obligation to provide pension benefits to same-sex partners, Judge Manuel Ventura Robles pointed out that "the court should make it a norm to apply the complementarity principle of international jurisdiction on human rights [matters]." He also indicated that "[the court's] jurisdiction was not established so that all cases would be submitted to it, or so that alleged victims win all cases under any circumstance." Likewise, Judge Vio Grossi indicated that the court should "guard, with particular resolve and zealousness, the limits of its actions as determined by the Convention and, in general, by international law.") Costa Rican judge Ventura did not hear the *Artavia* case, due to his nationality (see Inter-Am. Ct. H.R., Rules of Procedure of the Inter-American Court of Human Rights art. 19). *See also* Silva Abbott, *Un peligro para la dignidad humana del no nacido*, 6 (Chilean Law Professor Max Silva Abbott indicates that the court attempted to act as a continental constitutional tribunal during the implementation phase of the *Artavia* case). *See also* Blanco Donaire, *¿Aprueba la fecundación in vitro el test de razonabilidad?*, 32 (illustrating critique of the *Artavia* judgment by Costa Rican academics).

254. *See* Case of Artavia Murillo et al. ("In vitro fertilization") v. Costa Rica, Monitoring Compliance with Judgments, Order of the Inter-American Court of Human Rights, ¶ 26 (Inter-Am. Ct. H.R., Feb. 26, 2016), Dissenting Vote Judge Eduardo Vio Grossi.

255. *Id.* ¶ 17.

256. *Cf.* Lamm et al., *La Corte Interamericana de Derechos Humanos controla, sin concesión alguna, el cumplimiento de sus decisiones*, 9 (suggesting that artificial reproductive technologies have mobilized the commission and the court, which have taken a more "active" role than they normally do on other issues).

257. Case of Artavia Murillo et al. ("In vitro fertilization") v. Costa Rica, Monitoring Compliance with Judgments, Order of the Inter-American Court of Human Rights, ¶ 13 (Inter-Am. Ct. H.R., Feb. 26, 2016) (emphasis added).

258. *Id.* ¶ 14 (emphasis added).

259. *See also* Case of Gómez Murillo et al. v. Costa Rica, 19, 45.

260. *See* Vio Grossi, *Reflexión sobre la justicia interamericana en DD.HH.*

261. *See* Case of Artavia Murillo et al. ("In vitro fertilization") v. Costa Rica, Monitoring Compliance with Judgments, Order of the Inter-American Court of Human Rights, ¶¶ 21, 32 (Inter-Am. Ct. H.R., Feb. 26, 2016).

262. *Id.*

263. Cantón, *To Strengthen Human Rights, Change Organization of American States (Not the Commission)*, 3.

264. Corte Suprema de Justicia de la Nación, 14/02/2017, 368/1998 (34-M)/CS1 Ministerio de Relaciones y Culto "s/informe sentencia dictada en el caso 'Fontevecchia y D'Amico vs. Argentina' por la Corte Interamericana de Derechos Humanos" [Fallos: 340:47] (Arg.).

265. *See CSJ, Costa Rica (2016)*, ¶ III (Costa Rica). *See also* Case of Artavia Murillo et al. ("In vitro fertilization") v. Costa Rica, Monitoring Compliance with Judgments, Order of the Inter-American Court of Human Rights, ¶ 8 (Inter-Am. Ct. H.R., Feb. 26, 2016).

266. Piza Escalante, *La justicia constitucional en Costa Rica*, 210.

267. *See* Convenio entre el Gobierno de Costa Rica y la Corte Interamericana de Derechos Humanos, Ley No. 6889 art. 27 (original Spanish text says: "Las resoluciones de la Corte y, en su caso, de su Presidente, una vez comunicadas a las autoridades administrativas o judiciales correspondientes de la república, tendrán la misma fuerza ejecutiva y ejecutoria que las dictadas por los tribunales costarricenses").

268. *See, e.g.*, Compulsory Membership in an Association Prescribed by Law for the Practice of Journalism, S 81 (finding Costa Rican Law No. 4420 incompatible with the American Convention); Proposed Amendments of the Naturalization Provisions of the Constitution of Costa Rica (finding that the Costa Rica Constitution's naturalization requirements granting Latin Americans and Spanish citizens preferential status did not violate the American Convention's discrimination prohibitions).

269. *See* Avendaño, *Magistrado Luis Fernando Salazar: Es momento de que la Sala IV se haga a un lado* (judge who wrote the Constitutional Chamber's majority opinion says to the press that he will respect the Inter-American Court's decision to overturn the Constitutional Chamber's judgment). *See also* Avendaño, *Presidente de la Sala IV* (Chamber president Ernesto Jinesta tells the press that the Chamber should have never invalidated the executive decree).

270. *See* Case of Gómez Murillo et al. v. Costa Rica.

271. *Id.* ¶¶ 55, 56, 6(b)–(e) (under dispositions).

272. *Id.* ¶¶ 58–59, 6(f)–(g) (under dispositions).

273. *Id.* ¶ 61.

274. *Id.* ¶ 53, 7 (under dispositions).

275. *Id.* ¶¶ 13, 50.

276. *See* Case of Gómez Murillo et al. v. Costa Rica, *Opinion: Judge Vio Grossi*, 6 (Judge Vio Grossi noted the stark change in the state's position and observed that the unborn's right to life was left in a state of "defenselessness and vulnerability" with the new governmental representation before the court).

277. See *id.* at 9 n.40.

278. *See* Case of Gómez Murillo et al. v. Costa Rica, ¶ 18 (explaining the unusual procedural steps taken in the approval of the friendly settlement). *See also id., Opinion: Judge Vio Grossi*, 4 (pointing out that the court's approval of a friendly settlement through a judgment allowed the judgment to become binding on the state).

279. *See* Case of Gómez Murillo et al. v. Costa Rica, ¶¶ 6, 11, 14.

280. See *id., Opinion: Judge Vio Grossi* at 4–6, 7–9.

281. *See also* Case of Gómez Murillo et al. v. Costa Rica, ¶¶ 4–5 (resolution) (citing arts. 5.1, 7, 11.2, 17.2 and 24 but not art. 4). In addition, the *Gómez* judgment mentions that the plaintiffs themselves alleged a violation of art. 4(1) on the right to life, which the government of Costa Rica admitted to.

282. *See* Case of Gómez Murillo et al. v. Costa Rica, ¶¶ 19, 45.

283. *See* Ana Victoria Sánchez Villalobos and Others v. Costa Rica, ¶ 70. *See also* Case of Gómez Murillo et al. v. Costa Rica, ¶¶ 4–5 (resolution).

284. *E.g.*, Ana Victoria Sánchez Villalobos and Others v. Costa Rica, ¶ 1 (conclusions).

285. *See* Case of Gómez Murillo et al. v. Costa Rica, ¶¶ 5, 6(h), 9, 57, 62–64 (under dispositions). (Specifically, the court gave the government a deadline of six months to a year to formally report on a time line and specific steps taken to comply with the reparations—steps that the court would supervise. The court also invited petitioners to instruct the court on what measures they expected the state to take by the said deadline). *See also* Case of Gómez Murillo et al. v. Costa Rica, *Opinion: Judge Vio Grossi*, 3–4 (Judge Vio Grossi pointed out the judgment should have been considered *res judicata.*)

286. *See* Artavia Murillo v. Costa Rica, Case 12.361, Inter-Am. Comm'n H.R., Merits, Rep. No. 85/10 (2011), ¶ 110.

287. *See id.*, Explanation of Dissenting Opinion, ¶ 6.

288. *See* Artavia Murillo v. Costa Rica, Case 12.361, Inter-Am. Comm'n H.R., Merits, Rep. No. 85/10 (2011), ¶¶ 101–10.

289. *See* Artavia Murillo v. Costa Rica, 2, 49 (subtitle c).

290. *See id.* (García-Sayán, J., concurring), ¶ 8 (emphasis added).

291. *See* Case of Gómez Murillo et al. v. Costa Rica, *Opinion: Judge Vio Grossi*, 1.

292. *See* Paúl, *Admissibility of Evidence Before the Inter-American Court of Human Rights*, 653–76; Paúl, *Giro en Materia de Recurso de Revisión ante la Corte Interamericana*, 131–38 (commenting on the Inter-American Court's departure from consistent precedent in the case of *Bulacio v. Argentina* and in the *case of the Mapiripán massacre*). *See also* Case of Gómez Murillo et al. v. Costa Rica, *Opinion: Judge Vio Grossi*, 1 (unnumbered).

293. *See* Corte Suprema de Justicia de la Nación, 01/09/2015, "Recurso de hecho deducido por los actores en la causa L.E.H. y otros c/O.S.E.P. s/amparo" (Arg.) (rejecting any relevance of the *Artavia* judgment in Argentina, pointing out that the decision dealt with a full ban on IVF, whereas Argentina had legally authorized IVF with some permissible limitations).

294. *Oradores en Contra* (see Alejandro Pérez Hualde starting at 3:40).

295. ADPF No. 442, paras. 46–47.

296. *Id.* (citing *Artavia*, ¶¶ 263–64).

297. *See* ADPF No. 442 (emphasis added); *Advogada-Geral da União manifesta-se pela improcedência do pedido formulado pelo arguente*, 41–43.

298. *See* Artavia Murillo v. Costa Rica, ¶¶ 258–59, 262, 278, 326.

299. *See* Corte Suprema de Justicia de la Nación, 01/09/2015, "Recurso de hecho deducido por los actores en la causa L.E.H. y otros c/O.S.E.P. s/amparo" (Arg.).

300. *See* Corte Suprema de Justicia de la Nación, 01/09/2015, "Recurso de hecho deducido por los actores en la causa L.E.H. y otros c/O.S.E.P. s/amparo" (Arg.).

301. *See id.*, Voto ampliatorio Dr. Alejandro Pérez Hualde.

302. *See* Juzgado Federal de Salta No. 1, 8/7/2013, "Lodi Ortiz Andrea Melisa—Larran Cristian c/Swiss Medical s/amparo," Expdte. No. 61000007/13 (Arg.) (pointing out that federal supreme court judgments have no binding force in Argentinian provinces, and Inter-American courts have even less authority in provincial jurisdiction).

303. *Id.*

304. *See* Corte Suprema de Justicia, Sala Constitutional, Feb. 4, 2019, Amparo promovido por M. C. G.G. C/P.P.G., Director de la Clinica G." No. 3241/2010 (Para.). *See also* Tribunal de Apelación Penal de la Adolescencia, Acuerdo y Sentencia No. 12 (Para.).

305. *See* Tribunal de Apelación Penal de la Adolescencia, Acuerdo y Sentencia No. 12, 4–5 (Para.).

306. *See* Tribunal Constitucional, 28 agosto 2017, Requerimiento de inconstitucionalidad respecto del proyecto de ley que "regula la despenalización de la interrupción voluntaria del embarazo en tres causales," 89, 127 (Chile).

307. *See* Considerations Related to the Universal Ratification of the American Convention and Other Inter-American Human Rights Treaties.

308. *See IACHR Regrets Decision of Venezuela to Denounce the American Convention on Human Rights* (on Venezuela's withdrawal from the convention and withdrawal from the Inter-American Court jurisdiction).

309. *See* Artavia Murillo v. Costa Rica, ¶¶ 341, 381 (operative paragraph #7).

310. *See* Vasciannie, *Inter-American Commission on Human Rights*, 409.

311. *See, e.g.*, Maher v. Roe, Beal v. Doe, and Poelker v. Doe (US Supreme Court judgments finding no constitutional duty of American states to fund abortion).

312. See Signatories and Ratifications: American Convention on Human Rights.

313. *See* Carozza, *Anglo-Latin Divide and the Future of the Inter-American System of Human Rights*, 155–58 (explaining causes of historical reluctance on the part of English-speaking countries to accept international interference with their constitutional laws).

314. *Id.* at 164.

315. *See* Case of Gómez Murillo et al. v. Costa Rica, *Opinion: Judge Vio Grossi*, 6.

316. *See* Matter of B. regarding El Salvador, Provisional Measures, Order of the Inter-American Court of Human Rights, May 29, 2013.

317. *Id.*, ¶¶ 1, 4(ii)(e).

318. *See* Organization of American States, American Convention on Human Rights art. 46(1)(a) (on requirement of exhaustion of domestic remedies); *see also id.* (preamble) (reaffirming subsidiarity of the convention in "reinforcing or complementing the protection provided by the domestic law of the American states"). *See* Matter of B. regarding El Salvador, Provisional Measures, Order of the Inter-American Court of Human Rights, May 29, 2013, ¶ 17 (resolution point (1)).

319. *See* Gonzales v. Carhart, ¶ 1614 (the US Supreme Court upheld a similar finding reached by Congress regarding the partial-birth abortion procedure: "[P]artial-birth abortion is a gruesome and inhumane procedure that is *never medically necessary and should be prohibited*") (emphasis added).

320. *See* Sala de lo Constitucional de la Corte Suprema de Justicia, May 28, 2013, Amparo 310-2013 (El Sal.). *See* partial translation in Matter of B. regarding El Salvador, Provisional Measures, Order of the Inter-American Court of Human Rights, May 29, 2013, ¶ 10(xvii).

321. *See Florentín Meléndez Padilla (Former Rapporteurs)* (Florentín Meléndez was a member of the IACHR from 2004 to 2009; Judge Meléndez is also a former member and professor of the Inter-American Institute of Human Rights).

*See* Sala de lo Constitucional de la Corte Suprema de Justicia, May 28, 2013, Amparo 310-2013 (El Sal.), Voto disidente Florentín Meléndez.

322. Iraheta, *Magistrados: "En el caso Beatriz nos quisieron manipular."*

323. *See* Sala de lo Constitucional de la Corte Suprema de Justicia, May 28, 2013, Amparo 310-2013, ¶ VII(5)(C) (El Sal.).

324. *See* Sala de lo Constitucional de la Corte Suprema de Justicia, May 28, 2013, Amparo 310-2013 (El Sal.), Voto disidente en el caso B.C. Magistrado Florentín Meléndez.

325. *See* Sala de lo Constitucional de la Corte Suprema de Justicia, May 28, 2013, Amparo 310-2013, ¶ 8(c) and (e) (El Sal.); Matter of B. regarding El Salvador, Provisional Measures, Order of the Inter-American Court of Human Rights, August 19, 2013, ¶ 9.

326. *See* Sala de lo Constitucional de la Corte Suprema de Justicia, May 28, 2013, Amparo 310-2013 (El Sal.), Voto disidente Florentín Meléndez.

327. *See* Sala de lo Constitucional de la Corte Suprema de Justicia, May 28, 2013, Amparo 310-2013, ¶ I(1), I(2)(C)(a) (El Sal.).

328. *See id.* ¶ I(2)(C)(b).

329. *See id.* ¶ I(1), I(2)(C)(a).

330. *See* Matter of B. regarding El Salvador, Provisional Measures, Order of the Inter-American Court of Human Rights, May 29, 2013, ¶¶ 1, 3(v)(viii)(xi), 4; *see also* Matter of B. regarding El Salvador, Provisional Measures, Order of the Inter-American Court of Human Rights, August 19, 2013, ¶ 9.

331. *See* Sala de lo Constitucional de la Corte Suprema de Justicia, May 28, 2013, Amparo 310-2013 (El Sal.), ¶ I(2)(B)(b); *see* Matter of B. regarding El Salvador, Provisional Measures, Order of the Inter-American Court of Human Rights, May 29, 2013, ¶¶ 1, 2(iv); *see also* Matter of B. regarding El Salvador, Provisional Measures, Order of the Inter-American Court of Human Rights, August 19, 2013, ¶ 9.

332. *See* Matter of B. regarding El Salvador, Provisional Measures, Order of the Inter-American Court of Human Rights, May 29, 2013, ¶¶ 1, 4(2)(e).

333. *Id.* ¶ 4(ii)(b)–(e).

334. *See* Sala de lo Constitucional de la Corte Suprema de Justicia, May 28, 2013, Amparo 310-2013, ¶ I(1), I(2)(B)(i) (El Sal.).

335. *Id.*

336. *Denuncian a El Salvador ante la CIDH por caso de la joven "Beatriz."*

337. Colectivo Feminista para el Desarrollo Local de El Salvador, Agrupación Ciudadana por la Despenalización del Aborto Terapéutico, Ético y Eugenésico de El Salvador, Ipas, CEJIL, *Petición Inicial "Beatriz vs. Estado de El Salvador."*

338. *See CIDH le exige explicaciones a El Salvador por el caso de Beatriz.*

339. *See* Matter of B. regarding El Salvador, Provisional Measures, Order of the Inter-American Court of Human Rights, May 29, 2013, ¶ 14.

340. *See id.*

341. *Id.*

342. *Entrevista viernes 10/05/2013 Bloque #1 B, Entrevista Con: José Miguel Fortin (Dir. General de Medicina Legal) "El Aborto Terapéutico que Demanda Beatriz"* at 6:58. *See also* Tuttle, *Beatriz's Baby* (indicating that abortion lobbies exploit the least fortunate women in Latin America to promote abortion suits before international bodies).

343. *Entrevista viernes 10/05/2013 Bloque #1 B, Entrevista Con: José Miguel Fortin (Dir. General de Medicina Legal) "El Aborto Terapéutico que Demanda Beatriz"* at 8:50.

344. *Entrevista viernes 10/05/2013 Bloque #2 A, Entrevista Con: José Miguel Fortin (Dir. General de Medicina Legal) "El Aborto Terapéutico que Demanda Beatriz."*

345. *See* Sala de lo Constitucional de la Corte Suprema de Justicia, May 28, 2013, Amparo 310-2013 (El Sal.), Voto disidente Florentín Meléndez.

346. *See* Iraheta, *Magistrados: "En el caso Beatriz nos quisieron manipular."*

347. *See* Matter of B. regarding El Salvador, Provisional Measures, Order of the Inter-American Court of Human Rights, May 29, 2013, ¶ 14.

348. *El Salvador: UN Rights Experts Appeal to Government to Provide Life-Saving Treatment to Woman at Risk* (members of the expert group were Anand Grover, special rapporteur on the right of everyone to the enjoyment of the highest attainable standard of physical and mental health; Juan E. Méndez, special rapporteur on torture and other cruel, inhuman, or degrading treatment or punishment; Rashida Manjoo, special rapporteur on violence against women, its causes and consequences; and Kamala Chandrakirana, chairperson of the working group on the issue of discrimination against women in law and in practice). *See also El Salvador: Beatriz morirá si no se le practica un aborto.*

349. *See El Salvador: UN Rights Experts Appeal to Government to Provide Life-Saving Treatment to Woman at Risk.*

350. *Id.* (emphasis added).

351. *See* Orozco, *La reforma de la Comisión Interamericana de Derechos Humanos*, 6 (discussing usual procedural delays at the IACHR).

352. *See* Sala de lo Constitucional de la Corte Suprema de Justicia [Constitutional Chamber of Supreme Court of Justice], May 28, 2013, Amparo 310-2013 (El Sal.), Voto particular concurrente del Magistrado Rodolfo González Bonilla, ¶ I(2).

353. *Id.* ¶ I(2)(A).

354. *Id.* ¶ 3(xi)–(xii).

355. *See* Matter of B. regarding El Salvador, Provisional Measures, Order of the Inter-American Court of Human Rights, May 29, 2013, ¶ 3.

356. *Id.* ¶ 4(i).

357. *See* Sala de lo Constitucional de la Corte Suprema de Justicia [Constitutional Chamber of Supreme Court of Justice], May 28, 2013, Amparo 310-2013,

¶ VII(5)(C) (El Sal.). *See* partial translation in Matter of B. regarding El Salvador, Provisional Measures, Order of the Inter-American Court of Human Rights, May 29, 2013, ¶ 10(xvii).

358. *See* Sala de lo Constitucional de la Corte Suprema de Justicia, May 28, 2013, Amparo 310-2013 , ¶¶ I(2)(C)(b), VII(3)(D)(a) (El Sal.).

359. *See* Sala de lo Constitucional de la Corte Suprema de Justicia, May 28, 2013, Amparo 310-2013 (El Sal.), Voto particular concurrente del Magistrado Rodolfo González Bonilla, ¶ II(3).

360. Sala de lo Constitucional de la Corte Suprema de Justicia, May 28, 2013, Amparo 310-2013 (El Sal.) (see resolution paragraph).

361. *See* Sala de lo Constitucional de la Corte Suprema de Justicia, May 28, 2013, Amparo 310-2013 (El Sal.), Voto particular concurrente del Magistrado Rodolfo González Bonilla, ¶ IV(2).

362. *See* Sala de lo Constitucional de la Corte Suprema de Justicia, May 28, 2013, Amparo 310-2013, ¶ VII(5)(C) (El Sal.) (emphasis added).

363. *See* Sala de lo Constitucional de la Corte Suprema de Justicia, May 28, 2013, Amparo 310-2013 (El Sal.), Voto disidente Florentín Meléndez.

364. *Id.*

365. *See* Sala de lo Constitucional de la Corte Suprema de Justicia, May 28, 2013, Amparo 310-2013 (El Sal.) (see resolution paragraph under "Por tanto").

366. *See* Sala de lo Constitucional de la Corte Suprema de Justicia, May 28, 2013, Amparo 310-2013 (El Sal.), Voto disidente Florentín Meléndez.

367. *Id.*

368. *See* Sala de lo Constitucional de la Corte Suprema de Justicia, May 28, 2013, Amparo 310-2013, ¶ I(2)(C)(a) (El Sal.).

369. *Id.* ¶ VI(3).

370. *Id.* ¶¶ I(2)(D)(a), VII(3)(D)(c).

371. Código Penal, arts. 133–41 (El Sal.).

372. *See* Sala de lo Constitucional de la Corte Suprema de Justicia, May 28, 2013, Amparo 310-2013 , ¶ VI(3) (El Sal.).

373. *See* Sala de lo Constitucional de la Corte Suprema de Justicia, May 28, 2013, Amparo 310-2013, ¶ VII(5)(C) (El Sal.). *See* partial translation in Matter of B. regarding El Salvador, Provisional Measures, Order of the Inter-American Court of Human Rights, May 29, 2013, ¶ 4(ii)(b).

374. Matter of B. regarding El Salvador, Provisional Measures, Order of the Inter-American Court of Human Rights, May 29, 2013, ¶¶ 2(iv), (vi), 3(xi), 4(ii)(a) and (d), 8(c)(2), 8(e). *See* Tuttle, *Beatriz's Baby*.

375. *See* Matter of B. regarding El Salvador, Provisional Measures, Order of the Inter-American Court of Human Rights, May 29, 2013, ¶ 8(c) and (e). *See* Sala de lo Constitucional de la Corte Suprema de Justicia, May 28, 2013, Amparo 310-2013, ¶ VII(3)(C)(a) (El Sal.).

376. *See id.* ¶ VII(3)(D).

377. *See id.* ¶ VII(3)(C)(c).

378. *See id.* ¶ VII(3)(D)(b).

379. *See* Matter of B. regarding El Salvador, Provisional Measures, Order of the Inter-American Court of Human Rights, May 29, 2013, ¶¶ 8(f)–(h), 10 (viii), (xv)–(xvi).

380. *See Entrevista viernes 10/05/2013 Bloque #1 B, Entrevista Con: José Miguel Fortin (Dir. General de Medicina Legal) "El Aborto Terapéutico que Demanda Beatriz"* at 5:36.

381. *See Entrevista viernes 10/05/2013 Bloque #2 A, Entrevista Con: José Miguel Fortin (Dir. General de Medicina Legal) "El Aborto Terapéutico que Demanda Beatriz"* at 7:15.

382. *See Entrevista viernes 10/05/2013 Bloque #1 B, Entrevista Con: José Miguel Fortin (Dir. General de Medicina Legal) "El Aborto Terapéutico que Demanda Beatriz"* 0:59.

383. *Id.* at 5:00, 9:29 (adding that "taking the baby out of the mother's womb will not take away her lupus, will not take away her hypertension or reverse her kidney damage; her kidney damage will continue and when another lupus crisis occurs . . . she will be very ill, with or without the child").

384. *Entrevista viernes 10/05/2013 Bloque #3, Entrevista Con: José Miguel Fortin (Dir. General de Medicina Legal) "El Aborto Terapéutico que Demanda Beatriz."*

385. *See* Matter of B. regarding El Salvador, Provisional Measures, Order of the Inter-American Court of Human Rights, May 29, 2013, ¶¶ I(2)(B)(a), 2(v). *See also* Sala de lo Constitucional, Amparo 310-2013 (El Sal.), Voto particular concurrente del Magistrado Rodolfo González Bonilla, ¶ I(2)(A).

386. *See* Sala de lo Constitucional de la Corte Suprema de Justicia, May 28, 2013, Amparo 310-2013 (El Sal.), Voto particular concurrente del Magistrado Rodolfo González Bonilla, ¶ I(2)(A).

387. *Id.* ¶ I(2)(B). *See* Iraheta, *Magistrados: "En el caso Beatriz nos quisieron manipular."*

388. *See* Sala de lo Constitucional de la Corte Suprema de Justicia, May 28, 2013, Amparo 310-2013 (El Sal.), Voto particular concurrente del Magistrado Rodolfo González Bonilla, ¶ I(2)(B).

389. *Id.* ¶ IV(2).

390. See translation in Matter of B. regarding El Salvador, Provisional Measures, Order of the Inter-American Court of Human Rights, May 29, 2013, ¶ 10(xvi).

391. *See* Sala de lo Constitucional de la Corte Suprema de Justicia, May 28, 2013, Amparo 310-2013, ¶ VII(3)(B)(c) (El Sal.). *See also* Matter of B. regarding El Salvador, Provisional Measures, Order of the Inter-American Court of Human Rights, May 29, 2013, ¶ 10.

392. *See* Sala de lo Constitucional de la Corte Suprema de Justicia [Constitutional Chamber of Supreme Court of Justice], May 28, 2013, Amparo 310-2013, ¶ VII(4)(A) and (B) (El Sal.). *See* Matter of B. regarding El Salvador, Provisional

Measures, Order of the Inter-American Court of Human Rights, May 29, 2013, ¶ 10(xiv).

393. IACHR, *PM 114/13—B, El Salvador. See* Matter of B. regarding El Salvador, Provisional Measures, Order of the Inter-American Court of Human Rights, May 29, 2013, ¶ 3 (ix)–(xi).

394. Matter of B. regarding El Salvador, Provisional Measures, Order of the Inter-American Court of Human Rights, May 29, 2013, ¶ 3.

395. *Id.* ¶¶ 3(xi)–(xii), 4(i).

396. *Id.* ¶¶ 8, 9, 12–14.

397. *Id.* ¶ 17 (resolution point (1)).

398. *See* Matter of B. regarding El Salvador, Provisional Measures, Order of the Inter-American Court of Human Rights, May 29, 2013, ¶¶ 1, 4(ii)(e). *See* Sala de lo Constitucional de la Corte Suprema de Justicia [Constitutional Chamber of Supreme Court of Justice], May 28, 2013, Amparo 310-2013 (El Sal.), ¶ I(1), I(2)(B)(i). *See also* Matter of B. regarding El Salvador, Provisional Measures, Order of the Inter-American Court of Human Rights, May 29, 2013, ¶¶ 1, 4(ii)(c). *See also* Matter of B. regarding El Salvador, Provisional Measures, Order of the Inter-American Court of Human Rights, August 19, 2013 (see consideration point 4, indicating that in "the context of provisional measures the Court may consider only and strictly those arguments that are directly related to the extreme gravity, urgency and need to avoid irreparable damage to persons. Any other fact or argument can only be decided during consideration of the merits of a contentious case").

399. *See* Matter of B. regarding El Salvador, Provisional Measures, Order of the Inter-American Court of Human Rights, May 29, 2013, ¶¶ 15–16.

400. *See id.* ¶¶ 15–16.

401. *Id.* ¶ 17 (see resolution point (1)).

402. *See* Matter of B. regarding El Salvador, Provisional Measures, Order of the Inter-American Court of Human Rights, August 19, 2013, ¶ 6 (see consideration points).

403. *Id.* (see consideration points (6)(c), 7).

404. *Id.* (see consideration points (6)(d)–(h)).

405. *Id.* (see 6(b), 7, consideration point (6)).

406. *Id.* (see consideration points 6(a)–(b)).

407. *Id.* (see consideration point (6)(b)).

408. *Id.* (see consideration point 8).

409. *Id.* (see consideration point 8).

410. *Id.* (see consideration point 9).

411. *Id.* (see consideration points 10).

412. *Id.* (see consideration point 14).

413. *Id.* ¶ 14 (see also resolutory points 1–3).

414. Beatriz v. El Salvador, Petition 2003-13, Inter-Am. Comm'n H.R., Rep. No. 120/17, Admissibility.

415. *See* Matter of B. regarding El Salvador, Provisional Measures, Order of the Inter-American Court of Human Rights, August 19, 2013 (see consideration point 13).

416. *Id.* at 4.

417. *Id.* at ¶ 10.

418. *Id.* at 4.

419. *Id.* at 6.

420. *Id.* at 5.

421. *See* Organization of American States, American Convention on Human Rights art. 46(1).

422. Case of Duque v. Colombia, Opinion: Judge Ventura Robles, 2.

423. *See* Santiago Marzioni v. Argentina, ¶¶ 48–51.

THREE. Toward a Nonrestrictive Interpretation of the American Convention's Prenatal Right to Life from Conception

1. Vienna Convention on the Law of Treaties arts. 31–32. *See* Inter-Am. Ct. H.R., Restrictions to the Death Penalty, ¶¶ 48–50 (court's acceptance of interpretation rules established in the Vienna Convention). *See* American Convention on Human Rights arts. 29–31 (good faith and nonrestrictive interpretation).

2. Organization of American States, American Convention on Human Rights art. 29.

3. Organization of American States, American Convention on Human Rights art. 29 (Restrictions Regarding Interpretation: "No provision of this Convention shall be interpreted as: a. permitting any State Party, group, or person to suppress the enjoyment or exercise of the rights and freedoms recognized in this Convention or to restrict them to a greater extent than is provided for herein; b. restricting the enjoyment or exercise of any right or freedom recognized by virtue of the laws of any State Party or by virtue of another Convention to which one of the said states is a party; c. precluding other rights or guarantees that are inherent in the human personality or derived from representative democracy as a form of government; or d. excluding or limiting the effect that the American Declaration of the Rights and Duties of Man and other international acts of the same nature may have").

4. García Ramírez, *Relationship Between Inter-American Jurisdiction and States (National Systems)*, 130.

5. Barberis, *El derecho a la vida en el pacto de San José de Costa Rica*, 19.

6. Ventura Robles, "Los principales aportes del Juez Rodolfo E. Piza Escalante a la Corte Interamericana de Derechos Humanos (1979–1988)," 19.

7. *See* the following cases heard by the Inter-American Court of Human Rights: Artavia Murillo v. Costa Rica (Vio Grossi, J., dissenting), 10; Case of

Gómez Murillo et al. v. Costa Rica, *Opinion: Judge Vio Grossi*, 6. For more on the *pro homine* principle, *see* these cases heard by the same court: Ticona Estrada et al. v. Bolivia, ¶ 11; Raxcacó-Reyes v. Guatemala, ¶ 12; Acevedo-Jaramillo et al. v. Peru, ¶ 283; "Five Pensioners" v. Peru, ¶ 143.

8. *See* Juridical Condition and Rights of the Undocumented Migrants, ¶¶ 37, 78; Juridical Condition and Human Rights of the Child, ¶ 30 (application of *pro homine* principle to children and migrants). See also Tribunal Constitucional, 16 de octubre 2009, ONG "Acción de Lucha Anticorrupción" Sentencia del Tribunal Constitucional, § 3.2 ¶ 12 (Peruvian Constitutional Court's application of this principle to the human embryo).

9. *See, e.g.*, Constitución Política de la República de Honduras de 1982, art. 67 (Hond.).

10. Constitución Política del Perú, art. 2(1) (Peru).

11. *See* Constitución Política de la República de Honduras, art. 67 (Hond.).

12. *See* Constitución Política de los Estados Unidos Mexicanos, *as amended* to 2007, Transitorios art. Tercero, Diario Oficial de la Federación, 5 de febrero de 1917 (Mex.).

13. *See* Tribunal Constitucional, 16 de octubre 2009, ONG "Acción de Lucha Anticorrupción" Sentencia del Tribunal Constitucional, ¶¶ 24, 33–34.

14. Corte Suprema de Justicia de la Nación, 03/05/2002, "Portal de Belén—Asociación Civil sin Fines de Lucro c. Ministerio de Salud y Acción Social de la Nación s/amparo," 15 (Arg.); Tribunal Constitucional, 16 de octubre 2009, ONG "Acción de Lucha Anticorrupción" Sentencia del Tribunal Constitucional, ¶¶ 33–34; Corte Suprema de Justicia de la República de Honduras, Dictamen Decreto 54-2009, 9–10.

15. Tribunal Constitucional, 18 abril 2008, Requerimiento de inconstitucionalidad deducido en contra de algunas disposiciones de las "Normas Nacionales sobre Regulación de la Fertilidad," 139–40 (Chile). *See also* Corte Suprema de Justicia de la Nación, 03/05/2002, "Portal de Belén—Asociación Civil sin Fines de Lucro c. Ministerio de Salud y Acción Social de la Nación s/amparo," 4 (Arg.).

16. Jurisprudencia emitida por la Corte Interamericana de Derechos Humanos, 204.

17. *See, e.g.*, Villagrán-Morales v. Guatemala, ¶¶ 31(d), 144; Gómez-Paquiyauri brothers v. Peru, ¶ 2; Xákmok Kásek Indigenous Cmty. v. Para., ¶ 186; Case of Montero Aranguren et al. v. Venezuela, ¶ 63; Case of Zambrano Vélez et al. v. Ecuador, ¶ 78.

18. *See* Inter-Am. Ct. H.R., Servellón-García et al. v. Honduras, ¶ 54, citing Ituango Massacres v. Colombia, ¶ 244; Mapiripán Massacre v. Colombia, ¶ 152; Case of the girls Yean and Bosico v. Dominican Republic, ¶ 33.

19. Artavia Murillo v. Costa Rica, ¶ 223.

20. *Id.* ¶ 264.

21. *See, e.g.*, Manuel Ramos-Kuri, ed., *Artavia Murillo vs. Costa Rica* ¶ 2, 3; *Guanajuato Declaration about in Vitro Fertilization*, ¶¶ 2, 3 (declaration adopted by various experts in bioethics, medicine, philosophy, biology, law, academia, and the general sciences opposing the *Artavia* judgment's interpretation of the provision concerning the prenatal right to life).

22. *See* Carozza, *Anglo-Latin Divide and the Future of the Inter-American System of Human Rights*, 164.

23. *See* Juzgado Federal de Salta No. 1, 8/7/2013, "Lodi Ortiz Andrea Melisa—Larran Cristian c/Swiss Medical s/amparo," Expdte. No. 61000007/13 (Arg.).

24. *See* Corte Suprema de Justicia de la Nación, 01/09/2015, "Recurso de hecho deducido por los actores en la causa L.E.H. y otros c/O.S.E.P. s/amparo" (Arg.).

25. Organization of American States, American Convention on Human Rights art. 29(c) (emphasis added).

26. *Id.* art. 30. *See* The Word "Laws" in Article 30 of the American Convention on Human Rights, ¶ 35 (final resolution paragraph).

27. *Id.*

28. *See* Gender Identity, and Equality and Non-discrimination with regard to Same-Sex Couples, Concurring vote of Judge Humberto Sierra Porto, ¶¶ 26–29, 36.

29. *Id.* ¶¶ 20, 26–29.

30. *Id.* ¶¶ 27, 36.

31. *See* Nieto Navia, *Aspectos internacionales de la demanda contra la penalización del aborto*, 34.

32. Vienna Convention on the Law of Treaties art. 31(1) (emphasis added).

33. *Id.* art. 31(1) (good faith requirement).

34. *See* Artavia Murillo v. Costa Rica (Vio Grossi, J., dissenting) at 10.

35. *See Conclusions and Observations on the IACHR's Working Visit to El Salvador* (indicating that Commissioner Macaulay, in her capacity as IACHR rapporteur on the rights of women and rapporteur for El Salvador, urges El Salvador to reverse its full ban on elective abortion and to legalize abortion on at least three grounds).

36. *See* Murillo, *Elizabeth Odio, jueza electa en Corte Interamericana de Derechos Humanos: "El aborto no tiene por qué ser un crimen."*

37. Corte Constitucional, Sala Plena, mayo 10, 2006, Sentencia C-355/2006 (Colom.).

38. *Id.* §§ 6, 7.2.

39. Corte Constitucional, Sentencia T-388 of 2009 , I, 7, 7.3, para. 2 (Colom.).

40. *Id. See generally* Procuraduría Delegada para la Defensa de los Derechos de la Infancia, la Adolescencia y la Familia, Informe de Vigilancia a la Implementación de la Sentencia C-355 de 2006.

41. See chapter 1.

42. *See Carlos A. Dunshee de Abranches. Cf.* Organization of American States, *Actas y Documentos of the Interamerican Specialized Conference on Human Rights*, 408–9.

43. *See 75 Opiniones sobre el aborto* (where Judge García-Sayán supports legalization of abortion and condemns the Catholic Church for interfering with decriminalization debates). *See also* García-Sayán, *Muertes anunciadas, derecho a la vida* (where Judge García-Sayán refers to legalization and liberalization of abortion as a necessary "public health" measure that would benefit all and celebrates Mexico City's liberalization of abortion). *See* Zamora Castellanos, *Crisis en la Corte Interamericana de Derechos Humanos* (indicating that Judge Pérez Pérez supported the Latin American campaign for the right to abort on Facebook).

44. *See Audiencia pública: Caso Artavia Murillo y otros (fecundación in vitro) vs. Costa Rica, parte 4* (statement made at 2:14:00).

45. *Id.* at 00:04:05 onward.

46. *Id.* at 2:34:30 onward. *See also* Zamora Castellanos, *Crisis en la Corte Interamericana de Derechos Humanos* (commenting on García-Sayán's congratulatory greeting of Zegers-Hochschild at the hearings).

47. *See* Polo, *Tres jueces de Corte Interamericana asumen posición abortista en caso fecundación in vitro. See also* Zamora Castellanos, *Crisis en la Corte Interamericana de Derechos Humanos* (commenting on Judge Macaulay's sarcastic gesturing during the hearing); *Denuncian parcialidad de jueces de Corte IDH a favor del aborto.*

48. Soto, *Diputada Rita Cháves acusa a Corte de parcialidad en caso de FIV.*

49. Organization of American States, American Convention on Human Rights art. 1(2) ("For the purposes of this Convention, 'person' means every human being").

50. *See* Artavia Murillo v. Costa Rica, ¶ 256. Organization of American States, American Convention on Human Rights art. 4(1) (emphasis added).

51. Barberis, *El derecho a la vida en el pacto de San José de Costa Rica*, 20, 26.

52. *See* Nieto Navia, *Aspectos internacionales de la demanda contra la penalización del aborto*, 34.

53. Corte Suprema de Justicia, Sala Constitucional, marzo 15, 2000, Expdte. 95-001734-0007-CO (Costa Rica), § VI.

54. *See* Baby Boy v. United States (Marco Gerardo Monroy Cabra, comm'r, dissenting), paras. 5, 8.

55. Ação Direta de Inconstitucionalidade 3.510 Distrito Federal, 400–401 (Braz.) (original text in Portuguese states: "Ainda que se queira relativizar a força desse comando em face da expressão "em geral" nele abrigada, tal locução não afasta a idéia de que, para os efeitos legais, a vida começa na concepção, iniciada quer in utero, quer in vitro").

56. Gómez-Paquiyauri brothers v. Peru, ¶ 71; Castro Prison v. Peru, ¶ 61; Goiburú et al. v. Paraguay.

57. *See* Artavia Murillo v. Costa Rica, ¶¶ 222, 224–26, 231, 236, 252, 261, 269. See also ¶ 260 in the Spanish version (which mentions the unborn child among "other persons": "otras personas").

58. *See id.* ¶ 219.

59. *See id.* ¶¶ 173, 181–85 (where the court announces that it will analyze the meaning of the term *human being*, but simply fails to go beyond discussing its use as a synonym of *person*).

60. Entitlement of Legal Entities to Hold Rights Under the Inter-American Human Rights System, ¶¶ 7, 38.

61. *See id.* (Alberto Pérez Pérez, J., dissenting in part) ¶ 6.

62. *See generally* George and Tollefsen, *Embryo* (discussing ample evidence of the human embryo's membership in the human species).

63. *See* Corte Constitucional, Sala Plena, mayo 10, 2006, Sentencia C-355/2006 (Colom.), Salvamento de Voto del Magistrado Alvaro Tafur Galvis.

64. Corte Suprema de Justicia, Sala Constitucional, marzo 15, 2000, Expdte. 95-001734-0007-CO (Costa Rica), ¶ VI.

65. *See* Baby Boy v. United States, Dr. Marco Gerardo Monroy Cabra, dissenting.

66. *See* Artavia Murillo v. Costa Rica, ¶¶ 256, 264.

67. *See id.* (Vio Grossi, J., dissenting) 19 (suggesting that the rationale used by the majority was intended to legitimize elective abortion).

68. *See Oradores en Contra* (see Nestor Sagüés, 11/07/18, starting at 5:58).

69. *Oradores en Contra* (see Alejandro Pérez Hualde starting at 5:05).

70. *See* chapter 5.

71. Tribunal Constitucional, 14 de junio 2006, "José Fernando Roser Rohde c. Instituto Nacional de Higiene y Medicina Tropical 'Leopoldo Izquieta Pérez' y el Ministro de Salud S/Acción de Amparo" (Ecuador). *See* Tribunal Constitucional, 16 de octubre 2009, ONG "Acción de Lucha Anticorrupción" Sentencia del Tribunal Constitucional, ¶ 12 (Peru).

72. Tribunal Constitucional, 16 de octubre 2009, ONG "Acción de Lucha Anticorrupción" Sentencia del Tribunal Constitucional, ¶¶ 4, 12 (Peru).

73. *See* Corte Suprema de Justicia de la Nación, 03/05/2002, "Portal de Belén—Asociación Civil sin Fines de Lucro c. Ministerio de Salud y Acción Social de la Nación s/amparo" (Arg.).

74. Tribunal Constitucional Plurinacional, Feb. 5, 2014, Sentencia Constitucional Plurinacional 0206/2014, ¶ III(7)–(8).

75. *See* Artavia Murillo v. Costa Rica, ¶ 264. *See also* ¶ 220 (citing Baby Boy v. United States, para. 25) .

76. Baby Boy v. United States, paras. 18(e), 26.

77. *See* Artavia Murillo v. Costa Rica, ¶ 188.

78. *See id.* (Vio Grossi, J., dissenting) (Spanish version).

79. *See id.* 7–8.

80. *Id.* 8.
81. *Id.* I(B)(2)(b).
82. *Id.* II(B)(1).
83. Nieto Navia, *Aspectos internacionales de la demanda contra la penalización del aborto*, 33.
84. *See* Barberis, *El derecho a la vida en el pacto de San José de Costa Rica*, 20–21, 26.
85. *See* Signatories and Ratifications: American Convention on Human Rights (Dominican Republic also filed a declaration—not technically a reservation).
86. *See* Baby Boy v. United States, para. 19(e).
87. Protocol to the American Convention on Human Rights to Abolish the Death Penalty.
88. Tanner, *Interview with Judge Antônio A. Cançado Trindade*, 68, 177.
89. *See* Barberis, *El derecho a la vida en el pacto de San José de Costa Rica*, 20.
90. Corte Constitucional, Sala Plena, mayo 10, 2006, Sentencia C-355/2006, § 1.2 (Colom.).
91. *See* Corte Constitucional, Sala Plena, mayo 10, 2006, Sentencia C-355/2006 (Colom.), Salvamento de Voto del Magistrado Alvaro Tafur Galvis.
92. Tribunal Constitucional Plurinacional, Feb. 5, 2014, Sentencia Constitucional Plurinacional 0206/2014, ¶ III(7)–(8).
93. *Id.* ¶ III(7), (8), (9).
94. *Id.* ¶ III(7)–(8).
95. Discussed in chapter 2.
96. *See* Sala de lo Constitucional, Sala de lo Constitucional de la Corte Suprema de Justicia, May 28, 2013, Amparo 310-2013, ¶¶ VI(1)(A)(b), VII(5)(C), IV(2) (El Sal.).
97. *Id.* Voto disidente en el caso B.C. Magistrado Florentín Meléndez.
98. *See* Sala de lo Constitucional de la Corte Suprema de Justicia, May 28, 2013, Amparo 310-2013, ¶¶ V(1)(A), VI(1)(A) (El Sal.). *Id.* ¶ V(1)(A). *See also* Código Penal arts. 27, 134, 137 (El Sal.).
99. *See* Sala de lo Constitucional de la Corte Suprema de Justicia, May 28, 2013, Amparo 310-2013, ¶ V(1)(A) and (B)(a) (El Sal.).
100. *See id.*, Voto disidente en el caso B.C. Magistrado Florentín Meléndez.
101. *See* Sala de lo Constitucional de la Corte Suprema de Justicia, May 28, 2013, Amparo 310-2013 (El Sal.), Voto particular concurrente del Magistrado Rodolfo González Bonilla, ¶¶ II(2), II(4)(B), V.
102. *See* Sala de lo Constitucional de la Corte Suprema de Justicia, May 28, 2013, Amparo 310-2013, ¶¶ III(2), V, V(1)(B) (El Sal.). *See also* Voto particular concurrente del Magistrado Rodolfo González Bonilla, ¶ III(2), V, explaining that the fact that one right may take "conditioned precedence" over another in a particular situation does not mean that the latter is declared invalid or obliterated;

such precedence does not authorize the creation of exceptions to the latter. Both rights continue to have the same status *in abstracto* even though one or the other may prevail on a case-by-case basis.

103. *See* Tribunal Constitucional, 28 agosto 2017, Requerimiento de inconstitucionalidad respecto del proyecto de ley que "regula la despenalización de la interrupción voluntaria del embarazo en tres causales," 169–71 (Chile).

104. *See id.* 59–60, 89.

105. *Id.* 243–46 (concurring Judge Domingo Hernández Emparanza also clarifies that the Constitutional Court is not creating a right to abortion by upholding the three criminal exceptions).

106. *Id.* at 244, 246.

107. Corte Constitucional, Sala Plena, mayo 10, 2006, Sentencia C-355/2006 (Colom.), Salvamento de Voto de los Magistrados Marco Gerardo Monroy Cabra y Rodrigo Escobar Gil.

108. Ação Direta de Inconstitucionalidade 3.510 Distrito Federal, 401 (Braz.).

109. *Id.* at 594–95. (Original test in Portuguese states: "[E]ssa expressão 'em geral' permite que se excepcione a proteção que se deve, em princípio, dar de forma absoluta à vida desde o momento da concepção. Por isso assentei que o Código Penal brasileiro, no artigo 128, I, permita o aborto necessário, afastando a antijuridicidade.")

110. Acción de inconstitucionalidad 146/2007 y su acumulada 147/2007, Suprema Corte de Justicia de la Nación (Mex.), *Voto de minoría que formulan los Ministros Sergio Salvador Aguirre Anguiano, Mariano Azuela Güitrón y Guillermo I. Ortiz Mayagoitia en la acción de inconstitucionalidad 146/2007 y su acumulada 147/2007*, 98.

111. Acción de inconstitucionalidad 146/2007 y su acumulada 147/2007, 89 (Mex.).

112. García Ramírez, *La pena de muerte en la Convención Americana de Derechos Humanos en la jurisprudencia de la Corte Interamericana* (see section F) (emphasis added), indicating that, even though states could *choose* to reduce legal protection for prenatal life, the convention does not *require* them to do so. The original Spanish text is as follows: "La expresión utilizada en el Pacto de San José no implica, por supuesto, que la tutela de la vida *deba* diferirse hasta un momento posterior a la concepción: sólo es 'posible' hacerlo."

113. Baby Boy v. United States, para. 18(e)–(h); Artavia Murillo v. Costa Rica, ¶¶ 204–5, 208, 220–21.

114. Ação Direta de Inconstitucionalidade 3.510 Distrito Federal, 594 (Braz.). The original text in Portuguese is as follows: "O Brasil também, nessa conferência diplomática, se opôs à redação originária para que ficasse—como efetivamente ficou—a ressalva do 'em geral.' Ou seja, em regra, exatamente para remeter essa matéria a legislação de cada Estado soberano."

115. Signatories and Ratifications: American Convention on Human Rights (emphasis added).

116. *See* Acción de inconstitucionalidad 146/2007 y su acumulada 147/2007, 167 (Mex.) (original language states: "[E]sta expresion 'en general' en el texto de la Convencion, . . . otorga a los Estados un *margen* para adopter legislacion que permita la interrupcion del embarazo en determinadas circunstancias").

117. *Declaración sobre el Sistema Interamericano de Derechos Humanos; Chile, Argentina, Brasil, Colombia y Paraguay piden a la Corte Interamericana de DD.HH. respetar "margenes de autonomía" de los estados.*

118. *See* Case of Gómez Murillo et al. v. Costa Rica, *Opinion: Judge Vio Grossi*, 5. *See also* Order of Feb. 26, 2016, Dissenting Vote Judge Eduardo Vio Grossi, ¶ 25. *See also* Vio Grossi, *Reflexión sobre la justicia interamericana en DD.HH.* (pointing out the consistency of a margin-of-appreciation doctrine with the convention, the court's statute, and its rules of procedure).

119. *See* Case of Gómez Murillo et al. v. Costa Rica, *Opinion: Judge Vio Grossi*, 5. *See also* Vio Grossi, *Reflexión sobre la justicia interamericana en DD.HH.* (where he proposes a margin of appreciation for both economic, social, and cultural rights and moral, ethical issues, which in his view would make court decisions on this matter more democratic and representative of states parties' legislative intent).

120. Case of Lagos del Campo v. Peru, partially dissenting vote Judge Eduardo Vio Grossi, 19–20.

121. *See* Carozza, *Anglo-Latin Divide and the Future of the Inter-American System of Human Rights*, 168.

122. *Id.*

123. *See, e.g.*, Parrillo v. Italy, ¶ 215 (dealing with artificial reproductive technologies).

124. *See* S.H. v. Austria, ¶¶ 69, 76 (where two couples sued Austria before the European Court claiming a right to heterologous IVF, and the European Court indicated that states enjoy a wide margin of appreciation to limit certain practices, especially the use of IVF, which implies "sensitive moral and ethical issues" and over which there was no European consensus on the matter). *See also* Handyside v. The United Kingdom (articulating the margin-of-appreciation doctrine).

125. Vo v. France, ¶ 75.

126. *Id.* ¶ 82.

127. *Id.* ¶ 75.

128. Evans v. The United Kingdom, ¶ 77.

129. *See* European Parliament, Parliamentary Questions, Answer given by Mr. Dalli on behalf of the Commission. *See also* Puppinck, *Abortion in European Law* (for an overview of abortion and the European Court of Human Rights).

130. *Cf.* García G. and Verdugo R., *Radiografía Política del Sistema Interamericano*, 5 (for a critique of the absence of a margin-of-appreciation doctrine in the Inter-American Court of Human Rights, among things).

131. *See* Artavia Murillo v. Costa Rica, ¶¶ 169–70, 316.

132. *See* García G. and Verdugo R., *Radiografía Política del Sistema Interamericano*, 5, 27.

133. García-Sayán, *Inter-American Court and Constitutionalism in Latin America*, 1857.

134. *See* Organization of American States, *Actas y Documentos of the Inter-american Specialized Conference on Human Rights*, 121.

135. Organization of American States, American Convention on Human Rights art. 4(1).

136. *See* Barberis, *El derecho a la vida en el pacto de San José de Costa Rica*, 26 (pointing out that nonarbitrariness is an essential requirement to determine the lawfulness of any exceptions to the right to life).

137. Case of the Pueblo Bello Massacre v. Colombia, ¶ 120; Case of the Massacres of El Mozote and nearby places v. El Salvador, ¶ 145.

138. *See* Ferrer Mac-Gregor and González Domínguez, *Death Penalty, Amnesty Laws, and Forced Disappearances*, 77.

139. Organization of American States, American Convention on Human Rights art. 30 ("The restrictions that, pursuant to this Convention, may be placed on the enjoyment or exercise of the rights or freedoms recognized herein may not be applied except in accordance with laws enacted for reasons of general interest and in accordance with the purpose for which such restrictions have been established").

140. *See* The Word "Laws" in Article 30 of the American Convention on Human Rights, ¶¶ 35, 37; Case of Tristán Donoso v. Panama, ¶ 56; Case of Atala Riffo and daughters v. Chile, ¶ 164; Case of Zambrano Vélez et al. v. Ecuador, ¶ 85.

141. Case of Ortiz Hernández et al. v. Venezuela, ¶ 103; Case of Coc Max et al. (Massacre of Xamán) v. Guatemala, ¶ 107.

142. Case of Zambrano Vélez et al. v. Ecuador, ¶ 84. Case of Landaeta Mejías brothers et al. v. Venezuela, ¶¶ 134, 281; Case of Nadege Dorzema et al. v. Dominican Republic, ¶ 85.

143. Case of Nadege Dorzema et al. v. Dominican Republic, ¶ 85.

144. *See* Barberis, *El derecho a la vida en el pacto de San José de Costa Rica*, 26.

145. *See* Acción de inconstitucionalidad 146/2007 y su acumulada 147/2007, 161 (Mex.).

146. Acción de inconstitucionalidad 146/2007 y su acumulada 147/2007, Suprema Corte de Justicia de la Nación (Mex.), *Voto concurrente que formula el Ministro Genaro David Góngora Pimentel en la acción de inconstitucionalidad 146/2007 y su acumulada 147/2007*, 3.

147. Acción de inconstitucionalidad 146/2007 y su acumulada 147/2007, Suprema Corte de Justicia de la Nación, Proyecto de resolución, 8–9 (Mex.).

148. *See* Acción de inconstitucionalidad 146/2007 y su acumulada 147/2007, Suprema Corte de Justicia de la Nación (Mex.), *Intervención del Min-*

*istro Sergio Salvador Aguirre Anguiano en sesión extraordinaria celebrada el 25 de agosto de 2008*, 14.

149. *Id.* at 14–15.

150. *See Baby Boy supra* n.54, ¶ 14(c).

151. *See* Artavia Murillo v. Costa Rica (Vio Grossi, J., dissenting), 9.

152. *See* Corte Constitucional, Sala Plena, mayo 10, 2006, Sentencia C-355/2006 (Colom.), Salvamento de Voto del Magistrado Alvaro Tafur.

153. Vienna Convention on the Law of Treaties art. 31(2): "The context for the purpose of the interpretation of a treaty shall comprise, in addition to the text, including its preamble and annexes: (a) any agreement relating to the treaty which was made between all the parties in connexion with the conclusion of the treaty; (b) any instrument which was made by one or more parties in connexion with the conclusion of the treaty and accepted by the other parties as an instrument related to the treaty."

154. *See* Villagrán-Morales v. Guatemala, ¶¶ 31(d), 144.

155. Right to Information on Consular Assistance in the Framework of the Guarantees of the Due Process of Law, ¶ 135.

156. *Death Penalty in the Inter-American Human Rights System*, 12.

157. Gómez-Paquiyauri brothers v. Peru, ¶ 76.

158. *See* Xákmok Kásek Indigenous Cmty. v. Para., ¶ 186; Case of Montero Aranguren et al. v. Venezuela, ¶ 63 (see also Spanish version); Sawhoyamaxa Indigenous Community v. Paraguay, ¶ 150; Case of Baldeón-García v. Peru, ¶ 82–83; Villagrán-Morales v. Guatemala, ¶ 144; Case of the Pueblo Bello Massacre v. Colombia, ¶119–20; Case of the 19 Merchants v. Colombia, ¶ 153; Case of Myrna Mack Chang v. Guatemala, ¶ 152.

159. *See* Protocol to the American Convention on Human Rights to Abolish the Death Penalty.

160. Case of Human Rights Defender et al. v. Guatemala, ¶ 139.

161. *See* Case of the Yakye Axa Indigenous Community v. Paraguay, 176; Case of Velásquez Rodríguez v. Honduras, ¶ 174; Case of Rodríguez Vera et al. v. Colombia, ¶ 496; Case of García Ibarra et al. v. Ecuador, ¶ 98; Case of Landaeta Mejías brothers et al. v. Venezuela, ¶ 217.

162. See Mapiripán Massacre v. Colombia, ¶ 120.

163. See Case of Ximenes Lopes v. Brazil, Merits, ¶¶ 88–90, 150; Case of Velásquez Rodríguez v. Honduras, ¶¶ 166, 176.

164. *See* Corte Constitucional [C.C.] [Constitutional Court], Sala Plena, mayo 10, 2006, Sentencia C-355/2006, Salvamento de Voto del Magistrado Alvaro Tafur Galvis.

165. Case of Gonzales Lluy et al. v. Ecuador, ¶ 191.

166. Organization of American States, American Convention on Human Rights art. 2: "Domestic legal effects. Where the exercise of any of the rights or freedoms referred to in article 1 is not already ensured by legislative or other

provisions, the States Parties undertake to adopt, in accordance with their constitutional processes and the provisions of this Convention, such legislative or other measures as may be necessary to give effect to those rights or freedoms." *See also* Case of Hilaire, Constantine and Benjamin et al. v. Trinidad & Tobago, ¶ 112.

167. *See* Case of Ortiz Hernández et al. v. Venezuela, ¶ 100; Case of García Ibarra et al. v. Ecuador, ¶ 97; Gómez-Paquiyauri brothers v. Peru, ¶ 129; Case of the Massacres of El Mozote and nearby places v. El Salvador, ¶ 172; Case of the Barrios Family v. Venezuela, Merits, ¶ 48; Case of Zambrano Vélez et al. v. Ecuador, ¶ 81.

168. Case of Landaeta Mejías brothers et al. v. Venezuela, ¶ 216; Case of Yarce et al. v. Colombia, ¶ 181; Case of Human Rights Defender et al. v. Guatemala, ¶ 139 (original text in Spanish states: "un deber de medio o de comportamiento, no de resultado, de prevenir que particulares vulneren bienes protegidos por derechos plasmados en el tratado"); Case of Poblete Vilches et al. v. Chile, ¶¶ 184–85.

169. *See* Case of Human Rights Defender et al. v. Guatemala, ¶ 140; Case of the Garífuna Punta Piedra Community and its members v. Honduras, ¶ 261.

170. Sawhoyamaxa Indigenous Community v. Paraguay, ¶ 153.

171. *See* Artavia Murillo v. Costa Rica (Vio Grossi, J., dissenting), 10 (citing Inter-American Court judgments to that effect).

172. Case of Salvador Chiriboga v. Ecuador, Preliminary Objections and Merits, ¶ 122.

173. *See* Acción de inconstitucionalidad 146/2007, *Intervención del Ministro Sergio Salvador Aguirre Anguiano en sesión extraordinaria celebrada el 25 de agosto de 2008* (Mex.).

174. Case of Duque v. Colombia, ¶ 91 (referring to the right to equality and nondiscrimination).

175. *See Declaración del Secretario General de la OEA sobre la Epidemia del virus Zika.* In 2016, OAS secretary general Almagro advocated for the legalization of abortion where mothers were affected with the Zika virus, which for a short period of time became an epidemic in some Latin American and Caribbean countries. On that occasion, Almagro indicated that in cases of infected pregnant women, "the legal interruption of pregnancy would be justifiable" on the basis of "the risk to the life of the mother from the perspective of her dignity, the material conditions of her life and existence, but above all, *her ability to make autonomous decisions about* her life and health and *the future of her offspring* and the nuclear family." *See also* Juridical Condition and Rights of the Undocumented Migrants, ¶ 84.

176. Convention on the Rights of Persons with Disabilities arts. 10, 12. This convention uses language similar to that of the American Convention on the right to life (art. 10) and on equal recognition before the law (art. 12): "States Parties reaffirm that *every human being* has the inherent right to life and shall take all necessary measures to ensure its *effective enjoyment* by persons with disabilities on an *equal basis with others*"; "States Parties reaffirm that persons with disabilities have *the right to recognition everywhere as persons* before the law."

177. Corte Constitucional, Sala Plena, mayo 10, 2006, Sentencia C-355/2006 (Colom.), Salvamento de Voto de los Magistrados Marco Gerardo Monroy Cabra y Rodrigo Escobar Gil.

178. Comunicado No. 42, Expdte. T 6612909—Sentencia SU-096/18, 2.

179. *Id.* at 2–3.

180. *See* Corte Constitucional, Sala Plena, mayo 10, 2006, Sentencia C-355/2006 (Colom.), Salvamento de Voto de los Magistrados Marco Gerardo Monroy Cabra y Rodrigo Escobar Gil.

181. *Id.*

182. *Id.*

183. Gonzales v. Carhart, 550 U.S. 124 (2007) (Ginsburg, J., dissenting) (arguing that upholding a ban on partial-birth abortion without a health exception violates women's autonomy and equality).

184. Fourth UN Conference at Beijing, Declaration and Plan of Action, para. 277(c) (the Beijing Declaration condemned prenatal sex selection against female unborn children as a human rights violation, calling nations to "eliminate all forms of discrimination against the *girl child* which result in harmful and unethical practices such as *pre-natal* sex selection").

185. Case of Boyce et al. v. Barbados, ¶ 113.

186. *Id.* ¶¶ 50, 51, 60 (emphasis added).

187. Case of Hilaire, Constantine and Benjamin et al. v. Trinidad & Tobago, ¶ 105.

188. Case of Atala Riffo and daughters v. Chile, Merits, ¶ 151.

189. *See* The Right to Information on Consular Assistance in the Framework of the Guarantees of the Due Process of Law, ¶ 136.

190. *Death Penalty in the Inter-American Human Rights System*, ¶ 13.

191. *See* Ferrer Mac-Gregor and González Domínguez, *Death Penalty, Amnesty Laws, and Forced Disappearances*, 67, 82.

192. *See* Nieto Navia, *Aspectos internacionales de la demanda contra la penalización del aborto*, 34.

193. Organization of American States, American Convention on Human Rights art. 4(4). *See* Case of Boyce et al. v. Barbados, Preliminary, ¶ 51; Case of Raxcacó-Reyes v. Guatemala, ¶¶ 81–82 (where the court found that mandatory death penalty sentencing violates the American Convention because "the same penalty is imposed for conduct that can be vastly different, and where it is not restricted to the most serious crimes").

194. Nieto Navia, *Aspectos internacionales de la demanda contra la penalización del aborto*, 34 (citing the American Convention on Human Rights art. 4(5): "Capital punishment shall not be imposed upon persons who, at the time the crime was committed, were under 18 years of age or over 70 years of age; *nor shall it be applied to pregnant women*").

195. *See* Nieto Navia, *Aspectos internacionales de la demanda contra la penalización del aborto*, 33 (original text in Spanish states: "Nada de esto se da en un

aborto contra un ser que no ha cometido delitos, no ha sido juzgado, tiene menos de 18 años y no tiene por qué responder con su vida por los errores de sus padres").

196. Organization of American States, American Convention on Human Rights preamble.

197. Organization of American States, American Convention on Human Rights art. 3 ("Every person has the right to recognition as a person before the law").

198. *See* Case of Bámaca Velásquez v. Guatemala. *See* Case of the girls Yean and Bosico v. Dominican Republic, ¶ 179; Case of Bámaca Velásquez, ¶ 179.

199. Corte Constitucional, Sala Plena, mayo 10, 2006, Sentencia C-355/2006 (Colom.), Salvamento de Voto de los Magistrados Marco Gerardo Monroy Cabra y Rodrigo Escobar Gil a la Sentencia.

200. *Id.*

201. Anzualdo Castro v. Peru, ¶ 90.

202. Serrano-Cruz Sisters v. El Salvador (Ventura-Robles, J., dissenting).

203. Case of Bámaca Velásquez, ¶ 179.

204. *See* Juridical Condition and Human Rights of the Child (see n.1 in operative paragraphs).

205. *Id.* (see n.6 in operative paragraphs).

206. *See* Case of the "Juvenile Reeducation Institute" v. Paraguay (Judge A. A. Cançado Trindade, concurring), para. 9.

207. *See* Artavia Murillo v. Costa Rica, ¶ 222.

208. *See* Juridical Condition and Human Rights of the Child (see n.1 in operative paragraphs).

209. Juridical Condition and Human Rights of the Child (Judge A. A. Cançado Trindade, concurring), ¶ 6.

210. Contreras et al. v. El Salvador, ¶ 107; Inter-Am. Ct. H.R., "Other treaties" subject to the consultative jurisdiction of the court (64 American Convention on Human Rights), ¶¶ 14, 31, 37, 40, 41, 48. *See also* Villagrán-Morales v. Guatemala, ¶ 194, *Accord.* Restrictions on the Death Penalty, ¶ 24.

211. Case of the Sawhoyamaxa Indigenous Community v. Paraguay, ¶ 177; Villagrán-Morales v. Guatemala, ¶ 188; Juridical Condition and Human Rights of the Child, ¶ 42. *Cf.* Organization of American States, THE RIGHTS OF THE CHILD IN THE INTER-AMERICAN HUMAN RIGHTS SYSTEM, 7, 17.

212. Convention on the Rights of the Child, preamble (emphasis added). *See also* Declaration of the Rights of the Child, preamble.

213. *See* Rep. of the Working Group on a Draft Convention on the Rights of the Child, ¶ 37.

214. *See* Vienna Convention on the Law of Treaties art. 31(1).

215. *See* Artavia Murillo v. Costa Rica, ¶¶ 229–32.

216. *See, e.g.*, Alston, *Unborn Child and Abortion under the Draft Convention on the Rights of the Child* (pro-choice academic Philip Alston argues that legalized

abortion is compatible with the Convention on the Rights of the Child because the preamble has little interpretive value). *See* Vienna Convention on the Law of Treaties art. 31(2) (stipulating that the preamble is included in the treaty's text: "The context for the purpose of the interpretation of a treaty shall comprise, in addition to the *text, including its preamble and annexes*..." (emphasis added)).

217. Convention on the Rights of the Child arts. 6, 24(2)(d).

218. Derecho a la vida del producto de la concepción, 588 (Mex.).

219. *See* Corte Suprema de Justicia de la Nación, 03/05/2002, "Portal de Belén—Asociación Civil sin Fines de Lucro c. Ministerio de Salud y Acción Social de la Nación s/amparo," 5–6 (Arg.).

220. *See, e.g.*, Juzgado Federal de Salta No. 1, 8/7/2013, "Lodi Ortiz Andrea Melisa—Larran Cristian c/Swiss Medical s/amparo," Expdte. No. 61000007/13 (Arg.).

221. *See* Sala de lo Constitucional de la Corte Suprema de Justicia, May 28, 2013, Amparo 310-2013, ¶ IV(1)(C), ¶ VI(1)(A)(b) (El Sal.).

222. *See* Tribunal Constitucional, 18 abril 2008, Requerimiento de inconstitucionalidad deducido en contra de algunas disposiciones de las "Normas Nacionales sobre Regulación de la Fertilidad," 8, 32, 37 (Chile). *See* Tribunal Constitucional, 28 agosto 2017, Requerimiento de inconstitucionalidad respecto del proyecto de ley que "regula la despenalización de la interrupción voluntaria del embarazo en tres causales," 178–79 (Chile) (dissenting judges point out that legalization of abortion would violate the Convention on the Rights of the Child).

223. *See* Sala de lo Constitucional de la Corte Suprema de Justicia, May 28, 2013, Amparo 310-2013 (El Sal.), Voto disidente en el caso B.C. Magistrado Florentín Meléndez.

224. *Id.*

225. Adame Goddard, *Comentario a la sentencia sobre la protección de la vida desde el momento de la concepción*, 15, 23.

226. Convention on the Rights of the Child art. 6 (emphasis added). *See* Nieto Navia, *Aspectos internacionales de la demanda contra la penalización del aborto*, 44.

227. *See* Baby Boy v. United States (Dr. Luis Demetrio Tinoco Castro, dissenting).

228. *See* Rep. of the Working Group on a Draft Convention on the Rights of the Child, 4, 6.

229. Case of Coc Max et al. (Massacre of Xamán) v. Guatemala, ¶ 115. *See* Juridical Condition and Human Rights of the Child, ¶ 59.

230. *See* Mapiripán Massacre v. Colombia, ¶ 14; Gómez-Paquiyauri brothers v. Peru, ¶¶ 124, 171; Case of Bulacio v. Argentina, ¶ 138.

231. *See* Ituango Massacres v. Colombia, ¶ 244; Mapiripán Massacre v. Colombia, ¶ 152; Inter-Am. Ct. H.R., Case of the "Juvenile Reeducation Institute" v. Paraguay, ¶ 147; Inter-Am. Ct. H.R., Servellón-García et al. v. Honduras, ¶ 113.

232. Juridical Condition and Human Rights of the Child, ¶ 80.

233. *Michael Domingues v. United States,* ¶¶ 49, 85.

234. *Id.* ¶¶ 5, 85.

235. *Id.* ¶ 49.

236. *See* Villagrán-Morales v. Guatemala, ¶¶ 137–39.

237. *Id.*, Joint Concurring Opinion Of Judges A. A. Cançado Trindade and A. Abreu-Burelli, ¶ 2.

238. *See* Paúl, *American Convention on Human Rights,* 54–55 (noting the contradiction between the prohibition of a restrictive interpretation in *Villagrán* and the holding in *Artavia*).

239. Vienna Convention on the Law of Treaties art. 31(2)(b).

240. *See* Signatories and Ratifications: American Convention on Human Rights (Mexico filed the declaration twice: in 1981, at the time of ratification, and then in 2002, with virtually identical text (2002 addition between brackets)). See also in chapter 5 the account of Mexican Supreme Court jurisprudence holding that abortion is a matter of state law, not federal law (in contrast with the United States, where the federal Supreme Court assumed jurisdiction over the matter).

241. *See, e.g.*, SCJN (Mex.), Acción de inconstitucionalidad 146/2007 y su acumulada 147/2007, Suprema Corte de Justicia de la Nación (Mex.), *Intervención del Ministro Presidente Guillermo I. Ortiz Mayagoitia,* 431–37 (Mexican Supreme Court Judge Sergio Salvador Aguirre Anguiano, explains why the term "states" in this declaration does not refer to Mexican states, but to international states parties to the Convention).

242. Acción de inconstitucionalidad 146/2007 y su acumulada 147/2007, Suprema Corte de Justicia de la Nación (Mex.).

243. Acción de inconstitucionalidad 146/2007 y su acumulada 147/2007 (Mex.), *Voto de minoría que formulan los Ministros Sergio Salvador Aguirre Anguiano, Mariano Azuela Güitrón y Guillermo I. Ortiz Mayagoitia en la acción de inconstitucionalidad 146/2007 y su acumulada 147/2007,* 98–100.

244. *Id.*

245. American Declaration of the Rights and Duties of Man art. 1.

246. *CSJ, Costa Rica (2000)*, § VI.

247. American Declaration of the Rights and Duties of Man art. 7 (emphasis added).

248. *See* Baby Boy v. United States (Dr. Luis Demetrio Tinoco Castro, dissenting).

249. *See id.*

250. *See* Baby Boy v. United States (Dr. Marco Gerardo Monroy Cabra, dissenting), para. 9.

251. *See* Baby Boy v. United States, ¶ 14(a).

252. *See* Baby Boy v. United States (Dr. Luis Demetrio Tinoco Castro, dissenting).

253. *See* Baby Boy v. United States, ¶ 19(b).

254. *See id.* ¶ 19(g).

255. *Id.*

256. *See id.* ¶ 18(a)–(c).

257. *See* Artavia Murillo v. Costa Rica, ¶¶ 194–213.

258. *See* Baby Boy v. United States (Dr. Luis Demetrio Tinoco Castro, dissenting); *see also id.* (Dr. Marco Gerardo Monroy Cabra, dissenting), para. 3.

259. *See* Artavia Murillo v. Costa Rica (Dr. Luis Demetrio Tinoco Castro, dissenting).

260. *Id.*

261. *See* Baby Boy v. United States (Dr. Marco Gerardo Monroy Cabra, dissenting), para. 2.

262. *Id.*

263. *See id.* ¶ 3.

264. *See id.* para. 4.

265. *See id.* para. 9.

266. *See* Baby Boy v. United States (Dr. Luis Demetrio Tinoco Castro, dissenting).

267. *Id.*

268. *See* Vienna Convention on the Law of Treaties art. 31(1) ("A treaty shall be interpreted in good faith in accordance with the ordinary meaning to be given to the terms of the treaty in their context and in the light of its object and purpose").

269. *See* Corte Suprema de Justicia de la Nación, 01/09/2015, "Recurso de hecho deducido por los actores en la causa L.E.H. y otros c/O.S.E.P. s/amparo" (Arg.) (Alejandro Pérez Hualde, J., separate opinion).

270. Organization of American States, American Convention on Human Rights, preamble (emphasis added).

271. *See* Vienna Convention on the Law of Treaties art. 18. *See also* Damrosch and Murphy, *International Law*, 134–35 (citing commentators that regard article 18 as reflecting customary law). For further discussion on the Inter-American Commission's interpretation of US obligations under the American Convention, see chapter 1 of this volume, under Baby Boy v. United States, and chapter 3, on object and purpose of the American Convention regarding the prenatal right to life.

272. *See* Damrosch and Murphy, *International Law*, 134–35 (citing commentators that regard article 18 as reflecting customary law).

273. See *id.* 135 (citing Bradley, "Treaty Signature," 214–15).

274. Case of Montero Aranguren et al. v. Venezuela, ¶ 64; Case of Zambrano Vélez et al. v. Ecuador, ¶ 79.

275. *See* Artavia Murillo v. Costa Rica, ¶¶ 258, 263 ("the object and purpose of the expression 'in general' in article 4(1) of the Convention is to allow, as appropriate, an adequate balance between competing rights and interests").

276. *See* Case of Gómez Murillo et al. v. Costa Rica, *Opinion: Judge Vio Grossi*, 5.

277. *See* Artavia Murillo v. Costa Rica (Vio Grossi, J., dissenting), 7, 19–20.

278. *Id.* at 18.

279. *Id.* at 5.

280. *Id.* 7.

281. *See* Case of Gómez Murillo et al. v. Costa Rica, *Opinion: Judge Vio Grossi*, 5.

282. Buergenthal, *Commentary:* 121–36.

283. *See* Sala de lo Constitucional de la Corte Suprema de Justicia, May 28, 2013, Amparo 310-2013, ¶ I(1)(A)(b) (El Sal.).

284. *See* Corte Suprema de Justicia, Constituida en Tribunal de Amparo, Dec. 8, 2017, Amparo 1434-2017, 7–8 (Guat.).

285. Organization of American States, American Convention on Human Rights, preamble § 4 (note that paragraph 3 alludes to principles only rather than rights), arts. 2, 26, 29(b)–(c).

286. *Id.* arts. 31, 76–77.

287. *See* Inter-American Convention on the Prevention, Punishment and Eradication of Violence Against Women ("Convention of Belém do Pará"); Additional Protocol to the American Convention on Human Rights in the Area of Economic, Social and Cultural Rights (Protocol of San Salvador).

288. *See* Propuesta de Convención Interamericana de los Derechos Sexuales y los Derechos Reproductivos.

289. *See id.* arts. 18, 20.

290. *Id.* art. 25(2).

291. *See* Organization of American States, Inter-American Convention on the Elimination of All Forms of Discrimination Against Persons with Disabilities; Organization of American States, Inter-American Convention Against Racism, Racial Discrimination and Related Forms of Intolerance.

292. *See* Case of Gómez Murillo et al. v. Costa Rica, 1–2. *See also* Case of Duque v. Colombia, *Opinion: Judge Vio Grossi*, 10 (where Judge Vio Grossi pointed out that "the normative function in regards to the Convention, especially as it pertains to matters of conspicuous moral and ethical content, considered to constitute the basis of society, which involve legitimate ideological, moral, religious and ethical conceptions, belongs to states parties and not to the Court. Its exercise [by states parties] would, given the current institutional Inter-American landscape, be more democratic and give greater legitimacy to the norm that is eventually adopted").

293. See Letter from Minister of Popular Power for Foreign Affairs of the Bolivarian Republic of Venezuela to José Miguel Insulza, 3.

294. *Cf.* De Schutter and Tulkens, "Rights in Conflict" (discussing the European Court of Human Rights' treatment of conflicting rights under these situations).

295. Carozza, *Anglo-Latin Divide and the Future of the Inter-American System of Human Rights*, 164 (emphasis added). *See also* Shelton, "International Law on Protection of the Fetus" (where Professor Shelton, who then went on to become a member of the Inter-American Commission on Human Rights, points out that the American Convention stands out among other international human rights instruments in its explicit establishment of a prenatal right to life).

## FOUR. Evolutive Interpretation

1. Vienna Convention on the Law of Treaties art. 31(3)(b) ("There shall be taken into account, together with the context: . . . (b) any subsequent practice in the application of the treaty which establishes the agreement of the parties regarding its interpretation").

2. Artavia Murillo v. Costa Rica, ¶ 245.

3. *See* Duarte, *Análisis crítico a la sentencia de la Corte Interamericana de Derechos Humanos en el fallo sobre fertilización in vitro*, 123 (commenting on 1967 constitutions of Paraguay and Ecuador, which recognized constitutional protection for "the child, from conception").

4. *See* O.A.S., *Derecho de Familia y Niñez ("la Red")* (indicating that constitutional provisions recognizing a right to life from conception were adopted in 1980 in Chile (signed the American Convention in 1969, ratified it in 1990), in 1982 in Honduras (signed the American Convention in 1969, ratified it in 1977), in 1983 in El Salvador (signed the American Convention in 1969, ratified it in 1978), in 1985 in Guatemala (signed the American Convention in 1969, ratified it in 1978), in 1992 in Paraguay (signed the American Convention in 1969, ratified it in 1989), in 1993 in Peru (signed the American Convention in 1977, ratified it in 1978), in 2008 in Ecuador (signed the American Convention in 1969, ratified it in 1977), and in 2010 in Dominican Republic (signed the American Convention in 1977, ratified it in 1978). *See also* Signatories and Ratifications: American Convention on Human Rights.

5. CONSTITUCIÓN NACIONAL [CONST. NAC.] art. 75(23) (Arg.) (emphasis added).

6. *See* Rita Joseph, *Human Rights and the Unborn Child*, 213–17 (noting that article 1(2) of the convention states that the terms *person* and *human being* have identical meaning, thus preempting the use of the concept of "personhood" as an exclusionary tool).

7. *See* CONSTITUCIÓN POLÍTICA DE LA REPÚBLICA DE EL SALVADOR, art. 1 (El Sal.). *See also* Comm. on the Rights of the Child, *Consideration of Reports Submitted by States Parties Under Article 44 of the Convention: Second Periodic Reports of the States Parties Due in 1997: El Salvador*, ¶ 9.

8. *See* CONSTITUCIÓN POLÍTICA DE LA REPÚBLICA PARAGUAY, art. 4 (Para.). For an English translation, see Comm. on the Rights of the Child, *Consideration*

*of Reports Submitted by States Parties Under Article 44 of the Convention: Third Periodic Reports of States Parties Due in 2002; Paraguay*, ¶ 288.

9. *See* CONSTITUCIÓN POLÍTICA DEL PERÚ, art. 2(1) (Peru).

10. *See* CONSTITUCIÓN POLÍTICA DE LA REPÚBLICA DE GUATEMALA, art. 3 (Guat.).

11. *See* Corte Suprema de Justicia, Constituida en Tribunal de Amparo, Dec. 8, 2017, Amparo 1434-2017, 7–8 (Guat.).

12. *See* CONSTITUCIÓN POLÍTICA DE LA REPÚBLICA DE HONDURAS DE 1982, art. 67 (Hond.).

13. *See* CONSTITUCIÓN POLÍTICA DE LA REPÚBLICA DOMINICANA, art. 37 (Dom. Rep.).

14. CONSTITUCIÓN POLÍTICA DE LA REPÚBLICA DEL ECUADOR, art. 45 (Ecuador).

15. *See* CONSTITUCIÓN DE 1967, art. 30 (Ecuador).

16. *See* CONSTITUCIÓN POLÍTICA DE LA REPÚBLICA DE CHILE, art. 19(1) (Chile).

17. *See* Tribunal Constitucional, 18 abril 2008, Requerimiento de inconstitucionalidad deducido en contra de algunas disposiciones de las "Normas Nacionales sobre Regulación de la Fertilidad," 128 (Chile).

18. *Id.* ¶¶ 15, 17.

19. Corral, *El estatus del embrión humano en la sentencia sobre aborto del Tribunal Constitucional*; Díaz de Valdés, *The Chilean Constitutional Court's Abortion Decision.*

20. *See* Tribunal Constitucional, 28 agosto 2017, Requerimiento de inconstitucionalidad respecto del proyecto de ley que "regula la despenalización de la interrupción voluntaria del embarazo en tres causales," 103 (Chile).

21. Derecho a la vida del producto de la concepción, 588. *See* Derecho a la vida: Su protección constitucional, 589.

22. *See* CONSTITUCIÓN POLÍTICA DE LOS ESTADOS UNIDOS MEXICANOS, *as amended* 2007, art. 123 (emphasis added).

23. *See* Derecho a la vida del producto de la concepción, 588. *See* Derecho a la vida: Su protección constitucional, 589.

24. *See* Acción de inconstitucionalidad 146/2007 y su acumulada 147/2007 (Mex.), *Voto de minoría que formulan los Ministros Sergio Salvador Aguirre Anguiano, Mariano Azuela Güitrón y Guillermo I. Ortiz Mayagoitia en la acción de inconstitucionalidad 146/2007 y su acumulada 147/2007*, 11–32 (pointing out the court's lack of consensus on the abrogation of previous jurisprudence). *See also* Acción de inconstitucionalidad 146/2007 y su acumulada 147/2007 (Mex.), *Intervención del Ministro Sergio Salvador Aguirre Anguiano en sesión extraordinaria celebrada el 25 de agosto de 2008*, 9–10 (where Judge Sergio Aguirre Anguiano indicates that Jurisprudence 13/2002 was voted for by ten supreme court judges and therefore created precedent).

25. *See generally* Acción de inconstitucionalidad 146/2007 y su acumulada 147/2007 (Mex.), 1–208.

26. Acción de inconstitucionalidad 146/2007 y su acumulada 147/2007 (Mex.), 201–2 (original Spanish text is as follows: "considerando así al nasciturus como persona titular del derecho a la vida").

27. *See* Proyecto de Acción de inconstitucionalidad 146/2007 y su acumulada 147/2007, 312–13 (Mex.) (Mexican Supreme Court composition that upheld Mexico City's legalization of first-trimester abortions grants that "protection of human life from conception derives from . . . the American Convention on Human Rights").

28. Acción de inconstitucionalidad 146/2007 y su acumulada 147/2007 (Mex.), 428–29.

29. *See* Acción de inconstitucionalidad 146/2007 y su acumulada 147/2007 (Mex.), *Intervención del Ministro Sergio Salvador Agüirre Anguiano en sesión extraordinaria celebrada el 25 de agosto de 2008*, 15.

30. *See* Adame Goddard, *Comentario a la sentencia sobre la protección de la vida desde el momento de la concepción*, 603–43 (for more on the challenges to the Baja California and San Luis Potosí Amendments).

31. *See* Signatories and Ratifications: American Convention on Human Rights (Mexico ratified the American Convention in 1981).

32. Constitución Política del Estado Libre y Soberano de Baja California, art. 7; Constitución Política del Estado de Chiapas art. 4; CONSTITUCIÓN POLÍTICA DE CHIHUAHUA, art. 5 (Chihuahua was the first state to amend its constitution in 1994 to establish a right to life from conception); Constitución Política del Estado de Coahuila de Zaragoza, art. 173; Constitución Política del Estado Libre y Soberano de Colima, art. 1(I); Constitución Política del Estado Libre y Soberano de Durango, art. 1; Constitución Política del Estado de Guanajuato, art. 1; Constitución Política del Estado de Jalisco, art. 4; Constitución Política del Estado Libre y Soberano de Morelos, art. 2; Constitución Política del Estado de Nayarit, art. 7(XIII)(1); Constitución Política del Estado Libre y Soberano de Oaxaca, art. 12; Constitución Política del Estado Libre y Soberano de Puebla, art. 26(III)(IV); Constitución Política del Estado de Querétaro, art. 2; Constitución Política del Estado Libre y Soberano de Quintana Roo, art. 13; Constitución Política del Estado Libre y Soberano de San Luis Potosí, art. 16; Constitución Política del Estado de Sonora, art. 1; Constitución Política del Estado de Tamaulipas, art. 16; Constitución Política del Estado de Veracruz de Ignacio de la Llave, art. 4; Constitución Política del Estado de Yucatán, *as amended* 1 de abril de 2014, art. 1.

33. Constitución Política del Estado Libre y Soberano de Campeche, art. 6. *See* Pérez Hernández, Bartolini Esparza, et al., ABORTO: LA POLÍTICA DE UN ESTADO CLAUDICANTE, 45 (mentioning *Decreto No. 63* of 2010, which overturned the amendment).

34. Cabrera Martínez, *Diputados de Sinaloa aprueban ley a favor de la vida desde la concepción.*

35. *See* Pérez Hernández, Bartolini Esparza, et al., Aborto: La Política de un Estado Claudicante, 64–65 (describing interference by UN agencies opposing the state of Nuevo León's constitutional amendment recognizing a right to life from conception). *See Aprueban en Nuevo León derecho a la vida desde la concepción* (reporting on constitutional reform adopted in March 2019 that recognizes a "right to life from conception to natural death").

36. For more on constitutional challenges to state amendments on the right to life, *see* Ortiz Trujillo and Maqueda, "United Mexican States," 55–58.

37. *See* Adame Goddard, *Comentario a la sentencia sobre la protección de la vida desde el momento de la concepción*; Hoffman, *Turn-Around Victory; México: Suprema Corte ratifica blindaje de vida en 18 estados*; *Mexican Supreme Court Strikes Down State Pro-life Constitutional Amendment.*

38. Tozzi, *This Week's Pro-Life Victories in Mexico.*

39. *Id.*

40. Constitución Política del Estado de Chiapas, art. 14; Constitución Política de Chihuahua, art. 5; Constitución Política del Estado Libre y Soberano de Colima, art. 1(I); Constitución Política del Estado Libre y Soberano de Durango, art. 1; Constitución Política del Estado de Guanajuato, art. 1; Constitución Política del Estado de Jalisco, art. 4; Constitución Política del Estado Libre y Soberano de Morelos, art. 2; Constitución Política del Estado de Nayarit, art. 7(XIII)(1); Constitución Política del Estado Libre y Soberano de Oaxaca, art. 12; Constitución Política del Estado de Querétaro, art. 2; Constitución Política del Estado Libre y Soberano de San Luis Potosí, art. 16; Constitución Política del Estado de Tamaulipas, art. 16.

41. Constitución Política del Estado de Yucatán, art. 1; Constitución Política del Estado Libre y Soberano de Campeche, art. 6.

42. Constitución Política del Estado de Guanajuato, art. 1.

43. Constitución Política del Estado de Coahuila de Zaragoza, art. 173.

44. Constitución Política del Estado Libre y Soberano de Baja California, art. 7.

45. Constitución Política del Estado Libre y Soberano de Campeche, art. 6; Constitución Política del Estado de Chiapas, art. 4; Constitución Política del Estado Libre y Soberano de Puebla, art. 26(III) and (IV); Constitución Política del Estado de Querétaro, art. 2; Constitución Política del Estado Libre y Soberano de Quintana Roo, art. 13; Constitución Política del Estado de Sonora, art. 1; Constitución Política del Estado Libre y Soberano de San Luis Potosí, art. 16; Constitución Política del Estado de Tamaulipas, art. 16; Constitución Política del Estado de Veracruz de Ignacio de la Llave, art. 4; Constitución Política del Estado de Yucatán, *as amended* 01 de abril del 2014, art. 1.

46. Constitución Política del Estado de Querétaro, art. 2.

47. Constitución Política del Estado Libre y Soberano de San Luis Potosí, art. 16; Constitución Política del Estado de Sonora, art. 1.

48. *See* Constitución Política del Estado de Nayarit, *as amended* by Decreto de 16 de diciembre de 2010, art. 7(XIII)(1).

49. Constitución Política del Estado Libre y Soberano de Campeche, art. 6; Constitución Política del Estado Libre y Soberano de Durango, art. 1; Constitución Política del Estado de Jalisco, art. 4; Constitución Política del Estado de Nayarit, art. 7(XIII)(1); Constitución Política del Estado Libre y Soberano de Oaxaca, art. 12; Constitución Política del Estado de Sonora, art. 1; Constitución Política del Estado de Querétaro, art. 2; Constitución Política del Estado de Tamaulipas, art. 16; Constitución Política del Estado de Yucatán, art. 1.

50. *See* Signatories and Ratifications: American Convention on Human Rights (Argentina signed and ratified the American Convention in 1984). All of the Argentinian provincial constitutions referenced here were adopted after 1986, except for the Formosa Constitution, which was adopted in 1957). For dates of Argentinian provincial constitutions, see *Constituciones* on the InfoLEG website at INFOLEG.GOB.AR.

51. Art. 10, CONSTITUCIÓN DE LA PROVINCIA DE SALTA (Arg.); art. 18, CONSTITUCIÓN DE LA PROVINCIA DE CHUBUT (Arg.); art. 65(III)(1), CONSTITUCIÓN DE LA PROVINCIA DE CATAMARCA (Arg.); art. 13, CONSTITUCIÓN DE LA PROVINCIA DE SAN LUIS (Arg.); art. 4, CONSTITUCIÓN DE LA PROVINCIA DE CÓRDOBA (Arg.); arts. 40, 125, CONSTITUCIÓN DE LA PROVINCIA DE TUCUMÁN (Arg.).

52. Art. 16, CONSTITUCIÓN DE LA PROVINCIA DE ENTRE RÍOS (Arg.).

53. Art. 12, CONSTITUCIÓN DE LA PROVINCIA DE BUENOS AIRES (Arg.); art. 16, CONSTITUCIÓN DE LA PROVINCIA DE ENTRE RÍOS (Arg.).

54. Art. 14, CONSTITUCIÓN DE LA PROVINCIA DE TIERRA DEL FUEGO, ANTARTIDA E ISLAS DEL ATLÁNTICO SUR (Arg.); art. 16, CONSTITUCIÓN DE LA PROVINCIA DE ENTRE RÍOS (Arg.); arts. 40, 125, CONSTITUCIÓN DE LA PROVINCIA DE TUCUMÁN (Arg.); art. 15, CONSTITUCIÓN DE LA PROVINCIA DE CHACO (Arg.); Art. 13, CONSTITUCIÓN DE LA PROVINCIA DE SAN LUIS (Arg.); art. 4, CONSTITUCIÓN DE LA PROVINCIA DE CÓRDOBA (Arg.).

55. Art. 5, CONSTITUCIÓN DE LA PROVINCIA DE FORMOSA (Arg.).

56. Art. 16, CONSTITUCIÓN DE LA PROVINCIA DE SANTIAGO DEL ESTERO (Arg.).

57. Art. 18, CONSTITUCIÓN DE LA PROVINCIA DE CHUBUT (Arg.); art. 15, CONSTITUCIÓN DE LA PROVINCIA DE CHACO (Arg.); Art. 13, CONSTITUCIÓN DE LA PROVINCIA DE SAN LUIS (Arg.); arts. 4, 19, CONSTITUCIÓN DE LA PROVINCIA DE CÓRDOBA (Arg.).

58. Arts. 40, 125, CONSTITUCIÓN DE LA PROVINCIA DE TUCUMÁN (Arg.); art. 15, CONSTITUCIÓN DE LA PROVINCIA DE CHACO (Arg.); art. 13, CONSTITUCIÓN DE LA PROVINCIA DE SAN LUIS (Arg.); art. 4, CONSTITUCIÓN DE LA PROVINCIA DE CÓRDOBA (Arg.).

59. Art. 65, CONSTITUCIÓN DE LA PROVINCIA DE CATAMARCA (Arg.); art. 5, CONSTITUCIÓN DE LA PROVINCIA DE FORMOSA (Arg.).

60. CÓDIGO CIVIL, arts. 24, 101, 574, 592 (Arg.). *See also* CÓDIGO CIVIL, art. 63 (Arg.) (former civil code).

61. Código Civil, art. 19 (Arg.).

62. Código Civil, art. 70 (Arg.) (former civil code).

63. See Lafferriere, *El artículo 19 del nuevo Código Civil y el reconocimiento como persona del embrión humano no implantado* (discussing legislative intent to protect human life from the time of fertilization either inside or outside the maternal womb).

64. Corte Suprema de Justicia de la Nación, 11/01/2001, "T., S. c/Gobierno de la Ciudad de Buenos Aires s/amparo" (Arg.); Corte Suprema de Justicia de la Nación, 03/05/2002, "Portal de Belén—Asociación Civil sin Fines de Lucro c. Ministerio de Salud y Acción Social de la Nación s/amparo." *See* Quintana, *Persona y filiación en la legislación actual*, 14–15 (explaining proposals for Civil Code reform in Argentina).

65. Código de la Niñez y la Adolescencia, arts. 2, 12 (Costa Rica); Decreto No. 839, 16 de abril de 2009, Ley de Protección de la Niñez y Adolescencia, art. 3 (El Sal.); Código de la Niñez y Adolescencia, art. 12 (Hond.); Código de la Niñez y Adolescencia, art. 2 (Ecuador); Ley de Protección Integral de la Niñez y Adolescencia, arts. 2, 9 (Guat.); Código de la Niñez y la Adolescencia, art. 12 (Nicar.); Ley 14: Que Crea la Secretaría Nacional de Niñez, Adolescencia y Familia, art. 2(3) (Pan.).

66. *See* Código de la Niñez y la Adolescencia, art. 12 (Nicar.).

67. Código Civil de la República de Nicaragua, arts. 11, 19 (Nicar.).

68. Código de la Niñez y la Adolescencia, art. 9 (Para.).

69. Código de la Niñez y Adolescencia, art. 1 (Hond.). *Id.* at art. 12.

70. Ley de Política Nacional de Población, Decreto Legislativo No. 346, art. IV(1) (Peru).

71. Ley Nacional No. 25.929 de Derechos de Padres e Hijos durante el Proceso de Nacimiento, art. 2 (Arg.).

72. Decreto No. 839, 16 de abril de 2009, Ley de Protección de la Niñez y Adolescencia, arts. 3, 5, 16–17 (El Sal.).

73. *Id.* at arts. 5, 16.

74. Código de Familia, art. 344 (El Sal.).

75. Código de Salud, art. 48 (El Sal.).

76. *See* Código Niña, Niño y Adolescente, art. 5 (Bol.); *see also* previous Code Código del Niño, Niña y Adolescente, art. 2 (Bol.).

77. Código de la Niñez y la Adolescencia, art. 2 (Costa Rica).

78. Ley de Protección Integral de la Niñez y Adolescencia, art. 2 (Guat.).

79. Ley 14: Que Crea la Secretaría Nacional de Niñez, Adolescencia y Familia, art. 2(3) (Pan.).

80. Ley No. 3: Por la Cual se Aprueba el Código de Familia, art. 484 (Pan.).

81. Ley No. 2169: Que Establece la Mayoría de Edad, art. 3(a) (Para.). Ley No. 836/30: Código Sanitario, art. 22 (Para.).

82. *See* Comm. on the Rights of the Child, *Consideration of Reports Submitted by States Parties Under Article 44 of the Convention: Periodic Reports of States*

*Parties Due in 1997: Paraguay, Addendum* CRC/C/65/Add.12 ¶ 72 at 33 (citing Ley No. 903/81, art. 1 (Para.)).

83. Código de los Niños y Adolescentes, art. 1 (Peru).

84. Código de la Niñez y Adolescencia, art. 10 (Para.). Código de la Niñez y Adolescencia, art. 148 (Ecuador).

85. Ley No. 870, Código de Familia, arts. 316(a), 430, 479 (Nicar.).

86. *See* Decreto No. 267-2005, La Gaceta 30, 832 (Hond).

87. *See* Diario de Centro America, Órgano Oficial de la República de Guatemala, Acuerdo No. 21.

88. Congreso de la República de Perú, 2001, Dictamen recaído en el Proyecto de Ley No. 122/2001-cr, mediante el cual se propone declarar el día 25 de marzo de cada año como "Día del Niño por Nacer," art. 15.

89. *See* Signatories and Ratifications: American Convention on Human Rights (all Latin American and Caribbean children's codes or children's acts have been adopted after signature or ratification of the American Convention. The earliest children's codes were adopted in 1990 in Brazil and Honduras. El Salvador was the latest in 2010. The American Convention was ratified by Honduras in 1990, by Costa Rica and Nicaragua in 1998, by Peru in 2000, by Guatemala and Ecuador in 2003, and by El Salvador in 2010).

90. Código Niña, Niño y Adolescente, arts. 5, 16 (Bol.); *see also* Ley del Código del Niño, Niña y Adolescente, arts. 2, 13 (Bol.) (previous code); Código del Menor, arts. 3, 4 (Colom.); Código de la Niñez y la Adolescencia, art. 12 (Costa Rica); Código de la Niñez y Adolescencia, art. 20 (Ecuador); Decreto No. 839, 16 de abril de 2009, Ley de Protección de la Niñez y Adolescencia, art. 16 (El Sal.); Ley de Protección Integral de la Niñez y Adolescencia, art. 9 (Guat.); Código de la Niñez y Adolescencia, art. 12 (Hond.); Código de la Niñez y la Adolescencia, art. 12 (Nicar.); Código de la Niñez y Adolescencia, art. 9 (Para.); Código de los Niños y Adolescentes, art. 1 (Peru).

91. Código Civil, art. 75 (Chile); Código Civil, art. 91 (Colom.); Código Civil, art. 52 (Hond.); Código Civil, art. 13 (Nicar.); Código Civil, art. 1 (Peru); Código Civil, art. 73 (El Sal.).

92. *See* Código Civil, art. 91 (Colom.).

93. Lei 10.406, 10 de janeiro de 2002, Código Civil, art. 2 (Braz.) (original Portuguese text is as follows: "A personalidade civil da pessoa começa do nascimento com vida; mas a lei põe a salvo, desde a concepção, os direitos do nascituro"). *See also* Supremo Tribunal Federal, Explicação Ministro Ricardo Lewandowski, 248 (Braz.).

94. Lei 8.069, 13 de Julho de 1990, Estatuto Da Criança E Do Adolescente, art. 7 (Braz.).

95. Ley No. 3: Por la Cual Se Aprueba el Código de Familia, art. 489(1) (Pan.).

96. Código de Familia, art. 353 (El Sal.).

97. Código Sanitario, art. 15 (Para.).

98. Ley de Política Nacional de Población, art. IV(1) (Peru).

99. *See* art. 75(23), Constitución Nacional (Arg.).

100. Constituição Federal, arts. 201, 203 (Braz.).

101. Constitución Política de la Republica de Honduras de 1982, art. 123 (Hond.).

102. Decreto No. 839, 16 de abril de 2009, Ley de Protección de la Niñez y Adolescencia, arts. 16, 20 (El Sal.).

103. Código de Familia, arts. 346, 353–54 (El Sal.).

104. Código de la Niñez y Adolescencia, art. 12 (Hond.).

105. Ley de Protección Integral de la Niñez y Adolescencia, art. 9 (Guat.).

106. Código de la Niñez y Adolescencia, arts. 20, 25 (Ecuador).

107. Código de la Niñez y la Adolescencia, arts. 12, 34 (Nicar.).

108. Código de los Niños y la Adolescentes, art. 2 (Peru).

109. Ley de Protección de la Niñez y Adolescencia, art. 17 (El Sal.).

110. *Id.* art. 17 (El Sal.).

111. *Id.* art. 23 (El Sal.).

112. *Id.* art. 20 (El Sal.).

113. Ley No. 3: Por la Cual se Aprueba el Código de Familia, arts. 698–99 (Pan.).

114. Código de la Niñez y Adolescencia, art. 10 (Para.).

115. Código de la Niñez y la Adolescencia, art. 12 (Costa Rica).

116. *Id.* arts. 38, 51 (beneficiaries are required to attend related courses promoted by the governmental social services agency).

117. Lei 8.069, 13 de Julho de 1990, Estatuto da Criança e do Adolescente, art. 7 (Braz.).

118. *Id.* at art. 8.

119. *See* Código Niña, Niño y Adolescente, art. 16 (Bol.); *see also* Ley del Código del Niño, Niña y Adolescente, art. 13 (Bol.) (previous code).

120. *See* Código Niña, Niño y Adolescente, art. 24 (Bol.); *see also* Ley del Código del Niño, Niña y Adolescente, art. 15 (Bol.) (previous code).

121. Código del Menor, arts. 3–4 (Colom.); *see also* Ley 1098 de 2006, Código de la Infancia y la Adolescencia, art. 17 (Colom.).

122. Ley para la Protección de los Derechos de Niñas, Niños y Adolescentes (Mex.).

123. Constitución Política de los Estados Unidos Mexicanos, art. 123(A)(XV).

124. Ley General de Salud, art. III (Peru).

125. Código de la Niñez y la Adolescencia, art. 9 (Para.).

126. Código para el Sistema de Protección y los Derechos Fundamentales de Niños, Niñas y Adolescentes, art. 30 (Dom. Rep.).

127. Código Sanitario, arts. 15–16 (Para.) (see Title I, relating to the health of persons).

128. Código de Salud, art. 48 (El Sal.).

129. Ley No. 3: Por la Cual se Aprueba el Código de Familia, art. 493 (Pan.).

130. Comm. on the Rights of the Child, *Initial Reports of States Parties Due in 1992: Barbados, Addendum* ¶ 158.

131. Código de la Niñez y la Adolescencia, art. 50 (Costa Rica).

132. *Id.* art. 53.

133. Código Sanitario, arts. 16–17 (Chile).

134. Código de la Niñez y Adolescencia, arts. 25, 27 (Ecuador).

135. *Id.* art. 27.

136. Código de la Niñez y Adolescencia, art. 13 (Hond.).

137. Código Civil, art. 243, § 2 (Chile).

138. Código De Processo Civil, art. 877 (Braz.).

139. Código Sanitario, art. 21 (Para.).

140. Código de Familia, art. 211 (El Sal.).

141. Código Civil, art. 1527 (Bol.). *See also* Código de las Familias y del Proceso Familiar, art. 28 (Bol.).

142. Lei 8.069, 13 de Julho de 1990, Estatuto da Criança e do Adolescente, art. 26 (Braz.); *see also* Lei 10.406, 10 de janeiro de 2002, Código Civil, art. 1.609 (Braz.).

143. Código de Familia, arts. 84–85, 94 (Costa Rica).

144. Código de Familia, arts. 144, 146 (El Sal.).

145. Ley No. 3: Por la Cual se Aprueba el Código de Familia, art. 272 (Pan.).

146. Código de Familia, art. 83 (Costa Rica).

147. Código Civil, arts. 574, 592 (Arg.); Ley 1098 de 2006, Código de la Infancia y la Adolescencia, art. 82 (Colom.); Código para el Sistema de Protección y los Derechos Fundamentales de Niños, Niñas y Adolescentes, art. 63 (Dom. Rep.); Código de Familia, art. 96 (Hond.); Código Civil Federal, art. 359 (Mex.); Código Civil, art. 16 (Nicar.); Código Civil del Paraguay, art. 30 (Para.); Código Civil, arts. 365, 405 (Peru).

148. Código de Familia, art. 96 (Hond.).

149. Código Civil del Paraguay, art. 30 (Para.). Código Civil, art. 365 (Peru).

150. Lei No. 11.804, art. 2 (Braz.).

151. *See Lei dos alimentos gravídicos garante "pensão" durante a gestação* (explaining that the law guarantees that the biological father will pay the pregnant woman supplementary financial aid during her pregnancy).

152. Lei No 11.804, art. 6 (Braz.).

153. Ley No. 870, Código de Familia, arts. 316(a), 319 (Nicar.).

154. Código de la Niñez y Adolescencia, art. 161 (Para.).

155. Ley 1098 de 2006, Código de la Infancia y la Adolescencia, arts. 24, 111 (Colom.); Código de Familia, art. 96 (Costa Rica); Ley No. 14.908, art. 1 (Chile); Código para el Sistema de Protección y los Derechos Fundamentales de Niños, Niñas y Adolescentes, art. 173 (Dom. Rep.); Código de la Niñez y

Adolescencia, art. 148 (Ecuador); Código De Familia, art. 249 (El Sal.); Código Civil, art. 52 (Hond.); *see also* Código de la Niñez y Adolescencia, arts. 73–74 (Hond.); Ley No. 3: Por la Cual se Aprueba el Código de Familia, arts. 377(4), 493 (Pan.); Código de la Niñez y Adolescencia, art. 97, 161 (Para.); Código Civil, arts. 46, 414 (Peru); *see also* Código de los Niños y Adolescentes, art. 92 (Peru); Código de la Niñez y la Adolescencia, art. 46 (Uru.).

156. Código de la Niñez y Adolescencia, art. 148 (Ecuador).

157. Código Civil, arts. 46, 414 (Peru); Código de los Niños y Adolescentes, art. 92 (Peru).

158. Código de las Familias y del Proceso Familiar (Bol.).

159. Código de Familia, art. 96 (Costa Rica).

160. Ley No. 3: Por la Cual se Aprueba el Código de Familia, arts. 377(4), 493 (Pan.).

161. Código Civil, arts. 46, 414 (Peru). *See also* Ley No. 3: Por la Cual se Aprueba el Código de Familia, arts. 287–89 (Pan.); Ley No. 3: Por la Cual se Aprueba el Código de Familia, art. 289 (Pan.).

162. Código de Familia, art. 214 (Hond.).

163. Codigo de la Niñez y Adolescencia, arts. 2, 12 (Ecuador).

164. Ley No. 3: Por la Cual se Aprueba el Código de Familia, art. 697 (Pan.).

165. Código Sanitario, art. 19 (Para.).

166. Código Niña, Niño y Adolescente, arts. 48(c), 88(a) (Bol.). Article 88 states: "Se prohíbe la adopción de . . . Seres humanos por nacer" [the abortion of unborn human beings is prohibited]. Article 48 states: "Es nulo el consentimiento dado antes del nacimiento" [consent [for adoption] before birth is prohibited].

167. Ley General de Salud, arts. 320, 323, 326(II) (Mex).

168. Ley General de Salud, art. 7 (Peru).

169. Ley 1098 de 2006, Código de la Infancia y la Adolescencia, art. 64 (Colom.).

170. Código de la Niñez y Adolescencia, art. 64 (Hond.).

171. Código de la Niñez y Adolescencia, art. 163 (Ecuador).

172. Código de la Niñez y Adolescencia, art. 64 (Hond.).

173. Ley de Protección Integral de La Niñez Y Adolescencia, art. 19 (El Sal.).

174. Código Penal, art. 140 (El Sal.).

175. *Id.* art. 141.

176. Código de los Niños y Adolescentes, art. 1 (Peru).

177. Ley 599 de 2000, Código Penal, arts. 132–34 (Colom.).

178. Código Penal, art. 146 (Nicar.).

179. Código Penal de la República de Panamá, arts. 145, 147 (Pan.). *See also* Ley No. 3, de 15 de Enero de 2004, Que Prohíbe Toda Forma De Clonación Humana y Dicta Otras Disposiciones (Pan.) (banning human cloning in Panama); Código Penal [Cód. Pen.] [Criminal Code], art. 225(C) (Guat.).

180. Civil Codes of Bolivia (1975), Ecuador (1982), Paraguay (1988), Peru (1991), Chile (2000), Brazil (2002), and El Salvador (2004) were adopted after the adoption of the American Convention. Civil Codes of Argentina (1871), Colombia (1873), Panama (1916), Mexico (1928), Nicaragua (1929), and Honduras (1906) precede the signature or adoption of the American Convention, but their provisions regarding unborn children have not been derogated or substantially modified.

181. Código Civil, arts. 1, 663, 1008 (Bol.); Lei 10.406, art. 2 (Braz.); Código Civil, arts. 74–75 (Chile); Código Civil, art. 90 (Colom.); Código Civil, arts. 60–61 (Ecuador); Código Civil, arts. 72–73 (El Sal.); Código Civil, arts. 51–52 (Hond.); Código Civil Federal, art. 22 (Mex.); Código Civil, arts. 7, 13 (Nicar.); Código Civil de la República de Panamá, arts. 41–43 (Pan.); Código Civil, arts. 28, 37 (Para.); Código Civil, art. 1 (Peru).

182. Código Civil Federal, art. 22 (Mex.).

183. Código Civil, art. 1 (Peru).

184. Código Civil, art. 75 (Chile); Código Civil, art. 93 (Colom.); Código Civil, art. 61 (Ecuador); Código Civil, art. 73 (El Sal.); Código Civil, art. 52 (Hond.); Código Civil, art. 13 (Nicar.); Código Civil de la República de Panamá, art. 43 (Pan.).

185. Código Civil, art. 75 (Chile). *See also* Corte Suprema de Justicia, 30 agosto 2001, "Philippi Izquierdo c. Laboratorio Chile S.A."; Tribunal Constitucional, 18 abril 2008, Requerimiento de inconstitucionalidad deducido en contra de algunas disposiciones de las "Normas Nacionales sobre Regulación de la Fertilidad" (Chile).

186. *See* Código Civil, art. 75 (Chile). *See also* Código Civil, art. 61 (Ecuador).

187. Código Civil, arts. 54, 70, 3290 (Arg.). *See also* Código Civil, arts. 19, 24 (Arg.).

188. *See* Farfán Bertrán, "Protection of the Human Right to Life in the Republic of Argentina," 132–33.

189. Código Civil del Distrito Federal, art. 22 (Mex.).

190. Código Civil del Estado de Aguascalientes, art. 19; Código Civil del Estado de Baja California, art. 22; Código Civil para el Estado Libre y Soberano de Baja California Sur, arts. 22, 1201, 2231; Código Civil del Estado de Campeche, art. 26; Código Civil del Estado de Chiapas, art. 20; Código Civil del Estado de Chihuahua, art. 22; Código Civil para el Estado de Coahuila de Zaragoza, art. 31; Código Civil del Estado de Colima, art. 22; Código Civil del Estado de Durango, art. 22; Código Civil del Estado de Guanajuato, art. 21; Código Civil del Estado Libre y Soberano de Guerrero, art. 25; Código Civil para el Estado de Hidalgo, art. 22; Código Civil del Estado de Jalisco, art. 19; Código Civil para el Estado de Michoacán, art. 16, 30 de Julio de 1936 (1936 Code), art. 20 (2008 Code); Código Familiar para el Estado Libre y Soberano de

Morelos, art. 3; Código Civil del Estado de Nayarit, art. 22; Código Civil para el Estado de Nuevo León, art. 23; Código Civil para del Estado de Oaxaca, art. 21; Código Civil para el Estado Libre y Soberano de Puebla, art. 37; Código Civil del Estado de Querétaro, art. 22; Código Civil para el Estado de Quintana Roo, art. 428; Código Civil para el Estado de San Luis Potosí, art. 17; Código Civil del Estado de Sinaloa, art. 22; Código Civil para el Estado de Tabasco, art. 29; Código Civil para el Estado de Tamaulipas, art. 18; Código Civil para el Estado Libre y Soberano de Tlaxcala, art. 32; Código Civil del Estado de Veracruz, arts. 26, 28; Código Civil del Estado de Yucatán, art. 16.

191. *See* Comm. on the Rights of the Child, *Consideration of Reports Submitted by States Parties Under Article 44 of the Convention: Second Periodic Report; Suriname,* ¶ 43; Comm. on the Rights of the Child, *Consideration of Reports Submitted by States Parties Under Article 44 of the Convention: Initial Reports of States Parties Due in 1995; Addendum: Suriname,* ¶ 28 (indicating that, according to the country's civil code, an unborn child may be named as an heir (arts. 865, 927), may be granted usufruct (art. 791), and may receive gifts (art. 1689)).

192. Ley No. 824, 31 de diciembre de 1974 (Chile).

193. Código Civil, arts. 1680, 1861 (Para.).

194. Lei 10.406, Código Civil, art. 542 (Braz.); Código Civil, art. 63 (Ecuador); Código Civil, art. 75 (El Sal.); Código Civil Federal, art. 2357 (Mex.); Código Civil, art. 54 (Hond.).

195. Código Civil, art. 21 (Arg.); Código Civil, art. 28 (Para.).

196. Código Civil, arts. 1122, 1235 (Bol.); Código Civil, art. 93 (Colom.); Código Civil, arts. 31, 605 (Costa Rica); Código Civil, art. 63 (Ecuador); Código Civil, art. 75 (El Sal.); Código Civil, arts. 54, 1298 (Hond.); Código Civil de la República de Panamá, art. 44 (Pan.); Código Civil, art. 856 (Peru).

197. Código Civil, arts. 12, 15, 19 (Nicar.).

198. Código Civil, arts. 21, 2279(b) (Arg.); Código Civil, arts. 1, 663, 1008 (Bol.); Código Civil, art. 605 (Costa Rica); Código Civil, arts. 343, 356, 487 (Chile); Código Civil de la República Dominicana, arts. 906, 1049–50 (Dom. Rep.); Código Civil Federal, arts. 1314, 2357; Código Civil, art. 19 (Nicar.); Código Civil, art. 28 (Para.); Código Civil, arts. 805, 856 (Peru).

199. Código Civil, art. 90 (Colom.); Código Civil, art. 60 (Ecuador); Código Civil, art. 72 (El Sal.); Código Civil, art. 20 (Nicar.).

200. Código Civil Federal, art. 337 (Mex.).

201. Código Civil del Paraguay, art. 32 (Para.).

202. Código Civil, art. 101 (Arg.); Lei 10.406, 10 de janeiro de 2002, Código Civil, arts. 878, 1.779 (Braz.); Código Civil, art. 31 (Costa Rica); Código Civil, art. 390 (Ecuador); Código Civil, arts. 238, 486, 490 (El Sal.); Código Civil, arts. 414, 429, 544 (Hond.); Código Civil, arts. 12, 18, 306, 321, 377, 380 (Nicar.); Código Civil de la República de Panamá, art. 948 (Pan.); Código Civil del Paraguay, arts. 31, 37 (Para.); Código Civil, art. 617 (Peru).

203. Código Civil, arts. 343, 356, 487 (Chile); Código Civil, arts. 433–46, 575, 580 (Colom.); Código Civil, arts. 390, 526 (Ecuador); Código Civil, art. 486 (El Sal.); Código Civil, art. 544 (Hond.); Código Civil, arts. 306, 321 (Nicar.); Código Civil, art. 617 (Peru).

204. Lei 10.406, 10 de janeiro de 2002, Código Civil, art. 878 (Braz.); Código Civil, art. 663 (Bol.); Código Civil, arts. 484–85 (El Sal.); Código Civil del Paraguay, art. 40 (Para.).

205. Código Civil, arts. 365, 405 (Peru).

206. Lei 10.406, 10 de janeiro de 2002, Código Civil, arts. 1.798, 1.799 (Braz.); Ley No. 3: Por la Cual Se Aprueba el Código de Familia, arts. 287–88 (Pan.); Código Civil, art. 201 (Hond.). *See also* Comm. on the Rights of the Child, *Consideration of Reports Submitted by States Parties Under Article 44 of the Convention: Initial Reports of States Parties Due in 1995: Addendum, Suriname*, ¶ 28.

207. Código Civil, arts. 433–46, 575, 580 (Colom.); Código Civil, arts. 343, 356, 487 (Chile); Código Civil, art. 402 (Ecuador); Código Civil, art. 429 (Hond.); Código Civil, art. 306 (Nicar.); Código Civil, arts. 598, 805 (Peru).

208. Código Civil del Estado de México, art. 7.637 (Mex.); Código Civil del Estado de Querétaro, art. 2244 (Mex.).

209. Código Civil, arts. 343, 356, 487 (Chile); Código Civil, arts. 433–46, 575, 580 (Colom.); Código Civil, arts. 390, 526 (Ecuador); Código Civil, arts. 377, 380 (Nicar.); Código Civil, art. 486 (El Sal.).

210. *See, e.g.*, Constitución Política de la República de Honduras de 1982, art. 67 (Hond.).

211. *See* Constitución Política del Perú, art. 2 ¶ 1 (Peru): Constitución Política de la República de Honduras, art. 67 (Hond.); Tribunal Constitucional, 18 abril 2008, Requerimiento de inconstitucionalidad deducido en contra de algunas disposiciones de las "Normas Nacionales sobre Regulación de la Fertilidad"; Constitución Política de los Estados Unidos Mexicanos [C.P.], Transitorios art. Tercero (Mex.); T.C. (Peru), ONG "Acción de Lucha Anticorrupción," § 3.2 ¶ 12.

212. Constitución Política del Perú, art. 2(1) (Peru).

213. *See* Constitución Política de la República de Honduras, art. 67 (Hond.).

214. *See* Constitución Política de los Estados Unidos Mexicanos, Transitorios art. Tercero (Mex.).

215. *See* Tribunal Constitucional, 18 abril 2008, Requerimiento de inconstitucionalidad deducido en contra de algunas disposiciones de las "Normas Nacionales sobre Regulación de la Fertilidad."

216. *See* Corte Suprema de Justicia, Constituida en Tribunal de Amparo, Dec. 8, 2017, Amparo 1434-2017, 18.

217. Código Civil, art. 1(II) (Bol.); Código Civil, art. 1 (Peru).

218. Código Penal (Peru). (see Exposición de Motivos, Innovaciones Propuestas en la Parte Especial).

219. Código de los Niños y Adolescentes, art. 1 (Peru).

220. Código Civil Federal, art. 22 (Mex.).

221. Código Civil, art. 31 (Costa Rica).

222. Código Civil, art. 1 (Guat.); Código Civil de la República de Panamá, art. 41 (Pan.).

223. *See* Comm. on the Rights of the Child, *Consideration of Reports Submitted by States Parties Under Article 44 of the Convention: Second Periodic Report; Suriname*, ¶ 43; Comm. on the Rights of the Child, *Consideration of Reports Submitted by States Parties Under Article 44 of the Convention: Initial Reports of States Parties Due in 1995; Addendum: Suriname*, ¶ 28.

## FIVE. Evolutive Interpretation

1. Organization of American States, American Convention on Human Rights art. 4(1).

2. See Cabrera-García & Montiel-Flores v. Mexico, ¶ 234; Case of Boyce et al. v. Barbados, ¶ 122.

3. Case of Boyce et al. v. Barbados, ¶ 69.

4. Case of Salvador Chiriboga v. Ecuador ¶ 122.

5. Artavia Murillo v. Costa Rica, ¶ 245.

6. Gómez-Paquiyauri brothers v. Peru, ¶ 129; Case of the Massacres of El Mozote and nearby places v. El Salvador, ¶ 172; Case of the Barrios Family v. Venezuela, ¶ 48.

7. All translations are the author's unless official English translations are cited. The great majority of current criminal law provisions on abortion in Latin America and the Caribbean were adopted after each state's corresponding date of signature or ratification of the American Convention: 1970–73 in Costa Rica, Ecuador, El Salvador, and Guatemala; 1983–87 in Barbados, Argentina, Haiti, and Grenada; 1991–2000 in Peru, Honduras, Dominican Republic, and Colombia; 2000–present in Brazil (2004), Nicaragua (2007), Mexico (1931–2008), Paraguay (1997–2008), Panama (2007–2010), Chile (1874–2011), and Uruguay (1998–2012). Criminal code provisions on abortion of Bolivia (1972), Jamaica (1861), and Dominica (1873) precede their date of signature or ratification of the American Convention and are still effective today.

8. Código Penal, art. 88 (Arg.); Código Penal, arts. 121–28 (Braz.).

9. Código Penal, arts. 121–28 (Braz.); Código Penal, art. 110 (Costa Rica); Código Orgánico Integral Penal, ch. 2 § 1 (Ecuador).

10. Código Penal, tit. I, ch. II (El Sal.).

11. Comm. on the Rights of the Child, *Consideration of Reports Submitted by States Parties Under Article 44 of the Convention: Initial Reports of States Parties Due in 1993; Dominica*, ¶ 95–98.

12. Código Penal, tit. I, ch. III (Guat.); Código Penal Federal, tit. XIX, ch. VI (Mex.); Código Penal, tit. I, ch. I (Pan.).

13. Código Penal, tit. I, ch. I (Nicar.).

14. *See* Código Penal, libro I, tit. I (Peru).

15. *See* Código Penal, libro II, tit. XII (Uru.).

16. Código Penal, libro II, tit. VIII (Bol.).

17. Código Penal, libro II, tit. VII (Chile).

18. Criminal Code, § 247(2) (Gren.) (emphasis added).

19. Código Penal, art. 263 (Bol.).

20. Código Penal, art. 118 (Costa Rica).

21. Suriname Penal Code, arts. 309(1), 355 (Surin.).

22. Código Penal, art. 126 (Hond.).

23. Código Penal, art. 133 (Guat.); Código Penal Federal, art. 329 (Mex.).

24. Código Penal, L. 3.440/08, arts. 14(18), 109 (Para.).

25. Offences Against the Person Act, §§ 8, 56 (Dominica).

26. *See* Artavia Murillo v. Costa Rica, ¶¶ 181, 187; *Aborto*, in *Diccionario de la lengua española*; *Abortion*, in Miller-Keane Encyclopedia & Dictionary of Medicine, 12; *Mosby's Medical, Nursing, & Allied Health Dictionary*, 6 (defining *abortion* as "the spontaneous or induced termination of pregnancy before the fetus has developed to the stage of viability").

27. Código Penal, art. 137 (El Sal.); *see* Código Penal, art. 139 (Guat.); *see* Código Penal, art. 145 (Nicar.).

28. Código Penal Federal, art. 333 (Mex.).

29. *See, e.g.*, Código Penal Para el Estado de Morelos, art. 119 (Mex.) (notes that miscarriages are not punishable even if the mother's negligence is "notorious" in the state of Morelos).

30. *See* Decreto No. 216-03; Código Penal, art. 49 (Chile).

31. *See Ratifican ley que apunta a controlar casos de aborto* (reporting on passage of the bill and a pro-choice senator's statements that the bill's true purpose was to identify cases of illegal abortion and to prosecute women).

32. *See* Tribunal Constitucional, 28 agosto 2017, Requerimiento de inconstitucionalidad respecto del proyecto de ley que "regula la despenalización de la interrupción voluntaria del embarazo en tres causales" (Chile), 169–73, 176 (indicating that there has never been a prohibition of indirect abortion to save a mother's life in Chile).

33. *See id.* 173 (citing witness testimony by a maternal-fetal health specialist who noted the rarity of the situation, namely that, in 2014, only fifty-six childbirth-related maternal deaths occurred in Chile, of which twenty-two occurred after delivery).

34. *See, e.g.*, Sala de lo Constitucional, Nov. 20, 2007, Inconstitucionalidad 18-98, ¶ V(2)(A).

35. Código Penal, art. 137 (Guat.).

36. *See* Corte Suprema de Justicia, Constituida en Tribunal de Amparo, Dec. 8, 2017, Amparo 1434-2017, 8, 13 (Guat.).

37. Código Penal, L. 1.160/97, art. 349 (Para.); Código Penal, L. 3.440/08, art. 109 (3) (Para.); Offences Against the Person Act, § 8(1) (Dominica).

38. Código Penal, L. 3.440/08, art. 109 (4) (Para.) (the code's language specifically states that fetal death may legally occur only indirectly, not directly, under such circumstances: "No obra antijurídicamente el que produjera indirectamente la muerte de un feto, si esto, según los conocimientos y las experiencias del arte médico, fuera necesario para proteger de un peligro serio la vida de la madre").

39. Offences Against the Person Act, § 8(2) (Dominica).

40. Código Organico Integral Penal, art. 148 (Ecuador); Código Penal, art. 116 (Peru); Código Penal, art. 325 (Uru.).

41. Código Penal, arts. 125 (Braz.); Código Organico Integral Penal, art. 148 (Ecuador); Código Penal, art. 134 (El Sal.); Código Penal, art. 349 (Para.).

42. Ley No. 20.357, Tipifica Crímenes de Lesa Humanidad, art. 5(4).

43. *See* Código Penal, arts. 263–64 (Bol.); Código Penal, art. 135 (Guat.); Código Penal Federal, art. 330, Diario Oficial de la Federación, 14 de Agosto de 1931 (Mex.); Código Penal, art. 144 (Nicar.); Código Penal, art. 85 (Arg.); Código Penal, arts. 125, 126 (Braz.); L. 599, julio 24, 2000, 44097 Diario Oficial, art. 125–26 (Colom.); Código Penal, art. 118 (1) (Costa Rica); *see* Surin. Penal Code, art. 356 (Surin.).

44. Código Penal, art. 135 (Guat.); Código Penal, art. 144 (Nicar.); Código Penal Federal, art. 330, Diario Oficial de la Federación, 14 de Agosto de 1931 (Mex.).

45. Código Penal, art. 144 (Nicar.).

46. Código Penal, art. 143 (Pan.).

47. Código Orgánico Integral Penal, art. 147 (Ecuador); Código Penal, art. 143 (Pan.); Código Penal, art. 349 (Para.); Código Penal, art. 116 (Peru); Surin. Penal Code, arts. 309(1), 355 (Surin.).

48. Código Orgánico Integral Penal, art. 48(4) (Ecuador).

49. *See, e.g.*, Código Penal, art. 267 (Bol.).

50. Código Penal, art. 87 (Arg.); Código Penal, art. 268 (Bol.); Código Penal, arts. 342–43 (Chile); Código Penal, art. 139 (Guat.); Código Penal, art. 132 (Hond.); Código Penal, art. 118 (Peru).

51. Código Penal, art. 268 (Bol.); L. 599, julio 24, 2000, 44097 Diario Oficial, arts. 125–26 (Colom.); Código Orgánico Integral Penal, art. 48(4) (Ecuador); Código Penal, art. 137 (El Sal.); Código Penal, art. 145 (Nicar.).

52. Código Penal, art. 268 (Bol.).

53. Código Penal, art. 122 (Costa Rica); Código Penal, art. 118 (Peru).

54. Código Penal, art. 145 (Nicar.).

55. Código Penal, art. 143 (Pan.); Código Penal, art. 349 (Para.); Código Penal, art. 327 (Uru.).

56. Ley No. 1.674, Ley Contra La Violencia en La Familia o Domestica, art. 10 (Bol.); Ley No. 8589, Penalización de la Violencia Contra Las Mujeres, art. 8(c) (Costa Rica).

57. *Death Penalty in the Inter-American Human Rights System*, 37.

58. Comm. on the Rights of the Child, *Initial Reports of States Parties Due in 1993: Dominica*, ¶¶ 95–98.

59. *See* Offences Against the Person Act, §§ 72, 73 (Jam.).

60. L. 599, julio 24, 2000, 44097 DIARIO OFICIAL, arts. 125–26 (Colom.).

61. CÓDIGO PENAL, art. 148 (Nicar.); CÓDIGO PENAL, arts. 138–39 (El Sal.).

62. CÓDIGO PENAL, art. 124-A (Peru).

63. L. 599, julio 24, 2000, 44097 DIARIO OFICIAL, arts. 125–26 (Colom.); CÓDIGO PENAL, arts. 148–49 (Nicar.).

64. CÓDIGO PENAL, arts. 138–39 (El Sal.).

65. Código de La Niñez y Adolescencia, art. 131(2) and (6) (Ecuador).

66. Código de los Niños y Adolescentes, art. 1 (Peru).

67. CONSTITUCIÓN DE LA REPUBLICA DE ECUADOR, ch. 6, art. 66, 2008; CÓDIGO PENAL, art. 145 (Pan.); CÓDIGO PENAL, art. 225(c) (Guat.).

68. Ley No. 20.120, Sobre La Investigación Científica en el ser Humano, su Genoma, y Prohibe La Clonación Humana, arts. 5, 6, 10(2) and 17 (Chile).

69. CÓDIGO CIVIL, art. 57 (Arg.).

70. CÓDIGO CIVIL, art. 9 (Arg.).

71. *See* Decreto No. 839, 16 de Abril de 2009, Ley de Protección de la Niñez y Adolescencia, art. 19 (El. Sal.).

72. *See, e.g.*, Juzgado De Garantías (Cht.), "L. G. s/muerte dudosa" (Arg.) (conviction of an Argentinian abortion provider for causing the death of a pregnant woman and her unborn child).

73. *See* Tribunal Constitucional (Chile), Aug. 28, 2017, Requerimiento de inconstitucionalidad, 120.

74. *See* CIDH, *Derechos Humanos y Criminalización del Aborto en Sudamérica* at 27:05, 30:16 (reporting on 71 cases of abortion identified by law enforcement in Bolivia from 2006 to 2013, indicating that the great majority of these were not prosecuted).

75. *See, e.g.*, *Dictan prisión preventiva para doctor y enfermera* (reporting on arrest, prosecution, and conviction of an abortion provider and his nurse, as well as on the evidence found, i.e., abortion equipment, abortifacient drugs, fetal remains, and a dismembered fetus); *Honduras: Descubrimos las clínicas de la muerte en Comayagüela* (on related undercover investigation by journalists). *See* Cámara Nac. De Apelac. en lo Criminal y Correccional, sala 02, 26/01/17, "Birnie, Ronaldo Julián y otros s/procesamiento" (Arg.) (conviction of a group of individuals for illicit association to sell and distribute abortifacient drugs in Argentina). *See also* Schachar, *Guatemala Blocks Entry to Dutch Ship Providing Abortions* (reporting on detention of Dutch Women on Waves activists for distributing abortifacient drugs off the Guatemalan coast).

76. *See* Nuevo Código Procesal Penal [Criminal Procedure Code], art. 28(1) (Hond.).

77. *See* Código Penal, art. 128 (Hond.).

78. Código Penal, art. 263(2) (Bol.); Código Penal, art. 124 (Braz.); L. 599, julio 24, 2000, 44097 Diario Oficial, arts. 125–26 (Colom.); Código Orgánico Integral Penal, art. 149 (Ecuador); Código Penal, art. 119 (Costa Rica); Código Penal, art. 141 (Pan.); Surin. Penal Code, art. 355 (Surin.).

79. Código Penal, art. 88 (Arg.); Código Penal, art. 344 (Chile).

80. *See* Tribunal Constitucional, 28 agosto 2017, Requerimiento de inconstitucionalidad respecto del proyecto de ley que "regula la despenalización de la interrupción voluntaria del embarazo en tres causales," 13, 51 (Chile) (citing article 2 of the bill published in Boletín No. 9895-11, which reformed the criminal code yet kept penalties for any abortions outside of the three grounds established therein).

81. Código Penal, arts. 21–22 (Dom. Rep.); Código Penal, art. 133 (El Sal.); Code Pénal Haïtien, art. 262 (Haiti); Código Penal (Hond.); Criminal Code § 234 (Gren.); Comm. on the Rights of the Child, *Consideration of Reports Submitted by States Parties Under Article 44 of the Convention: Grenada*, ¶ 50, U.N. Doc. CRC/C/3/ADdd.55 (Nov. 28, 1997).

82. Código Penal, art. 143 (Nicar.); Código Penal, L. 3.440/08, art. 109(3) (Para.); Código Penal, art. 114 (Peru); Código Penal, art. 325 (Uru.).

83. Offences Against the Person Act, § 72 (Jam.).

84. Offences Against the Person Act, §§ 8, 56 (Dominica).

85. Código Penal, art. 88 (Arg.); Código Penal, art. 263 (Bol.); L. 599, julio 24, 2000, 44097 Diario Oficial, arts. 125–26 (Colom.); Criminal Code, § 247(1) (Gren.); Código Penal, art. 317 (Dom. Rep.); Código Penal, art. 133 (El Sal.); Código Penal, art. 135 (Guat.); Code Pénal, art. 262 (Haiti).

86. Código Orgánico Integral Penal, art. 149 (Ecuador); Código Penal, L. 641, ch. 2 (Nicar.); Código Penal, arts. 141–42 (Pan.); Código Penal, L. 3.440/08, art. 109(3) (Para.); Código Penal, art. 114 (Peru); Código Penal, art. 325 (Uru.); Código Penal, arts. 342–44 (Chile); Offences Against the Person Act, §§ 72, 73 (Jam.).

87. Offences Against the Person Act, § 57 (Dominica); Código Penal, art. 325 (Uru.); Código Penal, art. 267 (Bol.); Código Penal, art. 118(2) (Costa Rica); Offences Against the Person Act, § 72 (Jam.); Código Penal, art. 143 (Nicar.); Código Penal, art. 88 (Arg.); Código Penal, art. 115 (Peru); Surin. Penal Code, art. 357 (Surin.); Código Penal, art. 317 (Dom. Rep.); Código Orgánico Integral Penal, art. 149 (Ecuador); Código Penal, L. 3.440/08 art. 109(3) (Para.); Código Penal, art. 142 (Pan.); Código Penal, art. 135 (Guat.); Código Penal, art. 342 (Chile); Código Penal, art. 135 (El Sal.).

88. Código Penal, art. 317 (Dom. Rep.).

89. *See, e.g.*, Código Penal, arts. 349, 352 (Para.); Código Penal, art. 435 (Venez.); Código Penal, art. 86, 88 (Arg.); Código Penal, arts. 342–45 (Chile);

Código Penal, arts. 18, 317 (Dom. Rep.); Code Pénal, art. 262 (Haiti); Código Penal, art. 140 (Guat.); Surin. Penal Code, arts. 309(2), 358 (Surin.).

90. *See, e.g.*, Código Penal, art. 269 (Bol.); Surin. Penal Code, art. 309(2) (Surin.).

91. Offences Against the Person Act, § 73 (Jam.); Code Pénal, art. 262 (Haiti).

92. Código Penal, art. 127 (Hond.).

93. Código Penal, art. 381(4) (Costa Rica); Surin. Penal Code, art. 309(1) (Surin.).

94. Código Penal, art. 86 (Arg.); Código Penal, arts. 85, 86 (Arg.); Código Penal, arts. 47(1), 56, 69 (IV), 126 (Braz.); Código Penal, art. 135 (El Sal.); Código Penal, art. 140 (Guat.); Código Penal Federal, art. 331, Diario Oficial de la Federación, 14 de Agosto de 1931 (Mex.); *see* Código Penal, art. 143 (Nicar.); Código Penal, art. 117 (Peru); Surin Penal Code, art. 309(3) (Surin.).

95. Código Penal, art. 317 (Dom. Rep.).

96. Código Penal, art. 136 (El Sal.).

97. *See* Código Penal, art. 325 (Uru.).

98. Código Penal, art. 88 (Arg.); Código Penal, art. 263 (Bol.); Código Penal, art. 139 (Guat.); Code Pénal, art. 262 (Haiti).

99. Offences Against the Person Act, § 72 (Jam.).

100. Código Penal, L. 3.440/08, art. 109(3) (Para.).

101. Criminal Code, § 247(1) (Gren.).

102. Código Penal, art. 328(1) (Uru.); Código Penal, art. 265 (Bol.); Código Penal, art. 344 (Chile); Código Penal, art. 120 (Costa Rica).

103. Código Penal, art. 93(4) (Guat.); Código Penal, art. 328(1) (Uru.).

104. Código Penal Federal, art. 332, Diario Oficial de la Federación, 14 de Agosto de 1931 (Mex.).

105. *See* Decreto No. 144-83, 26 Sept. 1983, Código Penal, art. 129 (Hond.).

106. *See* Código Penal, art. 163 (Nicar.); Código Penal, art. 444 (Ecuador), and Código Orgánico Integral Penal, art. 148 (Ecuador) (not containing the *honoris causa* mitigating factor).

107. Código Penal, art. 120 (Peru).

108. Código Penal, art. 328(3) (Uru.).

109. Código Penal, art. 134 (Guat.).

110. Código Penal, art. 119 (Costa Rica).

111. Código Penal, art. 120 (Peru).

112. *See* Código Penal, art. 328(4) (Uru.); Caceres Sarubbi and Chavez de Talavera, *Paraguay*, 111.

113. Código Pena,l art. 127 (Braz.).

114. Código Penal, art. 85 (Arg.); Código Penal, art. 264 (Bol.); Código Penal, art. 118(2) (Costa Rica); Código Orgánico Integral Penal, art. 147 (Ecuador); Código Penal, art. 136 (Guat.); Código Penal, art. 349 (Para.); Código Penal, art. 115 (Peru); *see* Código Penal, art. 326 (Uru.).

115. *See, e.g.*, CÓDIGO PENAL, art. 349 (Para.).

116. *See, e.g.*, CÓDIGO PENAL, art. 86 (Arg.); CÓDIGO PENAL, art. 349 (Para.); CÓDIGO PENAL, arts. 18, 317 (Dom. Rep.); CODE PÉNAL, art. 262 (Haiti).

117. DECRETO-LEI No. 3.688, art. 20 (Braz.).

118. Offences Against the Person Act, § 56 (Dominica).

119. CÓDIGO PENAL, art. 317 (Dom. Rep.).

120. *See* Corte Suprema de Justicia de la Nación, 03/05/2002, "Portal de Belén—Asociación Civil sin Fines de Lucro c. Ministerio de Salud y Acción Social de la Nación s/amparo" (Arg.).

121. *Id.*

122. *See* Corte Suprema de Justicia, 30 agosto 2001, "Philippi Izquierdo c. Laboratorio Chile S.A."; Tribunal Constitucional, 18 abril 2008, Requerimiento de inconstitucionalidad deducido en contra de algunas disposiciones de las "Normas Nacionales sobre Regulación de la Fertilidad" (Chile).

123. CÓDIGO PENAL, art. 317 (Dom. Rep.).

124. Tribunal Constitucional, 18 abril 2008, Requerimiento de inconstitucionalidad deducido en contra de algunas disposiciones de las "Normas Nacionales sobre Regulación de la Fertilidad" (Chile).

125. Ley No. 20.418 fija normas sobre información, orientación y prestaciones en materia de regulación de la fertilidad, art. 4 (Chile). The original text is as follows: "En todo caso, no se considerarán anticonceptivos, ni serán parte de la política pública en materia de regulación de la fertilidad, aquellos métodos cuyo objetivo o efecto directo sea provocar un aborto.").

126. Tribunal Constitucional, 14 de junio 2006, "José Fernando Roser Rohde c. Instituto Nacional de Higiene y Medicina Tropical 'Leopold Izquieta Pérez' y el Ministro de Salud S/Acción de Amparo" (Ecuador).

127. Tribunal Constitucional, 16 de octubre 2009, ONG "Acción de Lucha Anticorrupción" Sentencia del Tribunal Constitucional, ¶ 12 (Peru).

128. Corte Suprema de Justicia de la República de Honduras, Dictamen Decreto 54-2009 (Hond.).

129. Secretaría de Salud, Acuerdo No. 2744 (21 de octubre 2009) (Hond.).

130. *See* Corte Suprema de Justicia, Constituida en Tribunal de Amparo, Dec. 8, 2017, Amparo 1434-2017, 11–12.

131. *See* Acceso a la justicia de mujeres víctimas de violencia sexual en Mesoamérica, ¶ 242.

132. Decreto No. 839, art. 19 (El. Sal.).

133. *See* Stith, *Nueva teoría constitucional y penal sobre el aborto en el derecho español*, 265 (contrasting *inexigibilidad* of criminal penalties for abortion in Spain and Germany to criminal defense grounds in American law, concluding that US law has no analogous defense to any criminal offense).

134. *See Decriminalize* (defining "[to] decriminalize" as "to remove or reduce the criminal classification or status of" or "to make (something that is illegal) legal by changing the law"; decriminalization of abortion on grounds of nonpun-

ishment of abortion in Latin America and the Caribbean is analogous to the first, rather than the second definition of "decriminalization").

135. *See* Tribunal Constitucional Plurinacional, Feb. 5, 2014, Sentencia 0206/2014, ¶ III(7), (8), (9) (Bol.) (distinguishing nonpunishment of abortions from a supposed right to abortion). *See also* Derecho a la vida del producto de la concepción (Mex.); Sala de lo Constitucional de la Corte Suprema de Justicia, Nov. 20, 2007, Inconstitucionalidad 18-98, ¶ V(A) (El Sal.).

136. *See* Tribunal Constitucional, 28 agosto 2017, Requerimiento de inconstitucionalidad respecto del proyecto de ley que "regula la despenalización de la interrupción voluntaria del embarazo en tres causales," 176–77 (Chile).

137. *See* Suprema Corte de Justicia de la Nación, Excusas absolutorias y excluyentes de responsabilidad, 592. The original text: "Las excusas absolutorias son causas que al dejar subsistente el carácter delictivo de la conducta o hecho tipificado como delito en la ley, impiden la aplicación de la pena, es decir, son aquellas en las que aun cuando se configure el delito, no permiten que se sancione al sujeto activo en casos específicos; en tanto que las excluyentes de responsabilidad se caracterizan por impedir que ésta surja. En otras palabras, en las citadas excluyentes la conducta tipificada en la ley no es incriminable desde el inicio; mientras que en las excusas absolutorias la conducta es incriminable, pero no sancionable, consecuentemente no relevan al sujeto activo de su responsabilidad en la comisión de la conducta típica, sino que determinan su impunibilidad."

138. *Id.*

139. Rep. of the Fourth World Conference on Women, para. 5.

140. *See* Javier Anzoátegui, *Muerte de una persona inocente* (analogy between nonpunishment of abortion and nonpunishable crime of robbery or fraud between close relatives in Argentinian law, where criminal penalties are waived even though the law recognizes that a crime has been committed). *See also* Alejandro Freeland, *¡Vengo a ejercer mi derecho a abortar!* (on distinction between a right to abortion and the exemption from criminal punishment for abortion of children conceived in rape in Argentina).

141. *See* Código Penal, art. 121 § 5 (Braz.).

142. *See* Código Penal, art. 165 (Nicar.) (eliminating "therapeutic" exception in Nicaragua, where the old criminal code required the opinion of at least three physicians and patient's consent).

143. *See* Tribunal Constitucional, 28 agosto 2017, Requerimiento de inconstitucionalidad respecto del proyecto de ley que "regula la despenalización de la interrupción voluntaria del embarazo en tres causales," 13, 247 (Chile).

144. Código Penal, art. 128 (Braz.).

145. Código Penal, art. 119 (Peru).

146. Código Penal, art. 86(1) (Arg.); Código Penal, art. 266 (Bol.); Código Penal, art. 121 (Costa Rica); Código Orgánico Integral Penal, art. 150(1) (Ecuador).

147. Código Penal, art. 328(3) (Uru.); Ley No. 18.987, Interrupción Voluntaria del Embarazo, art. 6(A) (Uru.).

148. Follow-Up Mechanism to the Belém do Pará Convention (MESECVI), Second Hemispheric Report on the Implementation of the Belém do Pará Convention, 40.

149. Código Penal Federal, art. 334 (Mex.).

150. Corte Constitucional, Sala Plena, mayo 10, 2006, Sentencia C-355/2006 (Colom.).

151. Medical Termination of Pregnancy Act, § 4(1)(a) and (5) (Barb.).

152. *Id.* § 6.

153. Código Penal, art. 144 (Pan.).

154. Código Penal, art. 266 (Bol.).

155. *See* Doe v. Bolton, 410 U.S. 179 (1973), where US Supreme Court mandated that any abortion restrictions must include a health exception regardless of the unborn child's gestational period. Health was broadly defined as allowing the consideration of nonmedical factors such as "emotional, psychological, familial, and the woman's age—relevant to the well-being of the patient." According to *Doe*, the applicability of the exception is to be determined by the woman and her physician, foreclosing any state oversight or enforcement of the exception over abortion providers.

156. Código Penal, art. 119 (Peru). *See also* Resolución Ministerial No. 486-2014, 526379, stating that health ministry regulations that define this exemption from criminal punishment as including situations of "risk of grave and permanent harm" to the mother's health. The regulations do stress that abortion should be a measure of last resort in such cases and that the guiding principle should be to protect both the mother and the unborn child's life and health. *But see* Guía Técnica Nacional para la Estandarización del Procedimiento de la Atención Integral de la Gestante en la Interrupción Voluntaria por Indicación Terapéutica del Embarazo Menor de 22 Semanas con Consentimiento Informado en el Marco de lo Dispuesto en el Artículo 119° del Código Penal, which sets forth the Peruvian national guidelines for therapeutic abortion, which regulate the medical protocols to follow for nonpunishment of abortions under exemptions for the life and health of the mother. The guidelines give a relatively liberal interpretation of the so-called therapeutic exemptions for criminal abortion. They do not at any point, however, mention these abortions as protected under constitutional law or under international human rights law; they make no reference to the American Convention either. *See also* Norma Técnica de Planificación Familiar, 34 (the Peruvian Technical Norms for Family Planning specifically indicate that "abortion shall not be considered a family planning method").

157. Código Penal, art. 86(1) (Arg.); Código Penal, art. 266 (Bol.); Código Penal, art. 121 (Costa Rica); Código Orgánico Integral Penal, art. 150(1) (Ecuador).

158. Ortiz Trujillo and Maqueda, "United Mexican States," 45.
159. Medical Termination of Pregnancy Act, § 6 (Barb.).
160. Criminal Code § 250(2) (Gren.).
161. Ley No. 18.987, Interrupción Voluntaria del Embarazo, art. 6(A) (Uru.).
162. Medical Termination of Pregnancy Act, § 4(1)(a) (Barb.).
163. *Id.* § 4(3). *See* Ortiz Trujillo and Maqueda, "United Mexican States," 44–46 (poverty may be a lawful ground for nonpunishment of abortion in the Mexican state of Yucatán).
164. Medical Termination of Pregnancy Act, § 6 (Barb.).
165. Código Penal, art. 266 (Bol.).
166. Corte Constitucional, Sala Plena, mayo 10, 2006,Sentencia C-355/2006, *supra* n.150 (Colom.).
167. *See, e.g.*, Código Penal, art. 142(1) (Pan.).
168. Medical Termination of Pregnancy Act, § 4(2) (Barb.); Código Penal, art. 266 (Bol.).
169. Código Penal, art. 128 (Braz.); Código Penal, art. 142(1) (Pan.); Ley No. 18.987, Interrupción Voluntaria del Embarazo, art. 6(C) (Uru.).
170. Código Penal, art. 128 (Braz.).
171. Lei No. 12.845, de 1º de Agosto de 2013, Dispõe sobre o atendimento obrigatório e integral de pessoas em situação de violência sexual [on the mandatory and comprehensive treatment of persons in situations of sexual violence] art. 3(IV) (Braz.).
172. Código Penal, art. 93(5) (Costa Rica).
173. *See* Follow-Up Mechanism to the Belém do Pará Convention (MESECVI), Second Hemispheric Report on the Implementation of the Belém do Pará Convention, 167.
174. Código Penal Federal, art. 333 (Mex.).
175. Decreto por el que reforman, derogan y adicionan diversas disposiciones de la Ley General de Víctimas, arts. 30(IX), 35. Executive regulations at the federal level have also authorized the abortion of those conceived in rape, the first of which became effective in 2009: the Norma Oficial Mexicana (Mexican Official Norm) NOM-046-SSA2-2005 on domestic, sexual, and gender violence against women, ordering authorities to provide emergency contraception to sexual assault victims. That regulation was amended in 2016 to mandate public health authorities to provide surgical abortions to alleged rape victims on request, including minors, with no judicial authorization or police report required. For further description and analysis of these regulations *see* Pérez Hernández, Bartolini Esparza, et al., Aborto: La Politica de un Estado Claudicante, 47–50.
176. Decreto por el que reforman, derogan y adicionan diversas disposiciones de la Ley General de Víctimas, art. 29.
177. Código Penal, art. 86(2) (Arg.).

178. *See* Farfán Bertrán, "Protection of the Human Right to Life in the Republic of Argentina," 139–40 (citing senate commission report on abortion exemptions).

179. Código Orgánico Integral Penal, art. 150(2) (Ecuador).

180. *See* Corte Suprema de Justicia de la Nación, 13/03/2012, "F.A.L. /s medida autosatisfactiva" [Fallos] (Arg.), Fallo F.A.L. (*see* "Considerando 29").

181. Pautas de Intervención en Abortos no Punibles, 1, 7.

182. *See* Corte Suprema de Justicia de la Nación, 13/03/2012, "F.A.L. /s medida autosatisfactiva" [Fallos] (Arg.), Fallo F.A.L. (see "Considerando 29").

183. *Argentina: Juristas: Fallo abortista de la Corte no aplica obligatoriamente* (Argentinian scholars on lack of binding effects of judgment on provinces other than Chubut and on *erga omnes* effects for *amparo* actions only); *see also Radio 10: El Puente*, an interview given by Supreme Court Justice Eugenio Raúl Zaffaroni in which Zaffaroni, who then went on to become an Inter-American Court judge, says, in regard to the F.A.L. decision: "No es obligatoria nuestra jurisprudencia en el resto de los tribunales" [our jurisprudence is not binding on the rest of the courts].

184. Decreto 1170-2012, del 21 de marzo de 2012, Poder Ejecutivo de la Provincia de Salta (accepting the F.A.L. judgment as a "recommendation" but clarifying that Supreme Court decisions apply only to parties to the dispute and have no effect on provincial authorities). *See also* Tozzi et al., *El activismo judicial en Latinoamérica*, 1–7.

185. *See* Iglesias, *Aborto no punible.*

186. *"Protocolo para la atención integral de las personas con derecho a la interrupción legal del embarazo" elaborado por el Programa Nacional de Salud Sexual y Procreación Responsable del Ministerio de Salud de la Nación (Selección)*, 53 (Protocol text and affidavit samples).

187. *See id.* 47 (*Resolución N° 02.233 del 25 de Octubre que deja sin efecto la Resolución N° 2095/2016 del Ministerio de Salud de la Provincia de Buenos Aires que aprobaba el "Protocolo para la atención integral de las personas con derecho a la interrupción legal del embarazo," aludiendo a motivos de revisión administrativa*, resolution rejecting the protocol's application in Buenos Aires). *See id.* 49 (initial resolution adopting the protocol in the province of Buenos Aires). *See also* Giunta and Mitre, *Argentina: Modificación del Código Civil y el impacto de la decisión de la Corte Suprema de la Nación.*

188. *See* Corte Constitucional, Sala Plena, mayo 10, 2006, Sentencia C-355/2006 (Colom.).

189. L. 599, julio 24, 2000, arts. 125–26 (Colom.).

190. Corte Constitucional, Sala Plena, mayo 10, 2006, Sentencia C-355/2006 (Colom.).

191. C.C. (Colom.), Sentencia T-585/10 (Colom.) (holding, among other things, that authorities may not require a police report where a request for abortion was made on the grounds of rape).

192. Código Penal, art. 144 (Pan.).

193. Ley No. 18.987, Interrupción Voluntaria del Embarazo, art. 6(C) (Uru.). *See* Código Penal, art. 328(2) (Uru.).

194. *See* Tribunal Constitucional, 28 agosto 2017, Requerimiento de inconstitucionalidad respecto del proyecto de ley que "regula la despenalización de la interrupción voluntaria del embarazo en tres causales," 4, 10–11 (citing article 3 of the bill, published in Boletín No. 9895-11).

195. *See id.* at 253.

196. CSJN (Arg.), Fallo F. A.L. (see "Considerando 29").

197. Medical Termination of Pregnancy Act, § 4(2) (Barb.).

198. Código Penal, art. 266 (Bol.). *See* Tribunal Constitucional Plurinacional, Feb. 5, 2014, Sentencia 0206/2014 (Bol.).

199. *Id.* at ¶ III(8)(8).

200. *Id.* at ¶ III(8)(8) and (9).

201. *See, e.g.*, Código Penal, art. 120(2) (Peru).

202. Ley No. 18.987, Interrupción Voluntaria del Embarazo, art. 6(B) (Uru.).

203. *See* Tribunal Constitucional, 28 agosto 2017, Requerimiento de inconstitucionalidad respecto del proyecto de ley que "regula la despenalización de la interrupción voluntaria del embarazo en tres causales," 4 (Chile) (citing article 2 of the bill, published in Boletín No. 9895-11).

204. See *id.* 247–50.

205. *See id.* 250–52.

206. Corte Constitucional, Sala Plena, mayo 10, 2006, Sentencia C-355/2006 (Colom.).

207. *See* Comunicado No. 42, Expdte. T 6612909—Sentencia SU-096/18, 2.

208. *Id.* 2–3.

209. *Id.* 3.

210. *Id.* 4–5.

211. Inteiro Teor do Acórdão, Argüição de Descumprimento de Preceito Fundamental 54, 4.

212.. *Id.*

213. *Cf.* de Santa Cruz Oliveira and Garoupa, *Stare Decisis and Certiorari Arrive to Brazil*, 556 (for more on the legal weight of Supreme Federal Court decisions).

214. *See* Inteiro Teor do Acórdão, Argüição de Descumprimento de Preceito Fundamental 54, 392, 396.

215. *Id.* at 246.

216. *Id.* at 247.

217. *Id.* at 267.

218. Código Penal Federal, art. 334 (Mex.); Código Penal, art. 144 (Pan.).

219. Código Penal, art. 144 (Pan.).

220. Medical Termination of Pregnancy Act, § 4(1)(b) (Barb.).

221. *Id.*

222. *Id.* at § 10.

223. *See* Follow-Up Mechanism to the Belém do Pará Convention (MESECVI), Second Hemispheric Report on the Implementation of the Belém do Pará Convention.

224. *See IACHR Urges El Salvador to End the Total Criminalization of Abortion* (where Commissioner Margarette Macaulay argues that decriminalization of abortion on four grounds—namely life, health, rape, and fetal disability—is required by international human rights law).

225. Ley que abroga Código del Sistema Penal/2018 (official act abolishing reformed Criminal Code). *See also Evo Morales aplaza nuevo Código Penal.*

226. *See Behind the scenes of Bolivia's Historic Abortion Law Change* (describing lobbying activities by Ipas and partnership with a national congresswoman).

227. *See* Proyecto de Ley 122/2017-2018, Código del Sistema Penal, art. 157 V(1) (Bol.).

228. *See Aprueban el artículo 153 del Código de Sistema Penal referido al aborto* (commenting on rejected proposals for broader economic exemptions for abortion, citing a congresswoman who promoted poverty as a ground for non-punishment of abortion). *See also* Peiró, *Insólito: Bolivia quiere legalizar el aborto "por pobreza"* (critiquing the bill's language that would have created exemptions for indigent women and women living in extreme poverty).

229. *See* Proyecto de Ley 122/2017-2018, art. 157 (VII).

230. *See El Presidente en ejercicio indicó que no se legalizó el aborto y reiteró que el artículo 205 protege la práctica profesional de los médicos*; *Bolivia lawmakers vote to ease right* [*sic*: word should be *Tight*] *abortion restrictions* (noting opposition from religious groups and public demonstrations by Catholic and evangelical churches in the country).

231. Ley Abrogatoria del Código del Sistema Penal Ley 1005 de 15 de diciembre de 2017 y Creación del Consejo Nacional de Reforma del Sistema Penal (see *Exposición de Motivos*).

232. *Id.*

233. *See* Código Penal, Art. 266 (Bol.).

234. *Asamblea Nacional negó la despenalización del aborto por violación en Ecuador.*

235. Ley No. 21.030, 14 de septiembre de 2017, Regula la despenalización de la interrupción voluntaria del embarazo en tres causales (this final version includes amendments made after the Constitutional court challenge).

236. *See* Tribunal Constitucional, 28 agosto 2017, Requerimiento de inconstitucionalidad respecto del proyecto de ley que "regula la despenalización de la interrupción voluntaria del embarazo en tres causales," 174 (citing World Health Organization statistics and noting exceptionally low maternal mortality rates in Chile). *See also* Koch, *Epidemiology of Abortion and Its Prevention in Chile*, 71 (showing that abortion-related maternal deaths decreased after Chile's adoption

of a full abortion ban in 1989, becoming "an exceptionally rare phenomenon in epidemiological terms").

237. *See* Tribunal Constitucional, 28 agosto 2017, Requerimiento de inconstitucionalidad respecto del proyecto de ley que "regula la despenalización de la interrupción voluntaria del embarazo en tres causales," 55, 168–69 (discussing Chile's full abortion ban since 1875; dissenting opinion pointing out that the health code did not permit abortion since 1931, as had been falsely stated, but permitted only a narrow therapeutic exception, far from a legislative intent to decriminalize direct abortion). *See id.* at 55 (indicating that the health code required authorization by three physicians in 1931 and was later modified to require the authorization of two physicians in 1967).

238. *See* Código Penal, art. 342 (Chile) (citing Ley No. 19927 art. 1(4), Enero 14, 2004, Diario Oficial [D.O.] (Chile)). *See also* Ley No. 18.826, 24 de agosto de 1989, Reemplázase el artículo 119 del Código Sanitario por el siguiente: "Artículo 119—No podrá ejecutarse ninguna acción cuyo fin sea provocar un aborto"; Código Sanitario, art. 119 (Chile). *See also* Tribunal Constitucional, 28 agosto 2017, Requerimiento de inconstitucionalidad respecto del proyecto de ley que "regula la despenalización de la interrupción voluntaria del embarazo en tres causales," 17, 169–71, 173 (where Chilean legislators and the dissenting judges interpret the health code provision to mean that only direct abortion had been prohibited therein and that indirect abortion for therapeutic purposes—that is, in situations of risk to the mother's life—had always been permitted in Chile).

239. *See, e.g., Triunfo pro-vida en Chile*; *Chile: Senate Defeats Pro-Abortion Bills. See Senado aprueba proyecto de aborto en tres causales tras maratónica jornada* (indicating the abortion bill passed by a narrow margin in the Chilean Senate).

240. *See* Tribunal Constitucional, 28 agosto 2017, Requerimiento de inconstitucionalidad respecto del proyecto de ley que "regula la despenalización de la interrupción voluntaria del embarazo en tres causales," 132–33, 172 (dissenting judges indicate that the bill allows direct abortion under this exemption because the exemption takes into account only the mother's life and interests, not the unborn child's; the relevant provision reads: ". . . so that the interruption of the pregnancy prevents risk to *her* life." They also point out that the law allows abortion to save the mother's life at any stage of pregnancy without factoring fetal viability into the medical analysis, even where delaying the abortion may be medically appropriate).

241. *See* Comisión Interamericana de Derechos Humanos, *Chile: Derechos sexuales y reproductivos.*

242. Rep. on Public Hearings from the 162nd Session.

243. *See* Constitución Política de la República de Chile, art. 19(1) (Chile). *See* Tribunal Constitucional, 28 agosto 2017, Requerimiento de inconstitucionalidad respecto del proyecto de ley que "regula la despenalización de la interrupción voluntaria del embarazo en tres causales," *supra* n.32 at 1–2, 134.

244. *See* Tribunal Constitucional, 28 agosto 2017, Requerimiento de inconstitucionalidad respecto del proyecto de ley que "regula la despenalización de la interrupción voluntaria del embarazo en tres causales," 86, 120.

245. *See id.* at 75–79, 86–89, 120–21.

246. *See id.* at 75–79, 86–89, 103–4, 120–21.

247. *See id.* at 48 and 147 (noting that binding precedent does not exist under Chilean constitutional law). *See* Corral, *El estatus del embrión humano en la sentencia sobre aborto del Tribunal Constitucional* (where Chilean law professor Hernán Corral Talciani points out that five judges disagreed with the majority on the finding that the human embryo lacked personhood and that, therefore, the holding may not create authoritative interpretation in this regard). *Cf.* Díaz de Valdés, *Chilean Constitutional Court's Abortion Decision* (where a law professor, the director of the Centre of Constitutional Justice at Universidad del Desarrollo, indicates that "it is hard to know whether there was a common rationale behind the 6–4 majority decision" because the judgment contained many separate opinions and minority votes).

248. *See* Tribunal Constitucional, 28 agosto 2017, Requerimiento de inconstitucionalidad respecto del proyecto de ley que "regula la despenalización de la interrupción voluntaria del embarazo en tres causales," 65–86, 87–88, 96–103.

249. *See id.* 60–62 (citing the judgment concerning the morning-after pill and the passage of a statute prohibiting abortifacients, suggesting that the precedent had been derogated because the morning-after pill was now being distributed by the government and commercially available).

250. *See id.* 62–64, 74–75, 89, 92, 102–3.

251. *See id.* 143–90, 163–64.

252. *See id.* 146–50, 165, 170.

253. *See id.* 164–65.

254. *See id.* 262 (original text is "atajo o 'pirueta' argumentativa").

255. *See id.* 51 (original Spanish text states: "en primer lugar, mantiene como delito el aborto").

256. *See id.* 239–40.

257. *See id.* 11–12, 125–34.

258. *See id.* 12, 131–34.

259. *See id.* 127.

260. *See id.* 13. *See* Singman and Gibson, *Planned Parenthood Under Investigation over Sale of Fetal Tissue.*

261. *See* Tribunal Constitucional, 28 agosto 2017, Requerimiento de inconstitucionalidad respecto del proyecto de ley que "regula la despenalización de la interrupción voluntaria del embarazo en tres causales," 12.

262. *See IACHR Welcomes Approval of Chilean Law Decriminalizing Abortion on Three Grounds*.

263. *Id.*

264. Comm. on the Elimination of Discrimination against Women, Concluding Observations on the Seventh Periodic Report of Chile, para. 39.

265. *See* Tribunal Constitucional, enero 18 de 2019, Rol No. 5572-18-CDS (Chile).

266. *See* Decreto 67 de junio de 2018, Aprueba reglamento para ejercer objeción de conciencia según lo dispuesto en el artículo 119 ter del Código Sanitario, arts. 2, 14, 29 (Chile).

267. *Id.* art. 13. *See also* Decreto con Fuerza de Ley 36, julio 10, 1980, Normas que se Aplicaran en los Convenios que celebren los Servicios de Salud.

268. *See* Decreto 67 de junio de 2018, Aprueba reglamento para ejercer objeción de conciencia según lo dispuesto en el artículo 119 ter del Código Sanitario, art. 24 (Chile).

269. Medical Termination of Pregnancy Act, § 13 (Barb.).

270. *Id.* § 4.

271. *Id.* § 4(2).

272. *Id.* § 12(b).

273. *Id.* §§ 8, 9, 14.

274. *See* Tribunal Constitucional, 28 agosto 2017, Requerimiento de inconstitucionalidad respecto del proyecto de ley que "regula la despenalización de la interrupción voluntaria del embarazo en tres causales," 7, 117 (identifying a duty of health care providers to provide the pregnant woman seeking an abortion with information on abortion alternatives).

275. *See id.* at 7.

276. *Id.* at 7–8.

277. *Id.* at 7–9 and 116 (indicating that counseling must be optional and nondissuasive).

278. *See id.* at 11–12, 125–34.

279. Procuraduría Delegada para la Defensa de los Derechos de la Infancia, la Adolescencia y la Familia, Informe de Vigilancia a la Implementación de la Sentencia C-355 de 2006, 188.

280. *Id.* at 125–26.

281. Ley No. 18.987, Interrupción Voluntaria del Embarazo, art. 3 (Uru.).

282. *Id.* art. 3.

283. Ley No. 18.987, Interrupción Voluntaria del Embarazo, art. 3 (Uru.).

284. *See, e.g.*, Medical Termination of Pregnancy Act, § 8(2) (Barb.); Código Penal, art. 128 (Braz.); Código Orgánico Integral Penal, art. 150 (Ecuador); Ley No. 18.987, Interrupción Voluntaria del Embarazo, art. 7 (Uru.).

285. Ley No. 18.987, Interrupción Voluntaria del Embarazo, art. 8 (Uru.).

286. Corte Constitucional, Sala Plena, mayo 10, 2006, Sentencia C-355/2006 (Colom.); L. 599, julio 24, 2000, arts. 125–26 (Colom.) (note the judgment's use of tendentious language referring to a younger child under fourteen years as "*woman* under fourteen years of age").

287. *See* Tribunal Constitucional, 28 agosto 2017, Requerimiento de inconstitucionalidad respecto del proyecto de ley que "regula la despenalización de la interrupción voluntaria del embarazo en tres causales," 5–7, 10–11.

288. *See id.* at 6, 53 (interpreting article 3 of the bill, published in Boletín No. 9895-11).

289. *See id.* at 4–6.

290. *See* Código Penal art. 263 (Bol.); Código Penal, art. 126 (Braz.).

291. Adam Gabbatt, *Jamaican Doctor Arrested for Performing Abortion on 12-Year-Old.*

292. Código Penal, art. 136 (El Sal.).

293. Código Penal, art. 126 (Braz.); Código Penal, art. 327 (Uru.).

294. *See* Ley No. 18.987, Interrupción Voluntaria del Embarazo (Uru.).

295. Letter from Tabaré Vázquez, Presidencia de la República Oriental del Uruguay, to Señor Presidente de la Asamblea General (Nov. 14, 2008) (Uru.).

296. *See* Ley No. 18.987, Interrupción Voluntaria del Embarazo, art. 6(A) (Uru.).

297. *Id.* art. 3.

298. *Id.* art. 6.

299. *Id.* art. 9.

300. *Id.* art. 1.

301. *Id.* arts. 10, 11 (institutional objection, however, is limited to health care institutions that conscientiously objected before the law became effective; objecting institutions must establish a referral mechanism in accordance with health department regulations).

302. *See* Franck, *Tribunal uruguayo suspende la aplicación de gran parte del decreto reglamentario del aborto por afectar el derecho a la objeción de conciencia.*

303. Ministerio de Salud & Presidencia Uruguay, *Interrupción Voluntaria Embarazo (IVE) 2013–2017.*

304. *Id.*

305. Rankin, *Controversial Ruling Threatens Abortion Access in Uruguay and Beyond.*

306. 1ª Turma afasta prisão preventiva de acusados da prática de aborto (majority opinion).

307. *See id.* (Judge Marco Aurelio's grounds for dissent, with which Fux concurred, were based on the following considerations: (1) the accused were first-time offenders, had a clean criminal background, were employed, and were permanent residents of the district in question; (2) to hold them in protective custody was disproportionate because even if the accused were convicted they could serve their sentence in open conditions; and (3) the accused made no attempt to escape when they were caught red-handed).

308. *See id.* at para. 25.

309. *Id.* at paras. 29–30.

310. *Id.* at paras. 32–48.
311. *See id.* at para 46.
312. *See id.* at para. 28.
313. *Cf.* Bruno, *Bringing Uniformity to Brazilian Court Decisions* (for more on Brazilian jurisprudence and binding effects of *súmula vinculante*).
314. ADPF No. 442.
315. Decisão de Convocação de Audiência Pública (reporting that Justice Rosa Weber schedules a public hearing on ADPF 442 regarding first-trimester abortion). *See ADPF 442, STF* (public hearing videos on Supreme Federal Court's official YouTube channel).
316. *See Advogada-Geral da União manifesta-se pela improcedência do pedido formulado pelo arguente*, 10, 20–22 (citing bills on liberalization or restriction of abortion).
317. *Id.* at 12 (original text in Portuguese says: "um critério excludente de tipicidade formal não estabelecido pelo legislador").
318. Decreto por el que reforman, derogan y adicionan diversas disposiciones de la Ley General de Víctimas (Mex.). *See* Código Penal Para el Estado de Aguascalientes, art. 101 (Mex.); Código Penal Para el Estado de Baja California, art. 132 (Mex.); Código Penal Para el Estado de Baja California Sur, art. 249 (Mex.); Código Penal Para el Estado de Chihuahua, art. 143 (Mex.); Código Penal Para el Estado de Coahuila (Mex.); Código Penal Para el Estado de Colima, art. 187 (Mex.); Código Penal Para el Estado Libre de México, art. 248 (Mex.); Código Penal Para el Estado de Guanajuato, art. 158 (Mex.); Código Penal Para el Estado de Guerrero, art. 116 (Mex.); Código Penal Para el Estado de Hidalgo, art. 154 (Mex.); Código Penal Para el Estado Libre y Soberano de Jalisco, art. 227 (Mex.); Código Penal Para el Estado de Michoacán, art. 285 (Mex.); Código Penal Para el Estado de Morelos, art. 115 (Mex.); Código Penal Para el Estado de Nayarit, art. 335 (Mex.); Código Penal Para el Estado de Nuevo León, art. 327 (Mex.); Código Penal Para el Estado de Oaxaca, art. 312 (Mex.); Código Penal de Defensa Social Para el Estado Libre y Soberano de Puebla, art. 339 (Mex.); Código Penal Para el Estado de Querétaro, art. 136 (Mex.); Código Penal de Defensa Social Para el Estado Libre y Soberano de Quintana Roo, art. 92 (Mex.); Código de Defensa Social Para el Estado de San Luis Potosí, art. 128 (Mex.); Código de Defensa Social Para el Estado de Sinaloa, art. 154 (Mex.); Código de Defensa Social Para el Estado de Sonora, art. 265 (Mex.); Código de Defensa Social Para el Estado de Tabasco, art. 130 (Mex.); Código de Defensa Social Para el Estado de Tamaulipas, art. 356 (Mex.); Código de Defensa Social Para el Estado de Yucatán, art. 389 (Mex.); Código de Defensa Social Para el Estado de Zacatecas, art. 310 (Mex.). *See, e.g.*, Código de Defensa Social Para el Estado de Chiapas, art. 178 (Mex.).
319. *See* Decreto por el que reforman, derogan y adicionan diversas disposiciones de la Ley General de Víctimas (Mex.) (The district had previously adopted

an act that created several provisions for nonpunishment of abortion in Mexico City ("health of the mother," rape, eugenic abortion, and error in artificial insemination), coined "Ley Robles" for its author, Rosario Robles Berlanga, governor of Mexico City at the time). *See also* Decreto que Reforma los Artículos 145 y 148 del Nuevo Código Penal para el Distrito Federal y se Adicionan los Artículos 16 bis 6 y 16 bis 7 a la Ley de Salud para el Distrito Federal, Gaceta Oficial de la Federación (the district then turned these into provisions for nonpunishment of abortion after the first trimester by amending its criminal code and health code again in 2003).

320. SCJN (Mex.), Acción de inconstitucionalidad 146/2007 y su acumulada 147/2007, 8–9.

321. *See id.* 1–208.

322. *See id.* 394.

323. *Id.* 174–75.

324. *See, e.g.*, Reforma y Adición al Artículo 7, Fracción XI, de la Constitución Política del Estado Libre y Soberano de Nayarit, 2–3 (see Exposición de Motivos).

325. *See* Pérez Hernández, Bartolini Esparza, et al., ABORTO: LA POLÍTICA DE UN ESTADO CLAUDICANTE, 108, 111 (citing government statistics provided by Mexico City's health secretariat; discussing their limited accuracy due to the lack of statistical reporting on the part of private abortion providers).

326. Barberis, *El derecho a la vida en el pacto de San José de Costa Rica*, 12.

327. *See* Inteiro Teor do Acórdão, Argüição de Descumprimento de Preceito Fundamental 54, 1 (2018 decision reiterating Constitutional Court's jurisprudence, invoking international obligations arising out of the CEDAW Convention).

328. Corte Constitucional, Sala Plena, mayo 10, 2006, Sentencia C-355/2006 (Colom.).

329. *See* Corte Constitucional, Sala Plena, marzo 17, 1994, Sentencia C-133/1994; Corte Constitucional, Sala Plena, enero 23, 1997, Sentencia C-013/1997 (Colom.); Corte Constitucional, Sala Plena, junio 20, 2001, Sentencia C-647/2001 (Colom.).

330. *See also* Corte Constitucional, Sala Plena, abril 24, 1997, Sentencia C-213/1997 (Colom.); Corte Constitucional, Sala Novena, mayo 18, 1998, Sentencia T-223/98 (Colom.); Corte Constitucional, Sala Tercera, julio 8, 2005, Sentencia T-727/05 (Colom.); Corte Constitucional, Sala Quinta, junio 16, 2005, Sentencia T-639/05 (Colom.); Corte Constitucional, Sala Novena, febrero 17, 2005, Sentencia T-128/05 (Colom.); Corte Constitucional, Sala Sexta, septiembre 9, 2004, Sentencia T-872/04 (Colom.); Corte Constitucional, Sala Novena, mayo 20, 2004, Sentencia T-501/04 (Colom.); Corte Constitucional, Sala Octava, enero 29, 2004, Sentencia T-063/04 (Colom.).

331. *See* Corte Constitucional, Sala Plena, mayo 10, 2006, Sentencia C-355/2006 (Colom.), Salvamento de Voto de los Magistrados Marco Gerardo Monroy Cabra y Rodrigo Escobar Gil. *See also* Mora Restrepo, *Justicia constitucional y arbitrariedad de los jueces*, 60–65 (jurisprudential and philosophical

critique of the Colombian Constitutional Court's decisions on abortion, explaining evolution of its jurisprudence); *Entrevista sobre el aborto con el Dr. Gabriel Mora-Restrepo, experto en Derecho Constitucional en Colombia* (for an academic critique of the C-355 holding).

332. *See* Corte Constitucional, Sala Plena, mayo 10, 2006, Sentencia C-355/2006, para. 7 (Colom.) The original text states: "[D]e las normas constitucionales e internacionales no se deduce un mandato de despenalización del aborto ni una prohibición a los legisladores nacionales para adoptar normas penales en este ámbito. De tal forma que el Congreso dispone de un amplio margen de configuración de la política pública en relación con el aborto."

333. *See* Corte Constitucional, Sala Plena, mayo 10, 2006, Sentencia C-355/2006 (Colom.).

334. *See* Corte Constitucional, Sala Plena, mayo 10, 2006, Sentencia C-355/2006 (Colom.), Salvamento de Voto de los Magistrados Marco Gerardo Monroy Cabra y Rodrigo Escobar Gil.

335. *See* L. 270, art. 48(2) (Colom.) (establishing that *sentencias de tutela* have binding effects on the parties only); L. 2591, art. 34 (Colom.) (requiring ratification of the Constitutional Court *en banc* for creation of jurisprudence). *See also* López Medina, *El Derecho de los Jueces*, 59–60 (explaining the relative legal weight and authoritativeness of *sentencias de tutela* in terms of creating *erga omnes* obligations).

336. *See* chapter 2 concerning Matter of B. regarding El Salvador, Provisional Measures.

337. Constitutional Court, Sentencia T-841/11 (Colom.).

338. *See* Constitutional Court, junio 9, 2016, Sentencia T-301/2016 (Colom.) (the plaintiff in that case requested a "feticide," given the fetus's advanced gestational age, on the grounds of her fetal disability (hydrocephaly)); Comunicado No. 42, Expdte. T 6612909—Sentencia SU-096/18. Here, according to dissenting opinions, the ground of fetal disability involved an uncertain diagnosis of a milder form of disability, namely brain malformations that might cause intellectual disability. Several medical providers declined to perform the procedure. The child was born on September 9, 2015, and survived until at least June 2016, when the decision was issued. *See also* Constitutional Court, Sentencia T-841/12 (Colom.) (mandating, among other things, that immediate abortions be provided within five days of a request, particularly abortions on disabled women, at a parent's request). *See also* the following judgments: Constitutional Court, Sentencia T-209/08 (Colom.); Constitutional Court, Sentencia T-988/07 (Colom.); Constitutional Court, Sentencia T-946/08 (Colom.); Constitutional Court, Sentencia T-585/10 (Colom.) (holding, among other things, that authorities may not require a police report where a request for abortion was made on the grounds of rape and that no medical report or opinion must be required in abortion requests involving the mother's health or life, even where the said medical information would address the risks of late-term abortions to a mother's health).

339. *See* Comunicado No. 42, Expdte. T 6612909—Sentencia SU-096/18, 3.

340. *Id.* at 7.

341. *Id.* at 3.

342. *Id.* (original language text is as follows: "[E]n ese sentido, las causales de despenalización del aborto establecidas por la sentencia C-355 de 2006, deben ajustarse a la protección de la vida del que está por nacer, la que se incrementa con el paso de las semanas de gestación y en particular a partir de la semana 24 cuando el feto alcanza su viabilidad autónoma").

343. *Id.* at 5.

344. *See* Constitutional Court, Sentencia T-946/08 (Colom.); Constitutional Court, Sentencia T-388/13 (Colom.) (limiting conscientious objection to physicians and excluding other medical and administrative personnel, as well as institutions that may object to abortions being performed on their premises, among other things).

345. *See* Corte Constitucional, febrero 28, 2012, Auto 038/12.

346. Comunicado No. 56.

347. *See* Constitutional Court, Sentencia T-627/12 (Colom.).

348. *See* Constitutional Court, Sentencia T-585/10, para. 19 (Colom.) (original text states: "[Resulta] innegable que, a partir de la Sentencia C-355 de 2006, surgió en Colombia *un verdadero derecho a la interrupción voluntaria del embarazo* en cabeza de las mujeres que se encuentran incursas *en las tres hipótesis despenalizadas*").

349. *Id.* para. 22 (original text states: "[Su] reconocimiento [implicó] el surgimiento de un conjunto de obligaciones de respeto y de garantía en cabeza del Estado y de los prestadores y promotores del servicio público de salud").

350. *See* Constitutional Court, junio 9, 2016, Sentencia T-301/2016 (see resolutory paragraph 3).

351. *See* Comunicado No. 42, Expdte. T 6612909—Sentencia SU-096/18, 1.

352. *Id.* at 2. The original text states: "La Corte Constitucional reitera los lineamientos establecidos en la sentencia C-355 de 2006, *sin ir más alla de las causales previstas en esta providencia* para aplicar la IVE y de las condiciones dispuestas para ello. Al mismo tiempo exhortó al Congreso de la República para que en ejercicio de su potestad de configuración legislativa, regule la materia."

353. *See* Corte Constitucional, Sala Plena, mayo 10, 2006, Sentencia C-355/2006, para. 7 (Colom.). *See also* Comunicado No. 42, Expdte. T 6612909—Sentencia SU-096/18, 2.

354. Corte Constitucional, Sala Plena, mayo 10, 2006, Sentencia C-355/2006 (Colom.) (see *Consideraciones Finales*).

355. Suprema Corte de Justicia de la Nación, Segunda Sala, 4 de Abril de 2018, Amparo en revisión 601/2017 (Mex.).

356. *Id.* at 2, 13, 33.

357. See Decreto por el que reforman, derogan y adicionan diversas disposiciones de la Ley General de Víctimas, arts. 30(IX), 35.

358. Suprema Corte de Justicia de la Nación [SCJN], Segunda Sala, 4 de Abril de 2018, Amparo en revisión 601/2017 (Mex.).

359. *Id.* at 7.

360. *Id.* at 8–9.

361. See Suprema Corte de Justicia de la Nación [SCJN], Primera Sala, 2 de Diciembre de 2015, Amparo en revisión 442/2015 (Mex.). The First Chamber of the Mexican Supreme Court had previously heard another *amparo en revisión* in 2015, involving a pregnant minor and her mother, whose partner had sexually assaulted the child. The minor was denied an abortion at almost twenty weeks gestation in the state of Hidalgo, due to the state's ninety-day statutory limit for abortions of those conceived in rape. The mother then took the pregnant child for an abortion in Mexico City, where the late-term abortion was authorized on the basis of health risks to the pregnant child. The mother of the pregnant child and her legal representatives initially pursued constitutional remedies, claiming that the state's failure to provide the abortion violated the national constitution. No request for the prosecution and conviction of the perpetrator was made in that *amparo* either. The girl's mother, however, eventually withdrew her claim, indicating that the whole process had negative psychological effects on the child and the entire family; therefore, the chamber never reached a finding on the claim's merits.

362. Suprema Corte de Justicia de la Nación, Segunda Sala, 4 de Abril de 2018, Amparo en revisión 601/2017, 23–30.

363. *Id.* 30–35.

364. *Id.* 37–50.

365. Tribunal Constitucional Plurinacional, Feb. 5, 2014, Sentencia 0206/2014, ¶ III(8)(7) (Bol.). *See also* chapter 2 section II(D)(6).

366. *Id.* at ¶ III(8)(8).

367. *Id.* at ¶ III(8)(7).

368. *Id.* at ¶ III(7), (8) and (9).

369. *Id.* at ¶ III(8)(7) (the judgment also cites relevant precedent protecting the human being from the moment of conception onward in Judgments 1112/2012, 1104/2012, 0424/2012 and 2567/2010).

370. *Id.* at ¶ III(8)(8) and (9).

371. *Id.*

372. *See* Tribunal Constitucional, 28 agosto 2017, Requerimiento de inconstitucionalidad respecto del proyecto de ley que "regula la despenalización de la interrupción voluntaria del embarazo en res causales," 51 (Chile).

373. *See* Tribunal Constitucional, 28 agosto 2017, Requerimiento de inconstitucionalidad respecto del proyecto de ley que "regula la despenalización de la interrupción voluntaria del embarazo en tres causales," 239–40, 243 (Chile) (concurring judge Domingo Hernández Emparanza clarifies that the Constitutional Court is not creating a right to abortion by upholding the three criminal punishment exemptions). *See also id.* 267–68 (where dissenting judge Romero Guzmán reaches a similar conclusion).

374. *See* Sala de lo Constitucional de la Corte Suprema de Justicia, Nov. 20, 2007, Inconstitucionalidad 18-98, ¶ V(1)(C) (El Sal.). *See also* Sala de lo Constitucional de la Corte Suprema de Justicia, May 28, 2013, Amparo 310-2013, ¶¶ V(1)(A), VI(1)(A) (El Sal.). *See* also Constitución Política de la República de El Salvador, art. 1 (El Sal.).

375. *See* Sala de lo Constitucional de la Corte Suprema de Justicia, Nov. 20, 2007, Inconstitucionalidad 18-98, ¶¶ V(1)(C), V(2)(A) (El Sal.). *See also* Sala de lo Constitucional de la Corte Suprema de Justicia, May 28, 2013, Amparo 310-2013, ¶¶ V(1)(A), VI(1)(A).

376. *See* Sala de lo Constitucional de la Corte Suprema de Justicia, Nov. 20, 2007, Inconstitucionalidad 18-98, ¶ VI (El Sal.).

377. *See* Sala de lo Constitucional de la Corte Suprema de Justicia, May 28, 2013, Amparo 310-2013, Voto particular concurrente del Magistrado Rodolfo Gonzalez Bonilla, ¶ III(3).

378. *See* Corte Suprema de Justicia, Constituida en Tribunal de Amparo, Dec. 8, 2017, Amparo 1434-2017, 13–14.

379. *Id.* at 14–15.

380. *Id.* at 15.

381. *Id.* at 16–17.

382. *Id.* at 15, 21.

383. *See, e.g., Listado actualizado* (describing seventeen legislative bills to provide pregnant women with welfare assistance, including financial, material and nonmaterial resources during pregnancy and after childbirth).

384. *See Proyecto de Ley, Interrupción Voluntaria del Embarazo*, arts. 3, 5–8, 10–11, 13.

385. *Id.* art. 3.

386. *Id.* arts. 3, 7, 18.

387. *Id.* art 16.

388. World Health Organization, *Safe Abortion*, 37–46.

389. *Id.* 40.

390. *Proyecto de Ley, Interrupción Voluntaria del Embarazo*, art. 14.

391. *Id.* arts. 11, 13.

392. *Id.* arts. 13, 15, 17.

393. *Id.* arts. 16, 19–21.

394. *Id.* art. 9. *See also Toller—Exposición sobre Proyecto de Ley de IVE* (pointing out the bill's reference to the language in Ley 26.061 and its corresponding regulation in Decreto 415/06).

395. *See Proyecto de Ley, Interrupción Voluntaria del Embarazo*, arts.12, 14.

396. *Id.* art. 23.

397. *See* Comm. on the Rights of the Child, *Concluding Observations on the Combined Fifth and Sixth Periodic Reports of Argentina*, para. 32(b) (the committee recommends that Argentina "[e]nsure access to safe abortion and post-abor-

tion care services for adolescent girls, ensuring that their views are always heard and given due consideration as part of the decision-making process"). *See also ONU felicitó a la Argentina por debatir el aborto y respaldó la legalización* (reporting on letter from working group's chair Ivana Radačić, encouraging legislators to adopt the bill and to reject religious arguments against abortion).

398. *See Annex: Public Hearings of the 168 Period of Sessions; Right to Sexual and Reproductive Health for Women in Argentina.*

399. *See* Canteros et al., *Aborto en Argentina y en la región.*

400. *See Joint Statement, IACHR Hearing on Abortion,* which reported that "[m]any of the arguments utilized against the legalization of abortion in the Chamber of Deputies [Argentina's lower house of Congress] make spurious claims regarding international human rights law. For this reason, [we] asked that the IACHR orient the legislative debate in Argentina and reinforce international standards regarding the right [to abortion]." *See also Annex: Public Hearings of the 168 Period of Sessions; Right to Sexual and Reproductive Health for Women in Argentina* (where IACHR supports abortion rights advocates' claims and urges Argentinian legislators to pass the abortion bill).

401. See *Oradores en Contra* (speeches that invoke the American Convention against legalization of abortion in Argentina include those by Nestor Pedro Sagüés, emeritus law professor at the University of Buenos Aires and author of multiple treatises on Argentinian constitutional law; Manuel García Mansilla, dean of Universidad Austral; María Inés Franck, law professor at Pontifical Catholic University of Argentina; and Marisa Herrera, Gregorio Badeni, and María Angélica Gelli, law professors at the University of Buenos Aires School of Law).

402. *See* Position statement, March 22, 2018 (Arg.).

403. *See Votos, Inforgrafía; Acta de votación, Sesión de la Cámara alta 08/08/2018.*

404. *See* Williams Becker and Lafferriere, *Análisis del predictamen de legalización del aborto* (referring to Bill 2492-D-2017).

405. *See* Sala de lo Constitucional de la Corte Suprema de Justicia, Nov. 20, 2007, Inconstitucionalidad 18-98, ¶ V(2)(A).

406. *See* Center for Reproductive Rights, The World's Abortion Laws.

407. *See* Tribunal Constitucional, 28 agosto 2017, Requerimiento de inconstitucionalidad respecto del proyecto de ley que "regula la despenalización de la interrupción voluntaria del embarazo en tres causales,"173.

408. *See* subsection above entitled "Indirect Abortion Distinguished" (explaining distinction between direct and indirect abortion). *See also* discussion in chapter 2 of provisional measures in *Beatriz.*

409. *See* Código Penal, arts. 342–45 (Chile); Código Penal, art. 317 (Dom. Rep.); Código Penal, arts. 133–41 (El Sal.); Code Pénal, art. 262 (Haiti); *see* Código Penal, arts. 126–32 (Hond.); Código Penal, arts. 143–49 (Nicar.); Suriname Penal Code, arts. 309(1), 355–58 (Surin.). *Cf.* U.N. Committee on the

Elimination of Discrimination Agnst [*sic*] Women, *Third Periodic Report of States Parties, Suriname*, 46. *See also Derecho de Familia y Niñez* (constitutional provisions recognizing a right to life from conception were adopted in 1980 in Chile (signed the American Convention in 1969, ratified it in 1990), in 1982 in Honduras (signed the American Convention in 1969, ratified it in 1977), in 1983 in El Salvador (signed the American Convention in 1969, ratified it in 1978), and in 2010 in Dominican Republic (signed the American Convention in 1977, ratified it in 1978)).

410. *See, e.g.*, Sala de lo Constitucional de la Corte Suprema de Justicia, Nov. 20, 2007, Inconstitucionalidad 18-98, ¶ V(2)(A)–(B) (El Sal.) (where El Salvador's Supreme Court distinguished between termination of pregnancy for therapeutic purposes and abortion, concluding that the first is not understood to be an abortion in that jurisdiction and is therefore legally allowed).

411. *See Comisión multipartidaria del Código Penal decide no despenalizar figura del aborto.*

412. *See* Offences Against the Person Act, § 8(1) (Dominica); Código Penal, art. 139 (Guat.); Código Penal, L. 3.440/08, art. 109 (4) (Para.).

413. Código Penal, L. 3.440/08, art. 109(4) (Para.). The code's language specifically says fetal death may legally occur only indirectly, not directly, under such circumstances: "Artículo 109. Muerte indirecta por estado de necesidad en el parto. No obra antijurídicamente el que causara *indirectamente* la muerte del feto mediante actos propios del parto si ello, según los conocimientos y las experiencias del arte médico, fuera *necesario* e *inevitable* para desviar un peligro serio para la vida o la salud de la madre" (emphasis added).

414. U.N., Dept. of Economic and Social Affairs, Population Division, *Abortion Policies*, vol. 1, p. 137.

415. National Assembly of the Republic of Nicaragua, La Gaceta, Diario Oficial [D.O.], Ley No. 603, at p. 224 (citing Código Penal, arts. 143–49 (Nicar.)).

416. *See* Código Penal, arts. 130–31 (1985) (Hond.).

417. *Id.*

418. *See* Decreto No. 13-85, 13 Feb. 1985, Código Penal (Hond.).

419. *See* Reglamento de Aplicación de la Ley del Seguro Social, art. 81 (Hond.).

420. *See* Code Pénal, art. 262 (Haiti); Comm. on the Elimination of Discrimination Against Women, *Consideration of Reports Submitted by States Parties Under Article 18 of the Convention on the Elimination of All Forms of Discrimination Against Women, Combined Initial, Second, Third, Fourth, Fifth, Sixth and Seventh Periodic Reports of States Parties: Haiti*, 89.

421. *See* Código Penal, art. 317 (Dom. Rep.). *See also* Comm. on the Elimination of Discrimination Against Women, *Consideration of Reports Submitted by States Parties Under Article 18 of the Convention on the Elimination of All Forms of Discrimination Against Women, Third Periodic Reports of States Parties: Suriname*, 48.

422. *"Grave Regression for Dominican Women and Girls' Right to Health"* (stating, "We urge Dominican authorities to repeal all restrictive legal provisions regarding abortion, especially in cases of risk to the health, including mental health, of the woman or girl, of rape and incest and of fatal impairment of the foetus," and regretting that "[t]he Dominican Republic did not seize this key moment of legislative amendment to reaffirm its commitment towards the elimination of gender discrimination in its legislation and to advance women's and adolescents' sexual and reproductive rights"). *See* Amaya, *Presidente de Dominicana pide que se permita el aborto en tres situaciones.*

423. *See* Tribunal Constitucional, Dec. 17, 2015, Sentencia TC/0599/15.

424. *Id.* 113–33.

425. *See Despite 20-Year Wait, New Penal Code Keeps Old Abortion Ban.*

426. *See* Estévez and Méndez, *Rechazan informe sobre penalización del aborto.*

427. *See No al aborto, ratifica comisión del CN que no lo despenalizó.*

428. *See Honduras Needs Progressive Reform of Abortion Law to Advance Women's Human Rights, Say UN Experts.*

429. *See Presidente de Honduras rechaza que el Parlamento despenalice el aborto.*

430 . *See Comisión multipartidaria del Código Penal decide no despenalizar figura del aborto.*

431. *See* Mejía, *Honduras: Congreso Nacional aprobo seguir con la penalización del aborto* (reporting a vote of 79–9, with 6 abstentions, in favor of the committee report rejecting the criminal code reform on abortion).

432. Colegio Médico de Honduras, Comisión de Ética y Práctica Médica, Oficio No. SAEC-32-2017.

433. *See* Malkin, *Supporters of El Salvador's Abortion Ban Foil Efforts to Soften It.*

434. *See IACHR Urges El Salvador to End the Total Criminalization of Abortion.*

435. *See* Sala de lo Constitucional de la Corte Suprema de Justicia, May 28, 2013, Amparo 310-2013, ¶¶ V(I)(A), VI(1)(A)(b) (El Sal.). *See id.*, Voto disidente en el caso B.C. Magistrado Florentín Meléndez.

436. Constitución Política de la República de El Salvador, arts. 1, 2 (El Sal.). *See* Sala de lo Constitucional de la Corte Suprema de Justicia, Sept. 21, 2011, Amparo 166-2009 (El Sal.).

437. *See* Sala de lo Constitucional de la Corte Suprema de Justicia, Nov. 20, 2007, Inconstitucionalidad 18-98, ¶ I(1) (El Sal.).

438. *Id.* at ¶ V(2)(A).

439. *Id.* at ¶¶ IV(1)(C), V(1).

440. *Id.* at ¶ IV(1)(C).

441. *Id.* at ¶¶IV(1)(C)–IV(2)(A), V(1), V(2)(B).

442. *Id.* at ¶¶IV(3), V(2).

443. *Id.* at ¶¶V(1), V(2)(B).

444. *See* Sala de lo Constitucional de la Corte Suprema de Justicia, April 13, 2011, Inconstitucionalidad 67-10 (El Sal.).

445. *Id.* at 2, 4, 5, 6.

446. *Id.* at 4–5, 6

447. *See* Sala de lo Constitucional de la Corte Suprema de Justicia, May 28, 2013, Amparo 310-2013, ¶¶ V(1)(A), VI(1)(A) (El Sal.).

448. *See id.* ¶ V(1)(A). *See also* CÓDIGO PENAL arts. 27, 134, 137 (El Sal.).

449. *See* Sala de lo Constitucional de la Corte Suprema de Justicia, Nov. 20, 2007, Inconstitucionalidad 18-98, ¶ V(1), V(2)(B), VI (2007) (El Sal.).

450. *See* CONSTITUCIÓN POLÍTICA DE LA REPÚBLICA DE GUATEMALA, art. 3 (Guat.). *See also* Corte Suprema de Justicia, Constituida en Tribunal de Amparo, Dec. 8, 2017, Amparo 1434-2017, 4–5, 7–8, 22–23 (Guat.).

451. *See* Corte Suprema de Justicia, Constituida en Tribunal de Amparo, Dec. 8, 2017, Amparo 1434-2017, 19–24 (Guat.).

452. *Id.* 2–3, 11–12.

453. *Id.* 8, 12.

454. *Id.* 12–14.

455. *Id.* 13–15. *See also* chapter 3.

456. *Id.* 4–5, 7–8, 22–23.

457. *Id.* 15, 21.

458. *Id.* 6–10.

459. *Id.* 16–17.

460. *Id.* 2–3, 11, 17.

461. *Id.* 17.

462. *Id.* 18.

463. Ley de Amparo, art. 43 (Guat.).

464. Vienna Convention on the Law of Treaties art. 31(3)(b) (emphasis added) ("any *subsequent* practice in the application of the treaty which establishes the agreement of the parties regarding its interpretation").

465. Baby Boy v. United States, paras. §§ 18(d)–(f).

466. *Id.* §§ 18(e)–(f), 26.

467. *Id.* § 18(e).

468. *See* Baby Boy v. United States, para. § 14(c) (those exemptions are no longer exonerating factors but only mitigating factors, as explained in previous sections, and in some jurisdictions they have been entirely abolished).

469. *See, e.g., Parlamento rechaza despenalización del aborto terapéutico* (indicating that an overwhelming majority of the Sandinista party voted no to the creation of a therapeutic abortion exception to the country's full abortion ban).

470. *See* Tanner, *Interview with Judge Antônio A. Cançado Trindade*, 68.

471. Bélanger and Flynn, *Persistence of Induced Abortion in Cuba*, 13–26.

472. *See Abortion in Latin America and the Caribbean.*

473. *Id.*

474. Código Penal, art. 432–36 (Venez.). Signatories and Ratifications: American Convention on Human Rights.

475. *See* Baby Boy v. United States, para. § 14(c).

476. *See* Gonzales v. Carhart, 550 U.S. 124 (2007).

477. *Accord.* Maher v. Roe, 432 U.S. 464 (1977); Beal v. Doe, 432 U.S. 438 (1977); Poelker v. Doe, 432 U.S. 519 (1977); Harris v. McRae, 448 U.S. 297 (1980); Williams v. Zbaraz, 448 U.S. 358 (1980); Webster v. Reproductive Health Services, 492 U.S. 490 (1989).

478. *See* Parliament of Can. Standing Senate Comm. on Human Rights, Enhancing Canada's Role in the OAS; Schabas, *Canadian Ratification of the American Convention on Human Rights*, 322–23 (indicating that "the most important" objection to Canada's ratification of the American Convention is the right-to-life provision and the possibility that it may limit abortion in the country). *Cf.* Carozza, *Anglo-Latin Divide and the Future of the Inter-American System of Human Rights*, 164 (indicating that, on its face, the American Convention is much more protective of the right to life of the unborn than the domestic law of Canada would allow given its very broad legal protection of a woman's right to terminate her pregnancy).

479. Parliament of Can. Standing Senate Comm. on Human Rights, *Canadian Adherence to the American Convention on Human Rights*, 42.

480. *Id.* 42–43.

481. *Id.* 43.

482. Blofield, *Women's Choices in Comparative Perspective*, 399–419 (describes some abortion laws in Italy, Portugal, and Spain, compared to some Chilean and Argentinian abortion laws, from an abortion rights perspective).

## SIX. Systemic and Historic Interpretation

1. Vienna Convention on the Law of Treaties arts. 31(3)(c).

2. Protocol Additional to the Geneva Conventions of 12 August 1949, and Relating to the Protection of Victims of Non-International Armed Conflicts (Protocol II) art. 6(4); Int'l Comm. of the Red Cross, Geneva Conventions of 12 August 1949: State Parties/Signatories (Additional Protocol II has been ratified by all Latin American and Caribbean states except Mexico). *See also* United Nations Declaration on Human Cloning; *accord.* Press Release, General Assembly, General Assembly Adopts United Nations Declaration on Human Cloning by Vote of 84–34–37, indicating that the declaration was supported by affirmative votes from Bolivia, Chile, Costa Rica, Dominican Republic, Ecuador, El Salvador, Guatemala, Haiti, Honduras, Mexico, Nicaragua, Panama, Paraguay, and Suriname, among others. The delegations of Dominica and Peru were absent from the vote. Argentina, Barbados, Colombia, and Uruguay abstained. Brazil and Jamaica voted against it.

3. American Convention on Human Rights.

4. *See* Rep. of the International Conference on Population and Development, 133–41. *See* Rep. of the Fourth World Conference on Women, 157.

5. *See* American Convention on Human Rights art. 64(1) (emphasis added). *See* González et al. ("Cotton Field") v. Mexico, ¶ 43.

6. Inter-Am. Ct. H.R., "Other treaties" subject to the consultative jurisdiction of the court (64 American Convention on Human Rights), ¶¶ 21, 44, 48.

7. *Id.*

8. *See* Nieto Navia, *Aspectos internacionales de la demanda contra la penalización del aborto*, 36 (where Judge Nieto Navia points out that the use of the jurisprudence of the European Court of Human Rights' or use of CEDAW committee decisions as a source of interpretation of the American Convention would be conspicuously inappropriate).

9. Vienna Convention on the Law of Treaties arts. 31(3)(c) (emphasis added).

10. *See* Artavia Murillo v. Costa Rica (Vio Grossi, J., dissenting), 17–18.

11. *Chile, Argentina, Brasil, Colombia y Paraguay piden a la Corte Interamericana de DD.HH. respetar "margenes de autonomía" de los estados.*

12. *See* Carozza, *Anglo-Latin Divide and the Future of the Inter-American System of Human Rights*, 162.

13. *See* Case of Gómez Murillo et al. v. Costa Rica, *Opinion: Judge Vio Grossi* (decrying the court's invocation of "normative bodies that are not binding for Costa Rica or for states parties to the Convention"). *See also* Case of Atala Riffo and daughters v. Chile (Pérez-Pérez, J., dissenting), ¶ 20. The lack of intellectual rigor in treaty interpretation by international human rights bodies in general is unfortunately not unique to the Inter-American system; scholars have made similar criticisms of other human rights bodies that monitor international human rights treaties. *See, e.g.*, Mechlem, *Treaty Bodies and the Interpretation of Human Rights*, 905 (pointing out that United Nations human rights treaty bodies often produce interpretations that suffer from methodological weaknesses and lack of coherence and analytical rigor).

14. Puppinck, *Abortion and the European Convention on Human Rights*, 147–52.

15. Odièvre v. France, ¶ 45.

16. A, B & C v. Ireland, ¶¶ 214, 227, 246, 249 (where the Grand Chamber of the European Court of Human Rights delivered judgment on a challenge to Ireland's full ban on abortion, which only allows a "life of the mother" exception). The court stated that even where recognized, abortion rights may be weighed against the unborn's child right to life. *Id.* ¶ 213. The court concluded that Ireland did not violate article 8 in regard to the first and second applicants because "Ireland struck a fair balance between the right of the first and second applicants to respect for their private lives and the rights invoked on behalf of the unborn." *Id.*

¶¶ 241–42. Moreover, the court reiterated that "[a] broad margin of appreciation" is given to European states in regard to abortion prohibitions, given the "acute sensitivity of the moral and ethical issues raised by the question of abortion" and "the importance of the public interest at stake," in this case the public interest being "the protection accorded under Irish law to the right to life of the unborn." *Id.* ¶ 233. This margin of appreciation, the court stated, could be narrowed by the existence of a European consensus to the contrary. *See id.* ¶ 234. However, the court did not consider that the European consensus "decisively narrows the broad margin of appreciation of the State."

17. *Silva Monteiro Martins Ribeiro v. Portugal*; *Jean-Jacques Amy v. Belgium.*

18. *See* Puppinck, *Abortion and the European Convention on Human Rights*, 145 (comprehensive analysis of European Court of Human Rights judgments on abortion).

19. *See* A, B & C v. Ireland.

20. Brüggemann v. Germany, ¶ 59.

21. *See* BUNDESVERFASSUNGSGERICHT, Feb. 25, 1975 (Ger.), 37, *translated in* Stith, *Construction vs. Development*, and in Jonas and Gorby, *West German Abortion Decision*, 605–84. *See* Rhonheimer and Carozza, *Fundamental Rights, Moral Law, and the Legal Defense of Life in a Constitutional Democracy*, 151. *See also* Judgment of May 28, 1993 (Ger.), 229. The German court indicated, however, that it was making no judgment about the nature or rights of the embryo prior to implantation because this matter was not at issue in the cases before it. *But see* Embryonenschutzgesetz, I: 2746 (general protection of the preimplantation embryo in German statutory law).

22. See BUNDESVERFASSUNGSGERICHT, Feb. 25, 1975 (Ger.), 37.

23. *Id.* 653.

24. Judgment of May 28, 1993 (Ger.), 18, 203–5.

25. Judgment of May 28, 1993 (Ger.), 251–52, *translated in* Stith, *Construction vs. Development.*

26. *Id.* 254.

27. *Id.* 252.

28. *See* U.N., Multilateral Treaties Deposited with the Secretary-General, 389–91.

29. *See* Vienna Convention on the Law of Treaties arts. 31(2)(b), 31(3).

30. Declaration of the Rights of the Child preamble; Convention on the Rights of the Child preamble, ¶ 6.

31. Convention on the Rights of the Child arts. 6, 24(2)(d). *See also* Abramson, *Violence against Babies*, 60 (indicating that the Convention on the Rights of the Child was intended to cover children during the entire prenatal period).

32. Human Rights Committee, General Comment No. 36 (2018) on article 6 of the International Covenant on Civil and Political Rights, on the Right to Life, ¶ 60 (emphasis added).

33. *See* Corte Constitucional, Sala Plena, mayo 10, 2006, Sentencia C-355/2006 (Colom.), Salvamento de Voto de los Magistrados Marco Gerardo Monroy Cabra y Rodrigo Escobar Gil (original Spanish text is as follows: "La interpretación armónica del Preámbulo y los artículos primero y sexto de la Convención en cita, lleva a concluir que la misma entiende que la expresión 'niño' comprende a los seres humanos no nacidos, y que respecto de ellos se extiende la protección especial de derechos que dispensa el Tratado, entre ellos el derecho a la vida").

34. Convention on the Rights of the Child art. 1 (defining "child" as "every human being below the age of eighteen"). *See also* Flood, "Does International Law Protect the Unborn Child?," 10 (noting that the definition of "child" in article 1 establishes a ceiling, but not a floor, regarding a child's age, thus tacitly including unborn children within its scope of protection).

35. *See* García Elorrio, "Protección de los niños no nacidos en el Sistema Jurídico Interamericano de Derechos Humanos," 105–7 (for a discussion of Latin American participation in the preparatory work of the 1959 Declaration on the Rights of the Child).

36. U.N. Comm. on the Rights of the Child, Reservations, Declarations and Objections to the Convention on the Rights of the Child.

37. *Id.*

38. Corte Suprema de Justicia de la Nación, 01/09/2015, "Recurso de hecho deducido por los actores en la causa L.E.H. y otros c/O.S.E.P. s/amparo" (Arg.).

39. *Id.*

40. *See* Juridical Condition and Human Rights of the Child, ¶ 29 (noting that "the various States of the hemisphere have adopted provisions in their legislation, both constitutional and regular, regarding the matter at hand; the Committee on the Rights of the Child has repeatedly referred to these provisions").

41. Ley No. 23.849, Apruébase la Convención sobre los Derechos del Niño, art. 2 (Arg.).

42. Comm. on the Rights of the Child, *Consideration of Reports Submitted by States Parties Under Article 44 of the Convention: Initial Reports of States Parties Due in 1994; Addendum: Argentina*, para. 41; *see also* Comm. on the Rights of the Child, *Consideration of Reports Submitted by States Parties Under Article 44 of the Convention: Periodic Reports of States Parties Due in 1998; Argentina*, para. 2 (noting Argentina's interpretive declaration upon ratification of the CRC that "the Article must be interpreted to the effect that a child means every human being from the moment of conception up to the age of 18").

43. Comm. on the Rights of the Child, *Consideration of Reports Submitted by States Parties Under Article 44 of the Convention: Fourth Periodic Reports of States Parties Due in 2006; Guatemala*, para. 41.

44. Comm. on the Rights of the Child, *Consideration of Reports Submitted by States Parties Under Article 44 of the Convention: Second Periodic Reports of States Parties Due in 1997; El Salvador*, para. 51.

45. Comm. on the Rights of the Child, *Consideration of Reports Submitted by States Parties Under Article 44 of the Convention: Fourth Periodic Reports of States Parties Due in 2007; Bolivia*, para. 192.

46. Comm. on the Rights of the Child, *Consideration of Reports Submitted by States Parties Under Article 44 of the Convention: Periodic Reports of States Parties Due in 1997; Addendum: Honduras*, para. 156.

47. Comm. on the Rights of the Child, *Consideration of Reports Submitted by States Parties Under Article 44 of the Convention: Periodic Reports of States Parties Due in 1997; Addendum: Peru*, paras. 137–38.

48. Comm. on the Rights of the Child, *Consideration of Reports Submitted by States Parties Under Article 44 of the Convention: Third Periodic Reports of States Parties Due in 2002; Paraguay*, paras. 127, 288–89.

49. Comm. on the Rights of the Child, *Consideration of Reports Submitted by States Parties Under Article 44 of the Convention: Initial Reports of States Parties Due in 1992; Addendum: Ecuador*, para. 66; Comm. on the Rights of the Child, *Consideration of Reports Submitted by States Parties Under Article 44 of the Convention: Fourth Periodic Reports of States Parties Due in 2007: Ecuador*, para. 524; Comm. on the Rights of the Child, *Consideration of Reports Submitted by States Parties Under Article 44 of the Convention: Second and Third Periodic Reports Due in 1997 and 2002; Ecuador*, para. 134.

50. Comm. on the Rights of the Child, *Consideration of Reports Submitted by States Parties Under Article 44 of the Convention: Periodic Reports of States Parties Due in 1997; Addendum: Honduras*, para. 156.

51. Comm. on the Rights of the Child, *Consideration of Reports Submitted by States Parties Under Article 8, Paragraph 1, of the Optional Protocol to the Convention on the Rights of the Child on the Involvement of Children in Armed Conflict: Initial Reports of States Parties Due in 2007; Colombia*, para. 89; Comm. on the Rights of the Child, *Third Periodic Reports of States Parties Due in 2003: Addendum: Colombia*, paras. 158–59.

52. Convention on the Rights of the Child art. 3(2). Comm. on the Rights of the Child, *Consideration of Reports Submitted by States Parties Under Article 44 of the Convention: Initial Reports of States Parties Due in 1992; Uruguay*, para. 67.

53. Comm. on the Rights of the Child, *Consideration of Reports Submitted by States Parties Under Article 44 of the Convention: Fourth Periodic Reports of States Parties Due in 2007; Bolivia*, para. 192; Comm. on the Rights of the Child, *Consideration of Reports Submitted by States Parties Under Article 12(1) of the Optional Protocol to the Convention on the Rights of the Child on the Sale of Children, Child Prostitution and Child Pornography: Initial Reports of States Parties Due in 2005: Costa Rica*, paras. 29, 32; Comm. on the Rights of the Child, *Consideration of Reports Submitted by States Parties Under Article 44 of the Convention: Third Periodic Reports of States Parties Due in 2002: Nicaragua*, para. 127; Comm. on the Rights of the Child, *Consideration of Reports Submitted by States Parties*

*Under Article 44 of the Convention: Periodic Reports of States Parties Due in 1997: Paraguay*, para. 173.

54. Comm. on the Rights of the Child, *Third and Fourth Periodic Reports of States Parties Due in 2008: Panama*, paras. 99, 259.

55. Acción de inconstitucionalidad 146/2007 y su acumulada 147/2007, Proyecto de resolución, 421.

56. *Id.* 424–26 (original text in Spanish is as follows: "la Convención sobre los Derechos del Niño consagra a favor del niño el derecho a la vida, entendido el término de 'niño' como todo ser humano desde el momento de su concepción hasta la edad de dieciocho años . . . prohíbe hacer distinción entre los niños por razón del nacimiento," "si la Convención otorga al niño el derecho intrínseco a la vida, además de reconocer que el mismo por su falta de madurez tanto física como mental, necesita protección legal y cuidados especiales tanto antes como después del nacimiento, no hay duda que tal derecho y protección comprende al producto de la concepción").

57. SCJN (Mex.), Acción de inconstitucionalidad 146/2007 y su acumulada 147/2007, Suprema Corte de Justicia de la Nación, *Voto de minoría que formulan los Ministros Sergio Salvador Aguirre Anguiano, Mariano Azuela Güitrón y Guillermo I. Ortiz Mayagoitia en la acción de inconstitucionalidad 146/2007 y su acumulada 147/2007*, 100–105 (Mex.).

58. Comm. on the Rights of the Child, *Second Periodic Reports of States Parties Due in 1997; Addendum: Guatemala*, para. 83.

59. *See* Comm. on the Rights of the Child, *Consideration of Reports Submitted by States Parties Under Article 44 of the Convention: Fourth Periodic Reports of States Parties Due in 2007; Nicaragua*, para. 93; *see also* Comm. on the Rights of the Child, *Consideration of Reports Submitted by States Parties Under Article 44 of the Convention: Third Periodic Reports of States Parties Due in 2002; Nicaragua*, para. 127.

60. *See* Comm. on the Rights of the Child, *Consideration of Reports Submitted by States Parties Under Article 44 of the Convention: Third Periodic Reports of States Parties Due in 2002; Paraguay*, para. 288.

61. Comm. on the Rights of the Child, *Consideration of Reports Submitted by States Parties Under Article 44 of the Convention: Initial Report of States Parties Due in 1992; Addendum: Venezuela*, paras. 69, 71.

62. Convention on the Rights of the Child art. 6.

63. Comm. on the Rights of the Child, *Consideration of Reports Submitted by States Parties Under Article 44 of the Convention: Third Periodic Reports of States Parties Due in 2004; Peru*, 60. *See also* Comm. on the Rights of the Child, *Consideration of Reports Submitted by States Parties Under Article 44 of the Convention: Periodic Reports of States Parties Due in 1997; Addendum: Peru*, para. 137.

64. Comm. on the Rights of the Child, *Consideration of Reports Submitted by States Parties Under Article 44 of the Convention: Periodic Reports of States Parties Due in 1997: Addendum: Peru*, para. 196.

65. Comm. on the Rights of the Child, *Consideration of Reports Submitted by States Parties Under Article 44 of the Convention: Initial Reports of States Parties Due in 1992; Addendum: Costa Rica,* para. 78.

66. Comm. on the Rights of the Child, *Consideration of Reports Submitted by States Parties Under Article 44 of the Convention: Periodic Reports of States Parties Due in 1997; Addendum: Honduras,* para. 161.

67. Comm. on the Rights of the Child, *Consideration of Reports Submitted by States Parties Under Article 44 of the Convention: Third and Fourth Periodic Reports of States Parties Due in 2008; Panama,* paras. 177–79, 298–304.

68. Comm. on the Rights of the Child, *Consideration of Reports Submitted by States Parties Under Article 44 of the Convention: Periodic Reports of States Parties Due in 1997; Chile,* para. 304; Comm. on the Rights of the Child, *Consideration of Reports Submitted by States Parties Under Article 44 of the Convention: Initial Reports of States Parties Due in 1993: Addendum, Chile,* para. 67.

69. Comm. on the Rights of the Child, *Consideration of Reports Submitted by States Parties Under Article 44 of the Convention: Second Periodic Reports of States Parties Due in 1997; El Salvador,* para. 147.

70. Comm. On the Rights of the Child, *Consideration of Reports Submitted by States Parties under Article 12(1) of the Optional Protocol to the Convention on the Rights of the Child on the Sale of Children, Child Prostitution and Child Pornography: Initial Reports of States Parties Due in 2005; Colombia,* para. 16; *see also* Comm. on the Rights of the Child, *Consideration of Reports Submitted by States Parties Under Article 8, Paragraph 1, of the Optional Protocol to the Convention on the Rights of the Child on the Involvement of Children in Armed Conflict: Initial Reports of States Parties Due in 2007; Colombia,* paras. 87–90; Comm. on the Rights of the Child, *Consideration of Reports Submitted by States Parties Under Article 44 of the Convention: Third Periodic Reports of States Parties Due in 2003; Addendum: Colombia,* paras. 229–30.

71. Comm. on the Rights of the Child, *Consideration of Reports Submitted by States Parties Under Article 44 of the Convention: Initial Reports of States Parties Due in 1997; Haiti,* para. 61.

72. Comm. on the Rights of the Child, *Consideration of Reports Submitted by States Parties Under Article 44 of the Convention: Initial Reports of States Parties Due in 1993; Dominica,* paras. 95–98.

73. Comm. on the Rights of the Child, *Consideration of Reports Submitted by States Parties Under Article 44 of the Convention: Initial Reports of States Parties Due in 1992; Grenada,* para. 50.

74. Comm. on the Rights of the Child, *Consideration of Reports Submitted by States Parties Under Article 44 of the Convention: Initial Reports of States Parties Due in 1997; Haiti,* para. 61.

75. Comm. on the Rights of the Child, *Consideration of Reports Submitted by States Parties Under Article 44 of the Convention: Initial Reports of States Parties Due in 1995; Suriname,* para. 29.

76. Comm. on the Rights of the Child, *Consideration of Reports Submitted by States Parties Under Article 44 of the Convention: Initial Reports of States Parties Due in 1997; Haiti*, para. 142.

77. Comm. on the Rights of the Child, *Consideration of Reports Submitted by States Parties Under Article 44 of the Convention: Initial Reports of States Parties Due in 1993; Dominica*, paras. 95–98.

78. *See* Rep. of the Comm. on the Rights of the Child, July 16, 2008.

79. Comm. on the Rights of the Child, *Consideration of Reports Submitted by States Parties Under Article 44 of the Convention: Initial Reports of States Parties Due in 1992; Brazil*, para. 283.

80. Comm. on the Rights of the Child, *Consideration of Reports Submitted by States Parties Under Article 44 of the Convention: Initial Reports of States Parties Due in 1992; Mexico*, paras. 35–36, 113, 138.

81. Convention on the Rights of the Child preamble, ¶ 6 (emphasis added).

82. *See* Declaration on the Rights of the Child, preamble.

83. *See Legislative History of the Convention on the Rights of the Child, 1978–1989: Article 1* (definition of a child), 33. The Polish draft established the convention's protection of all children without discrimination, including discrimination by birth, without defining the term: "*Every child, without any exception whatsoever*, shall be entitled to the rights set forth in this Convention, without distinction or discrimination on account of race, colour, sex, language, religion, political or other opinion, national or social origin, property, *birth or other status*, whether of himself or of his family." Germany seems to have understood birth or status as describing the situation of natural versus legitimate children, but no indication was given that that understanding excluded one relating to unborn versus born children.

84. *Id.* 54.

85. *Id.* 61.

86. *Id.* 75. *See also* Artavia Murillo v. Costa Rica, ¶ 232 (granting that the language limiting human rights protection starting at birth had been eliminated).

87. *See Legislative History of the CRC Convention on the Rights of the Child, 1978–1989: Article 1* (definition of a child), 305.

88. *See* Rep. of the Working Group on a Draft Convention on the Rights of the Child, ¶¶ 15, 43, 76, 77 (two proposals by Malta and Senegal to amend article 1 to define the child as any "human being" "from the moment of conception" were dropped upon the adoption of the text "before and after birth" in the preamble, which, as they indicated, implied the same recognition of childhood starting at conception).

89. *Id.* ¶ 37.

90. *Id.* at 116, ¶ 43. Article 21 of the draft convention stated: "Nothing in this Convention shall affect any provisions that are more conducive to the realization of the rights of the child and that may be contained in: a) the law of a State Party;

(or) b) any other international convention, treaty or agreement in force for that state; or c) customary international law."

91. *See* Rep. of the Working Group to the Commission on Human Rights, ¶ 6. *See also* Rep. of the Working Group on a Draft Convention on the Rights of the Child, 9 ¶ 30.

92. Rep. of the Working Group on a Draft Convention on the Rights of the Child, 10, ¶ 38. *See also* Rep. of the Working Group to the Commission on Human Rights, ¶ 6.

93. Rep. of the Working Group on a Draft Convention on the Rights of the Child, 10, ¶ 39.

94. *Id.* at 10, ¶ 35. *See also* Rep. of the Working Group to the Commission on Human Rights, ¶ 11.

95. Rep. of the Working Group to the Commission on Human Rights, 10, ¶ 30.

96. *See* Office of the United Nations High Commissioner for Human Rights, Legislative History of the Convention on the Rights of the Child, Volume II, 729.

97. *See* Rep. of the Working Group on a Draft Convention on the Rights of the Child, ¶¶ 17–18, 36.

98. *See id.* at 10, ¶ 36.

99. *See* Rep. of the Working Group to the Commission on Human Rights, ¶ 6.

100. *Id.*, ¶ 8, 10. *See* Rep. of the Working Group on a Draft Convention on the Rights of the Child, 10, ¶ 38. *See also* Rep. of the Working Group to the Commission on Human Rights, ¶ 6.

101. *See* Rep. of the Working Group to the Commission on Human Rights, ¶¶ 16–19.

102. Rep. of the Working Group on a Draft Convention on the Rights of the Child, ¶¶ 41, 43.

103. *Id.*, 4, 11, ¶¶ 4, 43 (the chairman who introduced this statement remains unnamed in the preparatory work records; the only chairman names mentioned for those sessions are Adam Lopatka from Poland and Anders Röhnquist from Sweden).

104. *Id.*, 143, ¶ 731.

105. *See* Artavia Murillo v. Costa Rica, ¶ 231–32, 244. Rep. of the Working Group on a Draft Convention on the Rights of the Child, Annex, ¶ 44 (the counsel's report explains why the working group's statement may be invalid and ineffective in interpreting the convention).

106. *Id.*

107. *See* Rep. of the Working Group on a Draft Convention on the Rights of the Child, 11, Annex, ¶¶ 44–47.

108. *Id.* 144.

109. Vienna Convention on the Law of Treaties art. 31(2): "The context for the purpose of the interpretation of a treaty shall comprise, in addition to the

text, including its preamble and annexes: (a) any agreement relating to the treaty which was made between *all the parties* in connexion with the conclusion of the treaty; (b) any instrument which was made by one or more parties in connexion with the conclusion of the treaty and *accepted by the other parties as an instrument related to the treaty*" (emphasis added).

110. U.N. Comm. on the Rights of the Child, Reservations, Declarations and Objections Relating to the Convention on the Rights of the Child.

111. *See* Rep. of the Working Group on a Draft Convention on the Rights of the Child, 10, ¶ 40 (Italy, a member of the said working group, actually expressed an understanding that "the concept of 'responsible motherhood,' affirmed in many modern judicial systems, was not against the protection of children before birth").

112. *See* Artavia Murillo v. Costa Rica, ¶ 231 (emphasis added).

113. American Convention on Human Rights art. 29.

114. *See* Juridical Condition and Human Rights of the Child, ¶ 21. *See also* Convention on the Rights of the Child art. 41 (article 41 of the Convention on the Rights of the Child contains a similar clause, which provides that nothing in the convention shall affect any national laws or provisions in other international treaties to which a state is party that "are more conducive to the realization of the rights of the child").

115. Additional Protocol to the American Convention on Human Rights in the Area of Economic, Social and Cultural Rights (Protocol of San Salvador) art. 15(3)(a)–(d).

116. Inter-American Convention on Support Obligations art. 2.

117. *Id.*

118. Geneva Convention Relative to the Protection of Civilian Persons in Time of War art. 14. *See* Int'l Comm. of the Red Cross, Geneva Conventions of 12 August 1949: State Parties/Signatories (the Geneva Convention (IV) has been ratified by all states parties to the American Convention).

119. Rome Statute of the International Criminal Court art. 6(d).

120. Inter-American Convention on the Prevention, Punishment and Eradication of Violence Against Women ("Convention of Belém do Pará"). *See also* Signatories and Ratifications: Inter-American Convention on the Prevention, Punishment and Eradication of Violence against Women "Convention of Belém do Pará."

121. *See* International Covenant on Economic, Social and Cultural Rights arts. 12(2)(a), 12(1) (including the reduction of stillbirths, reduction of infant mortality, and "the healthy development of the child" in the right "to the enjoyment of the highest attainable standard of physical and mental health"). *See also* U.N., Multilateral Treaties Deposited with the Secretary-General, 182–84 (the ICESCR has been ratified by all Latin American and Caribbean states except Haiti). *Accord.* Comm. on Econ., Soc. and Cultural Rights, *Substantive Issues Arising in the Implementation of the International Covenant on Economic, Social and*

*Cultural Rights: The Right to the Highest Attainable Standard of Health*, paras. 14, 22, 35 (tying children's right to health and development to maternal health).

122. *See* Convention on the Elimination of All Forms of Discrimination Against Women art. 12(2) ("States Parties shall ensure to women appropriate services in connexion with pregnancy"). *See* U.N., Multilateral Treaties Deposited with the Secretary-General, 157–59.

123. Acción de inconstitucionalidad 146/2007 y su acumulada 147/2007, 438–41.

124. *Id.* at 441.

125. *See* United Nations Declaration on Human Cloning.

126. *See General Assembly Adopts Declaration on Human Cloning by Vote of 84–34–37.*

127. Letter dated 2 April 2003 from the Permanent Representative of Costa Rica to the United Nations addressed to the Secretary-General.

128. *Declaración de Guácimo* (the declaration was signed by the presidents of Costa Rica, El Salvador, Guatemala, Honduras, Nicaragua, and Panama).

129. *Id.*

130. Universal Declaration of Human Rights art. 25(2).

131. *See id.* arts. 22, 25(1)–(2).

132. *See* Corte Constitucional, Sala Plena, mayo 10, 2006,, Sentencia C-355/2006 (Colom.), Salvamento de Voto de los Magistrados Marco Gerardo Monroy Cabra y Rodrigo Escobar Gil.

133. *See* Artavia Murillo v. Costa Rica, ¶ 224.

134. U.N. E.S.C., Comm'n on Human Rights, 2nd Sess. 35th meeting.

135. *Id.* 4–6.

136. *Id.* 6.

137. *Id.* 16.

138. Rep. of the Working Group on a Draft Convention on the Rights of the Child, Annex, ¶ 44. U.N. E.S.C., Comm'n on Human Rights, 2nd Sess. 35th meeting, 12–14 (citing language that would have protected the right to life "except in a case in which [taking a fetus's or embryo's life] is permitted by law" and "to prevent the birth of a child of unsound mind").

139. U.N. E.S.C., Comm'n on Human Rights, 2nd Sess. 35th meeting, 12–17.

140 International Covenant on Civil and Political Rights art. 6(1).

141. Bossuyt, *Guide to the "Travaux Préparatoires" of the International Covenant on Civil and Political Rights*, 119 (indicating that Uruguay and Colombia's proposal was accepted by a vote of 65–3).

142. *Id.* 121.

143. *Id.* 113–14, 120–21.

144. *Id.* 121.

145. *Id.*

146. *See* Artavia Murillo v. Costa Rica, ¶ 225.

147. *See* Bossuyt, *Guide to the "Travaux Préparatoires" of the International Covenant on Civil and Political Rights*, 121.

148. *See* International Covenant on Civil and Political Rights art. 6(5). U.N., Multilateral Treaties Deposited with the Secretary-General, 204–6. *See* Bossuyt, *Guide to the "Travaux Préparatoires" of the International Covenant on Civil and Political Rights*, 141.

149. Bossuyt, *Guide to the "Travaux Préparatoires" of the International Covenant on Civil and Political Rights*, 143.

150. *Id.* at 142.

151. *Id.* at 143.

152. *Id.* at 142–43.

153. Dinah Shelton, "International Law on Protection of the Fetus," 14.

154. *See* Protocol Additional to the Geneva Conventions of 12 August 1949, and Relating to the Protection of Victims of Non-International Armed Conflicts (Protocol II).

155. *See* Sala de lo Constitucional de la Corte Suprema de Justicia, May 28, 2013, Amparo 310-2013, ¶ VI(1)(A)(b).

156. *See id.*, *Voto disidente en el caso B.C. Magistrado Florentín Meléndez* [Dissenting vote in case of B.C. Justice Florentín Meléndez].

157. *See* Derecho a la vida del producto de la concepción (Mex.).

158. *Id.*

159. The Human Rights Committee, which monitors the ICCPR; the CEDAW Committee; the ICESCR Committee; the Committee against Torture; and even the CRC Committee on the Rights of the Child have repeatedly urged Latin American and Caribbean states, as well as other states that legally protected prenatal life, to create abortion rights. *See, e.g.*, Rep. of the Comm. on the Elimination of Discrimination Against Women, 19th Sess., para. 201, expressing "deep concern in connection with the reproductive health of Panamanian women and an apparent setback in the treatment of the right to abortion in cases where the pregnancy is the result of rape. . . . [The Committee] also recommends that Panamanian women who are pregnant as a result of rape should be granted the opportunity to seek termination of such pregnancies." *See also* Rep. of the Comm. on the Elimination of Discrimination Against Women, 15th Sess., para. 123, suggesting Paraguay should increase access to "safe" abortion, particularly for rural women and girls.

160. *See* Artavia Murillo v. Costa Rica, ¶ 226.

161. Human Rights Committee, General Comment No. 36 (2018) on Article 6 of the International Covenant on Civil and Political Rights, ¶¶ 8, 10.

162. *Id.* ¶ 8.

163. *See, e.g.*, San José Articles, art. 6 (the San José Articles are a declaration signed by a group of experts in international law, public health, science, medicine, and government, including Professor John Finnis of Oxford; former judge of the European Court of Human Rights Javier Borrego; Professor Carter Snead of UN-

ESCO's International Bioethics Committee; Lord Nicholas Windsor, member of the royal family of the United Kingdom; Hon. Luca Volonte, president of the European People's Party in the Parliamentary Assembly of the Council of Europe; and Robert P. George, McCormick Professor of Jurisprudence at Princeton University and former member of the President's Council on Bioethics).

164. Corte Constitucional, Sala Plena, mayo 10, 2006, Sentencia C-355/2006 (Colom.), Salvamento de Voto de los Magistrados Marco Gerardo Monroy Cabra y Rodrigo Escobar Gil.

165. *See* Tribunal Constitucional, 28 agosto 2017, Requerimiento de inconstitucionalidad respecto del proyecto de ley que "regula la despenalización de la interrupción voluntaria del embarazo en tres causales," 180 (Colom.).

166. *See* Baby Boy v. United States, §§ 18(e), 26.

167. *Id.* ¶ 27.

168. *See* Corte Constitucional, Sala Plena, mayo 10, 2006, Sentencia C-355/2006 (Colom.), Salvamento de Voto de los Magistrados Marco Gerardo Monroy Cabra y Rodrigo Escobar Gil. *Cf.* African Commission on Human and Peoples' Rights, *Protocol to the African Charter on Human and Peoples' Rights on the Rights of Women in Africa* art. 14(2)(c). (This is the only regional treaty that currently includes the term "abortion." Obviously it is not binding on Latin American states. This treaty, also known as the Maputo Protocol, authorizes abortion only under certain circumstances, in the absence of which the procedure would be illegal). *Cf.* African Commission on Human and Peoples' Rights, *Ratification Table* (thirty-six of the fifty-four African Union members have ratified or acceded to the Maputo Protocol). *Cf.* the notes section of the SAN JOSÉ ARTICLES, which points out that "[the Maputo Protocol] is highly contentious and in no way enjoys universal acceptance. . . . [T]he reason most often cited for non-accession is the abortion provision."

169. Press Release, General Assembly, Several Aspects of Sexual, Reproductive Health—Providing Information, Using Contraception, Abortion—Should Be "Decriminalized."

170. Corte Constitucional, Sala Plena, mayo 10, 2006, Sentencia C-355/2006 (Colom.), Salvamento de Voto de los Magistrados Marco Gerardo Monroy Cabra y Rodrigo Escobar Gil.

171. *Id.*

172. Corte Constitucional, Sala Plena, mayo 10, 2006, Sentencia C-355/2006 (Colom.), Salvamento de Voto del Magistrado Alvaro Tafur Galvis.

173. *See* Convention on the Elimination of Discrimination against Women art. 12(2).

174. *See* Corte Constitucional, Sala Plena, mayo 10, 2006, Sentencia C-355/2006 (Colom.), Salvamento de Voto de los Magistrados Marco Gerardo Monroy Cabra y Rodrigo Escobar Gil.

175. Rome Statute of the International Criminal Court art. 7(2)(f).

176. *See* Rep. of the International Conference on Population and Development; Rep. of the Fourth World Conference on Women. *See, e.g.*, U.N. Population Information Network, U.N. Population Division, *From Cairo to Beijing.*

177. *See* Rep. of the International Conference on Population and Development, para. 8.25, at 58–59. *Accord.* Rep. of the Fourth World Conference on Women, ch. 1, paras. 97, at 36; 106(j)–(k), at 39–40.

178. Rep. of the Fourth World Conference on Women, para. 106(k), at 40 (emphasis added).

179. Rep. of the International Conference on Population and Development, paras. 7.24, at 46; 8.25, at 58–59. *Accord.* Rep. of the Fourth World Conference on Women, para. 106(k) at 40 (quoting Rep. of the International Conference on Population and Development, para. 8.25, at 58–59).

180. Rep. of the International Conference on Population and Development, para. 8.25, at 58; Rep. of the Fourth World Conference on Women, para. 106(k), at 40. *See also Key Actions for the Further Implementation of the Programme of Action of the International Conference on Population and Development*, para. 63(ii) ("Governments should take appropriate steps to help women to avoid abortion, which in no case should be promoted as a method of family planning, and in all cases provide for the humane treatment and counseling of women who have had recourse to abortion").

181. Rep. of the International Conference on Population and Development, para. 8.25, at 58; Rep. of the Fourth World Conference on Women, para. 106(k), at 40.

182. Rep. of the International Conference on Population and Development, 42.

183. *Id.* para. 8.25, at 59; Rep. of the Fourth World Conference on Women, para. 106(k), at 40 (quoting Rep. of the International Conference on Population and Development, para. 8.25, at 59).

184. Rep. of the International Conference on Population and Development, para. 8.25, at 59; Rep. of the Fourth World Conference on Women, para. 106(k), at 40 (quoting Rep. of the International Conference on Population and Development, para. 8.25, at 59). *See also Key Actions for the Further Implementation of the Programme of Action of the International Conference on Population and Development*, para. 63(i).

185. Rep. of the International Conference on Population and Development, paras. 4.15, at 25; 4.23, at 26; Rep. of the Fourth World Conference on Women, paras. 115, at 49; 277(c), at 113.

186. Fourth United Nations Conference on Women, *Beijing Declaration and Platform for Action*, para. 277(c).

187. Rep. of the International Conference on Population and Development, 177.

188. Rep. of the Fourth World Conference on Women, ch. 5, para. 5, at 154.

189. *Id.*, ch. 5, para. 5, at 154.

190. *Id.* ch. 5, para. 5, at 155.

191. *Id.* para. 23, at 140.

192. *Id.* para. 8, at 157.

193. Rep. of the International Conference on Population and Development, para. 24, at 141.

194. Rep. of the International Conference on Population and Development, para. 26, at 142 (technically, reservations are filed in the adoption of treaties, not conferences; however, many states chose to call their written statements "reservations," perhaps to further clarify their opposition to the distortion of the proper understanding of reproductive rights terminology).

195. Rep. of the Fourth World Conference on Women, para. 11(b), at 158.

196. *Id.* 133.

197. U.N. General Assembly, Carta de fecha 11 de agosto de 2010 dirigida al Secretario General por el Encargado de Negocios interino de la Misión Permanente de El Salvador ante las Naciones Unidas, ¶ 2.

198. Rep. of the International Conference on Population and Development, para. 10, at 134.

199. Rep. of the Fourth World Conference on Women, para. 13, at 163.

200. Rep. of the International Conference on Population and Development, para. 14, at 136. *Accord.* Rep. of the Fourth World Conference on Women, ch. 5, para. 26, at 168.

201. Rep. of the International Conference on Population and Development, para. 5, at 137.

202. *Id.* para. 30, at 148. Rep. of the Fourth World Conference on Women, ch. 5, para. 28, at 169.

203. Rep. of the International Conference on Population and Development, para. 30, at 147.

204. *See* Herrmann, *Abortion Proponents Admit Defeat at Rio Conference.*

205. *See Copenhagen Declaration on Social Development and Programme of Action*, ch. 5, para. 5: "The Argentine Republic cannot accept the idea that reproductive health should include abortion, either as a service or as a method of birth control. This reservation, which is based on the universal nature of the right to life, extends to all references of this kind." *See also* Rep. of the World Summit on Sustainable Development, 140. At the 2002 World Summit on Sustainable Development in Johannesburg, Argentina submitted a declaration stating: "It is the understanding of the Argentine Republic that the provisions of the Plan of Implementation are inspired by a respect for human life and human dignity (principle 1 of the Rio Declaration) and that therefore nothing in the Plan can be interpreted as justifying any action that directly or indirectly jeopardizes the inviolability and sacredness of human life from the moment of conception." *See* U.N. Conference on Human Settlements (Habitat II), Istanbul Declaration on Settlements and the Habitat Agenda, 190.

206. Economic Commission for Latin America and the Caribbean, *Consenso de Montevideo sobre Población y Desarrollo*, 37–38 (Guatemala reservation).

207. U.N. Conference on Human Settlements (Habitat II), Istanbul Declaration on Settlements and the Habitat Agenda, 194.

208. *See* Regional Conference on Women in Latin America and the Caribbean, Aug. 6–9, 2007, Rep. of the Tenth Session, 29, 31–32; Regional Conference on Women in Latin America and the Caribbean, July 1–16, 2010, Rep. of the Eleventh Session, 37–38, 41.

209. Regional Conference on Women in Latin America and the Caribbean, Aug. 6–9, 2007, Rep. of the Tenth Session, 37.

210. *Id.* 39.

211. *Id.* 41.

212. Regional Conference on Women in Latin America and the Caribbean, July 1–16, 2010, Rep. of the Eleventh Session, 32.

213. U.N. Comm. on the Elimination of Discrimination Against Women, Women's Anti-Discrimination Committee Takes Up Report of Honduras.

214. *See* Press Release, General Assembly, Several Aspects of Sexual, Reproductive Health—Providing Information, Using Contraception, Abortion—Should Be "Decriminalized," Third Committee Told.

215. *Id.*

216. Vienna Convention on the Law of Treaties arts. 31(3)(a) and (b), 32.

217. *Id.* art. 32.

218. *See* Barberis, *El derecho a la vida en el pacto de San José de Costa Rica*, 15–16.

219. *Id.* 15–16, 18.

220. *See* Baby Boy v. United States, para. 21 (majority opinion).

221. *See id.* para. 5 (Marco Gerardo Monroy Cabra, comm'r, dissenting), para. 2 (Dr. Luis Demetrio Tinoco Castro, dissenting).

222. *See* Monroy Cabra, "Aplicación de la Convención Americana sobre Derechos Humanos en el orden jurídico interno," 135.

223. Baby Boy v. United States, para. 27.

224. Inter-American Yearbook on Human Rights, 97 (1968, indicating that twelve states signed the convention at the conference and subsequently ratified it: Colombia, Costa Rica, Chile, Ecuador, El Salvador, Guatemala, Honduras, Nicaragua, Panama, Paraguay, Uruguay, and Venezuela. Some did not sign the convention at the Specialized Human Rights Conference: the United States, Argentina, Brazil, Mexico, Peru, Dominican Republic, and Trinidad and Tobago. All of them, however, signed the convention later, with the exception of the United States, which signed but did not ratify the convention. Some countries were not represented at the conference: Barbados, Bolivia, Cuba, Haiti, and Jamaica, all of which, with the exception of Cuba, subsequently adhered to the convention.

225. *See* Minutes of the 2nd session of the committee I, 160.

226. *Id.* at 159.

227. *Id.* at 160.

228. *Id.* at 57. Original language is as follows: "Creemos que en cuanto al 'derecho a la vida,' se fortalecerían los conceptos universales de los derechos humanos si el texto interamericano fuera igual al que se adoptó en las Naciones Unidas, en el Artículo 6(1) del pacto." (The said ICCPR article states: "Every human being has the inherent right to life. This right shall be protected by law. No one shall be arbitrarily deprived of his life.")

229. *See* Artavia Murillo v. Costa Rica, ¶ 206.

230. Organization of American States, *Actas y Documentos of the Interamerican Specialized Conference on Human Rights, supra* n. 225 at 160.

231. *Id.* at 121, 159–60.

232. Baby Boy v. United States, para. 26

233. *See* Organization of American States, *Actas y Documentos of the Interamerican Specialized Conference on Human Rights*, 121, 159–60. The relevant paragraph in original language states: "Esta cláusula final es vaga y por eso no tendrá eficacia para impedir que los Estados Partes en la futura convención incluyan en sus leyes internas los más variados casos de aborto. Dicha cláusula podrá, por lo tanto, provocar dudas que dificulten no sólo la aceptación de este artículo, como su aplicación, si prevaleciera la redacción actual."

234. Organization of American States, *Actas y Documentos of the Interamerican Specialized Conference on Human Rights*, 121.

235. *Id.* at 121, 159–60.

236. *Id.* at 160.

237. *Id.* at 159.

238. *Id.* at 160.

239. *See* Artavia Murillo v. Costa Rica, ¶ 221.

240. Organization of American States, *Actas y Documentos of the Interamerican Specialized Conference on Human Rights*, 121.

241. *Id.* 441.

242. *Id.*

243. *Id.* (emphasis added).

244. *See* Baby Boy v. United States, para. 22 (majority opinion). *See* Organization of American States, *Actas y Documentos of the Interamerican Specialized Conference on Human Rights*, 121, 441.

245. *See* Artavia Murillo v. Costa Rica, ¶¶ 193, 223. *Id.* (Vio Grossi, J., dissenting) at 17.

246. *See id.* ¶ 212.

247. *See id.* ¶¶ 200, 206, 220–21. *See* Baby Boy v. United States, paras. 30–31. See also Antkowiak and Gonza, *American Convention on Human Rights*, 60.

Conclusion

1. Case of Hilaire, Constantine and Benjamin et al. v. Trinidad & Tobago, ¶ 112; Case of the Barrios Family v. Venezuela, ¶ 48.

2. *See* Tribunal Constitucional, 28 agosto 2017, Requerimiento de inconstitucionalidad respecto del proyecto de ley que "regula la despenalización de la interrupción voluntaria del embarazo en tres causales," 48 (Colom.) (pointing out that no country in the world has been exempt from deep-set differences on the issue of legalization of abortion).

3. Letter from Tabaré Vázquez, Presidencia de la República Oriental del Uruguay, where then-president Tabaré Vázquez states that "the Pact of San Jose of Costa Rica . . . contains explicit dispositions, such as its article 2 and article 4, which bind our country to protect a human being's life from conception. They also grant him the status of person. . . . If Uruguay wishes to follow a legal/political life different from that established by the American Convention, it ought to denounce the said Convention."

4. *See, e.g.*, Farfán Bertrán, *El caso "Artavia Murillo c. Costa Rica" a la luz de la teoría del control de convencionalidad*, 47.

5. Restrictions to the Death Penalty, ¶¶ 56, 57.

# BIBLIOGRAPHY

## Treaties and International Human Rights Instruments

Additional Protocol to the American Convention on Human Rights in the Area of Economic, Social and Cultural Rights (Protocol of San Salvador), Nov. 17, 1988, O.A.S.T.S. No. 69, 28 I.L.M. 161.

Charter of the Organization of American States, Apr. 30, 1948, 2 U.S.T. 2416, 119 U.N.T.S. 48.

Convention on the Elimination of All Forms of Discrimination Against Women, opened for signature Mar. 1, 1980, 1249 U.N.T.S. 13.

Convention on the Rights of Persons with Disabilities, G.A. Res. 61/106, U.N. Doc. A/RES/61/106 (Jan. 24, 2007), https://www.refworld.org/docid/45f973632.html.

Convention on the Rights of the Child, G.A. Res. 44/25, U.N. Doc. A/RES/44/25 (Nov. 20, 1989).

Declaration of the Rights of the Child, G.A. Res. 1386 (XIV), U.N. Doc. A/RES/1386 (XIV), Preamble (Nov. 20, 1959).

Geneva Convention Relative to the Protection of Civilian Persons in Time of War, Aug. 12, 1949, 6 U.S.T. 3516, 75 U.N.T.S. 287.

Inter-American Convention on Support Obligations, July 15, 1989, O.A.S.T.S. No. 71, 29 I.L.M. 75.

Inter-American Convention on the Prevention, Punishment and Eradication of Violence Against Women ("Convention of Belém do Pará"), June 9, 1994, 33 I.L.M. 1534.

International Covenant on Economic, Social and Cultural Rights, Dec. 16, 1966, 993 U.N.T.S. 3.

Organization of American States, American Convention on Human Rights, Nov. 22, 1969, O.A.S.T.S. No. 36, 1144 U.N.T.S. 123 (entered into force July 18, 1978).

Organization of American States, American Declaration of the Rights and Duties of Man, May 2, 1948, OAS/Ser.L/V/I.4, rev. 13.

Organization of American States, Inter-American Convention Against Racism, Racial Discrimination and Related Forms of Intolerance, June 5, 2013, O.A.S.T.S. No. A-68 (entered into force Nov. 11, 2017), http://www.oas.org/en/sla/dil/inter_american_treaties_A-68_racism.asp.

Organization of American States, Inter-American Convention on the Elimination of All Forms of Discrimination Against Persons with Disabilities, June 7, 1999, AG/RES. 1608 (XXIX-O/99) (entered into force Sept. 14, 2001), http://www.oas.org/juridico/english/treaties/a-65.html.

Protocol Additional to the Geneva Conventions of 12 August 1949, and Relating to the Protection of Victims of Non-International Armed Conflicts (Protocol II), June 8, 1977, 1125 U.N.T.S. 609.

Protocol to the American Convention on Human Rights to Abolish the Death Penalty, OEA/Ser.L.V/II.82 doc.6 rev.1, 80 (1992) (adopted at Asunción, Paraguay, June 8, 1990, at the twentieth regular session of the General Assembly; entered into force August 28, 1991).

Rome Statute of the International Criminal Court, opened for signature July 17, 1998, 2187 U.N.T.S. 90.

Rules of Procedure of the Inter-American Commission on Human Rights, Inter-Am. Comm'n on Human Rights (1960).

Rules of Procedure of the Inter-American Commission on Human Rights, Inter-Am. Comm'n on Human Rights (1980).

Rules of Procedure of the Inter-American Commission on Human Rights, Inter-Am. Comm'n on Human Rights Res. 1/2013.

San José Articles (Mar. 25, 2011), https://sanjosearticles.com/.

Signatories and Ratifications: American Convention on Human Rights, OAS, http://www.oas.org/dil/treaties_B-32_American_Convention_on_Human_Rights_sign.htm.Signatories and Ratifications: Inter-American Convention on the Prevention, Punishment and Eradication of Violence against Women "Convention of Belém do Pará," OAS, http://www.oas.org/juridico/english/sigs/a-61.html.

Statute of the Inter-American Commission on Human Rights, O.A.S. G.A. Res. 447 (IX) (Oct. 31, 1979).

Treaties, States Parties and Commentaries: Protocol II, Int'l Comm. of the Red Cross, http://www.icrc.org/ihl.nsf/WebSign?ReadForm&id=475&ps=P.

Universal Declaration of Human Rights, G.A. Res. 217 (III) A, U.N. Doc. A/RES/217(III) (Dec. 10, 1948).

United Nations Declaration on Human Cloning, G.A. Res. 59/280, U.N. Doc. A/RES/59/280 (Mar. 8, 2005).

Vienna Convention on the Law of Treaties 31–32, May 22, 1969, 8 I.L.M. 679, 1155 U.N.T.S. 331.

## OAS Documents

*About Us*, Inter-American Human Rights Institute, https://www.iidh.ed.cr/.

*Carlos A. Dunshee de Abranches, Brazil, 1964–1983*, in *Former IACHR Commissioners*, OAS, http://www.oas.org/en/iachr/mandate/composition.asp.

*Declaración del Secretario General de la OEA sobre la Epidemia del virus Zika* [OAS secretary general's declaration on the Zika virus epidemic], OAS (Apr. 26, 2016), http://www.oas.org/es/centro_noticias/comunicado_prensa.asp?sCodigo=C-051/16.

*Derecho de Familia y Niñez ("la Red")* [Family and juvenile law ("The network")], ORGANIZACIÓN DE LOS ESTADOS AMERICANOS (Feb. 25, 2014), http://www.oas.org/dil/esp/derecho_de_familia.htm.

Economic Commission for Latin America and the Caribbean (ECLAC), *Consenso de Montevideo sobre Población y Desarrollo* [Montevideo consensus on population and development], U.N. Doc. LC/L. 3697, http://repositorio.cepal.org/bitstream/handle/11362/21835/4/S20131037_es.pdf.

Follow-Up Mechanism to the Belém do Pará Convention (MESECVI), Second Hemispheric Report on the Implementation of the Belém do Pará Convention (April 2012), http://www.oas.org/en/mesecvi/docs/MESECVI-SegundoInformeHemisferico-EN.pdf.

*IACHR Strengthened*, ORGANIZACIÓN DE LOS ESTADOS AMERICANOS, http://www.oas.org/es/cidh/prensa/crisis-cidh.asp.

Inter-American Yearbook on Human Rights (1968), General Secretariat of the OAS, Washington, D.C. (1973).

Letter from Minister of Popular Power for Foreign Affairs of the Bolivarian Republic of Venezuela to José Miguel Insulza, Secretary General of the Organization of American States (Sept. 6, 2012), OAS, http://www.oas.org/DIL/Nota_República_Bolivariana_Venezuela_to_SG.English.pdf.

Minutes of the 2nd session of the committee I, Doc. 36, Nov. 11, 1969, in *Actas y Documentos of the Interamerican Specialized Conference on Human Rights*, OEA/Ser.K/XVI/1.2, 121 (Nov. 7–22, 1969).

Organization of American States, American Convention on Human Rights art. 4(1), Nov. 21, 1969, O.A.S.T.S. No. 36, 1144 U.N.T.S. 123 (entered into force July 18, 1978).

Organization of American States, THE RIGHTS OF THE CHILD IN THE INTER-AMERICAN HUMAN RIGHTS SYSTEM, OEA/Ser.L/V/II.133 (2d ed. 2009).

Organization of American States, *Actas y Documentos of the Interamerican Specialized Conference on Human Rights*, OEA/Ser.K/XVI/1.2, 121 (Nov. 7–22, 1969), https://www.oas.org/es/cidh/docs/enlaces/conferencia%20interamericana.pdf.

*Palabras pronunciadas por el doctor Rodolfo Piza Escalante, presidente de la Corte Interamericana de Derechos Humanos, con motivo de la instalación de la misma, en el Teatro Nacional de Costa Rica* [Speech by Doctor Rodolfo Piza Escalante, president of the Inter-American Court of Human Rights, on the occasion of the first session of the court, in the National Theater of Costa Rica] (Sept. 3, 1979), CORTE INTERAMERICANA DE DERECHOS HUMANOS, MEMORIA DE LA INSTALACIÓN (1999).

*Specialized Organizations*, O.A.S., http://www.oas.org/en/about/specialized_organizations.asp.

United Nations Documents

Callamard, Agnes (special rapporteur on extrajudicial, summary, or arbitrary executions), *Rep. on a Gender-Sensitive Approach to Arbitrary Killings*, U.N. Doc. A/HRC/35/23 (June 6, 2017), https://www.ohchr.org/en/issues/executions/pages/srexecutionsindex.aspx.

Comm. on Econ., Soc. and Cultural Rights, *Substantive Issues Arising in the Implementation of the International Covenant on Economic, Social and Cultural Rights: The Right to the Highest Attainable Standard of Health* (article 12 of the International Covenant on Economic, Social and Cultural Rights), U.N. Doc. E/C.12/2000/4 (Aug. 11, 2000).

Comm. on the Elimination of Discrimination Against Women, Concluding Observations on the Seventh Periodic Report of Chile, U.N. Doc. CEDAW/C/CHL/CO/7 (Mar. 14, 2018), https://tbinternet.ohchr.org/_layouts/treatybodyexternal/Download.aspx?symbolno=CEDAW%2fC%2fCHL%2fCO%2f7&Lang=en.

Comm. on the Elimination of Discrimination Against Women, *Consideration of Reports Submitted by States Parties Under Article 18 of the Convention on the Elimination of All Forms of Discrimination Against Women, Combined Initial, Second, Third, Fourth, Fifth, Sixth and Seventh Periodic Reports of States Parties: Haiti* (July 9, 2008), https://www.refworld.org/publisher,CEDAW,STATEPARTIESREP,HTI,48d769192,0.html.

Comm. on the Elimination of Discrimination Against Women, *Consideration of Reports Submitted by States Parties Under Article 18 of the Convention on the Elimination of All Forms of Discrimination Against Women, Third Periodic Reports of States Parties: Suriname* (June 9, 2005).

Comm. on the Rights of the Child, *Concluding Observations on the Combined Fifth and Sixth Periodic Reports of Argentina*, CRC/C/ARG/CO/5-6 (June 1, 2018).

Comm. on the Rights of the Child, *Consideration of Reports Submitted by States Parties Under Article 8, Paragraph 1, of the Optional Protocol to the Convention on the Rights of the Child on the Involvement of Children in Armed Conflict: Initial Reports of States Parties Due in 2007; Colombia*, U.N. Doc. CRC/C/OPAC/COL/1 (Oct. 21, 2009).

Comm. on the Rights of the Child, *Consideration of Reports Submitted by States Parties Under Article 44 of the Convention: Grenada*, U.N. Doc. CRC/C/3/ADdd.55 (Nov. 28, 1997).

Comm. on the Rights of the Child, *Consideration of Reports Submitted by States Parties Under Article 44 of the Convention: Fourth Periodic Reports of States Parties Due in 2007; Bolivia*, U.N. Doc. CRC/C/BOL/4 (Mar. 25, 2009).

Comm. on the Rights of the Child, *Consideration of Reports Submitted by States Parties Under Article 44 of the Convention: Fourth Periodic Reports of States Parties Due in 2007; Ecuador*, U.N. Doc. CRC/C/ECU/4 (July 10, 2009).

Comm. on the Rights of the Child, *Consideration of Reports Submitted by States Parties Under Article 44 of the Convention: Fourth Periodic Reports of States Parties Due in 2006; Guatemala,* 78 U.N. Doc. CRC/C/GTM/3-4 (Apr. 25, 2008).
Comm. on the Rights of the Child, *Consideration of Reports Submitted by States Parties Under Article 44 of the Convention: Fourth Periodic Reports of States Parties Due in 2007; Nicaragua,* U.N. Doc. CRC/C/NIC/4 (Mar. 22, 2010).
Comm. on the Rights of the Child, *Consideration of Reports Submitted by States Parties Under Article 44 of the Convention: Initial Reports of States Parties Due in 1994; Addendum: Argentina,* U.N. Doc. CRC/C/8/Add.17 (Dec. 22, 1994).
Comm. on the Rights of the Child, *Consideration of Reports Submitted by States Parties Under article 44 of the Convention: Initial Reports of States Parties Due in 1992; Addendum: Barbados,* U.N. Doc. CRC/C/3/Add.45 (1997).
Comm. on the Rights of the Child, *Consideration of Reports Submitted by States Parties Under Article 44 of the Convention: Initial Reports of States Parties Due in 1993; Addendum, Chile,* U.N. Doc. CRC/C/3/Add.18 (June 22, 1993).
Comm. on the Rights of the Child, *Consideration of Reports Submitted by States Parties Under Article 44 of the Convention: Initial Reports of States Parties Due in 1992; Addendum: Costa Rica,* U.N. Doc. CRC/C/3/Add.8 (Feb. 19, 1993).
Comm. on the Rights of the Child, *Consideration of Reports Submitted by States Parties Under Article 44 of the Convention: Initial Reports of States Parties Due in 1992; Addendum: Ecuador,* U.N. Doc. CRC/C/3/Add.44 (Sept. 24, 1996).
Comm. on the Rights of the Child, *Consideration of Reports Submitted by States Parties Under Article 44 of the Convention: Initial Reports of States Parties Due in 1995; Addendum: Suriname,* U.N. Doc. CRC/C/28/Add.11 (Feb. 13, 1998).
Comm. on the Rights of the Child, *Consideration of Reports Submitted by States Parties Under Article 44 of the Convention: Initial Report of States Parties Due in 1992; Addendum: Venezuela,* U.N. Doc. CRC/C/3/Add.54 (Sept. 22, 1997).
Comm. on the Rights of the Child, *Consideration of Reports Submitted by States Parties Under Article 44 of the Convention: Initial Reports of States Parties Due in 1992; Brazil,* U.N. Doc. CRC/C/3/Add.65 (Dec. 17, 2003).
Comm. on the Rights of the Child, *Consideration of Reports Submitted by States Parties Under Article 44 of the Convention: Initial Reports of States Parties Due in 1993; Dominica,* U.N. Doc. CRC/C/8/Add.48 (Oct. 15, 2003).
Comm. on the Rights of the Child, *Consideration of Reports Submitted by States Parties Under Article 44 of the Convention: Initial Reports of States Parties Due in 1992; Grenada,* U.N. Doc. CRC/C/3/Add.55 (Nov. 28, 1997).
Comm. on the Rights of the Child, *Consideration of Reports Submitted by States Parties Under Article 44 of the Convention: Initial Reports of States Parties Due in 1997; Haiti,* U.N. Doc. CRC/C/51/Add.7 (June 21, 2002).
Comm. on the Rights of the Child, *Consideration of Reports Submitted by States Parties Under Article 44 of the Convention: Initial Reports of States Parties Due in 1992; Mexico,* U.N. Doc. CRC/C/3/Add.11 (Feb. 10, 1993).

Comm. on the Rights of the Child, *Consideration of Reports Submitted by States Parties Under Article 44 of the Convention: Initial Reports of States Parties Due in 1995; Suriname*, U.N. Doc. CRC/C/28/Add.11 (Sept. 23, 1998).

Comm. on the Rights of the Child, *Consideration of Reports Submitted by States Parties Under Article 44 of the Convention: Initial Reports of States Parties Due in 1992; Uruguay*, U.N. Doc. CRC/C/3/Add.37 (Nov. 13, 1995).

Comm. on the Rights of the Child, *Consideration of Reports Submitted by States Parties Under Article 44 of the Convention: Periodic Reports of States Parties Due in 1997; Addendum: Honduras*, U.N. Doc. CRC/C/65/Add.2 (Feb. 20, 1998).

Comm. on the Rights of the Child, *Consideration of Reports Submitted by States Parties Under Article 44 of the Convention: Periodic Reports of States Parties Due in 1997; Addendum: Peru*, U.N. Doc. CRC/C/65/Add.8 (Aug. 3, 1998).

Comm. On the Rights of the Child, *Consideration of Reports Submitted by States Parties Under Article 44 of the Convention: Periodic Reports of States Parties Due in 1998; Argentina*, U.N. Doc. CRC/C/70/Add.10, (Feb. 26, 2002).

Comm. on the Rights of the Child, *Consideration of Reports Submitted by States Parties Under Article 44 of the Convention: Periodic Reports of States Parties Due in 1997; Chile*, U.N. Doc. CRC/C/65/Add.13 (June 25, 2001).

Comm. on the Rights of the Child, *Consideration of Reports Submitted by States Parties Under Article 44 of the Convention: Periodic Reports of States Parties Due in 1997; Paraguay, Addendum*, U.N. Doc. CRC/C/65/Add.12 (Mar. 15, 2001).

Comm. on the Rights of the Child, *Consideration of Reports Submitted by States Parties Under Article 44 of the Convention: Second and Third Periodic Reports Due in 1997 and 2002; Ecuador*, U.N. Doc. CRC/C/65/Add.28 (July 15, 2004).

Comm. on the Rights of the Child, *Consideration of Reports Submitted by States Parties Under Article 44 of the Convention: Second Periodic Reports of States Parties Due in 1997; Addendum: Guatemala*, U.N. Doc. CRC/C/65/Add.10 (Mar. 29, 2000).

Comm. on the Rights of the Child, *Consideration of Reports Submitted by States Parties Under Article 44 of the Convention: Second Periodic Reports of States Parties Due in 1997; El Salvador*, U.N. Doc. CRC/C/65/Add.25 (Oct. 22, 2003).

Comm. on the Rights of the Child, *Consideration of Reports Submitted by States Parties Under Article 44 of the Convention: Second Periodic Report; Suriname*, U.N. Doc. CRC/C/SUR/2 (Nov. 24, 2005).

Comm. on the Rights of the Child, *Consideration of Reports Submitted by States Parties Under Article 44 of the Convention: Third and Fourth Periodic Reports of States Parties Due in 2008; Panama*, U.N. Doc. CRC/C/PAN/3-4 (Jan. 27, 2011).

Comm. on the Rights of the Child, *Consideration of Reports Submitted by States Parties Under Article 44 of the Convention: Third Periodic Reports of States Parties Due in 2003; Addendum; Colombia*, U.N. Doc. CRC/C/129/Add.6 (Aug. 24, 2005).

Comm. on the Rights of the Child, *Consideration of Reports Submitted by S tates Parties Under Article 44 of the Convention: Third Periodic Reports of*

*States Parties Due in 2002; Nicaragua*, U.N. Doc. CRC/C/125/Add.3 (Oct. 15, 2004).

Comm. on the Rights of the Child, Comm. on the Rights of the Child, *Consideration of Reports Submitted by States Parties Under Article 44 of the Convention: Third Periodic Reports of States Parties Due in 2002; Paraguay*, U.N. Doc. CRC/C/PRY/3 (Mar. 27, 2009).

Comm. on the Rights of the Child, *Consideration of Reports Submitted by States Parties Under Article 44 of the Convention: Third Periodic Reports of States Parties Due in 2004; Peru*, CRC/C/125/Add.6 (May 24, 2005).

Comm. on the Rights of the Child, *Consideration of Reports Submitted by States Parties under Article 12(1) of the Optional Protocol to the Convention on the Rights of the Child on the Sale of Children, Child Prostitution and Child Pornography: Initial Reports of States Parties Due in 2005; Colombia*, U.N. Doc. CRC/C/OPSC/COL/1 (Dec. 3, 2009).

Comm. on the Rights of the Child, *Consideration of Reports Submitted by States Parties Under Article 12(1) of the Optional Protocol to the Convention on the Rights of the Child on the Sale of Children, Child Prostitution and Child Pornography: Initial Reports of States Parties Due in 2005; Costa Rica*, U.N. Doc. CRC/C/OPSC/CRI/1 (Dec. 23, 2005).

*Copenhagen Declaration on Social Development and Programme of Action*, World Summit for Social Development, U.N. Doc. A/CONF.166/9, ch. 5, para. 5 (Apr. 19, 1995).

*El Salvador: UN Rights Experts Appeal to Government to Provide Life-Saving Treatment to Woman at Risk*, United Nations Human Rights Office of the High Commissioner (Apr. 26, 2013), http://newsarchive.ohchr.org/EN/NewsEvents/Pages/DisplayNews.aspx?NewsID=13269&LangID=E.

Fourth United Nations Conference on Women, *Beijing Declaration and Platform for Action*, UN Women, https://www.unwomen.org/en/digital-library/publications/2015/01/beijing-declaration.

*"Grave Regression for Dominican Women and Girls' Right to Health"—UN Experts Call for the Criminal Code Reform to Be Dropped*, UNITED NATIONS HUMAN RIGHTS OFFICE OF THE HIGH COMMISSIONER (July 27, 2016), http://www.ohchr.org/EN/NewsEvents/Pages/DisplayNews.aspx?NewsID=20307&LangID=E#sthash.lg8U4pvB.dpuf.

*Honduras Needs Progressive Reform of Abortion Law to Advance Women's Human Rights, Say UN Experts*, UNITED NATIONS HUMAN RIGHTS OFFICE OF THE HIGH COMMISSIONER (Apr. 28, 2017), http://www.ohchr.org/EN/NewsEvents/Pages/DisplayNews.aspx?NewsID=21549&LangID=E#sthash.N4da1SoF.dpuf.

Human Rights Committee (HRC), General Comment No. 36 (2018) on Article 6 of the International Covenant on Civil and Political Rights, on the Right to Life, 30 Oct. 2018, CCPR/C/GC/36, https://tbinternet.ohchr.org/Treaties/CCPR/Shared%20Documents/1_Global/CCPR_C_GC_36_8785_E.pdf.

*Key Actions for the Further Implementation of the Programme of Action of the International Conference on Population and Development*, U.N. Doc. A/RES/S-21/2 (Nov. 8, 1999); GAOR, 21st Special Sess., Supp. No. 2, Annex (July 2, 1999).

*Latin America & Caribbean (Developing Only)*, WORLD BANK, http://data.worldbank.org/region/latin-america-and-caribbean.

*Legislative History of the Convention on the Rights of the Child, 1978–1989: Article 1 (Definition of a Child)*, [ST/]HR/1995/Ser.1/Article.1, U.N. CENTRE FOR HUMAN RIGHTS (Geneva, 1996), https://digitallibrary.un.org/record/216308?ln=en.

*Maternal Mortality in 2005: Estimates Developed by WHO, UNICEF, UNFPA, and the World Bank*, WORLD HEALTH ORGANIZATION (2007), http://www.who.int/whosis/mme_2005.pdf.

Office of the United Nations High Commissioner for Human Rights, Legislative History of the Convention on the Rights of the Child, Volume II, HR/PUB/07/1 (New York-Geneva, 2007).

Press Release, General Assembly, General Assembly Adopts United Nations Declaration on Human Cloning by Vote of 84–34–37, according to UN Press Release GA/10333 (Mar. 8, 2005).

Press Release, General Assembly, Several Aspects of Sexual, Reproductive Health—Providing Information, Using Contraception, Abortion—Should Be "Decriminalized," Third Committee Told, U.N. Press Release GA/SHC/4018 (Oct. 24, 2011).

Regional Conference on Women in Latin America and the Caribbean, July 1–16, 2010, Rep. of the Eleventh Session, U.N. Doc. LC/L.3309 (Apr. 1, 2011).

Regional Conference on Women in Latin America and the Caribbean, Aug. 6–9, 2007, Rep. of the Tenth Session, U.N. Doc. LC/G.2361(CRM.10/8) (Apr. 1, 2008).

Rep. of the Comm. on the Elimination of Discrimination Against Women, 15th Sess., Jan. 15–Feb. 2, 1996, para. 123, U.N. Doc. A/51/28; GAOR, 51st Sess., Supp. No. 38 (May 9, 1996).

Rep. of the Comm. on the Elimination of Discrimination Against Women, 19th Sess., June 22–July 10, 1998, para. 201, U.N. Doc. A/53/38/Rev.1; GAOR, 53d Sess., Supp. No. 38 (Aug. 21, 1998)

Rep. of the Comm. on the Rights of the Child, July 16, 2008, U.N. Doc. A/63/41; GAOR, 63d Sess., Supp. No. 41 (2008).

Rep. of the Fourth World Conference on Women, U.N. Doc. A/CONF.177/20/Rev.1, U.N. Sales No. 96.IV.13 XIII.I8 (1996).

Rep. of the International Conference on Population and Development, U.N. Doc. A/CONF.171/13/Rev.1, U.N. Sales No. 95.XIII.I8 (1995)

Rep. of the Working Group on a Draft Convention on the Rights of the Child, Comm'n on Human Rights, 45th Sess., Nov. 28, 1988–Dec. 9, 1988, Feb. 21, 1989–Feb. 23, 1989, U.N. Doc. E/CN.4/1989/48 (Mar. 2, 1989).

Rep. of the Working Group to the Commission on Human Rights, Comm'n on Human Rights, 38th Sess., U.N. Doc. E/CN.4/L.1542 (Mar. 10, 1980), http://hr-travaux.law.virginia.edu/document/crc/ecn4l1542/nid-175.
Rep. of the World Summit on Sustainable Development, U.N. Doc. A/CONF.199/20*, U.N. Sales No. E.03.II.A.I (2002).
U.N., Multilateral Treaties Deposited with the Secretary-General: Status as of 1 April 2009, U.N. Doc. ST/LEG/SER.E/26, U.N. Sales No. E.09.V.3 (2009).
U.N. Committee on the Elimination of Discrimination Against Women, *UN Committee on the Elimination of Discrimination Agnst* [sic] *Women: Third Periodic Report of States Parties, Suriname*, U.N. Committee on the Elimination of Discrimination Against Women (CEDAW), June 9, 2005, CEDAW/C/SUR/3, http://www.refworld.org/docid/43f3000d0.html.
U.N. Comm. on the Elimination of Discrimination Against Women, Women's Anti-Discrimination Committee Takes Up Report of Honduras; Child Labour, Working Conditions in Maquiladores Among Issues, U.N. Press Release WOM/1641 (July 26, 2007), http://www.un.org/News/Press/docs/2007/wom1641.doc.htm.
U.N. Comm. on the Rights of the Child (CRC), Reservations, Declarations and Objections Relating to the Convention on the Rights of the Child—Note by the Secretary-General, 11 July 1994, CRC/C/2/Rev.3, http://www.refworld.org/docid/3ae6aeda4.html.
U.N. E.S.C., Comm'n on Human Rights, 2nd Sess., 35th mtg. U.N. Doc. E/CN.4/SR/35 (1948), http://www.un.org/en/ga/search/view_doc.asp?symbol =E/CN.4/AC.1/SR.35.
U.N. General Assembly, Carta de fecha 11 de agosto de 2010 dirigida al Secretario General por el Encargado de Negocios interino de la Misión Permanente de El Salvador ante las Naciones Unidas [Letter dated Aug. 11, 2010, addressed to the secretary general from the interim business attache of the Permanent Mission of El Salvador before the United Nations], Aug. 16, 2010, A/64/894.
U.N. Population Information Network, U.N. Population Division, *From Cairo to Beijing: Women's Conference Amplifies ICPD* (Oct. 1995), http://www.un.org /popin/unfpa/taskforce/icpdnews/icpdnews9510/cairo.html.
U.N. Conference on Human Settlements (Habitat II), Istanbul Declaration on Settlements and the Habitat Agenda, June 3–14, 1996, U.N. Doc. A/CONF.165/14 (Aug. 7, 1996).
U.N., Dept. of Economic and Social Affairs, Population Division, volume 1 of *Abortion Policies: A Global Review* (United Nations Publications 2001), https://books.google.com/books/about/Abortion_Policies.html?id =gOr7AAAAMAAJ.
World Health Organization, *Safe Abortion: Technical and Policy Guidance for Health Systems* (2nd ed. 2012), https://www.who.int/reproductivehealth /publications/unsafe_abortion/9789241548434/en/.

## Inter-American Court Judgments, Advisory Opinions, and Resolutions

Acevedo-Jaramillo et al. v. Peru, Preliminary Objections, Merits, Reparations, and Costs, Inter-Am. Ct. H.R. (ser. C) No. 144 (Feb. 7, 2006).

Advisory Opinion OC-19/05, Inter-Am. Ct. H.R. (ser. A) No. 19 (Nov. 28, 2005).

Almonacid Arellano v. Chile, Inter-Am. Ct. H.R. (ser. C) No. 208 (Oct. 9, 2002).

Anzualdo Castro v. Peru, Preliminary Objection, Merits, Reparations, and Costs, Inter-Am. Ct. H.R. (ser. C) No. 202 (Sept. 22, 2009).

*Audiencia pública: Caso Artavia Murillo y otros (fecundación in vitro) vs. Costa Rica, parte 4* [Public Hearing: Case of Artavia Murillo and others (in vitro fertilization) v. Costa Rica. part 4], VIMEO, http://vimeo.com/49172353.

Boyce et al. v. Barbados, Preliminary Objection, Merits, Reparations and Costs, Judgment, Inter-Am. Ct. H.R. (ser. C) No. 169 (Nov. 20, 2007).

Cabrera-García & Montiel-Flores v. Mexico, Preliminary Objections, Merits, Reparations and Costs, Judgment, Inter-Am. Ct. H.R. (ser. C) No. 220 (Nov. 26, 2010).

Case of Artavia Murillo et al. ("In vitro fertilization") v. Costa Rica, Request for Provisional Measures, Provisional Measures, Order of the Inter-American Court of Human Rights (Inter-Am. Ct. H.R., March 31, 2014).

Case of Artavia Murillo et al. ("In vitro fertilization") v. Costa Rica, Monitoring Compliance with Judgments, Order of the Inter-American Court of Human Rights, ¶ 4 (Inter-Am. Ct. H.R., Feb. 26, 2016) [in Spanish only].

Case of Artavia Murillo et al. v. Costa Rica, Preliminary Objections, Merits, Reparations, and Costs, Judgment, Inter-Am. Ct. H.R. (ser. C) No. 257 (Nov. 28, 2012).

Case of Atala Riffo and daughters v. Chile, Merits, Reparations and Costs, Inter-Am. Ct. H.R. (ser. C) No. 239 (Feb. 24, 2012).

Case of Baena Ricardo et al. v. Panama, Merits, Reparations and Costs, Judgment, Inter-Am. Ct. H.R. (ser. C) No. 72 (Feb. 2, 2001).

Case of Baldeón-García v. Peru, Merits, Reparations and Costs, Inter-Am. Ct. H.R. (ser. C) No. 147 (April 06, 2006).

Case of Bámaca Velásquez v. Guatemala, Merits, Inter-Am. Ct. H.R. (ser. C) No. 70 (Nov. 25, 2000).

Case of Boyce et al. v. Barbados, Preliminary Objection, Merits, Reparations and Costs, Inter-Am. Ct. H.R. (ser. C) No. 169 (Nov. 20, 2007).

Case of Bulacio v. Argentina, Merits, Reparations and Costs, Judgment of September, Inter-Am Ct. H.R. (ser. C) No. 100 (Sep. 18, 2003).

Case of Caballero Delgado and Santana v. Colombia, Merits, Judgment, Inter-Am. Ct. H.R. (ser. C) No. 22 (Dec. 8, 1995).

Case of Coc Max et al. (Massacre of Xamán) v. Guatemala, Merits, Reparations and Costs, Judgment, Inter-Am. Ct. H.R. (ser. C) No. 356 (Aug. 22, 2018).

Case of Díaz-Peña v. Venezuela, Preliminary Objection, Merits, Reparations and Costs, Judgment, Inter-Am. Ct. H.R. (ser. C) No. 244 (June 26, 2012).

Case of Duque v. Colombia, Preliminary Objections, Merits, Reparations and Costs, Judgment, Inter-Am. Ct. H.R. (ser. C) No. 310 (Feb. 26, 2016).
Case of Fontevecchia and D'Amico v. Argentina, Merits, Reparations and Costs, Judgment, Inter-Am. Ct. H.R. (ser. C) No. 238 (Nov. 29, 2011).
Case of García Ibarra et al. v. Ecuador, Preliminary Objections, Merits, Reparations and Costs, Judgment, Inter-Am. Ct. H.R. (ser. C) No. 306 (Nov. 17, 2015).
Case of Gelman v. Uruguay, Inter-Am. Ct. H.R., Monitoring Compliance with Judgment, Order of the Inter-American Court of Human Rights of March 20 (2013).
Case of Genie Lacayo v. Nicaragua, Merits, Reparations and Costs, Judgment, Inter-Am. Ct. H.R. (ser. C) No. 30 (Jan. 29, 1997).
Case of Gómez Murillo et al. v. Costa Rica, Judgment, Inter-Am. Ct. H.R. (ser. C) No. 326 (Nov. 29, 2016) [Only in Spanish].
Case of Gonzales Lluy et al. v. Ecuador, Preliminary Objections, Merits, Reparations and Costs, Inter-Am. Ct. H.R. (ser. C) No. 298 (Sept. 1, 2015).
Case of Hilaire, Constantine and Benjamin et al. v. Trinidad & Tobago, Merits, Reparations and Costs, Inter-Am. Ct. H.R. (ser. C) No. 94 (Sept. 1, 2001).
Case of Human Rights Defender et al. v. Guatemala, Preliminary Objections, Merits, Reparations and Costs, Inter-Am. Ct. H.R. (ser. C) No. 283 (Aug. 28, 2014).
Case of Lagos del Campo v. Peru, Preliminary Objections, Merits, Reparations and Costs, Judgment, Inter-Am. Ct. H.R. (ser. C) No. 340 (Aug. 31, 2017) .
Case of Landaeta Mejías brothers et al. v. Venezuela, Preliminary Objection, Merits, Reparations and Costs, Inter-Am. Ct. H.R. (ser. C) No. 281 (Aug. 27, 2014).
Case of Loayza Tamayo v. Peru, Merits, Judgment, Inter-Am. Ct. H.R. (ser. C) No. 33 (Sept. 17, 1997).
Case of Montero Aranguren et al. (Detention Center of Catia) v. Venezuela, Preliminary Objection, Merits, Reparations and Costs, Judgment, Inter-Am. Ct. H.R. (ser. C) No. 150, (July 5, 2006).
Case of Myrna Mack Chang v. Guatemala, Merits, Reparations and Costs, Inter-Am Ct. H.R. (ser. C) No. 101 (Nov. 25, 2003).
Case of Nadege Dorzema et al. v. Dominican Republic, Merits, Reparations and Costs, Inter-Am. Ct. H.R. (ser. C) No. 251 (Oct. 24, 2012).
Case of Ortiz Hernández et al. v. Venezuela, Preliminary Objection, Merits, Reparations and Costs, Judgment, Inter-Am. Ct. H.R. (ser. C) No. 338 (Aug. 22, 2017).
Case of Palma Mendoza et al. v. Ecuador, Judgment, Inter-Am. Ct. H.R. (ser. C) No. 247 (Sept. 3, 2012).
Case of Perozo et al. v. Venezuela, Preliminary Objections, Merits, Reparations and Costs, Judgment, Inter-Am. Ct. H.R. (ser. C) No. 195 (Jan. 28, 2009).
Case of Poblete Vilches et al. v. Chile, Merits, Reparations and Costs, Inter-Am. Ct. H.R. (ser. C) No. 349 (Mar. 8, 2018).
Case of Rodríguez Vera et al. (The Disappeared from the Palace of Justice) v. Colombia, Preliminary Objections, Merits, Reparations and Costs, Judgment, Inter-Am. Ct. H.R. (ser. C) No. 287 (Nov. 14, 2014).

Case of Salvador Chiriboga v. Ecuador, Preliminary Objections and Merits, Inter-Am. Ct. H.R. (ser. C) No. 179 (May 6, 2008).
Case of the Barrios Family v. Venezuela, Merits, Reparations and Costs, Inter-Am. Ct. H.R. (ser. C) No. 237 (Nov. 24, 2011).
Case of the Garífuna Punta Piedra Community and its members v. Honduras, Preliminary Objections, Merits, Reparations and Costs, Inter-Am. Ct. H.R. (ser. C) No. 304 (Oct. 8, 2015).
Case of the "Juvenile Reeducation Institute" v. Paraguay, Preliminary Objections, Merits, Reparations and Costs, Inter-Am. Ct. H.R. (ser. C) No. 112 (Sept. 2, 2004).
Case of the girls Yean and Bosico v. Dominican Republic, Inter-Am. Ct. H.R. (ser. C) No. 130 (Sep. 8, 2005).
Case of the Massacres of El Mozote and nearby places v. El Salvador, Merits, Reparations and Costs, Inter-Am. Ct. H.R. (ser. C) No. 252 (Oct. 25, 2012).
Case of the 19 Merchants v. Colombia, Merits, Reparations and Costs, Inter-Am Ct. H.R. (ser. C) No. 109 (July 5, 2004).
Case of the Pueblo Bello Massacre v. Colombia, Merits, Reparations and Costs, Inter-Am. Ct. H.R. (ser. C) No. 140 (Jan. 31, 2006).
Case of the Pueblo Bello Massacre, Inter-Am. Ct. H.R. (ser. C) No. 140 (Jan. 31, 2006).
Case of the Yakye Axa Indigenous Community v. Paraguay, Merits, Reparations and Costs, Judgment, Inter-Am. Ct. H.R. (ser. C) No. 125 (June 17, 2005).
Case of Tristán Donoso v. Panama, Preliminary Objection, Merits, Reparations and Costs, Inter-Am. Ct. H.R. (ser. C) No. 193 (Jan. 27, 2009).
Case of Velásquez Rodríguez v. Honduras, Merits, Judgment, Inter-Am. Ct. H.R. (ser. C) No. 4 (July 29, 1988).
Case of Ximenes Lopes v. Brazil, Merits, Reparations and Costs, Judgment, Inter-Am. Ct. H.R. (ser. C) No. 149 (July 4, 2006).
Case of Zambrano Vélez et al. v. Ecuador, Merits, Reparations and Costs, Inter-Am. Ct. H.R. (ser. C) No. 166 (July 4, 2007).
Caso Artavia Murillo y otros ("fecundación in vitro") vs. Costa Rica: Reparaciones declaradas cumplidas [Case of Artavia Murillo ("in vitro fertilization") v. Costa Rica: Reparations that have been declared as complied with], Inter-American Court of Human Rights, http://www.corteidh.or.cr/docs/supervisiones/SCS/costarica/artavia/artaviac.pdf.
Castro Prison v. Peru, Merits, Reparations and Costs, Inter-Am. Ct. H.R. (ser. C) No. 160 (Nov. 25, 2006).
Cayara v. Peru, Preliminary Objections, Judgment, Inter-Am. Ct. H.R. (ser. C) No. 14 (Feb. 3, 1993).
Compulsory Membership in an Association Prescribed by Law for the Practice of Journalism (arts. 13, 29 of American Convention on Human Rights), Advisory Opinion OC-5/85, Inter-Am. Ct. H.R. (ser. A) No. 5 (Nov. 13, 1985).

Constitutional Court v. Peru, Merits, Reparations and Costs, Judgment, Inter-Am. Ct. H.R. (ser. C) No. 71 (Jan. 31, 2001).
Contreras et al. v. El Salvador, Merits, Reparations and Costs, Judgment, Inter-Am. Ct. H.R. (ser. C) No. 232 (Aug. 31, 2011).
Control de Convencionalidad, Cuadernillo de Jurisprudencia de la Corte Interamericana de Derechos Humanos No. 7, Corte Interamericana de Derechos Humanos, http://www.corteidh.or.cr/sitios/libros/todos/docs/cuadernillo7.pdf .
Control of Due Process in the Exercise of the Powers of the Inter-American Commission on Human Rights, Advisory Opinion OC-19/05, Inter-Am. Ct. H.R. (ser. A) No. 19 (Nov. 28, 2005).
Enforceability of the Right to Reply or Correction (arts. 14(1), 1(1), and 2 American Convention on Human Rights), Inter-Am. Ct. H.R., Advisory Opinion OC-7/86 (ser. A) No. 7 (1986).
Entitlement of Legal Entities to Hold Rights Under the Inter-American Human Rights System (Interpretation and scope of article 1(2), in relation to articles 1(2), 8, 11(2), 13, 16, 21, 24, 25, 29, 30, 44, 46, and 62(3) of the American Convention on Human Rights, as well as of article 8(1)(A) and (B) of the Protocol of San Salvador), Advisory Opinion OC-22/16 of Inter-Am. Ct. H.R. (ser. A) No. 22 (Feb. 26, 2016).
"Five Pensioners" v. Peru, Merits, Reparations and Costs, Inter-Am. Ct. H.R. (ser. C) No. 98 (Feb. 28, 2003).
Gender Identity, and Equality and Non-discrimination with regard to Same-Sex Couples: State Obligations in Relation to Change of Name, Gender Identity, and Rights Deriving from a Relationship between Same-Sex Couples, Advisory Opinion OC-24/17, Inter-Am. Ct. H.R. (ser. A) No. 24 (Nov. 24, 2017).
Goiburú et al. v. Paraguay, Merits, Reparations and Costs, Inter-Am. Ct. H.R (ser. C) No. 153 (Sept. 22, 2006).
Gómez-Paquiyauri brothers v. Peru, Merits, Reparations and Costs, Inter-Am. Ct. H.R. (ser. C) No. 110 (July 8, 2004).
González et al. ("Cotton Field") v. Mexico, Preliminary Objection, Merits, Reparations and Costs, Inter-Am. Ct. H.R. (ser. C) No. 205 (Nov. 16, 2009).
Inter-Am. Ct. H.R., "Other treaties" subject to the consultative jurisdiction of the court (64 American Convention on Human Rights), Advisory Opinion OC-1/82 (ser. A) No. 1 (Sept. 24, 1982).
Inter-Am. Ct. H.R., Rules of Procedure of the Inter-American Court of Human Rights, INTER-AMERICAN COURT OF HUMAN RIGHTS, https://www.oas.org/xxxivga/english/reference_docs/Reglamento_CorteIDH.pdf.
Interpretation of the American Declaration of the Rights and Duties of Man Within the Framework of Article 64 of the American Convention on Human Rights, Advisory Opinion OC-10/89, Inter-Am. Ct. H.R. (ser. A) No. 10 (July 14, 1989).

Ituango Massacres v. Colombia, Preliminary Objection, Merits, Reparations and Costs, Inter-Am. Ct. H.R. (ser. C) No. 148 (July 1, 2006).

Juridical Condition and Human Rights of the Child, Advisory Opinion OC-17/02, Inter-Am. Ct. H.R. (ser. A) No. 17 (Aug. 28, 2002).

Juridical Condition and Rights of the Undocumented Migrants, Advisory Opinion OC-18/03, Inter-Am Ct. H.R. (ser. A) No. 18 (Sep. 17, 2003).

Las Dos Erres Massacre v. Guatemala, Preliminary Objections, Merits, Reparations and Costs, Inter-Am. Ct. H.R. (ser. C) No. 211 (Nov. 24, 2009).

Las Palmeras v. Colombia, Merits, Judgment, Inter-Am. Ct. H.R. (ser. C) No. 90 (Dec. 6, 2001).

Mapiripán Massacre v. Colombia, Merits, Reparations and Costs, Inter-Am Ct. H.R. (ser. C) No. 134 (Sep. 15, 2005).

Matter of B. regarding El Salvador, Provisional Measures, Order of the Inter-American Court of Human Rights, Inter-Am. Ct. H.R. (August 19, 2013).

Matter of B. regarding El Salvador, Provisional Measures, Order of the Inter-American Court of Human Rights, Inter-Am. Ct. H.R. (May 29, 2013).

Nogueira de Carvalho et al. v. Brazil, Preliminary Judgments and Merits, Judgment, Inter-Am. Ct. H.R. (ser. C) No. 161 (Nov. 28, 2006).

Panel I, Diálogo jurisprudencial y control de convencionalidad: Una mirada comparada [Panel I, Jurisprudential dialogue and conventionality control: A comparative look], VIMEO (Oct. 11, 2013), http://vimeo.com/album/2565106/video/76720365.

Proposed Amendments of the Naturalization Provisions of the Constitution of Costa Rica, Advisory Opinion OC-4/84, Inter-Am. Ct. H.R. (ser. A) No. 4 (Jan. 19, 1984).

Provisional Measures Requested by the Inter-American Commission on Human Rights in the Matter of the Republic of Argentina, Reggiardo Tolosa Case, Order of the President of the Inter-American Court of Human Rights, Inter-Am. Ct. H.R. (Nov. 19, 1993), http://cidh.org/Ninez/Medprovisionaleseng.htm.

Raxcacó-Reyes v. Guatemala, Merits, Reparations and Costs, Inter-Am. Ct. H.R. (ser. C) No. 133 (Sep. 15, 2005).

Redilla Pacheco v. Mexico, Inter-Am. Ct. H. R. (ser. C) No. 65/05 (Oct. 12, 2005).

Request for Advisory Opinion (Letter from Ana Helena Chacón Echeverría, Costa Rican vice president, Marvin Carvajal Pérez, legal director [presidency], Eugenia Gutiérrez Ruiz, legal director [Foreign Affairs Ministry], to Chief Justice Roberto Caldas) (May 17, 2016), INTER-AMERICAN COURT OF HUMAN RIGHTS [in Spanish only], http://www.corteidh.or.cr/docs/solicitudoc/solicitud_17_05_16_esp.pdf.

Restrictions to the Death Penalty (Arts. 4(2) and 4(4) American Convention on Human Rights), Advisory Opinion OC-3/83, Inter-Am. Ct. H.R. (ser. A) No. 3 (Sept. 8, 1983).

The Right to Information on Consular Assistance in the Framework of the Guarantees of the Due Process of Law, Advisory Opinion OC-16/99, Inter-Am. Ct. H.R. (ser. A) No. 16 (Oct. 1, 1999).
Sawhoyamaxa Indigenous Community v. Paraguay, Merits, Reparations and Costs, Inter-Am. Ct. H.R. (ser. C) No. 146 (March 29, 2006).
Serrano-Cruz Sisters v. El Salvador, Merits, Reparations, and Costs, Judgment, Inter-Am. Ct. H.R. (ser. C) No. 120 (Mar. 1, 2005) (Ventura-Robles, J., dissenting).
Servellón-García et al. v. Honduras, Merits, Reparations and Costs, Inter-Am. Ct. H.R. (ser. C) No. 152 (Sep. 21, 2006).
Ticona Estrada et al. v. Bolivia, Merits, Reparations and Costs, Inter-Am. Ct. H.R. (ser. C) No. 191 (Nov. 27, 2008).
Vélez-Loor v. Panama, Preliminary Objections, Merits, Reparations and Costs, Judgment, Inter-Am. Ct. H.R. (ser. C) No. 218 (Nov. 23, 2010).
Villagrán-Morales v. Guatemala, Merits, Judgment, Inter-Am. Ct. H.R. (ser. C) No. 63 (Nov. 19, 1999).
The Word "Laws" in Article 30 of the American Convention on Human Rights, Advisory Opinion OC-6/86, Inter-Am. Ct. H.R. (ser. A) No. 6 (May 9, 1986).
Xákmok Kásek Indigenous Cmty. v. Para., Merits, Reparations and Costs, Judgment, Inter-Am. Ct. H.R. (ser. C) No. 214 (Aug. 24, 2010).

## IACHR Documents and Press Releases

Acceso a la justicia de mujeres víctimas de violencia sexual en Mesoamérica [Access to Justice for Women Victims of Sexual Violence in Mesoamerica], Inter-Am. Comm'n H.R., OEA/Ser.L/V/II, Doc. 63 (2011).
*Access to Maternal Health Services from a Human Rights Perspective*, Inter-Am. Comm'n H.R., OEA/Ser.L/V/II., Doc. 69 (July 7, 2010), http://cidh.org/women/SaludMaterna10Eng/MaternalHealthTOCeng.htm.
Ana Victoria Sanchez Villalobos and Others v. Costa Rica, Petition 12.361, Inter-Am. Comm'n H.R., Rep. No. 25/04, OEA/Ser.L./V/II.122 Doc. 5 rev. 1 (2004).
Andrews v. United States, Case 11.139, Inter-Am. Comm'n H.R., Rep. No. 57/96, OEA/Ser.L/V/II.95 Doc. 7 rev. (1997).
*Annex: Public Hearings of the 168 Period of Sessions; Right to Sexual and Reproductive Health for Women in Argentina*, IACHR (press release, May 11, 2018), http://www.oas.org/en/iachr/media_center/PReleases/2018/104A.asp.
Annual Report of the Inter-American Commission on Human Rights, OEA/Ser.L./V/11.50, doc. 13 rev. 1 (1980).
Annual Report of the Inter-American Commission on Human Rights 2002, ch. IV, Cuba, OEA/Ser.L./V/II.117, doc. 1 rev. 1 (March 7, 2003), http://www.cidh.org/annualrep/2002eng/chap.4c.htm.

Artavia Murillo v. Costa Rica, Case 12.361, Inter-Am. Comm'n H.R., Merits, Rep. No. 85/10 (2011).

Asunto Niña Mainumby respecto de Paraguay, Medidas Cautelares No. 178/15, Inter-Am. Comm. H.R., No. 22/2015 (June 8, 2015) [available in Spanish only], http://www.oas.org/es/cidh/decisiones/pdf/2015/mc178-15-es.pdf.

*Audiencia CIDH Nicaragua Derecho a la integridad personal de niñas y mujeres en Nicaragua* [IACHR hearing: Right to personal integrity of girls and women in Nicaragua], YouTube (Mar. 12, 2013), https://www.youtube.com/watch?v=oCiuKAJjDik.

Baby Boy v. United States, Case 2141, Inter-Am. Comm'n H.R., Report No. 23/81, Mar. 6, 1981, OEA/Ser.L/V/II.54, Doc. 9, rev. 1.

Banco de Lima v. Government of Peru, Case 10.169, Inter-Am. Comm'n H.R., Decision on Admissibility, Rep. No. 10/91, OEA/Ser.L/V/II.79, Doc. 22 (1991).

Beatriz v. El Salvador, Petition 2003-13, Inter-Am. Comm'n H.R., Rep. No. 120/17, Admissibility, Sept. 7, 2017, OEA/Ser.L/V/II.164 Doc. 141, http://www.oas.org/en/iachr/decisions/2017/ESAD2003-13EN.pdf .

Bendeck-Cohdinsa v. Honduras, Inter-Am. Comm'n H.R., Decision on Admissibility, Rep. No. 106/99 (1999).

Brief by *Rafael Nieto Navia and Three Law Professors* as Amici Curiae Supporting Costa Rica, Inter-Am. Comm'n H.R., Gretel Artavia Murillo v. Costa Rica (on file with author).

Brief for Asociación para la Defensa de la Vida [Association for the Defense of Life] and El Centro Iberoamericano de Estudios para la Familia [The Ibero-American Center for Family Studies] as Amici Curiae Supporting Respondents, Inter-Am. Comm'n H.R., Ana Victoria Sánchez v. Costa Rica.

Campos en los cuales han de tomarse medidas para dar mayor vigencia a los derechos humanos de acuerdo con lo prescrito por la Declaración Americana de los Derechos y Deberes del Hombre [Areas in Which Further Steps Ought to Be Taken to Give Human Rights Greater Effectiveness as Prescribed by the American Declaration of the Rights and Duties of Man], OAS/Ser.L/V/II/.27, Doc. 11 rev., 6 Marzo 1972 [in Spanish only], http://www.cidh.oas.org/annualrep/71sp/parte2.htm.

Case No. 9647 (United States), Res. 3/87, Inter-Am. Comm'n H.R., OEA/Ser.L/V/II.71, Doc. 9, rev. 1 (Mar. 27, 1987).

*CIDH presenta caso sobre Costa Rica a la Corte IDH* [IACHR presents case against Costa Rica before the IA Court], IACHR (press release, Feb. 16, 2016), http://www.oas.org/es/cidh/prensa/comunicados/2016/013.asp.

Comisión Interamericana De Derechos Humanos [IACHR], *Chile: Derechos sexuales y reproductivos* [Chile: Sexual and reproductive rights; video of 162 Periodo Extraordinario de Sesiones en Buenos Aires], YouTube (May 24, 2017), https://www.youtube.com/watch?v=cZul5ntxAA8.

Commissioner Felipe González, Address at the O.A.S. General Assembly, Peru (June 8, 2010), http://www.cidh.oas.org/Discursos/06.08.10eng.htm.

*Conclusions and Observations on the IACHR's Working Visit to El Salvador*, IACHR (press release, Jan. 29, 2018), http://www.oas.org/en/iachr/media_center/PReleases/2018/011A.asp.

Considerations Related to the Universal Ratification of the American Convention and Other Inter-American Human Rights Treaties, Inter-Am. Comm'n H.R., OEA/Ser.L/V/II.152 Doc. 21 (2014).

*The Death Penalty in the Inter-American Human Rights System: From Restrictions to Abolition*, Inter-Am. Comm. H.R. OEA/Ser.L/V/II Doc. 68 (Dec. 31, 2011), https://www.oas.org/en/iachr/docs/pdf/deathpenalty.pdf.

*Derechos Humanos y Criminalización del Aborto en Sudamérica* [Human Rights and criminalization of abortion in South America], CIDH (March 15, 2013), https://www.youtube.com/watch?v=kEPXNAWAvLU.

*Financial Resources*, IACHR (2016), http://www.oas.org/en/iachr/mandate /financial_resources.asp.

Gómez v. Costa Rica, Case 1368-04, Inter-Am. Comm'n H.R., Decision on Admissibility, Report No. 156/10, OEA/Ser.L./V/II.122 (2010).

*Human Rights Situation of Pregnant Women in the Americas*, Session: 156th Period of Sessions, YouTube (Oct. 20, 2015), https://www.youtube.com/watch?v=4S54REs0V4Y.

IACHR, *Third Report on the Situation of Human Rights in Colombia*, OEA/Ser.L/V/II.102, Doc. 9 rev. 1, 26 February 1999, http://www.cidh.oas.org/countryrep /Colom99en/table%20of%20contents.htm.

*IACHR and Inter-American Court Present a Joint Proposal for the Financing of the Inter-American System of Human Rights*, IACHR (press release, Oct. 4, 2016), http://www.oas.org/en/iachr/media_center/PReleases/2016/146.asp.

IACHR Annual Reports, OAS, http://www.oas.org/en/iachr/reports/annual.asp.

*IACHR Hearings and Other Public Events, Sessions by Topic, Rights of Women*, ORGANIZATION OF AMERICAN STATES, http://www.oas.org/es/cidh /audiencias/TopicsList.aspx?Lang=en&Topic=15.

*IACHR Regrets Decision of Venezuela to Denounce the American Convention on Human Rights* (press release, Sept. 12, 2012), http://www.oas.org/en/iachr/media_center/PReleases/2012/117.asp.

*IACHR Thanks Donors*, IACHR, http://www.oas.org/en/iachr/donantes/2013 /default.asp.

*IACHR Thanks the United States for Additional Financial Contribution*, IACHR (press release, Oct. 26, 2016), http://www.oas.org/en/iachr/media_center/PReleases/2016/158.asp.

*IACHR Urges All States to Adopt Comprehensive, Immediate Measures to Respect and Protect Women's Sexual and Reproductive Rights*, IACHR (press release, Oct. 23, 2017), http://www.oas.org/en/iachr/media_center/PReleases/2017/165.asp.

*IACHR Urges El Salvador to End the Total Criminalization of Abortion*, IACHR (press release, March 7, 2018), http://www.oas.org/en/iachr/media_center/PReleases/2018/042.asp.

*IACHR Welcomes Approval of Chilean Law Decriminalizing Abortion on Three Grounds*, OAS (press release, Sept. 5, 2017), http://www.oas.org/en/iachr/media_center/PReleases/2017/133.asp.

Inadmissibility Report 12.379, Mario Alfredo Lares-Reyes et al., Inter-Am. Comm'n H.R. (Feb. 27, 2002).

James Demers v. Canada, Petition 225-04, Inter-Am. Comm'n H.R., No. 85/06 (2007).

Letter from Ana Victoria Sánchez Villalobos, Plaintiff, Inter-Am. Comm'n on Human Rights Case 12.361, to Santiago A. Cantón, Exec. Sec'y, Inter-Am. Comm'n on Human Rights (Nov. 18, 2008).

Letter from Roberto F. Caldas (Inter-American Court chief justice) and James Cavallaro (Inter-American Commission president) to Luis L. Almagro Lemes (O.A.S. General Secretary), IACHR (sent on Sept. 30, 2016), http://www.oas.org/documents/spa/press/Carta-CIDH-30-dep-2016-esp.pdf.

Luis Godoy v. Argentina, Case 12.324, Inter-Am. Comm'n H.R., Decision on Merits, Rep. No. 66/12 (2012).

Manuela and family v. El Salvador, Petition 424-12, Inter-Am. Comm'n H.R., Rep. No. 29/17, Admissibility, March 18, 2017, OEA/Ser.L/V/II.161, Doc. 36, https://www.oas.org/en/iachr/decisions/2017/ESAD424-12EN.pdf.

Mevopal v. Argentina, Inter-Am. Comm'n H.R., Decision on Admissibility, Rep. No. 39/99 (1999).

Michael Domingues v. United States, Case 12.285, Inter-Am. Comm'n H.R., Rep. No. 62/02, Merits (2002).

*Paraguay: Violencia sexual*, Comisión Interamericana de Derechos Humanos, YouTube (Apr. 4, 2016), https://www.youtube.com/watch?v=jcTdc1SLnro.

Paulina del Carmen Ramírez Jacinto v. Mexico, Petition 161-02, Inter-Am. Comm'n H.R., No. 21/07 and Annex (2007).

*PM 43-10 "Amelia," Precautionary Measures Granted by the Commission during 2010*, OAS, http://www.oas.org/en/iachr/decisions/precautionary.asp.

*PM 114/13—B, El Salvador*, IACHR, http://www.oas.org/en/iachr/decisions/precautionary.asp#tab2013.

Public Hearings of the 96 Regular Session from Aug. 27 to Sept. 7, 2012, Inter-Am. Comm'n Human Rights, *Caso Artavia Murillo y otros (Fecundación in vitro) vs. Costa Rica, Parte 4* [Case of Artavia Murillo and others (IVF) v. Costa Rica, part 4], http://www.oas.org/es/cidh/audiencias/Hearings.aspx?Lang=es&Session=53.

Public Hearings of the 133 Period of Sessions, Inter-Am. Comm'n Human Rights, *In Vitro Fertilization, Costa Rica: Case 12.361 and Petitions 1368/04, 16/05, 678/06, 1191/06* (Oct. 28, 2008), http://www.oas.org/es/cidh/audiencias/.

*Recursos Financieros 2014*, IACHR, http://www.oas.org/es/cidh/mandato/finanzas/2014-Recursos-Financieros.pdf.
Rep. on Public Hearings from the 162nd Session, OAS (press release, June 27, 2017), http://www.oas.org/en/iachr/media_center/PReleases/2017/085.asp
Resolución de levantamiento de medidas cautelares 28/2018 [Resolution lifting precautionary measures 28/2018], Inter-Am. Comm'n H.R. (May 5, 2018), http://www.oas.org/es/cidh/decisiones/pdf/2018/28-18MC617-15-CR-Levantamiento.pdf.
Santiago Marzioni v. Argentina, Case 11.673, Inter-Am. Comm'n H.R., Rep. No. 39/96, OEA/Ser.L/V/II.95 Doc. 7 rev. (1997).
Tabacalera Boquerón v. Paraguy, Inter-Am. Comm'n H.R., Decision on Admissibility, Rep. No. 47/97, OEA/Ser.L./V/II.98, Doc. 6 rev. (1998).
*Thematic Hearing "Derechos sexuales y reproductivos de las mujeres en América del Sur"* IACHR, 158 period of sessions (June 7, 2016), YouTube, https://www.youtube.com/watch?v=CIobTDgLD2w.
*Thematic Hearing "Human Rights Situation of Women Deprived of Liberty due to Obstetric Emergencies During Pregnancy in El Salvador,"* IACHR, 156 period of sessions (Oct. 19, 2015) https://www.youtube.com/watch?v=h9Op-28nM2U.
*Thematic Hearing "Human Rights Situation of Women in Nicaragua,"* IACHR, 141 period of sessions (March 25, 2011), http://www.oas.org/es/cidh/audiencias/Hearings.aspx?Lang=es&Session=119.
*Thematic Hearing "Risks and Vulnerabilities Affecting Defenders of Women's Rights in the Americas,"* IACHR, 133 period of sessions (Oct. 28, 2008), http://www.oas.org/es/cidh/audiencias/Hearings.aspx?Lang=es&Session=9.
*Thematic Hearing "Situación de derechos humanos de las mujeres y las niñas en El Salvador*, IACHR, 147 period of sessions (March 16, 2013), https://www.youtube.com/watch?v=XRSAA7UWsko.
*What Is the IACHR?*, Inter-American Commission on Human Rights, http://www.cidh.oas.org/what.htm.

## National Court Decisions

1ª Turma afasta prisão preventiva de acusados da prática de aborto, Supremo Tribunal Federal (published Nov. 29, 2016) (Braz.), http://www.stf.jus.br/portal/cms/verNoticiaDetalhe.asp?idConteudo=330769.
Ação Direta de Inconstitucionalidade 3.510 Distrito Federal, Supremo Tribunal Federal Jurisprudência [S.T.F.J.], 2403-1, Relator: Ayres Britto, 28.05.2010, 137 (Braz.).
Acción de inconstitucionalidad 146/2007 y su acumulada 147/2007, Suprema Corte de Justicia de la Nación [SCJN] [Supreme Court] (Mex.).

Acción de inconstitucionalidad 146/2007 y su acumulada 147/2007, Suprema Corte de Justicia de la Nación [SCJN] [Supreme Court], *Intervención del Ministro Sergio Salvador Aguirre Anguiano en sesión extraordinaria celebrada el 25 de agosto de 2008* (Mex.).

Acción de inconstitucionalidad 146/2007 y su acumulada 147/2007, Suprema Corte de Justicia de la Nación [SCJN] [Supreme Court], *Voto concurrente que formula el Ministro Genaro David Góngora Pimentel en la acción de inconstitucionalidad 146/2007 y su acumulada 147/2007* (Mex.).

Acción de inconstitucionalidad 146/2007 y su acumulada 147/2007, Suprema Corte de Justicia de la Nación [SCJN] [Supreme Court], *Voto concurrente que formula el Ministro Sergio A. Valls en la acción de inconstitucionalidad 146/2007 y su acumulada 147/2007* (Mex.).

Acción de inconstitucionalidad 146/2007 y su acumulada 147/2007, Suprema Corte de Justicia de la Nación [SCJN] [Supreme Court], *Voto de minoría que formulan los Ministros Sergio Salvador Aguirre Anguiano, Mariano Azuela Güitrón y Guillermo I. Ortiz Mayagoitia en la acción de inconstitucionalidad 146/2007 y su acumulada 147/2007* (Mex.).

ADPF No. 442, Consultor Jurídico, https://www.conjur.com.br/dl/psol-stf-descriminalize-aborto-meses.pdf.

*Advogada-Geral da União manifesta-se pela improcedência do pedido formulado pelo arguente* [Attorney General presents on the impropriety of the plaintiff's request], Argüição de Descumprimento de Preceito Fundamental 442 Distrito Federal, ADVOCACIA-GERAL DA UNIÃO (Braz.), http://www.camara.gov.br/proposicoesWeb/fichadetramitacao?idProposicao=1050889.

Beal v. Doe, 432 U.S. 438 (1977).

Bundesverfassungsgericht [Federal Constitutional Court], Feb. 25, 1975, 39 BVerfGE 1 (First Senate 1975) (Ger.).

Cámara Nac. De Apelac. en lo Criminal y Correccional [National Court of Civil and Correctional Appeals of the Federal Capital], sala 02, 26/01/17, "Birnie, Ronaldo Julián y otros s/procesamiento," SAIJ: FA17260002 (Arg.).

Commonwealth of Mass. v. Kenneth Edelin, 371 Mass. 497 (1976).

Comunicado No. 42, Expdte. T 6612909—Sentencia SU-096/18, REPÚBLICA DE COLOMBIA, CORTE CONSTITUCIONAL (Oct. 17, 2018), http://www.corteconstitucional.gov.co/comunicados/No.%2042%20comunicado%2017%20de%20octubre%20de%202018.pdf.

Comunicado No. 56, Corte Constitucional [C.C.] [Constitutional Court], diciembre 10, 2015 (Colom.), http://www.corteconstitucional.gov.co/comunicados/No.%2056%20comunicado%2010%20de%20diciembre%20de%202015.pdf.

Corte Constitucional [C.C.] [Constitutional Court], junio 9, 2016, Sentencia T-301/2016, G.C. (t. Tercero) (Colom.).

Corte Constitucional [C.C.] [Constitutional Court], Sentencia T-209/08, G.C. (s. Novena) (Colom.).
Corte Constitucional [C.C.] [Constitutional Court], mayo 28, 2009, Sentencia T-388/09, G.C. (s. Octava) (Colom.).
Corte Constitucional [C.C.] [Constitutional Court], julio 22, 2010, Sentencia T-585/10, G.C. (s. Octava) (Colom.).
Corte Constitucional [C.C.] [Constitutional Court], agosto 10, 2012, Sentencia T-627/12, G.C. (s. Octava) (Colom.).
Corte Constitucional [C.C.] [Constitutional Court], Sentencia T-841/11, G.C. (s. Octava) (Colom.).
Corte Constitucional [C.C.] [Constitutional Court], octubre 2, 2008, Sentencia T-946/08, G.C. (t. Tercera) (Colom.).
Corte Constitucional [C.C.] [Constitutional Court], Sentencia T-988/07, G.C. (s. Séptima) (Colom.).
Corte Constitucional [C.C.] [Constitutional Court], febrero 28, 2012, Auto 038/12 (Colom.)
Corte Constitucional [C.C.] [Constitutional Court], febrero 17, 2005, Sentencia T-128/05, G.C. (s. Novena), (Colom.)
Corte Constitucional [C.C.] [Constitutional Court], mayo 18, 1998, Sentencia T-223/98, G.C. (s. Novena) (Colom.)
Corte Constitucional [C.C.] [Constitutional Court], mayo 20, 2004, Sentencia T-501/04, G.C. (s. Novena) (Colom.)
Corte Constitucional [C.C.] [Constitutional Court], enero 29, 2004, Sentencia T-063/04, G.C. (s. Octava) (Colom.).
Corte Constitucional [C.C.] [Constitutional Court], abril 24, 1997, Sentencia C-213/1997, G.C. (s. Plena) (Colom.).
Corte Constitucional [C.C.] [Constitutional Court], enero 23, 1997, Sentencia C-013/1997, G.C. (s. Plena) (Colom.).
Corte Constitucional [C.C.] [Constitutional Court], junio 20, 2001, Sentencia C-647/2001, G.C. (s. Plena) (Colom.).
Corte Constitucional [C.C.] [Constitutional Court], marzo 17, 1994, Sentencia C-133/1994, G.C. (s. Plena) (Colom.).
Corte Constitucional [C.C.] [Constitutional Court], Sala Plena, mayo 10, 2006, Sentencia C-355/2006, Gaceta de la Corte Constitucional [G.C.] (t. Tercero) (Colom.).
Corte Constitucional [C.C.] [Constitutional Court], junio 16, 2005, Sentencia T-639/05, G.C. (s. Quinta) (Colom.).
Corte Constitucional [C.C.] [Constitutional Court], septiembre 9, 2004, Sentencia T-872/04, G.C. (s. Sexta) (Colom.).
Corte Constitucional [C.C.] [Constitutional Court], julio 8, 2005, Sentencia T-727/05, G.C. (s. Tercera) (Colom.).
Corte Suprema de Justicia [C.S.J.] [Supreme Court], agosto 30, 2001, "Philippi Izquierdo c. Laboratorio Chile S.A.," Rol de la causa: 2186-2001 (Chile).

Corte Suprema de Justicia [C.S.J.] [Supreme Court], Sala Constitucional [Constitutional Chamber], marzo 15, 2000, Expdte. 95-001734-0007-CO, Gaceta Judicial [G.J.] (No. 45) (Costa Rica).

Corte Suprema de Justicia [C.S.J.] [Supreme Court], Sala Constitucional [Constitutional Chamber], Exp. 15-013929-0007-CO, Res. N. 2016001692, febrero 3, 2016, SISTEMA COSTARRICENSE DE INFORMACIÓN JURÍDICA (Costa Rica).

Corte Suprema de Justicia de la Nación [CSJN] [National Supreme Court of Justice], 13/03/2012, "F.A.L. /s medida autosatisfactiva" [Fallos] (Arg.).

Corte Suprema de Justicia de la Nación [CSJN] [National Supreme Court of Justice], 03/05/2002, "Portal de Belén—Asociación Civil sin Fines de Lucro c. Ministerio de Salud y Acción Social de la Nación s/amparo" [Fallos] (2001-D-(1-7)) (Arg.).

Corte Suprema de Justicia de la Nación (CSJN) [National Supreme Court of Justice], 14/02/2017, 368/1998 (34-M)/CS1 Ministerio de Relaciones y Culto "s/informe sentencia dictada en el caso 'Fontevecchia y D'Amico vs. Argentina' por la Corte Interamericana de Derechos Humanos" [Fallos: 340:47] (Arg.).

Corte Suprema de Justicia de la Nación [CSJN] [National Supreme Court of Justice], 11/01/2001, "T., S. c/Gobierno de la Ciudad de Buenos Aires s/amparo" [Fallos: 324:5], J.A. 2001-II-356 (Arg.).

Corte Suprema de Justicia de la Nación [CSJN] [National Supreme Court of Justice], 01/09/2015, "Recurso de hecho deducido por los actores en la causa L.E.H. y otros c/O.S.E.P. s/amparo" [Fallos: 338:779] (Arg.).

Corte Suprema de Justicia de la República de Honduras [Supreme Court of Honduras], Dictamen Decreto 54-2009 [Decision on decree 54-2009], 21 de junio 2012 (Hond.).

Corte Suprema de Justicia, Constituida en Tribunal de Amparo [Supreme Court of Justice, constituting *Amparo* Tribunal], Dec. 8, 2017, Amparo 1434-2017, CORTE SUPREMA DE JUSTICIA (2017) (Guat.).

Corte Suprema de Justicia, Sala Constitutional [Supreme Court of Justice, Constitutional Chamber], Feb. 4, 2019, Amparo promovido por M. C. G.G. C/P.P.G., Director de la Clinica G." No. 3241/2010, CORTE SUPREMA DE JUSTICIA (Para.).

Decisão de Convocação de Audiência Pública [Resolution calling a public hearing], Argüição de Descumprimento de Preceito Fundamental 442 Distrito Federal, SUPREMO TRIBUNAL FEDERAL (Braz.), http://www.stf.jus.br/arquivo/cms/audienciasPublicas/anexo/DespachoConvocatoriointerrupcaoGravidez.pdf.

Derecho a la vida: Su protección constitutional [Right to life: Its constitutional protection], Pleno de la Suprema Corte de Justicia de la Nación [SCJN] [Supreme Court], Semanario Judicial de la Federación y Gaceta, Novena Época, tomo XV, Febrero de 2002, Tesis P./J. 13/2002, Página 589 (Mex.).

Derecho a la vida del producto de la concepción: Su protección deriva de la Constitución Política de los Estados Unidos Mexicanos, de los tratados internacionales y de las leyes federales y locales [Right to life of the product of conception: His protection derives from the Constitution of the United States of Mexico, international treaties, and federal and local laws], Pleno de la Suprema Corte de Justicia de la Nación [SCJN] [Supreme Court *en banc*], Semanario Judicial de la Federación y Gaceta, Novena Época, tomo XV, Febrero de 2002, Jurisprudencia P./J. 14/2002, Página 588 (Mex.), http://observatoriointernacional.com/?p=504.

Doe v. Bolton, 410 U.S. 179 (1973).

ENTSCHEIDUNGEN DES BUNDESVERFASSUNGSGERICHTS [BVERFGE] [Federal Constitutional Court] May 29, 1974 (Ger.).

ENTSCHEIDUNGEN DES BUNDESVERFASSUNGSGERICHTS [BVERFGE] [Federal Constitutional Court] Oct. 22, 1974 (Ger.).

Gonzales v. Carhart, 550 U.S. 124 (2007).

Harris v. McRae, 448 U.S. 297 (1980).

Inteiro Teor do Acórdão, Argüição de Descumprimento de Preceito Fundamental 54, SUPREMO TRIBUNAL FEDERAL JURISPRUDÊNCIA [S.T.F.J.], Relator: Marco Aurélio, 12.04.2012, 4 (Braz.).

Judgment of May 28, 1993, 88 ENTSCHEIDUNGEN DES BUNDESVERFASSUNGSGERICHTS [BVERFGE] 203 (Second Senate), 1993 Europäische Grundrechte Zeitschrift [EuGRZ].

Jurisprudencia emitida por la Corte Interamericana de Derechos Humanos, Es vinculante para los jueces mexicanos siempre que sea más favorable a la persona [Inter-American Court Jurisprudence is Binding on Mexican judges as long as more favorable to the human persons], Pleno de la Suprema Corte de Justicia de la Nación [SCJN] [Supreme Court], Gaceta del Semanario Judicial de la Federación, Décima Época, tomo I, Abril de 2014, Tesis P./J. 21/2014 (10a.), Página 204 (Mex.).

Juzgado De Garantías (Cht.) (provincial lower court of ordinary jurisdiction), 23/01/17, "L. G. s/muerte dudosa," SAIJ: FA17150000 (Arg.).

Juzgado Federal de Salta No. 1 [Federal court of Salta N. 1], 8/7/2013, "Lodi Ortiz Andrea Melisa—Larran Cristian c/Swiss Medical s/amparo," Expdte. No. 61000007/13 (Arg.).

Maher v. Roe, 432 U.S. 464 (1977).

Poelker v. Doe, 432 U.S. 519 (1977).

Proyecto de Acción de inconstitucionalidad 146/2007 y su acumulada 147/2007, Suprema Corte de Justicia de la Nación [SCJN] [Supreme Court] (Mex.).

Roe v. Wade, 410 U.S. 113 (1973).

Sala de lo Constitucional de la Corte Suprema de Justicia [Constitutional Chamber of Supreme Court of Justice], April 13, 2011, Inconstitucionalidad 67-10, CENTRO DE DOCUMENTACIÓN JUDICIAL DE CORTE SUPREMA DE

JUSTICIA DE EL SALVADOR (2007) (El Sal.), http://www.csj.gob.sv/ResSalaConst.nsf/3904032ec36cbce60625767f000945eb/0a7cee6e086c6795062578a80080552d/$FILE/67-2010.pdf.

Sala de lo Constitucional de la Corte Suprema de Justicia [Constitutional Chamber of Supreme Court of Justice], May 28, 2013, Amparo 310-2013, CENTRO DE DOCUMENTACIÓN JUDICIAL DE CORTE SUPREMA DE JUSTICIA DE EL SALVADOR (2013) (El Sal.), http://www.jurisprudencia.gob.sv/DocumentosBoveda/D/1/2010-2019/2013/05/A00CC.PDF.

Sala de lo Constitucional de la Corte Suprema de Justicia [Constitutional Chamber of Supreme Court of Justice], Sept. 21, 2011, Amparo 166-2009, CENTRO DE DOCUMENTACIÓN JUDICIAL DE CORTE SUPREMA DE JUSTICIA DE EL SALVADOR (2011) (El Sal.), http://www.jurisprudencia.gob.sv/DocumentosBoveda/D/1/2010-2019/2011/09/92F11.PDF.

Sala de lo Constitucional de la Corte Suprema de Justicia [Constitutional Chamber of Supreme Court of Justice], Nov. 20, 2007, Inconstitucionalidad 18-98, CENTRO DE DOCUMENTACIÓN JUDICIAL DE CORTE SUPREMA DE JUSTICIA DE EL SALVADOR (2007) (El Sal.), http://www.jurisprudencia.gob.sv/DocumentosBoveda/D/1/2000-2009/2007/11/2EF3.PDF.

Suprema Corte de Justicia de la Nación [SCJN], Primera Sala, 2 de Diciembre de 2015, Amparo en revisión 442/2015 (Mex.).

Suprema Corte de Justicia de la Nación [SCJN], Segunda Sala, 4 de Abril de 2018, Amparo en revisión 601/2017 (Mex.).

Suprema Corte de Justicia de la Nación [SCJN] [Supreme Court], Excusas absolutorias y excluyentes de responsabilidad: Sus diferencias [Absolutory excuses and exculpatory factors: Their differences], Novena Época, tomo XV, Febrero de 2002, Tesis P./J. 11/2002, Página 592 (Mex.), https://sjf.scjn.gob.mx/SJFSist/Documentos/Tesis/187/187799.pdf.

Suprema Corte de Justicia de Mendoza [S.C.J. de Mza.] [Supreme Court of Mendoza], 30/07/2014, "L., E. H. c. OSEP s/acción de amparo," Expdte: 110.803 (Arg.), http://www2.jus.mendoza.gov.ar/listas/proveidos/vertexto.php?ide=3768538768.

Suprema Corte de Justicia del Uruguay [S.C.J.] [Uruguay Supreme Court of Justice], 22/02/2013, M. L., J. F. F., O.—Denuncia—Excepción de inconstitucionalidad arts 1, 2 y 3 de la ley 18831, No. 20/2013 (Uru.).

Supremo Tribunal Federal [S.T.F.], Explicação Ministro Ricardo Lewandowski, Argüição de Descumprimento de Preceito Fundamental Distrito Federal 54-8, Relator: Marco Aurélio, 31.07.2008 (Braz.), http://redir.stf.jus.br/paginadorpub/paginador.jsp?docTP=TP&docID=3707334.

Tribunal Constitucional [T.C.] [Constitutional Court], 14 de junio 2006, "José Fernando Roser Rohde c. Instituto Nacional de Higiene y Medicina Tropical 'Leopoldo Izquieta Pérez' y el Ministro de Salud S/Acción de Amparo," Caso No. 0014-2005-RA (Ecuador).

Tribunal Constitucional [T.C.] [Constitutional Court], Dec. 17, 2015, Sentencia TC/0599/15, TRIBUNAL CONSTITUCIONAL REPUBLICA DOMINICANA (2015) (Dom. Rep.), https://www.tribunalconstitucional.gob.do/content/sentencia-tc059915.
Tribunal Constitucional [T.C.] [Constitutional Court], 16 de octubre 2009, ONG "Acción de Lucha Anticorrupción" Sentencia del Tribunal Constitucional, Expdte. No. 02005-2009-PA/TC (Peru).
Tribunal Constitucional [T.C.] [Constitutional Court], enero 18 de 2019, Rol No. 5572-18-CDS /5650-18-CDS (Chile), https://www.tribunalconstitucional.cl/ver2.php?id=4168.
Tribunal Constitucional [T.C.] [Constitutional Court], 18 abril 2008, Requerimiento de inconstitucionalidad deducido en contra de algunas disposiciones de las "Normas Nacionales sobre Regulación de la Fertilidad," aprobadas por el Decreto Supremo No. 48, de 2007, del Ministerio de Salud, Rol de la causa: 740-07 (Chile).
Tribunal Constitucional [T.C.] [Constitutional Court], 28 agosto 2017, Requerimiento de inconstitucionalidad respecto del proyecto de ley que "regula la despenalización de la interrupción voluntaria del embarazo en tres causales," Boletín No. 9895-11 [Constitutional writ regarding the bill that "regulates the decriminalization of voluntary interruption of pregnancy under three grounds"], Rol No. 3729(3751)-17-CPT (Chile).
Tribunal Constitucional Plurinacional [Constitutional Plurinational Tribunal] Feb. 5, 2014, Sentencia Constitucional Plurinacional 0206/2014, Exp. 00320-2012-01-AIA (Bol.).
Tribunal de Apelación Penal de la Adolescencia [Juvenile Court of Appeals], Dec. 3, 2018, Acuerdo y Sentencia No. 12, CORTE SUPREMA DE JUSTICIA (Para.).
Webster v. Reproductive Health Services, 492 U.S. 490 (1989).
Williams v. Zbaraz, 448 U.S. 358 (1980).

## National and State Constitutions, Statutes, and Regulations

Acuerdo No. 21, Órgano Oficial de la República de Guatemala, Diario de Centro America, tomo CCLXI, abril de 1999.
Code Pénal [C. Pén] (Haiti).
Código Civil [Cód. Civ.] [Civil Code] (Arg.).
Código Civil (Bol.).
Código Civil [Cód. Civ.] [Civil Code] (Chile).
Código Civil [C.C.] [Civil Code] (Colom.).
Código Civil (Costa Rica).
Código Civil (Ecuador).
Código Civil (El Sal.).

Código Civil (Guat.).
Código Civil (Hond.).
Código Civil (Nicar.).
Código Civil (Para.).
Código Civil [Cód. Civ.] [Civil Code] (Peru).
Código Civil de la República de Nicaragua [Civil Code of the Republic of Nicaragua] (Nicar.).
Código Civil de la República de Panamá [Civil Code of the Republic of Panamá] (Pan.).
Código Civil de la República Dominicana [Civil Code of the Republic of Dominicana] (Dom. Rep.).
Código Civil del Distrito Federal [Civil Code for the Federal District], 26 de mayo de 1928 (Mex.).
Código Civil del Estado de Aguascalientes [Civil Code of the State of Aguascalientes], 7 de diciembre de 1947 (Mex.).
Código Civil del Estado de Baja California [Civil Code of the State of Baja California] de Enero de 1974 (Mex.).
Código Civil del Estado de Campeche [Civil Code of the State of Campeche], 17 de octubre de 1942 (Mex.).
Código Civil del Estado de Chiapas [Civil Code of the State of Chiapas], 2 de febrero de 1938 (Mex.).
Código Civil del Estado de Chihuahua [Civil Code of the State of Chihuahua], 23 de marzo de 1974 (Mex.).
Código Civil del Estado de Colima [Civil Code of the State of Colima], 25 de septiembre de 1954 (Mex.).
Código Civil del Estado de Durango [Civil Code of the State of Durango], 21 de abril de 2013 (Mex.).
Código Civil del Estado de Guanajuato [Civil Code of the State of Guanajuato], 14 de mayo de 1967 (Mex.).
Código Civil del Estado de Jalisco [Civil Code of the State of Jalisco], 25 de febrero de 1995 (Mex.).
Código Civil del Estado de México [Civil Code of the State of Mexico], 29 de abril de 2002 (Mex.).
Código Civil del Estado de Nayarit [Civil Code of the State of Nayarit] 22 de agosto de 1981 (Mex.).
Código Civil del Estado de Querétaro [Civil Code of the State of Querétaro], 21 de octubre de 2009 (Mex.).
Código Civil del Estado de Sinaloa [Civil Code of the State of Sinaloa], 25 de julio de 1940 (Mex.).
Código Civil del Estado de Veracruz [Civil Code of the State of Veracruz], 15 de septiembre de 1932 (Mex.).
Código Civil del Estado de Yucatán [Civil Code of the State of Yucatan], 31 de diciembre de 1993 (Mex.).

Código Civil del Estado Libre y Soberano de Guerrero [Civil Code of the Free and Sovereign State of Guerrero], Número 358, 2 de febrero de 1993 (Mex.).

Código Civil Federal [CC] [Federal Civil Code], Diario Oficial de la Federación [DOF], 28-01-2010 (Mex.).

Código Civil para el Estado de Coahuila de Zaragoza [Civil Code for the State of Coahuila de Zaragoza], 25 de junio de 1999 (Mex.).

Código Civil para el Estado de Hidalgo [Civil Code for the State of Hidalgo], 8 de octubre de 1940 (Mex.).

Código Civil para el Estado de Oaxaca [Civil Code for the State of Oaxaca], 25 de noviembre de 1944 (Mex.).

Código Civil para el Estado de Michoacán [Civil Code for the State of Michoacán], 30 de julio de 1936 (Mex.).

Código Civil para el Estado de Nuevo León [Civil Code of the State of Nuevo León], 6 de julio de 1935 (Mex.).

Código Civil para el Estado de Quintana Roo [Civil Code for the State of Quintana Roo], 8 de octubre de 1980 (Mex.).

Código Civil para el Estado de San Luis Potosí [Civil Code for the State of San Luis Potosí], 18 de abril de 1946 (Mex.).

Código Civil para el Estado de Tabasco [Civil Code for the State of Tabasco], 9 de abril de 1997 (Mex.).

Código Civil para el Estado de Tamaulipas [Civil Code for the State of Tamaulipas], 10 de enero de 1987 (Mex.).

Código Civil para el Estado Libre y Soberano de Baja California Sur [Civil Code for the Free and Sovereign State of Baja California], 19 de julio de 1996 (Mex.).

Código Civil para el Estado Libre y Soberano de Tlaxcala [Civil Code for the Free and Sovereign State of Tlaxcala], 20 de octubre de 1976 (Mex.).

Código Civil para el Estado Libre y Soberano de Puebla [Civil Code for the Free and Sovereign State of Puebla], 25 de enero de 2005 (Mex.).

Código de Defensa Social Para el Estado de Chiapas [C.P.] [Criminal Code for the State of Chiapas], Diario Oficial de la Federación [DO], 1 de mayo de 2013 (Mex.).

Código Penal de Defensa Social Para el Estado de San Luis Potosí [C.P.] [Criminal Code for the State of San Luis Potosí], Diario Oficial de la Federación [DO], 30 de septiembre de 2000 (Mex.).

Código de Defensa Social Para el Estado de Sinaloa [C.P.] [Criminal Code for the State of Sinaloa], Diario Oficial de la Federación [DO], 28 de octubre de 1992 (Mex.).

Código de Defensa Social Para el Estado de Sonora [C.P.] [Criminal Code for the State of Sonora], Diario Oficial de la Federación [DO], 24 de marzo de 1994 (Mex.).

Código de Defensa Social Para el Estado de Tabasco [C.P.] [Criminal Code for the State of Tabasco], Diario Oficial de la Federación [DO], 5 de febrero de 1997 (Mex.).

Código de Defensa Social Para el Estado de Tamaulipas [C.P.] [Criminal Code for the State of Tamaulipas], Diario Oficial de la Federación [DO], 20 de diciembre de 1986 (Mex.).
Código de Defensa Social Para el Estado de Yucatán [C.P.] [Criminal Code for the State of Yucatán], Diario Oficial de la Federación [DO], 30 de marzo de 2000 (Mex.).
Código de Defensa Social Para el Estado de Zacatecas [C.P.] [Criminal Code for the State of Zacatecas], Diario Oficial de la Federación [DO], 4 de agosto de 2012 (Mex.).
Código de Familia (Costa Rica).
Código de Familia (El Sal.).
Código de Familia (Hond.).
Código de la Niñez y Adolescencia [Childhood and Adolescence Code] (Ecuador).
Código de la Niñez y Adolescencia [Childhood and Adolescence Code] (Hond.).
Código de la Niñez y Adolescencia [Childhood and Adolescence Code] (Para.).
Código de la Niñez y la Adolescencia [Childhood and Adolescence Code] (Costa Rica).
Código de la Niñez y la Adolescencia [Childhood and Adolescence Code] (Nicar.).
Código de la Niñez y la Adolescencia [Childhood and Adolescence Code] (Uru.).
Código de las Familias y del Proceso Familiar, Ley No. 603 de 19 de noviembre de 2014, 28 (Bol.).
Código del Menor [Childhood Code] (Colom.).
Código de los Niños y Adolescentes (Peru).
Código de Proceso Civil [C.P.C.] [Code of Civil Process] (Braz.).
Código de Salud [Health Code] (El Sal.).
Código Familiar para el Estado Libre y Soberano de Morelos [Family Code for the Free and Sovereign State of Morelos], 6 de septiembre de 2006 (Mex.).
Código Niña, Niño y Adolescente, Ley No. 548 de 17 de julio de 2014 (Bol.).
Código Orgánico Integral Penal [Cód. Pen.] [Criminal Code] (Ecuador).
Código para el Sistema de Protección y los Derechos Fundamentales de Niños, Niñas y Adolescentes (Dom. Rep.).
Código Penal [Cód. Pen.] [Criminal Code] (Arg.).
Código Penal [Cód. Pen.] [Criminal Code] (Bol.).
Código Penal [Cód. Pen.] [Criminal Code] (Braz.).
Código Penal [Cód. Pen.] [Criminal Code] (Chile).
Código Penal [Cód. Pen.] [Criminal Code] (Costa Rica).
Código Penal [Cód. Pen.] [Criminal Code] (Dom. Rep.).
Código Penal [Cód. Pen.] [Criminal Code] (El Sal.).
Código Penal [Cód. Pen.] [Criminal Code] (Guat.).

Código Penal [Cód. Pen.] [Criminal Code] (Hond.).
Código Penal [Cód. Pen] [Criminal Code] (Nicar.).
Código Penal [Cód. Pen.] [Criminal Code] (Pan.).
Código Penal [Cód. Pen.] [Criminal Code] (Para.).
Código Penal [Cód. Pen.] [Criminal Code] (Peru).
Código Penal [Cód. Pen.] [Criminal Code] (Uru.).
Código Penal [Cód. Pen.] [Criminal Code] (Venez.).
Código Penal de Defensa Social Para el Estado Libre y Soberano de Puebla [C.P.] [Criminal Code of Social Defense for the Free and Sovereign State of Puebla], Diario Oficial de la Federación [DO], 24 de septiembre de 1986 (Mex.).
Código Penal de Defensa Social Para el Estado Libre y Soberano de Quintana Roo [C.P.] [Criminal Code of Social Defense for the Free and Sovereign State of Quintana Roo], Diario Oficial de la Federación [DO], 13 de diciembre de 2010 (Mex.).
Código Penal Federal [C.P.F.] [Federal Criminal Code] Diario Oficial de la Federación [D.O.], 14 de agosto de 1931 (Mex.).
Código Penal Para el Estado de Aguascalientes [C.P.] [Criminal Code for the State of Aguascalientes], Diario Oficial de la Federación [DO], 20 de mayo de 2013 (Mex.).
Código Penal para el Estado de Baja California [C.P.] [Criminal Code for the State of Baja California] Diario Oficial de la Federación [DO], 17 de diciembre de 2010 (Mex.).
Código Penal para el Estado de Baja California Sur [C.P.] [Criminal Code for the State of Baja California South], as amended, Boletín Oficial del Gobierno del Estado de Baja California Sur, 20 de marzo de 2005 (Mex.).
Código Penal Para el Estado de Chihuahua [C.P.] [Criminal Code for the State of Chihuahua], Diario Oficial de la Federación [DO], 27 de diciembre de 2006 (Mex.) (Oct. 13, 2013).
Código Penal Para el Estado de Coahuila [C.P.] [Criminal Code for the State of Coahuila], Diario Oficial de la Federación [DO], 28 de mayo de 1999 (Mex.).
Código Penal Para el Estado de Colima [C.P.] [Criminal Code for the State of Colima], Diario Oficial de la Federación [DO], 25 de noviembre de 2010 (Mex.).
Código Penal Para el Estado de Guanajuato [C.P.] [Criminal Code for the State of Guanajuato], Diario Oficial de la Federación [DO], 2 de noviembre de 2001 (Mex.).
Código Penal Para el Estado de Guerrero [C.P.] [Criminal Code for the State of Guerrero], Diario Oficial de la Federación [DO], 14 de noviembre de 1986 (Mex.).
Código Penal Para el Estado de Hidalgo [C.P.] [Criminal Code for the State of Hidalgo], Diario Oficial de la Federación [DO], 9 de junio de 1990 (Mex.).
Código Penal Para el Estado de Michoacán [C.P.] [Criminal Code for the State of Michoacán], Diario Oficial de la Federación [DO], 7 de julio de 1980 (Mex.).

Código Penal Para el Estado de Morelos [C.P.] [Criminal Code for the State of Morelos], Diario Oficial de la Federación [DO], 7 de noviembre de 1996 (Mex.).

Código Penal Para el Estado de Nayarit [C.P.] , 23 de diciembre de 2016, [Criminal Code for the State of Nayarit], Diario Oficial de la Federación [DO] (Mex.).

Código Penal Para el Estado de Nuevo León [C.P.] [Criminal Code for the State of Nuevo León], Diario Oficial de la Federación [DO], 5 de julio de 2011 (Mex.).

Código Penal Para el Estado de Oaxaca [C.P.] [Criminal Code for the State of Oaxaca], Diario Oficial de la Federación [DO], 9 de septiembre de 2006 (Mex.).

Código Penal Para el Estado de Querétaro [C.P.] [Criminal Code for the State of Querétero], Diario Oficial de la Federación [DO], 23 de julio de 1987 (Mex.).

Código Penal Para el Estado Libre de México [C.P.] [Criminal Code for the Free State of Mexico], Diario Oficial de la Federación [DO], 20 de marzo de 2000 (Mex.).

Código Penal Para el Estado Libre y Soberano de Jalisco [Criminal Code for the Free and Sovereign State of Jalisco], Diario Oficial de la Federación [DO], 2 de septiembre de 1982 (Mex.).

Código Sanitario [Cód. Sanit.] [Health Code] (Para.).

Código Sanitario [Cód. Sanit.] [Health Code] (Chile).

Congreso de la República de Perú, 2001, Dictamen recaído en el Proyecto de Ley No. 122/2001-cr, mediante el cual se propone declarar el día 25 de marzo de cada año como "Día del Niño por Nacer" [Decision on Bill No. 122/2001-cr on the proposal to declare March 25 of every year as the "Unborn Child's Day"], http://www2.congreso. gob.pe/sicr/ApoyComisiones /dictamenes0106.nsf/dictamenes/C75571EC32CEDA-980525700 D005691CF.

Constitución de la Provincia de Buenos Aires (Arg.).

Constitución de la Provincia de Catamarca (Arg.).

Constitución de la Provincia de Chaco (Arg.).

Constitución de la Provincia de Chubut (Arg.).

Constitución de la Provincia de Córdoba (Arg.).

Constitución de la Provincia de Entre Ríos (Arg.).

Constitución de la Provincia de Formosa (Arg.).

Constitución de la Provincia de Salta (Arg.).

Constitución de la Provincia de San Luis (Arg.).

Constitución de la Provincia de Santiago Del Estero (Arg.).

Constitución de la Provincia de Tierra del Fuego, Antartida e Islas del Atlántico Sur (Arg.).

Constitución de la Provincia de Tucumán (Arg.).

Constitución Política de los Estados Unidos Mexicanos [C.P.], Diario Oficial de la Federación [DO], 5 de febrero de 1917 (Mex.), http://www.diputados.gob.mx/LeyesBiblio/ref/cpeum_art.htm.
Constitución de 1967 (Ecuador).
Constitución Nacional [Const. Nac.] (Arg.).
Constitución Política de Chihuahua, 25 de mayo de 1921 (Mex.).
Constitución Política de Costa Rica (Costa Rica).
Constitución Política de la República de Chile [C.P.] (Chile).
Constitución Política de la República de El Salvador (El Sal.).
Constitución Política de la República de Guatemala (Guat.).
Constitución Política de la República de Honduras de 1982 (Hond.).
Constitución Política de la República del Ecuador (Ecuador).
Constitución Política de la República Dominicana (Dom. Rep.).
Constitución Política de la República Paraguay (Para.).
Constitución Política del Estado de Chiapas, 16 de agosto de 2013 (Mex.).
Constitución Política del Estado de Coahuila de Zaragoza, 19 de febrero de 1918 (Mex.).
Constitución Política del Estado de Guanajuato, 3 de septiembre de 1917 (Mex.).
Constitución Política del Estado de Jalisco, 21 de julio de 1917 (Mex.).
Constitución Política del Estado de Nayarit, 17 de febrero de 1918 (Mex.).
Constitución Política del Estado de Querétaro, 31 de marzo de 2008 (Mex.).
Constitución Política del Estado de Sonora, 29 de septiembre de 1917 (Mex.).
Constitución Política del Estado de Tamaulipas, 5 de febrero de 1921 (Mex.).
Constitución Política del Estado de Veracruz de Ignacio de la Llave, 25 de septiembre de 1917 (Mex.).
Constitución Política del Estado de Yucatán, 14 enero 1918 (Mex.), *as amended* 1 de abril de 2014.
Constitución Política del Estado Libre y Soberano de Baja California, Periódico Oficial, 16 de agosto de 1953 (Mex.).
Constitución Política del Estado Libre y Soberano de Baja California, 16 de agosto de 1953 (Mex.).
Constitución Política del Estado Libre y Soberano de Campeche, 29 de mayo de 1965 (Mex.).
Constitución Política del Estado Libre y Soberano de Colima, 20 de octubre de 1917 (Mex.).
Constitución Política del Estado Libre y Soberano de Durango, 1 de noviembre de 1917 (Mex.).
Constitución Política del Estado Libre y Soberano de Morelos, 20 de noviembre de 1930 (Mex.).
Constitución Política del Estado Libre y Soberano de Oaxaca, 4 de abril de 1922 (Mex.).
Constitución Política del Estado Libre y Soberano de Puebla, 2 de octubre de 1917 (Mex.).

Constitución Política del Estado Libre y Soberano de Quintana Roo, 12 de enero de 1975 (Mex.).
Constitución Política del Estado Libre y Soberano de San Luis Potosí, 20 de noviembre de 1996 (Mex.).
Constitución Política del Perú (Peru).
Constituição Federal [C.F.] [Constitution] (Braz.).
Convenio entre el Gobierno de la República de Costa Rica y la Corte Interamericana de Derechos Humanos [Agreement between the Costa Rican government and the Inter-American Court of Human Rights], Ley No. 6889 (Costa Rica), http://www.corteidh.or.cr/docs/otros/convenio.pdf.
Criminal Code (Gren.).
Decreto 1170-2012, del 21 de marzo de 2012, Poder Ejecutivo de la Provincia de Salta, Guías de procedimiento para la asistencia integral de víctimas de violencia sexual y atención de los abortos no punibles en hospitales públicos [Guidelines for comprehensive assistance to sexual violence victims and nonpunishment of abortions in public hospitals] (Arg.), http://test.e-legis-ar.msal.gov.ar/leisref/public/showAct.php?id=19703.
Decreto 67 de junio de 2018, Aprueba reglamento para ejercer objeción de conciencia según lo dispuesto en el artículo 119 ter del Código Sanitario [Approves regulation to assert conscientious objection under 119 of the Health Code], Biblioteca del Congreso Nacional de Chile (Chile), https://www.leychile.cl/Navegar?idNorma=1124446&idVersion=2018-11-07.
Decreto con Fuerza de Ley 36, julio 10, 1980, Normas que se Aplicaran en los Convenios que celebren los Servicios De Salud [Regulations for agreements entered into by Health Services], BIBLIOTECA DEL CONGRESO NACIONAL DE CHILE (Chile), https://www.leychile.cl/N?i=4198&f=1985-07-04&p=.
Decreto-Lei No. 3.688, De 3 De Outubre de 1941, Lei das Contravenções Penais [Criminal Offenses Act] 20 (Braz.), http://www.planalto.gov.br/ccivil_03/decreto-lei/del3688.htm.
Decreto No. 13-85, 13 Feb. 1985, Código Penal (Hond.).
Decreto No. 216-03, 12 de diciembre de 2003, https://www.leychile.cl/Navegar?idNorma=219014.
Decreto No. 267-2005, La Gaceta 30, 832 (28 de septiembre de 2005) (Hond.).
Decreto No. 839, 16 de abril de 2009, Ley de Protección de la Niñez y Adolescencia, 19 (El Sal.).
Decreto por el que reforman, derogan y adicionan diversas disposiciones de la Ley General de Víctimas; y se reforma el primer párrafo del artículo 182-R del Código Federal de Procedimientos Penales [Decree reforming, derogating and adding various provisions to the General Victim's Law; reforming first paragraph of article 182-R of the Federal Criminal Procedure Code], arts. 30(IX), 35. Diario Oficial de la Federación [D.O.], 3 de mayo de 2013 (Mex.), http://www.diputados.gob.mx/LeyesBiblio/ref/lgv/LGV_ref01_03may13.pdf.

Decreto que Reforma los Artículos 145 y 148 del Nuevo Código Penal para el Distrito Federal y se Adicionan los Artículos 16 bis 6 y 16 bis 7 a la Ley de Salud para el Distrito Federal [Decree reforming articles 145 and 148 of the new Criminal Code for the Federal District adding articles 16 bis, 6 and 16 bis 7 to the Federal District's Health Law], Gaceta Oficial de la Federación, 27 de enero de 2004 (Mex.).

Embryonenschutzgesetz (ESchG) [Law on the Protection of Embryos], Bundesgezetzblatt 1990 I: 2746 (Ger.).

Exec. Order No. 24029-S (1995) [Costa Rica Ministry of Health], http://www.ordenjuridico.gob.mx/fichaOrdenamiento.php?idArchivo=24212&ambito=estatal.

Guía Técnica Nacional para la Estandarización del Procedimiento de la Atención Integral de la Gestante en la Interrupción Voluntaria por Indicación Terapéutica del Embarazo Menor de 22 Semanas con Consentimiento Informado en el Marco de lo Dispuesto en el Artículo 119° del Código Penal [National technical guidelines for the standarization of the procedure for comprehensive care of the pregnant woman in voluntary interruption of pregnancy for therapeutic indications in gestation under 22 weeks according to section 119 of the Criminal Code], Resolución No. 486-2014/MINSA, 27 de junio de 2014 (Peru).

L. 270, marzo 7, 1996, 42.745 Diario Oficial [D.O.] (Colom.).

L. 599, julio 24, 2000, 44.097 Diario Oficial [D.O.] Colom.).

L. 2591, noviembre 19, 1991, 40195 Diario Oficial [D.O.] (Colom.).

Lei 10.406, 10 de janeiro de 2002, Código Civil [Cód. Civ.] [Civil Code] (Braz.). http://www.planalto.gov.br/ccivil_03/Leis/2002/L10406.htm.

Lei 8.069, 13 de Julho de 1990, Estatuto da Criança e do Adolescente (Braz.).

Lei No. 11.804, 5 de Novembro de 2008 (Braz.).

Lei No. 12.845, de 1º de Agosto de 2013, Dispõe sobre o atendimento obrigatório e integral de pessoas em situação de violência sexual [On the mandatory and comprehensive treatment of persons in situations of sexual violence] 3(IV) (Braz.), https://www.planalto.gov.br/ccivil_03/_ato2011-2014/2013/lei/l12845.htm.

Ley 14: Que Crea la Secretaría Nacional de Niñez, Adolescencia y Familia (Pan.).

Ley 599 de 2000, Código Penal (Colom.).

Ley 1098 de 2006, Código de la Infancia y la Adolescencia (Colom.).

Ley Abrogatoria del Código del Sistema Penal Ley 1005 de 15 de diciembre de 2017 y Creación del Consejo Nacional de Reforma del Sistema Penal, PL No. 464/2017-2018, Asamblea Legislativa Plurinacional de Bolivia (Jan. 9, 2018).

Ley de Amparo, Exhibición Personal y de Constitucionalidad [Statute on Amparo, personal exhibition and constitutionality writs] (Guat.).

Ley de Política Nacional de Población, Decreto Legislativo No. 346 (Peru).

Ley de Protección Integral de la Niñez y Adolescencia (Guat.).

Ley General de Salud (Mex).
Ley General de Salud, Ley No. 26842 (Peru).
Ley Nacional No. 25.929 de Derechos de Padres e Hijos durante el Proceso de Nacimiento: Declaración de Interés del Sistema Nacional de Información Mujer, por parte del Senado de la Nación; Declaración sobre Difusión del Parto Humanizado (Arg.).
Ley No. 1.674, Ley Contra La Violencia en La Familia o Domestica (Bol.).
Ley No. 3, de 15 de Enero de 2004, Que Prohíbe Toda Forma de Clonación Humana y Dicta Otras Disposiciones (Pan.), http://biblio.juridicas.unam.mx/libros/5/2292/73.pdf.
Ley No. 3: Por la Cual se Aprueba el Código de Familia, 17 de mayo de 1994 (Pan.).
Ley No. 14.908, 1 de septiembre de 2007, Diario Oficial [D.O.] (Chile).
Ley No. 18.826, 24 de agosto de 1989, Reemplázase el artículo 119 del Código Sanitario por el siguiente: "Artículo 119—No podrá ejecutarse ninguna acción cuyo fin sea provocar un aborto" [119 of the Health Code is replaced by the following: "Article 119—No act may be carried out for the purpose of provoking an abortion"] (Chile), http://www.leychile.cl/Navegar?idNorma=30202&buscar=ley+18.826.
Ley No. 18.987, Interrupción Voluntaria del Embarazo (Uru.).
Ley No. 20.120, Sobre la Investigación Científica en el ser Humano, su Genoma, y Prohibe la Clonación Humana (Chile).
Ley No. 20.357, 26 de junio de 2009, Tipifica Crímenes de Lesa Humanidad y Genocidio y Crímenes y Delitos de Guerra [Establishing crimes against humanity and genocide and war crimes and offenses] (Chile), https://www.leychile.cl/Navegar?idNorma=1004297.
Ley No. 20.418, Fija normas sobre información, orientación y prestaciones en materia de regulación de la fertilidad (Chile), https://www.leychile.cl/Navegar?idNorma=1010482.
Ley No. 21.030, 14 de septiembre de 2017, Regula la despenalización de la interrupción voluntaria del embarazo en tres causales [Regulates the decriminalization of voluntary interruption of pregnancy under three grounds], BIBLIOTECA DEL CONGRESO NACIONAL DE CHILE (Chile), https://www.leychile.cl/Navegar?idNorma=1108237&idVersion=2017-09-23.
Ley No. 23.849, Apruébase la Convención sobre los Derechos del Niño (Arg.).
Ley No. 824, 31 de diciembre de 1974, Diario Oficial [D.O.] (Chile).
Ley No. 836/30: Código Sanitario (Para.).
Ley No. 870, Código de Familia (Nicar.).
Ley No. 2169: Que Establece la Mayoría de Edad (Para.).
Ley No. 8589, Penalización de la Violencia Contra Las Mujeres [Criminalization of violence against women] (Costa Rica).
Ley para la Protección de los Derechos de Niñas, Niños y Adolescentes, 28(F), 29 de mayo de 2000 (Mex.).

Ley que abroga Código del Sistema Penal/2018, OBSERVATORIO INTERNACIONAL DE POLÍTICAS PÚBLICAS Y FAMILIA, https://observatoriointernacional.com/bolivia-persona-por-nacer-ley-que-abroga-codigo-del-sistema-penal2018/.

Medical Termination of Pregnancy Act (Act No. 4 of 1983) (Barb.).

National Assembly of the Republic of Nicaragua, La Gaceta, DIARIO OFICIAL [D.O.], Ley No. 603, Derogation of art. 165 of the current criminal code (Nov. 14, 2006).

Norma Técnica de Planificación Familiar [Technical norm on family planning], NT No. 032-MINSA/DGSP-V.01, 2005 (Peru).

Pautas de Intervención en Abortos no Punibles, Guía Técnica para la Atención Integral de los Abortos no Punibles [Intervention Guidelines in Nonpunishable Abortions, Technical Guide for Comprehensive Attention of Non-punishable Abortions] 1, 7 (2010) (Arg.), http://www.msal.gob.ar/images/stories/bes/graficos/0000000667cnt-Guia-tecnica-web.pdf.

*"Protocolo para la atención integral de las personas con derecho a la interrupción legal del embarazo" elaborado por el Programa Nacional de Salud Sexual y Procreación Responsable del Ministerio de Salud de la Nación (Selección)* ["Protocol for comprehensive care of persons with a right to interruption of pregnancy" created by the National Ministry of Health National Program on Sexual Health and Responsible Procreation], XII BOLETÍN JURÍDICO OBSERVATORIO DE LIBERTAD RELIGIOSA DE AMÉRICA LATINA Y EL CARIBE [B.J.O.L.R.A.L.C.], no. 2, 2016, at 47 (Chile).

PROYECTO DE LEY 122/2017-2018, CÓDIGO DEL SISTEMA PENAL [CÓD. PEN.] [CRIMINAL CODE] (Bol.).

*Proyecto de Ley, Interrupción Voluntaria del Embarazo* [Legislative Bill, Voluntary Interruption of Pregnancy] SENADO ARGENTINA, http://www.senado.gov.ar/micrositios/ive/4.

Reforma y Adición al Artículo 7, Fracción XI, de la Constitución Política del Estado Libre y Soberano de Nayarit y Cómputo y Declaratoria de Aprobación de la Reforma, Periódico Oficial, Órgano del Gobierno del Estado de Nayarit, 2–3 (2009) (Mex.), http://www.ordenjuridico.gob.mx/fichaOrdenamiento.php?idArchivo=24212&ambito=estatal.

Reglamento de Aplicación de la Ley del Seguro Social (Hond.), https://www.tsc.gob.hn/biblioteca/index.php/reglamentos/54-reglamento-de-aplicacion-de-la-ley-del-seguro-social.

Resolución Ministerial No. 486-2014, DIARIO OFICIAL EL PERUANO (28 de junio de 2014), http://www.unfpa.org.pe/Legislacion/PDF/20140627-MINSA-Aprueban-Guia-Tecnica-Interrupcion-Voluntaria-Embarazo.pdf.

Secretaría de Salud, Acuerdo No. 2744 (21 de octubre de 2009) (Hond.).

SURINAME PENAL CODE (Surin.).

The Offences Against the Person Act [TOAPA] (Dominica).

The Offences Against the Person Act [TOAPA] (Jam.)

## Books

Abramson, Bruce. *Violence against Babies: Protection of Pre- and Post-natal Children under the Framework of the Convention on the Rights of the Child.* Rev. ed. Provo, UT: World Family Policy Center, 2006.

Antkowiak, Thomas M., and Alejandra Gonza. *The American Convention on Human Rights: Essential Rights.* Oxford: Oxford University Press, 2017.

Baer, Karl Ernst von. *Epistola de Ovo Mammalium et Hominis Genesi.* Leipzig, 1827.

Barberis, Julio A. *El derecho a la vida en el pacto de San José de Costa Rica* [The right to life in the San José, Costa Rica, Pact]. In *Os Rumos Do Direito Internacional Dos Direitos Humanos: Ensaios Em Homanegem Ao Professor Antônio Augusto Cançado Trindade; Liber Amicorum Cançado Trindade*, edited by Renato Zerbini Ribeiro Leão, Andrew Drzemczewski, Jaime Ruiz de Santiago, José Flávio Sombra Saraiva, Christophe Swinarski, and Manuel E. Ventura Robles, 11–26. Porto Alegre, Brazil: Fabris, 2005. http://www.corteidh.or.cr/tablas/22962.pdf.

Becerra Ramírez, Manuel. "La jerarquía de los tratados en el orden jurídico interno: Una visión desde la perspectiva del derecho internacional" [The hierarchy of treaties in domestic law: An international law perspective]. *In Recepción nacional del derecho internacional de los derechos humanos y admisión de la competencia contenciosa de la Corte Interamericana*, by Mireya Castañeda Hernández and Sergio García Ramírez, edited by UNAM/Secretaría de Relaciones Exteriores Corte Interamericana de Derechos Humanos, 291–317. Mexico City: Instituto de Investigaciones Jurídicas UNAM, 2009. http://corteidh.or.cr/tablas/r28105.pdf.

Bossuyt, Marc J. *Guide to the "Travaux Préparatoires" of the International Covenant on Civil and Political Rights.* Dordrecht: Nijhoff, 1987.

Bradley, Curtis A. "Treaty Signature." In *The Oxford Guide to Treaties*, edited by Duncan B. Hollis, 208–19. Oxford: Oxford University Press, 2014.

Caceres Sarubbi, Carlos Agustín, and Carmen Viviana Chavez de Talavera. "Paraguay." In *Defending the Human Right to Life in Latin America*, edited by M. Laura Farfán Bertrán, William L. Saunders, and Jeanneane Maxon, translated by Noelia Estefanía Marchetti, 111. Washington, DC: Americans United for Life, 2012.

Cook, Rebecca J., Bernard M. Dickens, and Mahmoud F. Fathalla. *Reproductive Health and Human Rights: Integrating Medicine, Ethics, and Law.* Oxford: Oxford University Press, 2003.

Damrosch, Lori F., and Sean D. Murphy. *International Law: Cases and Materials.* 6th ed. St. Paul, MN: West Academic Publishing, 2014.

De Schutter, Olivier, and Françoise Tulkens. "Rights in Conflict: The European Court of Human Rights as a Pragmatic Institution." In *Conflicts between Fundamental Rights*, edited by Eva Brems, 169–216. Cambridge: Intersentia, 2008.

Dulitzky, Ariel. "50 años del sistema interamericano de derechos humanos: Una propuesta reflexión sobre cambios estratégicos necesarios" [50 years of the Inter-American human rights system: A proposed reflection about necessary strategic changes]. In *60 años después: Enseñanzas pasadas y desafíos futuros* [60 years later: Past lessons and future challenges], edited by Gonzalo Aguilar Cavallo, 491–501. Santiago, Chile: Centro de Estudios Constitucionales de Chile, 2008. http://www.utexas.edu/law/faculty/adulitzky/03-50Anos-Sistema-Interamericano.pdf.

Farfán Bertrán, María Laura. "The Protection of the Human Right to Life in the Republic of Argentina—The Guarantee of the Enforceability of the Whole System of Human Rights." In *Defending the Human Right to Life in Latin America*, edited by M. Laura Farfán Bertrán, William L. Saunders, and Jeanneane Maxon, translated by Noelia Estefanía Marchetti, 132–33. Washington, DC: Americans United for Life, 2012.

Ferrer Mac-Gregor, Eduardo. "Interpretación conforme y control difuso de convencionalidad: El nuevo paradigma para el juez mexicano" [Conformity of interpretation and diffuse conventionality control: The new paradigm for the Mexican judge]. In *Derechos humanos: Un nuevo modelo constitucional*, edited by Miguel Carbonell and Pedro Salazar, NN–NN. Mexico City: Unam, 2011. http://www.corteidh.or.cr/tablas/r29018.pdf.

Flood, Patrick J. "Does International Law Protect the Unborn Child?" In *Life and Learning XVI: Proceedings of the Sixteenth University Faculty for Life Conference at Villanova University*, 2006, edited by Joseph W. Koterski, 3-42. Washington, DC: University Faculty for Life, 2007.

García Elorrio, Aurelio. "Protección de los niños no nacidos en el Sistema Jurídico Interamericano de Derechos Humanos: La integración normativa con el *jus cogens*" [Protection of unborn children in the Inter-American juridical system: The normative integration of *jus cogens*]. In *Derechos humanos: 9 Casos Controversiales en América Latina*, edited by Jorge Scala, Aurelio F. García Elorrio, Héctor Hernández, Paola Scarinci de Delbosco, and Alexandra Loría Beeche, 2nd ed., 19–165. San José, Costa Rica: Promesa, 2009.

George, Robert P., and Christopher Tollefsen. *Embryo: A Defense of Human Life.* Princeton: Witherspoon Institute, 2008.

Joseph, Rita. *Human Rights and the Unborn Child.* Leiden: Nijhoff, 2009.

*Justicia, libertad y derechos humanos: Ensayos en homenaje a Rodolfo E. Piza Escalante.* San José, Costa Rica: Inter-American Institute for Human Rights, 2003.

López Medina, Diego Eduardo. *El Derecho de los Jueces.* 2nd ed. Bogotá: Legis Editores Universidad de los Andes, 2006.

Loudon, Irvine. *Death in Childbirth: An International Study of Maternal Care and Maternal Mortality, 1800–1950.* Oxford: Clarendon, 1993.

Monroy Cabra, Marco Gerardo. "Aplicación de la Convención Americana sobre Derechos Humanos en el orden jurídico interno." In *Derechos humanos en las Américas: Homenaje a la memoria de Carlos A. Dunshee de Abranches*, edited

by Organización de los Estados Americanos, NN–NN. Washington, DC: Organización de los Estados Americanos, 1984.
Mora Restrepo, Gabriel. *Justicia constitucional y arbitrariedad de los jueces*. Buenos Aires: Marcial Pons, 2009.
Ortiz Trujillo, Diana, and Santiago Maqueda. "United Mexican States." In *Defending the Human Right to Life in Latin America*, edited by M. Laura Farfán Bertrán, William L. Saunders, and Jeanneane Maxon, translated by Noelia Estefanía Marchetti, 35–66. Washington, DC: Americans United for Life, 2012.
Piza Escalante, Rodolfo. *La justicia constitucional en Costa Rica* [Constitutional justice in Costa Rica]. San José, Costa Rica: IJSA Investigaciones Jurídica, 2004.
Quintana, Eduardo Martin. *Persona y filiación en la legislación actual*. N.p.: Eder, 2015.
Ramos-Kuri, Manuel, ed. *Artavia Murillo vs. Costa Rica: Análisis crítico a la sentencia de la Corte Interamericana de Derechos Humanos en el fallo sobre fertilización in vitro*. Querétaro, Mexico: Centro de Investigación Social Avanzada A. C., 2017.
Sagüés, Néstor P. *El "control de convencionalidad" como instrumento para la elaboración de un ius comune interamericano* [Conventionality control as an instrument for the creation of an Inter-American *ius commune*]. N.p. [Mexico]: UNAM, 2014.
Shelton, Dinah. *Abortion and Protection of the Human Fetus: Legal Problems in Cross-Cultural Perspective*. Dordrecht: Nijhoff, 1987.
Shelton, Dinah. "International Law on Protection of the Fetus." In *Abortion and the Protection of the Human Fetus: Legal Problems in a Cross-Cultural Perspective*, edited by George F. Cole and Stanislaw J. Frankowski, 1–16. Dordrecht: Nijhoff, 1987.
Ventura Robles, Manuel E. "Los principales aportes del Juez Rodolfo E. Piza Escalante a la Corte Interamericana de Derechos Humanos (1979–1988)." In *Justicia, libertad y derechos humanos: Ensayos en homenaje a Rodolfo E. Piza Escalante*, 270–75. San José, Costa Rica: Instituto Interamericano de Derechos Humanos, 2003.

## Law Review/Legal Articles and Treatises

Alston, Philip, *The Unborn Child and Abortion under the Draft Convention on the Rights of the Child*, 12 HUM. RTS. Q. 156 (1990).
Antkowiak, Thomas M., *A Dark Side of Virtue: The Inter-American Court and Reparations for Indigenous Peoples*, 25 DUKE J. OF COMP. & INT'L L. 1 (2015).
Anzoátegui, Javier, *Muerte de una persona inocente*, 245 REVISTA JURIDICA LA LEY [L.L.] 1 (2012).

Bélanger, D., and A. Flynn, *The Persistence of Induced Abortion in Cuba: Exploring the Notion of an "Abortion Culture,"* 40 Stud. in Fam. Plan. 13 (2009).
Blanco Donaire, Wendy, *¿Aprueba la fecundación in vitro el test de razonabilidad jurídica?* [Does in vitro fertilization pass the reasonableness test?] 133 Revista de Ciencias Jurídicas 29 (2014) (Costa Rica), https://revistas.ucr.ac.cr/index.php/juridicas/article/viewFile/14165/13466.
Blofield, Merike. *Women's Choices in Comparative Perspective: Abortion Policies in Late-Developing Catholic Countries*, 40 Comparative Politics, no. 4, 2008, 399.
Bruno, Anna Silvia, *Bringing Uniformity to Brazilian Court Decisions: Looking at the American Precedent and at Italian Living Law*, 11 Electronic J. of Comp. L., no. 4, 2007, 1 (Neth.), http://www.ejcl.org/114/art114-3.pdf.
Buergenthal, Thomas, *The Advisory Practice of the Inter-American Human Rights Court*, 79 Am. J. Int'l L. 1 (1985).
Buergenthal, Thomas, *Commentary: The American Convention on Human Rights: Illusions and Hopes*, 21 Buff. L. Rev. 121 (1971).
Cantón, Santiago, *To Strengthen Human Rights, Change the Organization of American States (Not the Commission)*, 20 Hum. Rts. Brief 1 (2013).
Carozza, Paolo G., *From Conquest to Constitutions: Retrieving a Latin American Tradition of the Idea of Human Rights*, 25 Hum. Rts. Q. 281 (2003).
Carozza, Paolo G., *The Anglo-Latin Divide and the Future of the Inter-American System of Human Rights*, 5 Notre Dame J. of Int'l & Comp. L. 153 (2015).
Cassel, Douglass, *Regional Human Rights Regime and State Pushback: The Case of the Inter-American Human Rights System (2011–2013)*, 33 Hum. Rts. L.J. 1 (2013).
Castillo Córdova, Luis, *La Corte IDH, o El mito de la infalibilidad* [The IA Court, or The myth of infallibility], La Ley Gaceta Jurídica, Feb. 19, 2018, http://laley.pe/not/4878/la-corte-idh-o-el-mito-de-la-infalibilidad/.
Corral, Hernán, *El estatus del embrión humano en la sentencia sobre aborto del Tribunal Constitucional* [The status of the human embryo in the abortion judgment of the Constitutional Tribunal], Diario Constitucional.cl, Sept. 4, 2017, http://www.diarioconstitucional.cl/articulos/el-estatus-del-embrion-humano-en-la-sentencia-sobre-aborto-del-tribunal-constitucional.
Croxatto, Horacio B., and Fernando Zegers Hochschild, *Anticoncepción de emergencia, Ciencia y Moral* [Emergency contraception, science, and morality] in *Anticoncepción de emergencia: Antecedentes del debate* [Emergency contraception: Background of the debate], 95 Estudios Publicos [CEP] 400 (2004) (Chile).
Farfán Bertrán, M. Laura, *El caso "Artavia Murillo c. Costa Rica" a la luz de la teoría del control de convencionalidad: A propósito del debate sobre la legalización del aborto en la Argentina* [The Artavia Murillo v. Costa Rica judgment in light of conventionality control: About the debate on abortion legalization in Argentina], IV Jurisprudentia Argentina [J.A.] 47 (2018) (Arg.).

Ferrer Mac-Gregor, Eduardo, *Eficacia de la sentencia interamericana y la cosa juzgada internacional: Vinculación directa hacia las partes (*res judicata*) e indirecta hacia los estados parte de la Convención Americana (*res interpretata*) (sobre el cumplimiento del caso Gelman vs. Uruguay)* [Efficacy of the Inter-American judgment and the international *res judicata*: Direct relation to the parties (*res judicata*) and indirect relation to states parties to the American Convenion (*res interpretata*) (on compliance with the Gelman v. Uruguay case)], 11 ESTUDIOS CONSTITUCIONALES, no. 2, 2013, at 641, http://www.corteidh.or.cr/tablas/r31255.pdf.

Ferrer Mac-Gregor, Eduardo, and Pablo González Domínguez, *Death Penalty, Amnesty Laws, and Forced Disappearances: Three Main Topics of the Inter-American* Corpus Juris *in Criminal Law*, 5 NOTRE DAME J. OF INT'L & COMP. L. 63 (2015).

García G., José Francisco, and Sergio Verdugo R., *Radiografía Política del Sistema Interamericano* [Political X-ray of the Inter-American system of human rights], 7 LIBERTAD Y DESARROLLO, Dec. 2011, at 12.

García Ramírez, Sergio, *El control judicial interno de convencionalidad* [The domestic judicial conventionality control], 28 IUS REVISTA DEL INSTITUTO DE CIENCIAS JURÍDICAS DE PUEBLA 123 (2011), http://www.corteidh.or.cr/tablas/r27771.pdf.

García Ramírez, Sergio, *La pena de muerte en la Convención Americana de Derechos Humanos en la jurisprudencia de la Corte Interamericana* [The death penalty in the American Convention on Human Rights in the jurisprudence of the Inter-American Court], 114 BOLETÍN MEXICANO DE DERECHO COMPARADO 1021 (2005), https://revistas.juridicas.unam.mx/index.php/derecho-comparado/article/view/3853/4820.

García Ramírez, Sergio, *The Relationship Between Inter-American Jurisdiction and States (National Systems): Some Pertinent Questions*, 5 NOTRE DAME J. OF INT'L & COMP. L., no. 1, 2015, at 115.

García-Sayán, Diego, *Exámenes del horizonte* [Assessments from the horizon] in *La reforma de la Comisión Interamericana de Derechos Humanos* [Inter-American Commission on Human Rights reform], 19 APORTES DPLF: REVISTA DE LA FUNDACIÓN PARA EL DEBIDO PROCESO 54 (2014), http://perso.unifr.ch/derechopenal/assets/files/obrasportales/op_20140508_03.pdf.

García-Sayán, Diego, *The Inter-American Court and Constitutionalism in Latin America*, 89 TEX. L. REV. 1835 (2011).

Henríquez Herrera, Ian, *Comentario al fallo de la Corte Interamericana de Derechos Humanos en el caso Artavia Murillo y otros* [Commentary on the judgment by the Inter-American Court of Human Rights in Artavia Murillo et al.], III REVISTA INTERNACIONAL DE DERECHOS HUMANOS 55 (2013) (Arg.).

Hitters, Juan Carlos, *El control de convencionalidad y el cumplimiento de las sentencias de la Corte Interamericana* [Conventionality control and compliance with Inter-American Court judgments], 10 ESTUDIOS CONSTITUCIONALES, no. 2, 2013, at 535. http://www.scielo.cl/scielo.php?script=sci_arttext&pid =S0718-52002012000200014.

Hitters, Juan Carlos, *Un avance en el control de convencionalidad: El efecto* erga omnes *de las sentencias de la Corte Interamericana* [A step forward for conventionality control: The *erga omnes* effect of Inter-American Court judgments], 11 ESTUDIOS CONSTITUCIONALES, no. 2, 2013, at 695, http://revistas .pucp.edu.pe/index.php/pensamientoconstitucional/article/viewFile /8959/9367.

Jardim de Santa Cruz Oliveira, Maria Angela, and Nuno Garoupa, *Stare Decisis and Certiorari Arrive to Brazil: A Comparative Law and Economics Approach,* 26 EMORY INT'L L. REV. 556 (2012).

Jonas, Robert E., and John D. Gorby, *West German Abortion Decision: A Contrast to Roe v. Wade,* 9 J. MARSHALL J. OF PRAC. & PROC. 551 (1976).

Koch, Elard, *The Epidemiology of Abortion and Its Prevention in Chile,* 30 ISSUES IN L. & MED., no. 1, 2015, at 71.

Lafferriere, Jorge Nicolás, *El artículo 19 del nuevo Código Civil y el reconocimiento como persona del embrión humano no implantado* [Article 19 of the new Civil Code and the recognition of the nonimplanted human embryo as a person], LA LEY: REVISTA DE DERECHO DE FAMILIA Y PERSONA [DFyP] (2014), Nov. 1, 2014.

Lafferriere, Jorge Nicolás, *La Corte Interamericana de Derechos Humanos y un injusto fallo sobre el embrión humano ante las biotecnologías* [The Inter-American Court of Human Rights and an unjust ruling on the human embryo before biotechnology], 2 REVISTA DE DERECHO DE FAMILIA Y LAS PERSONAS [DFyP] 179 (2013) (Arg.).

Lamm, Eleonora et al., *La Corte Interamericana de Derechos Humanos controla, sin concesión alguna, el cumplimiento de sus decisiones* [The Inter-American Court of Human Rights controls compliance with its decisions with no concessions], LA LEY [L.L.] (2016).

Márquez Luzardo, Carmen María, *La denuncia de la Convención Americana sobre Derechos Humanos y otros casos paradigmáticos: Los precedentes de Trinidad y Tobago, Perú y Venezuela* [The denunciation of the American Convention on Human Rights and other paradigmatic cases: The precedents of Trinidad and Tobago, Peru, and Venezuela], VIII CUESTIONES JURÍDICAS 27 (2014) (Venez.).

Mechlem, Kerstin, *Treaty Bodies and the Interpretation of Human Rights,* 42 VAND. J. TRANSNAT'L L. 905 (2009).

Meier García, Eduardo, *Nacionalismo Constitucional y Derecho Internacional de los Derechos Humanos* 9 ESTUDIOS CONSTITUCIONALES, no. 2, 2011, at 329, http://www.scielo.cl/scielo.php?script=sci_arttext&pid=S0718 -52002011000200008.

Nieto Navia, Rafael, *Aspectos internacionales de la demanda contra la penalización del aborto* [International aspects of the lawsuit against criminalization of abortion] 9 REVISTA PERSONA Y BIOÉTICA, no. 1, 2005, at 21(Colom.).

Nogueira Alcalá, Humberto, *Diálogo interjurisdiccional, control de convencionalidad y jurisprudencia del Tribunal Constitucional en el período 2006–2011* [Interjurisdictional dialogue, conventionality control, and constitutional court jurisprudence from 2006 to 2011], 10 ESTUDIOS CONSTITUCIONALES, no. 2, 2012, at 57, http://www.scielo.cl/scielo.php?script=sci_arttext&pid =S0718-52002012000200003.

Paúl, Álvaro, *Admissibility of Evidence before the Inter-American Court of Human Rights*, 13 REVISTA DIREITO GV 653 (2017).

Paúl, Álvaro, *The American Convention on Human Rights: Updated by the Inter-American Court*, 20 IURIS DICTIO 53 (2017).

Paúl, Álvaro, *Giro en Materia de Recurso de Revisión ante la Corte Interamericana* [Twist on the Remedy of Revision Before the Inter-American Court], 4 REVISTA CHILENA DE DERECHO Y CIENCIA POLÍTICA 131 (2013), http://ssrn .com/abstract=2333818.

Pereyra Zabala, Gastón, *El control de convencionalidad en el sistema interamericano de derechos humanos* [Conventionality control in the Inter-American system of human rights], 6 REVISTA DE DERECHO 155 (2011) (Uru.), http://revistas .ucu.edu.uy/index.php/revistadederecho/article/download/802/796.

Puppinck, Grégor, *Abortion and the European Convention on Human Rights*, 3 IRISH J. LEGAL STUD., no. 2, 2013, at 142.

Puppinck, Grégor, *Abortion in European Law: Human Rights, Social Rights and the New Cultural Trend*, 4 AVE MARIA INT'L L.J. 29 (2015).

Rabbi Baldi Cabanillas, Renato, and Eugenia Fléming Cánepa, *El caso "Artavia Murillo vs. Costa Rica" de la CIDH: Las técnicas de fertilización asistida, el estatuto del embrión y sus efectos en el derecho interno* [The IACt case of Artavia Murillo v. Costa Rica: Reproductive technologies, the embryo's legal status, and its effects in domestic law] in SILVIA PALACIO DE CAEIRO, TRATADO DE DERECHOS HUMANOS Y SU INFLUENCIA EN EL DERECHO ARGENTINO, XI LA LEY [L.L.] 551 (2015) (Arg.).

Rhonheimer, Martin, and Paolo G. Carozza, *Fundamental Rights, Moral Law, and the Legal Defense of Life in a Constitutional Democracy* 43 AM. J. JURIS. 135 (1998).

Rocha da Silva, Alice, and Andrea de Quadros Dantas Echeverria, *Tentativas de contenção do ativismo judicial da Corte Interamericana de Direitos Humanos* [Attempts to contain judicial activism in the Inter-American Court of Human Rights], 5 BRAZILIAN JOURNAL OF PUBLIC POLICY 392 (2015).

Sagüés, Néstor P., *Obligaciones internacionales y control de convencionalidad* [International duties and conventionality control], 8 ESTUDIOS CONSTITUCIONALES, no. 1, 2010, at 117, http://www.corteidh.or.cr/tablas/28053-11.pdf.

Schabas, William A., *Canadian Ratification of the American Convention on Human Rights*, 16 NETH. Q. HUM. RTS. 315 (1998).

Shelton, Dinah, *Abortion and Right to Life in the Inter-American System: The Case of Baby Boy*, 2 HUM. RTS. L.J. 309 (1981).

Shelton, Dinah, *The Rules and the Reality of Petition Procedures in the Inter-American Human Rights System*, 5 Notre Dame J. Int'l & Comp. L. 1 (2015).

Silva Abbott, Max, *El caso Artavia Murillo vs. Costa Rica: Análisis crítico y posibles efectos regionales*, 6 Derecho Público Iberoamericano 13 (2015) (Chile).

Silva Abbott, Max, *Un peligro para la dignidad humana del no nacido: El caso Artavia Murillo y el control de convencionalidad* [A danger for the unborn's human dignity: The Artavia Murillo case and conventionality control], XII Jornadas Internacionales de Derecho Natural 2 (2016) (Arg.), http://bibliotecadigital.uca.edu.ar/repositorio/ponencias/peligro-dignidad-humana-no-nacido-abbott.pdf.

Stith, Richard, *Construction vs. Development: Polarizing Models of Human Gestation*, 24 Kennedy Inst. Ethics J. 345 (2014).

Stith, Richard, *If Dorothy Had Not Had Toto to Pull Back the Wizard's Curtain: The Fabrication of Human Rights as a World Religion*, 44 Val. U. L. Rev. 847 (2010).

Stith, Richard, *Nueva teoría constitucional y penal sobre el aborto en el derecho español*, 39 Revista de Ciencias Sociales 219 (1994) (Chile).

Stith, Richard, and J. H. H. Weiler, *Can Treaty Law Be Supreme, Directly Effective and Autonomous—All at the Same Time? (An Epistolary Exchange)*, 34 N.Y.U.J. Int'l L. & Pol. 729 (2002).

Tanner, Lauri R., *Interview with Judge Antônio A. Cançado Trindade: A Court of Human Rights*, XVI Ann. Surv. Int'l & Comp. L. 165 (2010).

Tozzi, Piero A., et al., *El activismo judicial en Latinoamérica: Análisis a raíz de la reciente jurisprudencia argentina proaborto* [Judicial Activism in Latin America: Analysis Following the Recent Argentinian Proabortion jurisprudence] 13 El Derecho [E.D.] 1 (2013).

Vasciannie, Stephen, *The Inter-American Commission on Human Rights: Reform and the Question of Universality*, 21(2) ILSA J. of Int'l & Comp. L., no. 2, 2015, at 409.

Vio Grossi, Eduardo, *Jurisprudencia de la Corte Interamericana de Derechos Humanos: ¿Del control de convencionalidad a la supranacionalidad?* [Jurisprudence of the Inter-American Court of Human Rights: From *control de convencionalidad* to supranationality?] XXI Anuario de Derecho Constitucional Latinoamericano 93 (2015) (Colom.).

Weiler, J. H. H., *The Transformation of Europe*, 100 Yale L.J. 2403 (1991).

## Press Articles

*Abogada afirma que el estado miente a la CIDH sobre el caso de la "Niña Mainumby,"* ABC Color (Aug. 15, 2015), http://www.abc.com.py/edicion-impresa/locales/abogada-afirma-que-el-estado-miente-a-la-cidh-sobre-el-caso-de-la-nina-mainumby-1398155.html.

Agrawal, Priya, *Maternal Mortality and Morbidity in the United States of America*, 93 Bull. of the World Health Org., no. 3, Mar. 2015, at 133, http://www.who.int/bulletin/volumes/93/3/14-148627/en/.

Amaya, Luis Alejandro, *Presidente de República Dominicana pide que se permita el aborto en tres situaciones* [President of Dominican Republic seeks to allow abortion in three situations], CNN (Dec. 20, 2016), http://cnnespanol.cnn.com/2016/12/20/presidente-de-republica-dominicana-pide-que-se-permita-el-aborto-en-tres-situaciones/.

*Aprueban el artículo 153 del Código de Sistema Penal referido al aborto* [Approval of article 153 of the Criminal Code system regarding abortion], El Deber (Sept. 29, 2017), https://www.eldeber.com.bo/bolivia/Aprueban-el-articulo-153-en-que-el-aborto-no-es-penado-20170928-0098.html.

*Aprueban en Nuevo León derecho a la vida desde la concepción* [Right to life from conception approved in Nuevo León], Informador.mx (Mar. 7, 2019, 2:43 AM), https://www.informador.mx/mexico/Aprueban-en-Nuevo-Leon-derecho-a-la-vida-desde-la-concepcion-20190307-0016.html.

Aréchaga, Ignacio, *Despotismo ilustrado de hoy* [Today's enlightened despotism], El Sónar Blog (Feb. 6, 2018), http://elsonar.aceprensa.com/author/pivars/page/6/.

*Asamblea Nacional negó la despenalización del aborto por violación en Ecuador* [National Assembly rejected abortion decriminalization for rape in Ecuador], El Universo (Sept. 17, 2019), https://www.eluniverso.com/noticias/2019/09/17/nota/7522780/aborto-violacion-ecuador-asamblea-nacional.

Avendaño, Carlos, *Fecundación in vitro: Trámite exprés* [In vitro fertilization: Fast-track procedure], Diario Extra (Costa Rica) (Mar. 15, 2011), https://web.archive.org/web/20110319215920/http://www2.diarioextra.com/2011/marzo/15/opinion04.php.

Avendaño, Manuel, *Magistrado Luis Fernando Salazar: Es momento de que la Sala IV se haga a un lado* [Judge Luis Fernando Salazar: It's time for the IV Chamber to step aside], La Nación (Mar. 1, 2016), http://www.nacion.com/nacional/salud-publica/Magistrado-Fernando-Salazar-IV-FIV_0_1545845518.html.

Avendaño, Manuel, *Presidente de la Sala IV: Decreto era "suficiente" para regular la FIV en Costa Rica* [President of the IV Chamber: Decree was "appropriate" to regulate IVF in Costa Rica], La Nación (Feb. 26, 2016), http://www.nacion.com/nacional/salud-publica/Presidente-Constitucional-Decreto-FIV-Costa_0_1545045555.html.

Baklinski, Pete, *NPR Says El Salvador Mom Was Charged for "Having an Abortion"—but Evidence Shows She Murdered Her Newborn*, LIFE SITE (Oct. 3, 2014), https://www.lifesitenews.com/news/npr-says-el-salvador-mom-was-charged-for-having-an-abortion-but-evidence-sh.

*Bolivia Lawmakers Vote to Ease Right* [*sic*: the word should be *Tight*] *Abortion Restrictions*, AP News (Dec. 6, 2017), https://apnews.com/0d5423c6da774216812fb5edca503a8c.

Cabrera Martínez, Javier, *Diputados de Sinaloa aprueban ley a favor de la vida desde la concepción*, El Universal (Sept. 28, 2018), http://www.eluniversal.com.mx/estados/diputados-de-sinaloa-aprueban-ley-favor-de-la-vida-desde-la-concepcion.

*Chile, Argentina, Brasil, Colombia y Paraguay piden a la Corte Interamericana de DD.HH. respetar "margenes de autonomía" de los estados* [Chile, Argentina, Brazil, Colombia, and Paraguay ask the Inter-American Court of HR to respect states' "margin of autonomy"], 24 Horas (April 23, 2019), https://www.24horas.cl/internacional/chile-argentina-brasil-colombia-y-paraguay-piden-a-la-corte-interamericana-de-ddhh-respetar-margenes-de-autonomia-de-los-estados-3256287.

*CIDH Extends Deadline for Approval of Law for In-Vitro Fertilization in Costa Rica*, Inside Costa Rica (Feb. 24, 2011), http://insidecostarica.com/dailynews/2011/february/24/costarica11022402.htm.

*Denuncian a El Salvador ante la CIDH por caso de la joven "Beatriz"* [El Salvador denounced before IACHR for case of young woman "Beatriz"], BBC Mundo (Nov. 29, 2013), http://www.bbc.com/mundo/ultimas_noticias/2013/11/131129_ultnot_denuncia_contra_el_salvador_ante_la_cidh_bd.

*Denuncian parcialidad de jueces de Corte IDH a favor del aborto* [Inter-American Court judges' bias in favor of abortion denounced], Aciprensa (Oct. 3, 2012), http://www.aciprensa.com/noticias/denuncian-parcialidad-de-jueces-de-corte-idh-a-favor-del-aborto-22790/.

*Despite 20-Year Wait, New Penal Code Keeps Old Abortion Ban*, Dominican Today (Dec. 15, 2016), http://www.dominicantoday.com/dr/local/2016/12/15/61709/Despite-20-year-wait-new-Penal-Code-keeps-old-abortion-ban.

Díaz, Luis, *Radio Fides interpondrá recurso de amparo por censura a campaña contra FIV* [Fides Radio appeals censorship of campaign against IVF], La Nación (June 28, 2011, 4:39 PM), https://www.nacion.com/archivo/radio-fides-interpondra-recurso-de-amparo-por-censura-a-campana-contra-fiv/C5HV3NZMQRA5VGP53D7KDHROPU/story/.

Díaz de Valdés, José Manuel, *The Chilean Constitutional Court's Abortion Decision: More Questions than Answers*, Int'l J. Const. Blog (Aug. 5, 2018), http://www.iconnectblog.com/2018/08/i-connect-symposium-the-chilean-constitutional-courts-abortion-decision-more-questions-than-answers.

*Dictan prisión preventiva para doctor y enfermera* [Temporary imprisonment ordered for doctor and nurse], El Heraldo (Feb. 10, 2015), http://www.elheraldo.hn/sucesos/793708-219/dictan-prisi%C3%B3n-preventiva-para-doctor-y-enfermera.

*El Presidente en ejercicio indicó que no se legalizó el aborto y reiteró que el artículo 205 protege la práctica profesional de los médicos* [The acting president indicated that abortion was not legalized and reiterated that article 205 protects medical practice], VICEPRESIDENCIA DEL ESTADO PLURINACIONAL DE BOLIVIA (Dec. 15, 2017), https://www.vicepresidencia.gob.bo/El-presidente-en-ejercicio-indico-que-no-se-legalizo-el-aborto-y-reitero-que-el.

*Entrevista sobre el aborto con el Dr. Gabriel Mora-Restrepo, experto en Derecho Constitucional en Colombia* [Interview on abortion with Dr. Gabriel Mora Restrepo, Constitutional Law expert in Colombia], ACIPRENSA (Sept. 27, 2012), https://www.aciprensa.com/Docum/documento.php?id=514.

Estévez, Alicia, and Ámbar Méndez, *Rechazan informe sobre penalización del aborto* [Report on abortion criminalization rejected], LISTIN DIARIO (July 12, 2017), https://www.listindiario.com/la-republica/2017/07/12/473645/rechazan-informe-sobre-penalizacion-del-aborto.

*Evo Morales aplaza nuevo Código Penal* [Evo Morales rejects new Criminal Code], TELESUR (Jan. 21, 2018), https://www.telesurtv.net/news/evo-morales-aplaza-nuevo-codigo-penal-conspiracion-derecha-20180121-0035.html.

Freeland, Alejandro, *¡Vengo a ejercer mi derecho a abortar. Médico, proceda ya!* [I come to exercise my right to have an abortion. Doctor, proceed now!], TODOSOBRELACORTE.COM, https://todosobrelacorte.wordpress.com/2012/03/13/vengo-a-ejercer-mi-derecho-a-abortar-medico-proceda-ya/.

Gabbatt, Adam, *Jamaican Doctor Arrested for Performing Abortion on 12-Year-Old*, GUARDIAN (July 13, 2012), http://www.guardian.co.uk/world/2012/jul/13/doctor-arrested-illegal-abortion-jamaica.

García Sayán, Diego, *Muertes anunciadas, derecho a la vida* [Deaths announced, the right to life], LAREPUBLICA.PE, http://www.larepublica.pe/atando-cabos/13/03/2009/muertes-anunciadas-derecho-la-vida.

Hoffman, Matthew, *Turn-Around Victory: Mexican Supreme Court Upholds State Pro-life Laws*, LIFE SITE NEWS (May 3, 2013), http://www.lifesitenews.com/news/turn-around-victory-mexican-supreme-court-upholds-state-pro-life-laws/.

*Honduras: Descubrimos las clínicas de la muerte en Comayagüela* [We discovered death clinics in Comayaguela], EL HERALDO (Feb. 2, 2015), http://www.elheraldo.hn/alfrente/790945-209/honduras-descubrimos-las-cl%C3%ADnicas-de-la-muerte-en-comayag%C3%BCela.

Iglesias, Mariana, *Aborto no punible: La mayoría de las provincias no cumple el fallo de la Corte* [Legal abortion: Most provinces do not meet the court's decision], CLARÍN (Mar. 13, 2013), http://www.clarin.com/sociedad/mayoria-provincias-cumple-fallo-Corte_0_881911861.html.

Iraheta, Oscar, *Magistrados: "En el caso Beatriz nos quisieron manipular"* [Magistrates: "They tried to manipulate us in the Beatriz case"], EL SALVADOR

.COM (July 17, 2013), http://www.elsalvador.com/articulo/sucesos/magistrados-caso-beatriz-nos-quisieron-manipular-36770.

Kassembaum, N. J., et al., *Global, Regional, and National Levels and Causes of Maternal Mortality During 1990–2013: A Systematic Analysis for the Global Burden of Disease Study 2013*, 384 LANCET 980 (2014), https://doi.org/10.1016/S0140-6736(14)60696-6.

Koch, Elard, *The Epidemiology of Abortion and Its Prevention in Chile*, 30 ISSUES IN L. & MED., no. 1, 2015, at 71.

Koch, Elard, et al., *Women's Education Level, Maternal Health Facilities, Abortion Legislation and Maternal Deaths: A Natural Experiment in Chile from 1957 to 2007*, 7 PLOS ONE, no. 5, May 4, 2012, e36613, https://doi.org/10.1371/journal.pone.0036613.

*Lei dos alimentos gravídicos garante "pensão" durante a gestação* [Prenatal alimony law ensures "pension" during gestation], DOURADO NEWS (March 14, 2013), http://www.douradosnews.com.br/noticias/brasil/lei-dos-alimentos-gravidicos-garante-pensao-durante-a-gestacao/494129/.

*Levantan censura a anuncios católicos sobre fecundación in vitro en Costa Rica* [Censorship lifted from Catholic ads on in vitro fertilization in Costa Rica], ACIPRENSA (Apr. 24, 2012, 4:02 PM), http://www.aciprensa.com/noticias/levantan-censura-a-anuncios-catolicos-sobre-fecundacion-in-vitro-en-costa-rica/.

López Garelli, Sanie, *Liberan a la madre de la niña paraguaya embarazada*, CNN (June 23, 2015), http://cnnespanol.cnn.com/2015/06/23/liberan-a-la-madre-de-la-nina-paraguaya-embarazada/.

López Garelli, Sanie, *Prueba de ADN confirma que padrastro embarazó a la niña paraguaya de 11 años*, CNN (Oct. 9, 2015), http://cnnespanol.cnn.com/2015/10/09/prueba-de-adn-confirma-que-padrastro-embarazo-a-la-nina-paraguaya-de-11-anos/.

Madrigal, Luis Miguel, *Costa Rica consulta a Corte IDH si es necesaria legislación que regule uniones homosexuales* [Costa Rica asks the IA Court if it needs legislation to regulate same-sex unions], EL MUNDO.CR (May 17, 2016), https://www.elmundo.cr/costa-rica-consulta-a-corte-idh-si-es-necesaria-legislacion-que-regule-uniones-homosexuales/.

Malkin, Elizabeth, *Supporters of El Salvador's Abortion Ban Foil Efforts to Soften It*, N.Y. TIMES (April 26, 2018), https://www.nytimes.com/2018/04/26/world/americas/abortion-ban-salvador.html.

Martin, Nina, *U.S. Has the Worst Rate of Maternal Deaths in the Developed World*, NPR (May 12, 2017, 10:28 AM), https://www.npr.org/2017/05/12/528098789/u-s-has-the-worst-rate-of-maternal-deaths-in-the-developed-world.

May, Huberth, *El Estado incumple la sentencia FIV* [The state fails to comply with the IVF judgment], LA NACIÓN (Costa Rica) (Aug. 16, 2013), http://www.nacion.com/opinion/foros/incumple-sentencia-FIV_0_1360263964.html.

McFadden, Robert, *Kenneth C. Edelin, Doctor at Center of Landmark Abortion Case, Dies at 74*, N.Y. TIMES (Dec. 30, 2013), http://www.nytimes.com/2013/12/31/us/kenneth-c-edelin-physician-at-center-of-landmark-abortion-case-dies-at-74.htm.

Mejía, Alvaro, *Honduras: Congreso Nacional aprobo seguir con la penalizacion del aborto* [Honduras: National Congress approved continuing to punish abortion], EL HERALDO (May 4, 2017), https://www.elheraldo.hn/pais/1068167-466/honduras-congreso-nacional-aprob%C3%B3-seguir-con-la-penalizaci%C3%B3n-del-aborto.

*Mexican Supreme Court Strikes Down State Pro-life Constitutional Amendment*, LIFE SITE NEWS (April 30, 2013), http://www.lifesitenews.com/news/mexican-supreme-court-strikes-down-state-pro-life-constitutional-amendment/.

*México: Suprema Corte ratifica blindaje de vida ante aborto en 18 estados* [Mexico: Supreme Court ratifies protection of life against abortion in 18 states], ACIPRENSA (May 3, 2013), http://www.aciprensa.com/noticias/mexico-suprema-corte-ratifica-blindaje-de-vida-ante-aborto-en-18-estados-53077/#.UZpmmWzD8dU.

Morello, Carol, *Pompeo Cuts OAS Funds over Advocacy of Legal Abortion*, WASH. POST (March 26, 2019), https://www.washingtonpost.com/world/national-security/pompeo-cuts-oas-funds-over-advocacy-of-legal-abortion/2019/03/26/4ea5314d-d7e0-48de-b636-e552447430b0_story.html?noredirect=on&utm_term=.daac7dcbd274.

*Mujer comprende que vida comienza en concepción y retira demanda contra Costa Rica* [Woman understands that life begins at conception and withdraws suit against Costa Rica], ACIPRENSA (Dec. 11, 2008), http://www.aciprensa.com/noticia.php?n=23767.

Murillo, Álvaro, *Costa Rica ofrece a CIDH posible arreglo en aborto terapéutico*, LA NACIÓN (June 7, 2015), http://www.nacion.com/nacional/politica/Pais-CIDH-posible-arreglo-terapeutico_0_1492250790.html.

Murillo, Álvaro, *Elizabeth Odio, jueza electa en Corte Interamericana de Derechos Humanos: "El aborto no tiene por qué ser un crimen"* [Elizabeth Odio, elected judge at the Inter-American Court of Human Rights: "Abortion should not be a crime"], LA NACIÓN (June 20, 2015), https://www.nacion.com/el-pais/politica/elizabeth-odio-jueza-electa-en-corte-interamericana-de-derechos-humanos-el-aborto-no-tiene-por-que-ser-un-crimen/PDZ2GIMXWRBDHLT2MHZBGBH3OY/story/.

*Nicaragua propone someter a reforma la Convención Americana sobre Derechos Humanos* [Nicaragua proposes amending the American Convention on Human Rights], LAPRENSA (Mar. 7, 2013, 5:15 PM), http://www.laprensa.com.ni/2013/03/07/poderes/137338-nicaragua-propone-someter-a.

*Niña de 11 años dio a luz* [Eleven-year-old child gives birth], ABC COLOR (Aug.13, 2015), http://www.abc.com.py/nacionales/nina-de-11-anos-dio-a-luz-hoy-1397642.html.

*No al aborto, ratifica comisión del CN que no lo despenalizó* [No to abortion, congressional commission confirms that it did not decriminalize it], HONDUDIARIO.COM (May 2, 2017), http://hondudiario.com/2017/05/03/no-al-aborto-ratifica-comision-del-cn-que-no-lo-despenalizo/.

*ONU felicitó a la Argentina por debatir el aborto y respaldó la legalización* [U.N. congratulates Argentina for debating abortion and supports its legalization], ÁMBITO.COM (June 13, 2018), https://www.ambito.com/onu-felicito-la-argentina-debatir-el-aborto-y-respaldo-la-legalizacion-n4024525.

*Parlamento rechaza despenalización del aborto terapéutico* [Parliament rejects decriminalization of therapeutic abortion], EL NUEVO DIARIO (Nov. 13, 2007, 4:13 PM), http://www.elnuevodiario.com.ni/politica/2072-parlamento-rechaza-despenalizacion-aborto-terpeuti/.

Peiró, Claudia, *Insólito: Bolivia quiere legalizar el aborto "por pobreza"* [Astounding: Bolivia wants to legalize abortion "for poverty"], INFOBAE (Mar. 17, 2017), https://www.infobae.com/america/america-latina/2017/03/17/insolito-bolivia-quiere-legalizar-el-aborto-por-pobreza/.

Picq, Manuela, *Is the Inter-American Commission of Human Rights Too Progressive?* AL JAZEERA (June 9, 2012), http://www.aljazeera.com/indepth/opinion/2012/06/2012658344220937.html.

*Presidente de Honduras rechaza que el Parlamento despenalice el aborto* [Honduras President rejects Parliament decriminalization of abortion], EL NUEVO HERALD (Apr. 25, 2017), http://www.elnuevoherald.com/noticias/mundo/america-latina/article146785944.html.

Ramos, David, *CIDH favorece a ONGs pro aborto y discrimina a las que defienden la vida, denuncian* [IACHR favors pro-abortion NGOs and discriminates against those that defend life, complaint], ACIPRENSA (Nov. 23, 2016), https://www.aciprensa.com/noticias/cidh-favorece-a-ongs-pro-aborto-y-discrimina-a-las-que-defienden-la-vida-denuncian-15409/.

Rankin, Lauren, *Controversial Ruling Threatens Abortion Access in Uruguay and Beyond*, REWIRE.NEWS (March 14, 2017), https://rewire.news/article/2017/03/14/controversial-ruling-threatens-abortion-access-uruguay-beyond/.

*Ratifican ley que apunta a controlar casos de aborto* [Ratification of bill intended to control abortion cases], ABC COLOR (Nov. 3, 2017), http://www.abc.com.py/edicion-impresa/politica/ratifican-ley-que-apunta-a-controlar-casos-de-aborto-1646351.html.

Schachar, Natalie, et al., *Guatemala Blocks Entry to Dutch Ship Providing Abortions*, REUTERS (Feb. 24, 2017), http://www.reuters.com/article/us-guatemala-abortion-idUSKBN163080?utm_source=email+marketing+Mailigen&utm_campaign=News+3.1.17&utm_medium=email.

Schumacher-Matos, Edward, *Abortion or Infanticide in El Salvador?*, NPR OMBUDSMAN (Nov. 10, 2014), http://www.npr.org/sections/ombudsman/2014/11/10/361207588/abortion-or-infanticide-in-el-salvador.

*Senado aprueba proyecto de aborto en tres causales tras maratónica jornada* [Senate approves bill on three grounds for abortion after marathon-like session], 24 HORAS (July 19, 2017), http://www.24horas.cl/nacional/senado-aprueba-proyecto-de-aborto-en-tres-causales-tras-maratonica-jornada-2451532.

Silva Abbott, Max, *Jurisdicción de Corte Interamericana* [Inter-American Court jurisdiction], EL MERCURIO—BLOGS (Jan. 4, 2013), http://www.elmercurio.com/blogs/2013/01/04/8118/Jurisdiccion-de-Corte-Interamericana.aspx.

Singman, Brooke, and Jake Gibson, *Planned Parenthood Under Investigation by Justice Department over Sale of Fetal Tissue*, FOX NEWS (Dec. 7, 2017), http://www.foxnews.com/politics/2017/12/07/planned-parenthood-under-investigation-by-justice-department-over-sale-fetal-tissue.html.

Soto, Jimena, *Diputada Rita Cháves acusa a Corte de parcialidad en caso de FIV* [Congresswoman Rita Chaves accuses Court of bias in IVF case], CRHOY (Sept. 6, 2012), http://www.crhoy.com/diputada-acusa-a-corte-de-parcialidad-en-caso-de-fiv/.

Tozzi, Piero, *This Week's Pro-life Victories in Mexico*, TURTLE BAY AND BEYOND (May 3, 2013), http://www.turtlebayandbeyond.org/2013/abortion/this-weeks-pro-life-victories-in-mexico/.

*Trends in Maternal Mortality: 1990 to 2008*, WORLD HEALTH ORGANIZATION (2010), http://apps.who.int/iris/bitstream/10665/44423/1/9789241500265_eng.pdf.

*Triunfo pro-vida en Chile: Rechazan aborto terapéutico* [Pro-life victory in Chile: Therapeutic abortion rejected], ACIPRENSA (April 9, 2012), https://www.aciprensa.com/noticias/triunfo-pro-vida-en-chile-rechazan-aborto-terapeutico.

Tuttle, Ian, *Beatriz's Baby*, NATIONAL REVIEW (June 13, 2013), http://www.nationalreview.com/article/350917/beatrizs-baby-ian-tuttle.

Vásquez, Ian, *La Corte Interamericana se debilita* [The Inter-American Court is weakened], EL COMERCIO (Feb. 6, 2018), https://elcomercio.pe/opinion/mirada-de-fondo/corte-interamericana-costa-rica-ddhh-matrimonio-debilita-ian-vasquez-noticia-494971.

Vio Grossi, Eduardo, *Reflexión sobre la justicia interamericana en DD.HH.* [Reflections on Inter-American human rights justice], EL MERCURIO BLOGS (Jan. 3, 2016), http://www.elmercurio.com/blogs/2016/01/03/38243/Reflexion-sobre-la-justicia-interamericana-en-DDHH.aspx.

Zamora Castellanos, Fernando, *Crisis en la Corte Interamericana de Derechos Humanos* [Crisis at the Inter-American Court of Human Rights], EL IMPARCIAL (Nov. 20, 2013), http://www.elimparcial.es/mundo/crisis-en-la-corte-interamericana-de-derechos-humanos-130920.html.

## Other

*75 Opiniones sobre el aborto: Un tema para hablar, una agenda para discutir* [75 opinions on abortion: A topic to talk about, an agenda to discuss], PROMSEX (2011), http://www.corteidh.or.cr/tablas/28123.pdf .

A, B & C v. Ireland, 2010-VI Eur. Ct. H.R. 210.

*Abortion, in* CATECHISM OF THE CATHOLIC CHURCH §§ 2370–75, http://www.vatican.va/archive/ENG0015/__P7Z.HTM.

*Abortion in Latin America and the Caribbean*, GUTTMACHER INSTITUTE (May 2016), https://www.guttmacher.org/sites/default/files/factsheet/ib_aww-latin-america.pdf.

*Aborto en Centroamérica: Una región donde se acumula la injusticia*, FEMINISTAS EN RESISTENCIA HONDURAS (Sept. 29, 2010), http://feministascontraelgolpehn.blogspot.com/2010/09/aborto-en-centroamerica-una-region.html.

*About Planned Parenthood Global*, PLANNED PARENTHOOD, https://www.plannedparenthood.org/about-us/planned-parenthood-global/who-we-are.

*Acta de votación, Sesión de la Cámara alta 08/08/2018* [Voting record, High Chamber Session 8/8/18], SENADO ARGENTINA, http://www.senado.gov.ar/micrositios/ive/4#fechaEvento2042.

Adame Goddard, Jorge, *Comentario a la sentencia sobre la protección de la vida desde el momento de la concepción, La protección de la vida desde el momento de la concepción en las constituciones locales* [Commentary on the judgment on protection of life from conception: Protection of life from the momento of conception in local constitutions], INSTITUTO DE INVESTIGACIONES JURÍDICAS (UNAM) 1 (2012).

*ADPF 442, STF*, YOUTUBE, https://www.youtube.com/user/STF/search?query=adpf+442.

*Advogada-Geral da União manifesta-se pela improcedência do pedido formulado pelo arguente* [Attorney General presents on the impropriety of the plaintiff's request], Argüição de Descumprimento de Preceito Fundamental 442 Distrito Federal, ADVOCACIA-GERAL DA UNIÃO (Braz.), http://www.camara.gov.br/proposicoesWeb/fichadetramitacao?idProposicao=1050889.

African Commission on Human and Peoples' Rights, *Protocol to the African Charter on Human and Peoples' Rights on the Rights of Women in Africa*, Sept. 13, 2000, CAB/LEG/66.6, reprinted in Martin Semalulu Nsibirwa, *A Brief Analysis of the Draft Protocol to the African Charter on Human and Peoples' Rights on the Rights of Women*, 1 AFR. HUM. RTS. L.J. 40 (2001).

African Commission on Human and Peoples' Rights, *Ratification Table: Protocol to the African Charter on Human and Peoples' Rights on the Rights of Women in Africa*, https://au.int/sites/default/files/treaties/37077-sl-PROTOCOL%20TO%20THE%20AFRICAN%20CHARTER%20ON%20HUMAN%20AND%20PEOPLE%27S%20RIGHTS%20ON%20THE%20RIGHTS%20OF%20WOMEN%20IN%20AFRICA.pdf.

Alliance Defending Freedom, Brief of *Amici Curiae*, Inter-Am. Ct. H.R., FN 39, http://www.adfmedia.org/files/ivf-costaricaamicus-english.pdf.
Andújar de Zamora, Miryan, *Instrumentalización del embrión humano: Ante los deseos de los adultos y la falta de límites en los avances biotecnológicos* [Instrumentalization of the human embryo: Before the desires of adults and the lack of limits on biotechnological advances], CENTRO DE BIOÉTICA, PERSONA Y FAMILIA (Jan. 18, 2013), https://centrodebioetica.org/instrumentalizacion-del-embrion-humano-ante-los-deseos-de-los-adultos-y-la-falta-de-limites-en-los-avances-biotecnologicos/.
*Argentina: Juristas: Fallo abortista de la Corte no aplica obligatoriamente* [Argentina: Lawyers: Court abortion ruling does not necessarily apply], VIDA HUMANA INTERNACIONAL (Mar. 19, 2012), http://vidahumana.org/bk-vhi/vida-humana-internacional/item/1707-argentina-juristas-fallo-abortista-de-la-corte-no-aplica-obligatoriamente.
*Behind the Scenes of Bolivia's Historic Abortion Law Change*, IPAS (Dec. 18, 2017), https://ipas.org/news/2017/December/behind-the-scenes-of-bolivias-historic-abortion-law-change.
Brüggemann v. Germany, App. No. 6959/75, 3 Eur. Ct. H.R. Rep. 244 (1981).
Canteros, Laura Salomé, et al., *Aborto en Argentina y en la región: Entrevista a Luz Patricia Mejía, exrelatora sobre los Derechos de las Mujeres y presidenta de la CIDH* [Abortion in Argentina and in the region: interview with Luz Patricia Mejía, former rapporteur on women's rights and IACHR president], NODAL (May 24, 2018, 3:15 PM), https://www.nodal.am/2018/05/aborto-en-argentina-y-en-la-region-entrevista-a-luz-patricia-mejia-exrelatora-sobre-los-derechos-de-las-mujeres-comisionada-y-presidenta-de-la-cidh/.
Carranza Latrubesse, Gustavo, *Las perplejidades de los derechos humanos (a propósito del fallo de la Corte IDH en el caso Artavia Murillo y otros c. Costa Rica)* [The perplexities of human rights (with regard to the IACHR ruling in the case Artavia Murillo and Others v. Costa Rica)], Academia Nacional de Derecho y Ciencias Sociales de Cordoba, Jan. 14, 2012, http://bicentenario.unc.edu.ar/acaderc/las-perplejidades-de-los-derechos-humanos-a-proposito-del-fallo-de-la-corte-idh-en-el-caso-artavia-murillo-y-otros-vs.-costa-rica.
Center for Reproductive Rights, THE WORLD'S ABORTION LAWS (2018), http://worldabortionlaws.com/map/.
*The Center's Cases*, THE CENTER FOR REPRODUCTIVE RIGHTS, http://reproductiverights.org/en/archive/cases?issue=All&region=49.
*Chile: Senate Defeats Pro-abortion Bills*, PARLIAMENTARY NETWORK FOR CRITICAL ISSUES (May 2012), http://www.pncius.org/newsletter.aspx?id=59.
*CIDH le exige explicaciones a El Salvador por el caso de Beatriz* [IACHR demands explanations from El Salvador regarding the Beatriz case], CEJIL (April 8, 2015), https://www.cejil.org/es/cidh-le-exige-explicaciones-salvador-caso-beatriz.

Colectivo Feminista para el Desarrollo Local de El Salvador, Agrupación Ciudadana por la Despenalización del Aborto Terapéutico, Ético y Eugenésico de El Salvador, Ipas, CEJIL [Feminist Collective for local development of El Salvador; Citizens Group for the Decriminalization of Therapeutic, Ethical and Eugenic Abortion of El Salvador; Ipas; CEJIL], *Petición Inicial "Beatriz vs. Estado de El Salvador"* [Initial petition "Beatriz v. State of El Salvador"] (Nov. 29, 2013).

Colegio Médico de Honduras, Comisión de Ética y Práctica Médica, Oficio No. SAEC-32-2017 (May 9, 2017), https://s3.amazonaws.com/cmh-core/DOC/PDF/Posicion-despenalizacion-aborto-cmh-2017.pdf.

*Comisión multipartidaria del Código Penal decide no despenalizar figura del aborto* [Multiparty commission on Criminal Code decides not to decriminalize abortion], TELEPRENSA (May 4, 2017), https://www.teleprensa.com/honduras/comision-multipartidaria-del-codigo-penal-decide-no-despenalizar-figura-del-aborto.html.

*Composition of the Court*, EUROPEAN COURT OF HUMAN RIGHTS, https://www.echr.coe.int/Pages/home.aspx?p=court/judges&c=.

*Comunicado de Prensa*, MINISTERIO DE RELACIONES EXTERIORES, REPÚBLICA DEL PARAGUAY (May 13, 2015), http://www.mre.gov.py/v2/Noticia/2773/comunicado-de-prensa.

*Comunicado de Prensa No. 2*, MINISTERIO DE RELACIONES EXTERIORES, REPÚBLICA DEL PARAGUAY (May 21, 2015), http://www.mre.gov.py/v2/Noticia/2802/comunicado-de-prensa-n-2.

*Comunicado de Prensa*, MINISTERIO DE RELACIONES EXTERIORES, REPÚBLICA DEL PARAGUAY (June 11, 2015), http://www.mre.gov.py/v2/Noticia/2876/comunicado-de-prensa.

*Conceive*, OXFORD DICTIONARIES, https://en.oxforddictionaries.com/thesaurus/conceive.

*Constituciones*, INFOLEG, http://infoleg.gov.ar/basehome/constituciones.htm.

*Declaración de Guácimo, XV Cumbre de Presidentes Centroamericanos* [Guácimo Declaration, 15th Summit of Central American Presidents], GOBIERNO DE LA REPÚBLICA DE GUATEMALA, https://www.minex.gob.gt/MDAA/DATA/MDAA/20101108164849396 1994-08-20%20%20XV%20REUNION%20ORDINARIA%20(Costa%20Rica).pdf.

*Declaración sobre el Sistema Interamericano de Derechos Humanos* [Declaration on the Inter-American System on Human Rights], April 2, 2019.

*Decriminalize*, MERRIAM-WEBSTER LEGAL DICTIONARY (Dec. 28, 2015, 6:50 PM), https://www.merriam-webster.com/dictionary/decriminalize#legalDictionary.

*Diccionario de la lengua española* [Dictionary of the Spanish language], REAL ACADEMIA ESPAÑOLA, http://lema.rae.es/drae/?val=aborto.

The Economist Currency Converter, THE ECONOMIST, http://www.economist.com/markets/currency/fullconverter.cfm

*El Salvador 2016 Human Rights Report*, U.S. Dept. of State (April 4, 2017), https://www.justice.gov/sites/default/files/pages/attachments/2017/03/06/dos-hrr_2016_el_salvador.pdf.

*El Salvador: Beatriz morirá si no se le practica un aborto* [Beatriz will die if she doesn't get an abortion], Amnesty International (last visited Aug. 22, 2017), https://www.es.amnesty.org/actua/acciones/elsalvador-beatriz/.

*Entrevista viernes 10/05/2013 Bloque #1 B, Entrevista Con: José Miguel Fortin (Dir. General de Medicina Legal) "El Aborto Terapéutico que Demanda Beatriz,"* HECHOS A.M. CANAL 12, YouTube (May 10, 2013), https://www.youtube.com/watch?v=pvybGil7qnY.

*Entrevista viernes 10/05/2013 Bloque #2 A, Entrevista Con: José Miguel Fortin (Dir. General de Medicina Legal) "El Aborto Terapéutico que Demanda Beatriz,"* HECHOS A.M. CANAL 12, YouTube (May 10, 2013), https://www.youtube.com/watch?v=3Ef4dzH4VUE.

*Entrevista viernes 10/05/2013 Bloque #3, Entrevista Con: José Miguel Fortin (Dir. General de Medicina Legal) "El Aborto Terapéutico que Demanda Beatriz,"* HECHOS A.M. CANAL 12, YouTube (May 10, 2013), https://www.youtube.com/watch?v=pi6OChd7BdE.

European Parliament, Parliamentary Questions, Answer given by Mr. Dalli on behalf of the Commission, 30 April 2012, E-002933/2012, OJ C 240 E, 21/08/2013, http://www.europarl.europa.eu/sides/getAllAnswers.do?reference=E-2012-002933&language=EN.

Evans v. The United Kingdom, 2007-I Eur. Ct. H.R. 355.

*Fernando Zegers-Hochschild, MD*, Int'l Comm. Monitoring Assisted Reprod. Tech., http://www.icmartivf.org/zegers-hochschild.html.

*Florentín Meléndez Padilla (Former Rapporteur)*, Organization of American States, http://www.oas.org/en/iachr/pdl/mandate/composition.asp.

Franck, María Inés, *Costa Rica: Por segunda vez llevada a la Corte Interamericana con motivo de la FIV* [For the second time, Costa Rica taken to the Inter-American Court over IVF], Observatorio Internacional de Políticas Públicas y Familia (Feb. 2016), http://observatoriointernacional.com/?p=2392.

Franck, María Inés, *Tribunal uruguayo suspende la aplicación de gran parte del decreto reglamentario del aborto por afectar el derecho a la objeción de conciencia* [Uruguayan court suspends the application of most of a regulatory decree for affecting the right to conscientious objection], Observatorio Internacional de Políticas Públicas y Familia (Oct. 2014), http://observatoriointernacional.com/?p=1866.

*The Gift of a Child*, *in* Catechism of the Catholic Church §§ 2373–79, http://www.vatican.va/archive/ccc_css/archive/catechism/p3s2c2a6.htm.

Giunta, Laura, and Agustina Mitre, *Argentina: Modificación del Código Civil y el impacto de la decisión de la Corte Suprema de la Nación*, Defendiendo Vidas (2015), https://aul.org/wp-content/uploads/2019/02/2015-11-Argentina

-Modificación-del-Código-Civil-y-el-impacto-de-la-decisión-de-la-Corte-Suprema-de-la-Nación.pdf.

Glass v. United Kingdom, 2004-II Eur. Ct. H.R. 25.

*Gobiernos de América Latina: Denunciar la Convención Americana de Derechos Humanos* [Latin American Governments: Denounce the American Convention of Human Rights] (online petition), CHANGE.ORG (last visited Jan. 11, 2014), http://tinyurl.com/amn5hpl.

*Guanajuato Declaration about in Vitro Fertilization* (April 20, 2013), http://declaraciondeguanajuato.org/english.php.

Handyside v. The United Kingdom, App. No. 5493/72, A24 Eur. Ct. H.R. 1 (1976).

Herrmann, Timothy, *Abortion Proponents Admit Defeat at Rio Conference*, C-FAM (June 20, 2012), http://www.c-fam.org/fridayfax/volume-15/abortion-proponents-admit-defeat-at-rio-conference.html.

*Human Rights: Paraguay Has Failed to Protect a 10-Year Old* [*sic*] *Girl Child Who Became Pregnant after Being Raped, Say UN Experts*, UNITED NATIONS HUMAN RIGHTS, OFFICE OF THE HIGH COMMISSIONER (May 11, 2015), http://www.ohchr.org/EN/NewsEvents/Pages/DisplayNews.aspx?NewsID=15944&LangID=E.

*IACHR Demands Explanations from El Salvador over Beatriz Case*, CEJIL, https://cejil.org/en/iachr-demands-explanations-salvador-over-beatriz-case.

*I/A Court History*, CORTE INTERAMERICANA DE DERECHOS HUMANOS, http://www.corteidh.or.cr/historia-en.cfm.

*Inter-American Commission on Human Rights to Hear Beatriz case against El Salvador*, IPAS (April 14, 2015), https://ipas.org/news/2015/April/inter-american-commission-on-human-rights-to-hear-beatriz-case-against-el-salvador.

INTER-AMERICAN INSTITUTE OF HUMAN RIGHTS, http://www.iidh.ed.cr/.

Int'l Comm. of the Red Cross, Geneva Conventions of 12 August 1949: State Parties/Signatories, http://www.icrc.org/ihl.nsf/.

Jean-Jacques Amy v. Belgium, App. No. 11684/85, A28 Eur. Ct. H.R. 7 (1988).

*Joint Statement, IACHR Hearing on Abortion: Legalization Is a Human Rights Imperative*, CELS (May 9, 2018), https://www.cels.org.ar/web/en/2018/05/audiencia-sobre-aborto-en-la-cidh-legalizarlo-es-un-imperativo-de-derechos-humanos/.

*La Corte sostuvo que la Corte Interamericana de Derechos Humanos no puede revocar sentencias del Máximo Tribunal argentino* [The Court held that the Inter-American Court cannot revoke judgments of the highest Argentinian court], CENTRO DE INFORMACIÓN JUDICIAL (Feb. 14, 2017), http://www.cij.gov.ar/nota-24822.html.

*Legisladores de toda América piden a la OEA que no se promueva el aborto con dinero de sus países* [Legislators from all over America ask the OAS not to promote abortion with their money], POLITICAL NETWORK FOR VALUES (April 5, 2019), http://politicalnetworkforvalues.org/2019/04/congreso-hemisferico-parlamentarios-aborto-oea/.

Letter dated 2 April 2003 from the Permanent Representative of Costa Rica to the United Nations addressed to the Secretary-General, U.N. Doc. A/58/73 (Apr. 17, 2003).

Letter from James Lankford, Thom Tillis, Michael B. Enzi, Michael S. Lee, James M. Inhofe, John Kennedy, Roy Blunt, Ted Cruz and Joni K. Ernst, U.S. senators, to Mike Pompeo, sec'y of state, U.S. Dep't of State (Dec. 21, 2018), *in* Martin M. Barillas, *9 Senators Seek to Halt US Funding to Pro-abortion Orgs in Latin America*, LIFE SITE NEWS, https://www.lifesitenews.com/news/9-senators-seek-to-halt-us-funding-to-pro-abortion-orgs-in-latin-america.

Letter from Tabaré Vázquez, Presidencia de la República Oriental del Uruguay [Presidency of Oriental Republic of Uruguay], to Señor Presidente de la Asamblea General [Mr. President of Uruguay General Assembly] (Nov. 14, 2008) (Uru.), *in* Leslie Van Rompaey et al., *Veto al aborto, Estudios interdisciplinarios sobre las 15 tesis del Presidente Tabaré Vázquez*, UNIVERSIDAD DE MONTEVIDEO (2012), at 10, https://www.um.edu.uy/docs/veto_al_aborto.pdf.

Letter from Tom Farer, Robert Goldman, Dinah Shelton, James Cavallaro, presidents and members of the Comm'n, and Douglas Cassel, U.S. nominee to the Comm'n, to Mike Pompeo, Sec'y of state, U.S. Dep't of State (Feb. 13, 2019), GLOBAL AMERICANS, https://theglobalamericans.org/wp-content/uploads/2019/02/Pompeo.IACHR_.2.13.19.pdf.

Letter [from Sen. Mike Lee and Sen. Marco Rubio] to State Department to fully implement the Organization of American States (OAS) Revitalization and Reform Act of 2013 (2013), SCRIBD, https://www.scribd.com/document/326377092/Letter-to-State-Department-to-fully-implement-the-Organization-of-American-States-OAS-Revitalization-and-Reform-Act-of-2013.

*Listado actualizado: Proyectos de ley para cuidar las dos vidas* [Updated list: Legislative bills to save both lives], MATERNIDAD VULNERABLE, CENTRO DE BIOÉTICA, PERSONA Y FAMILIA (Sept. 10, 2018), http://www.maternidadvulnerable.com.ar/2018/09/10/proyectos-de-ley-para-cuidar-las-dos-vidas/.

*Mexico Declaration, American Declaration Regarding the Independence and Self-Determination of Peoples on Matters Relating to Life, Family and Religious Freedom*, CONGRESO HEMISFÉRICO DE PARLAMENTARIOS (2017), https://www.declaraciondemexico.com/declaration-of-mexico/.

MILLER-KEANE ENCYCLOPEDIA & DICTIONARY OF MEDICINE, NURSING, & ALLIED HEALTH (5th ed., W.B. Saunders 1992).

Ministerio de Salud & Presidencia República Oriental del Uruguay, *Interrupción Voluntaria Embarazo (IVE) 2013–2017* [Voluntary interruption of pregnancy, 2013–2017], MINISTERIO DE SALUD PÚBLICA (March 2018) (Uru.).

*Mosby's Medical, Nursing, & Allied Health Dictionary* (6th ed. 2002).

Odièvre v. France, App. No. 42326/98, 38 Eur. Ct. H.R. Rep. 43 (2004).

*Opinión sobre las sentencias de la #CIDH–Parte 1–FEB 11–1/4 | Willax*, YouTube (Feb. 11, 2018), https://www.youtube.com/watch?v=KUlLM_J53EI&t=30s.

*Oradores en Contra* [Speakers against], Senado Argentina, http://www.senado.gov.ar/micrositios/ive/4#fechaEvento2042.

Ornelas Duarte, Aracely, *Análisis crítico a la sentencia de la Corte Interamericana de Derechos Humanos en el fallo sobre fertilización in vitro, in* Centro de Investigación Social Avanzada (CISAV), Artavia Murillo vs. Costa Rica, 123.

Orozco, J. Jesus, *La reforma de la Comisión Interamericana de Derechos Humanos* [Reform of the Inter-American Commission on Human Rights], 19 Aportes DPLF: Revista de la Fundación para el Debido Proceso 8 (2014), http://perso.unifr.ch/derechopenal/assets/files/obrasportales/op_20140508_03.pdf.

*Our Work*, Ipas (2019), https://www.ipas.org/our-work.

Ovelar, Diputado [Congressman] Eber, *Debatirán sobre el aborto en una audiencia pública* [Abortion will be debated in a public hearing], Honorable Camara de Diputados, Congreso Nacional, República del Paraguay (May 18, 2015), http://publications.gc.ca/collections/collection_2011/sen/yc32-0/YC32-0-372-4-eng.pdf.

Oviedo, Jorge, *Costa Rica después de la sentencia de la CIDH en Artavia Murillo* [Costa Rica after the ruling of the IACHR in Artavia Murillo], Feb. 2014, Observatorio Internacional de Políticas Públicas y Familia (Arg.), http://observatoriointernacional.com/?p=1576.

P. & S. v. Poland, App. No. 57375/08, Eur. Ct. H.R. (2008).

*Paraguay: UN Experts Deplore Government's Failure to Protect 10-Year-Old Rape Survivor*, UN News (May 11, 2015), http://www.un.org/apps/news/story.asp?NewsID=50826#.WG7V3mwizIU.

Parliament of Can. Standing Senate Comm. on Human Rights, Enhancing Canada's Role in the OAS: Canadian Adherence to the American Convention on Human Rights, No. 2/37-446S (2003), http://www.parl.gc.ca/Content/SEN/Committee/372/huma/rep/rep04may03-e.pdf.

Parrillo v. Italy, App. No. 46470/11, 2015-V Eur. Ct. H.R. 141 (2015).

*Paulina: Five Years Later*, Center for Reproductive Rights (June 1, 2005), https://reproductiverights.org/document/paulina-five-years-later.

Pérez Hernández, Candido, Marcelo Bartolini Esparza, et al., Aborto: La Política de un Estado Claudicante (LXIII Legislatura de la H. Cámara de Diputados eds., 2017) (Mex.).

*Pompeo Announces Expansion of Pro-life "Mexico City Policy"*—EWTN News Nightly 2019-03-26, YouTube (Mar. 26, 2019), https://www.youtube.com/watch?v=Z48JjLyVvtY&index=14&list=PL9CQlldupc5_STtOyJ3gnmbEWyFDpRzw-&t=2s.

Position statement, March 22, 2018, ACADEMIA NACIONAL DE MEDICINA (Arg.), https://www.acamedbai.org.ar/pdf/declaraciones/Academia%20Nacional%20de%20Medicina%20(3).pdf?mkt_hm=6&utm_source=email_marketing&utm_admin=893&utm_medium=email&utm_campaign=Declaracin_de_la_Academia_Nacional_de_Medicina_ante_proyectos_de_aborto.

Procuraduría Delegada para la Defensa de los Derechos de la Infancia, la Adolescencia y la Familia, Informe de Vigilancia a la Implementación de la Sentencia C-355 de 2006, Bogota, D.C., diciembre de 2012, http://convencioninteramericana.org/wp-content/uploads/2016/04/Propuesta_Convencion.pdf.

PROPUESTA DE CONVENCIÓN INTERAMERICANA DE LOS DERECHOS SEXUALES Y LOS DERECHOS REPRODUCTIVOS, CONVENCIÓN AMERICANA DE DERECHOS SEXUALES Y REPRODUCTIVOS, http://convencioninteramericana.org/wp-content/uploads/2016/04/Propuesta_Convencion.pdf.

*"Protocolo para la atención integral de las personas con derecho a la interrupción legal del embarazo" elaborado por el Programa Nacional de Salud Sexual y Procreación Responsable del Ministerio de Salud de la Nación (Selección)* ["Protocol for comprehensive care of persons with a right to interruption of pregnancy" created by the National Ministry of Health National Program on Sexual Health and Responsible Procreation], XII BOLETÍN JURÍDICO OBSERVATORIO DE LIBERTAD RELIGIOSA DE AMÉRICA LATINA Y EL CARIBE [B.J.O.L.R.A.L.C.], no. 2, 2016, at 53 (Chile).

*Radio 10: El Puente* [Interview with Eugenio Raúl Zaffaroni, Supreme Court justice who then went on to become an Inter-American Court judge] (Mar. 14, 2012), http://www.radio10.com.ar/.

S.H. v. Austria, App. No. 57813/00, 2011-V Eur. Ct. H.R. 29 (2010).

*Silva Monteiro Martins Ribeiro v. Portugal*, App. No. 16471/02, Eur. Ct. H.R. (2004).

*Special Procedures of the Human Rights Council*, UNITED NATIONS HUMAN RIGHTS, OFFICE OF THE HIGH COMMISSIONER, http://www.ohchr.org/EN/HRBodies/SP/Pages/Welcomepage.aspx.

*Steps for Performing Manual Vacuum Aspiration Using the Ipas MVA Plus and EasyGrip Cannulae*, IPAS (2019), https://www.ipas.org/resources/steps-for-performing-manual-vacuum-aspiration-using-the-ipas-mva-plus-and-easygrip-cannulae.

*Testimony of Dr. Ken Edelin, Associate Dean, Boston University [School] of Medicine*, UNITED STATES SENATE COMMITTEE ON THE JUDICIARY (June 23, 2005), http://www.judiciary.senate.gov/imo/media/doc/Edelin%20Testimony%20062305.pdf.

*Toller—Exposición sobre Proyecto de Ley de IVE (CD 22/18, en revisión Senado, 24.7.2918)*, MATERNIDAD VULNERABLE, CENTRO DE BIOÉTICA, PERSONA Y FAMILIA (July 26, 2018), http://www.maternidadvulnerable.com.ar/2018/07/26/fernando-toller-2/.

*Tres jueces de Corte Interamericana asumen posición abortista en caso fecundación in vitro* [Three Inter-American Court judges adopt proabortion position in in vitro fertilization case], PROVIDA DE HONDURAS (Sept. 11, 2012), https://providahn.org/tres-jueces-de-corte-interamericana-asumen-posicion-abortista-en-caso-fecundacion-in-vitro/.

*Votos, Inforgrafía* [Voting information], DIPUTADOS ARGENTINA, https://www.hcdn.gob.ar/prensa/noticias/2018/despenalizacion-aborto/inforgrafia.html.

Vo v. France, App. No. 53924/00, 2004-VIII, 2004-VIII Eur. Ct. H.R. 67 (2004).

Williams Becker, Alejandro, and Jorge Nicolás Lafferriere, *Análisis del predictamen de legalización del aborto* [Analysis of preliminary report on abortion legalization], MATERNIDAD VULNERABLE, CENTRO DE BIOÉTICA, PERSONA Y FAMILIA (June 8, 2018) (Arg.), https://www.maternidadvulnerable.com.ar/2018/06/08/analisis-del-predictamen-de-legalizacion-del-aborto/.

*Woman-Centered, Comprehensive Abortion Care Trainer's Manual, 2nd edition*, IPAS, https://www.ipas.org/resources/woman-centered-comprehensive-abortion-care-trainers-manual-second-edition.

# INDEX

LIGIA DE JESÚS CASTALDI

is professor of law at Ave Maria School of Law. She has worked for several international governmental human rights agencies, including UNICEF's regional office for Latin America and the Caribbean and the Inter-American Commission on Human Rights.

www.ingramcontent.com/pod-product-compliance
Ingram Content Group UK Ltd.
Pitfield, Milton Keynes, MK11 3LW, UK
UKHW020838290926
15470UKWH00004B/1412

9 780268 107659